D0984345

INJUNCTIONS AND
SPECIFIC PERFORMANCE

INJUNCTIONS AND
SPECIFIC PERFORMANCE

ROBERT J. SHARPE

B.A., LL.B., D. Phil.

Of the Ontario Bar
Professor of Law, University of Toronto

TORONTO
CANADA LAW BOOK LIMITED
1983

ISBN: 0 88804 017 2

PREFACE

My aim in writing this book has been to provide an accurate account of the present state of the law with respect to injunctions and specific performance, and at the same time to contribute to the process of elaborating sound theoretical principles to govern the award of these remedies. An attempt has been made to identify their advantages and disadvantages and to identify a rationale which will put historical factors in proper perspective. I have tried to isolate remedial issues from questions of substantive law. Because the remedies examined cover such a broad spectrum of substantive law issues, an attempt must be made to draw a distinction between right and remedy if the subject is to be at all manageable. A strict distinction between right and remedy is perhaps not possible, if only because measuring the appropriateness of a remedy requires reference to the nature of the right being protected. However, I hope that I have been able to show that there are identifiable issues of remedial choice which deserve discrete analysis. My starting point is the assumption that a right has been violated or threatened and that the task of the court is to formulate the appropriate remedial response.

Despite the importance of the subject, systematic treatment of remedial issues is a relatively recent development. In the case of injunctions and specific performance, analysis has tended to focus on principles which evolved in the pre-Judicature Act era of a dual-court system. Recently, however, both courts and commentators have begun to rationalize these remedies in more modern terms, questioning their availability in some instances while extending it in others. It is surely time to formulate principles governing remedial choice which focus on the particular advantages of one remedy or another rather than simply to follow criteria which evolved before the fusion of law and equity. This also means that equitable and legal remedies should be looked at as a whole. To this end, I have worked closely with Professor S.M. Waddams, whose book *The Law of Damages* is published simultaneously with this as a companion volume.

I wish to thank the University of Toronto and the Social Sciences and Humanities Research Council for enabling me to spend a sabbatical year at the University of Oxford during which much of the work on this book was done. I also thank Magdalen College and the Bodleian Law Library for helping to make my year a pleasant and productive one. I have benefited from discussions with many friends and colleagues. This book is in large measure a product of my Remedies course at the Faculty of Law, University of Toronto, and I sincerely thank my students for many insightful comments. I am especially grateful to Professor S.M. Waddams with whom I have worked in close collaboration.

Robert J. Sharpe

Toronto
September 1983.

TABLE OF CONTENTS

TABLE OF CASES

xliii

xlv

TABLE OF STATUTES

CANADA

PART 1

INJUNCTIONS

CHAPTER 1

GENERAL PRINCIPLES

1. Forms of Injunctive Relief

(1) Mandatory injunctions

1   A mandatory injunction is one which requires the defendant to act positively. A mandatory injunction may be given to remedy past wrongs and require the defendant to undo some wrong he has committed. Such orders are restorative in nature, requiring the defendant to take whatever steps are necessary to repair the situation in a manner consistent with the plaintiff's rights. In other cases, mandatory injunctions look to the future and require the defendant to carry out some unperformed duty to act. In either class of case, although the general principles governing the availability of injunctive relief apply, the very fact of requiring a positive course of action raises special problems.[1]

(2) Prohibitive injunctions

2   The most common form of injunction is the prohibitive order which restrains the defendant from committing a specified act. Prohibitive injunctions are the subject of most of Part I of this book, and the particular problems of appropriateness, definition and enforceability are dealt with in the pages which follow. Prohibitive injunctions are also frequently granted to restrain breaches of contract, a matter discussed in detail in Chapter 9.

3   The courts have favoured prohibitive relief over mandatory relief. Prohibitive injunctions have always been seen to be more readily granted than mandatory injunctions, and an injunction restraining breach of a negative covenant is granted in circumstances in which the courts would hesitate to award specific performance.[2] A negative obligation is readily defined and readily enforceable. Ordinarily, it will be less intrusive to restrain the defendant from continuing a certain act, than to require him to perform some positive act. However, it should not be overlooked that the burden imposed by a prohibitive order is often substantial and a negative order often may amount in practical terms to an order requiring a certain course of action.[3]

---

[1] See, *infra*, §50 *et seq*.

[2] *Infra*, Chapter 9.

[3] *Infra*, §§54, 378.

(3) Interlocutory injunctions

4   Injunctions may be classified according to the time at which they are granted. Pre-trial relief in the form of *ex parte*, interim, and interlocutory injunctions raise the difficult issue of balancing the plaintiff's need for immediate protection against the defendant's right to a full hearing at trial on the merits before any order is made. The problems of interlocutory injunctions are addressed in Chapter 2.

(4) Quia timet injunctions

5   Another temporal classification is suggested by *quia timet* injunctions, granted before any harm has actually been suffered, and this issue is addressed in this chapter under the heading "Prematurity".

2. Inadequacy of Damages

(1) Historical factors

6   The traditional rule is that an injunction will be granted only where damages would provide an inadequate remedy.[4] The reason for this is largely historical. Injunctions are an equitable remedy, and the pre-Judicature Act dual-court structure imposed limitations on equitable jurisdiction. While the "common" injunction was used as a potent device to force parties in common law actions to abide by equitable principles,[5] common law remedies remained predominant, and the specific remedies of injunction and specific performance were limited to those special circumstances where the common law remedy of damages was seen to be inadequate. Law and equity have been fused and a single court now administers both, but the imprint of history has not been erased.

7   It is not possible to define inadequacy of damages in a precise way. It is a vague principle which takes shape depending upon the context. It means one thing when used with respect to interlocutory injunctions,[6] another in nuisance actions,[7] and still another where an injunction is sought to restrain a breach of contract.[8]

---

[4] See, *e.g.*, *London & Blackwall Ry. Co. v. Cross* (1886), 31 Ch. D. 354 (C.A.), at p. 369, *per* Lindley, L.J.: "The very first principle of injunction law is that *prima facie* you do not obtain injunctions to restrain actionable wrongs, for which damages are the proper remedy."

[5] See Eden, *Law of Injunctions* (London, Butterworth & Son, 1821).

[6] *Infra*, §§165-178.

[7] *Infra*, Chapter 3

[8] *Infra*, Chapter 9.

8   Indeed, as seen in Chapters 4 and 9 respectively, where injunctions are sought to restrain interference with property rights or to restrain breach of negative covenants, injunctions are in fact so
strongly favoured that it is more accurate to say that the injunction is
the presumed remedy. Because the phrase "inadequacy of damages"
has varying meaning in varying contexts, detailed discussion of its effect is best postponed and presented in the various chapters dealing
with these particular applications of specific relief.

9   It can be argued that the historical rationale for the inadequacy of
damages principle, to the extent that it implies a presumption in favour of one remedy or another, has long since disappeared, and that
an effort should now be made to explain the choice between injunction or damages in more satisfactory terms. A "non-hierarchical"[9]
scheme governing the selection of remedies, dependent upon the relative advantages and disadvantages of each in the given substantive
law context, with no presumptions favouring one remedy over the
other, is to be preferred. It is suggested that the discussion in various
parts of this book of the treatment of inadequacy of damages leads to
the conclusion that despite the continued use of the traditional language of the pre-Judicature Act system, these jurisdictional constraints removed more than one hundred years ago have less
influence than the language would suggest.[10] As is the case with specific performance,[11] in deciding whether to grant injunctions, modern
courts are less and less willing to be bound by tradition alone, and
more and more willing to base their decisions on the relative advantages and disadvantages of damages or an injunction. The courts do
seem to be moving steadily closer to a "non-hierarchical" scheme of
remedy selection.

---

[9] The phrase is used by Fiss, *The Civil Rights Injunction* (Bloomington, Indiana University Press, 1978). See, especially, at p. 6, arguing for a "non-hierarchical conception of remedies, where there is no presumptive remedy, but rather a context-
specific evaluation of the advantages and disadvantages of each form of relief." See
also at p. 91: "the choice of remedy should not turn on generalized propositions —
couched in the obscure but colorful language of history — about which remedies
are favoured and which are disfavoured. It should instead turn upon an apprecia-
tion of the technical advantages of each remedy and a judgment, made in light of
the substantive claim, about the desirability of the allocation of power that is implicit in each remedial system."

[10] For an express judicial recognition of this, see *Evans Marshall & Co. Ltd. v. Bertola S.A.*, [1973] 1 W.L.R. 349 (C.A.), at p. 379, *per* Sachs, L.J.:

The standard question in relation to the grant of an injunction, "Are damages
an adequate remedy?", might perhaps, in the light of the authorities of recent
years, be rewritten: "Is it just, in all the circumstances, that a plaintiff should be
confined to his remedy in damages?"

[11] See, *infra*, §§529-549, where inadequacy of damages is discussed in that context.

(2) Advantages of injunctive relief

10   In the discussion of inadequacy of damages and specific performance in Chapter 7, it is suggested that the underlying rationale of remedy selection in the contractual setting is the protection of the plaintiff's expectation interest in a manner which minimizes the burden upon the defendant. Because injunctions are granted in such a variety of substantive law settings, it is difficult to suggest an analogous principle here.

11   However, it is possible to identify certain advantages injunctions often have over damages, as well as to identify certain problems inherent in injunctive relief but not found where damages are awarded. The prime advantage of any form of specific relief is that it avoids the risks inherent in damage assessment. This feature of specific relief in the contractual setting is discussed in Chapter 7.[12] Similar principles apply to injunctions and are discussed below in this chapter[13] and as well in Chapter 4.[14] The more difficult the accurate assessment in money terms of the impact upon the plaintiff of the defendant's wrong, the more likely the court is to grant an injunction. As seen in Chapter 4, where property rights are at stake, although damages in terms of market value loss are often readily calculable, a remedy reflecting only market value is ordinarily seen as inappropriate to reflect the nature of the plaintiff's substantive right. Hence, damages based on market value, which might be quite appropriate in another setting, may be said to be "inadequate".

(3) Balance of burden and benefit

12   An important factor in determining the relative advantages of damages and injunctions is to consider not only the protection of the plaintiff's position but also the burden to be imposed upon the defendant. Specific remedies are relatively more intrusive than are damage awards. A specific remedy requires that a certain course of conduct be followed. The cost or burden the remedy imposes is an important factor which the courts do take into account, and ordinarily, the remedy which achieves satisfaction of the plaintiff's substantive rights in the least burdensome way will be preferred.

13   An important and familiar aspect of the discretion determining the availability of equitable remedies and the calculation of the adequacy

---

[12] *Infra*, §529.

[13] *Infra*, §§17, 18.

[14] *Infra*, especially at §368.

of damages is the balancing of the burden the remedy imposes on the defendant against the benefit it confers on the plaintiff, and consideration of the relative costs of specific relief and damage awards.[15] To the extent that these matters can be quantified, the more the burden an injunction imposes on a defendant exceeds the benefit it would confer on the plaintiff, the less likely the plaintiff is to be awarded an injunction, whether prohibitive or mandatory.[16] Closely related is the weighing of the burden an injunction imposes against the likely amount of a damages award. The more the cost of an injunction to a defendant exceeds the amount of damages which would be assessed against him, the less likely the court is to grant an injunction.[17] Equally, the more difficult it is to put a dollar value on the plaintiff's loss, the more likely the court is to simply award an injunction.[18]

14 The discretion to award injunctions cannot be reduced to a simple balance of burden and benefit, and any attempt to devise a precise calculus would be unwarranted and unwise. However, it does remain that the weighing of the relative cost of an injunction is one important factor in determining the award of injunctive relief. Again, this is a theme which is developed in specific contexts in various parts of this book.[19]

(4) Post-judgment bargaining

15 Consideration of the possibility of post-judgment bargaining provides a useful focus for discussion. It is possible, and indeed in some cases likely, that the plaintiff will sell his right to enforce the injunction,[20] and the price the defendant will have to pay will turn

---

[15] See, *e.g.*, *Kelk v. Pearson* (1871), L.R. 6 Ch. App. 809 at p. 812, *per* James, L.J.

[16] *National Provincial Plate Glass Ins. Co. v. Prudential Ass'ce Co.* (1877), 6 Ch. D. 757 at p. 761, *per* Jessel, M.R.: "the injury to the Defendants will be out of all comparison to the injury to the plaintiffs". See also *Jacomb v. Knight* (1863), 3 De G.J. & S. 533, 46 E.R. 743; *Edleston v. Crossley & Sons Ltd.* (1868), 18 L.T. 15 (Ch.) *cf. McManus v. Cooke* (1887), 35 Ch. D. 681; *Milward v. Redditch Local Board of Health* (1873), 21 W.R. 429.

[17] *Cadwell and Fleming v. C.P.R.* (1916), 37 O.L.R. 412 (H.C.), at p. 423, *per* Clute, J.: "the probable expense of restoration would be very much greater than the payment of damages".

[18] *Gilpinville Ltd. v. Dumaresq*, [1927] 1 D.L.R. 730 (N.S.S.C.). *Cf. Senior v. Pawson* (1866), L.R. 3 Eq. 330 at p. 336, refusing an injunction where a "much larger amount would be done by granting this mandatory injunction" than by awarding damages.

[19] See, *e.g.*, *infra*, §§52-58, 376-378, 385-390, 404, 426-434.

[20] The economic analysis which explores the way rights may be bought and sold is discussed, *infra*, §§ 410-424.

partly on the cost to him of complying with the decree. The more valuable the lost opportunity and added costs imposed by the injunction, the more the defendant will be prepared to pay for his release, and the more the shrewd plaintiff will be able to extract from him. This amount, in many cases, may bear virtually no relation to the actual value the plaintiff placed upon his right prior to the infringement by the defendant and may simply reflect the costs the injunction imposes on the defendant.

16   The reported cases suggest that the courts are in fact very conscious of this factor, particularly in the context of mandatory injunctions. In a 19th century case, where the plaintiff sought mandatory injunction to compel a defendant to pull down a building which interfered with the plaintiff's light, but where clearly the extent of interference was minimal, the court refused to grant a mandatory injunction which would have had the effect of delivering "the Defendants to the Plaintiff bound hand and foot, in order to be made subject to any extortionate demand that he may by possibility make".[21] In a House of Lords decision dealing with a claim for an injunction based upon interference with light, this intention by the court "not to allow an action for the protection of ancient lights to be used as a means of extorting money" was referred to, and Lord Macnaghten went on to state:

> . . . there is quite as much oppression on the part of those who invoke the assistance of the Court to protect some ancient lights, which they have never before considered of any great value, as there is on the part of those who are improving the neighbourhood by the erection of buildings that must necessarily to some extent interfere with the light of adjoining premises.[22]

17   Yet, other cases have held that an infringement of property rights requires an injunction to enable the plaintiff to vindicate the veto power his property interest gives him over use by another of what is

---

[21] *Isenberg v. East India House Estate Co. Ltd.* (1863), 3 De. G.J. & S. 263 at p. 273, 46 E.R. 637, *per* Westbury, L.C. See also *Senior v. Pawson* (1866), L.R. 3 Eq. 330 at p. 336, *per* Page Wood, V.C.: "I do not think I ought to make a decree which would enable an extortionate price to be obtained for the injury sustained by the Plaintiff." In both cases, the defendant had tried to bargain with the plaintiff who beforehand had made a substantial demand. In other cases, the courts have stayed a mandatory injunction explicitly to enable the parties to bargain: *Krehl v. Burrell* (1878), 7 Ch. D. 551 at p. 554, where Jessel, M.R., commented that the amount the plaintiff had demanded "does not appear to me to come at all within the description of extortion, especially considering the enormous benefit which would accrue to the Defendant by allowing this expensive building to remain." See also *Gilpinville Ltd. v. Dumaresq*, *supra*, footnote 18.

[22] *Colls v. Home & Colonial Stores Ltd.*, [1904] A.C. 179 (H.L.), at p. 193.

his.[23] A possible rationale for distinguishing these cases is explored in Chapter 4,[24] but for present purposes, the important point is that the effect of an injunction will be to protect the plaintiff's right, whatever its nature, as if it were his property. That is, the plaintiff will not be required to take substituted relief in the form of compensatory damages measured on an objective basis by the court for the infringement or loss of his right, but rather will be able to prevent its infringement unless he is paid his own price. The risk of over- or undercompensation inherent in any award of damages is thereby avoided, and if the plaintiff is to be given money in substitution for his right, the amount required will be fixed by the plaintiff himself based upon his own subjective valuation rather than by the court on an objective or market value basis.

18   The defendant, it is often said, is not entitled to commit a wrong and expect that he can simply pay damages for it.[25] Thus, in a 19th century case in which a mandatory injunction was sought requiring the demolition of a wall which interfered with the plaintiff's light, the Court of Appeal upheld the mandatory injunction, and Jessel, M.R., said that the granting of a mandatory injunction did not mean that the injury could not be compensated, but that "if it were not granted, the Defendant would be allowed practically to deprive the Plaintiff of the enjoyment of his property if he would give him a price for it."[26] Even where damages could be assessed for an invasion of the plaintiff's property rights, the courts still tend to award injunctive relief, and avoid the result where the plaintiff's "comfort is to be taken away, not at his own estimate, but at the value which a jury might put on it."[27] In *Goodson v. Richardson*[28] the defendant committed a deliberate and continuing trespass by laying water-pipes along a

---

[23] *Infra*, §18. See also *Kelsen v. Imperial Tobacco Co.*, [1957] 2 Q.B. 334 at p. 347, *per* McNair, J., granting a mandatory injunction in a purely commercial setting to vindicate the plaintiff's right to exploit his property for what it was worth: "both parties have in pursuance of what they claimed to be their business interests attempted to bring commercial pressure to bear one upon the another . . .".

[24] *Infra*, §430.

[25] See *e.g.*, *Krehl v. Burrell* (1878), 7 Ch. D. 551 at p. 554, *per* Jessel, M.R., referring to Lord Cairns' Act and the possibility of awarding damages rather than an injunction: "It never could have been meant to invest the Court of Chancery with a new statutory power . . . to compel people to sell their property without their consent at a valuation."

[26] *Smith v. Smith* (1875), L.R. 20 Eq. 500 at p. 504, *per* Jessel, M.R.

[27] *Dent v. Auction Mart Co.* (1866), L.R. 2 Eq. 238 at p. 247, *per* Page Wood, V.C.

[28] (1874), L.R. 9 Ch. App. 221. See also *Marriott v. East Grinstead Gas & Water Co.*, [1909] 1 Ch. 70.

highway, the title of which was held by the plaintiff. Although the plaintiff did not have unlimited rights with respect to the soil in that the upper surface had been dedicated to the public as a highway, and thus the burying of the pipes in the highway interfered in no way with his enjoyment, still, the court held, the defendant had committed a deliberate trespass and

> . . . it is enough to say that the very fact that no interference of this kind can lawfully take place without his consent, and without a bargain with him, gives his interest in this land, even in a pecuniary point of view, precisely the value which that power of veto upon its use creates, when such use is to any other person desirable and an object sought to be obtained.[29]

(5) Equitable damages

19   The courts have thus refused to permit damages in lieu of injunction to be used as a general act of expropriation to benefit the defendant who has invaded the plaintiff's rights. However, inflexible application of this principle would produce awkward results. In cases where the burden imposed on the defendant is out of all proportion to the harm the plaintiff has suffered, the courts have quite properly balked at granting an injunction, but have been able through carefully constructed damage awards still to reflect the property interest of the plaintiff.[30]

20   In *Wrotham Park Estate Co. Ltd. v. Parkside Homes Ltd.*[31] it was held that it was preferable to award damages rather than require the demolition of houses constructed in violation of a restrictive covenant. Although the plaintiffs failed to demonstrate a diminution in the market value of their property caused by the violation of the restrictive covenant, the court held it would be wrong "that the plaintiffs should receive no compensation and that the defendants should be left in undisturbed possession of the fruits of their wrongdoing"[32] and concluded that "a just substitute for a mandatory injunction would be such a sum of money as might reasonably have been demanded by the plaintiffs from [the defendants] as a quid pro quo for relaxing the covenant."[33] This was calculated on the basis of a percentage of the

---

[29] *Ibid*, at p. 224, *per* Lord Selborne, L.C.
[30] See Waddams, *The Law of Damages* (1983), §§956-962. See also Sharpe and Waddams, "Damages for Lost Opportunity to Bargain", 2 Ox. J.L.S. 290 (1982).
[31] [1974] 1 W.L.R. 798 (Ch.).
[32] *Ibid.*, at p. 812, *per* Brightman, J.
[33] *Ibid.*, at p. 815.

profit gained by the defendant in developing the site in violation of the covenant.[34]

21   In other cases, equitable damages may be measured to adjust recovery to suit particular circumstances where the plaintiff is entitled to something but not all. In *Bracewell v. Appleby*,[35] the plaintiffs had delayed in asserting their rights and had allowed the defendants to build in violation of a restriction. They were "treated as being willing to accept a fair price" and not "as if they were in the extremely powerful bargaining position which an interlocutory injunction would have given them." The award was made reflecting the amount "which the plaintiffs would accept as compensating them for loss of amenity and increased user, and which at the same time, whilst making the . . . land a viable building plot would not be so high as to deter the defendant from building at all."[36]

22   These cases of "equitable" damages reflect an attempt by the court to approximate the bargain that might have been struck had the plaintiff obtained an injunction before the defendant had spent any time or effort, thereby vindicating the plaintiff's right to bargain, while avoiding what are seen to be the unjustifiably harsh consequences of awarding injunctive relief.

(6) Other factors

(a) Insolvency

23   Insolvency of the defendant is a factor which may be taken into account in assessing whether a damages award would be inadequate for the purposes of injunctive relief. Interlocutory injunctions are now awarded restraining disposition of assets pending trial where necessary to protect the plaintiff's right to enforce his money judgment after the trial.[37] In other cases, the defendant's lack of means is often referred to as a factor favouring injunctive relief.[38] Insolvency does,

---

[34] In a Canadian case, *Arbutus Park Estates Ltd. v. Fuller* (1976), 74 D.L.R. (3d) 257 (B.C.S.C.), the defendant had built a garage in violation of a covenant requiring him to have plans approved by the plaintiffs. Although the defendant made no direct profit, he did save the cost of having such plans prepared, and the court awarded that amount in the form of damages on the ground that the plaintiffs could easily have insisted that the defendant retain an architect to prepare aesthetically appropriate plans for the garage.

[35] [1975] Ch. 408.

[36] *Ibid.*, at pp. 419-20, *per* Graham, J.

[37] *Infra*, §201 et seq.

[38] *Infra*, §551. See also *Evans Marshall & Co. Ltd. v. Bertola S.A.*, [1973] 1 W.L.R. 349 (C.A.), at p. 380; *Rosen v. Pullen* (1981), 126 D.L.R. (3d) 62 (Ont. H.C.J.).

however, raise difficult problems, particularly in the context of specific performance, and more detailed consideration is postponed until Chapter 7 where its impact on the availability of both injunctions and specific performance is dealt with.

(b) Avoiding multiplicity of suits

24   A remedy in damages may be inadequate where the award relates only to past wrongdoing, but the wrong continues. Avoiding a succession of suits is a traditional equitable justification for specific relief.[39] In the case of continuing wrongs, damages awarded for past wrongs may be seen as inadequate on the grounds that the plaintiff must sue repeatedly for each cause of action that accrues. The effect of an injunction is to stop the wrongful conduct entirely and thereby avoid the need for a succession of actions. Although specific mention is not often made in modern cases of this rationale for injunctive relief, it remains an important consideration.

25   It should be noted, however, that the objective of avoiding a multiplicity of suits can be met without awarding an injunction. Courts do have the power to award "damages in lieu of an injunction" compensating the plaintiff for prospective wrongs.[40] Such awards are discussed in the companion volume to this book[41] and are also discussed in various parts of this book as an alternative to an injunction.[42] As such awards are possible, the possibility of multiplicity of suits for future wrongs does not necessarily lead to the conclusion that an injunction should be ordered.

3. Supervision

(1) Continuing judicial direction

26   It is often said that where the obligation of the defendant requires performance of an ongoing or complex nature, the court will not grant an injunction, thereby undertaking the task of supervision.

27   The difficulty of supervision and the court's reluctance to make an order which will require further judicial direction or intervention is a familiar theme, especially in mandatory injunction cases. In an early Ontario case where the Attorney-General sought a mandatory injunction to require the repair of certain roads, Blake, C., held that:

---

[39] *Infra*, §555.
[40] *Supra*, §§19-22.
[41] Waddams, *supra*, footnote 30, §§1101-1104.
[42] See *e.g.*, *supra*, §§19-22; *infra*, §§369-371.

To admit such a jurisdiction would be, in effect, to constitute this court the general superintendent of roads throughout the province; for, if it be our duty to direct the defendants to repair this particular highway, it must be equally our duty to grant relief in every other case of neglect — which is, I think, absurd.[43]

28   Similarly, in *Powell Duffryn Steam Coal Co. v. Taff Vale Ry. Co.*[44] the plaintiff was held entitled to run its trains over part of the defendant's line, but none the less was refused a mandatory injunction on the grounds that:

It is not the practice of this Court to compel by injunction either a company or an individual to do a continuous act which requires the continuous employment of people . . . Where what is required is not merely to restrain a party from doing an act of wrong, but to oblige him to do some continuous act involving labour and care, the Court has never found its way to do this by injunction.[45]

29   The supervision problem is a genuine one, and the considerations it involves are also examined in the context of specific performance.[46] It is not intended here to suggest that the supervision problem should be ignored, but neither should it be given undue emphasis. Quite clearly, the courts have not been stopped from making orders requiring supervision where necessary. The decision in *Vane v. Lord Barnard*[47] demonstrates that even in the 18th century, when the courts were especially reluctant to award decrees involving supervision, such orders could be made. Lord Barnard had settled his estate on a trust for his son, reserving to himself a life interest, but later "having taken some displeasure against his son, got *two hundred* workmen together, and of a sudden, in a few days, stript the castle of the lead, iron, glass-doors, and boards, etc., to the value of £3,000."[48] Presumably, the castle would have been in danger of permanent harm and the son had no right of entry to effect repairs necessary to protect his vested interest. The court held that a mandatory injunction should be awarded requiring

. . . that the castle should be repaired, and put into the same condition it was in, in *August* 1714; and for that purpose a commission was to issue

---

[43] *A.-G. v. Weston Plank Road Co.* (1853), 4 Gr. 211 (C.A.), at p. 218. For a more modern statement, see *McKenzie Barge & Marine Ways Ltd. v. District of North Vancouver* (1964), 44 D.L.R. (2d) 382 (B.C.C.A.).

[44] (1874), L.R. 9 Ch. App. 331.

[45] *Ibid.*, at p. 335, *per* James, L.J.

[46] *Infra*, §§558-576.

[47] (1716), 2 Vern. 738, 23 E.R. 1082.

[48] *Ibid.*

to ascertain what ought to be repaired, and a master to see it done at the expense and charge of the defendant, Lord *Barnard* . . .[49]

30   The appointment of a commissioner and involvement of a master, at the expense of the defendant, to assist in the task of supervision shows that where necessary, techniques have long been available to enable the court to see justice done through the carrying out of complex obligations, and at the same time minimize the burden imposed upon the court itself. Modern rules of court typically provide that the court may require the act to be done by some other party at the defendant's expense in the case of disobedience.[50]

31   There are in fact many reported cases awarding decrees requiring ongoing performance, and possible further judicial involvement to supervise compliance. In *Lane v. Newdigate*,[51] the court paid lip service to the practice then in vogue of using only negative language, but at the same time made a positive decree by restraining the defendant from further "impeding, obstructing, or hindering, the Plaintiff . . . by continuing to keep the said canals, or the banks, gates, locks, or works, of the same respectively, out of good repair".[52]

32   An Ontario court adopted a similar verbal approach in order to force a railway company to meet its obligation to make available for sale on its cars a certain class of cheaper workmen's tickets, rather than offering them at inconvenient times and places.[53] The defendant was "restrained from running cars upon which these tickets are not kept for sale, and this restriction is coupled with a declaration that they are bound to sell them on their cars".[54] The propriety of the decree was confirmed by the Supreme Court of Canada.[55] Similarly, in another case an order was made enjoining the defendant from allowing to remain unperformed, work necessary to erect a pump and supply houses on adjacent land with water.[56] The jurisdiction to award a

---

[49] *Ibid.* Unfortunately, the order was not enforced, and after Lord Barnard's death, proceedings were taken to charge his estate with the damages: see discussion in 2 Eq. Ca. Abr. at p. 759, 22 E.R. 644.

[50] See, *e.g.*, Rule 579 of the Ontario Rules of Practice.

[51] (1804), 10 Ves. Jun. 192, 32 E.R. 818.

[52] *Ibid.*, at p. 194. See, *infra*, §51, for discussion of the circuitous form of wording.

[53] *City of Hamilton v. Hamilton Street Ry. Co.* (1904), 8 O.L.R. 642 (H.C.J.), affd 10 O.L.R. 594 (C.A.), affd 39 S.C.R. 673.

[54] 8 O.L.R. at p. 646, *per* Street, J.

[55] *Supra*, footnote 53. *Cf. City of Kingston v. Kingston, Portsmouth and Cataraqui Electric Ry. Co.* (1898), 25 O.A.R. 462, refusing an injunction against operating a railway except in compliance with an agreement, and *A.-G. ex rel. Jarvis v. International Bridge Co.* (1875), 22 Gr. 298, where a similar verbal ploy was rejected.

[56] *Cooke v. Chilcott* (1876), 3 Ch. D. 694. See also *Strelley v. Pearson* (1880), 15 Ch. D. 113, where Fry, J., stated that there was jurisdiction to enjoin the defendant from ceasing to pump water out of a mine.

mandatory injunction to restore a building removed from mortgaged premises was asserted in an early Ontario case.[57] There are reported instances of mandatory injunctions to effect repairs,[58] construct a fence,[59] build a wall and repair a footpath,[60] vote shares as directed by the beneficial owner, [61] and redirect mail to the proper recipient.[62]

33   Unfortunately, too little has been made of these cases where the court has been willing to enforce ongoing obligations or complex duties which may well involve it in further proceedings to enforce the order. Perhaps the most notable example of the court's willingness to enforce such a duty, and undertake the possibility of future litigation is the "moving mountain" case, *Kennard v. Cory Bros.*[63] In that case, a coal-mine operator in South Wales had tipped vast quantities of colliery refuse, estimated to weigh 500,000 tons, on a hillside without taking steps to drain away water descending from further up the hill. Water running down the hill had a lubricating effect, and a serious slide occurred. Two actions were brought, the first by the Attorney-General, in public nuisance, the second by the owner of certain lands damaged by the slide. At an early stage, expert advisors were consulted, and it was agreed that the parties would jointly pay the cost of remedial drainage works to avoid a further slide, the cost of such works ultimately to be borne by the loser. Both actions were tried together, and both plaintiffs were successful. The trial judge, Sargant, J., awarded the following relief: (1) a declaration of the defendants' liability for the past and any future slide; (2) a perpetual injunction restraining further tipping; (3) an inquiry as to the plaintiff's damages; and (4) liberty to the plaintiff to apply, in case of apprehended damage, for a mandatory injunction to compel the defendants "to do and execute such works as might be necessary to protect permanently the plaintiffs' buildings or otherwise to abate the nuisance caused by the acts of the defendant company or to keep open the present works".[64]

34   This order, which clearly contemplated an ongoing involvement by the court to ensure that the plaintiff's rights were protected, was re-

---

[57] *Meyers v. Smith* (1869), 15 Gr. 616.

[58] *Lane v. Newdigate, supra,* footnote 51; *infra,* §§33-38.

[59] *Masson v. Grand Junction Ry. Co.* (1879), 26 Gr. at p. 289*n* (C.A.).

[60] *A.-G. v. Roe,* [1915] 1 Ch. 235.

[61] *Puddephatt v. Leith,* [1916] 1 Ch. 200.

[62] *Hermann Loog v. Bean* (1884), 26 Ch. D. 306 (C.A.).

[63] [1922] 1 Ch. 265, affd [1922] 2 Ch. 1 (C.A.).

[64] [1922] 1 Ch. at p. 267, relating what had been done on an earlier application.

versed by the Court of Appeal, but restored by the House of Lords,[65] although the appeal was argued on substantive rather than remedial points. Later, the plaintiffs reapplied for a mandatory injunction as there was blockage in the drainage works designed to alleviate the buildup of water and consequent lubricating effect conducive to further slides. The defendants argued that the court could not supervise such an order and should not impose a continuing obligation to repair, and that the plaintiff should rather be awarded damages, measured either by the cost of effecting the maintenance and repairs, the drains being in fact on the plaintiff's land, or by the diminution in market value of the plaintiff's land represented by the capital cost of maintaining these drainage works. Sargant, J., rejected the defendants' arguments and awarded a mandatory injunction and his order was upheld by the Court of Appeal.[66] The order was, he explained, framed rather narrowly "to avoid casting upon [the defendants] a burden greater than was absolutely necessary for the reasonable protection of the plaintiffs", and he had avoided a broadly worded order that "the defendants should do works, to be ascertained if necessary by the report of some engineer appointed for the purpose, which would have the result of rendering the tips permanently innocuous apart from any continuing process of maintenance or repair."[67]

35   In the Court of Appeal, Lord Sterndale, M.R., referred to the question of superintendence, but added "I do not find that there is any objection in principle to the imposition of such an obligation upon a wrongdoer."[68] Scrutton, L.J., held that while there was a "general rule" against making orders

> . . . to do undefined works which may require continuous supervision in the sense of continuous applications to see whether the undefined works ordered to be done are or are not being carried out . . . [still] . . . the Court has never defined in one way or the other, and perhaps cannot define, exactly where it will draw the line as to which order it will make and as to which order it will not make.[69]

Scrutton, L.J., also noted that orders had been made on occasion although

> "it cannot be foreseen at the time when the order is made exactly what maintenance will be required, and when and though that involves that

---

[65] *A.-G. v. Cory Brothers & Co. Ltd.*, [1921] 1 A.C. 521 (H.L.).
[66] *Supra*, footnote 63.
[67] [1922] 1 Ch. at pp. 274-5.
[68] [1922] 2 Ch. at p. 13.
[69] *Ibid.*, at pp. 20-21.

applications from time to time may have to be made to the Court to supervise the carrying out of the order."[70]

36　　　The case bears close examination. Although by no means typical, it does demonstrate the possibility of the court imposing an ongoing obligation, and openly allowing for repeated applications for further specific direction as to the nature of work to be done. The order avoided the guesswork and likely inadequacy of a damages award, as well as the extraordinary expenditure which would have been imposed by a general mandatory order requiring the defendant to dispose of the problem once and for all. The court refused to be bound by choice between these extremes and opted instead for an approach which it knew might involve further litigation, presumably because the threat of harm to the plaintiff was sufficiently grave to warrant this expenditure of judicial time and effort.

37　　　The description of the disinclination of the court to award specific relief in cases requiring supervision as a practice or rule of thumb, rather than a firm rule, is noted as well in the discussion of specific performance.[71] This same approach was echoed more recently in a mandatory injunction case where it was stated that while the jurisdiction will be exercised only in exceptional circumstances, "it cannot be regarded as an absolute and inflexible rule that the court will never grant an injunction requiring a person to do a series of acts requiring the continuous employment of people over a number of years."[72]

38　　　*A.-G. v. Birmingham, Tame and Rea District Drainage Board*[73] provides another example of ongoing involvement by the court to provide an equitable remedy where the dispute does not admit of a simple immediate solution. The Attorney-General sought an injunction restraining the defendant board from discharging sewage into the river Tame in contravention of the Public Health Act, 1875. In 1899, the plaintiff applied for an interlocutory injunction which was dismissed, but on the basis of the defendants' undertaking to conduct their operations under the supervision of an engineer agreed to by the parties. That engineer prepared a report, and upon the defendants' undertaking to carry out his recommendations with reasonable dispatch, the trial was adjourned for several months. A further adjournment was granted to allow the defendants to continue imple-

---

[70] *Ibid.*, at p. 21.

[71] *Infra*, Chapter 7.

[72] *Gravesham Borough Council v. British Railways Bd.*, [1978] Ch. 379 at p. 405, *per* Slade, J.

[73] [1910] 1 Ch. 48 (C.A.), affd [1912] A.C. 788 (H.L.).

mentation of the recommendations. A considerable amount of money was spent by the defendants over a seven-year period trying to improve the quality of its effluent, but the plaintiff was still not satisfied with the results, and decided to bring the matter on for trial. Kekewich, J., granted an injunction. The defendant board appealed, and asked for a stay to enable it to carry out further extensive works. The appeal was adjourned from time to time, during which a further considerable sum was spent by the defendants. When the matter came on before the Court of Appeal there was a conflict in evidence as to the sufficiency of the purification effect of these works, and the court appointed an expert to inquire and report. That report was favourable to the defendants, and was accepted by the Court of Appeal. In the circumstances, the Court of Appeal held that it should accept the defendants' undertaking to use their best endeavours to prevent further breach of the Act, and discharge the injunction. This would

> . . . while removing the sword over the heads of the defendants [in the shape of a perpetual injunction], and while enabling them to discharge their duties without the prejudice created by such an injunction, impose upon them such obligations as the statute desires should be imposed upon them and will give to the plaintiffs all such rights as they ought to have.[74]

The order was, according to Farwell, L.J., "beneficial to all parties" in that it did "no harm to the plaintiffs, because it avoids the cumbrous and unsatisfactory motion for a writ of sequestration, in which the applicant is hampered by the fact that he has to prove wilful disobedience to the order".[75] On further appeal to the House of Lords, the right of the Court of Appeal to hear further evidence, order the appraiser's report without consent of both parties and dissolve the injunction was upheld. The Court of Appeal was entitled to look at the changes which had occurred between the trial and appeal, just as the trial judge might have postponed the injunction to await the results of the works undertaken by the defendant. As Lord Gorell put it, "there was nothing to prevent the Court of Appeal from discharging or moulding the injunction as it thought fit in the circumstances".[76] The House of Lords did vary the order to make the obligation of the defendants even more specific, requiring that the defendants should undertake that the existing results as described by the experts be maintained.

[74] [1910] 1 Ch. at p. 56, *per* Cozens-Hardy, M.R.
[75] *Ibid.*, at p. 62.
[76] [1912] A.C. at p. 806 (H.L.).

(2) Problems of definition

39   Supervision involves a problem of definition, and here, injunctions perhaps pose more of a problem than does specific performance where often the parties themselves have by their agreement provided the detailed elaboration of what is required of the defendant. Quite clearly, in formulating injunction orders, the courts should avoid vague or ambiguous language which fails to give the defendant proper guidance or which in effect postpones determination of what actually constitutes a violation of the plaintiff's rights.[77] It is unfair to the defendant to do nothing more than warn him not to do anything wrong, and resolve the important questions of detail on a contempt application.[78] When an issue is "ripe for decision between the parties"[79] the courts should decide then and there.

40   Still, it has often been said that for negative injunctions, a general form is to be used,[80] provided it gives sufficient guidance, and orders prohibiting the defendant from acting "in the manner hitherto pursued by him or in any other manner so as to cause a nuisance"[81] and "in the manner complained of by the plaintiffs in this motion or otherwise so as to cause a nuisance"[82] have been approved by appellate courts.[83]

41   Rather more specificity is required for mandatory orders, not only so that the defendant will have a clear idea of what he is required to do, but also so that the court will be able to assess accurately the burden its order imposes.[84] A mandatory order insists upon a positive course of action, the burden of which may be difficult to assess unless the details of the obligation are defined. For example, one can estimate the burden imposed by an order forbidding the further dis-

---

[77] *Low v. Innes* (1864), 4 De G. J. & S. 286 at pp. 295-6, 46 E.R. 929, *per* Westbury, L.C.; *A.-G. v. Staffordshire County Council*, [1905] 1 Ch. 336 at p. 342, *per* Joyce, J.

[78] See *Cother v. Midland Ry. Co.* (1848), 2 Ph. 469 at p. 471, 41 E.R. 1025, *per* Cottenham L.C.

[79] *Parker v. First Avenue Hotel Co.* (1883), 24 Ch. D. 282 (C.A.), at p. 285, *per* Cotton, L.J.

[80] *Parkers Dye Works Ltd. v. Smith* (1914), 20 D.L.R. 500, 32 O.L.R. 169 (S.C. App. Div.); *Alex Pirie & Sons Ltd. v. Earl of Kintore*, [1906] A.C. 478 (H.L.), at p. 482; *Savage v. MacKenzie* (1961), 25 D.L.R. (2d) 175 (N.B.S.C. App. Div.).

[81] *Beamish v. Glenn* (1916), 28 D.L.R. 702, 36 O.L.R. 10 (S.C. App. Div.).

[82] *Thompson-Schwab v. Costaki*, [1956] 1 W.L.R. 335 (C.A.).

[83] Compare, however, *Kennaway v. Thompson*, [1981] Q.B. 88 (C.A.), discussed, *infra*, §§ 389, 395.

[84] *Redland Bricks Ltd. v. Morris*, [1970] A.C. 652 (H.L.); *Fishenden v. Higgs & Hill Ltd.* (1935), 153 L.T. 128 (C.A.), at p. 142, *per* Maugham, L.J.

charge of a pollutant into a river. Depending on the circumstances, the defendant may have to move, change his method, or perhaps devote his property to another use. On the other hand, an order requiring the defendant to clean up a river he has polluted might well impose a burden which could not be measured at the time such an order was made. The court could not accurately balance the advantage to be gained against the burden imposed.

42   It was this very consideration which played an important role in the decision of the House of Lords in *Redland Bricks Ltd. v. Morris*.[85] There, an excavation on the defendants' land undermined the support for the plaintiffs' property. A slip occurred and further slippage was likely if support was not restored. An injunction was awarded requiring the defendants to "take all necessary steps to restore the support to the [plaintiffs'] land within a period of six months".[86] The value of the plaintiffs' land was estimated to be about £1,500, whereas the expense required to restore support was said to be in the region of £30,000. The order was upheld on appeal but reversed by the House of Lords, one of the main grounds being that the order failed "to see that the defendant knows exactly in fact what he has to do and this means not as a matter of law but as a matter of fact, so that in carrying out an order he can give his contractors the proper instructions."[87]

43   However, Lord Upjohn, who delivered the unanimous judgment, apparently did not reject the possibility that a proper order could be made in such a case, and said that the judge "might have ordered the appellants to carry out the remedial works described by the respondents' expert in his evidence though it would have to be set out in great detail."[88] Such an order would, however, have imposed an unacceptable burden on the defendant, given the disproportionate expense. However,

> . . . the order in fact imposed went much further; it imposed an unlimited and unqualified obligation upon the appellants, and I do not know how they could have attempted to comply with it. The expenditure of the sum of £30,000 which I have just mentioned would not necessarily have complied with it for though it would in all probability have prevented any further damage it was not guaranteed to do so and that is what in effect the mandatory order of the learned judge required.[89]

---

[85] *Supra*, footnote 84.
[86] *Supra*, footnote 84, at p. 656.
[87] *Supra*, at p. 666.
[88] *Supra*, at p. 667.
[89] *Supra*, at p. 667.

44   Thus, the decision rests not so much on the impossibility of making
a mandatory order enforcing an obligation of a detailed and complex
nature, but rather on the point that at the time the order is made, the
court should be in a position to assess the cost of compliance. As already noted, in many cases it may be difficult at the date of trial to
say exactly what must be done and it may be that time and further
applications to the court to clarify and specify the details of the defendants' obligation are required. Thus, to the extent that *Redland
Bricks* can be taken to stand for the proposition that the court must
resolve the entire issue once and for all at the hearing, it does impose
a significant constraint on the availability of mandatory injunctions.

45   On the other hand, as already noted, other courts have taken a
more flexible approach on this issue.[90] One problem is that committal
proceedings are admittedly a "most inconvenient and disagreeable"[91]
form for the resolution of questions of details of the defendants' performance. However, the form need not determine the substance.
While coercive measures are the ultimate threat for wilful failure to
comply, they are the last resort, and detailed questions of obligation
and compliance can be resolved without an order of imprisonment.[92]
If necessary, the court can make an order by which it implicitly undertakes to review the circumstances and the obligation imposed as
matters proceed. In the *Kennard* case, the court refused to restrict itself to a narrow choice between no injunction or an injunction which
was too vague.[93] It is not uncommon in nuisance cases to make orders which extend leave to apply, or suspend operation pending the
defendants' attempts to abate the problem.[94] Such orders recognize
the impracticality of attempting to dispose finally of the litigation at
the trial, and the need in appropriate circumstances to afford the
plaintiff the injunction to which he is entitled rather than deny it on
grounds of judicial inconvenience or expense.

46   If the court is prepared, in effect, to keep the suit alive, creative
use can be made of mandatory as well as negative injunction orders.
The initial order decides only what is then ripe for decision, and as

---

[90] *Supra*, §§33-38.

[91] *Hackett v. Baiss* (1875), L.R. 20 Eq. 494 at p. 499, *per* Jessel, M.R.

[92] See *A.-G. B.C. ex rel. Eaton v. Haney Speedways Ltd.* (1963), 41 D.L.R. (2d) 85
(B.C.S.C.); *Ireson v. Holt Timber Co.* (1913), 18 D.L.R. 604 at p. 614, 30 O.L.R.
at p. 218 at pp. 229-30 (S.C. App. Div.), *per* Riddell, J.A.; *Elliot v. North Eastern
Ry. Co.* (1863), 10 H.L.C. 333 at p. 359, 11 E.R. 1055.

[93] *Supra*, §§33-36.

[94] *Infra*, §§391-394.

matters proceed, supplementary direction or qualifications as to the defendants' obligation can be made.

(3) Supervision — conclusion

47   In Chapter 7, the added judicial costs of specific relief in the contractual setting are discussed.[95] A specific order involves a risk that subsequent proceedings may be required to force the defendant to comply, or to assess the adequacy of his compliance efforts. Courts prefer orders which are final. It is argued in Chapter 7 that refusing specific relief because of supervision problems rests on a desire to avoid undue expenditure of judicial resources on the dispute which would result from repeated applications to the court to ensure compliance.

48   There are many situations however in which the courts do undertake an ongoing role in the regulation and management of the litigant's affairs. In family law, custody and access orders are subject to ongoing review. Maintenance orders involve not only the imposition on the defendant of an ongoing obligation of indefinite duration, but also the reservation of the power to alter the nature of that obligation should circumstances change. In the commercial area, orders appointing receivers directly involve the court in the management of the most complex business arrangements. Similarly, the jurisdiction to protect infants and the mentally incompetent often involves repeated application to the court for directions, as does the more familiar jurisdiction concerning the administration of estates and trusts. Even with damages, questions of detail are often left to be resolved by a master on the basis of principles established by the trial judgment.

49   In all of these situations, there is a recognition of the impossibility or impracticality of trying to resolve the matter once and for all on one single application, and a willingness to incur the cost of ongoing judicial involvement. There is really no reason why, in appropriate cases, a similar approach cannot be adopted in the case of injunctions. Where an injunction is an appropriate and preferred remedy, it is surely harsh to deprive the plaintiff of its benefit out of fear of litigation costs, unless those costs are so great as to outweigh the advantage of affording appropriate remedial relief.

---

[95] *Infra*, §§568-576.

4. Mandatory Injunctions

50   There are certain special considerations which apply in the case of mandatory injunctions which can be examined most conveniently in this introductory chapter.

51   At one time, the court of equity was reluctant to grant mandatory injunctions, but there was never an absolute rule against such orders.[96] By the early 19th century, chancery regularly issued mandatory injunctions, although a curiously circuitous verbal form of order was commonly used.[97] A defendant enjoined from permitting a building to remain standing was, however, in no doubt at all that positive action on his part was called for. By the end of the 19th century, this lip service to former doubts as to the propriety of a directly mandatory order was abandoned.[98] While the formalism has gone, the caution remains, and repeating what was expressed in an early case, it is often said that a mandatory injunction will not be granted "except in cases in which extreme, or at all events very serious, damage will ensue from [the court's] interference being withheld."[99]

52   Still, it seems equally clear that the discretion to award mandatory injunctions is governed by the same principles which apply to any form of injunctive relief,[100] and the analysis is altered only by the fact that a mandatory order requires the defendant to undertake a positive course of action. This is significant in two respects. First, the imposition of an obligation to act positively affects the balance of burden and benefit familiar in all injunction cases. Secondly, requiring positive acts raises the issues examined in the preceding section on definition and the court's reluctance to become involved in ongoing supervision of complex obligations.

---

[96] See, *e.g.*, *Lane v. Newdigate* (1804), 10 Ves. Jun. 192 at p. 194, 32 E.R. 818, where Lord Eldon doubted his power to order repairs but made an order restraining the defendant from "farther impeding, obstructing, or hindering, the Plaintiff . . . by continuing to keep the said canals, or the banks, gates, locks, or works, of the same respectively, out of good repair. . .".

[97] *Supra*, footnote 96. See *e.g.*, *Baxter v. Bower* (1875), 33 L.T. 41 (C.A.); see also *Farwell v. Wallbridge* (1851), 2 Gr. 332, where this form of order was described as objectionable but established in practice; *Saunders v. William Richards Co.* (1901), 2 N.B. Eq. 303.

[98] In *Jackson v. Normanby Brick Co.*, [1899] 1 Ch. 438 (C.A.), Lindley, M.R., stated at p. 439 that it would be "better for the Court to say in plain terms what it means, and in direct words to order the buildings to be pulled down and removed."

[99] *Durell v. Pritchard* (1865), L.R. 1 Ch. App. 244 at p. 250.

[100] See *Hermann Loog v. Bean* (1884), 26 Ch. D. 306 (C.A.), at p. 314; *Puddephatt v. Leith*, [1916] 1 Ch. 200.

(1) Burden and benefit

53   If an injunction is granted before the defendant has commenced his wrongful activity, the burden it imposes on the defendant is relatively low. He is faced with an order requiring him to respect the plaintiff's rights, and he will have incurred no cost and expended no effort before he is stopped. More often, however, the defendant will have committed a wrong or at least be well on the way, and an injunction in favour of the plaintiff will, on account of costs already incurred, impose more of a burden than would be represented only by the cost of stopping itself. Some, if not all, of the costs incurred by the defendant in reliance on the belief that he would not be stopped are lost. A mandatory order imposes an obligation to take positive steps to set matters right, and hence involves not only forgoing the benefit of costs already incurred, but also the imposition of the additional costs which will be incurred by that positive course of action. To the extent that the availability of injunctive relief is determined by a balance of burden and benefit, mandatory injunctions are often relatively costly remedies, and for that reason, more difficult to obtain.

54   On the other hand, it is easy to overstate the added burden imposed by a mandatory order. Prohibitive orders often have the practical effect of requiring a positive course of action. In nuisance cases, for instance, a negative injunction restraining the continuation of a nuisance in effect usually requires the defendant to take positive steps to correct a situation, and these steps may be extremely costly. As will be seen in Chapter 4, courts do take this factor into account in nuisance cases, but the concern over cost or burden is usually the focus of more explicit concern where mandatory relief is sought.

55   There are many examples illustrating judicial concern for the costliness of mandatory injunctions as a determining factor. Thus, for example, in *Haggerty v. Latreille*,[101] the Ontario Court of Appeal refused to award a mandatory injunction to compel the defendant to remove a large amount of fill interfering with the plaintiff's shore line "in view of the comparatively trifling injury which has been caused to the appellant [plaintiff] and the very considerable expense that the respondents [defendants] would be put to if a mandatory order were granted".[102] Similarly, in a decision of the British Columbia Court of Appeal,[103] the court refused to award a mandatory injunction requir-

---

[101] (1913), 14 D.L.R. 532, 29 O.L.R. 300 (S.C. App. Div.).
[102] *Ibid.*, at p. 541 D.L.R., pp. 311-12 O.L.R., *per* Meredith, C.J.O.
[103] *Clark v. McKenzie*, [1930] 2 D.L.R. 843 (B.C.C.A.).

ing the defendant to remove a building which had been inadvertently erected so as to encroach upon the plaintiff's lot line. The cost to the defendant of removal was $1,500; the value of the land affected $15; and the value of the plaintiff's entire lot only $1,000.[104]

56   It is not suggested that cost or burden should not be considered, but merely that it is inappropriate to direct undue attention to this factor in mandatory cases as significantly higher costs are often imposed by prohibitive injunctions when considerably less concern is expressed.[105]

57   Where a mandatory injunction is not restorative but rather sought to enforce some positive duty to act, expenditures already made and foregone if an injunction is granted are unlikely to be involved. However, the balance of burden and benefit may still be relevant. For example, in *A.-G. v. Colchester Corp.*,[106] the plaintiff sued for a mandatory injunction to require the defendant to comply with a duty allegedly imposed by an ancient franchise to run a ferry. The evidence disclosed that the ferry could be run only at a loss, and Lord Goddard C.J., held that "it would seem to be inequitable to order the [defendant] to continue working it".[107]

58   The significance of balancing burden and benefit and the different treatment accorded prohibitive and mandatory injunctions is well illustrated by the cases dealing with express negative covenants. Where the defendant has expressly undertaken not to do something, a prohibitive injunction stopping him from so behaving will be readily granted.[108] In such cases, the courts have said that as the defendant agreed with his "eyes open"[109] not to do what he is being stopped from doing, he cannot complain of the burden an injunction would impose. However, where the plaintiff sues after the defendant has violated his agreement and where a mandatory order is required, different considerations are brought to bear, even though the plaintiff still bases his claim upon an express negative covenant. In one case, the court acknowledged the fact that a prohibitive injunction would be readily available but went on to say that "where, however, the act has been done, and the question is whether or not a mandatory injunction should be granted, slightly different considerations

---

[104] Encroachment cases are discussed further, *infra*, §434.

[105] *Infra*, §378; *supra*, §54.

[106] [1955] 2 Q.B. 207.

[107] *Ibid.*, at p. 217.

[108] *Doherty v. Allman* (1878), 3 App. Cas. 709, discussed, *infra*, Chapter 9.

[109] *Ibid.*, at p. 720, *per* Cairns, L.C.

obviously apply."[110] The court went on to hold that "if the granting of a mandatory order would inflict damage upon the defendant out of all proportion to the relief which the plaintiff ought to obtain, the Court will, in my opinion, and ought, in my judgment, to refuse it."[111] A similar principle has been acted on in several other cases.[112]

(2) Deliberateness of defendant's conduct

59   The discretion to grant or withhold mandatory injunctions, however, involves more than a balance of burden and benefit. In the first place, it would be wrong to put undue emphasis on the state of affairs existing at the time of the trial. If the defendant would have been stopped by a prohibitive injunction from interfering with the plaintiff's rights before his own conduct made restorative measures necessary, it by no means follows that he should be in a better position having accomplished his wrong. The plaintiff should hardly be at a disadvantage simply because the defendant raced ahead with his wrongful conduct.[113] While it is clear that where circumstances require positive acts to put matters right, the added cost to the defendant is a material consideration, it is also appropriate to consider the extent of his blameworthiness for the existence of the state of affairs which have altered the situation so as to make the injunction so costly. The defendant who has acted in reliance on a *bona fide* but mistaken belief that his activity would not invade the plaintiff's rights will not be treated the same as the defendant who has acted in a high-handed or deliberate fashion. Similarly, a defendant who has behaved negligently will be given less consideration than one who has behaved without fault.

60   Thus, in *Redland Bricks Ltd. v. Morris*,[114] the House of Lords held

---

[110] *Sharp v. Harrison*, [1922] 1 Ch. 502 at p. 512, *per* Astbury, J.

[111] *Ibid.*, at p. 515.

[112] *Bowes v. Law* (1870), L.R. 9 Eq. 636; *Kilbey v. Haviland* (1871), 19 W.R. 698 (Ch.); *Shepherd Homes Ltd. v. Sandham*, [1971] Ch. 340. *Cf.*, however, *Charrington v. Simons & Co.*, [1971] 2 All E.R. 588 (C.A.); *Manners v. Johnson* (1875), 1 Ch. D. 673.

[113] This may constitute grounds for an interlocutory mandatory injunction: *infra*, §191. See also *Luganda v. Service Hotels*, [1969] 2 Ch. 209 (C.A.), at p. 220, *per* Denning, M.R., granting an interlocutory mandatory injunction reinstating a tenant:

> They were wrong to take the law into their own hands. If the management had not changed the lock . . . the court would have granted an injunction to prevent the management from locking him [the plaintiff] out. They should not be in a better position by wrongfully locking him out . . . "In a court of equity, wrongful acts are no passport to favour."

[114] [1970] A.C. 652 (H.L.)

that a mandatory injunction should not be awarded against the defendant who had inadvertently undermined support for his neighbour's property requiring restoration works, estimated to cost £30,000, to save a market garden plot valued at about £1,500. The House of Lords emphasized that the defendants "did not act either wantonly or in plain disregard of their neighbours' rights"[115] and that they had retained engineers and geologists to advise them prior to commencing their operations. Delivering the unanimous judgment of the House of Lords, Lord Upjohn held that:

> . . . the amount to be expended under a mandatory order by the defendant must be balanced . . . against the anticipated possible damage to the plaintiff and if, on such balance, it seems unreasonable to inflict such expenditure . . . then the court must exercise its jurisdiction accordingly.[116]

Lord Upjohn emphasized the distinction, however, between a defendant who "has acted reasonably, though in the event wrongly," and one who has acted "without regard to his neighbour's rights, or has tried to steal a march on him or has tried to evade the jurisdiction of the courts".[117]

61   By contrast, in *Gross v. Wright*[118] the Supreme Court of Canada upheld a mandatory order requiring the demolition of a party wall built to an uneven thickness where it appeared that the defendant had deliberately deceived the plaintiff and gained access to his property to construct the wall in a manner which violated an agreement between the parties and which very much favoured the defendant. Although on the plaintiff's side the wall had been constructed in a manner consistent with the agreement, the defendant had reduced its thickness on his own side. Thus, it could hardly be said that the loss to the plaintiff was substantial, but still the court held that given the deliberate and deceitful nature of the defendant's conduct an order requiring the wall to be brought down was appropriate.

62   Similarly, in an Irish case often cited in this context, *Woodhouse v. Newry Navigation Co.*,[119] the court somewhat reluctantly awarded a mandatory injunction which clearly imposed a cost on the defendants out of all proportion to the benefit accruing to the plaintiff, on the

---

[115] *Ibid.*, at p. 663.

[116] *Ibid.*, at p. 666.

[117] *Ibid.*

[118] [1923] S.C.R. 214, [1923] 2 D.L.R. 171. See also *Esso Petroleum Co. Ltd. v. Kingswood Motors (Addlestone) Ltd.*, [1974] Q.B. 142.

[119] [1898] 1 I.R. 161 (C.A.).

grounds that a wilful or at least reckless trespass had been committed. Orders such as these have an almost punitive aspect and are made perhaps as much to act as a lesson to others as to do justice to the plaintiff. As discussed above,[120] such orders may in practical terms have the effect of conferring a windfall gain upon the plaintiff as a result of post-judgment bargaining.

(3) Plaintiff's vigilance

63   Another factor relevant to assessing the fairness of imposing the burden of a mandatory order is the plaintiff's vigilance.[121] The defendant who acts in the face of a firm warning that the plaintiff intends to assert his rights is quite clearly less entitled to plead that the burden of restoring matters ought not to be imposed upon him, than if he had proceeded innocently and without warning.[122] Similarly, a plaintiff who fails to assert his rights in the face of conduct he later complains of can be said to have lulled the defendant into the belief that he will not be stopped, and is thereby less entitled to insist that the defendant bear the burden of restoration.[123] Mere delay is not enough — "quiescence is not acquiesence"[124] — the delay must be such as induced some act of the defendant rendering it inequitable to later impose the burden of restorative measures upon him.[125]

64   It has sometimes been said that in the face of early and clear protest by the plaintiffs, and especially after the commencement of proceedings, the defendant proceeds at his own peril, and orders requiring the demolition of works undertaken after such warning are not at all uncommon.[126]

65   It has been held, however, that the plaintiffs need not seek an interim injunction to prevent the defendants from proceeding.[127] One

---

[120] *Supra*, §§15-16.

[121] See, *infra*, §§82-102, for discussion of delay and laches.

[122] *Grand Junction Canal Co. v. Shugar* (1871), L.R. 6 Ch. App. 483.

[123] *Young v. Star Omnibus Co. Ltd.* (1902), 86 L.T. 41 (Ch.); *Gaskin v. Balls* (1879), 13 Ch. D. 324 (C.A.); *Stanley v. Earl of Shrewsbury* (1875), L.R. 19 Eq. 616.

[124] *Woodhouse v. Newry Navigation Co.*, *supra*, footnote 119, at p. 170, *per* Fitz Gibbon, L.J.; *Gale v. Abbott* (1862), 6 L.T. 852 (Ch.).

[125] *Infra*, §§84-87. Where the plaintiff stands by because he is unaware of the effect the defendant's conduct will have, a mandatory injunction may still be granted: see, *e.g.*, *Baxter v. Bower* (1875), 33 L.T. 41 (C.A.).

[126] *Smith v. Day* (1880), 13 Ch. D. 651 (C.A.). See also the interlocutory cases discussed, *infra*, §191.

[127] *Wrotham Park Estate Co. Ltd. v. Parkside Homes Ltd.*, [1974] 1 W.L.R. 798 (Ch.); *Gale v. Abbott* (1862), 6 L.T. 852 (Ch.).

important reason why the plaintiff may not seek interlocutory relief is that he would be required to give an undertaking in damages.[128] If the right upon which he relies is uncertain or if the equities are evenly balanced, protection gained by an interlocutory injunction comes at a considerable risk and price to the plaintiff. The effect of saying that the plaintiff need not necessarily have sought interlocutory relief is to shift the risk of proceeding to the defendant. It is not clear, however, that the costs of delay produced by the uncertainty of the legal position should inevitably be borne by the party undertaking the activity. The issue, of course, arises only where the plaintiff wins in the end, so that the uncertainty has been resolved in the plaintiff's favour. However, to the extent that the courts are already prepared to take into account the burden on the defendant imposed by mandatory relief, and the reasonableness of the defendant's conduct in proceeding with a building or construction, it would appear consistent also to consider the degree of resoluteness exhibited by the plaintiff in asserting his rights. It is suggested, then, that the plaintiff's failure to seek interim relief, if explained for no other reason than a desire to avoid having to give an undertaking in damages, is a factor which ought to be taken into account in determining the appropriateness of mandatory relief at the trial.

5. The Problem of Prematurity

66   All injunctions are future looking in the sense that they are intended to prevent or avoid harm rather than compensate for an injury already suffered. When the plaintiff has already suffered harm, although the remedial focus is often on the future, what has happened in the past provides the basis for assessing the appropriateness of the remedy.[129] The court is able to see from what has already happened the nature and extent of the future threat posed by the defendant's conduct, and is able to assess the appropriateness of injunctive relief on the basis of that experience. The situation has crystallized in the sense that the defendant's course of conduct is settled, its effect upon the plaintiff is known, and the relative benefits to the plaintiff, and the burdens an injunction would impose on the defendant, can be assessed.

67   Where the harm to the plaintiff has yet to occur the problems of prediction are encountered. Here, the plaintiff sues *quia timet* — be-

---

[128] *Infra*, §§173-178.

[129] For a theoretical discussion of the problems of remedial prediction, see Leubsdorf, "Remedies for Uncertainty", 61 Boston U.L. Rev. 132 (1981).

cause he fears — and the judgment as to the propriety of injunctive relief must be made without the advantage of actual evidence as to the nature of harm inflicted on the plaintiff. The court is asked to predict that harm will occur in the future and that the harm is of a type that ought to be prevented by injunction. Thus, while all injunctions involve predicting the future, the label *quia timet* and the problem of prematurity relate to the situation where the difficulties of prediction are more acute in that the plaintiff is asking for injunctive relief before he has suffered any of the harm to be prevented by the injunction.

68   The jurisdiction to award *quia timet* injunctions is undoubted.[130] It is said to be "an illustration of the rule that prevention is better than cure"[131] especially where the cure in the form of damages may be uncertain, and the courts have extolled their preventive function:

> No part of the jurisdiction of the old Court of Chancery was considered more valuable than that exercise of jurisdiction which prevented material injury being inflicted, and no subject was more frequently the cause of bills for injunction than the class of cases which were brought to restrain threatened injury as distinguished from injury which was already accomplished.[132]

69   All the same, despite this apparent enthusiasm, the courts have adopted a cautious approach when asked to award an injunction prior to actual harm being suffered, and have said that there must be a high degree of probability that the harm will in fact occur.

70   One of the leading cases in this area, *Fletcher v. Bealey*,[133] provides striking illustration of this cautious approach. The plaintiff manufactured high quality white paper and required pure water for the process. The defendant had leased property upstream on the banks of the same river from which the plaintiff drew water and the defendant used this plot to dump a waste product from its alkali manufac-

---

[130] See, *e.g.*, *Crowder v. Tinkler* (1816), 19 Ves. Jun. 617 at p. 622, 34 E.R. 645; *B.C. Telephone Co. v. Morrison*, [1921] 1 W.W.R. 694 (B.C.S.C.); *Steeves Dairy v. Twin City Co-op. Milk Producers Ass'n*, [1926] 1 D.L.R. 130 (B.C.S.C.), at p. 140, *per* Macdonald, J.: "if the intention to do the act complained of be proved to exist or if an act is threatened, which, in the opinion of the Court, if completed, would give a ground of action, there is a foundation for the exercise of the jurisdiction." In *Scott Rur. Mun. v. Edwards*, [1934] S.C.R. 332, [1934] 3 D.L.R. 793, the Supreme Court of Canada upheld a *quia timet* injunction for the reasons given by the Saskatchewan Court of Appeal where Martin, J.A., said at p. 796: "If a fair case of prospective injury is made out the Court has jurisdiction to interfere before waste has actually been committed."

[131] *Re Anderson-Berry*, [1928] Ch. 290 (C.A.), at p. 307, *per* Sargant, L.J.

[132] *Frearson v. Loe* (1878), 9 Ch. D. 48 at p. 65, *per* Jessel, M.R.

[133] (1885), 28 Ch. D. 688.

turing process. There was no doubt that if the defendant proceeded
to deposit this refuse at the present rate, sooner or later there would
ooze from the heap a pernicious liquid which would find its way into
the river and make the water totally unsuitable for the plaintiff's purposes. The sole defence to the plaintiff's claim for an injunction was
that the action was premature — the defendant admitted what the
plaintiff alleged, but asserted that it had no intention of allowing the
harmful liquid to pass into the river.

71   The plaintiff's case was a sympathetic one. The defendant had
taken only a ten-year lease on the property. In that time enough
waste would accumulate to pose a threat, and the defendant might
well have left leaving no one to guard against the risk. The plaintiff
sought not to enjoin all dumping of waste, but only an order preventing the defendant from dumping "in any way so as to pollute the
water to his injury."[134] Thus, arguably, if the defendant were true to
his word, the injunction would give solace to the plaintiff without
causing the defendant any harm.

72   However, the defence succeeded, and an injunction was refused
with costs, on the grounds that the threatened harm was insuffi-
ciently immediate to justify injunctive relief. Pearson, J., held that
there must be not only "proof of imminent danger" but also "proof
that the apprehended damage will, if it comes, be very substantial",
and that the damage would, if it did come, arise under circumstances
in which "it will be impossible for the Plaintiff to protect himself
against it"[135] without the injunction.

73   Other cases have used similar language describing the required imminence and gravity of threatened harm which would justify the
award of an injunction.[136] In *Earl of Ripon v. Hobart*,[137] an early 19th
century case still often cited, Lord Brougham, L.C., indicated that
"the law will guard against risks which are so imminent that no prudent person would incur them" even though damage was not absolutely certain, and that the decision involves to some extent
"balancing the magnitude of the evil against the chances of its
occurrence".[138] Other cases have referred to the need to show "extreme probability";[139] "that there must be such a great probability,

---

[134] *Ibid.*, at p. 690.
[135] *Ibid.*, at p. 698.
[136] See, *e.g.*, *Oak Bay v. Gardner* (1914), 17 D.L.R. 802 (B.C.C.A.).
[137] (1834), 3 My. & K. 169, 40 E.R. 65.
[138] *Ibid.*, at p. 176.
[139] *A.-G. v. Kingston-on-Thames Corp.* (1865), 34 L.J. Ch. 481.

that, in the view of ordinary men, using ordinary sense, the injury would follow";[140] there must be a "strong case of probability that the apprehended mischief will in fact arise."[141]

74   Arguably, *Fletcher v. Bealey* and the other cases which take a similar line represent an unduly restrictive approach. In such cases, the plaintiff typically suffers a real and legitimate fear of injury, and an injunction could be seen merely as a warning to the defendant to avoid inattention to the possibility of harm.

75   It is suggested, however, that the cautious approach exemplified by *Fletcher v. Bealey* can be justified particularly in the nuisance area. While the test has been posed in terms of the temporal imminence of harm, it is submitted that this is not the only, or necessarily best, way to describe the analysis which is suggested by the results reached. What the court does look for is the information necessary to predict with confidence not only that the harm will occur, but also other relevant circumstances which will then exist. In other words, the court must be satisfied that the relevant factors which bear upon the granting of injunctive relief have crystallized. Cases in which *quia timet* injunctions have been granted may be taken to suggest that the notion of crystallization is an appropriate way to describe the state of affairs the courts require before granting injunctive relief. Thus, in *Hooper v. Rogers*,[142] the Court of Appeal rejected the argument that an injunction would be premature even though the plaintiff had failed to show that damage was imminent in a temporal sense. Referring to the older cases, Russell, L.J., explained "I do not regard the use of the word 'imminent' in those passages as negativing a power to grant a mandatory injunction in the present case; I take the use of the word to indicate that the injunction must not be granted prematurely."[143] Similarly, injunctions to protect the plaintiff's right to trade, or prevent patent or copyright infringement, are regularly granted without concern as to the length of time which would intervene before the harm would occur if an injunction were not granted.[144] In such cases, the nature of the threat is clear; its impact

---

[140] *Pattisson v. Gilford* (1874), L.R. 18 Eq. 259 at p. 264, *per* Jessel, M.R.

[141] *Nevers v. Lilley* (1909), 4 N.B. Eq. 104 at p. 111, *per* Barker, C.J. Similar expressions are found in *A.-G. v. Manchester Corp.*, [1893] 2 Ch. 87; *A.-G. v. Nottingham Corp.*, [1904] 1 Ch. 673; *Peatt v. Rhode* (1892), 2 B.C.R. 159 (S.C.).

[142] [1975] Ch. 43 (C.A.).

[143] *Ibid.*, at p. 49. The word "premature" has often been used to describe when *quia timet* relief will be refused, including one decision by the Supreme Court of Canada: *Matthew v. Guardian Ass'ce Co.* (1918), 58 S.C.R. 47 at p. 61, 45 D.L.R. 32 at p. 42, *per* Anglin, J.

[144] *Hendriks v. Montagu* (1881), 17 Ch. D. 638 (C.A.). See, *e.g.*, *American Cyanamid*

on the plaintiff and the effect of an injunction on the defendant can be measured. *Quia timet* injunctions have been ordered to prevent threatened strike action,[145] and in a British Columbia case, the nuisance cases were distinguished: "the means of proof are more readily available and it is doubtful that we should apply the same standard of proof to other torts where technical evidence is not a part of the method of proof."[146]

76   In most cases, the definition of the plaintiff's right and the degree of remedial protection it is to be afforded is not static, but is rather determined by circumstances existing at the time the harm occurs. This is especially true in nuisance cases, so frequently the subject of injunction and *quia timet* applications, where the remedial choice is merely one aspect of resolving the problem of competing land uses.[147] Nuisance is by definition a relative concept, and is affected by many variables. Although the harm feared may constitute a nuisance if all relevant factors remain constant, the court should be satisfied of the constancy of those factors before awarding an injunction which effectively determines the situation once and for all.

77   A related matter is the weighing of the benefit the injunction confers on the plaintiff against the cost it imposes on the defendant.[148] Again, this assessment can be made only where the court has a firm grasp on the actual effect the harm will have on the plaintiff at the time it occurs, and the cost alleviating or avoiding that harm will impose upon the defendant. If the situation is still fluid or uncertain, an injunction granted prematurely may impose unjustified costs on the defendant, and of course, this is particularly the case where the plaintiff seeks a mandatory injunction.[149]

78   Another consideration is that making *quia timet* injunctions too readily available could stifle development and innovation. Change by some almost always threatens others, and legal rights take shape and colour depending on the actual circumstances. As noted, this is expecially true in nuisance cases where neither the nature of the substantive right nor the choice of remedy are determined by any absolute

---

Co. v. Ethicon Ltd., [1975] A.C. 396 (H.L.).

[145] *Foundation Co. of Canada Ltd. v. McGloin* (1963), 42 D.L.R. (2d) 209, [1964] 1 O.R. 350 (H.C.J.).

[146] *Holland America Cruises N.V. v. Gralewicz* (1975), 60 D.L.R. (3d) 512 (B.C.S.C.), at p. 522, *per* Bouck, J.

[147] See, *infra*, Chapter 4.

[148] *Supra*, §§12, 13.

[149] *Redland Bricks Ltd. v. Morris*, [1970] A.C. 652 (H.L.), discussed, *supra*, §§42-44, 60.

standard but rather on the basis of the reasonableness of competing uses and the extent of harm suffered. The potentially stifling effect of *quia timet* injunctions is quite clearly a factor which the courts have taken into account. Even an injunction which does not stop the defendant absolutely but requires him to act in a manner consistent with the plaintiff's rights may often have an unnecessarily severe chilling effect on legitimate development. Since the plaintiff can still sue before harm is actually suffered, as it was put in a 19th century case, an injunction "hanging over the heads of the Defendants would be much more likely to prejudice them, than refusing the motion would be likely to prejudice the Plaintiff."[150] The general law already sets out what the defendant can and cannot do, and an injunction even in general terms not only poses a threat of immediate contempt proceedings but may also effectively freeze the parties' rights prematurely.

79   Thus, the existing law reflects the notion that from the point of view of accommodating changes in economic and industrial activity, as well as other forms of socially desirable activity, all of which involve change and impose risks, it is important to be able to postpone as long as possible, up to the point where harm is actually sustained, the award of injunctive relief.[151] The point was made in rather poetic terms by James, L.J.:

It would have been wrong . . . in the reign of *Henry* VI to have inter-

---

[150] *Haines v. Taylor* (1847), 2 Ph. 209 at p. 210, 41 E.R. 922, *per* Cottenham, L.C.

[151] See, *e.g.*, *British Canadian Securities Ltd. v. Corp. of the City of Victoria* (1911), 19 W.L.R. 242 (B.C.S.C.) (proposed public convenience). See especially the cases dealing with proposed smallpox hospitals where there was conflicting evidence as to whether adjacent residents would contract the disease, and where the general benefit to society of having such hospitals was emphasized: *Baines v. Baker* (1752), Amb. 158, 27 E.R. 105; *A.-G. v. Manchester Corp.*, [1893] 2 Ch. 87; *A.-G. v. Nottingham Corp.*, [1904] 1 Ch. 673; *Shuttleworth v. Vancouver Gen'l Hospital*, [1927] 2 D.L.R. 573 (B.C.S.C.). The decision of Fitz Gibbon, L.J., in *A.-G. v. Rathmines & Pembroke Joint Hospital Bd.*, [1904] 1 I.R. 161 (C.A.), at pp. 171-2, was often cited:

A sentiment of danger and dislike, however natural and justifiable — certainty that the Hospital will be disagreeable or inconvenient — proof that it will abridge a man's pleasure, or make him anxious — the inability of the Court to say that no danger will arise — none of these, accompanied by depreciation of property, will discharge the burden of proof which rests on the plaintiff, or can justify a precautionary injunction, restraining an owner's use of his own land upon the ground of apprehended nuisance to his neighbours.

Arguably, where a risk produced by this sort of activity is incurred for the general social welfare, the cost of this risk — here, diminution in the plaintiff's property value — should not be borne by the plaintiff alone, but compensated through compulsory purchase-type legislation.

fered with the further use of sea coal in *London*, because it had been ascertained . . . or predicted . . . that by the reign of Queen *Victoria* both white and red roses would have ceased to bloom in the *Temple Gardens*. If some picturesque haven opens its arms to invite the commerce of the world, it is not for this Court to forbid the embrace, although the fruit of it should be the sights, and sounds, and smells of a common seaport and shipbuilding town, which drive the Dryads and their masters from their ancient solitudes.[152]

80   Another consideration is the "floodgates of litigation". If injunctions are given too readily on the basis of what is feared, the plaintiff will be encouraged to sue early on, thus imposing the cost of perhaps unnecessary litigation on society as well as on the unsuccessful defendant.[153] There is a strong policy in the law favouring settlement of disputes without litigation, and the principle that an injunction will not be granted simply because it does no harm to the honest and law-abiding defendant[154] is perhaps justified by the desire to save the cost and social friction inherent in litigation.

81   The guarded approach to *quia timet* injunctions does make it difficult for the plaintiff properly to time his action. On the one hand, if the plaintiff sues too early, his action will be dismissed as premature.[155] On the other hand, if he waits until harm materializes, the defendant will complain that an injunction should not be awarded because of the expenditure already incurred.[156] However, it

---

[152] *Salvin v. North Brancepeth Coal Co.* (1874), L.R. 9 Ch. App. 705 at pp. 709-10.

[153] It seems to be accepted that the plaintiff who fails because his action was premature will ordinarily have to pay the defendant's costs: see, *e.g.*, *Lemos v. Kennedy Leigh Development Co. Ltd.* (1961), 105 Sol. Jo. 178 (C.A.).

[154] *Law Society of Upper Canada v. MacNaughton*, [1942] O.W.N. 551 (C.A.) (interlocutory injunction refused); [1943] O.W.N. 229 (injunction refused at trial); *Bridlington Relay Ltd. v. Yorkshire Electricity Board*, [1965] Ch. 436 at p. 445, *per* Buckley, J.: "it would be wrong for this court in quia timet proceedings to grant relief by way of injunction to compel this defendant to do something which it appears to be willing to do without the imposition of an order of the court." *Cf. Newson v. Pender* (1884), 27 Ch. D. 43 (C.A.), granting an interlocutory injunction to stop a building which the plaintiff alleged would interfere with his light despite the defendant's undertaking to tear it down if found to be in the wrong at trial.

[155] Although it would appear that a declaratory order may be granted: *Litchfield-Speer v. Queen Anne's Gate Syndicate (No. 2) Ltd.*, [1919] 1 Ch. 407.

[156] See *Birmingham Canal Co. v. Lloyd* (1812), 18 Ves. Jun. 515, 34 E.R. 413, where the defendants gave notice of their proposed construction, the plaintiff warned that he would sue for damages, the defendants spent £2,000 on the works, and the plaintiff then sued for an injunction. The action was dismissed, *per* Lord Eldon, L.C.: "They ought to have commenced their opposition when they could have done so with justice". *Cf. Hendriks v. Montagu* (1881), 17 Ch. D. 638 (C.A.), at p. 646, *per* James, L.J.: "Of course, defendants in these cases always do say 'you are too early' in one case, and 'you are too late' in the other, but plaintiffs are never too early

is clear that a plaintiff is not required to sue when he is bound to lose merely to warn the defendant,[157] and so long as the plaintiff has asserted his rights promptly, even a mandatory injunction will not be refused simply because the plaintiff did not sue for an interlocutory injunction which would require him to undertake to pay damages to the defendant in the event he were unsuccessful.[158]

6. Delay

(1) Introduction

82   A plaintiff, once entitled to an injunction or specific performance, may lose that right on account of delay in asserting his claim. Because the principles governing the treatment of delay are the same whether the remedy sought is specific performance or an injunction, it is convenient to discuss in one place the matter of delay as it affects both remedies. The treatment of delay as a factor determining the availability of specific relief is characteristic of most equitable doctrines: the courts apply general principles rather than specific rules, leaving wide scope for discretion in particular cases.

83   Consideration of delay is an aspect of the more general principle which takes into account the injustice of awarding relief against a party who will be prejudiced on account of a change of position related to acts or omissions of the party seeking relief.[159]

84   Delay in asserting one's rights may, of course, have evidentiary significance. It is often said that a reasonable person is unlikely to sleep on a well-founded claim. However, it has for long been clearly established that a combination of delay and prejudice to the defendant is required to deprive the plaintiff of a specific remedy to which he is otherwise entitled.[160] In a decision of the Supreme Court of Canada, Duff, J., described the principle as follows:

---

when the Court is satisfied that the thing which the plaintiff dreads is really and substantially threatened to be done, as in this case."

[157] *Infra*, §§100-102.

[158] *Supra*, §§63-65; *infra*, §100.

[159] See, *e.g.*, *infra*, §§772-790, discussing election of remedies in the context of specific performance.

[160] *Lindsay Petroleum Co. v. Hurd* (1874), L.R. 5 P.C. 221; *Lamare v. Dixon* (1873), L.R. 6 H.L. 414 at p. 421, *per* Lord Chelmsford: "quiescence is not acquiescence"; *Archbold v. Scully* (1861), 9 H.L.C. 360 at pp. 363, 388, 11 E.R. 769; *Erlanger v. New Sombrero Phosphate Co.* (1878), 3 App. Cas. 1218 at p. 1279; *Taylor v. Wallbridge* (1879), 2 S.C.R. 616; *Shorb v. Public Trustee* (1954), 11 W.W.R. (N.S.) 132 (Alta. S.C. App. Div.); *Blundon v. Storm*, [1972] S.C.R. 135, 20 D.L.R. (3d) 413; *Canada Trust Co. v. Lloyd*, [1968] S.C.R. 300, 66 D.L.R. (2d) 722, motion to

The doctrine of laches, it has been frequently said, is not a technical doctrine, and in order to constitute a defence there must be such a change of position as would make it inequitable to require the defendant to carry out the contract or the delay must be of such a character as to justify the inference that the plaintiffs intended to abandon their rights under the contract or otherwise to make it unjust to grant specific performance.[161]

85   And as Megarry, V.C., explained more recently in a case where there had been a lengthy delay, but no apparent prejudice to the defendant on that account: "If specific performance was to be regarded as a prize, to be awarded by equity to the zealous and denied to the indolent, then the plaintiffs should fail. But whatever might have been the position over a century ago that was the wrong approach today."[162]

86   Prejudice of this nature on account of delay is peculiar to the context of specific relief, and difficult to imagine in the case of monetary relief. The burden of specific relief on the defendant may increase because of changes induced by the plaintiff's conduct. Rarely will it be more onerous to pay damages later rather than sooner.[163]

87   In this area terminology has not been used consistently. The words laches, acquiescence and waiver are all used with varying meaning. Formerly, laches appears to have referred to simple delay unaccompanied by prejudice[164] whereas acquiescence was used to describe the

---

vary judgment refused [1968] S.C.R. vii; *Gutheil v. Rur. Mun. of Caledonia No. 99* (1964), 48 D.L.R. (2d) 628 (Sask Q.B.); *Landreville v. The Queen (No. 2)*, [1977] 2 F.C. 726, 75 D.L.R. (3d) 380 (T.D.).

[161] *Bark-Fong v. Cooper* (1913), 49 S.C.R. 14 at p. 23, 16 D.L.R. 299 at p. 305. This paraphrases the often-cited statement of the principle of laches in *Lindsay Petroleum Co. v. Hurd, supra*, footnote 160, at pp. 239-40, *per* Sir Barnes Peacock:

Now the doctrine of laches in Courts of Equity is not an arbitrary or a technical doctrine. Where it would be practically unjust to give a remedy, either because the party has, by his conduct, done that which might fairly be regarded as equivalent to a waiver of it, or where by his conduct and neglect he has, though perhaps not waiving that remedy, yet put the other party in a situation in which it would not be reasonable to place him if the remedy were afterwards to be asserted, in either of these cases, lapse of time and delay are most material. . . . Two circumstances, always important in such cases, are, the length of the delay and the nature of the acts done during the interval, which might affect either party and cause a balance of justice or injustice in taking the one course or the other, so far as relates to the remedy.

[162] *Lazard Brothers & Co. Ltd. v. Fairfield Properties Co. (Mayfair) Ltd.* (1978), 121 Sol. Jo. 793 (Ch.).

[163] Although the argument is sometimes made in restitution cases that the defendant is prejudiced having spent money he thought he would not have to pay the plaintiff: see Fridman and McLeod, *Restitution* (Toronto, Carswell, 1982), p. 606.

[164] *Milward v. Earl Thanet* (1801), 5 Ves. Jun. 720n, 31 E.R. 824n, *per* Lord Alvanley,

situation of delay combined with a change of position making it inequitable to grant specific relief.[165] However, acquiescence is also sometimes used to describe the more complete defence equivalent to release or waiver barring the plaintiff from suing at all,[166] where the plaintiff stands by while his rights are infringed, "in such a manner as really to induce the person committing the act, and who might otherwise have abstained from it, to believe that he consents to its being committed".[167] Acquiescence, in this sense, is equivalent to waiver and affects the very existence of the substantive right, rather than just the availability of a specific remedy. The focus here will be on the effect of delay which has less drastic effect and which is relevant to the issue of remedial choice, that is, delay sufficient to deprive the plaintiff of specific relief, but not to bar his action altogether.

(2) Length of delay

88   It follows from the basic principle which governs delay that it is impossible to define generally what period of delay is required; delay will not be material unless productive of or accompanied by some prejudice to the defendant. In this sense, delay as a factor determining the availability of specific relief differs markedly from statutory limitation periods which set fixed and arbitrary limits within which

---

M.R.: "A party cannot call upon a Court of Equity for a specific performance unless he has shewn himself ready, desirous, prompt, and eager." See also *Eads v. Williams* (1854), 24 L.J. Ch. 531 at p. 535, *per* Lord Cranworth, L.C.: "specific performance is relief which this Court will not give, unless in cases where the parties seeking it come as promptly as the nature of the case will permit."

[165] See also Meagher, Gummow and Lehane, *Equity: Doctrines and Remedies* (Sydney, Butterworths, 1975), pp. 664-5, for discussion of the various meanings attributed to acquiescence.

[166] See Brunyate, *Limitation of Actions in Equity* (London, Stevens & Sons Ltd., 1932), p. 189: "Where lapse of time is an element in the more general defence that the plaintiff has released or waived his right or has elected not to assert them or is estopped from asserting them, then lapse of time is said to operate by way of acquiescence"; *Willmott v. Barber* (1880), 15 Ch. D. 96; *Anderson v. Municipality of South Vancouver* (1911), 45 S.C.R. 425. The view that there are different rules for legal and equitable rights was satisfactorily disposed of in *Habib Bank Ltd. v. Habib Bank AG Zurich*, [1981] 2 All E.R. 650 (C.A.), at p. 666, *per* Oliver, L.J.: "such distinctions are both archaic and arcane and . . . in the year 1980 they have but little significance for anyone but a legal historian."

[167] *De Bussche v. Alt* (1878), 8 Ch. D. 286 (C.A.), at p. 314, *per* Thesiger, L.J. See also *Duke of Leeds v. Earl of Amherst* (1846), 2 Ph. 117 at p. 123, 41 E.R. 886; *Archbold v. Scully* (1861), 9 H.L.C. 360 at p. 383, 11 E.R. 769, *per* Lord Wensleydale: "If a party, who could object, lies by and knowingly permits another to incur an expense in doing an act under the belief that it would not be objected to, and so a kind of permission may be said to be given to another to alter his condition, he may be said to acquiesce".

claims must be brought. A claim brought after the time fixed will be barred whether or not there has been actual prejudice to the defendant. Delay as a factor governing the availability of specific relief operates quite differently. There are no fixed periods, and actual prejudice is the governing factor. In some cases, specific relief may be refused after a short delay,[168] in others it may be granted despite a long delay,[169] as justice in the actual circumstance of the case requires.

89   However, certain cases may perhaps be identified which are more likely to be productive of prejudice after only a short period of delay. Obviously these are situations where matters are not standing still, and where immediate decisions are being taken by the defendant which might reasonably be influenced by the position taken by the plaintiff. Any case in which the defendant is presently spending resources on the very matter of which the plaintiff complains falls into this category. The most obvious examples are cases in which the defendant is proceeding with some building which violates the plaintiff's rights.[170] Another category is one in which the parties are engaged in speculative dealings. Where wide fluctuations of price may be expected over short periods of time, prompt action is called for, and courts will not permit the plaintiff to hesitate and thereby gain a risk-free period of speculation at the defendant's expense.[171]

---

[168] See, *e.g.*, *Edgar v. Caskey (No. 2)* (1912), 7 D.L.R. 45 (Alta. S.C.), refusing specific performance of a contract for the sale of a speculative property after a delay of only a few weeks.

[169] See *e.g.*, *Canada Trust Co. v. Lloyd*, [1968] S.C.R. 300, 66 D.L.R. (2d) 722, motion to vary judgment refused [1968] S.C.R. vii (delay of 43 years); *Fitzgerald v. Masters* (1956), 95 C.L.R. 420 (Aust. H.C.) (delay of over 20 years).

[170] *Supra*, §53.

[171] *Huxham v. Llewellyn* (1873), 21 W.R. 570 (Ch.), at p. 571, *per* Selborne, L.C. (delay of five months in instituting suit for specific performance of colliery lease): "this was not a reasonable time. If it were held otherwise it would enable the plaintiff to keep the defendant in suspense for an indefinite time"; *Glasbrook v. Richardson* (1874), 23 W.R. 51 (Ch.); *Ernest v. Vivian* (1863), 33 L.J. Ch. 513 at p. 517, *per* Kindserley, V.C.: "it is not equitable to allow him to wait till it is ascertained that the persons in possession have succeeded or may have been ruined, and if the subject result in profit, to ask to put that in his pocket, if in loss, to repudiate the loss"; *Mills v. Haywood* (1877), 6 Ch. D. 196 (C.A.), at p. 202, *per* Cotton, L.J.; *Clegg v. Edmondson* (1857), 8 De G.M.&G. 787 at p. 814, 44 E.R. 593 (partnership action involving a mining property), *per* Knight Bruce, L.J.: "[The plaintiff] should shew himself in good time willing to participate in possible loss as well as profit, not play a game in which he alone risks nothing"; *Pollard v. Clayton* (1855), 1 K.& J. 461 at p. 480, 69 E.R. 540, *per* Page Wood, V.C.: "Those who seek specific performance of contracts relating to such commodities [fluctuating day-to-day in market price] must be unusually vigilant and active in asserting their rights"; *Walker v. Brown*

(3) Excuses for delay

90   On the other hand, many factors may make it difficult for the defendant to link any prejudicial change of position with delay by the plaintiff. In certain cases, the defendant's own conduct will effectively lengthen the period within which the plaintiff has to decide whether to commence and prosecute proceedings. Any negotiations or equivocations by the defendant indicating that the plaintiff's position may be accepted without resort to litigation will tend to excuse the plaintiff who hesitates.[172]

91   It is also clear that a plaintiff cannot be charged with delay unless he has knowledge, or the means of knowledge, of his right to proceed against the defendant.[173] On the other hand, the plaintiff may be barred by delay where he fails to follow up his suspicions even though he has never actually acquired full knowledge of his right of action.[174] Similarly, a plaintiff's delay may be excused where he hesitates to sue because of genuine doubt as to whether or not the defendant's conduct amounts to an actionable wrong.[175] It is sometimes said that want of knowledge as an excuse extends only to want of knowledge of facts and not to their legal effect,[176] but where the plaintiff reasonably hesitates in asserting his rights because of genuine doubt as to whether he does have a cause of action, his delay may be excused.[177] Any other rule would encourage the immediate litigation of possibly frivolous claims. In some cases, it may be necessary for the plaintiff to accumulate evidence of repeated breaches to

---

(1868), 14 Gr. 237 at pp. 243-4, *per* VanKoughnet, C.: "Men are not allowed thus to sleep upon their bargains, and at any future time, when it may be to their own advantage to do so, rouse themselves, and complain to the Court, that the opposite parties refuse to carry them out." *Cf. Fitzgerald v. Masters* (1956), 95 C.L.R. 420 (Aust. H.C.), at p. 433, *per* Dixon, C.J., and Fullagar, J., holding that increase in value over a period of lengthy delay would not bar specific performance, and also suggesting that the defendant could be compensated for any money actually spent on the property.

[172] *A.-G. v. Colney Hatch Lunatic Asylum* (1868), L.R. 4 Ch. App. 146 at p. 160, *per* Hatherley, L.C.: "it is impossible for the Court to say that persons are to be discouraged from entering into negotiations and arrangements at the peril of being told if all that is attempted to be done fails, they are too late in coming here, and the case is remediless."

[173] *Lindsay Petroleum Co. v. Hurd, supra,* footnote 160, at pp. 241-2

[174] *Erlanger v. New Sombrero Phosphate Co., supra,* footnote 160; *cf. Betjemann v. Betjemann,* [1895] 2 Ch. 474 (C.A.).

[175] *Shaw v. Applegate,* [1977] 1 W.L.R. 970 (C.A.), at p. 976, *per* Buckley, L.J.

[176] *Stafford v. Stafford* (1857), 1 De G. & J. 193 at p. 202, 44 E.R. 697.

[177] *Holder v. Holder,* [1968] Ch. 353 (C.A.), at p. 406, *per* Sachs, L.J.; *Shaw v. Applegate, supra,* footnote 175.

make out his cause of action, and in those cases, the delay required to mount a case will not defeat his right to specific relief.[178]

92   Should the defendant be responsible for suppression of facts giving rise to the plaintiff's right, his misconduct will provide the plaintiff with an answer if a plea of delay is made. Thus, for example, in an early Ontario case,[179] the plaintiff had been out of the jurisdiction and left his affairs in the hands of an agent who had been induced to agree to a dismissal of a specific performance bill by misrepresentations made by the defendant. The plaintiff returned several years later, discovered the true facts, brought another action, and was awarded specific performance.

(4) Nature of prejudice

93   The most common form of alteration of position by the defendant productive of prejudice if specific relief is given, will be the incurring of some expense or liability, or perhaps the forgoing of an opportunity to mitigate.[180] Injunction cases dealing with the situation of the defendant who has spent money erecting buildings or improving property have already been noted.[181] In specific performance cases, the defendant may have agreed to resell the subject property in the belief that the plaintiff was not going to insist upon specific performance; a decree in the plaintiff's favour will face the defendant with liability to the subsequent purchaser.[182]

94   Where the contract involves speculative property, the purchaser may be tempted to delay suing to gain a risk-free hedge. Damages will be measured by the difference between contract and breach date value.[183] Specific performance will have the effect of giving compliance date value. If delay is permitted, the plaintiff will wait to see whether the item he has bargained for goes up in value. If it does, he can prosecute his action for specific performance; if its value declines

---

[178] *Lee v. Haley* (1869), L.R. 5 Ch. App. 155.

[179] *Larkin v. Good* (1870), 17 Gr. 585.

[180] *Hill v. Buffalo & Lake Huron Ry. Co.* (1864), 10 Gr. 506; *VanWagner v. Terryberry* (1855), 5 Gr. 324; *Moir v. Palmatier* (1900), 13 Man. R. 34 (K.B.); *cf. Greyhound Corp. v. Greyhound Car & Truck Rental Ltd.*, (1962), 35 D.L.R. (2d) 13, [1962] O.R. 988 (H.C.J.), ordering an injunction in a passing-off action but refusing costs where the plaintiff had delayed and the defendant had made expenditures.

[181] *Supra*, §§53, 89.

[182] For a case dealing with this issue see *Deveney v. Crampsey* (1967), 62 D.L.R. (2d) 244, [1967] 1 O.R. 647 (C.A.), revd [1969] S.C.R. 267, 2 D.L.R. (3d) 161.

[183] Waddams, *supra*, footnote 30, §§65-110.

below the breach date price he can still claim damages.[184] In several cases, the courts have deprecated such behaviour, and declined specific relief on the grounds of delay.[185] Usually, however, in these cases the defendant had resold, and the significance of the speculative nature of the bargained-for item was to reduce the period of time within which the plaintiff must act. Arguably, the defendant who has not resold suffers no prejudice beyond having to fulfil his bargain. It may be, however, that even where the defendant has not resold, it is possible to identify prejudice which would preclude specific relief.[186] The very fact that the defendant is left in an uncertain position, at risk as to price fluctuations and unsure whether to take advantage of other opportunities, will usually represent sufficient prejudice to make specific relief in favour of the plaintiff inappropriate.

(5) Delay and problems of proof

95   It has also been held that a defence of delay on equitable principles may be made out where the effect of delay is to make the defendant's case more difficult to prove.[187] In principle this seems difficult to justify on the doctrine of laches.[188] Limitation statutes applying generally to "actions" will include actions formerly brought in equity for a specific remedy, and the same limitation period should apply whether the plaintiff seeks damages, specific performance, or an injunction.[189] The purpose of limitation statutes is to guard against

---

[184] *Ibid.*

[185] *Supra*, footnote 171; *Orsi v. Morning* (1971), 20 D.L.R. (3d) at p. 26 at p. 42, [1971] 3 O.R. at p. 186 at p. 202 (H.C.J.), affd D.L.R. *loc. cit.* p. 49, O.R. *loc. cit.* p. 209 (C.A.), *per* Fraser, J.: "the purchasers were seeking to keep the vendors bound and themselves free without making more than a negligible investment"; *Di Giulio v. Boland*, [1957] O.W.N. 233 (H.C.J.), vard 13 D.L.R. (2d) 510, [1958] O.R. 384 (C.A.); *Smith v. Hughes* (1903), 5 O.L.R. 238 (H.C.J.); *McGreevy v. Hodder* (1912), 8 D.L.R. 755, 23 O.W.R. 699 (H.C.); *Edgar v. Caskey (No. 2)* (1912), 7 D.L.R. 45 (Alta. S.C.).

[186] *Harris v. Robinson* (1892), 21 S.C.R. 390, would appear to be such a case.

[187] *McIlreith v. Payzant* (1893), 25 N.S.R. 377 (C.A.); *Hughes v. Schofield*, [1975] 1 N.S.W.L.R. 8 (S.C.), citing a dictum from *Watt v. Assets Co. Ltd.*, [1905] A.C. 317 (H.L.), at p. 329. Spry, *The Principles of Equitable Remedies*, 2nd ed. (London, Sweet & Maxwell, 1980), cites loss of evidence as a "common case" at p. 219, and a "classic" case at p. 406.

[188] Brunyate, *supra*, footnote 166, at pp. 244-9, points out that the rule was derived to deal with cases not subject to any limitation period, and that it should not apply where there is a limitation period.

[189] *Taylor v. Davies* (1917), 41 D.L.R. 510 at p. 522, 41 O.L.R. 403 at p. 421 (S.C. App. Div.), *per* Meredith, C.J.O., affd [1920] A.C. 636, 51 D.L.R. 75 (P.C.). Legislation of this type usually contains an express saving provision to preserve the equitable doctrine of delay. See, *e.g.*, Limitations Act, Ont.:

stale claims and it would be hard to justify a shorter period on account of faded memories and lost evidence simply because a certain form of remedy is sought. The point of attaching special significance to delay in the context of specific relief is that because of the very nature of the remedy, delay may be productive of a kind of prejudice not inflicted by a damages award. Prejudice of that sort is not present merely because the defendant has a more difficult time putting his case together on account of the plaintiff's delay. However, in some jurisdictions claims for specific performance and injunctions are not covered by legislation.[190] In such cases, there is an established equitable doctrine that the statutory period may be applied by analogy.[191] Where a limitation period does apply, there seems no basis for applying this equitable doctrine. Thus, it is suggested that the better view is that where delay has merely made the defendant's case more difficult to prove, no case for laches is made out, and mere delay of that sort should not deprive the plaintiff of a specific remedy to which he is otherwise entitled. In jurisdictions where claims to specific relief are excluded from limitation provisions, the former doctrine of applying a statute of limitations by analogy may still be resorted to.

(6) Sale of land and possession

96   In sale of land cases, taking possession by the plaintiff prior to completion will be an important factor and may make delay irrelevant. In one case, it was said that where "all that needs to be done is for the legal title to be perfected . . . laches or delay is not a bar."[192] This is sometimes put on the basis of the equitable title acquired by the plaintiff,[193] but might also be justified simply on the grounds that the defendant suffers no prejudice. Ordinarily, there will be little if any doubt about the intentions of the plaintiff who has taken possession pursuant to the contract but has yet to receive the actual legal title, nor will the defendant in such a case ordinarily be able to show

---

2. Nothing in this Act interferes with any rule of equity in refusing relief on the ground of acquiescence, or otherwise, to any person whose right to bring an action is not barred by virtue of this Act.

[190] See, e.g., Limitation Act, 1939, U.K., s. 2(7), which expressly excludes claims for specific performance and injunctions.

[191] Brunyate, supra, footnote 166; Williams, Limitation of Actions in Canada, 2nd ed. (Toronto, Butterworths, 1980), at pp. 38-9.

[192] Williams v. Greatrex, [1957] 1 W.L.R. 31 (C.A.), at p. 36, per Denning, L.J.; Corp. of County of Huron v. Kerr (1868), 15 Gr. 265; Lewis v. Jay, [1934] 3 D.L.R. 228, [1934] O.R. 307 (C.A.); O'Keefe v. Taylor (1851), 2 Gr. 95.

[193] Williams v. Greatrex, supra, footnote 192.

prejudice.[194] Indeed, delay should bar the defence rather than the action. If he had any intention of disputing the plaintiff's title or right under the contract, the defendant should surely have taken steps to have the plaintiff removed.

97   On the other hand, where the plaintiff is in possession under an instalment payment contract, and defaults, plainly the vendor is entitled to possession. However, the plaintiff's default should not bar a specific performance action where he tenders the amount due before the vendor retakes possession, although the cases would seem to conflict on this point.[195]

(7) Delay and equitable damages

98   In some cases, it has been held that delay on the plaintiff's part and the resulting prejudice to the defendant may be significant enough to disentitle the plaintiff to specific relief, yet not so serious as to disallow an award of damages which reflects to some extent the value an injunction would have, had it been applied for on time.[196] A good example is *Bracewell v. Appleby*[197] where the plaintiffs, who had delayed, were denied a mandatory injunction requiring the demolition of a structure erected by the defendant in violation of a restriction. Such an order would have put the defendants in the position of being obliged to either tear down the building or pay a large sum to buy out the plaintiffs. The court held, however, that the plaintiffs were entitled to damages measured by the amount they might reasonably have accepted had they asserted their claim at the outset as compensation from the defendant for release from the restriction.

---

[194] *Cf.* where the plaintiff's possession is other than under the contract: *Porter v. Hale* (1894), 23 S.C.R. 265; *Mills v. Haywood* (1877), 6 Ch. D. 196 (C.A.), Spry, *supra*, footnote 187, suggests at p. 216 that "the better view is that this distinction is usually not critical".

[195] *Battell v. Hudson's Bay Co.* (1908), 9 W.L.R. 296 (Sask. Full Ct.), surely misapplies *Wallace v. Hesslein* (1898), 29 S.C.R. 171. In the former case, despite a lengthy delay, the purchaser tendered the full amount due under an instalment payment contract. In the latter, the purchaser was unable to pay the amount due, and it would have worked a hardship on the vendor had his action for possession been refused and the purchaser's counterclaim for specific performance allowed.

[196] *Senior v. Pawson* (1866), L.R. 3 Eq. 330; *Sayers v. Collyer* (1884), 28 Ch. D. 103 (C.A.) at p. 110; *cf. Malhotra v. Choudhury*, [1980] Ch. 52 (C.A.), taking delay into account in fixing equitable damages.

[197] [1975] Ch. 408.

(8) Interlocutory injunctions

99   On interlocutory applications, delay has somewhat different implications. The evidentiary factor becomes much more significant. To succeed, the plaintiff must show a substantial risk of irreparable harm in the period leading up to trial.[198] The very fact of delay by the plaintiff, quite apart from any question of prejudice to the defendant, may often serve as evidence that the risk is not significant enough to warrant interlocutory relief.[199] Also, refusal of interlocutory relief in no way precludes the court from awarding a final injunction after a full hearing when the evidentiary value of the near delay may be considerably less significant.[200]

100   A difficult and related question is whether a plaintiff's failure to seek interlocutory relief will affect his chances of securing a permanent injunction at trial. This is particularly important where a mandatory injunction is sought and where the defendant has expended resources after the action was commenced and before judgment.[201] The cases would seem to hold that it is not necessary for the plaintiff to have applied for interlocutory relief to succeed in securing a mandatory injunction.[202] So long as his objection is put forcefully, and the defendant is put on notice that the plaintiff objects to the action he is taking, mandatory relief may still be granted.[203]

101   This rule strongly favours the plaintiff, and it is suggested that there is a case for saying that the plaintiff's failure to seek an interlocutory order should be given more weight. If the plaintiff applies for and is awarded an interlocutory injunction, he will have to undertake

---

[198] *Infra*, Chapter 2.

[199] *Supra*, §84.

[200] *Johnson v. Wyatt* (1863), 2 De G.J. & S. 18 at p. 25, 46 E.R. 281, *per* Turner, L.J.:

> . . . to justify the Court in refusing to interfere at the hearing of a cause there must be a much stronger case of acquiescence than is required upon an interlocutory application, for at the hearing of a cause it is the duty of the Court to decide upon the rights of the parties, and the dismissal of the bill upon the ground of acquiescence amounts to a decision that a right which has once existed is absolutely and for ever lost.

[201] *Supra*, §§63-65.

[202] *Wrotham Park Estate Co. Ltd. v. Parkside Homes Ltd.*, [1974] 1 W.L.R. 798 (Ch.); *cf. Shaw v. Applegate*, [1977] 1 W.L.R. 970 (C.A.), at p. 978, *per* Buckley, L.J., and p. 981, *per* Goff, L.J.

[203] *Gaskin v. Balls* (1879), 13 Ch. D. 324 (C.A.), granting a mandatory injunction requiring the demolition of a building which violated a restrictive covenant where the plaintiff objected, but where the defendant completed construction before any action was commenced. Compare *Blundon v. Storm*, [1972] S.C.R. 135, 20 D.L.R. (3d) 413, applying a similar principle in a partnership action.

to bear any damages the injunction causes the defendant should the defendant succeed at trial.[204] In a doubtful case, the risk the undertaking represents may be substantial. If the plaintiff does not apply for an interlocutory injunction but merely commences an action, he bears no risk for damages caused by the injunction in the event he loses, and the risk of proceeding in the face of his protest shifts to the defendant. In this sense, the defendant who stops work but succeeds at trial will be much better off if the plaintiff did get an interlocutory injunction. Any damages he sustained by virtue of the injunction must be borne by the plaintiff, while the defendant who stops in face of the plaintiff's protest but then wins will have to bear the cost of the delay himself.

102   As noted in the section dealing with *quia timet* injunctions,[205] the decision whether or not to proceed is often a difficult one, and is closely related to the defence of delay. On the one hand, the law does not want to encourage litigation, and discourages plaintiffs from bringing actions prematurely. On the other hand, defendants who act and are not met with immediate protest are allowed to plead delay and change of position. The plaintiff's choice is delicate — he must time his action carefully, avoiding the risk of having his action dismissed as either premature or having been brought too late.

7. Other Discretionary Factors

(1) Clean hands

103   The maxim "he who comes to equity must come with clean hands" is colourful but potentially misleading in so far as it suggests a general power to scrutinize all aspects of the plaintiff's behaviour and refuse relief if it offends. The "clean hands" maxim is best understood as a very general catch-all phrase encompassing many discretionary factors better considered in more precise terms.[206] By itself, it

---

[204] *Infra*, §§173-178.

[205] *Supra*, §81.

[206] Spry, *supra*, footnote 187, at p. 6: "the maxim which states the requirement of clean hands cannot properly be regarded as setting out a rule which is either precise or capable of satisfactory operation", and at p. 231: "The maxims that a plaintiff in equity must approach the court with clean hands and that he who seeks equity must do equity are often used in a purely rhetorical manner in cases where the refusal of relief may better be justified on more precise grounds"; Chafee, *Some Problems of Equity* (Ann Arbor, University of Michigan Law School, 1950), pp. 1-102, especially at p. 94:

    . . . The clean hands maxim is not peculiar to equity, but is simply a picturesque

has really no analytical value, although, as will be seen, it has some-times been employed as if it did.

104   The phrase seems to hark back to an age when the Chancellor dis-pensed justice according to conscience and the morality of each par-ticular case, and yet, as long ago as 1787, it was laid down that the clean hands maxim "does not mean a general depravity; it must have an immediate and necessary relation to the equity sued for; it must be a depravity in a legal as well as in a moral sense."[207]

105   In the early 19th century Lord Brougham repeated this point per-haps more emphatically when he said:

> . . . that general fraudulent conduct signifies nothing; that general dis-honesty of purpose signifies nothing; that attempts to overreach go for nothing; that an intention and design to deceive may go for nothing, un-less all this dishonesty of purpose, all this fraud, all this intention and design, can be connected with the particular transaction, are not only connected with the particular transaction, but must be made to be the very ground upon which this transaction took place, and must have given rise to this contract.[208]

106   In *City of Toronto v. Polai*,[209] a trial judge refused an injunction to enforce a municipal by-law on the grounds that by virtue of a selec-tive enforcement policy, the plaintiff city came to the court with "un-clean hands". This was reversed on appeal[210] on the grounds that the public interest in enforcement of the by-law was paramount and not affected by the city's conduct, and it was said: "The misconduct charged against the plaintiff as a ground for invoking the maxim

---

phrase applied by equity judges to a general principle running through damage actions as well as suits for specific relief. This principle is that the plaintiff's fault is often an important element in the judicial settlement of disputes, as well as the defendant's fault.

. . . this principle of plaintiff's fault has rather weak unifying qualities. It can better be described as a string around a loose bundle of separate defenses which somewhat resemble each other.

[207] *Dering v. Earl of Winchelsea* (1787), 1 Cox 318 at pp. 319-20, 29 E.R. 1184, *per* Eyre, C.B.

[208] *Attwood v. Small* (1838), 61 Cl. & Fin. 232 at pp. 447-8, 7 E.R. 684. See also *Moody v. Cox*, [1917] 2 Ch. 71 (C.A.), at p. 87, *per* Scrutton, L.J.: "I think the ex-pression 'clean hands' is used more often in the text-books than it is in the judg-ments"; *Meyers v. Casey* (1913), 17 C.L.R 90 (Aust. H.C.), at p. 124, *per* Isaacs, J.: "No Court of equity will aid a man to derive advantage from his own wrong, and this is really the meaning of the maxim."

[209] (1968), 3 D.L.R. (3d) 498, [1969] 1 O.R. 655 (H.C.J.).

[210] 8 D.L.R. (3d) 689, [1970] 1 O.R. 483 (C.A.), affd [1973] S.C.R. 38, 28 D.L.R. (3d) 638. Compare *Homex Realty and Development Co. Ltd. v. Village of Wyoming*, [1980] 2 S.C.R. 1011 at pp. 1034-5, 116 D.L.R. (3d) 1 at p. 28, *per* Estey, J., dis-cussing a similar doctrine with respect to the prerogative remedy of *certiorari*.

against him must relate directly to the very transaction concerning which the complaint is made, and not merely to the general morals or conduct of the person seeking relief".[211]

107   These principles, it is submitted, are sound, and wrongdoing by the plaintiff will not deprive him of a specific remedy to which he is otherwise entitled unless it bears directly upon the appropriateness of the remedy.[212] If it does, refusal of relief will almost certainly be justifiable on some other more precise basis than the "clean hands" maxim. It is, of course, not uncommon for the "clean hands" principle to be referred to more loosely.[213] Usually the decision to refuse the remedy is amply justifiable on more precise grounds, but sometimes the maxim has been applied with very unfortunate results.[214]

Industrial property cases

108   It has been held in several cases that a plaintiff will be refused injunctive relief to protect copyright or trademark rights, or in passing-off actions, where he has been guilty of public deception.[215] This is sometimes related to the "clean hands" doctrine but the better view is that such misconduct affects the very substantive right sued upon.[216] The equitable maxim may have been applied in some cases

---

[211] 8 D.L.R. (3d) at pp. 699-700, [1970] 1 O.R. at pp. 493-4, *per* Schroeder, J.A.

[212] See, *e.g.*, *Argyll v. Argyll*, [1967] Ch. 302 at pp. 331-2, where Ungoed-Thomas, J. , held that a former spouse was not to be denied an injunction restraining the divulging of matrimonial confidences because her misconduct led to the breakdown of the marriage, or even because she herself had disclosed other unrelated confidences: "A person coming to Equity for relief . . . must come with clean hands; but the cleanliness required is to be judged in relation to the relief that is sought." See also *Melvin v. Melvin* (1975), 58 D.L.R. (3d) 98 (N.B. S.C. App. Div.).

[213] See, *e.g.*, *Hubbard v. Vosper*, [1972] 2 Q.B. 84 (C.A.), at p. 101, *per* Megaw, L.J. The doctrine has been applied to deny injunctive relief against unlawful picketing in labour disputes: *C.P.R. v. United Transportation Union, Local 144* (1970), 14 D.L.R. (3d) 497 (B.C.S.C.) (company deceptive in negotiations); *Pacific Trollers Ass'n v. United Fishermen & Allied Workers' Union* (1974), 46 D.L.R. (3d) 156 (B.C.S.C.) (plaintiff unlicensed to do activity in question). *Cf. A.-G. Can. v. Whitelock* (1973), 37 D.L.R. (3d) 757 (B.C.S.C.), at p. 762, *per* Berger, J.: "The doctrine of clean hands is essential to the sound development of labour law . . ." but refusing to apply the doctrine against the Crown.

[214] See *Litvinoff v. Kent* (1918), 34 T.L.R. 298 (Ch.), where a tenant was refused an injunction to restrain his landlord from locking him out, although it was held that the landlord had no right to do so, on the grounds that the plaintiff had been spreading revolutionary propaganda.

[215] *Lee v. Haley* (1869), L.R. 5 Ch. App. 155 at pp. 158-9; *Post v. Marsh* (1880), 16 Ch. D. 395; *Leather Cloth Co. Ltd. v. American Leather Cloth Co. Ltd.* (1863), 4 De G. J. & S. 137, 46 E.R. 868, 11 H.L.C. 523; *Mrs. Pomeroy Ltd. v. Scalé* (1907), 24 R.P.C. 177.

[216] Chafee, *supra*, footnote 206; *Ford v. Foster* (1872), L.R. 7 Ch. App. 611. *Cf. Ket-*

because the relief sought is an equitable remedy. However, if the claim had been for damages, the action would also have been dismissed on the basis that the plaintiff lacked the legal right to sue.[217] Hence, once it is determined that the deception of which the plaintiff has been guilty does not bear upon his right to sue, an injunction otherwise available should not be refused.

109   A similar doctrine arises in cases where the plaintiff seeks to protect copyright in obscene or immoral works. It has been consistently held that no injunctive relief will be granted[218] and again, the reasoning may be confused with a general "clean hands" doctrine. Once again, however, the reason for refusing relief is not some general equitable discretion, but simply that no copyright exists in such works.[219] Indeed, the courts have noted that the result of refusing injunctive relief is not to suppress such works but in fact to permit them to be published in more than one version.[220] The real reason for denying the remedy has nothing to do with any general equitable power to protect the public, but rests more simply upon the absence of a legal right.

(2) "He who seeks equity"

110   Another maxim the effect of which can sometimes be mistaken is "he who seeks equity must also do equity". This maxim, in fact, has little to do with the conduct of the parties prior to trial, and merely indicates that relief at trial may often be given on terms. Its effect was explained in a mid-19th century English case in terms which have been consistently applied:

> . . . it is a rule which . . . takes for granted the whole question in dispute. The rule . . . cannot *per se* decide what terms the Court should impose upon the Plaintiff as the price of the decree it gives him. It decides in the abstract that the Court giving the Plaintiff the relief to which he is entitled will do so only upon the terms of his submitting to give the Defendant such corresponding rights (if any) as he also may be entitled to in respect of the subject-matter of the suit; what these rights are must be determined *aliunde* by strict rules of law, and not by any arbitrary deter-

---

tles & Gas Appliances Ltd. v. Anthony Hordern & Sons Ltd. (1934), 35 S.R. (N.S.W.) 108 (S.C.).

[217] *Supra*, footnote 216.

[218] *Southey v. Sherwood* (1817), 2 Mer. 435, 35 E.R. 1006; *Glyn v. Weston Feature Film Co.*, [1916] 1 Ch. 261; *Lawrence v. Smith* (1822), Jac. 471, 37 E.R. 928.

[219] *Stockdale v. Onwhyn* (1826), 5 B. & C. 174, 108 E.R. 65.

[220] *Southey v. Sherwood*, *supra*, footnote 218, where the document in question was a manuscript which the plaintiff did not want published at all. By refusing the injunction, the court ensured that it would reach the public.

mination of the Court. The rule, in short, merely raises the question what those terms (if any) should be.[221]

Indeed, the maxim "he who seeks equity" is not often encountered with respect to specific remedies, although as noted,[222] the power to modify, qualify and condition performance is an important aspect of specific relief.

8. Jurisdiction

(1) Effect of the Judicature Act

111   One issue which often emerges when injunctions are sought in novel situations is the effect of the Judicature Act upon the power of the court to grant an injunction. It is surely odd that there should still be discussion of this issue in the modern cases.[223] Whatever the origin of the substantive cause, there surely can be no doubt that if an injunction best satisfies the goal of providing an appropriate remedy, it will be granted.

112   Where the question of the effect of the Judicature Act is discussed, one approach is to distinguish between using an injunction to create a new right, and using an injunction to provide a new remedy for pre-existing rights. This was explained in 1883 by Cotton, L.J., as follows:

> [The effect of the Judicature Acts is] to superadd to what would have

---

[221] *Hanson v. Keating* (1844), 4 Hare 1 at pp. 4-5, 67 E.R. 537, *per* Wigram, V.C. See also *United States of America v. McRae* (1867), L.R. 3 Ch. App. 79 at pp. 88-9, *per* Lord Chelmsford, L.C.: "the equity to be observed by a person seeking equity must be some equity which is involved in the subject of the suit"; *Calvin v. Hartwell* (1837), 5 Cl. & Fin. 484 at p. 522, 7 E.R. 488; *Paul v. Ferguson* (1868), 14 Gr. 230; *Taylor v. Brown* (1877), 25 Gr. 53; *Botsford v. Crane* (1877), 17 N.B.R. 154 (C.A.); *Richards v. Collins* (1912), 9 D.L.R. 249 at p. 254, 27 O.L.R. 390 at p. 398 (Div. Ct.), *per* Riddell J.:

> It is a well recognised principle of equity: "He who seeks equity must do equity." In many instances this contains a pun on the word "equity," and means nothing more than "He who seeks the assistance of a Court of Equity must, in the matter in which he so asks assistance, do what is just as a term of receiving such assistance." "Equity" means "Chancery" in one instance, and "Right" or "Fair Dealing" in the other.

[222] *Infra*, §§391-397; Chapter 11.

[223] The preoccupation with the traditional demarcation between law and equity is encountered less frequently in Canada than in England and Australia, "for various reasons, not the least of which has been the continued existence of a vigorous and able Chancery bar in both countries": Girard, Book Review of Spry's *Equitable Remedies*, 2nd ed., 19 U.W.O.L. Rev. 381 (1981), at p. 385, noting also that the House of Lords has tried to redress this situation in *United Scientific Holdings Ltd. v. Burnley Borough Council*, [1978] A.C. 904.

been previously the remedy, a remedy by way of injunction, altering therefore not in any way the rights of parties so as to give a right to those who had no legal right before, but enabling the Court to modify the principle on which it had previously proceeded in granting injunctions, so that where there is a legal right the Court may, without being hampered by its old rules, grant an injunction where it is just or convenient to do so for the purpose of protecting or asserting the legal rights of the parties.[224]

113   This suggests that so long as the plaintiff asserts a recognized legal or equitable right, there is jurisdiction to grant an injunction even if one has not been granted in the past in similar cases. It also suggests that the remedy can be applied in novel ways.

114   It is, however, perhaps the case that the language of the Judicature Act — that the court can award an interlocutory injunction wherever "just and convenient"[225] — is misleading. The provision does not constitute a mandate to award injunctions in the absence of a substantive right, however appealing the plaintiff's case may seem or however "just and convenient" an injunction might be.[226] This is not to say that the common law is frozen and that new causes of action cannot be recognized, but merely that such developments are to occur directly by conscious alteration to substantive rules.

115   On the other hand, a narrower view has often been suggested, to the effect that the Judicature Act was purely procedural in effect so that a modern court cannot award an injunction unless some pre-Judicature Act court would have had the power to do so.[227] In the

---

[224] *North London Ry. Co. v. Great Northern Ry. Co.* (1883), 11 Q.B.D. 30 (C.A.), at p. 39. *Cf.* the more restrictive view expressed by Brett, L.J., at pp. 36-7.

[225] See, *e.g.*, Judicature Act, Ont., s. 19(1). Most provisions of this type apply only to interlocutory orders. Compare, however, the English Supreme Court Act, 1981, s. 37(1), which now applies the "just and convenient" phrase to both final and interlocutory orders.

[226] See *Beddow v. Beddow* (1878), 9 Ch. D. 89 at p. 93, *per* Jessel, M.R., stating that the effect of the Judicature Act is to give the court "unlimited power to grant an injunction . . . according to sufficient legal reasons and on settled legal principles." See also *Aslatt v. Corp. of Southampton* (1880), 16 Ch. D. 143 at p. 148; *Richardson v. Methley School Board*, [1893] 3 Ch. 510 at p. 515. In *Chief Constable of Kent v. V*, [1982] 3 All E.R. 36 (C.A.), Lord Denning, M.R., suggested that the change in the English Act, *supra*, footnote 225, extends the power to grant injunctions to any case where to do so would be "just and convenient", subject only to the plaintiff having standing to apply.

[227] See, *e.g.*, *Harris v. Beauchamp Brothers*, [1894] 1 Q.B. 801 (C.A.), at p. 809; *Morgan v. Hart*, [1914] 2 K.B. 183 (C.A.) (both receiver cases). See also Meagher, Gummow and Lehane, *op. cit.*, *supra*, footnote 165, at p. 453. In *Gouriet v. Union of Post Office Workers*, [1978] A.C. 435 (H.L.), at p. 516, Lord Edmund-Davies stated that the section dealing with interlocutory relief "dealt only with procedure and had nothing to do with jurisdiction." *Cf. Rasu Maritima S.A. v. Perusahaan*, [1978] Q.B. 644 (C.A.), at pp. 659-60, *per* Lord Denning, M.R.

end, there is little practical difference between these views, and even if the second technical and seemingly more restrictive view were adopted, there would be few cases in which there is not jurisdiction to grant an injunction. Common law courts were empowered to award injunctions in 1854,[228] and this power has been relied upon to justify the award of injunctions in cases where a court of equity would not have done so before the Judicature Act. Thus, in defamation cases, although equity held itself without jurisdiction to grant injunctive relief, injunctions have been justified on the basis that a common law court did have jurisdiction to award such an injunction from 1854.[229] The disadvantage of this narrow and backward-looking view is that it requires minute analysis of pre-Judicature Act jurisdiction. This, it is submitted, is contrary to the whole spirit of the Judicature Act which was surely that legal and equitable principles were to be applied together and that the modern court was not to be tied by pre-Judicature Act jurisdictional constraints.[230]

116   The *Mareva* and *Anton Piller*[231] lines of cases show that the modern court is free to develop novel remedial solutions while adhering to the principle that injunctions are not to be used to create new substantive rights. These cases suggest that jurisdiction to award injunctions should not be given a narrow meaning, and that an injunction will not be barred merely because it was not the practice to grant one in the past.

117   On the other hand, there are many examples where courts have quite properly refused injunctive relief on the grounds that the plaintiff established no recognized cause of action.[232] This has often ari-

---

[228] Common Law Procedure Act, 1854, U.K., ss. 79, 82.
[229] *Quartz Hill Consolidated Gold Mining Co. v. Beall* (1882), 20 Ch. D. 501 (C.A.); *Bonnard v. Perryman*, [1891] 2 Ch. 269 (C.A.). *Cf.*, however, Meagher, Gummow and Lehane, *op. cit.*, *supra*, footnote 165, at pp. 453-4, suggesting that because *quia timet* injunctions could not be granted at law, and because equity would not grant injunctions in defamation actions at all, there is still no power to award an injunction *quia timet* in a defamation action.
[230] See also, *A.J. Bekhor Ltd. v. Bilton*, [1981] Q.B. 923 (C.A.), at p. 953, *per* Stephenson, L.J.: "How far those authorities imprison the courts a century later or fossilise their practice is a question which cannot be answered without considering the *Anton Piller* and *Mareva* lines of cases." Spry, *op. cit.*, *supra*, footnote 187, at p. 312, suggests that as the jurisdiction to award injunctions "given jurisdiction over the person of the defendant . . . has always been without limit. . ." and hedged only by discretionary principles, a preference for the procedural analysis of the Judicature Act does not curtail the actual jurisdiction to award injunctive relief.
[231] *Mareva Compania Naviera S.A. v. International Bulkcarriers Ltd.*, [1975] 2 Lloyd's Rep. 509 (C.A.); *Anton Piller KG v. Manufacturing Processes Ltd.*, [1976] Ch. 55 (C.A.); *infra*, Chapter 2.
[232] See, *e.g.*, *Weir v. Saskatchewan Amateur Softball Ass'n* (1978), 90 D.L.R. (3d) 707 (Sask. Q.B.)

sen, for example, in cases where the plaintiff sued to restrain the use of a name, either his own[233] or that of his house[234] or organization[235] or firm,[236] in circumstances where the defendant's conduct did not constitute passing-off or any other actionable wrong. The use of the name may cause inconvenience and annoyance to the plaintiff, but unless there is a basis in substantive law to support the suit, an injunction should not be awarded.[237]

118   The need for a justiciable substantive cause of action to support injunctive relief has been reiterated in two recent decisions of the House of Lords. In *Siskina v. Distos Compania Naviera S.A.*,[238] the House of Lords limited the exercise of the jurisdiction to award *Mareva* injunctions on this basis. It held that a *Mareva* injunction was merely ancillary to a substantive claim, and could not be awarded unless the plaintiff's substantive cause of action fell within the court's jurisdiction. Similarly, in *Bremer Vulkan Schiffbau und Maschinen Fabrik v. South India Shipping Corp. Ltd.*[239] the House of Lords refused to uphold an injunction restraining the defendant from proceeding with a long-delayed arbitration on the ground that in the circumstances, the plaintiff had no right enforceable in the courts.

119   It should be added, however, that in the end, it is often difficult to make a strict distinction between recognizing new rights, and affording new remedial solutions to existing rights. Neither common law nor equity developed by first defining rights in a strict sense. Both systems tended to develop in response to specific problems rather than by way of general definition, and the plaintiff could be said to have a right if the court, whether common law or equity, decided to give him a remedy.

---

[233] *Earl Cowley v. Countess Cowley*, [1901] A.C. 450 (H.L.); *Zumpano v. Zumpano*, [1979] 2 W.W.R. 652 (B.C.S.C.) (divorced father refused injunction to restrain wife from changing name of children).

[234] *Day v. Brownrigg* (1878), 10 Ch. D. 294 (C.A.).

[235] *Grand Lodge, A.O.U.W. v. Supreme Lodge, A.O.U.W.* (1907), 17 Man. R. 360 (K.B.).

[236] *Street v. Union Bank of Spain and England* (1885), 30 Ch. D. 156; *Levy v. Walker* (1879), 10 Ch. D. 436 (C.A.).

[237] There are many other cases turning on the plaintiff's failure to make out a substantive cause of action. See *Paton v. British Pregnancy Advisory Service Trustees*, [1979] Q.B. 276 (refusing a husband's application for an injunction to restrain his wife from having a lawful abortion); *White v. Mellin*, [1895] A.C. 154 (H.L.) (plaintiff unable to show actual damage in trade libel case).

[238] [1979] A.C. 210 (H.L.), discussed, *infra*, §126.

[239] [1981] A.C. 909 (H.L.), discussed, *infra*, §§483-487.

(2) Foreign elements

120   Claims for injunctions against foreign parties present jurisdictional constraints which are not encountered in the case of claims for money judgments. In the case of a money claim, the courts need not limit assumed jurisdiction to cases where enforceability is ensured. Equity, however, acts *in personam* and the effectiveness of an equitable decree depends upon the control which may be exercised over the person of the defendant. If the defendant is physically present, it will be possible to require him to do, or permit, acts outside the jurisdiction.[240] The courts have, however, conscientiously avoided making orders which cannot be enforced. The result is that the courts are reluctant to grant injunctions against parties not within the jurisdiction, and the practical import of rules permitting service *ex juris* in respect of injunction claims is necessarily limited. Rules of court are typically limited to cases where it is sought to restrain the defendant from doing anything *within the jurisdiction.*[241] As a practical matter the defendant who is "doing anything within the jurisdiction" will usually be physically present within the jurisdiction to allow ordinary service.

121   Situations do arise, however, where the activities of a foreign defendant do constitute conduct within the jurisdiction which can be restrained. In several cases, service out of the jurisdiction has been upheld in respect of claims for injunctions to restrain circulation or repetition of libellous material originating outside the jurisdiction.[242] Similarly, service has been permitted where the claim against the foreigner is to restrain him from infringing a patent or trademark within the jurisdiction,[243] or from taking legal proceedings within the jurisdiction to wind up a company.[244]

122   The question of enforceability must always be faced. If the foreign defendant is a corporation with some presence and property within the jurisdiction, there will be little difficulty. It was held in an English

---

[240] See, *e.g.*, *Cook Industries Inc. v. Galliher*, [1979] Ch. 439 (order to permit inspection of flat in Paris).

[241] See, e.g., Rule 25(i) of the Ontario Rules of Practice.

[242] *Tozier v. Hawkins* (1885), 15 Q.B.D. 680 (C.A.); *Dunlop Rubber Co. v. Dunlop*, [1921] 1 A.C. 367 (H.L.); *Alexander & Co. Ltd. v. Valentine & Sons (1907) Ltd.* (1908), 25 T.L.R. 29 (C.A.); compare, however, *De Bernales v. New York Herald*, [1893] 2 Q.B. 97n, discussed, *infra*, §125. Note, however, that an interlocutory injunction will only rarely be granted in defamation cases: *infra*, §§ 440-448.

[243] *Infra*, footnotes 245, 246, 248.

[244] *Lisbon-Berlyn (Transvaal) Gold Fields Ltd. v. Heddle* (1884), 52 L.T. 796 (Ch.); see also, *Overton & Co. v. Burn, Lowe, & Sons* (1896), 74 L.T. 776 (Ch.).

case,[245] for example, that service of a writ claiming an injunction to restrain infringement of a trademark should be upheld as the defendant company had branch offices in the jurisdiction rendering enforcement through sequestration possible.

123   However, where the defendant has no assets within the jurisdiction, or is an individual who remains outside the jurisdiction, the courts have been more cautious. Although the claim for an injunction against such a party may come within the letter of the rule, the tendency is to decline jurisdiction on discretionary grounds. [246]

124   In one case[247] an order for service on an individual in Ireland was upheld where "the defendant has not filed any affidavit shewing that he never comes to England; and if the injunction is granted, it can be enforced, whenever he comes within the jurisdiction." However, this was later interpreted[248] "to mean that if the defendant, who was an Irishman, was shewn to be in the habit of coming to *England*, then of course he could be reached by means of the injunction; if he had been altogether living in *Ireland* the case might have been different".

125   The second general principle which emerges from the cases is that the claim for the injunction must both be *bona fide* and emerge from a substantive cause of action justiciable in the court. The first aspect of this principle is that the courts guard against parties claiming an injunction merely to bring the case within the rule. Perhaps the best known example is *De Bernales v. New York Herald*[249] where an English plaintiff commenced an action for libel against an American newspaper and subsequently amended the writ to include a claim for injunction to restrain the defendant from any repetition. Leave to serve *ex juris* was refused on the grounds that the claim for an injunction was not *bona fide*, there being no evidence of any apprehended

---

[245] *Re Burland's Trade-mark* (1889), 41 Ch. D. 542. See also *Re Liddell's Settlement Trusts*, [1936] 1 Ch. 365 (C.A.).

[246] See *Marshall v. Marshall* (1888), 38 Ch. D. 330 (C.A.), holding that a passing-off action should be left to the Scottish Court although the defendant, an individual, had agents and servants within the jurisdiction, as the English court would be unable to enforce an order against him directly. See also *Kinahan v. Kinahan* (1890), 45 Ch. D. 78. Cf. *Badische Anilin und Soda Fabrik v. Henry Johnson & Co. and Basle Chemical Works*, [1896] 1 Ch. 25 (C.A.), where the English plaintiff was permitted to serve a Swiss manufacturer *ex juris* as a "necessary and proper party" in an action brought against both the English purchasers and the Swiss manufacturer for an injunction for breach of a trademark.

[247] *Tozier v. Hawkins, supra*, footnote 242, at p. 681, *per* Brett, M.R.

[248] *Re Burland's Trade-mark, supra*, footnote 245, at p. 545, *per* Chitty, J.

[249] *Supra*, footnote 242.

repetition of the libel, and that the injunction would be ineffective against the foreign defendant in any event.[250]

126   The second aspect of this principle is that the injunction must not be merely ancillary to some other claim which is not justiciable within the court. The House of Lords has recently held in *Siskina v. Distos Compania Naviera S.A.*[251] that a claim for a *Mareva* injunction to restrain a foreign defendant from removing assets from the jurisdiction does not fall within the rule if the English courts lack jurisdiction over the substantive claim. The "thing that it is sought to restrain the foreign defendant from doing . . ." within the jurisdiction must, according to the House of Lords, "amount to an invasion of some legal or equitable right belonging to the plaintiff in this country and enforceable here by a final judgment for an injunction."[252] In the case of a *Mareva* injunction, the claim for injunctive relief relates merely to interlocutory relief to protect the plaintiff's chances of recovering judgment in the event he succeeds on his substantive claim. Were such an injunction allowed in the circumstances of the *Siskina* case, its practical effect would often be to force the foreigner to come to the jurisdiction to defend an action ordinarily justiciable in a foreign court only to protect or obtain release of his assets. The courts have consistently refused to allow such a claim to be advanced "for the purpose of enabling the plaintiff to prosecute within [the jurisdiction] a claim which ought to be prosecuted elsewhere."[253]

---

[250] See also *Watson & Sons v. Daily Record Ltd.*, [1907] 1 K.B. 853 (C.A.); *English & American Machinery Co. v. Campbell Machine Co.* (1895), 39 Sol. Jo. 449 (Ch.); *Postlethwaite v. McWhinney* (1903), 6 O.L.R. 412 (H.C.J.).

[251] [1979] A.C. 210 (H.L.).

[252] *Ibid.*, at p. 256, *per* Lord Diplock.

[253] *Phelan v. Famous Players Canadian Corp.*, [1937] 2 D.L.R. 223 at pp. 225-7, [1937] O.W.N. 93 at pp.95-7 (H.C.J.). See also *Marshall v. Dominion Manufacturers Ltd.* (1914), 6 O.W.N. 385 (H.C.); *Rosler v. Hilbery*, [1925] Ch. 250 (C.A.); compare *Sears v. Meyers* (1893), 15 P.R. (Ont.) 381, where a foreign plaintiff was refused leave to serve a foreign defendant with a writ claiming upon a foreign judgment and asking for an interim injunction restraining the defendant from dealing with his lands. Compare, however, *Société Générale de Paris v. Dreyfus Brothers* (1885), 29 Ch. D. 239, revd on other grounds 37 Ch. D. 215 (C.A.), where the court refused to set aside service of a writ claiming an injunction to restrain the defendants from receiving or dealing with a fund in which the plaintiff held a property interest.

CHAPTER 2

INTERLOCUTORY INJUNCTIONS

1. The Standard for Interlocutory Injunctions[1]

(1) Introduction

127   The injunction is a flexible and drastic remedy. As will be seen in the chapters which follow, injunctions are not restricted to any area of substantive law, and are readily enforceable through the court's contempt power.

    The injunction can also be the speediest of remedies. It may be granted before trial, a feature which is almost unique in the array of available remedies, and one which makes the choice of injunctive relief all the more appealing in view of the relatively slow pace at which a civil action can be prosecuted. This chapter explores the appropriate considerations in the granting of interlocutory injunctions.

(2) Ex parte injunctions

128   There are three sorts of interlocutory restraining orders which are made.[2] In cases of urgency, an injunction may be granted *ex parte*, to restrain the defendant from committing the alleged violation of the plaintiff's rights for a stated period to allow for notice, filing of material, and a contested application.[3] There is some divergence in the

---

[1] The first part of this chapter is a modified version of Sharpe, "Interlocutory Injunctions: The Post-*American Cyanamid* Position", Chapter 8 in *Studies in Civil Procedure*, Gertner, ed. (Toronto, Butterworths, 1979).

[2] As pointed out by McRuer, C.J.H.C., in *Century Engineering Co. Ltd. v. Greto* (1960), 26 D.L.R. (2d) 300 at p. 304, [1961] O.R. 85 at p. 89 (H.C.J.):

    It is well established in practice that there are three sorts of interlocutory restraining orders that a Court may make: an interim order made *ex parte* and for a specific time only; an interim order made on notice but for a specific time, often in order to give the opposite party an opportunity to prepare a reply; and an order restraining the defendant until the trial or other disposition of the action.

It is also possible to obtain an interim order pending an appeal from a trial judgment either granting or staying an injunction, but this will be granted only with extreme caution and reluctance: see *Laboratoire Pentagone Ltée v. Parke, Davis & Co.*, [1968] S.C.R. 269, 70 D.L.R. (2d) 191; *Steinberg's Ltée v. Comité Paritaire de l'Alimentation au Détail, Région de Montréal*, [1968] S.C.R. 163, 66 D.L.R. (2d) 193; *Adrian Messenger Services v. Jockey Club Ltd. (No. 2)* (1972), 26 D.L.R. (3d) 287, [1972] 2 O.R. 619 (C.A.); compare, however, *Montana Mustard Seed Co. Inc. v. Continental Grain Co. (Canada) Ltd. (No 2)* (1974), 42 D.L.R. (3d) 624 (Sask. C.A.), where an injunction was granted pending appeal from an order dissolving an interlocutory injunction.

[3] In some cases, however, an *ex parte* injunction until trial may be ordered: see, *infra*, footnote 5; see also *Canadian Pacific Airlines Ltd. v. Hind* (1981), 122 D.L.R. (3d) 498, 32 O.R. (2d) 591 (H.C.J.); *Syndicat des Employés du Transport de Montréal (C.S.N.) v. A.-G. Que.*, [1970] S.C.R. 713, 17 D.L.R. (3d) 174, where an order, granted pursuant to legislation conferring jurisdiction to enjoin strikes which imperil public health or safety, was upheld although made *ex parte* and hav-

case-law as to the role played by the judge on the contested application. The better view, it is submitted, is that reflected by the Ontario cases which indicate that judges are to deal with the matter, "not as a mere appeal from the former order, but as an original substantive application. . . . the question on such a motion is not alone whether the order ought or ought not to have been made, but also whether, having been made, it should be rescinded or varied".[4] Other cases suggest rather more deference ought to be shown to the initial order and that, although it is unnecessary to present new facts or show non-disclosure on the *ex parte* application, the injunction will not be dissolved if it appears the first judge did consider all facts and arguments, even though the second judge might have decided the case differently.[5] This difference may merely reflect the fact that, in some jurisdictions, the practice is that an *ex parte* injunction continues until trial unless the defendant moves against it, whereas elsewhere, the normal practice is explicitly to limit *ex parte* injunctions for a stated period in the expectation that a contested application will follow.[6] It is submitted that the latter practice is much to be preferred and, as recently said by the Manitoba Court of Appeal, "in no case should an *ex parte* injunction be given for an indefinite period. It should be limited until the shortest possible time so that notice can be given to the parties affected by it. . . . [E]very *ex parte* injunction should be interim".[7]

129   To justify an *ex parte* injunction, there must be such urgency that the delay necessary to give notice might entail serious and irreparable injury to the plaintiff.[8] Granting an injunction before the plaintiff's right has been established at trial often entails a serious risk of infringing the rights of the defendant.[9] That risk is signifi-

---

ing a duration of over two months. Legislation often restricts the availability of *ex parte* injunctions in labour matters: see, *infra*, §§192-195.

[4] *Howland v. Dominion Bank* (1892), 15 P.R. 56 (Ont. C.A.), at p. 63, affd 22 S.C.R. 130, *per* MacLennan, J.A.

[5] *Gulf Islands Navigation Ltd. v. Seafarers Int'l Union of North America* (1959), 18 D.L.R. (2d) 216 (B.C.S.C.), affd loc. cit. p. 625 (C.A.).

[6] *Ibid.*

[7] *Griffin Steel Foundries Ltd. v. Canadian Ass'n of Industrial, Mechanical & Allied Workers* (1977), 80 D.L.R. (3d) 634 (Man. C.A.), at p. 640, *per* O'Sullivan, J.A.

[8] See, *e.g.*, *Gulf Islands Navigation Ltd. v. Seafarers Int'l Union of North America*, *supra*, footnote 5, at p. 218, *per* Wilson, J.: "The first enquiry to be made in all cases is — 'why did you not give notice?' — and if the answer elicited does not reveal extraordinary urgency, the application must be refused." See also *Scarr v. Gower* (1956), 2 D.L.R. (2d) 402 (B.C.C.A.); *Launch! Research & Development Inc. v. Essex Distributing Co.* (1977), 4 C.P.C. 261 (Ont. H.C.J.).

[9] *Infra*, §134.

cantly heightened if an injunction is granted without even giving the defendant notice and an opportunity to be heard. For this reason, the courts are especially cautious in granting *ex parte* injunctions. More important is the obligation on counsel to see that full and frank disclosure is made of all material facts.[10] Failure to make full disclosure has been dealt with severely, and will almost always result in the injunction being set aside as a punitive measure on the motion to continue once the defendant has been served.[11] An "interim" injunction usually refers to an order made on notice, but after limited argument and only for a specific time, usually to permit the defendant to cross-examine on the affidavits filed by the plaintiffs or to file his own material in reply.[12] An "interlocutory" injunction usually refers to an order restraining the defendant until trial or other disposition of the action,[13] and it is this type of injunction which is the subject of the bulk of this chapter.

(3) Balance of risks

130   Canadian judges have tended to eschew general statements of principle when deciding interlocutory injunction applications, and emphasis has been placed on the desirability of a healthy measure of discretion. The importance of the flexibility which broad discretion entails is properly seen as being all the more essential where the court is called upon to make a drastic order without the benefit of a full trial.

131   In dealing with interlocutory injunction applications, judges have used what might be called a checklist of factors. Typically, the courts have looked to the items on the list — the relative strength of the cases, irreparable harm, the balance of convenience, the preserva-

---

[10] *Massie & Renwick Ltd. v. Underwriters' Survey Bureau Ltd.*, [1937] S.C.R. 265, [1937] 2 D.L.R. 213. See cases cited, *infra*, footnote 11.

[11] *Capital Manufacturing Co. v. Buffalo Specialty Co.* (1912), 1 D.L.R. 260, 3 O.W.N. 553 (H.C.); *Herman v. Klig*, [1938] 3 D.L.R. 755, [1938] O.W.N. 270 (H.C.J.); *Scarr v. Gower, supra*, footnote 8; *Launch! Research & Development Inc. v. Essex Distributing Co., supra*, footnote 8; *McCharles v. Wyllie* (1927), 32 O.W.N. 202 (H.C.); *Baldwin v. Chaplin* (1913), 12 D.L.R. 387, 4 O.W.N. 1574 (H.C.); *Monocrest Kitchens Ltd. v. Evans* (1967), 63 D.L.R. (2d) 553 (B.C.S.C.). In *C.P.R. United Transportation Union, Local 144* (1970), 14 D.L.R. (3d) 497 (B.C.S.C.), it was held that any inaccuracy was fatal, even where the facts were not relevant to the decision to grant the *ex parte* injunction. Compare *Coles Bakery Ltd. v. Bakery & Confectionery Workers' Int'l Union of America* (1962), 36 D.L.R. (2d) 772 (B.C.S.C.).

[12] *Supra*, footnote 2.

[13] *Supra*, footnote 2.

tion of the *status quo* — and have avoided statements of general principle. Properly applied, the traditional approach affords a desirable measure of flexibility. Its weakness, however, is the lack of a focus and framework within which the various factors operate. The checklist does not itself articulate a precise standard against which the various considerations are to be measured. How do the various factors on the checklist relate to each other? Does each item represent a hurdle which must always be surmounted by the applicant, or may weakness on one item be compensated by strength on another? The judge is left to cope with this sort of problem in each single instance: the checklist technique tends to sacrifice definition of approach in the cause of flexibility. While the checklist has usually produced sound results, the want of a standard has caused certain problems. The very looseness in this approach provoked the House of Lords[14] to prescribe a more rigid, systematic formula which, as will be seen, has brought with it certain problems of its own.

132   It is suggested that a specific test or simple formula is bound to prove inadequate to describe results which courts should reach. It is difficult, dangerous and, perhaps, undesirable to attempt to lay down explicit formulations or guidelines. The decision properly depends very much upon the particular circumstances before the court. However, it is suggested that it is essential that there be a focus for decision-making in interlocutory injunction applications.

133   The problem posed by interlocutory injunction applications may, it is submitted, best be understood in terms of balancing the relative risks of granting or withholding the remedy. These risks may be simply stated as follows. The plaintiff must show a threat to his rights produced by the combination of the defendant's conduct and the delay until trial. The risk to the plaintiff in such cases is that, if an immediate remedy is withheld, his rights will be so impaired by the time of trial and final judgment that it will be too late to afford him complete relief.

134   Against this risk to the plaintiff must be balanced the risk of harm to the defendant, should the injunction be granted. This risk is inherent in that the court, on an interlocutory application, can only guess what the result at trial will be. It may well transpire that, although the plaintiff now appears to have a reasonable prospect of success, he

---

[14] *American Cyanamid Co. v. Ethicon Ltd.*, [1975] A.C. 396. The House of Lords was also reacting against the conscious practice of using the interlocutory injunction as a device to obtain a quick and relatively cheap resolution of the merits: Prescott, Note, 91 L.Q. R. 168 (1975).

may lose in the end. At this early stage of the proceedings, the pressure of chambers work may mean that the judge hearing the application will have less time to sift the factual and legal issues than he would have at trial. It will only be in exceptional cases that he will have the benefit of hearing *viva voce* evidence.[15] Usually, the case will be presented on affidavits. Without the benefit of pleadings and full discovery, the factual and legal issues may well be only roughly defined and, perhaps, not even fully investigated by the parties themselves. It will often be difficult, and sometimes impossible, to predict accurately the final result. Although it may now seem that the plaintiff will win, in the end the defendant may well prevail. Accordingly, inherent in the exercise lies a risk of harming the defendant by enjoining him from pursuing a course he may ultimately show he had every right to follow.

135   It is suggested, then, that the task of the court is to balance the risk of harm to the defendant, inherent in granting remedial relief before the merits of the dispute can be fully explored, against the risk that the plaintiff's rights will be significantly impaired in the time awaiting the trial.[16]

---

[15] See, for example, the Judicature Act, Ont., s. 20(4), which specifically provides for the *viva voce* cross-examination of deponents in cases involving labour disputes, discussed, *infra*, §193.

[16] Lord Diplock's decision in the *American Cyanamid* case, *supra*, footnote 14, at p. 406, appears to recognize, to some extent, that the central issue to be faced on applications for interlocutory injunctions is the balancing of risks:

> The object of the interlocutory injunction is to protect the plaintiff against injury by violation of his right for which he could not be adequately compensated in damages recoverable in the action if the uncertainty were resolved in his favour at the trial; but the plaintiff's need for such protection must be weighed against the corresponding need of the defendant to be protected against injury resulting from his having been prevented from exercising his own legal rights for which he could not be adequately compensated under the plaintiff's undertaking in damages if the uncertainty were resolved in the defendant's favour at the trial. The court must weigh one need against another and determine where "the balance of convenience" lies.

Leubsdorf, "The Standard for Preliminary Injunctions", 91 Harv. L. Rev. 525 (1978), at p. 542, presents an attempt to achieve a more precise calibration which is based upon a development of the following model:

> The court, in theory, should assess the probable irreparable loss of rights an injunction would cause by multiplying the probability that the defendant will prevail by the amount of the irreparable loss that the defendant would suffer if enjoined from exercising what turns out to be his legal right. It should then make a similar calculation of the probable irreparable loss of rights to the plaintiff from denying the injunction. Whichever course promises the smaller probable loss should be adopted.

It is submitted that, while this formulation provides a valid theoretical statement of

136   In the following sections, the various items on the "checklist" are analyzed in light of the reformulation of the standard for interlocutory relief attempted in the 1975 decision of the House of Lords in *American Cyanamid*.[17]

(4) Strength of the plaintiff's case

137   The first question the court asks is, "What is the relative strength of the plaintiff's case?" This question may be phrased in various ways: prior to the *American Cyanamid* decision, the formulation most in vogue was, "Has the plaintiff demonstrated a strong *prima facie* case?"[18] This probably means no more than, if the court had to decide finally the matter on the merits, on the basis of the material before it, would the plaintiff succeed? There are three possible answers to this question.

---

the approach which should be taken, it will only be the rare case that produces "irreparable loss of rights" susceptible to precise calculation, and that the weighing of factors inevitably involves a significant subjective element which can be described, but not quantified.

[17] *Supra*, footnote 14. The impact of the *Cyanamid* case has been discussed in the following: Baker, "Interlocutory Injunctions — a Discussion of the 'New Rules' ", 42 Sask. L. Rev. 53 (1977); Prescott, *supra*, footnote 14; Hammond, "Interlocutory Injunctions: Time for a new Model?", 30 U. of T. L.J. 240 (1980); Gray, "Interlocutory Injunctions Since Cyanamid", 40 Camb. L.J. 307 (1981); Rogers and Hately, "Getting the Pre-Trial Injunction", 60 Can. Bar Rev. 1 (1982).

[18] See, for example, *J.T. Stratford & Son Ltd. v. Lindley*, [1965] A.C. 269 (H.L.), at p. 307; *Preston v. Luck* (1884), 27 Ch. D. 497 (C.A.), at p. 506; *Smith v. Grigg, Ltd.*, [1924] 1 K.B. 655 (C.A.), at p. 659; *Cavendish House (Cheltenham) Ltd. v. Cavendish-Woodhouse, Ltd.* (1968), [1970] R.P.C. 234 (C.A.), at p. 235; *Street Ry. Advertising Co. v. Toronto Ry. Co.* (1904), 3 O.W.R. 849; *Trustee of N. Brenner & Co. Ltd. v. Brenner* (1923), 25 O.W.N. 415 (H.C.); *Richter v. Koskey and Adler*, [1953] 4 D.L.R. 509, [1953] O.W.N. 746 (H.C.J.); *286880 Ontario Ltd. v. Parke* (1974), 52 D.L.R. (3d) 535, 6 O.R. (2d) 311 (H.C.J.); *Pike v. Council of Ontario College of Art* (1972), 29 D.L.R. (3d) 544, [1972] 3 O.R. 808 (H.C.J.); *Contractors Equipment & Supply (1965) Ltd. v. Local 914* (1965), 54 D.L.R. (2d) 726 (Man. C.A.). This formulation has, however, not been uniform. Many cases ask whether the plaintiff has shown that there is "a substantial question to be investigated" (*e.g.*, *Home Oil Distributors Ltd. v. A.-G. B.C.*, [1939] 1 D.L.R. 573 (B.C.C.A.) at p. 576); that there is a "fair question" (*e.g.*, *Wheatley v. Ellis*, [1944] 3 W.W.R. 462 (B.C.C.A.), at p. 463); that there is a "serious question to be tried" (*e.g.*, *LaForest & Cochrane v. Carriere* (1921), 21 O.W.N. 265 (H.C.), at p. 266); or that there is "a substantial question to be tried" (*e.g.*, *Gladstone Petroleums Ltd. v. Husky Oil (Alberta) Ltd.* (1969), 9 D.L.R. (3d) 415 (Sask. Q.B.), at p. 418). It is submitted, however, that, to the extent that these formulations represent a variation from the *prima facie* case test, they present situations in which the assessment of the merits is difficult, and that, because of the inability at the preliminary stage to come to a conclusion on the merits, the case must turn on the balance of convenience, as indicated in the text, *infra*, §139. Compare, however, Baker, *supra*, footnote 17, at pp. 54-8.

138   (1) If the plaintiff does demonstrate a strong *prima facie* case, the likelihood of the ultimate success will weigh heavily in his favour. Clearly, however, the strong possibility of ultimate success is not, and should not be, conclusive. This approach would ignore the risk inherent in basing the decision solely upon a preliminary assessment of the strength of the case. It is possible that this preliminary assessment, based upon incomplete evidence and argument, is wrong, and accordingly, the other factors, discussed below, must also be taken into account.

139   (2) If the court is unable to come to a conclusion at this stage as to the strength of the plaintiff's case, the decision will have to turn upon other factors.[19] Inability to assess the plaintiff's case will usually result from the uncertainties of affidavit evidence, especially where affidavits conflict and where questions of credibility arise. It would be unfair, in such cases, to say that the plaintiff ought to be automatically foreclosed from obtaining an interlocutory injunction. The defendant would then always put up a smoke-screen of conflicting affidavits, the plaintiff's rights would be taken without trial, and perjury would be rewarded if not encouraged. Accordingly, in such cases the courts have traditionally turned to consider and to rest the decision on other factors.

140   (3) If the court can say, at this preliminary stage, that the plaintiff has not made out a strong *prima facie* case, the tendency has been to say that no injunction prior to trial should be granted.[20] If it appears

---

[19] *Dwyre v. Ottawa* (1898), 25 O.A.R. 121 at p. 130, *per* Moss, J.A.:

> The rules governing applications of this kind are well settled. Where the legal right is not sufficiently clear to enable the Court to form an opinion it will generally be governed in deciding an application for an interim injunction by considerations of the relative convenience and inconvenience which may result to the parties from granting or withholding the order.

See also: *Playter v. Lucas* (1921), 69 D.L.R. 514, 51 O.L.R. 492 (H.C.); *Thompson v. Cheeseworth* (1920), 18 O.W.N. 419 (H.C.); *Lido Industrial Products Ltd. v. Melnor Manufacturing Ltd.*, [1968] S.C.R. 769, 69 D.L.R. (2d) 256; *Evans Marshall & Co. Ltd. v. Bertola S.A.*, [1973] 1 W.L.R. 349 (C.A.); *McLaren v. Caldwell* (1880), 5 O.A.R. 363 at pp. 367-8; *Maker v. Davanne Holdings Ltd.*, [1955] 1 D.L.R. 728, [1954] O.R. 935 (H.C.J.); *Toronto Transit Com'n v. Aqua Taxi Ltd.*, [1955] O.W.N. 857 (H.C.J.); *Steel Art Co. Ltd. v. Hrivnak* (1979), 105 D.L.R. (3d) 716, 27 O.R. (2d) 136 (H.C.J.).

[20] See, for example, the following dictum of Heald, J., in *Salada Foods Ltd. v. W.K. Buckley Ltd. (No. 2)* (1973), 9 C.P.R. (2d) 35 (Fed. Ct. T.D.), at p. 38:

> The judicial principles governing the granting of interlocutory injunctions establish that the applicant must make out a fair or a clear *prima facie* case or his application should be rejected. The applicant must also establish irreparable injury; if the applicant's injury in the event of final success is compensable by dam-

likely that the plaintiff will fail on the merits at the trial, the argument goes, there can be no justification in giving him a temporary remedy, as he has nothing from which he needs to be protected. This third possible answer points to the difficulty, from the plaintiff's point of view, which can result from undue emphasis on the apparent strength of the case. Indeed, it was this very point which prompted the House of Lords to reconsider this entire area in the *American Cyanamid* case.

141   In *American Cyanamid*,[21] after an eight-day hearing on a complex factual issue, the English Court of Appeal set aside an interlocutory injunction. The plaintiff alleged that the defendant's proposed introduction of a synthetic, absorbable, surgical suture would violate the plaintiff's patent which was said to protect such sutures formed from a "polyhydroxyacetic ester". The claim and defence raised a complex factual issue concerning the meaning of "polyhydroxyacetic ester". Dealing with a complex factual question without the refinement pro-

---

ages, an injunction will not issue. If the applicant makes out both those requisites, and the other party also shows a fighting case, the Court must then decide whether the balance of convenience lies in granting or refusing the injunction, and as to this the burden of proof lies on the applicant.

This is described by Hammond, *supra*, footnote 17, at p. 240, as the "classical model involving, sequentially, an inquiry as to whether the plaintiff had demonstrated a sufficient probability of right, and, assuming that threshold test was met, further inquiry as to the adequacy of damages or other relief, and what the relative position of the parties would be if interlocutory relief was not (prospectively) granted." Other cases taking the same approach are: *Cradle Pictures (Canada) Ltd. v. Penner* (1975), 63 D.L.R. (3d) 440, 10 O.R. (2d) 444 (H.C.J.); *Richter v. Koskey and Adler, supra*, footnote 18; *Bain v. Bank of Canada, and Woodward*, [1935] 4 D.L.R. 112 (B.C.C.A.); *Blue Funnel Motor Line Ltd. v. City of Vancouver*, [1918] 3 W.W.R. 405 (B.C.S.C.); *Mugford v. St. John's Truckmen's Protective Union, Hearn and Billard*, [1955] 5 D.L.R. 644 (Nfld. S.C.). Compare, however, *Hubbard v. Vosper*, [1972] 2 Q.B. 84 (C.A.), and *Evans Marshall & Co. Ltd. v. Bertola S.A., supra*, footnote 19, at p. 378, where Sachs, L.J., indicated that, while the general rule required the plaintiff to establish a "reasonable *prima facie* case which could lead to success", and failure to do so was "a factor which may normally weigh heavily against granting an interlocutory injunction", the absence of the *prima facie* case did not, as a matter of law, preclude the court from granting interim relief.

In *Beecham Group Ltd. v. Bristol Laboratories Pty Ltd.* (1968), 118 C.L.R. 618 at p. 622, *per curiam*, the Australian High Court set out a more flexible standard. It was held that, while the relative strengths of the claim and defence should be considered, the degree of probability of the plaintiff's success required will vary depending upon the circumstances: "How strong the probability needs to be depends, no doubt, upon the nature of the rights he asserts and the practical consequences likely to flow from the order he seeks". See Cornwell and Sturzenegger, "Interlocutory Injunctions: A Serious Question to be Tried?", 8 Sydney L. Rev. 207 (1977).

[21] [1974] F.S.R. 312 (C.A.).

duced by pleading and discovery, and without the benefit of oral evidence, poses obvious difficulties. However, it was undertaken by the Court of Appeal, which reversed the chambers' judge on the grounds that the plaintiff had failed to establish a strong *prima facie* case. The court did not consider the balance of convenience or other factors,[22] and applied the strength of the plaintiff's case as a threshold test. Failure on the first question meant certain failure for the entire application.

142   On appeal to the House of Lords,[23] the initial decision to grant the interlocutory injunction was restored. Lord Diplock gave the unanimous decision and was particularly critical of what he considered to be undue emphasis on the strength of the plaintiff's case at the interlocutory stage. He suggested that terms such as *"prima facie* case" are inappropriate, and that the court should merely satisfy itself that the plaintiff has a case worthy of trial:[24] "The court no doubt must be satisfied that the claim is not frivolous or vexatious; in other words, that there is a serious question to be tried." Lord Diplock emphasized the difficulty of undertaking a preliminary trial of the matter upon affidavit material and said, in effect, that a preliminary attempt to predict the ultimate outcome was so fraught with danger and difficulty that it ought not to be undertaken at all.

143   Lord Diplock went on to set out a step-by-step formula as the appropriate way to determine whether an interlocutory injunction should be granted.[25] More detailed consideration of each step follows under specific headings, but it will facilitate discussion of the strength of case factor to summarize the formula here. *First*, as indicated, the court is to ask whether the plaintiff has presented a case which is not frivolous or vexatious, but which presents a serious case to be tried. *Second*, will damages provide the plaintiff with an adequate remedy? If so, no injunction should be granted. If not, *third*, would the plaintiff's undertaking in damages provide adequate compensation to the defendant, should he succeed at trial, for loss sustained because of the interlocutory injunction? If so, then there is a strong case for an interlocutory injunction. *Fourth*, where there is doubt as to the adequacy of the respective remedies in damages, the case

---

[22] *Ibid.*, at p. 333, *per* Russell, L.J.: "if there be no prima facie case on the point essential to entitle the plaintiff to complain of the defendants' proposed activities, that is the end of the claim to interlocutory relief."

[23] *American Cyanamid Co. v. Ethicon Ltd.*, [1975] A.C. 396 (H.L.).

[24] *Ibid.*, at p. 407.

[25] *Ibid.*, at pp. 407-8.

turns on the balance of convenience. *Fifth*, at this point, according to Lord Diplock, weight may be placed on the court's prediction of ultimate success, but only in certain cases. It is only where:

> the extent of the uncompensatable disadvantage to each party would not differ widely . . . [that] it may not be improper to take into account in tipping the balance the relative strength of each party's case as revealed by the affidavit evidence adduced on the hearing of the application. This, however, should be done only where it is apparent upon the facts disclosed by the evidence as to which there is no credible dispute that the strength of one party's case is disproportionate to that of the other party. The court is not justified in embarking upon anything resembling a trial of the action upon conflicting affidavits in order to evaluate the strength of either party's case.[26]

144   In other words, the strength of case consideration of the traditional approach is stood on its head. Under the *Cyanamid* approach, the strength of the case comes into play, initially, only to the extent of determining that the plaintiff's claim is not frivolous or vexatious. The core test to be applied is balance of convenience. It is only where the court cannot properly assess balance of convenience that the relative strength of the parties' cases may be taken into account and then, only where one side of the case is clearly stronger.

145   On the facts presented to the House of Lords, it is not at all difficult to understand this reluctance to engage in the attempt to predict the final outcome of that particular case. The hearing was expected to take twelve days, and would have involved a mass of technical and conflicting evidence. In such circumstances, it is neither surprising nor inappropriate to discount entirely the strength of case factor. By dispelling the notion that a strong *prima facie* case is an essential prerequisite to interlocutory relief, the decision conforms with a sensitive balance-of-risk approach.

146   However, it is quite another matter to deprecate reliance on a preliminary assessment in all cases. The particular difficulty of one case ought not to be taken as establishing a principle of general application, especially in an area of the law which has heretofore borne flexibility as its hallmark.

147   If the decision whether to grant preliminary injunctive relief does indeed turn on an assessment of the relative risks of harm, as suggested here, it seems incontrovertible that the plaintiff's chance of ultimate success is a directly relevant factor. The likelihood of the plaintiff's success or failure relates both to the extent of the risk that

---

[26] *Ibid.*, at p. 409.

there will be any legal harm which calls for a remedy in favour of the plaintiff,[27] and to the extent of the risk that an injunction may prevent the defendant from pursuing a course of conduct he had every right to follow. If relevant, the strength of a case should be considered, unless there is some compelling reason to disregard it. It is submitted that *Cyanamid* overstates the difficulty in accurately assessing the strength of the case on an incomplete record.

148   Neither in England nor Canada, does there appear to be evidence of poor quality of decisions on the merits at the interlocutory stage.[28] On the contrary, there is every indication that one of the virtues of the interlocutory application is that it provides a quick, inexpensive and reliable determination which usually avoids the necessity of further litigation.[29]

149   The difficulty of assessing the strength of a case varies widely according to the circumstances. In virtually all cases, the court should exercise caution in the weight it attaches to its preliminary assessment, but this is to say no more than that the risk to the defendant must be carefully weighed.

150   Where the chance of accurate prediction is higher, as for example, where the result turns on the construction of a statute or the legal consequence of admitted facts, the court hearing the preliminary application is in a very good position to predict the result. Moreover, procedural differences in Canada, notably the more frequent resort to the right to cross-examine on affidavits, will often place a Cana-

---

[27] Prescott, *supra*, footnote 14, at p. 171: "If it be pertinent to ask: 'Will the plaintiff suffer irreparable damage if no injunction is granted now?' it ought to be permitted to require also: "How sure are we that he will ultimately suffer legal damage at all?' "

[28] Prescott, *supra*, at p. 169:

> The practical effect of this doctrine [of basing the decision in part on the strength of the case] was that interlocutory motions for an injunction became a cheap and speedy means of testing the strengths of the parties' respective cases. That the standard of justice done on motion was high is demonstrated by the fact that in only a very few cases was the result at the trial different from that arrived at on motion. Indeed, in practice the parties usually elected to settle on the basis of the interlocutory finding without going to trial at all.

See also Leubsdorf, *supra*, footnote 16, at p. 555: "Perhaps the most manageable part of the preliminary injunction decision is estimating the likelihood of various results at final judgment."

[29] In *Fellowes & Son v. Fisher*, [1976] Q.B. 122 (C.A.), at p. 129, Lord Denning, M.R., noted that by virtue of the practice of considering the merits in some detail, "in 99 cases out of 100 [the matter] goes no further".

dian judge on firmer ground, even when dealing with conflicting evidence.[30]

151   It is submitted, therefore, that the suggested elimination of the relative strength of the case as a factor is regrettable, and indeed the recent English and Canadian cases indicate that the stricture of the *Cyanamid* case will not be observed at the practical level.

152   While *Cyanamid* has been followed in several Canadian[31] and English cases,[32] it has been rejected as being an inappropriate revision

---

[30] In *Toronto Marlboro Major Junior "A" Hockey Club v. Tonelli* (1975), 67 D.L.R. (3d) 214 at p. 227, 11 O.R. (2d) 664 at p. 677 (H.C.J.), Morden, J., noted that the reluctance of the House of Lords to "make a decision on facts which are in dispute and given by way of affidavits which have not been tested by oral cross-examination" does not apply with the same strength in jurisdictions which allow cross-examination upon affidavits as a right, even where the cross-examination does not take place in the presence of the court. This point was also emphasized in *Chitel v. Rothbart* (1982), 141 D.L.R. (3d) 268, 39 O.R. (2d) 513 (C.A.).

[31] It has been described as being "honest in its approach and should be applicable in most cases" in light of the "evidentiary problems facing the Courts on interim injunction motions" by the Ontario Divisional Court in *Yule, Inc. v. Atlantic Pizza Delight Franchise (1968) Ltd.* (1977), 80 D.L.R. (3d) 725 at p. 733, 17 O.R. (2d) 505 at p. 513 (H.C.J.), and applied in several other cases: see, *e.g.*, *Labelle v. Ottawa Real Estate Board* (1977), 78 D.L.R. (3d) 558, 16 O.R. (2d) 502 (H.C.J.); *Baker v. Gay and Mayes* (1978), 20 N.B.R. (2d) 643 (S.C.); *Thomas Lindsay Ltd. v. Lindsay* (1975), 64 D.L.R. (3d) 761 (B.C.S.C.); *Abouna v. Foothills Provincial General Hospital Board* (1975), 65 D.L.R. (3d) 337 (Alta. S.C.T.D.), at p. 345; *Bernard v. Valentini* (1978), 83 D.L.R. (3d) 440, 18 O.R. (2d) 656 (H.C.J.); *Hamlet of Baker Lake v. Minister of Indian Affairs and Northern Development*, [1979] 1 F.C. 487, 87 D.L.R. (3d) 342 (T.D.); *Wald v. Pape* (1978), 92 D.L.R. (3d) 378, 22 O.R. (2d) 163 (H.C.J.), affd 108 D.L.R. (3d) 373, 28 O.R. (2d) 27 (Div. Ct.); *Aspotogan Ltd. v. Lawrence* (1976), 14 N.S.R. (2d) 501 (S.C. App. Div.); *Erickson v. Wiggins Adjustments Ltd.*, [1980] 6 W.W.R. 188 (Alta. C.A.); *Re Greenpeace Foundation of British Columbia and Minister of Environment* (1981), 122 D.L.R. (3d) 179 (B.C.S.C.); *McFetridge v. Nova Scotia Barristers' Society* (1981), 122 D.L.R. (3d) 627 (N.S.S.C.), revd 123 D.L.R. (3d) 475 (S.C. App. Div.); *Steel Art Co. Ltd. v. Hrivnak* (1979), 105 D.L.R. (3d) 716, 27 O.R. (2d) 136 (H.C.J.); *A.-G. Ont. v. Harry* (1979), 93 D.L.R. (3d) 332, 22 O.R. (2d) 321 (H.C.J.); *Hebert v. Shawinigan Cataractes Hockey Club* (1978), 94 D.L.R. (3d) 153, 22 O.R. (2d) 654 (H.C.J.); *Turf Care Products Ltd. v. Crawford's Mowers & Marine Ltd.* (1978), 95 D.L.R. (3d) 378, 23 O.R. (2d) 292 (H.C.J.), leave to appeal to Div. Ct. refused D.L.R. *loc. cit.*, O.R. *loc. cit.*; *Sheddon v. Ontario Major Junior Hockey League* (1978), 83 D.L.R. (3d) 734, 19 O.R. (2d) 1 (H.C.J.).

[32] For a comprehensive review of the post-*Cyanamid* English cases, see Gray, *supra*, footnote 17. For examples of cases following *Cyanamid*, see *Hubbard v. Pitt*, [1976] Q.B. 142 (C.A.); *Catnic Components Ltd. v. Stressline Ltd.*, [1976] F.S.R. 157 (C.A.); *Potters-Ballotini Ltd. v. Weston-Baker*, [1977] R.P.C. 202 (C.A.); *Howe Richardson Scale Co. Ltd. v. Polimex-Cekop and National Westminster Bank Ltd.*, [1978] 1 Lloyd's Rep. 161 (C.A.); *Re Lord Cable*, [1977] 1 W.L.R. 7 (Ch.). It has also been followed in New Zealand: *Phillip Morris (New Zealand) Ltd. v. Liggett & Myers Tobacco Co. (New Zealand) Ltd.*, [1977] 2 N.Z.L.R. 35 (S.C.); but see Harris, "Interim and Interlocutory Injunctions; Assessment of Probability of Success", [1979] N.Z.L.J. 525.

of the traditional approach in several instances.[33] Even when the case is followed, there has also been a subtle tendency to elevate the standard to be met by the plaintiff on the merits, whatever lip-service is paid to *Cyanamid*.[34] Some cases interpret "not frivolous or vexatious" to mean something close to "a reasonable prospect of success".[35] It has been suggested in an English case that "frivolous or vexatious" should be read as requiring a higher probability of success

---

[33] *American Cyanamid* was not followed in *Cradle Pictures (Canada) Ltd. v. Penner* (1975), 63 D.L.R. (3d) 440, 10 O.R. (2d) 444 (H.C.J.); *A.-G. Ont. v. Grabarchuk* (1976), 67 D.L.R. (3d) 31, 11 O.R. (2d) 607 (Div. Ct.); *Niagara Frontier Caterers Ltd. v. Lukey* (1975), 24 C.P.R. (2d) 280 (Ont. H.C.J.); *Indal Ltd. v. Halko* (1976), 28 C.P.R. (2d) 230, (Ont. H.C.J.); *Weider & Weider Sports Equipment Co. Ltd. v. Dominion Mail Order Products Corp.* (1976), 30 C.P.R. (2d) 87 (Ont. H.C.J.); *Toronto Marlboro Major Junior "A" Hockey Club v. Tonelli, supra,* footnote 30, at pp. 226-8 D.L.R., pp. 676-8 O.R.; *Mercator Enterprises Ltd. v. Harris and Mainland Investments Ltd.* (1978), 29 N.S.R. (2d) 691 (S.C. App. Div.); *Canadian Javelin Ltd. v. Sparling* (1978), 4 B.L.R. 153 (Fed. Ct. T.D.), affd 91 D.L.R. (3d) 64 (C.A.), leave to appeal to S.C.C. refused 24 N.R. 571n; *Lambair Ltd. v. Aero Trades (Western) Ltd.* (1978), 87 D.L.R. (3d) 500 (Man. C.A.), leave to appeal to S.C.C. refused October 4, 1978. See also cases cited, *infra,* §§154-162. In *Camellia Tanker Ltd. S.A. v. Int'l Transport Workers Federation*, [1976] I.C.R. 274 (Ch.), affd *loc. cit.* p. 290 (C.A.), at p. 292, Megaw, L.J., observed that while he did not find it "necessary for the decision of this appeal to add to the discussion [of *Cyanamid*] . . . I do not believe that it was intended to overrule *J.T. Stratford & Son Ltd. v. Lindley*, [1965] A.C. 269 [which employed the *prima facie* case test] or to disapprove of the reasoning or the approach of the House of Lords in that case, including what was done therein on the assessment of affidavit evidence." See also *Bryanston Finance Ltd. v. De Vries (No. 2)*, [1976] 1 Ch. 63 (C.A.); *Lewis v. Heffer*, [1978] 1 W.L.R. 1061 (C.A.). *American Cyanamid* has not been followed in Australia: see *Firth Industries Ltd. v. Polyglas Engineering Pty. Ltd.* (1975), 6 A.L.R. 212 (H.C.). It has also been rejected in South Africa: *Beecham Group Ltd. v. B-M Group (Pty.) Ltd.*, [1977] R.P.C. 220 (S.C.).

See also Prescott, *supra,* footnote 14; Wilson, "Granting an Interlocutory Injunction", 125 New L.J. 302 (1975); Gore, "Interlocutory Injunction — A Final Judgment?", 38 Mod. L. Rev. 672 (1975); Elias, "Pickets and Interlocutory Injunctions", 34 Camb. L.J. 191 (1975).

[34] See, *e.g., Heathview Developments Ltd. v. Credit Foncier* (1982), 37 O.R. (2d) 262 (H.C.J.). In *Bernard v. Valentini, supra,* footnote 31, at pp. 442-3 D.L.R., p. 659 O.R., Cory, J., held that the *Cyanamid* test should apply, but at the same time stated that the facts strongly favoured the plaintiff: "It would be difficult and perhaps impossible in light of the chronology of events and the undisputed facts to come to any other conclusion, at least until the time of trial."

[35] See, for example, *Carlton Realty Co. Ltd. v. Maple Leaf Mills Ltd.* (1978), 93 D.L.R. (3d) 106 at p. 111, 22 O.R. (2d) 198 at p. 203 (H.C.J.), *per* Steele, J.: "The *American Cyanamid* case sets standards that appear in their words to be more lenient than the words '*prima facie* case' or 'probability of success'. I am of the opinion that there is not serious difference. Surely a serious question to be tried equates to a *prima facie* case." See *Hayter Motor Underwriting Agencies Ltd. v. R.B.H.S. Agencies Ltd.*, [1977] 2 Lloyd's Rep. 105 (C.A.); *Rasu Maritima S.A. v. Perusahaan*, [1978] Q.B. 644 (C.A.); *Losinska v. Civil and Public Services Ass'n*, [1976] I.C.R. 473 (C.A.).

than when the same phrase is used in relation with applications to strike out an action.[36] Similarly, it has been held that where the facts are not in dispute, greater weight should be placed on the merits.[37]

153   It is submitted that the problems of assessing the probable outcome in one type of case should not, and will not, preclude the court from weighing in the balance its perception of the likely result, so long as there is a cautious awareness of the inherent risk of inaccuracy at an early stage.

154   In certain cases, it is essential, as a matter of justice, that the strength of the case be the predominant consideration. In many cases the rights of the parties are, in fact, finally determined on the motion for an interlocutory injunction. Classic examples are cases involving picketing[38] and covenants in restraint of trade.[39] While a fully satisfactory determination may be possible only after pleadings, discovery and *viva voce* trial, the simple fact is that events will not wait for elaborate pre-trial proceedings and that the parties need an immediate determination.

155   Indeed, in cases falling within this category, factors other than the strength of the case are truly irrelevant. The risk-balancing standard is misplaced in this context. The court is not engaged in balancing the risk of prejudice to the plaintiff's rights pending trial against the risk that the defendant will be successful at trial. There will be no trial. To suggest that balance of convenience should prevail, and that the strength of the case should be disregarded, is to base the decision upon irrelevant factors, while ignoring that which should govern. Difficulty in deciding does not justify judicial abdication.

156   The difficulty which is produced by ignoring the strength of the case has been illustrated in several cases. In *Fellowes & Son v. Fisher*,[40] the English Court of Appeal was faced with an application by an employer to restrain until trial its former employee from breaching a non-competition covenant. Lord Denning, M.R., Browne, L.J., and Sir John Pennycuick all frankly confessed the diffi-

---

[36] *Mothercare Ltd. v. Robson Books Ltd.*, [1979] F.S.R. 466 (H.C.J.).

[37] *Smith v. Inner London Education Authority*, [1978] 1 All E.R. 411 (C.A.); *Office Overload Ltd. v. Gunn*, [1977] F.S.R. 39 (C.A.); *Alfred Dunhill Ltd. v. Sunoptic S.A.*, [1979] F.S.R. 337 (C.A.).

[38] *Infra*, §160. Provincial legislation affecting injunctions in labour matters is discussed, *infra*, §§192-195. In England, see Trade Union and Labour Relations Act 1974, ss. 13, 17, am. 1975, c. 71, Sch. 16, Pt. III, s. 6.

[39] *Infra*, §§156-159.

[40] [1976] Q.B. 122 (C.A.).

culty and frustration caused by the *Cyanamid* formulation. Lord Denning said flatly that a case, such as the one before him, could not properly be decided without consideration of the merits. The "special factors" qualification tacked on to the end of Lord Diplock's litany, Lord Denning suggested, allowed him, in the context of this case, to consider the strength of the claim and the defence.[41]

157   Sir John Pennycuick acknowledged his duty to follow the decision of the House of Lords, but confessed that the "principles laid down by Lord Diplock . . . present certain difficulties".[42] He observed that where the result turns upon the construction of a written instrument, the judge hearing the interlocutory application is entirely competent to assess the prospect of success, and suggested that this prediction "represents a factor which can hardly be disregarded in determining whether or not it is just to give interlocutory relief ".[43] After coping as best he could with the balance of convenience approach, his Lordship suggested that the House of Lords "may not have had this class of case in mind in the patent action before them", and indicated that he would "welcome further guidance from the House of Lords"[44] as to the applicability of the *Cyanamid* test to a case of the type before him. Browne, L.J., struggled with the balance of convenience approach and added: "I confess that I cannot see how the 'balance of convenience' can be fairly or reasonably considered without taking *some* account as *a* factor of the relative strength of the parties' cases."[45]

158   Subsequent cases hold that *Cyanamid* does not alter the onus on the plaintiff to show a strong *prima facie* case to obtain an interlocutory injunction to restrain a breach of a covenant in restraint of trade.[46] In many, if not most, cases involving covenants in restraint of

---

[41] *Infra*, §185.

[42] *Fellowes & Son, supra*, footnote 40, at p. 141.

[43] *Fellowes & Son, supra*, at p. 141

[44] *Fellowes & Son, supra*, at pp. 141-2.

[45] *Fellowes & Son, supra*, at p. 138.

[46] *Cantol Ltd. v. Brodi Chemicals Ltd.* (1978), 94 D.L.R. (3d) 265, 23 O.R. (2d) 36 (H.C.J.); *Creditel of Canada Ltd. v. Faultless* (1977), 81 D.L.R. (3d) 567, 18 O.R. (2d) 95 (H.C.J.); *W.R. Grace & Co. of Canada Ltd. v. Sare* (1980), 111 D.L.R. (3d) 204, 28 O.R. (2d) 612, (H.C.J.); *Erickson v. Wiggins Adjustments Ltd.*, [1980], 6 W.W.R. 188 (Alta C.A.); *Weight Watchers of Manitoba Ltd. v. Peters* (1979), 6 Man. R. (2d) 44 (Q.B.); *Drake Int'l Inc. v. Wortmann* (1980), 108 D.L.R. (3d) 133, 27 O.R. (2d) 707 (Div. Ct.); *Thomas Marshall (Exports) Ltd. v. Guinle*, [1979] F.S.R. 208 (H.C.J.); *Office Overload Ltd. v. Gunn*, [1977] F.S.R. 39 (C.A.). Compare, however, *Thomas Lindsay Ltd. v. Lindsay* (1975), 64 D.L.R. (3d) 761 (B.C.S.C.), and *Cascade Imperial Mills Ltd. v. Kunsman*, [1978] 4 W.W.R. 677 (B.C.S.C.), applying *Cyanamid*.

trade, the final decision, for practical purposes, is the one made on the interlocutory application. Indeed, reasonableness as to the duration of the life of the covenant is one of the tests of its validity.[47] Accordingly, to be at all valid, the life of the covenant may often have to be shorter than the time it will take to get the case tried. Even if the life of the covenant exceeds the time it takes to complete pre-trial proceedings and work through the queue for trial, the crucial period for both parties will usually be the first year or so.

159   Moreover, in these cases, it will almost never be possible to say that the claim is frivolous or vexatious. On the other hand, it will usually be quite feasible to predict with reasonable accuracy whether or not the covenant would be upheld at trial. It is surely wrong to say that the application should turn solely upon the balance of convenience, and that the result should be the same where the covenant is probably good as where it is probably bad.

160   A similar problem is posed by cases involving picketing. Here, there can be little doubt that, in virtually every case, the matter will be resolved at the interlocutory stage and there will be no trial.[48] Indeed, Lord Diplock himself has said that, in such cases, it is acceptable to consider the merits. In *N.W.L. Ltd. v. Woods*,[49] his Lordship modified the *Cyanamid* principle as follows:

> Where, however, the grant or refusal of the interlocutory injunction will have the practical effect of putting an end to the action because the harm that will have been already caused to the losing party by its refusal is complete and of a kind for which money cannot constitute any worthwhile recompense, the degree of likelihood that the plaintiff would have succeeded in establishing his right to an injunction if the action had gone to trial is a factor to be brought into the balance by the judge in weighing the risks that injustice may result from his deciding the application one way rather than the other.[50]

161   In the end, it seems that Lord Diplock's attempt in *Cyanamid* virtually to exclude consideration of the merits has been unsuccessful.[51]

---

[47] See, for example, *Eastes v. Russ*, [1914] 1 Ch. 468 (C.A.); *Cameron v. Canadian Factors Corp. Ltd.*, [1971] S.C.R. 148, 18 D.L.R. (3d) 574.

[48] The provisions of the Judicature Act, Ont., s. 20(4), providing for *viva voce* cross-examination, would seem clearly to contemplate a decision based upon the merits in situations involving picketing in furtherance of a labour dispute. In England, Parliament has, since the *Cyanamid* decision, specifically provided that regard is to be had to the merits: see Employment Protection Act 1975, c. 71, Sch. 16, Pt. III, s. 6, adding s. 17(2) to the Trade Union and Labour Relations Act 1974.

[49] [1979] 1 W.L.R. 1294 (H.L.), at p. 1306.

[50] *Ibid.*, at p. 1307.

[51] See also *Hadmor Productions Ltd. v. Hamilton*, [1983] A.C. 191 (H.L.), at pp. 223-4, *per* Lord Diplock.

Although there is some indication that the *N.W.L.* case was intended to have narrower application,[52] the category of case in which the matter will end at the interlocutory stage is quite broad. It will include picketing cases,[53] cases involving restrictive covenants,[54] threatened winding-up proceedings,[55] and probably other cases as well.[56] As already noted, *Cyanamid* has been rejected where the facts are not in dispute,[57] and in other cases, the standard of case required has been subtly elevated.[58] *Cyanamid* has also been explicitly rejected as appropriate in actions against public authorities[59] and in a case involving the internal affairs of a political party.[60] It has been held inappropriate in defamation cases[61] and does not appear to apply to breach of confidence cases.[62] Applications for interlocutory mandatory injunctions have also been excepted from its reach.[63] The Ontario Courts[64] have opted for the previous practice in patent actions,

---

[52] See *Porter v. Nat'l Union of Journalists*, [1980] I.R.L.R 404 (H.L.).

[53] *Cf. Hubbard v. Pitt*, [1976] Q.B. 142, where the Court of Appeal applied *Cyanamid*. For a criticism and a discussion of the substantive issues at stake in the case, see Elias, *supra*, footnote 33; Wallington, "Injunctions and the 'Right to Demonstrate' ", 35 Camb. L.J. 82 (1976).

[54] *Supra*, §§156-159.

[55] In *Bryanston Finance Ltd. v. De Vries (No. 2)*, [1976] Ch. 63 at p. 81, *per* Sir John Pennycuick, the Court of Appeal held the *Cyanamid* approach inappropriate where the application was for an injunction to prevent the prosecution of a winding-up petition: "I do not think that the decision [*Cyanamid*] should be read as applicable to motions which, though interlocutory in form, seek relief which will finally determine the issue in the action and more particularly motions seeking to stop proceedings in limine." Leave to appeal was refused by the House of Lords, *loc. cit.* p. 81.

[56] *Athlete's Foot Marketing Associates Inc. v. Cobra Sports Ltd.*, [1980] R.P.C. 343 (Ch.). Rogers and Hately, *supra*, footnote 17, at p. 17 observe: "The breadth of potential application of Lord Diplock's amended version of *American Cyanamid* has yet to be established, but it clearly offers a route for returning to the former reliance on the test of a strong *prima facie* case where the courts most want and need it."

[57] *Supra*, §152.

[58] *Supra*, §152.

[59] *Smith v. Inner London Education Authority*, [1978] 1 All E.R. 411 (C.A.).

[60] *Lewis v. Heffer*, [1978] 1 W.L.R. 1061 (C.A.).

[61] *Infra*, §443.

[62] *Bestobell Paints Ltd. v. Bigg*, [1975] F.S.R. 421 (H.C.J.); *Woodward v. Hutchins*, [1977] 2 All E.R. 751 (C.A.); *Lennon v. News Group Newspapers Ltd.*, [1978] F.S.R. 573 (C.A.).

[63] *De Falco v. Crawley Borough Council*, [1980] Q.B. 460 (C.A.).

[64] See *Teledyne Industries Inc. v. Lido Industrial Products Ltd.* (1977), 79 D.L.R. (3d) 446, 17 O.R. (2d) 111 (Div. Ct.), affd 86 D.L.R. (3d) 446, 19 O.R. (2d) 740 (C.A.); Hayhurst, "Annual Survey of Canadian Law, Industrial Property", 11 Ottawa L. Rev. 391 (1979), at pp. 436-40.

namely, that where infringement is disputed and the validity of the patent has not been established by a court decision, an injunction will not be granted if the defendant undertakes to account. It has been recognized that in trade mark and passing-off cases, the hearing on the interlocutory application will very often end the action, and that it is accordingly necessary to consider the merits with greater scrutiny than suggested by the *American Cyanamid* test.[65]

162   This list of exceptions makes it apparent that *Cyanamid* has failed to set an appropriate standard applicable to all cases, and the impact of the decision, in practical terms, is marginal.[66] It is suggested that the position may be summarized as follows.

163   The weight to be placed upon the preliminary assessment of the relative strength of the plaintiff's case is a delicate matter which will vary depending upon the context and circumstances. As the likely result at trial is clearly a relevant factor, the judge's preliminary assessment of the merits should, as a general rule, play an important part in the process. However, the weight to be attached to the preliminary assessment should depend upon the degree of predictability which the factual and legal issues allow. If the judge is of the view that the plaintiff is unlikely to succeed, but cannot say that the claim is frivolous or vexatious, he should still go on to consider the other factors, rather than dismiss the application at the threshold. This is a positive and helpful aspect of the *Cyanamid* case which should not be forgotten. However, the judge's negative impression of the plaintiff's chances of ultimate success should be taken into account, along with all other considerations. By the same token, even if the plaintiff's case looks very strong — a factor which should definitely weigh in his favour — the other factors should still be considered. If assessment of the merits is impracticable because of conflicting evidence or questions of credibility, the matter will have to be decided solely on the basis of the balance of convenience and the irreparable harm factors.

164   In certain situations, the issue is not balancing risks, but deciding the case in a final way. In those cases, the balance of risk approach should be abandoned as inappropriate. If it is apparent, as a practical

---

[65] *Newsweek Inc. v. British Broadcasting Corp.*, [1979] R.P.C. 441 (C.A.), *Athlete's Foot Marketing Associates Inc. v. Cobra Sports Ltd.*, *supra*, footnote 56.

[66] Rogers and Hately, *supra*, footnote 17, at pp. 14-15 and 21: "Whether or not the *American Cyanamid* test is applied, a strong legal case cannot but help persuade the court that an injunction is deserved." Gray, *supra*, footnote 17, concludes, after reviewing more than one hundred post-*Cyanamid* cases, that *Cyanamid* has in fact had little effect in diminishing the weight attached to the merits of the case at the interlocutory stage.

matter, that the interlocutory injunction will be the final determination of the dispute, then the judge must make the best of a difficult situation and base his decision solely on his assessment of the merits.

(5) Irreparable harm to the plaintiff

165 An essential factor in determining the appropriateness of an interlocutory injunction is "irreparable harm", a phrase familiar in equity jurisprudence. The remedies of Chancery were traditionally withheld, unless the plaintiff could show that the ordinary legal remedy in damages would be inappropriate or inadequate. In the context of preliminary injunctive relief, the phrase is given a more specific meaning, namely that the plaintiff, before the trial, must risk some injury which cannot be compensated or remedied other than through the granting of an interlocutory injunction.[67] The rationale for requiring the plaintiff to show irreparable harm is readily understood. If damages will provide adequate compensation, and the defendant is in a position to pay them, then ordinarily there will be no justification in running the risk of an injunction pending the trial. While it is easy to see why this requirement should be imposed, it is difficult to define exactly what is meant by irreparable harm.

166 The means of the defendant is an important, but not decisive, factor.[68] The courts have recognized that a rule which required the decision to grant an interlocutory injunction to be made on the basis of the wealth of either party could operate unjustly. It has been accepted, for example, that the inability of individual trade union

---

[67] *Cartwright & Sons Ltd. v. Carswell Co. Ltd.* (1958), 14 D.L.R. (2d) 596, [1958] O.W.N. 123 (H.C.J.); *Montreuil v. Ontario Asphalt Block Paving Co.* (1911), 2 O.W.N. 1512 (H.C.J.); *Cohen v. Congregation of Hazen Ave. Synagogue* (1918), 46 N.B.R. 152 (S.C.); *C.P.R. v. Canadian Northern Ry.* (1912), 7 D.L.R. 120 (Alta. S.C.); *Radenhurst v. Coate* (1857), 6 Gr. 139.

[68] *Cf. Hubbard v. Pitt,* [1976] Q.B. 142 (C.A.), where the inability of the defendant to satisfy a damage award was considered an important factor favouring an injunction. See Gray, *supra,* footnote 17 at pp. 330-3; *Alfred Dunhill Ltd. v. Sunoptic S.A.,* [1979] F.S.R. 337 (C.A.), at pp. 374-5, *per* Megaw, L.J.; *Apple Corps v. Lingasong Ltd.,* [1977] F.S.R. 345 (H.C.J.), at p. 351, *per* Megarry, V.-C.:

This argument seems to me to lead towards the conclusion that whenever affluent plaintiffs claim an interlocutory injunction against defendants with slender resources, the balance of convenience points towards granting the injunction. I would reject any such conclusion. I accept that there are circumstances in which the means of the defendant will be relevant in considering whether to grant an injunction but I do not think the term "balance of convenience" was ever intended to produce the result that the prosperous could go far to obtaining interlocutory injunctions against defendants of modest means merely by pointing to the financial disparity.

members, named as defendants, to satisfy a damage award should not invariably result in an injunction being granted against them.[69]

167   Typical cases in which irreparable harm is likely to be found are those where the act complained of (or, where the defendant's interests are being considered, the effect of an injunction) would put the party out of business, deprive him of his livelihood, or cause irrevocable damage to reputation or professional standing.[70]

168   In appropriate cases, the defendant can avoid an injunction by undertaking to account.[71] For example, in an Ontario case,[72] the plaintiff sought an injunction preventing the distribution of a film. The injunction was refused on the basis that the defendant keep full records of all revenue gained from the distribution of the film. In another Ontario case,[73] the plaintiff sought an injunction to restrain unlawful interference with its customers. An injunction was granted, prohibiting further solicitation, but also requiring the defendant to file a bond to protect the plaintiff's claim for damages with respect to customers the defendant had already contracted with.

169   Some cases involve interests which are obviously difficult to evaluate in money terms,[74] and yet the court may still be reluctant to grant injunctive relief. Where the public interest is at stake, the calculation of irreparable harm becomes more difficult, as interests in addition to those of the immediate parties must be considered.[75] In many

---

[69] Gray, *supra*, footnote 17, at pp. 328-9; *Beaverbrook Newspapers Ltd. v. Keys*, [1978] I C.R. 582 (C.A.).

[70] See, *e.g.*, *Fellowes & Son v. Fisher*, [1976] Q.B. 122 (C.A.); *Geometrics & Geometrics Services (Canada) Ltd. v. Smith* (1975), 65 D.L.R. (3d) 62, 11 O.R. (2d) 112 (H.C.J.); *Creditel of Canada Ltd. v. Faultless* (1977), 81 D.L.R. (3d) 567, 18 O.R. (2d) 95 (H.C.J.); *Sky Petroleum Ltd. v. V.I.P. Petroleum Ltd.*, [1974] 1 W.L.R. 576 (Ch.), and cases cited, *infra*, §660; Rogers and Hately, *supra*, footnote 17, at pp. 18-19.

[71] See the industrial property cases, *supra*, §161; *Lambair Ltd. v. Aero Trades (Western) Ltd.* (1978), 87 D.L.R. (3d) 500 (Man. C.A.), leave to appeal to S.C.C. refused October 4, 1978; *International Chemalloy Corp. v. Kawecki Berylco Industries Inc.* (1977), 3 C.P.C. 53 (Ont. H.C.J.).

[72] *Cemasco Management Ltd. v. Analysis Film Releasing Corp.* (1979), 98 D.L.R. (3d) 573, 24 O.R. (2d) 389 (H.C.J.).

[73] *Nelson Burns & Co. Ltd. v. Gratham Industries* (1981), 34 O.R. (2d) 558 (H.C.J.).

[74] See, *e.g.*, *Lewis v. Heffer*, [1978] 1 W.L.R. 1061 (C.A.), a case involving the functioning of a national political party, *per* Lane, L.J.: "In the political context which exists in this case there can be no question of quantifying anyone's loss in terms of cash."

[75] *Beaverbrook Newspapers Ltd. v. Keys*, *supra* footnote 69; *British Broadcasting Corp. v. Hearn*, [1978] 1 All E.R. 111 (C.A.); *Smith v. Inner London Education Authority*, [1978] 1 All E.R 411 (C.A.), at p. 422, *per* Browne, L.J.

cases, consideration of the public interest may be a powerful influence, depending on the circumstances, either in favour of[76] or against an interlocutory injunction.[77]

170   It is exceptionally difficult to define irreparable harm precisely. Courts regularly and routinely assess monetary awards for non-pecuniary injuries where this is necessary. On the other hand, the courts have sometimes been prepared to view what otherwise seem readily calculable losses as "irreparable" for the purposes of interlocutory relief.[78]

171   In the context of preliminary relief, the test is a relative and flexible one which, it is submitted, necessarily involves an evaluation of the other factors. Indeed, it has been held that an interlocutory injunction may be granted even where "irreparable" harm has not been demonstrated.[79] These cases do not represent a departure from principle, but rather suggest that the "irreparable harm" requirement can only be defined in the context of the risk-balancing exercise. If the plaintiff's case looks very strong, harm may appear to be more "irreparable" than where the plaintiff has only an even chance of success. While judges seldom explicitly acknowledge that there is an "overflow" effect produced by strength or weakness of other factors, it cannot be doubted that, as a practical matter, it exists.[80] The

[76] See, *e.g.*, *A.-G. Ont. v. Yeotes* (1979), 93 D.L.R. (3d) 332, 22 O.R. (2d) 321, 111 D.L.R. (3d) 488, 28 O.R. (2d) 577 (H.C.J.) (trial), revd on merits 120 D.L.R. (3d) 128, 31 O.R. (2d) 589 (C.A.), leave to appeal to S.C.C. refused 37 N.R. 356n; *Detroit & Windsor Subway Co. v. Blyth* (1980), 116 D.L.R. (3d) 708, 30 O.R. (2d) 216 (H.C.J.); see also, *infra*, Chapter 3, where injunctions to enforce public rights are discussed.

[77] The best example is provided by the defamation cases, discussed, *infra*, §440 *et seq.* See also *Air Canada v. Maley* (1976), 69 D.L.R. (3d) 180 (Fed. Ct. T.D.); *Roussel-Uclaf v. G.D. Searle & Co. Ltd.*, [1977] F.S.R. 125 (H.C.J.), at p. 132, *per* Graham, J., indicating *obiter*, that a court would never grant an interlocutory injunction in a patent action where the result would be to deprive the public temporarily of a life-saving drug.

[78] See, *e.g.*, *Turf Care Products Ltd. v. Crawford's Mowers & Marine Ltd.* (1978), 95 D.L.R. (3d) 378 at p. 381, 23 O.R. (2d) 292 at p. 295 (H.C.J.), leave to appeal to Div. Ct. refused D.L.R. *loc. cit.*, O.R. *loc. cit.*, *per* Lerner, J., granting an interlocutory injunction to restrain the defendant from disposing of property subject to a security interest: "To deny the plaintiff the injunction it requests and force it to seek damages in lieu of recovery of the goods, would render its special endorsement useless and require it instead to prove its damages." See also *Hoskin v. Price Waterhouse Ltd.* (1982), 35 O.R. (2d) 350 (H.C.J.), restraining an allegedly improvident sale by a receiver to protect a guarantor's interest.

[79] *Playter v. Lucas* (1921), 69 D.L.R. 514, 51 O.L.R. 492 (H.C.); *Terra Communications Ltd. v. Communicomp Data Ltd.* (1973), 41 D.L.R. (3d) 350, 1 O.R. (2d) 682 (H.C.J.); *Thomas Lindsay Ltd. v. Lindsay* (1975), 65 D.L.R. (3d) 761 (B.C.S.C.).

[80] See *Hubbard v. Vosper*, [1972] 2 Q.B. 84 (C.A.), at pp. 97-8, *per* Megaw, L.J.:

important point is that irreparable harm has not been given a definition of universal application: its meaning takes shape in the context of each particular case.

172   In *American Cyanamid*, Lord Diplock restated the need for the plaintiff to show irreparable harm as the second step in his formula. The question to be asked, said Lord Diplock, was the following. Assuming that the plaintiff succeeds in the end in establishing his right to a permanent injunction, will damages be adequate compensation for the loss sustained between the time of the application and the trial? "If damages in the measure recoverable at common law would be adequate remedy and the defendant would be in a financial position to pay them, no interlocutory injunction should normally be granted, however strong the plaintiff's claim appeared to be at that stage."[81] If damages are an adequate remedy, running the risk of restraining the defendant unjustifiably pending the trial is simply not warranted.

(6) Irreparable harm to the defendant — the plaintiff's undertaking in damages

173   Concomitant with the question of irreparable harm is the requirement of the plaintiff's undertaking in damages. It is well established that as a condition of obtaining an interlocutory injunction, the plaintiff must give an undertaking to pay to the defendant any damages that the defendant sustains by reason of the injunction, should the plaintiff fail in the ultimate result.[82]

One can readily imagine a case in which the plaintiff appears to have a 75 per cent. chance of establishing his claim, but in which the damage to the defendant from the granting of the interlocutory injunction, if the 25 per cent. defence proved to be right, would be so great compared with the triviality of the damage to the plaintiff if he is refused the injunction, that an interlocutory injunction should be refused. To my mind it is impossible and unworkable to lay down different standards in relation to different issues which fall to be considered in an application for an interlocutory injunction. Each case must be decided on a basis of fairness, justice and common sense in relation to the whole issues of fact and law which are relevant to the particular case.

[81] *American Cyanamid Co. v. Ethicon Ltd.*, [1975] A.C. 396 (H.L.), at p. 408.

[82] *Griffith v. Blake* (1884), 27 Ch. D. 474 (C.A.); *Vieweger Construction Co. Ltd. v. Rush & Tompkins Construction Ltd.*, [1965] S.C.R. 195, 48 D.L.R. (2d) 509; *Smith v. Day* (1882), 21 Ch. D. 421 (C.A.); *Bedell v. Gefaell (No. 2)*, [1938] 4 D.L.R. 443, [1938] O.R. 726 (C.A.); *Cummings v. Hydro-Electric Power Com'n of Ontario* (1965), 54 D.L.R. (2d) 583, [1966] 1 O.R. 605 (H.C.J.); *Griffin Steel Foundries Ltd. v. Canadian Ass'n of Industrial, Mechanical & Allied Workers* (1977), 80 D.L.R. (3d) 634 (Man. C.A.). British Columbia Supreme Court Rule 45(6) provides:

174 The Crown has been held exempt from this requirement where it sues to enforce what is, *prima facie*, the law of the land,[83] although the normal requirement of an undertaking applies to the Crown where it sues to enforce its own proprietary rights.[84]

175 In a recent Ontario case,[85] the Attorney-General gave an undertaking in damages when obtaining an interlocutory injunction to restrain the defendants from selling lands alleged to have been subdivided in contravention of planning legislation. The injunction was made permanent at trial, but the trial judgment was reversed on appeal. The defendants applied to the trial judge for inquiry as to damages, but the inquiry was refused on the grounds that the Attorney-General had an arguable case, had sued to protect the public and prevent public injury, and that the defendants had only succeeded because of a "loop-hole". In dismissing the defendant's application for an inquiry, Montgomery, J., stated that "the defendants have their subdivision; let them make their profit on it and not at the expense of the defenders of the public interest".[86]

176 It has also been held that there is a discretion in the court to relieve the plaintiff from the obligation to give an undertaking in special circumstances. In one case,[87] Lord Denning held that an impecunious plaintiff should not be denied injunctive relief before trial because of her inability to give a meaningful undertaking. In a British Columbia case[88] where the plaintiff appeared to have a strong case against a municipality, was impecunious and unable to give a meaningful undertaking, and where there seemed to be doubt as to whether the municipality would sustain any damage, the plaintiff was relieved of the normal obligation to give an undertaking. In other cases, it has been held that evidence of the plaintiff's substance to en-

---

Unless the Court otherwise orders, an order for an interlocutory or interim injunction shall contain the applicant's undertaking to abide by any order which the Court may make as to damages.

[83] *F. Hoffmann-La Roche & Co. and Attorney-General v. Secretary of State for Trade and Industry*, [1975] A.C. 295 (H.L.); *Corp. of Delta v. Nationwide Auctions Inc.* (1979), 100 D.L.R. (3d) 272 (B.C.S.C.). Compare *Manitoba Dental Ass'n v. Byman and Halstead* (1962), 34 D.L.R. (2d) 602 (Man. C.A.), holding that the plaintiff, entitled by statute to sue for an injunction restraining unauthorized practice, could still be required to give an undertaking.

[84] *F. Hoffmann-La Roche & Co.*, *supra*, footnote 83.

[85] *A.-G. Ont. v. Harry* (1982), 132 D.L.R. (3d) 73, 35 O.R. (2d) 248 (H.C.J.).

[86] *Ibid.*, at p. 77 D.L.R., p. 251 O.R.

[87] *Allen v. Jambo Holdings Ltd.*, [1980] 1 W.L.R. 1252 (C.A.), at p. 1257; *cf.*, however, *De Falco v. Crawley Borough Council*, [1980] Q.B. 460 (C.A.).

[88] *Corp. of Delta v. Nationwide Auctions Inc.*, *supra*, footnote 83.

sure the utility of his undertaking is relevant.[89] Thus, there is no
inflexible rule which inevitably requires that an undertaking be giv-
en, or which states that the decision turns on the means of the plaintiff to provide a secure undertaking. However, an undertaking is the
usual requirement, and it would appear that the plaintiff's case will
be very much weaker if he is of insufficient substance to ensure its
worth. In case of doubt, security by way of bond or payment into
court may be ordered.[90]

177   Should the plaintiff lose at trial, the defendant's request for an inquiry as to damages will be granted, unless there are special circumstances which dictate otherwise.[91] While damages have been refused
where the defendant succeeded on technical grounds, or where the
plaintiff sued in the public interest,[92] the courts have been reluctant
to deprive a successful defendant of his right to be compensated. It
has been held that, where the plaintiff discontinues his action prior to
trial, he is taken to admit to having no right to an injunction, and an
assessment of damages will be ordered.[93] The appropriate procedure
is for the defendant to apply to the trial judge for an order directing
an inquiry as to the damages the defendant has suffered.[94] There is

---

[89] *American Cyanamid Co.*, *supra*, footnote 81, at p. 408. In *Cambridge Credit Corp.
Ltd. v. Surfers' Paradise Forests Ltd.*, [1977] Qd. R. 261 (S.C.), it was specifically
held that evidence as to the substance of the plaintiff and the worth of his undertaking was relevant and admissible.

[90] *Wishart v. Knox* (1967), 65 D.L.R. (2d) 216 (Sask. C.A.); *Delap v. Robinson*
(1898), 18 P.R. (Ont.) 231 (non-resident required to post security).

[91] *Vieweger Construction Co. Ltd. v. Rush & Tompkins Construction Ltd.*, *supra*,
footnote 82.

[92] *Supra*, §§174, 175. See also *Vieweger Construction Co. Ltd.*, *supra*, at p. 207
S.C.R., p. 519 D.L.R., *per* Spence, J.: "There are examples of plaintiffs who are
public bodies and who acted in the public interest to hold the situation in *statu quo*
until the rights were determined. There are other cases where the defendant, although he succeeded upon technical grounds, certainly had been guilty of conduct
which did not move the Court to exercise its discretion in his favour." For an example of the former, see *Upper Canada College v. City of Toronto* (1917), 40 O.L.R.
483 (H.C.). For examples of the latter, see *Montreal Street Ry. Co. v. Ritchie*
(1889), 16 S.C.R. 622; *Ireson v. Holt Timber Co.* (1913), 18 D.L.R. 604, 30 O.L.R.
209 (S.C. App. Div.); *Douglass v. Bullen* (1913), 12 D.L.R. 652, 4 O.W.N. 1587
(H.C.); *Board of Trustees of Wasaga Beach v. Fielding*, [1947] O.R. 321 (H.C.),
affd [1947] O.R. 1012 (C.A.); *Merchants Gas Co. Ltd. v. Hall*, [1956] O.W.N. 820
(H.C.J.); *Baud Corp. N.V. v. Brook* (1972), 25 D.L.R. (3d) 374 (Alta. S.C.), affd
40 D.L.R. (3d) 418 (C.A.), affd 89 D.L.R. (3d) 1 (S.C.C.).

[93] *Wm. Halliday Contracting Co. Ltd. v. Nicols*, [1952] 4 D.L.R. 75, [1952] O.W.N.
229 (H.C.J.); *Bird Construction Co. Ltd. v. Paterson* (1960), 23 D.L.R. (2d) 182
(Alta. S.C. App. Div.); *Newcomen v. Coulson* (1878), 7 Ch. D. 764.

[94] *Sherk v. Horwitz* (1973), 39 D.L.R. (3d) 17, [1973] 3 O.R. 979 (H.C.J.); *Aspotogan
v. Lawrence* (1976), 14 N.S.R. (2d) 501 (S.C. App. Div.) (approving this practice,

little authority on how such damages are to be assessed. In a patent infringement case,[95] the British Columbia Court of Appeal held that the defendant had to establish that the damage for lost sales was the direct result of the injunction, and that, where the evidence indicated that orders had been cancelled because of the plaintiff's threatened proceedings against the defendant's customers, proof of damages was lacking. Thus, it would appear that to recover on the undertaking, the defendant must be able to establish clearly that the loss claimed flowed directly from the injunction.

178   In *American Cyanamid*, the question of irreparable harm to the defendant was the third item in Lord Diplock's formula, to be considered once the plaintiff had shown an arguable case and that he would suffer irreparable harm if denied an injunction: "If damages in the measure recoverable under such an undertaking would be an adequate remedy and the plaintiff would be in a financial position to pay them, there would be no reason upon this ground to refuse an interlocutory injunction."[96] This proposition might perhaps be put more positively. Where the defendant's potential damages appear to be readily calculable, and where the plaintiff is able to demonstrate a real risk of irreparable harm, a strong case for an interlocutory injunction has been made on this ground alone. Even in cases where calculation of harm to the defendant will be complex or difficult, the risk of harm to the defendant is still minimized to the extent that money can put the defendant in the position he would have been in had the injunction not been granted.

(7) Balance of convenience

179   Under the rubric of "balance of convenience", the courts have considered an indefinable array of elements. This factor formed Lord Diplock's fourth proposition in *American Cyanamid*: "It is where there is doubt as to the adequacy of the respective remedies in damages available to either party or to both, that the question of balance of convenience arises." The factors here are so various that it "would be unwise to attempt even to list [them] . . . let alone to suggest the relative weight to be attached to them". However, Lord Diplock

---

but assessing damages on appeal in light of the complexity and length of proceedings); *Norstrant v. Drumheller* (1920), 51 D.L.R. 373 (Alta. S.C. App. Div.) (striking out a counterclaim for such damages); *Bird Construction Co. Ltd. v. Paterson, supra*, footnote 93.

[95] *International Pediatric Products Ltd. v. Lambert* (1967), 66 D.L.R. (2d) 157 (B.C.C.A.).

[96] [1975] A.C. 396 (H.L.), at p. 408.

suggested two general principles. Where all else is equal, "it is a counsel of prudence to . . . preserve the status quo". Secondly, his Lordship observed that the assessment of where the balance of convenience lies is significantly affected by the "extent to which the disadvantages to each party would be incapable of being compensated in damages in the event of his succeeding at the trial".[97] The questions of "irreparable harm" and balance of convenience are closely linked, but balance of convenience also relates to matters difficult to quantify in monetary terms. Apart from, and in addition to, the risks of monetary loss and gain, what will be the relative impact upon the parties of granting or withholding the injunction? Does the benefit the plaintiff will gain from preliminary relief outweigh the convenience to the defendant of withholding relief? Is the inconvenience to the defendant, should the injunction be granted, more substantial than the inconvenience the plaintiff will suffer if relief is withheld?[98]

180   It seems clear that the other factors influence the weight to be given to balance of convenience. If the plaintiff's case looks very strong, he may well succeed, although the injunction would cause greater inconvenience to the defendant than withholding preliminary relief would cause the plaintiff. On the other hand, where an assessment of the case is impracticable and the damages question balanced, an assessment of balance of convenience will be determinative. It is impossible to develop a precise calculus or calibration of such a question beyond restating the nature of the risk-balancing exercise that is involved.

(8) Preservation of the status quo

181   This phrase is frequently used[99] to describe the purpose of an interlocutory injunction although it adds little or nothing to the analysis, and in fact, may produce a possible source of confusion.[100] Properly

---

[97] *Ibid.* at pp. 408-9.

[98] It is often said that "the defendant's interests must receive the same considerations as the plaintiff's". See, for example, *Chesapeake and Ohio Ry. Co. v. Ball*, [1953] O.R. 843 (H.C.), at p. 855, appeal quashed *loc. cit.* p. 877; *Terra Communications Ltd. v. Communicomp Data Ltd.* (1973), 41 D.L.R. (3d) 350, 1 O.R. (2d) 682 (H.C.J.).

[99] For a thorough discussion of the historic underpinning of the *status quo* factor and the interaction between the courts of law and equity, see Leubsdorf, *supra*, footnote 16, at pp. 527-40.

[100] The use of "*status quo*" as a factor is criticized in Wright and Miller, *Federal Practice and Procedure* (St. Paul, West Publishing Co., 1973), §2948, p. 466. See also "Injunctions", Developments in the Law, 78 Harv. L. Rev. 994 (1965), at p. 1058:

understood, the phrase merely restates the basic premise of granting an interlocutory injunction, namely, that the plaintiff must demonstrate that unless an injunction is granted, his rights will be nullified or impaired by the time of trial. In many ways *status quo* is an inappropriate, and potentially misleading, description of this principle. If the plaintiff sues *quia timet*,[101] a literal application of the *status quo* principle would suggest that he should always succeed. Similarly, if the defendant has already embarked upon the course of conduct of which the plaintiff complains, the *status quo* at the time of the application would preclude relief. Plainly, neither of these propositions can stand: interlocutory *quia timet* injunctions are frequently and properly refused, and the *status quo* has been defined as relating to the situation before the defendant commenced his course of conduct.[102] The proper application of the *status quo* factor, then, merely rephrases the basic question the plaintiff must answer: does the threat to his rights meet the basic test for interim relief?[103]

"The concept *status quo* lacks sufficient stability to provide a satisfactory foundation for judicial reasoning. The better course is to consider directly how best to preserve or create a state of affairs in which effective relief can be awarded to either party at the conclusion of the trial." See also Leubsdorf, *supra*, footnote 16, at p. 546:

"Emphasis on preserving the status quo is a habit without a reason. To freeze the existing situation may inflict irreparable injury on a plaintiff deprived of his rights or a defendant denied the right to innovate. The status quo shibboleth cannot be justified as a way to limit interlocutory judicial meddling, because a court interferes just as much when it orders the status quo preserved as when it changes it.

For an example of the unhelpfulness of the concept, see *Babic v. Milinkovic* (1972), 25 D.L.R. (3d) 752 (B.C.C.A.).

[101] *Supra*, §66 *et seq.*

[102] *Fellowes & Son v. Fisher*, [1976] Q.B. 122 (C.A.), at p. 141, *per* Sir John Pennycuick; Gray, *supra*, footnote 17, at pp. 336-7; *Alfred Dunhill Ltd. v. Sunoptic S.A.*, [1979] F.S.R. 337 (C.A.), at p. 376, *per* Megaw, L.J.:

For that [consideration of the status quo] to be of any help, it is necessary to answer the question: Existing when? Before what point of time? For the answer may be different, according as you look at the existing state of things at the date when the defendant did the act, or the first act which is alleged to have been wrongful; or the date when the plaintiff first learned of that act, or the date when the plaintiff ought first to have been aware of that act; or the date when the plaintiff first complained to the defendant; or the date when he issued his writ. I think the relevant point of time for purposes of the status quo may well vary in different cases.

[103] The *status quo* consideration has also been applied as a device to determine the balance of convenience. It is sometimes said that, all other things being equal, the correct course in achieving balance of convenience is to favour the *status quo* at the time the application is heard: *American Cyanamid Co. v. Ethicon Ltd.*, [1975] A.C. 396 (H.L.), at p. 408. Compare *Dwyre v. Ottawa* (1898), 25 O.A.R. 121, at p. 130, *per* Moss, J.A.: "where the inconvenience seems to be equally divided as between

182   It is often said that an interlocutory injunction should not be granted where it would have the effect of granting the whole relief claimed in the action.[104] However, it has also been said, quite properly it is submitted, that this is not an inflexible rule,[105] and as already noted, there are many instances in which it is quite obvious that, for all practical purposes, the interlocutory order finally disposes of the action.[106]

183   Interlocutory injunctive relief will not normally be granted where there is no prospect for a specific remedy being granted at the trial. The rationale underlying interlocutory injunctions is the need to protect the plaintiff's ultimate right to an appropriate remedy, and it will ordinarily be unnecessary to grant interlocutory relief unless there is at least some prospect of specific relief being granted at trial. The courts have, for example, declined to grant an interlocutory injunction to protect the plaintiff's position in respect of a matter within the jurisdiction of an administrative board or tribunal on the grounds that no final injunction could be granted in such a case by a court.[107] However, it is also clear that this principle must be applied flexibly. For example, it is now well established that an injunction to restrain disposition of assets pending trial may be granted.[108] Here, there is no possibility of an injunction being granted at the trial, and yet, interlocutory relief is seen as appropriate since the same rationale, namely, protecting the plaintiff's position to obtain satisfactory remedial protection at trial, may be applied. Similarly, in cases involving long-term contracts, courts have seen fit to grant interlocutory injunctions although they were dubious that either specific performance or a final injunction would be awarded at the trial.[109]

(9) Other factors

184   Lord Diplock concluded his formula in the *American Cyanamid*

---

the parties, the injunction will not be granted"; *Ferguson and Lawson v. Paterson Steamships Ltd.*, [1950] 4 D.L.R. 525, [1950] O.W.N. 546 (H.C.J.).

[104] *Dodd v. Amalgamated Marine Workers' Union* (1923), 93 L.J. Ch. 65 (C.A.); *New Brunswick Telephone Co. Ltd. v. Relph* (1979), 107 D.L.R. (3d) 727 (N.B.C.A.), at p. 731; *Board of Eston-Elrose School Unit No. 33 of Sask. v. Sask. Teachers' Federation* (1970), 14 D.L.R. (3d) 471 (Sask. Q.B.).

[105] *Woodford v. Smith*, [1970] 1 W.L.R. 806 (Ch.).

[106] *Supra*, §§154-161.

[107] *Stevenson v. Air Canada* (1982), 132 D.L.R. (3d) 406, 35 O.R. (2d) 68 (H.C.J.). See further, *infra*, §§344-348.

[108] *Infra*, §201 *et seq.*

[109] See, *e.g.*, *Evans Marshall & Co. v. Bertola S.A.*, [1973] 1 W.L.R. 349 (C.A.), at p. 380. See also cases cited, *infra*, §660.

case by stating, "I would reiterate that, in addition to those to which I have referred, there may be many other special factors to be taken into consideration in the particular circumstances of individual cases. *The instant appeal affords one example of this*"[110] (emphasis added).

185   Lord Denning, M.R., has suggested, almost with tongue in cheek, that the "special factors" qualification provides an escape from Lord Diplock's entire approach.[111] However, it seems clear from the context, and from the application of the "special factors" consideration to the facts of *Cyanamid* itself, that this was intended only to qualify the suggested approach for determining the balance of convenience.[112]

(10) Conclusion

186   Although reference has been made throughout the discussion to the *American Cyanamid* formula, it now seems clear that it will not be applied automatically or mechanically by the courts. As already noted,[113] Lord Diplock himself has recanted from the assertion that consideration of the merits should never play an important role. The seeming rigidity of the remaining items in the formula is also regrettable,[114] as Lord Diplock's reasons suggest a much more

---

[110] *Supra*, footnote 103, at p. 409.

[111] In *Fellowes & Son v. Fisher, supra*, footnote 102, at pp. 132-3, Lord Denning, M.R., referred to the exclusion of the *prima facie* case test and commented as follows:

> I find it impossible to reconcile this statement with the statements in the House 10 years ago in *J.T. Stratford & Son Ltd. v. Lindley* [1965] A.C. 269. Yet the House did not even mention *J.T. Stratford & Son Ltd. v. Lindley*. I do not like to suggest that this was per incuriam. When I last made so bold as to make such a suggestion in *Broome v. Cassell & Co. Ltd.* [1971] 2 Q.B. 354; [1972] A.C. 1027, it was regarded as a piece of lèse-majesté. The House of Lords never does anything per incuriam. So what are we to do with two statements of principle by the House which are not reconcilable the one with the other?

> . . . . .

> Where then is the reconciliation to be found? Only in this: the House did say, at p. 409:
> "there may be many other special factors to be taken into consideration in the particular circumstances of individual cases."
> That sentence points the way.

See also *Bryanston Finance Ltd. v. De Vries (No. 2)*, [1976] Ch. 63 (C.A.), at p. 78, *per* Buckley, L.J., for a broad view of the "special factors" consideration.

[112] *Hubbard v. Pitt*, [1976] Q.B. 142 (C.A.), *per* Stamp, L.J.: "it appears to me clear beyond peradventure that Lord Diplock was there referring to special factors affecting the balance of convenience and not to special factors enabling the court to ignore the general principles there laid down".

[113] *Supra*, §160.

[114] "The remedy by interlocutory injunction is so useful that it should be kept flexible

inflexible step-by-step approach than has been employed in the past. The terms "irreparable harm", "*status quo*", "balance of convenience" do not have a precise meaning. They are more properly seen as guides which take colour and definition in the circumstances of each case. More importantly, they ought not to be seen as separate, water-tight categories. These factors relate to each other, and strength on one part of the test ought to be permitted to compensate for weakness on another. It is not clear that the *Cyanamid* approach allows for this, and the decision suggests a misleadingly mechanical approach. The Manitoba Court of Appeal has quite properly held that "it is not necessary . . . to follow the consecutive steps set out in the *American Cyanamid* judgment in an inflexible way; nor is it necessary to treat the relative strength of each party's case only as a last step in the process".[115]

187   The traditional "checklist" approach permits the individual judge to analyze all the factors coherently. It does not, however, require him to do so, and the flexibility, which permits one judge to weigh and balance the risks accurately, allows another to depart from the central question and allows for uncertainty and unevenness in approach. The checklist does not specifically relate the factors to one another, and while it provides a valuable guide in coming to the proper result, it has failed to articulate clearly an appropriate overall approach.

188   Treating the checklist as a "multi-requisite test"[116] will often produce results which do not reflect the balance of risks and do not mini-

---

and discretionary. It must not be made the subject of strict rules.": *Hubbard v. Vosper*, [1972] 2 Q.B. 84 (C.A.), at p. 96, *per* Lord Denning, M.R. See also Leubsdorf, *supra*, footnote 16, at p. 526: "any standard applicable to cases arising from every area of the law can scarcely be more than a means of orientation".

[115] *Lambair Ltd. v. Aero Trades (Western) Ltd.* (1978), 87 D.L.R. (3d) 500 (Man. C.A.), at p. 508, leave to appeal to S.C.C. refused October 4, 1978, *per* Matas, J.A. See also *Robert Reiser & Co. Inc. v. Nadore Food Processing Equipment Ltd.* (1977), 81 D.L.R. (3d) 278, 17 O.R. (2d) 717 (H.C.J.); Rogers and Hately, *supra*, footnote 17, at p. 18: "it is apparent from the cases that no such fixed order is adhered to by the courts". Several English cases also take this view: see *Potters-Ballotini Ltd. v. Weston-Baker*, [1977] R.P.C. 202 (C.A.); *Catnic Components Ltd. v. Stressline Ltd.*, [1976] F.S.R. 157 (C.A.); *Mothercare Ltd. v. Robson Books Ltd.*, [1979] F.S.R. 466 (H.C.J.), at p. 473; *per* Megarry, V.-C.: "literalness may strangle reason; and there is high authority for saying that, however eminent the judge, the words of the judgment ought not to be construed as if they were part of an Act of Parliament".

[116] This term was employed, but not applied, by Cory, J., in *Yule, Inc. v. Atlantic Pizza Delight Franchise (1968) Ltd.* (1977), 80 D.L.R. (3d) 725 at p. 730, 17 O.R. (2d) 505 at p. 510 (Div. Ct.).

mize the risk of non-compensable harm. The most notable instance of this result has been the tendency to refuse an interlocutory injunction at the threshold, and without further inquiry, in cases where the judge forms the view that the plaintiff does not have a strong *prima facie* case.[117] Although other aspects of the *American Cyanamid* decision are regrettable, the rejection of the need to show a *prima facie* case as a threshold test in this sense is to be welcomed.

189   The checklist of factors which the courts have developed — relative strength of the case, irreparable harm, and balance of convenience — should not be employed as a series of independent hurdles. They should be seen in the nature of evidence relevant to the central issue of assessing the relative risks of harm to the parties from granting or withholding interlocutory relief.

2. Interlocutory Mandatory Injunctions

190   As noted above,[118] courts have tended to grant prohibitive injunctions more readily than mandatory injunctions. Requiring a positive course of action has been seen to be more difficult to justify. Especially difficult to obtain are interlocutory mandatory injunctions.[119] This, it is submitted, is readily explicable, even if the same principles guiding the award of prohibitive interlocutory injunctions are to be applied. A mandatory order is usually restorative in effect.[120] The plaintiff is asking the court to order the defendant to take the necessary positive action to put the situation back to what it should be. Usually, that can be achieved at trial. A negative order will stop the defendant from taking further action pending trial, and the plaintiff will almost always be able to secure complete restorative relief notwithstanding the delay. As the defendant would be required on an interlocutory basis to take positive action, the potential inconvenience to him is usually substantial. It is a rare case, indeed, where the risk of harm to him will be less significant than the risk to the plaintiff resulting from the court staying its hand until trial.

191   However, it is also clear that interlocutory mandatory orders can be made in appropriate cases.[121] Where the risk of harm to the plain-

---

[117] *Supra*, §140.

[118] *Supra*, §50 *et seq.*

[119] See, *e.g.*, *Toronto Brewing and Malting Co. v. Blake* (1882), 2 O.R. 175 (H.C.J.), at p. 183, *per* Proudfoot, J.: "I think there is no doubt of the general proposition that the Court has the right to interfere by mandatory injunction on an interlocutory application. But where that is done the right must be very clear indeed."

[120] *Supra*, §§52-54.

[121] See *e.g.*, *Mearns v. Corp. of Town of Petrolia* (1880), 28 Gr. 98; *Wyman and Mos-*

tiff is substantial and can only be alleviated by requiring positive steps at the interlocutory stage, such an order is appropriate. For example, in one old case,[122] the defendant had placed inflammable material on his property so as to cause a substantial and immediate risk of injury to the plaintiff. An interim mandatory order was granted. In more recent cases, interlocutory orders containing a mandatory component have been granted where seen as necessary to permit a plaintiff to continue carrying on business pending trial.[123] Also, if the defendant is seen to "steal a march" on the court by racing ahead with wrongful conduct after he knows of the plaintiff's intention to seek the court's assistance in stopping him, an interlocutory mandatory decree may be made to require the defendant to put the situation back to where it would have been but for his precipitous action.[124] Such orders are virtually punitive in effect, as they turn not un the need to protect the plaintiff pending trial (when a demolition order could still be made), but rather in a desire to vindicate the process of the court.

3. Labour Injunctions

192   Injunctions are frequently granted to enjoin unlawful strikes and tortious conduct committed in the course of labour disputes. The use of the injunction in this context is a fruitful source of controversy.[125]

---

crop Realty Ltd. v. Vancouver Real Estate Board (No. 3) (1956), 26 W.W.R. 188 (B.C.S.C.); *Pratt v. Scheveck*, [1926] 4 D.L.R. (3d) 1169 (Sask C.A.); *80 Wellesley St. East Ltd. v. Fundy Bay Builders Ltd.* (1972), 25 D.L.R. (3d) 386, [1972] 2 O.R. 280 (C.A.); *Sutton v. Vanderburg*, [1946] 3 D.L.R. 714, [1946] O.R. 497 (H.C.J.); *Cyprus Anvil Mining Corp. v. White Pass and Yukon Corp. Ltd.*, [1980] 6 W.W.R. 526 (B.C.S.C.), affd *loc. cit.* p. 536 (C.A.); *C.P.R. v. Gaud*, [1949] 2 K.B. 239 (C.A.); *Allport v. Securities Co. Ltd.* (1895), 72 L.T. 533 (Ch.); *Luganda v. Service Hotels*, [1969] 2 Ch. 209 (C.A.). For early examples, see *Ryder v. Bentham* (1750), Ves. Sen. Supp. 242, 28 E.R. 513 (Ch.); *Robinson v. Lord Byron* (1785), 1 Bro. C.C. 588, 28 E.R. 1315 (Ch.). In *Astro Exito Navegacion S.A. v. Southland Enterprise Co. Ltd.*, [1982] 3 W.L.R. 296 (C.A.), an interim mandatory injunction which had the effect of specifically enforcing a contract was awarded.

[122] *Hepburn v. Lordan* (1865), 2 H. & M. 345, 71 E.R. 497, vacated on consent 11 Jur. N.S. 254 *sub nom. Hepburn v. Lesdan.*

[123] See, *e.g.*, *Prairie Hospitality Consultants Ltd. v. Renard International Hospitality Consultants Ltd.* (1980), 118 D.L.R. (3d) 121 (B.C.S.C.); cases cited, *infra*, §660.

[124] *Daniel v. Ferguson*, [1891] 2 Ch. 27 (C.A.); *Von Joel v. Hornsey*, [1895] 2 Ch. 774 (C.A.); *Ruskin v. Canada All-News Radio Ltd.* (1979), 7 B.L.R. 142 (Ont. H.C.J.).

[125] Frankfurter and Greene, *The Labour Injunction* (New York, Macmillan Co., 1930); Carrothers, *The Labour Injunction in British Columbia* (Toronto, C.C.H. Canadian Ltd., 1956); Krever, "The Labour Injunction in Ontario: Procedure and Practice", in Carrothers and Palmer, *Report of a Study on the Labour Injunction in Ontario* (Toronto, Ontario Department of Labour, 1966).

In some provinces, many of the issues have been addressed through reforming legislation.[126] The difficult questions of substantive labour law which are raised cannot be addressed in a general book on specific remedies, but certain points may be made in the present context.

193   Procedurally, labour disputes provide, perhaps, the clearest example of situations in which the interlocutory injunction will effectively decide the entire dispute. In such cases, the balance of convenience approach is particularly inappropriate. Rarely will the matter proceed beyond the interlocutory stage, and the limited scope for factual inquiry available on ordinary interlocutory injunction hearings may be particularly inappropriate. In Ontario,[127] legislation specifically precludes the granting of *ex parte* injunctions in labour matters except in exceptional cases, and goes on to provide for special procedural provisions where labour injunctions are sought. Affidavit evidence must be confined to statements within the knowledge of the deponent, and the court is expressly required to permit *viva voce* cross-examination on such affidavits.[128] The right of immediate appeal to the Court of Appeal is also provided for. Thus, the legislation contemplates a truncated form of expedited trial at a very preliminary stage in the recognition that the court's decision often, if not always, will effectively determine the rights of the parties. Several provinces expressly limit the availability of *ex parte* orders,[129] and in British Columbia, the court has power to award injunctions in labour matters only in cases involving immediate and serious danger to individuals or property.[130]

194   As noted above,[131] it has been recognized in England that the *American Cyanamid* test is inappropriate in the context of a trade dispute for the very reason that the injunction will often end the litigation. Thus, even in the absence of legislation, courts may be expected to dispose of interlocutory injunction applications in labour matters on the merits rather than on a balance of convenience.

195   Provincial legislation sometimes also provides for extensive remedial powers at the hands of provincial labour relations boards.[132] The

---

[126] *Infra*, §§193, 194.

[127] Judicature Act, Ont., s. 20.

[128] Failure to observe this requirement goes to the court's jurisdiction to make an order: *Texpack Ltd. v. Rowley* (1971), 24 D.L.R. (3d) 675, [1972] 2 O.R. 93 (C.A.).

[129] Labour Act, Alta., s. 147; Judicature Act, N.B., s. 34; Queen's Bench Act, Sask., s. 20.

[130] Labour Code, B.C., s. 32.

[131] *Supra*, §160.

[132] Labour Code, B.C., ss. 28-32. See also Labour Relations Act, Ont., s. 92, dis-

Supreme Court of Canada has held that Nova Scotia legislation permitting the board to issue a cease and desist order in relation to an illegal work stoppage does not violate the constitutional restrictions imposed on provincially established tribunals.[133] In British Columbia, the Legislature has taken more drastic action, and conferred upon the provincial Labour Relations Board nearly exclusive jurisdiction with respect to such remedial relief.[134] It has often been suggested that the special expertise and tailor-made powers of labour relations boards may be more appropriate than the traditional judicial powers in the delicate balancing of interests which inevitably occurs in this context.[135]

4. Injunctions Restraining Disposition of Assets Pending Trial

(1) Proprietary claims

196   Interlocutory injunctions are frequently granted to restrain disposition of an asset where the plaintiff asserts a specific or proprietary claim in respect of that asset. If the plaintiff sues for specific performance of an agreement of sale, an interlocutory injunction may be granted, restraining the defendant from defeating the plaintiff's claim by disposing of the property in question before trial.[136] Similarly, even where the plaintiff asserts a money claim, an interlocutory injunction may be granted to protect the claim where the plaintiff has some proprietary right in the money or right to trace that particular fund.[137] The basis for injunctive relief here is to prevent dissipation or destruction of the property which is the subject-matter of the suit.

197   Where the plaintiff sues for specific performance, his claim will of-

---

cussed in *Consolidated-Bathurst Packaging Ltd. v. Canadian Paperworkers Union Local 595*, [1982] O.L.R.B. Rep. 1274.

[133] *Tomko v. Labour Relations Board (Nova Scotia)*, [1977] 1 S.C.R. 112, 69 D.L.R. (3d) 250.

[134] Labour Code, B.C., ss. 28-32. *Cf. Better Value Furniture (CHWK) Ltd. v. Vancouver Distribution Centre Ltd.* (1981), 122 D.L.R. (3d) 12 (B.C.C.A.), leave to appeal to S.C.C. refused 38 N.R. 449n, holding that the exclusive jurisdiction of the Board is confined to complaints under the Labour Code, a collective agreement or the regulations.

[135] See, *e.g.*, the comments of Laskin, C.J.C., in the *Tomko* case, *supra*, footnote 133, at pp. 122-3 S.C.R., p. 257 D.L.R., quoted, *infra*, §346.

[136] *London & County Banking Co. v. Lewis* (1882), 21 Ch. D. 490 (C.A.).

[137] *Trustee of N. Brenner & Co. Ltd. v. Brenner* (1923), 25 O.W.N. 415 (H.C.). Compare *Mills and Mills v. Petrovic* (1980), 118 D.L.R. (3d) 367, 30 O.R. (2d) 238 (H.C.J.), granting an injunction restraining disposition of the defendant's own property where there was strong evidence that the defendant had defrauded the plaintiff of other property.

ten be protected against sale to a third party by filing or registration of his notice or *lis pendens*.[138] It will, however, still be appropriate for the court to award an injunction if the plaintiff shows that a *lis pendens* will not afford adequate protection.[139] In cases involving the sale of chattels or other interest not subject to a registration scheme, an interlocutory injunction may be the only way to protect the claim against sale to a third party.[140]

(2) Fraudulent conveyances

198   There is a well-established jurisdiction to award an injunction restraining disposition of assets pending trial in fraudulent conveyance cases at the suit of a creditor, even before the creditor has obtained his money judgment. Before any fraud has been committed, the court will hesitate to restrain a defendant from dealing with his property at the instance of an ordinary creditor.[141] However, once there has actually been a fraudulent disposal of the property aimed at defeating the plaintiff's claim, the court will enjoin further dealings in the property so as to protect the plaintiff's rights.[142]

199   In order to secure such an injunction, the plaintiff must show he is a creditor, although, as noted, it is unnecessary that he has actually obtained a judgment.[143] Presumably, the plaintiff must establish a *prima facie* case of indebtedness.[144] Secondly, the plaintiff will have to show that a fraud has been committed, and again, as the matter arises at the interlocutory stage, it will be sufficient if the court is satisfied that there is a strong indication that the conveyance may have been fraudulent.[145] The acceptance of a general jurisdiction to award *Mareva* injunctions to protect claims from being defeated by devious means will,[146] of course, render this well-established, but relatively narrow, jurisdiction less significant.

---

[138] *Hadley v. London Bank of Scotland* (1865), 3 De G. J. & S. 63, 46 E.R. 562 (Ch.), refusing an injunction.

[139] *Supra*, footnote 136.

[140] See, *e.g. Hart v. Herwig* (1873), 8 Ch. App. 860 (ship); *Preston v. Luck* (1884), 27 Ch. D. 497 (C.A.) (patent).

[141] *Campbell v. Campbell* (1881), 29 Gr. 252 at pp. 254-5, *per* Boyd, C. See, however, the *Mareva* cases discussed, *infra*, §201 *et seq.*

[142] *Ibid.*; *Toronto Carpet Co. v. Wright* (1912), 3 D.L.R. 725 (Man. K.B.); *City of Toronto v. McIntosh* (1977), 16 O.R. (2d) 257 (H.C.J.); *Robert Reiser & Co. Inc. v. Nadore Food Processing Equipment Ltd.* (1977), 81 D.L.R. (3d) 278, 17 O.R. (2d) 717 (H.C.J.).

[143] *Robert Reiser & Co.*, *supra*, footnote 142.

[144] *Robert Reiser & Co.*, *supra*.

[145] *Robert Reiser & Co.*, *supra*.

[146] *Infra*, §201 *et seq.*

(3) Plaintiff's entitlement established

200   In some cases, there may be a delay between the date on which the plaintiff's entitlement to relief is determined, and the date upon which the precise amount of the judgment is established so that an enforceable judgment becomes available. Here, if the plaintiff is able to show that the defendant is likely to take steps to evade the judgment, the argument in favour of injunctive relief is particularly strong. As the defendant's liability on the merits has been established, he cannot complain that he is being improperly hampered by an injunction which restricts his freedom to dispose of his property. Such orders have been made in cases where the plaintiff's cost award has yet to be taxed.[147] Another appropriate situation might well be cases where judgment has been entered by default, but where unliquidated damages must be assessed. Similarly, it has been suggested that where the plaintiff sues on a foreign judgment, and there is no apparent reason to doubt the enforceability of that judgment, the plaintiff should be in the stronger position to claim interlocutory relief as the merits have already been examined.[148]

(4) Mareva injunctions

201   Until 1975, it was firmly established that an interlocutory injunction would not be granted before trial to restrain the defendant from disposing of his assets in order to protect the claim of an ordinary creditor.[149] An injunction restraining the defendant from dealing with his property before judgment constitutes a form of pre-trial execution. While the courts have always allowed a plaintiff, who asserts a specific or proprietary claim, to call upon the equitable jurisdiction of the court to protect his claim pending determination of his right at trial,[150] pre-trial execution of an unsecured or non-proprietary claim

---

[147] *Cummins v. Perkins*, [1899] 1 Ch. 16 (C.A.); *Faith Panton Property Plan Ltd. v. Hodgetts*, [1981] 1 W.L.R. 927 (C.A.).

[148] *Hunt v. BP Exploration Co. (Libya) Ltd.*, [1980] 1 N.Z.L.R. 104 (S.C.), at p. 120, *per* Barker, J.

[149] See *Lister & Co. v. Stubbs* (1890), 45 Ch. D. 1 (C.A.), affd *loc. cit.* p. 11 (C.A.), at p. 13, *per* Cotton, L.J.:

> I know of no case where, because it was highly probable that if the action were brought to a hearing the plaintiff could establish that a debt was due to him from the defendant, the defendant has been ordered to give security until that has been established by the judgment or decree.

Mills v. Northern Ry. of Buenos Ayres Co. (1870), 5 Ch. App. 621; *Beddow v. Beddow* (1878), 9 Ch. D. 89; *Robinson v. Pickering* (1881), 16 Ch. D. 660 (C.A.). The Canadian cases to the same effect are cited, *infra*, footnote 158.

[150] *Supra*, §§196, 197.

has been treated quite differently. Pre-trial execution is authorized by statute in many jurisdictions, but except for the specific cases already discussed, was not available under ordinary common law or equitable principles.[151]

202 Clearly, pre-trial execution of any kind poses definite problems. Attachment of assets or interference with disposition of assets will often constitute a serious interference with the defendant's affairs. That interference may be more readily justified where the plaintiff's right is specifically related to the asset in question. However, where the plaintiff asserts a general claim and looks to the assets only as a means of satisfying a likely or possible monetary judgment against the defendant, interference with the defendant's assets is more difficult to justify. Unless strictly limited to cases where the plaintiff's prospect of ultimate success is strong and to cases where the defendant is bent on flouting the court's process, restraining the defendant's freedom to deal with his property upon the filing of an unsecured claim could well produce serious injustice.

203 On the other hand, it is equally difficult to justify the invariable refusal of such relief. The rationale underlying the ordinary interlocutory injunction is surely met where the plaintiff is able to show that he has a strong case on the merits, and that if the defendant is not stopped, the plaintiff's right to an appropriate remedy at trial will be lost. The purpose of interlocutory injunctive relief is to prevent the effective destruction of the plaintiff's rights in the period of delay awaiting trial. If the risk that the plaintiff's right will be destroyed exceeds the risk that the defendant may be unduly interfered with, an interlocutory injunction is justified.[152] That purpose is surely met where the plaintiff can demonstrate that his money judgment will be rendered useless if the defendant is not prevented from arranging his affairs so as to evade the reach of the court's process.

204 Despite a long line of authority which suggested that an application for such an interlocutory injunction must fail,[153] the English courts, led by Lord Denning, began in 1975 to move away from the invariable refusal of injunctive relief in these cases. The *Mareva* injunction takes its name from one of the early cases[154] which dealt

---

[151] See Gertner, "Prejudgment Remedies: A Need for Rationalization", 19 Osgoode Hall L.J. 503 (1981), for discussion of the relationship between injunctive relief of the type described and other prejudgment remedies.

[152] *Supra*, §§133-135.

[153] *Supra*, footnote 149.

[154] *Mareva Compania Naviera S.A. v. International Bulkcarriers Ltd.*, [1975] 2 Lloyd's

with a shipowner's claim for hire under a time-charter. The defendant was a foreign corporation, and, the court found, unless restrained from removing money then on deposit to its credit in a London bank, there was every reason to believe that the plaintiff's claim would be defeated. The Court of Appeal therefore upheld an *ex parte* injunction forbidding the defendant from disposing of its property within, or removing such property outside the jurisdiction.

205   Following the *Mareva* case itself, *ex parte* injunctions became commonly used to protect large shipping claims.[155] As an international financial, shipping, and marine insurance centre, London is the focal point of a vast number of shipping transactions. Very often, the parties are foreign, one-ship operations. Payment of insurance proceeds, charter or freight charges are processed through London managers, banks and brokers, and after a loss giving rise to claims, or even where claims for hire are asserted, may be the defendant's only exigible asset. If such funds are not frozen in England by a *Mareva* injunction, they will disappear from the effective reach of English process, and legitimate claims will go unsatisfied.[156] The *Mareva* injunction has been a most welcome development in shipping circles, is in daily use in England, and undoubtedly has prevented a large number of defendants from flouting the process of the English courts.[157] As the following discussion will show, such injunctions are by no means limited to the shipping area, and are regularly awarded in a wide variety of substantive law areas where the plaintiff is able to show a serious risk of dissipation of assets which would unjustly deprive him of the fruits of his victory.

206   In Canada, despite a long line of earlier authority to the effect that no interlocutory injunction to restrain disposition of assets pending trial could be awarded,[158] it is now well established that the courts are

---

Rep. 509 (C.A.). The first reported case was *Nippon Yusen Kaisha v. Karageorgis*, [1975] 1 W.L.R. 1093 (C.A.).

[155] By 1979, there were said to be about twenty such injunctions granted each month: *Third Chandris Shipping Corp. v. Unimarine S.A.*, [1979] Q.B. 645 (C.A.) at p. 650, *per* Mustill, J.

[156] The background is given by Kerr, J., in *Siskina v. Distos Compania Haviera S.A.*, [1979] A.C. 210 (H.L.), at pp. 215-16.

[157] In *Third Chandris Shipping Corp. v. Unimarine S.A.*, *supra*, footnote 155, at p. 657, counsel arguing for the defendant acknowledged that it "would be very hard to find any one in the City who would not say that the *Mareva* injunction does not serve a very useful purpose". Lord Denning has described the *Mareva* injunction as "the greatest piece of judicial law reform in my time" (*The Due Process of Law* (London, Butterworths, 1980), at p. 134).

[158] *Burdett v. Fader* (1903), 6 O.L.R. 532 (H.C.J.); *Ferguson v. Ferguson* (1916), 29

prepared to follow Lord Denning's lead and to grant *Mareva* injunctions on the same basis as that established by the English courts. In *Chitel v. Rothbart*,[159] the Ontario Court of Appeal held that, while caution was required, these injunctions could be awarded. MacKinnon, A.C.J.O., concluded that the "Mareva injunction is here and here to stay and properly so, but it is not the rule — it is the exception to the rule".[160] Judgments of the Manitoba,[161] New Brunswick[162] and Nova Scotia[163] appeal courts have also approved the granting of such injunctions, again following the English lead.[164] In New Brunswick, a rule of court specifically empowers the court to grant such injunctions.[165]

(a) Domestic defendants

207   The early cases were clearly put on a basis of the particular problems posed by foreign defendants who theoretically fell within the court's jurisdiction, but who could easily stultify its effect. Unless they were prevented from removing their assets, they could effectively put themselves beyond the reach of the domestic court by a simple telephone call or telex message. Indeed, it was on the basis that claims against foreigners who could remove their assets should be put in a different category that the Court of Appeal held itself justified to depart from the well-established rule refusing restraint on disposition of assets pending trial.[166]

D.L.R. 364 (Man. K.B.); *Bedell v. Gefaell (No. 2)*, [1938] 4 D.L.R. 443, [1938] O.R. 726 (C.A.); *Bradley Bros. (Oshawa) Ltd. v. A to Z Rental Canada, Ltd.* (1970), 14 D.L.R. (3d) 171, [1970] 3 O.R. 787 (C.A.); *O.S.F. Industries Ltd. v. Marc-Jay Investments Inc.* (1978), 88 D.L.R. (3d) 446, 20 O.R. (2d) 566 (H.C.J.); *Christie v. Fraser* (1904), 10 B.C.R. 291 (Full Court).

[159] (1982), 141 D.L.R. (3d) 268, 39 O.R. (2d) 513 (C.A.).

[160] *Ibid.*, at p. 290 D.L.R., p. 534 O.R.

[161] *Feigelman v. Aetna Financial Services Ltd.* (1982), 143 D.L.R. (3d) 715 (Man. C.A.), leave to appeal to S.C.C. granted 46 N.R. 266n.

[162] *Humphreys v. Buraglia* (1982), 135 D.L.R. (3d) 535 (N.B.C.A.).

[163] *Parmar Fisheries Ltd. v. Parceria Maritima Esperanca L. DA.* (1982), 141 D.L.R. (3d) 498 (N.S.S.C.T.D.).

[164] See also *BP Exploration Co. (Libya) Ltd. v. Hunt* (1980), 114 D.L.R. (3d) 35 (N.W.T. S.C.); *Elesguro Inc. v. Ssangyong Shipping Co. Ltd.* (1980), 117 D.L.R. (3d) 105 (Fed. Ct. T.D.); *Liberty National Bank & Trust Co. v. Atkin* (1981), 121 D.L.R. (3d) 160, 31 O.R. (2d) 715 (H.C.J.); *Bank of Montreal v. Page Properties Ltd.* (1981), 120 D.L.R. (3d) 672, 32 O.R. (2d) 9 (Div. Ct.); *Canadian Pacific Airlines Ltd. v. Hind* (1981), 122 D.L.R. (3d) 498, 32 O.R. (2d) 591 (H.C.J.). For discussion of the Canadian cases see Gertner, *supra*, footnote 151; McAllister, "Mareva Injunctions" (1982), 28 C.P.C. 1; Stockwood, " 'Mareva' Injunctions", 3 Adv. Q. 85 (1981-82).

[165] Rule 40.03.

[166] See *Rasu Maritima S.A. v. Perusahaan*, [1978] Q.B. 644 (C.A.), at p. 659, per Lord Denning, M.R. (the first case to be fully argued before the Court of Appeal).

208   Gradually, however, the courts have moved away from the position that *Mareva* injunctions are available only against foreigners.[167]
In one case,[168] the defendant was served in England and had certain
contacts there, but was a foreigner and likely to depart with his assets
on short notice. An injunction was awarded although he had been
served within the jurisdiction. In a later case,[169] an injunction was
granted against an English defendant, who had gone abroad, on the
grounds that there had been shown a real risk that he might remove
his assets so as to defeat the claim. Then, in 1980, Lord Denning
held:

> ... that a *Mareva* injunction can be granted against a man even though
> he is based in this country if the circumstances are such that there is a
> danger of his absconding, or a danger of the assets being removed out of
> the jurisdiction or disposed of within the jurisdiction, or otherwise dealt
> with so that there is a danger that the plaintiff, if he gets judgment, will
> not be able to get it satisfied.[170]

That result has now been codified in England and it is now provided
by statute that:

> The power of the High Court . . . to grant an interlocutory injunction
> restraining a party to any proceedings from removing from the jurisdic-
> tion of the High Court, or otherwise dealing with, assets located within
> that jurisdiction shall be exercisable in cases where that party is, as well
> as in cases where he is not, domiciled, resident or present within that
> jurisdiction.[171]

In one case,[172] it was suggested that, despite the legislation, removal
from the jurisdiction remains the basis of the jurisdiction, and that
the power to restrain dealing with assets within the jurisdiction was
inserted to prevent the defendant from transferring his assets to a
third party who would in turn remove them from the jurisidiction on
his behalf.[173] The dictum of Lord Denning just cited,[174] suggests a

---

[167] *Cf. Gebr. Van Weedle Scheepvaart Kantoor B.V.* v. *Homeric Marine Services Ltd.*,
[1979] 2 Lloyd's Rep. 117 (Q.B.); *Faith Panton Property Plan Ltd.* v. *Hodgetts*,
[1981] 1 W.L.R. 927 (C.A.), at p. 937, *per* Brandon, L.J., stating that *Mareva* has
"never yet . . . applied to a case like the present one in which no foreign element of
any kind exists". The case was decided before the enactment of the 1981 legislation, and an injunction was granted on other grounds: *supra*, footnote 147.

[168] *Chartered Bank* v. *Daklouche*, [1980] 1 W.L.R. 107, (C.A.).

[169] *Barclay-Johnson* v. *Yuill*, [1980] 1 W.L.R. 1259 (Ch.).

[170] *Rahman (Prince Abdul)* v. *Abu-Taha*, [1980] 1 W.L.R. 1268 (C.A.), at p. 1273.

[171] Supreme Court Act 1981 (U.K.), s. 37(3).

[172] *A.J. Bekhor & Co. Ltd.* v. *Bilton*, [1981] Q.B. 923 (C.A.), at pp. 941-2, *per* Ackner, L.J.

[173] *Ibid.*, at p. 947, *per* Griffiths, L.J.

[174] *Supra*, footnote 170.

broader jurisdiction, and Lord Denning reiterated this view in *Z Ltd. v. A-Z and AA-LL*, where, referring to the statute, he said: "Those words 'otherwise deal with' are in my opinion to be given a wide meaning. They are not to be construed as ejusdem generis with 're-moving from the jurisdiction'."[175] After referring to an unreported case in which the Court of Appeal had restrained disposition within the jurisidiction, Lord Denning added: "The *Mareva* jurisdiction ex-tends to cases where there is a danger that the assets will be dissi-pated in this country as well as by removal out of the jurisdiction."[176]

209   On principle, it seems difficult to justify restricting the injunction to cases where there is a risk of removal of assets from the jurisdic-tion, whether under the statute or otherwise. Admittedly, it was the foreign element which was used to justify departure from the earlier cases denying the possibility of any form of pre-trial restraint on dis-position of assets.[177] However, once relief is available to protect against removal to foreign parts, is seems difficult to deny it in a purely domestic setting.

210   Removal of assets to foreign places is only one way in which a de-fendant can flout the jurisdiction of the court and avoid meeting his obligation to the plaintiff by concealing or fraudulently placing his assets beyond the reach of ordinary process. The underlying princi-ple of the *Mareva* injunction is to protect the plaintiff from having his right destroyed pending trial, and, it is suggested, if the plaintiff makes out a compelling case that this is likely to occur, it should not matter what surreptitious means have been chosen by the defendant. The Canadian courts appear willing to grant *Mareva* injunctions against domestic defendants restraining dealing with assets within the jurisdiction.[178] In one case,[179] the defendant had actually been impris-oned, and there was no suggestion that he had the intention or means to have assets removed from the jurisdiction, but the court did not hesitate to award injunctive relief.

(b) Test for the Mareva injunction

211   The standards to be applied in determining whether the plaintiff

---

[175] [1982] 2 W.L.R. 288 (C.A.), at p. 293.

[176] *Ibid.*, at p. 294.

[177] *Rasu Maritima S.A. v. Perusahaan, supra*, footnote 166.

[178] *Liberty National Bank & Trust Co. v. Atkin* (1981), 121 D.L.R. (3d) 160, 31 O.R. (2d) 715 (H.C.J.).

[179] *Canadian Pacific Airlines Ltd. v. Hind* (1981), 122 D.L.R. (3d) 498, 32 O.R. (2d) 591 (H.C.J.).

should obtain a *Mareva* injunction were set out by the English Court of Appeal in *Third Chandris Shipping Corp. v. Unimarine S.A.*,[180] and these have been regularly applied:

212   (i) The plaintiff should make full and frank disclosure of all matters in his knowledge which are material for the judge to know.[181]

Because such injunctions are invariably sought *ex parte*, the obligation of full and frank disclosure is especially important. The court's order may have serious effects upon the defendant's business, even if only for a matter of days until he is able to bring his own application against the order, and the courts have repeatedly stressed the importance of frank disclosure by the plaintiff at the *ex parte* hearing.[182]

213   (ii) The plaintiff should give particulars of his claim against the defendant, stating the ground of his claim and the amount thereof, and fairly stating the points made against it by the defendant.[183]

While it is difficult to be precise about the strength of case the plaintiff must demonstrate, it is clear that the courts have proceeded cautiously, recognizing the risk of substantial harm and inconvenience which may be caused to the defendant. The *Mareva* injunction is one which calls for careful scrutiny of the merits of the claim, and refusal of injunctive relief unless there is a good prospect of success at trial.[184] English courts have held, on the other hand, that the standard applied on summary judgment applications is inappropriate.[185] Thus, a plaintiff will not be denied his injunction simply because there is a triable issue, and he need not necessarily make out a case which would be strong enough to justify awarding him judgment then and there.

---

[180] [1979] Q.B. 645 (C.A.). The quotations which follow are at pp. 668-9, *per* Lord Denning, M.R.

[181] *Ibid.*, at p. 668.

[182] A *Mareva* injunction will be set aside for failure to disclose all the facts on the *ex parte* application: *Chitel v. Rothbart* (1982), 141 D.L.R. (3d) 268, 39 O.R. (2d) 513 (C.A.); *Negocios Del Mar S.A. v. Doric Shipping Corp. S.A.*, [1979] 1 Lloyd's Rep. 331 (C.A.). See also, *supra*, §129.

[183] *Third Chandris Shipping Corp.*, *supra*, footnote 180, at p. 668.

[184] An injunction was denied in *Etablissement Esefka International Anstalt v. Central Bank of Nigeria*, [1979] 1 Lloyd's Rep. 445 (C.A.), where there was doubt as to the plaintiff's claim. See also *Bakarim v. Victoria P. Shipping Co. Ltd.*, [1980] 2 Lloyd's Rep. 193 (Q.B.); *Bank of Montreal v. Page Properties Ltd.* (1981), 120 D.L.R. (3d) 672, 32 O.R. (2d) 9 (Div. Ct.). The *American Cyanamid* test has been held inapplicable to such cases: *Chitel v. Rothbart*, *supra*, footnote 182; *Canadian Pacific Airlines Ltd. v. Hind*, *supra*, footnote 179, at p. 503 D.L.R., p. 596 O.R., *per* Grange, J.: "There must be a very strong case and a real danger of disposition of the only assets which will satisfy the judgment."

[185] *Rasu Maritima S.A. v. Perusahaan*, [1978] Q.B. 644 (C.A.), at p. 661.

214   (iii) The plaintiff should give some grounds for believing that there
is a risk of the assets being removed before the judgment or award is
satisfied.[186]

The court will not grant an injunction merely because the defendant
is foreign, but will examine such factors as the nature of its operations, the stringency of company law under which it is incorporated,
and the existence of reciprocal enforcement legislation.[187] Again, it is
difficult to be precise here, but the courts certainly have denied injunctions where the plaintiff failed to establish a serious risk that the
defendant was going to deprive him of the fruits of his judgment.[188]

215   (iv) The plaintiff must, of course, give an undertaking in damages —
in case he fails in his claim or the injunction turns out to be unjustified.
In a suitable case this should be supported by a bond or security: and
the injunction only granted on it being given, or undertaken to be
given.[189]

The requirement of the undertaking is nothing more than a normal
incident of interlocutory injunctive relief.[190] However, in at least one
case, [191] an impecunious plaintiff has been awarded a *Mareva* injunction without having to file such an undertaking.

216   (v) The plaintiff should give some grounds for believing that the defendant has assets here.[192]

It has been held in England that the plaintiff satisfies the requirement
by pointing to the existence of a bank account, even if its present
state is in overdraft.[193] From the point of view of protecting the defendant's legitimate interests, this is perhaps the least important of
all criteria for the *Mareva* injunction, as a defendant who has no assets within the jurisdiction is hardly affected. Still, courts have always been unwilling to grant useless orders. In one case, an
injunction was refused where the defendant had no assets presently

---

[186] *Third Chandris Shipping Corp.*, *supra*, at p. 669.

[187] *Third Chandris Shipping Corp.*, *supra*, at p. 669.

[188] See, *e.g.*, *Etablissement Esefka International Anstalt v. Central Bank of Nigeria*,
[1979] 1 Lloyd's Rep. 445 (C.A.).

[189] *Third Chandris Shipping Corp.*, *supra*, at p. 669.

[190] *Supra*, §§173-177.

[191] *Allen v. Jambo Holdings Ltd.*, [1980] 1 W.L.R. 1252 (C.A.), at p. 1257, *per* Lord
Denning, M.R.: "I do not see why a poor plaintiff should be denied a *Mareva* injunction just because he is poor, whereas a rich plaintiff would get it."

[192] *Third Chandris Shipping Corp.*, *supra*, at p. 668.

[193] *Third Chandris Shipping Corp.*, *supra*, at p. 673, *per* Lawton, L.J.: "Large over-
drafts, such as commercial undertakings have, are almost always secured in some
way. The collateral security may represent substantial assets."

in the jurisidiction, but where the plaintiff suggested that assets would be coming into the jurisdiction subsequently.[194]

217   It is clear, of course, that even where the plaintiff succeeds at the *ex parte* stage, the defendant may move against the injunction upon being notified of its existence.[195] Thus, although these injunctions raise serious questions of due proces, to the extent that the plaintiff must make out a strong case, and the defendant is given an early opportunity to put forth his own version, the risk of harming the defendant seems justified when put against the risk to the plaintiff and certainty that many plaintiffs must have been deprived of their rights by evasive defendants before the courts developed the jurisdiction to award *Mareva* injunctions.

218   Obviously, however, the *Mareva* injunction is subject to abuse, especially since it is almost invariably granted *ex parte*. The English judges have cautioned against routine applications to gain security or perhaps merely to inconvenience the defendant where there is no real risk that he is about to dissipate his assets.[196] Similarly, Canadian judges have emphasized the extraordinary nature of the relief afforded by the *Mareva* injunction, and have not hesitated to set aside orders which did not meet the standard enunciated in *Third Chandris Shipping Corp.*[197]

(c) Form of order

219   *Mareva* injunctions have taken various forms.[198] The usual order made by the English courts is wide in scope, restraining the defen-

---

[194] *Cybel Inc. of Panama v. Timpuship* (C.A., unreported) referred to by Grant, "The Mareva Injunction Four Years On", 130 New L.J. 985 (1980), at p. 986.

[195] In *Z Ltd. v. A-Z and AA-LL*, [1982] 2 W.L.R. 288 (C.A.), at p. 309, Kerr, L.J., suggested that the practice of invariably inserting a return date in the *ex parte* order should be avoided:

     . . . While it must of course always be clear that it is open to the defendant, or any third party affected by the order, to apply to have it varied or discharged on short notice, and even ex parte in extreme cases, reliance on such means of adjustment should only be a secondary consideration. The primary consideration should be at the stage of the ex parte application, and what then appears to be the appropriate order.

[196] *Ibid.*, at p. 306, *per* Kerr, L.J.

[197] See, *e.g.*, *Erie Manufacturing Co. (Canada) v. Rogers* (1981), 24 C.P.C. 132 (H.C.J.); *Chitel v. Rothbart* (1982), 141 D.L.R. (3d) 268, 39 O.R. (2d) 513 (C.A.). See also *supra*, §129; *Negocios Del Mar S.A. v. Doric Shipping Corp. S.A.*, [1979] 1 Lloyd's Rep. 331 (C.A.), setting aside an injunction served to freeze a disputed payment where the full facts had not been disclosed.

[198] See *Cretanor Maritime Co. Ltd. v. Irish Marine Management Ltd.*, [1978] 1 W.L.R. 966 (C.A.).

dant from removing assets from the jurisdiction, or otherwise disposing of or dealing with assets within the jurisdiction, including the specified asset, so that assets remain within the jurisdiction equal to the amount of the plaintiff's claim. While the plaintiff does have to show grounds for believing that the defendant has some assets within the jurisdiction in order to obtain the injunction in the first place, in its ordinary form, the injunction is not restricted to those assets. The effect of the order has been described as "ambulatory"[199] in that it covers assets which might come into the defendant's control in the jurisdiction after the date of the order. The effectiveness of the jurisdiction obviously should not be stifled by overly specific orders, but on the other hand, it is difficult to justify restraining disposition of assets in an amount in excess of the plaintiff's claim, and the more specific the order, the less likely it is to interfere unjustifiably with the defendant's affairs.

220 One of the difficult problems is whether the injunction should specify a maximum amount. From the defendant's point of view, a limitation to the amount of the plaintiff's claim seems only fair. It is difficult to justify freezing assets above the amount required to secure the plaintiff's claim, thereby causing unnecessary hardship. On the other hand, if such an order is made in the first instance, enforcement problems may often arise where the defendant's assets are spread about. A bank, required to freeze an account, would have no way of determining whether the defendant had other assets elsewhere up to the stated amount to satisfy the injunction. There would appear to be no fixed rule on this point, and properly so. The plaintiff should be as specific as possible as to the defendant's assets, and where the injunction relates to a particular fund, it should be limited in amount. Where, however, there are accounts at two or more banks, the preferable practice is that suggested by Kerr, L.J., in *Z Ltd. v. A-Z*:

> In such cases it will be unavoidable, as it seems to me, that the first paragraph of the order should restrain the defendant in general terms up to the "maximum sum" in question, but that the second paragraph should then qualify the first by providing that, so far as any such accounts are concerned, the defendant is not to be entitled to draw upon any of them except to the extent to which any of them exceed the maximum sum referred to in the first paragraph. The effect of this will be to restrain the defendant generally up to the desired amount, but at the same time to

---

[199] *Ibid.*, at p. 973, *per* Buckley, L.J. *Cf.*, however, *Z Ltd. v. A-Z and AA-LL*, *supra*, footnote 195, at p. 313, *per* Kerr, L.J.

make some more qualified, though precise, provision about the extent to which any of the defendant's bank accounts are to be frozen. An order drafted in this form will achieve the general restraint which it is desired to impose on the defendant, who will know the value of the assets which he has within the jurisdiction, and will also at the same time enable the banks to know precisely what they may or may not permit the defendant to do in relation to any accounts of his which they may hold.[200]

(d) Chattels

221   *Mareva* injunctions have been granted restraining the removal from the jurisdiction of a chattel the value of which greatly exceeded the plaintiff's claim.[201] One argument here is that the burden the injunction imposes on the defendant may be unreasonable. In the *Rasu Maritima* case,[202] an injunction was refused, partly on this basis. The plaintiff sought to restrain removal of equipment to be used in the construction of a large plant. The detention of the equipment would have caused serious loss. It was not being removed from the jurisdiction in order to evade the claim, and, moreover, was going through Germany where it could also be seized. There was difficulty in determining title to the goods, and their scrap value was a "drop in the ocean"[203] compared with the size of the plaintiff's claim. As security would only be for the scrap value, the court held that it would not be proper to interfere with the construction of the plant by awarding an injunction. However, in shipping cases where *in rem* proceedings are taken to arrest ships, the regular practice is for security in a suitable amount to be given in order to obtain the release of the ship. A similar practice could readily be adopted in *Mareva* injunction cases, and has been advocated by Lord Denning.[204] In one case,[205] the English Court of Appeal dismissed an application to dissolve an injunction where the defendant had made no attempt to reach such an arrangement with the plaintiff, but argued that the detention of its aircraft caused enormous expense and loss. Lord Denning has stated that there was nothing wrong with making an order which would impose such a burden on the defendant as to force them to post security for

---

[200] *Supra*, footnote 195, at p. 311.

[201] Cases cited, *infra*, footnotes 202 and 205. See also *C.B.S. United Kingdom v. Lambert*, [1983] Ch. 37 (C.A.).

[202] *Rasu Maritima S.A. v Perusahaan*, [1978] Q.B. 644 (C.A.).

[203] *Ibid.*, at p. 663, *per* Lord Denning, M.R.

[204] *Infra*, footnotes 205 and 206.

[205] *Allen v. Jambo Holdings Ltd.*, [1980] 1 W.L.R. 1252 (C.A.).

the claim in order to secure the right to remove and use their chattel.[206] In the event of an abusive refusal by the plaintiff to agree to the release of the chattel upon security being posted, presumably the court would vary or perhaps even dissolve the injunction.

(e) Characterization of order and priorities

222   There is conflicting English authority on whether a *Mareva* injunction operates *in rem* or *in personam*. In *Cretanor Maritime Co. Ltd. v. Irish Marine Ltd.*,[207] the Court of Appeal rejected Lord Denning's description of the *Mareva* injunction as a form of attachment, and held that: "A *Mareva* injunction, however, even if it relates only to a particularised asset . . . is relief in personam. It does not effect a seizure of any asset. It merely restrains the owner from dealing with the asset in certain ways."[208] Thus, the court held, it does not affect the ranking of creditors' claims. In that case, it followed that a debenture holder entitled to security in the assets subject to a *Mareva* injunction can have the injunction set aside to the extent that it prevents him from realizing on his security. Although a receiver, appointed after the injunction has been granted, is subject to its terms, as he stands in the shoes of the defendant and is bound to respect the injunction, a creditor with a secured interest should not be prevented from realizing his security, and accordingly does have standing to move against the injunction, even though the injunction was granted before the creditor's security interest crystallized.[209]

223   However, in a subsequent case,[210] Lord Denning stated that the effect of a *Mareva* injunction is to attach the asset itself, and that the injunction operates *in rem*. However, he hastened to add that it does

---

[206] *Rasu Maritima S.A. v. Perusahaan, supra*, footnote 202, at p. 662, *per* Lord Denning, L.J.: "[There is] no objection in principle to an order being made in respect of assets: in the expectation that this will compel the defendant, as a matter of business, to provide security". *Cf. Cretanor Maritime Co. Ltd. v. Irish Marine Management Ltd., supra*, footnote 198, at pp. 974-5, *per* Buckley, L.J.: "In what circumstances it is justifiable for the court to lend its authority in the exercise of a discretionary jurisdiction and one based fundamentally on equitable principles to bringing pressure to bear upon a party in this way is, I think, still open to debate."

[207] *Supra*, footnote 198.

[208] *Cretanor Maritime Co., supra*, at p. 974, *per* Buckley, L.J.

[209] It has also been held that a *Mareva* injunction will not affect insurance moneys which have been assigned to mortgages under a mortgage created before the application: *W. Angliss & Co. (Australia) Pty. Ltd. v. Pinos Shipping Co.* (1978, unreported), referred to in Grant, "The Mareva Injunction Four Years On", 130 New L.J. 985 (1980), at p. 986.

[210] *Z Ltd. v. A-Z and AA-LL*, [1982] 2 W.L.R. 288 (C.A.), at p. 295.

not give a charge or priority in favour of any particular creditor. Lord Denning was addressing the problem of how a bank, not a party to the proceedings, could be bound by the injunction. The *in rem* characterization made it easier to justify holding the bank bound, thus making the injunction more effective.

224   Thus, it would seem, there is no real difference in substance between these conflicting views as to the *in rem* or *in personam* characterization of the injunction, as there is no dispute that the injunction affords no priority. As the result sought by Lord Denning, namely binding third parties to the injunction, can be justified without resorting to the *in rem* label,[211] and as that label has connotations which do not apply to the *Mareva* injunction, it is submitted that it is preferable to regard the *Mareva* injunction as a form of *in personam* relief.

225   A further point which follows from the fact that a *Mareva* injunction is not an actual seizure of assets is that the defendant may be permitted to meet *bona fide* expenses from money subject to the order.[212] The purpose of the injunction is to prevent the defendant from improperly putting his assets beyond the court's reach. A defendant who disputes the plaintiff's claim and wishes to meet *bona fide* liabilities as they fall due is clearly not attempting to evade the effect of a judgment. To prevent him from meeting such obligations would be to "rewrite the . . . law of insolvency",[213] and would put unsecured creditors who obtain *Mareva* injunctions in a preferred position over others.[214] This could produce a scramble to the court and as well, would operate very harshly on the defendant. As Goff, J., put it:

> It does not make commercial sense that a party claiming unliquidated damages should, without himself proceeding to judgment, prevent the defendant from using his assets to satisfy his debts as they fall due and so put him in the position of having to allow his creditors to proceed to judgment with consequent loss of credit and of commercial standing.[215]

Accordingly, it has been held that even where the amount of the payment will exhaust the defendant's assets and thereby defeat the

---

[211] See Chapter 6.

[212] *Iraqi Ministry of Defence v. Arcepey Shipping Co. S.A.*, [1980] 2 W.L.R. 488 (Q.B.).

[213] *Ibid.*, at p. 494, *per* Goff, J.

[214] See also *Bank of Montreal v. James Main Holdings Ltd.* (1982), 26 C.P.C. 266 (Ont. H.C.J.), affd 28 C.P.C. 157 (Div. Ct.); *Quinn v. Marsta Cession Services Ltd.* (1982), 133 D.L.R. (3d) at p. 112*n*, 37 O.R. (2d) 373 (H.C.J.).

[215] *Iraqi Ministry of Defence, supra*, footnote 212, at p. 495.

plaintiff's claim, such a payment must be allowed if made *bona fide* in the ordinary course of business or to provide for ordinary living expenses.[216] The practice is for the defendant to move for variation of the injunction, and the burden will be with him to satisfy the court that the variation will not conflict with the purpose of the *Mareva* injunction.[217] Even this, however, may cause the defendant and other creditors serious inconvenience as an application to the court will be required before the defendant can meet ordinary payments. A better solution is for the original order to provide that payments made in the regular course of business by the defendant may be made.[218]

(f) Commercial paper

226   *Mareva* injunctions have been refused where it is sought to enjoin payments on negotiable commercial paper.[219] The rationale is simply that commercial dealings depend upon reliance on negotiable instruments — in one *Mareva* case they were described as the "life blood of commerce"[220] — and that interference with payment in the ordinary course would have highly undesirable consequences. In one English case,[221] a *Mareva* injunction was refused, although the defendant was to be the immediate recipient of the proceeds of a bank guarantee amounting to an irrevocable letter of credit, and the money was to be paid in Greece, plainly beyond the reach of the English courts. On the other hand, the courts have indicated that a *Mareva* injunction might be granted where fraud is involved,[222] and of course, it will often be possible to impose an injunction upon the fruits of the payment itself once made.

(g) Interests of third parties

227   The English courts have taken into account the interests of third parties which may be affected by a *Mareva* injunction. The main con-

---

[216] *Iraqi Ministry of Defence, supra,* at p. 495.

[217] *A v. C (No. 2) (Note),* [1981] Q.B. 961.

[218] *Van Brugge v. Arthur Frommer Int'l Ltd.* (1982), 35 O.R. (2d) 333 (H.C.J.).

[219] *Montecchi v. Shimco (U.K.) Ltd.,* [1979] 1 W.L.R. 1180 (C.A.); *Intraco Ltd. v. Notis Shipping Corp.,* [1981] 2 Lloyd's Rep. 256 (C.A.).

[220] *Intraco Ltd., supra,* footnote 219, at p. 257. See also *R. D. Harbottle (Mercantile) Ltd. v. National Westminster Bank Ltd.,* [1978] Q.B. 146.

[221] *Intraco Ltd., supra,* and see *Rosen v. Pullen* (1981), 126 D.L.R. (3d) 62 (Ont. H.C.J.).

[222] *Intraco Ltd., supra.*

cern has been the expense a party may be put to by such an injunction. Banks are particularly affected where an injunction may require a detailed and costly search of bank records to determine the whereabouts and amount of the defendant's assets on deposit. It has been held that the plaintiff must bear these costs.[223] The plaintiff's obligation in this regard has been described as a promise to indemnify, implicit in the application for the injunction and insistence that the bank comply.[224] Also, it has been held that the court may require a specific undertaking from the plaintiff to meet such expenses as a condition of granting the injunction.[225] Similarly, in a shipping case, it was held that the injunction should be made conditional upon the plaintiff undertaking to bear the costs the injunction imposed upon a port authority by restraining removal of a ship.[226] It is clear that these are but instances of a more general principle, and that plaintiffs may be required to compensate other third parties affected in similar ways.[227]

228   In another shipping case,[228] an injunction restraining the defendants from removing cargo from a ship owned by a third party was discharged on appeal, on the ground that the order would interfere with the owner and crew: "I regard it as absolutely intolerable that the fact that one person has a claim for a debt against another, that third parties should be inconvenienced in this way, not only to affect their freedom of trading but their freedom of action generally speaking."[229]

229   Banks are particularly and routinely affected by *Mareva* injunctions. The English Court of Appeal, in *Z Ltd. v. A-Z*[230] laid down a number of guidelines which may be summarized as follows. The bank is required to comply with the injunction upon notice, even if it has not yet been served on the defendant to make it binding on him.

---

[223] *Searose Ltd. v. Seatrain U.K. Ltd.*, [1981] 1 W.L.R. 894 (Q.B.); *Z Ltd. v. A-Z and AA-LL*, [1982] 2 W.L.R. 288 (C.A.).

[224] *Z Ltd.*, *supra*, footnote 223, at p. 297, *per* Lord Denning, M.R.

[225] *Z Ltd.*, *supra*, at p. 297; *Searose Ltd.*, *supra*, footnote 223.

[226] *Clipper Maritime Co. Ltd. of Monrovia v. Mineralimportexport*, [1981] 1 W.L.R 1262 (Q.B.).

[227] See *Project Development Co. Ltd. S.A. v. K.M.K. Securities Ltd.*, [1982] 1 W.L.R. 1470 (Q.B.), requiring the plaintiff to indemnify an intervener for the cost of moving to vacate an order to permit it to set off a claim against money held to the defendant's credit.

[228] *Galaxia Maritime S.A. v. Mineralimportexport*, [1982] 1 W.L.R. 539 (C.A.)

[229] *Ibid.*, at p. 542, *per* Eveleigh, L.J.

[230] *Supra*, footnote 223.

The bank incurs no liability to the defendant for dishonouring cheques in compliance with the injunction. However, the bank may honour letters of credit or bank guarantees or cheques, which it has guaranteed by cheque card to third parties, since it bears direct liability to such third parties. The bank may be required to search its record to determine accounts and amounts in those accounts standing to the defendant's credit. However, it will not be bound to break confidence by disclosure, but merely required to freeze the account. The plaintiff should provide the most specific information possible which should be incorporated in the order.[231] The plaintiff must also indemnify the bank for any expense it is put to. Where the defendant is allowed certain amounts for living or other legitimate expenses, the order should specify the amounts, and the bank is not to be put on inquiry into the purpose of withdrawals or payments made within those limits. Joint accounts are not caught by a general order, but may be bound by the injunction if the court so directs. Specific assets held as security or in safe keeping are not caught unless provision is made in the order. Finally, according to Eveleigh, L.J., the bank will not be held liable for contempt should it violate the injunction, unless there is a wilful breach of its terms.[232]

(h) Discovery

230   In some cases, the plaintiff may have grounds for believing that the defendant does have assets within the jurisdiction, but have insufficient particulars of the whereabouts of such assets to make the injunction effective. It has been held that, in such a case, the court may order discovery in aid of the injunction.[233] Such discovery cannot be justified under the rules of court, as the matter to be examined does not relate to the substantive issue between the parties, but the English Court of Appeal has held that there is an inherent power "to make all such ancillary orders as appear to the court to be just and

---

[231] Supreme Court Practice, 1982, 29/1/11E:

> . . . great care and precision are necessary in drawing the terms of such an injunction; so as to particularize the fund, the moneys, the account, the goods or the other assets affected thereby and so as to avoid placing innocent third parties, such as banks, at the risk of being in or committing a contempt of court if they should perhaps unwittingly commit a breach of the injunction. A *Mareva* injunction should by its terms be free from doubt and should be clear, precise and definite in its operation.

[232] *Infra*, §508.

[233] *A.J. Bekhor & Co. Ltd. v. Bilton*, [1981] Q.B. 923 (C.A.); *A v. C (No. 2) (Note)*, [1981] Q.B. 961; *Z Ltd. v. A-Z and AA-LL*, *supra*, footnote 223.

convenient, to ensure that the exercise of the *Mareva* jurisdiction is effective to achieve its purpose".[234] However, at the same time, the court recognized that it was:

> . . . as important that it should not exceed its powers to interfere in the lives of private citizens and to compel them to make public what they may wish to keep private, as that it should use them to the full to protect and enforce private and public rights and restrain their destruction or infringement. Injustice comes from abuse of power, judicial power included, as well as from failure to exercise it.[235]

231   It was held that, although the defendant had been evasive and had attempted to mislead the court, an order for discovery could not be made which was aimed at unravelling the defendant's past dealings in order to punish him, rather than to determine the present whereabouts of his property for the purpose of enforcing the injunction. An order for cross-examination on the defendant's affidavit was later made,[236] however, and in Canada, where leave is often not required, cross-examination may often be the most practicable procedural device. The possibility of making a discovery order will be important in cases where the defendant has not yet filed an affidavit, and where the plaintiff can show the need to obtain details as to a fund, account, or other property upon which the injunction is to operate so as to make it effective.[237]

(i) Jurisdiction

232   Many *Mareva* cases pose jurisdictional problems. It is no bar to injunctive relief that the defendant is physically outside the territory of the court's jurisdiction.[238] An order restraining acts within the jurisdiction can be made. However, it has been held by the House of Lords in the *Siskina* case,[239] that to obtain a *Mareva* injunction

---

[234] *A.J. Bekhor, supra*, footnote 233, at p. 940, *per* Ackner, L.J.

[235] *A.J. Bekhor, supra*, at p. 951. Lord Denning, however, apparently takes a different view: see *Z Ltd., supra*, footnote 223, at p. 299. *Cf. RHM Foods Ltd. v. Bovril Ltd.*, [1982] 1 All E.R. 673 (C.A.), holding that discovery prior to pleading can only be awarded in aid of an interlocutory injunction in exceptional cases.

[236] *A.J. Bekhor, supra*, at p. 955.

[237] See also Black, "The Sheriff to the Aid of *Mareva*, or Vice Versa", 131 New L.J. 770 (1981), at p. 771, discussing an unreported English case where the court made an order requiring the defendant to " 'permit the sheriff . . . his officers, servants or agents to enter upon the land and buildings (named) forthwith for the purpose only of taking an inventory of all chattels personal' ".

[238] *Supra*, §120.

[239] *Siskina v. Distos Compania Naviera S.A.*, [1979] A.C. 210 (H.L.); see also §126, *supra*.

against a foreign defendant, the plaintiff must have a substantive course of action justiciable in the English courts. The mere presence of assets is not, by itself, sufficient to support jurisdiction. There is nothing in English or Canadian law similar to the American *quasi-in rem* jurisdiction.[240] Thus, where the defendant is outside the jurisdiction, the plaintiff must be able to satisfy the forum's service *ex juris* requirements. Both in England and in Canada, service *ex juris* rules permit service where an injunction is claimed without any specification as to the nature of the substantive cause.[241] However, the House of Lords held, in the *Siskina* case, that a *Mareva* injunction is necessarily ancillary to a substantive cause. The plaintiff does not claim a final injunction, but merely seeks interlocutory relief to protect his ultimate right to execute on a money judgment, and the House of Lords held that a plaintiff cannot obtain jurisdiction over a foreigner merely by pointing to assets within the jurisdiction against which he hopes to be able to execute.

5. Anton Piller Injunctions

(1) Introduction

233   In *Anton Piller KG v. Manufacturing Processes Ltd.*[242] the English Court of Appeal upheld the propriety of a practice then current[243] in industrial property cases of awarding a novel and innovative form of *ex parte* injunction. These orders give the plaintiff access to the defendant's premises to inspect documents and remove items belonging to the plaintiff. They are made where the plaintiff has demonstrated a strong case, and where it is clear that the defendants are rogues who would flout the ordinary process of the court and effectively deprive the plaintiff of his remedy. Injunctions of this type have been given the name of the *Anton Piller* case, and are frequently granted in England.[244] These orders have been made in Canada[245] and as with

---

[240] See Sharpe, *Interprovincial Product Liability Litigation* (Toronto, Butterworths, 1982), pp. 28-30, for discussion of this in the Canadian context.

[241] *Supra*, §120.

[242] [1976] Ch. 55 (C.A.).

[243] The only earlier reported case was *E.M.I. Ltd. v. Pandit*, [1975] 1 W.L.R. 302 (Ch.).

[244] See cases cited, *infra*, §§234-248. See also Dockray, "Liberty to Rummage — a Search Warrant in Civil Proceedings", [1977] P.L. 369; Bridge, "Inspection of Premises and Preservation of Evidence in Copyright Cases: A Procedural Innovation in the English Courts", 16 Law Teacher 166 (1982).

[245] Hayhurst, "The Anton Piller Order", 6 Can. Bus. L.J. 2 (1981), referring to unre-

the *Mareva* line of authority, the Canadian courts appear ready to follow suit, and to award this exceptional and extraordinary form of relief in appropriate cases.

234   Most of the English cases have involved the problems posed by patent and copyright "pirates".[246] Sophisticated and relatively cheap modern recording and copying equipment has facilitated illegal reproduction and yielded large profits. While plaintiffs can discover and enjoin particular retailers, this often proves ineffectual. Illicit materials are simply transferred to other outlets, and the source remains unknown. The beneficial aspects of *Anton Piller* orders in such circumstances are clear, and this judicial innovation has often provided a remedy where other less drastic measures would surely have been ineffectual.[247]

235   In the *Anton Piller* case itself,[248] the problem was one of confidential design information, defection and industrial espionage. The plaintiff was able to show that the defendant was involved in a scheme to obtain confidential drawings and designs and that unless immediate relief was given without prior notice to the defendants, there was a substantial risk that the drawings and information would be sent to Germany and used by a rival manufacturer. The plaintiffs applied for and obtained an *ex parte* injunction restraining the infringement of copyright and breach of confidence, and ordering the defendants to "permit one or two of the plaintiffs and one or two of their solicitors to enter the defendants' premises for the purpose of inspecting documents, files or things, and removing those which belonged to the plaintiffs."[249] The Court of Appeal recognized the drastic nature of the relief afforded by this order. Shaw, L.J., said that the jurisdiction "is to be resorted to only in circumstances where the normal processes of the law would be rendered nugatory if some immediate and effective measure was not available."[250] Ormrod, L.J.,

---

ported Canadian cases; *Bardeau Ltd. et al. v. Crown Food Services Equipment Ltd.* (1982), 38 O.R. (2d) 411 (H.C.J.). Orders are made in other Commonwealth jurisdictions as well: see Cato, "Anton Piller Orders", [1980] N.Z.L.J. 357.

[246] Orders have also been made against "bootleggers": see *Ex p. Island Records Ltd.*, [1978] Ch. 122 (C.A.), discussed, *infra*, §§314-317.

[247] See, *e.g. Ex p. Island Records Ltd.*, *supra*, footnote 246, at p. 133, *per* Lord Denning, M.R., describing the problem and extolling the utility of the injunction:

The effect of these ex parte orders has been dramatic. When served with them, the shopkeepers have acknowledged their wrongdoing and thrown their hand in. So useful are these orders that they are in daily use — not only in cases of infringement of copyright, but also in passing-off cases, and other cases.

[248] *Supra*, footnote 242.

[249] *Ibid.*, at p. 61.

[250] *Ibid.*, at p. 62.

set out three essential preconditions which have subsequently been adopted by other courts:

> First, there must be an extremely strong prima facie case. Secondly, the damage, potential or actual, must be very serious for the applicant. Thirdly, there must be clear evidence that the defendants have in their possession incriminating documents or things, and that there is a real possibility that they may destroy such material before any application inter partes can be made.[251]

236 The element of surprise is essential in these cases, and like the *Mareva* orders, they must necessarily be made *ex parte*. The fact that the defendant will be subjected to a significant interference without having been heard means that the court must be very cautious, and that a heavy onus rests upon counsel applying for such orders to be fully candid.

(2) Disclosure and privilege

237 Subsequent cases have refined the scope of *Anton Piller* orders. In a Court of Appeal decision involving pirated pop music, a term in the order requiring the defendant to disclose the name of his suppliers was described as a "legitimate extension".[252] The obligation to provide like information was imposed in another case upon the owner of a fishing vessel which allegedly had been involved in an illicit fishing expedition,[253] and in another, a bank which had unwittingly been used as an instrument for fraud was required to disclose confidential information which might assist the plaintiff in tracing its funds.[254]

238 This branch of the *Anton Piller* order, however, was curtailed in England by the decision of the House of Lords in *Rank Film Distributors Ltd. v. Video Information Centre*,[255] holding that where there arises a serious possibility of criminal proceedings, the defendant is justified in invoking the common law privilege against self-incrimination and refusing to provide details as to his sources of supply and distribution chain. In many cases, as in the *Rank* case itself, there will be a distinct possibility of criminal conspiracy charges.[256]

---

[251] *Ibid.*, at p. 62.

[252] *E.M.I. v. Sarwar and Haidar*, [1977] 3 F.S.R. 146 (C.A.).

[253] *Loose v. Williamson*, [1978] 1 W.L.R. 639 (Ch.).

[254] *Bankers Trust Co. v. Shapira*, [1980] 1 W.L.R. 1274 (C.A.).

[255] [1982] A.C. 380 (H.L.).

[256] In *Rank*, it was said that the threat of a prosecution under the Copyright Act itself would not be sufficient since there was virtual identity between the "petty" offence and the civil action: at p. 441 *per* Lord Wilberforce. *Cf. Ocli Optical Coatings Ltd. v. Spectron Optical Coatings Ltd.*, [1980] F.S.R. 227 (C.A.); and *Snugkcoat Ltd. v.*

239   In England, Parliament has reversed the *Rank* case by legislation[257] which removes the privilege in the case of orders made in intellectual property and passing-off cases, but provides that any statement or admission made is not admissible in criminal proceedings for a related offence.

240   In Canada, the position is unclear. Both federal and provincial legislation abolish the common law privilege and replace it with an obligation to answer coupled with the limited protection against the use of such information in subsequent proceedings.[258] If this legislation applies, the position in Canada would be as it now is in England by virtue of the English legislation. However, it could be argued that since these provisions apply only to a "witness", they do not govern and that the common law privilege is left intact. On the other hand, the obligation to disclose in an *Anton Piller* case is sometimes fulfilled by swearing an affidavit in the action, and it may perhaps be viewed as an aspect of the discovery process. Canadian courts have applied the statutory curtailment of the common law privilege to discovery as well as to the obligation to produce documents.[259] However, viewing a defendant responding to the requirements of an *Anton Piller* order as a "witness" may perhaps strain the meaning of that word.[260] Another point is that the Evidence Acts require that the

---

Chaudhry, [1980] F.S.R. 286, where the appeal court refused to uphold the privilege on the grounds that the risk of prosecution was insignificant. Possible offences in this area in Canada are discussed by Hayhurst, *supra*, footnote 245.

[257] Supreme Court Act, 1981, s. 72.

[258] Canada Evidence Act, R.S.C. 1970, c. E-10, s. 5, is a typical provision. The protection against subsequent use is also found in the Charter of Rights and Freedoms, s. 13.

[259] *Chambers v. Jaffray* (1906), 12 O.L.R. 377 (Div. Ct.); *Klein v. Bell*, [1955] S.C.R. 309, [1955] 2 D.L.R. 513 (where the B.C. Act was held *ultra vires* because it was too broadly worded. *Cf. Bell v. Montreal Trust Co.* (1956), 4 D.L.R. (2d) 475 (B.C.S.C.), affd 6 D.L.R. (2d) 589 (C.A.), upholding the redrafted version and applying it to the same action).

[260] It might be argued that the result in the cases referred to, *supra*, footnote 259, turns on the fact that it was expressly provided in provincial rules of court that a party being examined for discovery is to be treated in the same manner as a "witness" at trial: *Cf. Campbell v. Aird*, [1941] 2 D.L.R. 807 (Alta. S.C.T.D.), reviewing the previous Alberta cases, and see cases collected by Sopinka and Lederman, *The Law of Evidence in Civil Cases* (Toronto, Butterworths, 1974), pp. 226-7. However, it is submitted that in light of *Klein v. Bell, supra*, footnote 259, although interpreting the statute to provide no protection rather than abolish the privilege, this is unduly restrictive: at p. 317 S.C.R., p. 520 D.L.R., *per* Rand, J.: "A witness, in a broad sense, is one who, in the course of juridical processes, attests to matters of fact; and in the multiplying procedures directed to the elicitation of such matters, the object of the statute, dealing as it does with a basic right, would be defeated by limiting its protection to part only of coerced disclosure."

witness request the protection of the Act. It is not at all clear how this could be done in the case of an *Anton Piller* order although it may not now be required in light of s. 13 of the Charter of Rights and Freedoms. In the end, it seems unlikely that the legislation would apply and this would mean that the common law position expressed in the *Rank* case would govern.[261]

241   If it is applicable, the actual impact of the *Rank* decision is unclear. While the House of Lords rejected the argument that the obligation to disclose information should be put in the order, leaving it to the defendant to object, it was expressly noted that "in due course, no doubt, forms of order will be worked out which will enable the orders to be as effective as practicable while preserving the defendant's essential rights."[262] English judges have responded and devised techniques to avoid the full impact of the *Rank* decision. In one case, a term was inserted in the order requiring the plaintiff's solicitor to advise the defendant of his rights.[263] Another practice, more doubtful in light of what was said in *Rank*,[264] is to grant an order requiring disclosure upon the plaintiff undertaking not to use such information in criminal proceedings.[265]

242   In Canada, even if the more limited statutory exception applies, now altered by the Charter to remove the need for the defendant to ask for the protection of the statute,[266] serious problems remain. Whether or not the statute does apply, the defendant may have to make an immediate decision whether or not he should comply with the order. At the very least, it is submitted that a provision should be inserted notifying him of his rights and requiring the plaintiff's repre-

---

[261] Hayhurst, *supra*, footnote 245, suggests that *Anton Piller* orders are not covered by the Evidence Acts.

[262] *Supra*, footnote 255, at p. 443, *per* Lord Wilberforce. Compare the Court of Appeal decision in *Rank*, *loc. cit.* p. 416, *per* Bridge, L.J.,

   . . . that the only satisfactory practice will be, when the court invited to make an *Anton Piller* order can see from the strength of the applicant's evidence that the proposed defendant is in danger of self-incrimination, to abstain from making any order ex parte requiring immediate answers to questions or disclosure of documents. The practical consequence of this view may well be that whenever the evidence in a copyright case is strong enough to justify the making of an *Anton Piller* order it will also give rise to apprehension of self-incrimination on the part of the defendant so that the ex parte order will effectively have to be limited to authorising the search for and seizure of infringing copies.

[263] See Staines, Notes of Cases, 41 Mod. L.R. 580 (1981), at p. 584, referring to an unreported case.

[264] See, e.g., at pp. 442-3, *per* Lord Wilberforce.

[265] *Sony Corp. v. Anand*, [1981] 7 F.S.R. 398 (H.C.J.).

[266] *Cf. Tass v. The King*, [1947] S.C.R. 103 at p. 105, [1947] 1 D.L.R. 497 at p. 499.

sentatives to draw this to the defendant's attention when executing the order.[267]

(3) Scope

243   A dubious extension of the *Anton Piller* practice was made in *Yousif v. Salama*.[268] The plaintiff's claim was for a commission arising out of a trading partnership, and the defendants had indicated their intention to defend strenuously. The plaintiff feared that one defendant might destroy certain important records, especially that defendant's desk diary which, the plaintiff asserted, constituted evidence of his claim. By a majority, the Court of Appeal upheld an *ex parte* injunction giving the plaintiff access to the documents in question, to be copied and returned to the defendant. Lord Denning, M.R., observed that "instead of having to speculate or try to get evidence from elsewhere, it should all be available in the files. It can do no harm to the defendant at all. If he is honest, he will produce the documents in any case. If he is dishonest, that is all the more reason why the order should be made."[269]

244   Donaldson, L.J., dissenting, described the evidence of any intent to destroy the documents as "flimsy in the extreme" and added "I have considered, of course, whether, as was suggested in argument, it can rightly be said that no harm is done to an honest man by asking discovery from him when eventually he would have to be ordered to give it. I think that great harm is done. The people of this country are entitled not to have their privacy and their property invaded by a court order except in very exceptional circumstances."[270] It is one thing to justify a significant invasion of the defendant's privacy where there is strong evidence of an intent to flout the ordinary process and effectively deprive the plaintiff of his rights, but quite another to grant such drastic relief where there is no more than a possibility that the defendant might destroy evidence which might assist the plaintiff in making out his case.

245   A plaintiff who has been wronged is entitled to a remedy, but not at all costs. Other competing values come into play. Even a wrongdoer is entitled to certain basic protections, and it is difficult to justify

---

[267] Such a term was said to be required in *Bardeau Ltd. v. Crown Food Services Equipment Ltd.* (1982), 36 O.R. (2d) 355 (H.C.J.). For consideration of the sort of provision which might be included, see Hayhurst, *supra*, footnote 245.

[268] [1980] 1 W.L.R. 1540 (C.A.).

[269] *Ibid.*, at p. 1542.

[270] *Ibid.*, at p. 1544.

giving the plaintiff liberty to rummage[271] into the defendant's private affairs unless there is compelling evidence that the defendant is bent on flouting the process of the court by refusing to abide by the ordinary procedure of discovery. In one case,[272] Lawton, L.J., expressed concern that *Anton Piller* orders were being used as a means to convert the adversarial process into an inquisitorial one:

> It has to be remembered by all concerned that we do not have in this country an inquisitorial procedure for civil litigation. Our procedure is accusatorial. Those who make charges must state right at the beginning what they are and what facts they are based upon. They must not use *Anton Piller* orders as a means of finding out what sort of charges they can make.[273]

246   *Anton Piller* orders have been judicially described as "draconian" on several occasions[274] and they are obviously drastic measures. Civil procedure rules provide for discovery of documents, inspection and preservation of property, as well as oral discovery. *Anton Piller* orders go far beyond the usual discovery process. Inevitably, in some cases the plaintiff will see much that is confidential and privileged. In one case, an *ex parte* order was granted but then set aside where the plaintiff, who was in competition with the defendant, might have gained commercial advantage from having access to its rival's records.[275] As the judge observed, "it is impossible to limit the ambit of any inspection so as to prevent, however innocently, the inspector from getting an inside view of somebody else's business and works."[276]

247   More significant is the fact that the order virtually amounts to a search warrant. Lord Denning has been at pains to point out the distinction between *Anton Piller* orders and search warrants, and in the *Anton Piller* case itself, he explained the difference:

> [T]he order sought in this case is not a search warrant. It does not authorise the plaintiffs' solicitors or anyone else to enter the defendants' premises against their will. It does not authorise the breaking down of any doors, nor the slipping in by a back door, nor getting in by an open door or window. It only authorises entry and inspection by the permission of the defendants. The plaintiffs must get the defendants' permis-

---

[271] For discussion on this point, see Dockray, *supra*, footnote 244.

[272] *Hytrac Conveyors Ltd. v. Conveyors Int'l*, [1983] 1 W.L.R. 44 (C.A.).

[273] *Ibid.*, at p. 47.

[274] See, *e.g.*, *Thermax Ltd. v. Schott Industrial Glass Ltd.*, [1981] F.S.R. 289 (H.C.J.), at p. 291, *per* Browne-Wilkinson, J.: *E.M.I. Ltd. v. Pandit*, [1975] 1 W.L.R. 302 (Ch.), at p. 304, *per* Templeman, J.; *Yousif v. Salama*, [1980] 1 W.L.R. 1540 (C.A.), at p. 1544, *per* Donaldson, L.J.

[275] *Thermax Ltd. v. Schott Industrial Glass Ltd.*, *supra*, footnote 274.

[276] *Ibid.*, at p. 298, *per* Browne-Wilkinson, J.

sion. But it does do this: It brings pressure on the defendants to give permission. It does more. It actually orders them to give permission — with, I suppose, the result that if they do not give permission, they are guilty of contempt of court.[277]

The distinction between an order conferring coercive powers and one requiring permission to be given on pain of contempt is subtle to say the least,[278] especially in light of the fact, as Lord Denning himself pointed out, that the defendant refuses permission at his peril:

> It puts them in peril not only of proceedings for contempt, but also of adverse inferences being drawn against them; so much so that their own solicitor may often advise them to comply.[279]

(4) Conclusion

248   Thus, the pressure such an order puts upon the defendant cannot be minimized. It is respectfully submitted that repeated references in English cases to the argument that the innocent defendant has nothing to fear, and that the guilty defendant should be subjected to such invasions[280] represent an unfortunate departure from the usual respect afforded procedural safeguards. Such arguments could justify the invasion of many fundamental rights. A broad power to grant injunctions is not a mandate to the judiciary to right all wrongs at the expense of other basic values,[281] and it is respectfully submitted that excessive zeal in this area is apt to attract criticism which will impair the ability of the courts to use injunctions in innovative ways in other areas.[282]

---

[277] *Supra*, footnote 242, at p. 60.

[278] The English practice is to insert a provision giving the defendant leave to move to set aside the order. This does not, however, excuse non-compliance in the meanwhile. In *Hallmark Cards Inc. v. Image Arts Ltd.* (1976), 73 Law Soc. Gaz. 596 (C.A.), the defendant refused the plaintiff access and moved to set aside the order. Buckley, L.J., observed that the defendants were entitled to apply to have the order discharged, but that until the affidavits had been filed so that the matter could be heard, the proper course was to leave the injunction in place. If the defendants were successful, although they had violated the order while it stood, "one could not conceive that they would be liable to any penalties while it stood."

[279] *Anton Piller, supra*, footnote 242, at p. 61.

[280] *Supra*, §243; *E.M.I. Ltd. v. Sarwar and Haidar*, [1977] 3 F.S.R. 146 (C.A.), at p. 147, *per* Lord Denning, M.R.; *Loose v. Williamson*, [1978] 1 W.L.R. 639 at p. 641, *per* Goulding, J.

[281] *Cf. Entick v. Carrington* (1756), 19 St. Tr. 1030 at p. 1067, *per* Camden, C.J. (quoted in Dockray, *supra*, footnote 244, at p. 388): "What would the parliament say, if the judges should take upon themselves to mould an unlawful power into a convenient authority, by new restrictions? That would be, not judgment, but legislation."

[282] *Cf. Rank Film Distributors Ltd. v. Video Information Centre, supra*, footnote 255, at p. 439, *per* Lord Wilberforce, stating that these orders were "an illustration of the adaptability of equitable remedies to new situations."

CHAPTER 3

INJUNCTIONS TO ENFORCE PUBLIC RIGHTS

1. Introduction

249   Injunctions are primarily private law remedies, but also play an important role in public law. While a general account of administrative law remedies is beyond the scope of this book, an analysis of the role played by injunctions in public and administrative law is called for.

250   American experience with the injunction as a means of judicial implementation of broadly worded constitutional guarantees provides a dramatic contrast to the more conservative Anglo-Canadian practice. The "structural" civil rights injunction has been a potent remedial vehicle whereby it is declared "that henceforth the court will *direct* or *manage* the reconstruction of the social institution, in order to bring it into conformity with the constitution".[1] The civil rights injunction amounts, in effect, to a detailed legislative enactment.[2] English and Canadian judges have deliberately avoided such an active role. Lord Diplock has recently spoken of the need to remember "the difference between private law and public law"[3] when injunctions are applied for, and the sentiment expressed by an Ontario judge in 1924 reflects accurately the traditional Anglo-Canadian judicial attitude: "Government by injunction is a thing abhorrent to the law of England and of this Province."[4]

251   The enactment of the Charter of Rights and Freedoms, however, calls for a more adventurous response. The Charter expressly provides in s. 24 that "anyone whose rights or freedoms, as guaranteed by this Charter, have been infringed or denied may apply to a court of competent jurisdiction to obtain such remedy as the court considers appropriate and just in the circumstances." It can hardly be doubted that often, injunctions will be "appropriate and just in the circumstances". While one might expect Canadian judges to be less adventurous than their American brethren, there can be little doubt that injunctions, both in negative and mandatory form, will play an important role in the implementation of the rights guaranteed by the Charter.

252   Although Canadian and English courts have been cautious in their use of injunctions in the public law area, as will be seen from what follows, injunctions have often been employed in the enforcement of public rights, and a leading English text suggests that "its capacity for growth has not been fully exploited."[5]

---

[1] Fiss, *The Civil Rights Injunction* (Bloomington, Indiana University Press, 1978), p. 37.

[2] For examples of the detailed, statute-like injunctions issued in such cases, see Fiss, *Injunctions* (Mineola, N.Y., Foundation Press, 1972).

[3] *Gouriet v. Union of Post Office Workers*, [1978] A.C. 435 (H.L.), at p. 496.

[4] *Robinson v. Adams*, [1925] 1 D.L.R. 359 at p. 365, 56 O.L.R. 217 at p. 224 (S.C. App. Div.), *per* Middleton, J.A. The phrase "government by injunction" was a campaign slogan in the 1896 American presidential election, raised in protest against the use of an injunction to crush a railway strike and the American Railway Union: Fiss, *supra*, footnote 1, at p. 23.

[5] de Smith, *Judicial Review of Administrative Action*, 4th ed. by Evans (London, Stevens & Sons Ltd., 1980), p. 474. For general accounts of injunctions as administrative law remedies see de Smith, *supra*, pp. 429-74 and Wade, *Administrative Law*, 5th ed. (Oxford, Clarendon Press, 1982), pp. 515-22.

2. Injunctions at the Suit of the Attorney-General

253   There is a well-established jurisdiction to award injunctions at the suit of the Attorney-General to enjoin public wrongs.[6] The Attorney-General is said to invoke the *parens patriae* jurisdiction when suing in the public interest.[7] There is a substantial body of law involving injunctions to restrain corporations and statutory or public bodies from exceeding their powers.[8] The jurisdiction was especially appropriate with respect to corporations or bodies exercising public functions, but was not limited to these.[9] Modern examples are much less frequent, perhaps because other instruments of regulatory control are more prevalent, but there is no doubt that the power to issue such injunctions remains.

254   Another important aspect of the *parens patriae* jurisdiction relates to charities, and injunctions at the suit of the Attorney-General to control management of charities to protect funds is well recognized.[10]

255   Often, the Attorney-General acts completely on his own initiative and commences proceedings himself. A private litigant can also initiate proceedings, taken in the name of the Attorney-General "on the

---

[6] See de Smith, *supra*, footnote 5, p. 432 *et seq.*; Edwards, *The Law Officers of the Crown* (1964), Chapter 14. A provincial Attorney-General is a proper party to sue in the public interest, even where the wrong involves a violation of federal law: *A.-G. v. Niagara Falls International Bridge Co.* (1873), 20 Gr. 34; *People's Holding Co. v. A.-G. Que.*, [1931] S.C.R. 452, [1931] 4 D.L.R. 317.

[7] The chapter of Professor Edwards' book, *supra*, footnote 6, is entitled "The Guardian of the Public Interest".

[8] *A.-G. v. Manchester Corp.*, [1906] 1 Ch. 643; *A.-G. v. Mersey Ry. Co.*, [1907] A.C. 415 (H.L.); *A.-G. v. De Winton*, [1906] 2 Ch. 106; *A.-G. v. West Gloucestershire Water Co.*, [1909] 2 Ch. 338 (C.A.); *A.-G. v. Oxford, Worcester & Wolverhampton Ry. Co.* (1854), 2 W.R. 330 (Ch.); *London County Council v. A.-G.*, [1902] A.C. 165 (H.L.); *A.-G. v. Fulham Corp.*, [1921] 1 Ch. 440; *A.-G. v. Niagara Falls International Bridge Co.*, *supra*, footnote 6.

[9] *Prestney v. Colchester Corp.* (1882), 21 Ch. D. 111; *Clinch v. Financial Corp.* (1868), 4 Ch. App. 117. Where an individual sued, however, special damage had to be shown: *Ware v. Regent's Canal Co.* (1858), 3 De G. & J. 212, 44 E.R. 1250 (Ch.); *London Ass'n of Shipowners and Brokers v. London and India Docks Joint Committee*, [1892] 3 Ch. 242 (C.A.); *Marriott v. East Grinstead Gas & Water Co.*, [1909] 1 Ch. 70.

[10] *Re Belling*, [1967] Ch. 425; *Hauxwell v. Barton-upon-Humber Urban District Council*, [1974] Ch. 432. In *A.-G. v. Compton* (1842), 1 Y. & C.C.C. 417 at p. 427, 62 E.R. 951, Knight Bruce, V.-C., said that where

. . . property affected by a trust for public purposes is in the hands of those who hold it devoted to that trust, it is the privilege of the public that the Crown should be entitled to intervene by its officer for the purpose of asserting, on behalf of the public generally, that public interest and that public right which probably no individual could be found willing effectually to assert, even if the interest were such as to allow it.

relation of " the private party, if the Attorney-General consents to such action being brought. Many of the cases to be examined here are relator actions.[11]

256   In relator proceedings, the private party has carriage of the action, and is responsible for the costs.[12] However, the Attorney-General has the right to supervise the conduct of the action. The Attorney-General is entitled to review and approve the pleadings, and to be consulted on other pre-trial proceedings, including discovery. He has the right to stay the action, or take it over himself if he deems it appropriate. The courts have refused to review the Attorney-General's decision to grant or withhold his consent to relator proceedings.[13] So long as the Attorney-General is properly named, the decision to grant or withhold injunctive relief appears unaffected by whether the action was brought on the Attorney-General's own initiative, or as a relator action. The problem of standing, posed where an individual sues in respect of a public wrong without the fiat of the Attorney-General, is discussed under a separate heading below.[14]

(1) Public nuisance

257   The role of the Attorney-General in suing in the public interest to enjoin public nuisances is of great antiquity[15] and continues to have importance. Definition of what constitutes a public nuisance is a difficult aspect of substantive law.[16] Lord Denning's explanation has been quoted with approval by Canadian courts:

> The classic statement of the difference [between public and private nuisance] is that a public nuisance affects Her Majesty's subjects generally, whereas a private nuisance only affects particular individuals. But this does not help much . . . I prefer to look to the reason of the thing and to say that a public nuisance is a nuisance which is so widespread in its range or so indiscriminate in its effect that it would not be reasonable to expect one person to take proceedings on his own re-

---

[11] Relator actions are discussed in de Smith, *supra*, footnote 5, at pp. 449-50; Edwards, *supra*, footnote 6, at p. 286 *et seq.*

[12] *A.-G. v. Vivian* (1826), 1 Russ. 226, 38 E.R. 88.

[13] *Infra*, §328.

[14] *Infra*, §290 *et seq.*

[15] Edwards, *supra*, footnote 6.

[16] Fleming, *The Law of Torts*, 5th ed. (Sydney, Law Book Co. Ltd., 1977), p. 393: "Far from susceptible of exact definition, it has become a catch-all for a multitude of ill-assorted sins, linking offensive smells, crowing roosters, obstructions of rights of way, defective cellar-flaps, street queues, lotteries, houses of ill-fame and a host of other rag-ends of the law."

sponsibility to put a stop to it, but that it should be taken on the responsibility of the community at large.[17]

258 The term has been used to describe a wide variety of public wrongs, ranging from interference with uses of land similar to private nuisance but affecting many people, to cases involving a more general interference with public convenience, health or safety, including interference with rights of way on highways[18] and rights of navigation on public waterways,[19] and many other public annoyances.[20]

259 The use of the remedy of injunction with respect to private nuisances is examined in detail in Chapter 4. There, it is seen that although the injunction is the primary remedy, difficult issues of remedial choice do arise, and damages rather than an injunction are sometimes appropriate. In the case of public nuisance, there is much less scope for choice of remedy.[21] If the Attorney-General establishes that a public nuisance exists, it is difficult to imagine a court awarding damages rather than an injunction.[22] In some cases, however, the courts may refuse a remedy altogether, and the extent of the court's discretion where the Attorney-General sues is considered below under a separate heading.[23]

260 In some circumstances, an individual occupier specially affected may sue with respect to a public nuisance.[24] There, damages in place of an injunction may be awarded, but as seen from the discussion on standing,[25] there will be relatively few cases where a private plaintiff is able to sue in respect of a public nuisance if it does not also constitute a private nuisance. Where an individual does sue in respect of a public nuisance, it would seem that the remedial principles discussed

---

[17] *A.-G. ex rel. Glamorgan County Council and Pontardawe Rural District Council v. P.Y.A. Quarries Ltd.*, [1957] 1 All E.R. 894 (C.A.), at p. 908; *A.-G. B.C. ex rel. Eaton v. Haney Speedways Ltd.* (1963), 39 D.L.R. (2d) 48 (B.C.S.C.); *A.-G. Ont. v. Orange Productions Ltd.* (1971), 21 D.L.R. (3d) 257, [1971] 3 O.R. 585 (H.C.J.).

[18] See, *e.g.*, *Newell v. Smith* (1971), 20 D.L.R. (3d) 598 (N.S.S.C.T.D.).

[19] See, *e.g.*, *A.-G. Can. v. Brister*, [1943] 3 D.L.R. 50 (N.S.S.C.).

[20] See, *e.g.*, *A.-G. Ont. v. Orange Productions Ltd.*, *supra*, footnote 17.

[21] At common law, public nuisance could be prosecuted as a misdemeanour: Smith and Hogan, *Criminal Law*, 4th ed. (London, Butterworths, 1978), p. 764. For an example of a prosecution in Canada, see *The Queen v. Lord* (1864), 1 P.E.I.R. 245 (S.C.). Some public nuisances may still be prosecuted: Criminal Code, s. 176.

[22] *A.-G. v. Wimbledon House Estate Co. Ltd.*, [1904] 2 Ch. 34 at p. 44, *per* Farwell, J.

[23] *Infra*, §§261-265.

[24] *Infra*, §308 *et seq*.

[25] *Ibid*.

in Chapter 4 with respect to the choice between damages and an injunction will apply.[26]

(2) Discretion

261   It has often been said that the Attorney-General is not entitled to an injunction as of right,[27] and there are several cases in which the Attorney-General has been refused injunctive relief on discretionary grounds.[28] However, the nature of the discretion to be exercised in such cases appears to differ from that applied in cases between private litigants simply because the court is required to weigh the public interest.

262   The court will rarely conclude that the public interest in having the law obeyed is outweighed by the hardship an injunction would impose upon the defendant.[29] It seems clear that where the Attorney-General sues to restrain breach of a statutory provision, and where he is able to establish a substantive case, the courts will be very reluctant to refuse him on discretionary grounds.[30] In one case, it was held that "the general rule no longer operates; the dispute is no longer one between individuals, it is one between the public and a small section of the public refusing to abide by the law of the land."[31] In another case,[32] Devlin, J., held that although the court retains a discretion, once the Attorney-General has determined that injunctive relief is the most appropriate mode of enforcing the law, "this court, once a clear breach of the right has been shown, should only refuse the application in exceptional circumstances."[33]

---

[26] *Infra*, §372 *et seq.*

[27] *A.-G. v. Birmingham, Tame, and Rea District Drainage Board*, [1910] 1 Ch. 48 (C.A.), at p. 61, affd [1912] A.C. 788 (H.L.), *per* Farwell, L.J.: "It is for the Attorney-General to determine whether he should commence litigation, but it is for the Court to determine what the result of that litigation shall be". See also *Associated Minerals Consolidated Ltd. v. Wyong Shire Council*, [1975] A.C. 538 (P.C.), at p. 559, *per* Lord Wilberforce: "even in cases where relief is being sought by the Attorney-General in the public interest . . . the granting of an injunction is discretionary", and *A.-G. v. Wellington Colliery Co.* (1903), 10 B.C.R. 397 (S.C.). The refusal of the courts to review the Attorney-General's discretion to consent to relator proceedings is discussed, *infra*, §328.

[28] *A.-G. v. Sheffield Gas Consumers Co.* (1853), 3 De G.M. & G. 304, 43 E.R. 119; *A.-G. v. Cambridge Consumers Gas Co.* (1868), L.R. 4 Ch. App. 71; *A.-G. v. Kerr and Ball* (1914), 79 J.P. 51 (K.B.); *A.-G. v. Mayor, Aldermen & Corp. of Kingston-on-Thames* (1865), 13 W.R. 888; *A.-G. v. Grand Junction Canal Co.*, [1909] 2 Ch. 505.

[29] *A.-G. v. Colney Hatch Lunatic Asylum* (1868), L.R. 4 Ch. App. 146.

[30] *A.-G. v. Premier Line Ltd.*, [1932] 1 Ch. 303.

[31] *Ibid.*, at p. 313, *per* Eve, J.

[32] *A.-G. v. Bastow*, [1957] 1 Q.B. 514.

[33] *Ibid.*, at p. 523. Edwards, *supra*, footnote 6, at p. 293, suggests that any of the fol-

263   It has also been held that where the Attorney-General sues to restrain a breach of the law, actual damage need not be shown, on the
theory that Parliament is taken to have declared the harm injurious,
and the public is injured automatically by any breach of the law.[34] Injunctions have not infrequently been granted to restrain activity
which, although it appeared to have been generally beneficial to the
community, was strictly illegal.[35]

264   Delay by the Attorney-General in commencing suit would appear
to be a relevant factor if it prejudices the position of the defendant.[36]
However, its effect must be considered in light of the fact that the
Attorney-General asserts the public interest. This was recently explained by Lord Wilberforce as follows:

---

lowing "exceptional circumstances" would justify the court in refusing an injunction:
    . . . first, where bad faith on the part of the relator was disclosed; secondly,
    where it was shown that an injunction was likely to prove ineffective or would
    cause injustice; or, finally, where evidence was adduced at the hearing which was
    not within the knowledge or contemplation of the Attorney-General when grant-
    ing his fiat and which might place a different complexion on the whole situation.

[34] *A.-G. v. ex rel. Warwickshire County Council v. London & North Western Ry. Co.*,
[1900] 1 Q.B. 78 (C.A.); *A.-G. v. Shrewsbury (Kingsland) Bridge Co.* (1882), 21
Ch. D. 752; *A.-G. v. Cockermouth Local Board* (1874), L.R. 18 Eq. 172. See also
Manitoba Dental Ass'n v. Byman and Halstead (1962), 34 D.L.R. (2d) 602 (Man.
C.A.).

[35] See, *e.g.*, *A.-G. v. Fulham Corp.*, [1921] 1 Ch. 440; *A.-G. v. Harris*, [1961] 1 Q.B.
74 (C.A.). Cf. *A.-G. v. Sheffield Gas Consumers Co.* (1853), 3 De G.M. & G. 304
at pp. 311-12, 43 E.R. 119, *per* Knight Bruce, L.J. (applied in *A.-G. v. Cambridge
Consumers Gas Co.*, *supra*, footnote 28):
    Where, however, the public interest purports to be asserted, it is not wholly im-
    material, at least upon an interlocutory application, to look into the motives from
    which, or under which, the matter is brought forward. Now, in the present case,
    though the Attorney-General's name is used, it is impossible not to see that the
    suit has been instituted more from regard to private than to public good. If the
    public interest clearly required the immediate interposition of the Court, that
    might not be material. But we find, as a fact, that the majority of the Town
    Council is in favour of what the Defendants are proposing to do; and on a ques-
    tion of discretion, it is impossible, with reference to a community of this descrip-
    tion, not to look with some degree of attention at what the governing body of the
    borough think on the subject.

[36] *Associated Minerals Consolidated Ltd. v. Wyong Shire Council*, *supra*, footnote 27;
A.-G. v. Sheffield Gas Consumer Co., *supra*, footnote 35. Doubts as to the applicability of laches to the Attorney-General are expressed in *A.-G. ex rel. Monmouth-
shire County Council v. Scott*, [1905] 2 K.B. 160 (C.A.); *A.-G. v. Wimbledon
House Estates Co. Ltd.*, [1904] 2 Ch. 34 at p. 42. See also de Smith, *supra*, footnote
5, at pp. 438-9. In *A.-G. v. South Staffordshire Waterworks Co.* (1909), 25 T.L.R.
408 (Ch.), it was held that delay could not defeat the Attorney-General's claim for
an injunction to restrain an excess of statutory power as lapse of time could not
confer a right to avoid a statute. To the same effect is *Shaughnessy Heights Property Owners' Ass'n v. Northup* (1958), 12 D.L.R. (2d) 760 (B.C.S.C.).

It is necessary . . . to base the granting or denial of equitable relief on broader grounds than would normally apply as between private citizens. . . . the courts are somewhat slower to deny the Attorney-General, as the custodian of the public rights, relief on [the ground of delay] than in the case of an individual. The injury to a public interest by denial of relief, its extent and degree of irremediability, must be weighed against any loss which the defendant may have sustained by the plaintiff standing by while the defendant incurs expense or, if such is the case, misleading the defendant into supposing that its activities were or would be permitted . . . .[37]

265   The courts have regarded hardship arguments with great scepticism where public rights are involved.[38] In so holding they have dealt with an even hand, for as will be seen in Chapter 4, hardship on public authorities is not often accepted as a reason for denying injunctive relief to which the plaintiff is otherwise entitled.[39]

3. Criminal Law and Statutory Prohibitions

(1) Historical

266   The accepted traditional doctrine was that equity had no jurisdiction with respect to the criminal law, and that injunctive relief could not be had to enforce compliance.[40] This extended even to libel,

---

[37] *Associated Minerals Consolidated Ltd. v. Wyong Shire Council, supra*, footnote 27, at p. 560.

[38] For example, mandatory injunctions requiring the demolition of buildings erected in contravention of municipal by-laws have frequently been awarded. See *City of Toronto v. Copses*, [1934] O.W.N. 215 (H.C.J.); *City of Niagara Falls v. Mannette*, [1943] O.W.N. 599 (C.A.); *Re Hewitson and Hughes* (1980), 119 D.L.R. (3d) 117, 31 O.R. (2d) 536 (H.C.J.); *Township of Shuniah v. Richard* (1982), 136 D.L.R. (3d) 638, 37 O.R. (2d) 471 (H.C.J.); *Township of North Himsworth v. St. Denis* (1982), 17 M.P.L.R. 224 (Ont. C.A.). In *Long v. Roberts* (1965), 55 D.L.R. (2d) 195, [1966] 1 O.R. 771 (H.C.J.), a ratepayer was awarded a mandatory injunction for the removal of a building despite the fact that the local building inspector had (wrongly) granted a permit. See also, *City of Toronto v. Polai* (1969), 8 D.L.R. (3d) 689, [1970] 1 O.R. 483 (C.A.), affd [1973] S.C.R. 38, 28 D.L.R. (3d) 638, and *Bradbury v. Enfield London Borough Council*, [1967] 1 W.L.R. 1311 (C.A.), at p. 1324, *per* Lord Denning, M.R.: "Even if chaos should result, still the law must be obeyed." Compare the more restrained approach where injunctions are sought against Crown servants: *infra*, §349 *et seq.*, especially §362. Compare also *Harold Stephen & Co. Ltd. v. Post Office*, [1977] 1 W.L.R. 1172 (C.A.).

[39] *Infra*, especially at §§372 and 403.

[40] Maitland, *Equity* (London, Stevens & Sons, 1909), p. 19: "The Court of Chancery kept very clear of the province of crime"; *Gee v. Pritchard* (1818), 2 Swans. 402 at p. 413, 36 E.R. 670, *per* Lord Eldon, L.C.: "I have no jurisdiction to prevent the commission of crimes". In *Ramsay v. Aberfoyle Manufacturing Co.* (1935), 54 C.L.R. 230 (Aust. H.C.), Latham, C.J., said, at p. 239: "A court of equity has no general duty to 'enforce the law', either at the suit of the Attorney-General or of private persons"; and McTiernan, J., observed at pp. 255-6: "The provisions of the

which had the criminal law as its origin. Chancery was said to have no jurisdiction to grant injunctive relief in defamation actions.[41] One reason for the refusal to become involved with the administration of criminal justice may have been the unfortunate experience of the Star Chamber, which had dealt with such matters ostensibly on the same prerogative authority to see justice done that was the underpinning of equitable jurisdiction.[42] After the abolition of the Star Chamber, the administration of criminal law became the exclusive preserve of the common law courts, and the type of equitable discretion so familiar in other areas of the law has never been employed in the criminal law.

267   The jurisdictional impediment to injunctive relief to enforce the criminal law was removed by the Common Law Procedure Act, 1854.[43] Still, injunctions which merely supplemented the penalties provided for already existing offences, were unheard of until the 20th century. As late as 1894 in *Institute of Patent Agents v. Lockwood*,[44] the House of Lords maintained the traditional equitable refusal to become embroiled in the administration of criminal law. An injunction was sought to restrain an unregistered patent agent from practising in contravention of a statute which stipulated a £20 penalty. Lord Herschell thought that the submission that the defendant should be subjected to the additional expense of proceedings in the High Court, and be made subject not to the summary procedure and fine provided by statute, but to civil proceedings possibly leading to imprisonment, was so out of the question that it was "scarcely necessary to do more than state the contention to shew that it is impossible that it can be supported."[45] However, the practice of enforcing by injunction statutory prescriptions, especially those regulatory in na-

---

law for the trial and punishment of offenders are not to be supplanted or supplemented by this remedy." In *Robinson v. Adams*, [1925] 1 D.L.R. 359 at p. 365, 56 O.L.R. 217 at p. 225 (S.C. App. Div.), Middleton, J.A., stated: "It is safe to say that the Court of Chancery never granted an injunction in aid of the criminal law, or as supplementing the criminal law, if it was found to be inefficient."

[41] *St. James's Evening Post* (1742), 2 Atk. 469, 26 E.R. 683. The modern law relating to injunctions in defamation actions is discussed, *infra*, §440 *et seq*.

[42] "Developments in the Law — Injunctions", 78 Harv. L. Rev. 994 (1965), at p. 1013.

[43] See *Quartz Hill Consolidated Gold Mining Co. v. Beall* (1882), 20 Ch. D. 501 (C.A.).

[44] [1894] A.C. 347 (H.L.).

[45] *Ibid.*, at p. 362. Although it was a Scottish case, and although the Attorney-General was not joined, it seems clear that the decision of the House of Lords rests on the general proposition that the statutory penalty and procedure should be exclusive.

ture, has become increasingly common.[46] The more traditional granting of injunctive relief, noted above,[47] to keep statutory bodies and corporations within the limits of their powers perhaps provided an analogue and a starting point.

(2) Enjoining "flouters"

268   Although English cases are more common, there are also many Canadian decisions in which injunctions have been granted to enforce penal legislation. The most common situation is one in which the law has been "flouted", and the statutory penalty has proved to be an inadequate sanction.[48] In one of the leading English cases, *A.-G. v. Harris*,[49] the defendants had been convicted 95 and 142 times respectively of selling flowers in the street outside a public cemetery, contrary to a century-old statute. Although, the court noted, this activity caused no harm to the public — indeed, the flower stall was a positive benefit to many visitors to the cemetery — still, Sellers, L.J., observed: "It cannot, in my opinion, be anything other than a public detriment for the law to be defied, week by week, and the offender to find it profitable to pay the fine and continue to flout the law."[50]

269   There is now considerable authority in favour of injunctions in such cases in Canada.[51] An Alberta court granted an injunction enjoining the unauthorized practice of dentistry, although there was no evidence of actual harm from the practice in question, on the grounds that there had been open, continuous, flagrant and profit-

---

[46] Statutory provision for the enforcement of municipal by-laws by way of injunction is common. For cases discussing such legislation, see *City of Vancouver v. Kessler* (1963), 39 D.L.R. (2d) 564 (B.C.S.C.), affd 45 D.L.R. (2d) 535 (C.A.); *One Chestnut Park Road Ltd. v. City of Toronto*, [1964] S.C.R. 287, 43 D.L.R. (2d) 390; *Re City of Dartmouth and S.S. Kresge Co. Ltd.* (1965), 54 D.L.R. (2d) 155 (N.S.S.C.), revd on other grounds 58 D.L.R. (2d) 229 (S.C. App. Div.). By-laws have also been enforced without express statutory authorization: *A.-G. v. Ashborne Recreation Ground Co.*, [1903] 1 Ch. 101; *City of Toronto v. Solway* (1919), 49 D.L.R. 473, 46 O.L.R. 24 (S.C. App. Div.). But see *Devonport Corp. v. Tozer*, [1903] 1 Ch. 759 (C.A.), where a local authority was held to lack standing.

[47] *Supra*, §§253, 254.

[48] *A.-G. v. Harris*, [1961] 1 Q.B. 74 (C.A.); *A.-G. v. Premier Line Ltd.*, [1932] 1 Ch. 303; *A.-G. v. Sharp*, [1931] 1 Ch. 121 (C.A.).

[49] *Supra*, footnote 48.

[50] *Ibid.*, at p. 86, *per* Sellers, L.J.

[51] Cases cited, *infra*, footnotes 52-56; *Hamilton and Milton Road Co. v. Raspberry* (1887), 13 O.R. 466 (H.C.J.), granting an injunction to enforce a toll although a statutory remedy was provided. Compare, however, the discussion of injunctions to enforce true criminal offences, *infra*, §§272, 273.

able violation of the statute for which the statutory penalties were completely ineffective.[52] More recently in Ontario, a trucking company which persistently operated without the required licence notwithstanding numerous convictions was enjoined at the suit of the Attorney-General, the court holding that such relief was appropriate "where the law as contained in a public statute is being flouted."[53] The Alberta Court of Appeal[54] has held that an injunction may be awarded at the suit of the Attorney-General to prevent further violations of the Lord's Day Act where the facts demonstrated[55] "an open and continuous disregard of an imperative public statute and its usual sanctions which is unlikely to be thwarted without the intervention of the Court."

270   The rationale in this type of case seems clear: despite the absence of actual or threatened injury to persons or property, the public's interest in seeing the law obeyed justifies equitable intervention where the defendant is a persistent offender who will not be stopped by the penalties provided by statute.[56]

---

[52] *A.-G. Alta. ex rel. Rooney v. Lees and Courtney*, [1932] 3 W.W.R. 533 (Alta. S.C.). For similar cases dealing with unauthorized professional practice, see *A.-G. v. Churchill's Veterinary Sanatorium Ltd.*, [1910] 2 Ch. 401; *A.-G. v. Weeks*, [1932] 1 Ch. 211 (C.A.); *A.-G. v. George C. Smith Ltd.*, [1909] 2 Ch. 524; *Manitoba Dental Ass'n v. Byman and Halstead* (1962), 34 D.L.R. (2d) 602 (Man. C.A.); *Institute of Patent Agents v. Lockwood*, *supra*, footnote 44; *Public Accountants Council for Province of Ontario v. Premier Trust Co.* (1963), 42 D.L.R. (2d) 411, [1964] 1 O.R. 386 (H.C.J.) (professional body lacking standing to sue for injunction); *Ass'n of Professional Engineers of Ontario v. Canadian Council of Professional Certification* (1979), 106 D.L.R. (3d) 132, 27 O.R. (2d) 259 (H.C.J.) (refusing an injunction to restrain a rival body from conferring designations which might confuse the public).

[53] *A.-G. Ont. v. Grabarchuk* (1976), 67 D.L.R. (3d) 31 at p. 36, 11 O.R. (2d) 607 at p. 612 (Div. Ct.), *per* Reid, J.

[54] *A.-G. Alta. v. Plantation Indoor Plants Ltd.* (1982), 133 D.L.R. (3d) 741 (Alta. C.A.), leave to appeal to S.C.C. granted *loc. cit.*

[55] *Ibid.*, at p. 747, *per* McClung, J.A.

[56] In *A.-G. Ont. v. Yeotes* (1980), 111 D.L.R. (3d) 488 at pp. 496-7, 28 O.R. (2d) 577 at p. 585 (H.C.J.), vard 120 D.L.R. (3d) 128, 31 O.R. (2d) 589 (C.A.), leave to appeal to S.C.C. refused 37 N.R. 356*n*, Montgomery, J., gave the following summary, based primarily on the *Chaudry* case, *infra*, footnote 57:

    (1) Where the rights of the public are involved by reason of the illegal action of the defendant, there is jurisdiction to grant an injunction at the instance of the Attorney-General notwithstanding the fact that there are other remedies available, if such remedies are inadequate.

    (2) The conduct in question need not be restricted to acts which constitute an invasion of any right of property, but can extend to a mere invasion of the community's general right to have laws obeyed.

    (3) By virtue of the fact that the conduct necessarily involves the public, the dispute no longer is between individuals and therefore engenders an exception

(3) Danger to public safety

271   Another class of case is where there is an immediate threat or danger to public safety which would not be met by the ordinary process or procedure prescribed by statute. The leading example is *A.-G. v. Chaudry* [57] where the defendants had violated building and fire safety regulations in altering the construction of a hotel, and the evidence showed a serious risk to the safety of hotel patrons. Summary proceedings under the statute (which could lead to an order prohibiting occupancy of the premises) were delayed in the magistrates' court, and the Court of Appeal upheld an immediate interlocutory injunction. In other cases, injunctions have been granted to restrain the erection of buildings which would constitute a permanent infraction of by-laws or legislation,[58] as well as to forbid an act which would irreparably damage the environment.[59]

(4) Criminal offences proper

272   The extent to which injunctive relief may be had to prevent violations of the criminal law proper — in Canada, an offence created under Parliament's criminal law power — as distinct from statutory or regulatory offences is uncertain. The traditional refusal of equity to become involved in the criminal law evolved with truly criminal of-

---

to the general rule that the punishment prescribed by a statute is to be the only remedy.

(4)   The authority of the Court is discretionary, but cognizance must be given to the fact that the action is brought by the Attorney-General and therefore the injunction will be refused only in exceptional circumstances.

(5)   Deliberate and persistent breaches of the law are facts which also go to the question of the exercise of discretion unless the matter is too trivial, or injustice would be caused, or there is good reason for refusing to enforce the general right of the public to have laws obeyed.

See also *United Nurses of Alberta v. A.-G. Alta.* (1980), 124 D.L.R. (3d) 64 (Alta. Q.B.).

[57] [1971] 3 All E.R. 938 (C.A.).

[58] *A.-G. v. Wimbledon House Estate Co. Ltd.*, [1904] 2 Ch. 34, and *A.-G. v. Ashborne Recreation Ground Co.*, [1903] 1 Ch. 101, restraining building which would constitute a permanent and continuing violation of municipal by-laws. See also *Cooney v. Ku-ring-gai Corp.* (1963), 114 C.L.R. 582 (Aust. H.C.).

[59] See, *e.g.*, *A.-G. ex rel. Bedfordshire County Council v. Howard United Reformed Church Trustees*, [1976] A.C. 363 (H.L.) (injunction restraining demolition of listed building); *Kent County Council v. Batchelor (No. 2)*, [1979] 1 W.L.R. 213 (Q.B.), at p. 220, *per* Talbot, J., where a tree preservation order was enforced by injunction although the statute provided only for a fine: "It is not just a case of taking action to prevent a criminal offence. It is a case of preventing interference with the areas of natural beauty which they [the plaintiffs] have sought by their tree preservation orders to preserve."

fences in mind, before the age of regulation and the proliferation of statutory offences. There is a strong body of case-law in Ontario to the effect that an injunction will not be granted to restrain Criminal Code offences.[60] These cases arose in the context of labour disputes where a property owner sought to enjoin conduct amounting to watching and besetting.[61] In the leading case, *Robinson v. Adams*, a decision of the Ontario Court of Appeal, Middleton, J.A., said:

> The equitable jurisdiction of a civil Court cannot properly be invoked to suppress crime. Unlawful acts which are an offence against the public, and so fall within the criminal law, may also be the foundation of an action based upon the civil wrong done to an individual, but when Parliament has, in the public interest, forbidden certain acts and made them an offence against the law of the land, then, unless a right to property is affected, the civil Courts should not attempt to interfere and forbid by their injunction that which has already been forbidden by Parliament itself.[62]

More recently, an injunction to prevent an illegal abortion was refused, although primarily on the grounds of standing.[63]

273   On the other hand, in a decision of the Manitoba Court of Appeal, it was said that this line of authority did not apply where the Attorney-General sued as plaintiff.[64] Reliance was placed on the dictum of Hodgins, J.A., in another Ontario Court of Appeal decision, *A.-G. Ont. v. Canadian Wholesale Grocers Ass'n*,[65] suggesting that the Attorney-General did have the right to sue to restrain the carrying out of any criminal conspiracy in restraint of trade as defined by the Criminal Code. It is submitted, however, that the analysis of the

---

[60] *Robinson v. Adams*, [1925] 1 D.L.R. 359, 56 O.L.R. 217 (S.C. App. Div.); *Dallas v. Felek*, [1934] O.W.N. 247 (C.A.); *Rubenstein v. Kumer*, [1940] 2 D.L.R. 691, [1940] O.W.N. 153 (H.C.J.); *Stewart v. Baldassari* (1930), 38 O.W.N. 431 (H.C.); *Canada H.W. Gossard Co. Ltd. v. Tripp* (1967), 66 D.L.R. (2d) 139, [1968] 1 O.R. 230 (H.C.J.); *Mid-West Television Ltd. v. S.E.D. Systems Inc.*, [1981] 3 W.W.R. 560 (Sask. Q.B.).

[61] *Cf. Springhead Spinning Co. v. Riley* (1868), L.R. 6 Eq. 551, holding, in a similar context, that the employer's property rights were affected and that an injunction was not precluded because it also enforced a penal statute.

[62] *Supra*, footnote 60, at pp. 364-5 D.L.R., p. 224 O.L.R.

[63] *Dehler v. Ottawa Civic Hospital* (1979), 101 D.L.R. (3d) 686, 25 O.R. (2d) 748 (H.C.J.), affd 117 D.L.R. (3d) 512n, 29 O.R. (2d) 677n (C.A.), leave to appeal to S.C.C. refused D.L.R. *loc. cit.* The issue of standing is discussed, *infra*, §290 *et seq.* See also *Paton v. British Pregnancy Advisory Service Trustees*, [1979] Q.B. 276; *Whalley v. Whalley* (1981), 122 D.L.R. (3d) 717 (B.C.S.C.). *Cf. Re Simms and H* (1979), 106 D.L.R. (3d) 435 (N.S. Fam. Ct.), appointing a guardian *ad litem* of the unborn infant in a pending injunction proceeding.

[64] *Re R. and Odeon Morton Theatres Ltd.* (1974), 42 D.L.R. (3d) 471 (Man. C.A.).

[65] [1923] 2 D.L.R. 617 at p. 647, 53 O.L.R. 627 at p. 656 (S.C. App. Div.).

Manitoba Court of Appeal is open to question. First, there is no indication in *Robinson v. Adams*[66] that the decision rested on the plaintiff's want of standing, although admittedly that could provide alternate justification for the result. Secondly, in the *Canadian Wholesale Grocers* case, no injunction was in fact granted, and the dictum of Hodgins, J.A., was distinctly a minority view. Both Meredith, C.J.O., and Ferguson, J.A., held that no injunction would be granted had an offence been made out "because the public can be protected by proceeding against the respondents by indictment."[67] Where the public interest requires, it is possible for Parliament to include specific statutory authorization for such injunctions, as in the present Combines Investigation Act,[68] and it is argued below[69] that the more serious the offence, the more difficult it becomes to justify an inherent power to award injunctions.

(5) Are injunctions appropriate?

274   Appealing as first seems the proposition that the courts must use the injunctive power to see to it that the law is obeyed, powerful arguments, both substantive and procedural, have been raised against the practice, and it may require re-evaluation. In the *Gouriet* case, Viscount Dilhorne said that "Great difficulties may arise if 'enforcement' of the criminal law by injunction became a regular practice."[70] Lord Wilberforce added that the jurisdiction to grant such injunctions " — though proved useful on occasions — is one of great delicacy and is one to be used with caution."[71] Lord Diplock provided the following caveat:

> It is in my view appropriate to be used only in the most exceptional of cases. It is not accurate to describe it as preventive justice. It is a deterrent and punitive procedure; but this is characteristic too of the enforcement of criminal law through the ordinary courts of criminal jurisdiction. The very creation by Parliament of a statutory offence

---

[66] *Supra*, footnote 60.

[67] *Supra*, footnote 60, at p. 629 D.L.R., p. 639 O.L.R., *per* Meredith, C.J.O.

[68] S. 29.1, S.C. 1974-75, c. 76, s. 10. The Judicature Act, Ont., s. 19(2), permits the Supreme Court to enjoin publications that are "obscene, immoral, or otherwise injurious to public morals" but was held *ultra vires* as legislation in respect of criminal law: *A.-G. Ont. v. Koynok*, [1941] 1 D.L.R. 548, [1940] O.W.N. 555 (H.C.J.). *Cf. A.-G. Man. v. Rosenbaum*, [1930] 1 D.L.R. 152 (Man. K.B.), upholding a provincial statute authorizing an injunction to restrain fraudulent trading in securities. English statutes empowering the Attorney-General to seek injunctive relief are discussed in de Smith, *supra*, footnote 5, at p. 453.

[69] *Infra*, §285.

[70] *Gouriet v. Union of Post Office Workers*, [1978] A.C. 435 (H.L.), at p. 490.

[71] *Ibid.*, at p. 481.

constitutes a warning to potential offenders that if they are found guilty by a court of criminal jurisdiction of the conduct that is proscribed, they will be liable to suffer punishment up to a maximum authorised by the statute. When a court of civil jurisdiction grants an injunction restraining a potential offender from committing what is a crime but not a wrong for which there is redress in private law, this in effect is warning him that he will be in double jeopardy, for if he is found guilty by the civil court of committing the crime he will be liable to suffer punishment of whatever severity that court may think appropriate, whether or not it exceeds the maximum penalty authorised by the statute and notwithstanding that he will also be liable to be punished again for the same crime if found guilty of it by a court of criminal jurisdiction. Where the crime that is the subject matter of the injunction is triable on indictment the anomalies involved in the use of this exceptional procedure are enhanced. The accused has the constitutional right to be tried by jury and his guilt established by reference to the criminal standard of proof. If he is proceeded against for contempt of court he is deprived of these advantages.[72]

275   Except to the extent that it adds to the penalty to be paid, such an injunction is redundant. The offence itself constitutes an injunction against the defendant's behaviour. In an early Canadian case, counsel for the Attorney-General seeking an injunction to restrain breach of a statute was asked: "You have an injunction from the highest Court in the land now standing in the books . . . When you have got that, why do you come to this Court for a further injunction?"[73] The effect of such an injunction is to legislate an increased and indefinite penalty for an existing offence. Violation of the injunction constitutes contempt and a heavy fine or imprisonment[74] will likely result. The Legislature must have considered the gravity of the offence in specifying a maximum penalty, and, it is argued, it is for the Legislature, not the courts, to raise the price to be paid for violation. Very often, legislation provides explicitly for increased penalties for repeat offences, and in such cases it can hardly be said that the "flouter" was not contemplated. This argument has found favour with some courts,[75] but recently has more often been rejected.[76] In one of the

---

[72] *Ibid.*, at p. 498.

[73] *A.-G. v. Wellington Colliery Co.* (1903), 10 B.C.R. 397 (S.C.), at p. 399, *per* Irving, J.

[74] In *Kent County Council v. Batchelor* (1976), 33 P. & C.R. 185 (C.A.), contempt conviction was reversed by the Court of Appeal, but all three judges (Lord Denning, M.R., Shaw and Stephenson, L.JJ.) stated that a penalty of one month imprisonment would not be inappropriate, whereas the statute contravened provided only for a fine.

[75] *A.-G. v. Wellington Colliery Co.*, *supra*, footnote 73; *Institute of Patent Agents v. Lockwood*, [1894] A.C. 347 (H.L.).

[76] *Cf. A.-G. v. Harris*, [1961] 1 Q.B. 74 (C.A.), at pp. 93-4, *per* Pearce, L.J.:
    It is not, of course, desirable that Parliament should habitually rely on the

leading English cases, there had actually been an unsuccessful attempt to have the penalty increased before injunction proceedings
were taken.[77] Judges have spoken of the High Court's "inherent
power to secure by injunction obedience to the law by everyone in
the land".[78] The source of such a sweeping power is not altogether
clear, and the dicta from the *Gouriet* decision cited above suggest
that Parliament's sanctions ordinarily ought not to be supplemented
by the court.

276   In favour of such orders, one traditional equitable argument,
rarely employed,[79] is that an injunction will avoid a multiplicity of
proceedings. More importantly, it can be argued that injunctive relief is granted not so much to enforce the particular legislation or regulatory standard, but rather to uphold a general respect for the law.
In *A.-G. v. Harris*, Pearce, L.J., although conscious of the dangers
involved, observed that "a breach with impunity by one citizen leads
to a breach by other citizens, or to a general feeling that the law is
unjustly partial to those who have the persistence to flout it. Moreover, a breach of one law leads to a breach of another."[80] On this
theory, the court is in fact acting to remedy something not contemplated when the legislation was drafted and the penalty established.
More is at stake than a readjustment of a penalty to make it an effective deterrent: the court is in fact attempting to protect more generally the proposition that the law should be obeyed and to preclude a
persistent offender from casting general disrespect upon the legal regime. Moreover, the view that inadequate or ineffective legislative
sanctions should not be supplemented by the award of injunctions is
difficult to defend in cases such as *Chaudry*[81] where there was actual

---

High Court to deter the law breaker by other means than the statutory penalties
instead of taking the legislative step of making the penalties adequate to prevent
the offence which it has created. Especially is this so where the offences are of a
trivial nature. Yet it is, on the other hand, highly undesirable that some member
of the public should with impunity flout the law and deliberately continue acts
forbidden by Parliament.

[77] *Ibid.*, at p. 86.

[78] *Hammersmith London Borough Council v. Magnum Automated Forecourts Ltd.*,
[1978] 1 W.L.R. 50 (C.A.), at p. 55, *per* Lord Denning, M.R. See also *A.-G. v.
Chaudry*, [1971] 3 All E.R. 938 (C.A.), at p. 947, *per* Lord Denning, M.R.: "the
High Court always has reserve power to enforce the law so enacted by way of an injunction or declaration or other suitable remedy. The High Court has jurisdiction
to ensure obedience to the law whenever it is just and convenient so to do."

[79] *A.-G. v. Wimbledon House Estate Co. Ltd.*, [1904] 2 Ch. 34 at p. 42, *per* Farwell, J.

[80] *Supra*, footnote 76, at p. 95.

[81] *Supra*, footnote 78.

physical harm threatened by the defendant's course of conduct, or in cases where permanent or irreparable damage to the environment or public amenities might be caused.[82]

277   The second area of concern produced by the granting of such injunctions is procedural.[83] The differences between civil proceedings for an injunction and criminal proceedings are obvious. Procedural safeguards available in criminal or even *quasi*-criminal proceedings will not be available in a civil action for an injunction. Differences are especially marked for indictable offences triable by jury. However, even for summary offences, important protections — the right to silence and the criminal burden of proof — are lost in a civil action for injunction.[84] The defendant can be compelled to answer questions on discovery and subpoenaed by the plaintiff at trial; interlocutory injunctions may be granted on affidavit evidence where *viva voce* cross-examination may be unavailable, and perhaps even awarded on a "balance of convenience" standard.[85] Although the penalty will not be imposed until further violation, the award of an injunction amounts to conviction without trial, and there is certainly some element of double jeopardy to be faced.[86]

278   The double jeopardy argument has been scorned by Lord Denning, M.R., who has said: "The reply to [one who raises this argument] is simple: 'All the more reason why you should not break the law. You will then be in no jeopardy. If you do break it, you will not be punished twice over. Whichever court deals with you, it will

---

[82] *A.-G. v. Wimbledon House Estate Co. Ltd.*, *supra*, footnote 79; *A.-G. v. Ashborne Recreation Ground Co.*, [1903] 1 Ch. 101; *Cooney v. Ku-ring-gai Corp.* (1963), 114 C.L.R. 582 (Aust. H.C.); *A.-G. ex rel. Bedfordshire County Council v. Howard United Reformed Church Trustees*, [1976] A.C. 363 (H.L.); *Kent County Council v. Batchelor (No. 2)*, [1979] 1 W.L.R. 213 (Q.B.).

[83] Mentioned in *Gouriet, supra*, footnote 70. See also de Smith, *supra*, footnote 5, at p. 457.

[84] It may be, however, that the defendant in a civil action is able to benefit from the procedural guarantees of the Charter of Rights and Freedoms. Although strictly not "charged with an offence" as required by s. 11, the defendant may argue either that the Crown should not be able to short-circuit the rights guaranteed by s. 11 by bringing injunction proceedings rather than launching a prosecution, or that such rights are also protected by the "fundamental justice" guarantee of s. 7.

[85] In *A.-G. Ont. v. Grabarchuk* (1976), 67 D.L.R. (3d) 31, 11 O.R. (2d) 607 (Div. Ct.), the "balance of convenience" test was properly rejected for this class of case, but *cf. Harder v. N.Z. Tramways and Public Passenger Transport Authorities Employees Industrial Union of Workers*, [1977] 2 N.Z.L.R. 162 (S.C.).

[86] In *Gouriet v. Union of Post Office Workers*, [1978] A.C. 435 (H.L.), Lord Diplock specifically referred to the double jeopardy problem at pp. 499-500, as did Viscount Dilhorne at pp. 490-1.

take into consideration the punishment which has been, or can be, inflicted by the other.' "[87]

279   It is not clear, however, how a court would take into account the indefinite possibilities offered by a contempt conviction, and, indeed, the Alberta Court of Appeal has suggested that the contempt would be a distinct wrong and that the offender would deserve punishment for flouting the court's order, as well as separate punishment for violation of the statute.[88]

280   Still, it can be argued that the effect of such an injunction is merely to put the defendant on notice that much more severe consequences will flow from any further violation, and that by being put on notice he is not deprived of his right to a criminal trial. The fact that the injunction itself constitutes only a warning perhaps renders procedural deprivation more acceptable. Moreover, as the purpose behind such an injunction seems to be the maintenance of a general respect for the law, contempt proceedings are perhaps appropriate in that the offender who persists in the face of such warning from the court is violating the court's order as well as the statute.

281   Such arguments would be more compelling if the courts had exercised restraint in awarding injunctions against persons accused but not yet convicted. In several cases, injunctions have been granted before criminal proceedings were brought or completed. In a British Columbia case, an injunction was awarded despite grave doubt as to the constitutional validity of the by-law about to be violated.[89] In an Australian case, an injunction was granted to restrain an allegedly immoral theatrical performance before any charges had been laid.[90] The dissenting judge pointed out, correctly, it is submitted:

> . . . the appellants claim that what they propose to do will not constitute any offence and express their willingness to abide the event of prosecution. It seems to me to be utterly wrong for a civil court officiously to intervene and thereby to deny them the opportunity of proving their point or suffering the consequences.[91]

A finding that the defendant's conduct did constitute an offence

---

[87] *Ex p. Island Records Ltd.*, [1978] Ch. 122 (C.A.), at p. 135.

[88] *A.-G. Alta. v. Plantation Indoor Plants Ltd.* (1982), 133 D.L.R. (3d) 741 (Alta. C.A.), at p. 745, leave to appeal to S.C.C. granted *loc. cit.*

[89] *Kent District v. Storgoff and A.-G. B.C.* (1962), 40 W.W.R. 278 (B.C.S.C.). It was subsequently held that the by-law was *ultra vires*: *Kent District Corp. v. Storgoff and A.-G. B.C.* (1962), 41 W.W.R. 301 (B.C.S.C.).

[90] *A.-G. v. Huber* (1971), 2 S.A.S.R. 142 (S.C.); *cf. A.-G. v. Twelfth Night Theatre*, [1969] Qd. R. 319 (S.C.).

[91] *A.-G. v. Huber, supra*, footnote 90, at p. 166, *per* Bray, C.J.

could seriously prejudice his defence in criminal proceedings,[92] and if the defendant successfully avoided the injunction, it is by no means clear that a subsequent criminal proceeding would be barred.[93]

282   In Canada, where the Crown is appealing an acquittal it has been held that the defendant is entitled to rely on the verdict, and that no injunction should be granted.[94] However, in an English case where an appeal from a conviction in a Sunday closing case was pending before the Divisional Court, Lord Denning held that the court should not be precluded from acting, and his language suggests a broad power to intervene before any criminal proceedings are taken:

> When there is a plain breach of the Act I do not think that the authorities concerned need wait at all for finality anywhere. They can take proceedings in the High Court before any other proceedings are even started. It is open to the court in its discretion to grant an injunction straightaway, at all events when the breach of the law is plain and where there appears to be an intention by the defendants to continue with the breach.[95]

283   In an earlier case, it had been held proper to order an injunction prior to any resort to the ordinary criminal process where it is clear beforehand both that an offence has been or will be committed and that the offender can be stopped only through resort to the injunction.[96] In the *Chaudry* case,[97] imminent threat to public safety was said to justify the court's refusal to await the outcome in the magistrates' court.

284   It is submitted that especially where the defendant has never been convicted and where he asserts a defence to the alleged infraction, it is both unfair and dangerous to decide the question of guilt or innocence on affidavit evidence in an interlocutory application, unless there is some serious and immediate threat to public safety.

---

[92] While the accused would not be deprived of the right to a full trial, defending an injunction application would have serious procedural implications: see, *supra*, §277.

[93] The possibility of such abuse is discussed in the Australia Law Reform Commission's *Access to Courts: 1. Standing: Public Interest Suits*, Working Paper No. 7 (Sydney, 1977), pp. 57-8.

[94] *Re R. and Odeon Morton Theatres Ltd.* (1974), 42 D.L.R. (3d) 471 (Man. C.A.).

[95] *Stafford Borough Council v. Elkenford Ltd.*, [1977] 2 All E.R. 519 (C.A.), at p. 527. See also *Thanet District Council v. Ninedrive Ltd.*, [1978] 1 All E.R. 703 (Ch.), granting an injunction to restrain the operation of a Sunday market although *mandamus* proceedings were pending, and although the judge felt that the defendant's case was not "wholly unarguable". *Cf. A.-G. v. Cleaver* (1811), 18 Ves. Jun. 211, 34 E.R. 297, refusing to grant an injunction restraining a public nuisance where an indictment had been preferred.

[96] *A.-G. v. Smith*, [1958] 2 Q.B. 173.

[97] *A.-G. v. Chaudry*, [1971] 3 All E.R. 938 (C.A.).

285   The more serious the offence, the more difficult it is to justify the use of injunctions at all. The penalties attached to serious offences are usually flexible enough to permit the imposition of a severe penalty for repeat offenders. A heavy sentence will satisfy the desire to maintain respect for the law. Procedural deprivations are severe, especially where the defendant would have the right to jury trial in ordinary criminal proceedings. Moreover, there is an extensive and elaborate body of criminal law devoted to inchoate offences and threatened harm which surely should not be overridden by the discretionary power to grant injunctions. The law of arrest, conspiracy, incitement and attempt deals with the difficult issue of when coercive measures may properly be taken to nip crime in the bud. There is also the ancient power of binding-over which, although subject to many of the problems found with injunctions, can still be resorted to.[98]

(6) Violations of statutes without penalty

286   Injunctions have also been granted where the defendant is violating a statute which prescribes no penalty. In *A.-G. Ont. v. Harry*,[99] an injunction was granted restraining completion of conveyances of real property under a "checkerboard" scheme which the court found would violate the subdivision control requirements of the Ontario Planning Act. The Attorney-General was said to sue "as *parens patriae* to preclude transfer of the subject lands to innocent purchasers",[100] and the court found it appropriate to grant the injunction, thereby preventing the lands from being put on the market, possibly to the detriment of innocent purchasers and at the risk of considerable litigation.

287   More dubious, however, is another recent Ontario case[101] where the Attorney-General was awarded an injunction to end an illegal strike, although statutory provisions restricting the grounds for la-

---

[98] See Williams, "Preventive Justice and the Courts", [1977] Crim. L.R. 703. For discussion of the binding-over power see Grunis, "Binding-Over to Keep the Peace and be of Good Behaviour in England and Canada", [1976] Public Law 16, and Williams, *Keeping the Peace* (London, Hutchinson & Co. Ltd., 1967), pp. 87-113, pointing out that the power has often been employed in politically sensitive areas.

[99] (1979), 93 D.L.R. (3d) 332, 22 O.R. (2d) 321 (H.C.J.) (interlocutory injunction); *A.-G. v. Yeotes* (1980), 111 D.L.R. (3d) 488, 28 O.R. (2d) 577 (H.C.J.) (trial); 120 D.L.R. (3d) 128, 31 O.R. (2d) 589 (C.A.), allowing an appeal on the merits. Leave to appeal to the Supreme Court of Canada was refused 37 N.R. 356n.

[100] 111 D.L.R. (3d) at p. 493, 28 O.R. (2d) at p. 582, *per* Montgomery, J.

[101] *A.-G. Ont. v. C.U.P.E.* (1981), 119 D.L.R. (3d) 428, 31 O.R. (2d) 618 (H.C.J.).

bour injunctions were not satisfied,[102] on the theory that such provisions do not apply where the Attorney-General sues as guardian of the public interest. Presumably, the Legislature considered the public interest when enacting the statutory limitations, and it is difficult to see why they should be swept aside because the Attorney-General is plaintiff.

(7) Restraining or assisting police investigations

288   The courts have cautiously avoided interference with police discretion, and there has been an understandable reluctance to grant injunctions at the suit of one suspected of an offence which would impede the investigative efforts of the police.[103] This is usually put on the basis that if the plaintiff's activities are lawful, damages will provide an adequate remedy,[104] but the more important consideration is undoubtedly the reluctance to interfere with police investigations. In an Ontario case,[105] an injunction to prevent the police from "harassing" the plaintiff in the operation of an adult private film club was refused. Lerner, J., found that the plaintiff had failed to make out a substantive case of wrongdoing, but added that even if the police were wrong in their activity, injunctive relief should be refused:

> Interlocutory injunctions are an extraordinary procedure not to be lightly permitted except in exceptional circumstances. To exercise them in relation to policing duties would have this Court act in a supervising function by the instrument of injunction or a restraining order of police conduct. I do not consider that the function of this Court in these circumstances.[106]

289   In England, injunctive relief has been awarded to assist police in-

---

[102] *Supra*, §193.

[103] In addition to the cases cited, *infra*, see *Re Copeland and Adamson* (1972), 28 D.L.R. (3d) 26, [1972] 3 O.R. 248 (H.C.J.) (*mandamus*); *Morgenthaler et al. v. Ackroyd et al.* (1983), 20 A.C.W.S. (2d) 473 (Ont. H.C.J.); and see, *infra*, §362, discussing an injunction to restrain the enforcement of unconstitutional statutes.

[104] *Greenback Investments (Hamilton) Ltd. v. O'Connell* (1972), 29 D.L.R. (3d) 164 at pp. 166-7, [1972] 3 O.R. 656 at pp. 658-9 (H.C.J.), *per* O'Driscoll, J.:

> In the event the plaintiff company, through its servants and agents, is in fact carrying on a lawful business, I am confident that it can be adequately recompensed in damages; in the event the plaintiff is not carrying on a lawful business, then to grant the relief sought would amount to a direction that under no circumstances could Police Officers obtain search warrants and pursue their duties under the *Police Act* and the relevant sections of the *Criminal Code* . . .

[105] *286880 Ontario Ltd. v. Parke* (1974), 52 D.L.R. (3d) 535, 6 O.R. (2d) 311 (H.C.J.).

[106] *Ibid.*, at p. 542 D.L.R., p. 318 O.R.

vestigations. It is submitted that such orders would be objectionable in Canada, and that police powers should be founded firmly in legislation or established common law principles. In *West Mercia Constabulary v. Wagener*,[107] an injunction was awarded to the police to freeze a bank account into which it was alleged the proceeds of a crime had been paid. However little sympathy one might have for the defendant in such a case, there are obvious dangers inherent in extending police powers by injunction. The order was claimed not on behalf of the victims of the alleged crime to protect their proprietary rights, but to assist the police in overcoming an admitted gap in their investigative powers. The result was confirmed by *Chief Constable of Kent v. V*,[108] a decision of the English Court of Appeal. It is submitted that the courts should be especially hesitant to exercise their discretion to award injunctions to supplement the investigative powers of the police.[109] Although Lord Denning has described those who would deny the police such powers by way of injunction as "timorous souls",[110] it is submitted that the better view is that expressed by Slade, L.J., in dissent, namely, that if the police seek such additional powers, they should be sought from Parliament rather than the court.[111]

4. Standing

290   In the cases just examined, the Attorney-General has either commenced or lent his name to the proceedings. Where injunctions are sought by private individuals to restrain public nuisances or wrongs, the issue of standing arises.[112] The law has not favoured the private enforcement of public rights unless the issue of public rights is incidental to some private cause of action asserted by the plaintiff.

(1) Public bodies

291   Legislation often confers upon public bodies such as municipalities the right to sue to enforce their own regulations or by-laws by way of

---

[107] [1982] 1 W.L.R. 127 (Q.B.).

[108] [1982] 3 All E.R. 36 (C.A.).

[109] For criticism of the *Wagener* decision, see Feldman, "Injunctions in Fraud Investigations", 98 L.Q.R. 190 (1982).

[110] *Supra*, footnote 108, at p. 39.

[111] *Supra*, footnote 108, at p. 48.

[112] See Thio, *Locus Standi and Judicial Review* (Singapore, University Press, 1971); Stein, *Locus Standi* (Sydney, Law Book Co., 1979); de Smith, *supra*, footnote 5, at pp. 409-21, pp. 450-61.

injunction.[113] In a recent British Columbia case,[114] it was held that a *quasi*-public body, a marketing board exercising powers pursuant to both provincial and federal legislation, could sue to enforce compliance with the marketing scheme, but on the basis that it sued on behalf of the producers to protect private proprietary interests. Municipalities have been refused standing to sue for injunctions restraining public nuisances affecting their members,[115] although legislation alters this position in England.[116] Professional bodies have been denied standing to enjoin unauthorized practice unless specific provision for injunctive relief is made by statute.[117] In these cases, it is submitted, standing rules seem especially narrow and it is hard to see why a public body charged with the responsibility for enacting or enforcing delegated legislation should not be able to sue if injunctive relief is otherwise appropriate.

(2) Criminal law

292   The *Gouriet* case[118] reaffirms the principle that unless he suffers some special damage, an ordinary member of the public has no standing to claim an injunction for a breach of the criminal law. It is for the Attorney-General, and for the Attorney-General alone, to determine whether, in the public interest, injunctive relief should be

---

[113] For cases discussing such legislation, see *City of Vancouver v. Kessler* (1963), 39 D.L.R. (2d) 564 (B.C.S.C.), affd 45 D.L.R. (2d) 535 (C.A.); *One Chestnut Park Road Ltd. v. City of Toronto*, [1964] S.C.R. 287, 43 D.L.R. (2d) 390; *Re City of Dartmouth and S.S. Kresge Co. Ltd.* (1965), 54 D.L.R. (2d) 155 (N.S.S.C.), revd on other grounds 58 D.L.R. (2d) 229 (S.C. App. Div.). By-laws have also been enforced without express statutory authorization: *A.-G. v. Ashborne Recreation Ground Co.*, [1903] 1 Ch. 101; *City of Toronto v. Solway* (1919), 49 D.L.R. 473, 46 O.L.R. 24 (S.C. App. Div.). But see *Devonport Corp. v. Tozer*, [1903] 1 Ch. 759 (C.A.), where a local authority was held to lack standing.

[114] *Re B.C. Tree Fruit Marketing Board and Pacific Produce Co. Ltd.* (1979), 96 D.L.R. (3d) 645 (B.C.S.C.).

[115] *St. Lawrence Rendering Co. v. City of Cornwall*, [1951] 4 D.L.R. 790, [1951] O.R. 669 (H.C.J.); *Prestatyn Urban District Council v. Prestatyn Raceway Ltd.*, [1970] 1 W.L.R. 33 (Ch.).

[116] de Smith, *supra*, footnote 5, at pp. 452-8.

[117] *Institute of Patent Agents v. Lockwood*, [1894] A.C. 347 (H.L.); *Public Accountants Council for Province of Ontario v. Premier Trust Co.* (1963), 42 D.L.R. (2d) 411, [1964] 1 O.R. 386 (H.C.J.); *Ass'n of Professional Engineers of Ontario v. Canadian Council of Professional Certification* (1979), 106 D.L.R. (3d) 132, 27 O.R. 259 (H.C.J.). Cf. *A.-G. Alta. ex rel. Rooney v. Lees and Courtney*, [1932] 3 W.W.R. 533 (Alta. S.C.); *A.-G. v. Churchill's Veterinary Sanatorium Ltd.*, [1910] 2 Ch. 401; *A.-G. v. Weeks*, [1932] 1 Ch. 211 (C.A.); *A.-G. v. George C. Smith Ltd.*, [1909] 2 Ch. 524; *Manitoba Dental Ass'n v. Byman and Halstead* (1962), 34 D.L.R. (2d) 602 (Man. C.A.).

[118] *Gouriet v. Union of Post Office Workers*, [1978] A.C. 435 (H.L.).

sought. An ordinary member of the public with insufficient interest to sue in his own name must, according to *Gouriet*, obtain the Attorney-General's consent to relator proceedings,[119] and, it would seem, the decision of the Attorney-General to grant or withhold his fiat for such proceedings is one which the courts will not review.[120]

293   In *Gouriet*, the plaintiff, a member of the National Association for Freedom, took immediate action when it was announced that the defendant Union of Post Office Workers had decided to join an international protest against apartheid and boycott South African postal communications during the coming week.[121] The boycott would have violated the Post Office Act, 1953, which made it an offence, punishable by up to two years imprisonment, to detain or delay any postal packet in the course of transmission. The legislation explicitly denied a private right of action.[122] Gouriet sought the Attorney-General's consent to relator proceedings. The Attorney-General refused, and Gouriet issued a writ in his own name. His application for an interlocutory injunction was refused because he lacked standing. The next day, a Saturday, a special sitting of the Court of Appeal was arranged, and the court granted an interim injunction for three days, granted leave to join the Attorney-General as defendant, and adjourned the proceedings so that all parties could be heard. The Attorney-General subsequently appeared, but refused to explain his decision to refuse his consent to proceedings, asserting that it was a matter of prerogative, unreviewable by the court. The majority of the Court of Appeal accepted that the court could not go behind the Attorney-General's decision, but held that an individual was entitled to ask for declaratory relief, and that an interlocutory injunction could be granted to maintain the *status quo* until the trial of the de-

---

[119] In *Grant v. St. Lawrence Seaway Authority* (1960), 23 D.L.R. (2d) 252, [1960] O.R. 298 (C.A.), it was held (disapproving *Turtle v. City of Toronto* (1924), 56 O.L.R. 252 (S.C. App. Div.)), that the Attorney-General could not properly be added as a defendant where he had refused to consent to relator proceedings. See also *St. Lawrence Rendering Co. v. City of Cornwall, supra*, footnote 115, refusing an amendment to add the Attorney-General with his consent after the evidence had been completed.

[120] *London County Council v. A.-G.*, [1902] A.C. 165 (H.L.), at p. 168; *Grant v. St. Lawrence Seaway Authority, supra*, footnote 119.

[121] For a good account of the background, see Lunny, "Comment", 12 U. British Columbia L. Rev. 320 (1978).

[122] *Cf. John Fairfax Ltd. v. Australian Postal Com'n*, [1977] 2 N.S.W.L.R. 124 (C.A.); *John Fairfax & Sons Ltd. v. Australian Telecommunications Com'n*, [1977] 2 N.S.W.L.R. 400 (C.A.), finding a private right to claim an injunction under the relevant Australian legislation.

claratory action.[123] Lord Denning took a bolder approach, and, describing the Attorney-General's submission as a "direct challenge to the rule of law",[124] held that Gouriet was entitled to claim injunctive relief on his own behalf.

294   In the House of Lords, Gouriet did not argue that the Attorney-General's decision could be reviewed. Rather, he rested his case on the assertion that if refused by the Attorney-General, even as a private citizen not particularly affected, he should be granted standing. The House of Lords unanimously rejected the argument, and the Attorney-General's screening role was not only upheld on authority, but also welcomed in principle.

295   Lord Wilberforce made reference to the delicacy and political sensitivity of such actions, and described the usefulness of the role of the Attorney-General:

> . . . [T]o apply to the court for an injunction at all against the threat of a criminal offence, may involve a decision of policy with which conflicting considerations may enter. Will the law best be served by preventive action? Will the grant of an injunction exacerbate the situation? (Very relevant this in industrial disputes.) Is the injunction likely to be effective or may it be futile? Will it be better to make it clear that the law will be enforced by prosecution and to appeal to the law-abiding instinct, negotiations, and moderate leadership, rather than provoke people along the road to martyrdom? All these matters . . . and the exceptional nature of this *civil* remedy, point the matter as one essentially for the Attorney-General's preliminary discretion.
>
> . . . . .
>
> The very fact, that, as the present case very well shows, decisions are of the type to attract political criticism and controversy, shows that they are outside the range of discretionary problems which the courts can resolve. Judges are equipped to find legal rights and administer, on well-known principles, discretionary remedies. These matters are widely outside those areas.[125]

296   In the Court of Appeal, Lord Denning had asked the following question:

> Are the Courts to stand idly by? Is the Attorney-General the final arbiter as to whether the law should be enforced or not?

---

[123] *Gouriet v. Union of Post Office Workers*, [1977] Q.B. 729 (C.A.). Lawton and Ormrod, L.JJ., formed the majority. The Court of Appeal's decision was followed in *Harder v. N.Z. Tramways and Public Passenger Transport Authorities Employees Industrial Union of Workers*, [1977] 2 N.Z.L.R. 162 (S.C.), where the plaintiff was awarded an injunction to end an illegal strike of public transit workers.

[124] *Gouriet, ibid.*, at p. 758.

[125] [1978] A.C. at pp. 481-2.

. . . . .

All we are asked to do is to make an order on the union saying that it must obey the Act of Parliament. Surely no objection could be taken by anyone in the land to an order in that form.[126]

297   In the House of Lords Lord Diplock answered, deprecating the "unaccustomed degree of rhetoric in this case", and asserting that indeed it was the job of the courts "to stand idly by until their aid is invoked by someone recognised by law as entitled to claim the remedy in justice that he seeks."[127]

298   The question of standing is a difficult matter of administrative and constitutional law[128] which can be covered only briefly in a book on specific remedies. Two factors appear to motivate the cautious common law approach to the question of standing which arises when an ordinary member of the public seeks a remedy with respect to a matter of general public interest. First of all, there seems to be fear of a flood of unnecessary litigation that might result from affording broad rights of standing. Secondly, the fear of the politicization of the judicial process, reflected in *Gouriet*, but less frequently referred to explicitly, has also played an important role. It would appear that the judges have feared that permitting ordinary members of the public to raise public law issues in which they have no particular interest may unnecessarily involve the courts in political controversies and disputes. Before considering the desirability of applying *Gouriet* in Canada, it will be useful to consider the special standing rules which have emerged in Canadian constitutional litigation.

(3) Constitutional cases

299   Recent decisions of the Supreme Court of Canada indicate a departure from this traditional view in the constitutional context. In *Thorson v. A.-G. Can.*,[129] the Supreme Court of Canada held that the plaintiff, suing as an ordinary taxpayer, did have standing to

---

[126] *Supra*, footnote 123, at pp. 736-8. Lord Denning's enthusiam for private suits to enforce the criminal law was not unwavering. See *Thorne v. B.B.C.*, [1967] 1 W.L.R. 1104 (C.A.), at p. 1109, *per* Lord Denning, where an individual was denied standing to sue for an injunction to restrain the B.B.C. from broadcasting what was alleged to be racist propaganda which violated the Race Relations Act, 1965: "It is a fundamental rule that the court will only grant an injunction at the suit of a private individual to support a legal right", adding that the plaintiff should be denied standing because he did not have "any legal right in himself personally in this matter."

[127] *Supra*, footnote 118, at p. 496.

[128] For more complete discussion, see references, *supra*, footnote 112.

[129] [1975] 1 S.C.R. 138, 43 D.L.R. (3d) 1.

claim a declaration contesting the constitutionality of an Act of Parliament. The majority judgment, written by Laskin, J., discounted the traditional floodgates argument, pointing out that the courts retain an overriding discretion to refuse standing, that the sanction of costs is an effective deterrent, and that the experience of ratepayer cases in which an exception to the normal rules of standing had long been recognized,[130] were all factors which indicated that the fear of a flood of litigation was somewhat unreal. In *Thorson*, the Attorney-General of Canada refused the plaintiff's request to take proceedings, and there was doubt as to whether any provincial Attorney-General had the power to raise the constitutionality of the legislation as it in no way affected or conflicted with provincial powers. Thus, to deny standing to the plaintiff was to deny the possibility of judicial review because the Act imposed no penalties, sanctions or other measures which by themselves would raise a litigable issue. Laskin, J., refused to countenance a situation in which "a question of constitutionality should be immunized from judicial review by denying standing to anyone to challenge the impugned statute."[131] While *Thorson* could be explained on the rather narrow grounds that standing was necessary to enable the constitutionality of legislation to be examined, the second Supreme Court decision on the issue, *Nova Scotia Board of Censors v. McNeil*,[132] takes a broader view. There, an ordinary member of the public was given standing to sue for a declaration that provincial legislation authorizing censorship of movies was *ultra vires* although clearly such legislation was in some sense regulatory in nature and provided an opportunity for those directly affected by the board's decisions, namely, film exchanges, theatre owners and operators, to contest the legislation. The court held that in light of the "apparently unlimited power in the Board to determine what members of the public may view . . . the challenged legislation . . . strikes at the members of the public in one of its central aspects",[133] and the individual was allowed to proceed.

300   In the *Borowski* case,[134] the court held that a private individual had standing to sue for a declaration that the therapeutic abortion provi-

---

[130] See, *e.g.*, *MacIlreith v. Hart* (1908), 39 S.C.R. 657. English law is less generous to ratepayers: de Smith, *supra*, footnote 5, at p. 462.

[131] *Supra*, footnote 129, at p. 145 S.C.R., p. 7 D.L.R.

[132] [1976] 2 S.C.R. 265, 55 D.L.R. (3d) 632.

[133] *Ibid.*, at p. 271 S.C.R., p. 637 D.L.R.

[134] *Minister of Justice of Canada v. Borowski*, [1981] 2 S.C.R. 575, 130 D.L.R. (3d) 588.

sions of the Criminal Code were inoperative because of conflict with
the Canadian Bill of Rights, again on the basis that as the impugned
provisions were exculpatory, there was "no reasonable way in which
that issue can be brought into court unless proceedings are launched
by some interested citizen."[135] Martland, J., for the majority, summarized the effect of *Thorson* and *McNeil*:

> I interpret these cases as deciding that to establish status as a plain-
> tiff in a suit seeking a declaration that legislation is invalid, if there is a
> serious issue as to its invalidity, a person need only to show that he is
> affected by it directly or that he has a genuine interest as a citizen in
> the validity of the legislation and that there is no other reasonable and
> effective manner in which the issue may be brought before the Court.
> In my opinion, the respondent has met this test and should be permit-
> ted to proceed with his action.[136]

(4) Application of constitutional cases

301   While these cases provide a convincing basis to expand standing
rules, their impact outside the constitutional context is still
uncertain.[137] In one case,[138] the Manitoba Court of Appeal held that
an individual did have standing on the *Thorson* principle to sue for
an injunction to restrain a municipality from using a pesticide without complying with a statutory requirement for an environmental impact review. However, for the most part, the Supreme Court
decisions have not been taken to confer a wide discretion to afford
individual standing outside the realm of constitutional law. The Supreme Court of Canada has not dealt with the issue outside the constitutional context, but lower court decisions have tended to favour
the traditional restrictive approach.[139] For example, a recent British

---

[135] *Ibid.*, at p. 597 S.C.R., p. 606 D.L.R., *per* Martland, J.

[136] *Ibid.*, at p. 598 S.C.R., p. 606 D.L.R.

[137] For discussion, see Mullan, "Standing after McNeil", 8 Ottawa L. Rev. 32 (1976).

[138] *Stein v. City of Winnipeg* (1974), 48 D.L.R. (3d) 223 (Man. C.A.).

[139] *Rosenberg v. Grand River Conservation Authority* (1976), 69 D.L.R. (3d) 384, 12
O.R. (2d) 496 (C.A.), leave to appeal to S.C.C. refused October 19, 1976; *Re Pim
and Minister of Environment* (1978), 94 D.L.R. (3d) 254, 23 O.R. (2d) 45 (H.C.J.);
Re Canadians for Abolition of Seal Hunt and Minister of Fisheries and Environment
(1980), 111 D.L.R. (3d) 333 (Fed. Ct. T.D.); *Re Islands Protection Society and The
Queen* (1979), 98 D.L.R. (3d) 504 (B.C.S.C.), at p. 512, *per* Murray, J.: "I am of
the view that the principles laid down in those cases should be confined to constitutional cases"; *Re University of Manitoba Students' Union Inc. and A.-G. Man.*
(1979), 101 D.L.R. (3d) 390 (Man. Q.B.); *Re Village Bay Preservation Society and
Mayne Airfield Inc.* (1982), 136 D.L.R. (3d) 729 (B.C.S.C.). *Cf.*, however,
Bedford Service Com'n v. A.-G. N.S. (1976), 72 D.L.R. (3d) 639 (N.S.S.C. App.
Div.), revd [1977] 2 S.C.R. 269, 80 D.L.R. (3d) 767n; *Lord Nelson Hotel Ltd. v.*

Columbia decision[140] refused to apply the constitutional decisions to allow a private group concerned about the well-being of whales to sue for an injunction to enjoin a Minister from issuing a licence for the importation of whales, holding that the plaintiff would not "suffer special damage peculiar to itself from the interference with the public right."[141]

302   It seems especially unlikely that the rationale of *Thorson, McNeil* and *Borowski* could be applied to *Gouriet*-type cases where the legality of the defendant's conduct can readily be litigated after the fact by way of an ordinary prosecution. The issue is not whether standing must be conferred to enable access to the courts, but rather whether somewhat extraordinary preventative measures should be taken.

303   However, the result in *Gouriet* has been criticized by academic writers and others,[142] and it is perhaps less than certain that it would be followed in Canada. It can be argued that even accepting the delicate nature of the jurisdiction to enjoin breaches of the criminal law, the courts are capable of exercising the discretion traditionally possessed by the Attorney-General to decide whether injunctive relief would be appropriate, and that the power of the Attorney-General to immunize without explanation cannot be justified. Parliamentary control over the Attorney-General in such matters may well be more illusory than real, and decisions affecting public rights, especially relating to the law and its enforcement, ought to be made openly and in a reasoned way. The courts are used to handling delicate matters involving public interest, and from the perspective of public trust and confidence in the administration of justice, there may be advantages in permitting the courts to act notwithstanding the Attorney-General's disinterest in particular cases.

City of Halifax (1972), 33 D.L.R. (3d) 98 (N.S.S.C. App. Div.) (adjacent property owner found to have standing to enjoin rezoning). *King v. Liquor Control Board of Ontario* (1981), 125 D.L.R. (3d) 661, 33 O.R. (2d) 816 (H.C.J.), recognizes the standing of a tavern owner for a declaration, injunction and damages on the grounds that he had been subjected to unconstitutional pricing practices. For a similar case, see *Re Strelioff and Operator of Liquor Store in Town of Inuvik* (1982), 135 D.L.R. (3d) 561 (N.W.T.S.C.).

[140] *Re Greenpeace Foundation of British Columbia and Minister of Environment* (1981), 122 D.L.R. (3d) 179 (B.C.S.C.).

[141] *Ibid.*, at p. 184, *per* Callaghan, J.

[142] Australia Law Reform Commission, *supra*, footnote 93; Feldman, "Injunctions and the Criminal Law", 42 Mod. L.R. 369 (1979); Mercer, "The Gouriet Case: Public Interest Litigation in Britain and Canada", [1979] Public Law 214; Flick, "Relator Action: The Injunction and the Enforcement of Public Rights", 5 Monash L. Rev. 133 (1978); Hartley, "Gouriet: The Constitutional Issue", 41 Mod L.R. 58 (1978).

304   On the other hand, whatever view one might take on standing generally, it is submitted that the *Gouriet*-type case presents one of the most difficult situations in which to support the individual's right to sue.[143] One might well consider it desirable as a general matter to afford liberal access to the courts where legal issues of public importance are raised, and still doubt the wisdom of letting Gouriet sue, on the basis that the criminal law aspects of these injunctions give rise to special problems. There is surely something to be said for giving the Attorney-General the power to control such applications. Courts have remarkably little control over the Attorney-General's discretion to launch criminal proceedings proper, and it is difficult to see why more control should be given in the case of applications for injunctions. Perhaps some judicial control over abusive or over-zealous commencement of proceedings is called for,[144] but it has rarely been suggested that the normal day to day, case-by-case discretion involved in ordinary criminal proceedings should be a matter for judicial intervention.[145] Although the law allows private prosecutions[146] (a much less serious matter than a preventative injunction), even there, the Attorney-General is given a general and unreviewable power of superintendence.[147]

305   The judgment to be exercised in determining whether injunctive proceedings are appropriate is a political one in the broad sense: what is the best way, given the circumstances, to ensure respect for the law? What impact will an injunction have, especially if there is a serious risk of non-compliance? Plainly, an injunction will not always be the best way to guarantee respect for the law, but the courts would be placed in an awkward position if forced to say that the activity is illegal, but that problems of enforcement render injunctive relief impolitic.

306   Given the nature and extent of remedial protection afforded by an injunction, there may be good reason to adopt more stringent standing requirements than in a situation where a non-coercive remedy

---

[143] The possibility that *Gouriet* might be restricted to criminal law injunction suits is discussed by Bogart, "Comment", 56 Can. Bar Rev. 331 (1978). In *Gouriet*, Lord Denning, M.R., relied on *Thorson*, but Lord Wilberforce said that it was "unimpressive support." See [1978] A.C. at p. 480.

[144] *Cf. Rourke v. The Queen*, [1978] 1 S.C.R. 1021, 76 D.L.R. (3d) 193.

[145] *Cf.* Davis, *Discretionary Justice: A Preliminary Inquiry* (Baton Rouge, Louisiana State University Press, 1969) pp. 222-4.

[146] See Burns, "Private Prosecutions in Canada: The Law and a Proposal for Change", 21 McGill L.J. 269 (1975).

[147] *Ibid.*, at pp. 283-5.

such as a declaration is sought. An injunction is a recognition that coercive measures may be employed to protect the plaintiff's entitlement to some specific right. While it is no longer accurate, if it ever was, to say that injunctions should be awarded only to protect property rights,[148] it is still the case that the award of an injunction does confer a property-type protection on the plaintiff.[149] While all citizens have an interest in seeing that the law is obeyed, it is difficult to see the case for conferring on all members of the public a right to have the law obeyed of the strength achieved by an injunction.[150] Because the individual possesses no "right" in the injunction sense to have the law obeyed, the plaintiff must be someone who can claim to represent the public at large. However, this argument is based on the nature of remedial protection conferred by injunctions and need not preclude individual standing where only declaratory relief is claimed. The tendency to assimilate rules for standing in declaration cases with those for injunction cases is, it is submitted, regrettable.

(5) Protection of private interests

307 The *Gouriet* rule is subject to certain exceptions. As noted above, an individual may have standing where he can show "special damage". Conceivably, the courts could interpret the vague "special damage" requirement so as to water down the effect of requiring the Attorney-General's consent. Thus, Lord Denning has suggested that had Gouriet himself alleged that he was in regular communication with South Africa he would have had sufficient standing to insist that postal facilities be kept open.[151]

308 The classic statement of the principle that an individual who suffers "special damage" may sue is that of Buckley, J., in *Boyce v. Paddington Borough Council*:

> A plaintiff can sue without joining the Attorney-General in two cases: first, where the interference with the public right is such as that some private right of his is at the same time interfered with (e.g., where an obstruction is so placed in a highway that the owner of premises abutting upon the highway is specially affected by reason that the obstruction interferes with his private right to access from and to his premises to and from the highway); and, secondly, where no private

---

[148] *Infra*, Chapter 5.

[149] This concept is discussed at greater length, *infra*, Chapters 4 and 5.

[150] See *Orpen v. Roberts*, [1925] S.C.R. 364 at p. 370, [1925] 1 D.L.R. 1101 at p. 1106, *per* Duff, J.

[151] Denning, *The Discipline of Law* (London, Butterworths, 1979), p. 143.

right is interfered with, but the plaintiff, in respect of his public right, suffers special damage peculiar to himself from the interference with the public right.[152]

309   The first category adds little in that it merely identifies situations in which a private right independently held by the plaintiff overlaps or coincides with some violation of public right. The second category, that of "special damage" is ill-defined and raises a difficult issue of substantive law.[153] Some cases have held that the plaintiff must suffer damage different in kind, and not just in degree, from that suffered by the rest of the community,[154] but this has been much criticized,[155] and other decisions appear to be more generous.[156] It has been held in Newfoundland[157] that purely consequential or economic losses do not constitute "special damage" but this appears unnecessarily restrictive, and again, other cases appear to take a more generous view.[158]

310   Most of the cases defining the scope of the "special damage" requirement have arisen in the context of public nuisance suits, and the scope afforded by the courts has often been criticized as being unduly restrictive.[159] It has been noted that "the more widespread the damage occasioned by illegality, and therefore the greater the need for an injunction to restrain the defendant, the more difficult it is for the plaintiff to establish 'special damage'. Everyone else is in the same boat."[160]

311   On the other hand, the maxim that equity had no criminal jurisdic-

---

[152] [1903] 1 Ch. 109 at p. 114, revd [1903] 2 Ch. 556 (C.A.), restd [1906] A.C. 1 (H.L.).

[153] Fridman, "The Definition of Particular Damage in Nuisance", 2 U. West. Aust. L. Rev. 490 (1951-53); Thio, *supra*, footnote 112, pp. 170-83; Estey, "Public Nuisance and Standing to Sue", 10 Osgoode Hall L.J. 563 (1972); Zamir, *The Declaratory Judgment* (London, Stevens, 1962), pp. 270-81.

[154] Estey, *supra*, footnote 153, especially at p. 568 (where this view is criticized). See also *St. Lawrence Rendering Co. v. City of Cornwall*, [1951] 4 D.L.R. 790, [1951] O.R. 669 (H.C.J.).

[155] Estey, *supra*, footnote 153; Australia Law Reform Commission, *supra*, footnote 93.

[156] See, *e.g.*, *Turtle v. City of Toronto* (1924), 56 O.L.R. 252 (S.C. App. Div.).

[157] *Hickey v. Electric Reduction Co. of Canada* (1970), 21 D.L.R. (3d) 368 (Nfld. S.C.). See also *McRae v. British Norwegian Whaling Co. Ltd.* (1929), 12 Nfld. L.R. 274.

[158] *Rainy River Navigation Co. v. Ontario & Minn. Power* (1914), 17 D.L.R. 850, 26 O.W.R. 752 (S.C. App. Div.); *Drake v. Sault Ste. Marie Pulp and Paper Co.* (1898), 25 O.A.R. 251.

[159] de Smith, *supra*, footnote 5, at p. 452.

[160] Australia Law Reform Commission, *supra*, footnote 93, at p. 18.

tion never precluded Chancery from enjoining conduct which interfered with individual rights coincidentally with the commission of some offence.[161] Similarly, where a statute merely confirms or re-enacts an existing duty or right without excluding the normal private law remedies, injunctive relief is available.[162]

312   In some situations, a statute creating an offence may be read as also conferring a private right of action on a certain individual or class of individuals, in contemplating the right of those individuals to seek on their own behalf the usual private law remedies to vindicate their rights.[163] In such cases, the standing requirement is satisfied. Although the individual is enforcing a public right, as the duty has been imposed for the benefit of persons in his situation, he has the correlative right to prevent the injury which would be occasioned by contravention of the statute.

313   An important consideration is surely the regulatory and statutory framework which accompanies the statutory prescription. The Canadian courts appear unwilling to find a civil cause of action based on a breach of statute where the "statute . . . itself provides comprehensively for remedies for its breach."[164]

314   The body of case-law dealing with the issue of whether a statute which creates an offence is to be read as permitting an individual to sue is notoriously difficult.[165] A series of recent English decisions indicates the problems in the context of injunctions. In the first, *Ex p. Island Records*,[166] the plaintiffs, a group of performers and recording companies, sued for an *Anton Piller* injunction[167] which would have had the effect of enforcing the Dramatic and Musical Performers' Protection Act, 1958, which made it an offence to record live performances without the performer's consent, punishable by up to two

---

[161] *Springhead Spinning Co. v. Riley* (1868), L.R. 6 Eq. 551; *Emperor of Austria v. Day and Kossuth* (1861), 3 De G.F. & J. 217, 45 E.R. 861.

[162] *Cooper v. Whittingham* (1880), 15 Ch. D. 501; *Stevens v. Chown*, [1901] 1 Ch. 894. In *A.-G. Can. v. Ewen* (1895), 3 B.C.R. 468 (Full Ct.), it was held that a statute making it an offence to pollute did not preclude the award of an injunction at the suit of the Attorney-General.

[163] See, *e.g., Argyll v. Argyll*, [1967] Ch. 302; *Warder v. Cooper*, [1970] 1 Ch. 495.

[164] *Board of Governors of Seneca College v. Bhadauria*, [1981] 2 S.C.R. 181 at p. 189, 124 D.L.R. (3d) 193 at p. 200, *per* Laskin, C.J.C.

[165] See Fleming, *supra*, footnote 16, at p. 122 *et seq.*; *Cutler v. Wandsworth Stadium Ltd.*, [1949] A.C. 398 (H.L.); *Orpen v. Roberts*, [1925] S.C.R. 364, [1925] 1 D.L.R. 1101; *The Queen in right of Canada v. Saskatchewan Wheat Pool* (1983), 143 D.L.R. (3d) 9 (S.C.C.).

[166] [1978] Ch. 122 (C.A.).

[167] *Supra*, §233 *et seq.*

years in prison and a fine of £20 for each copy made. There is no copyright in live performances,[168] and the decision to exclude live performances from the Copyright Act was apparently taken deliberately.[169] No one can sympathize with the defendants who were selling "bootleg" recordings and exploiting this gap in the law to profit from the talent and efforts of the plaintiffs. The Court of Appeal held, by a majority,[170] that an injunction should be awarded. Lord Denning, M.R., said that the criminal law was a "broken reed" in such cases, there being no police resources to enforce the statute and accordingly, "the courts must allow a private individual himself to bring an action against the offender — in those cases where his private rights and interests are specially affected by the breach."[171]

315   Lord Denning was prepared to give the notion of a "private right" broad meaning: "has the plaintiff a particular right which he is entitled to have protected? To this the answer which runs through all the cases is this: A man who is carrying on a lawful trade or calling has a right to be protected from any unlawful interference with it".[172]

316   However reprehensible the conduct of defendants might be, the decision to award injunctive relief raises certain difficult issues. For better or worse, Parliament failed to confer copyright protection on performances. Yet the result of granting injunctive relief is to do just that. Armed with an injunction or even the threat of an injunction, performers would be able to deal with "bootleggers," just as if they had copyright in their performances.[173] It may well be that performers should have this protection, but granting an injunction based on the offence is to obliterate a distinction drawn deliberately by the Legislature.[174]

---

[168] This was accepted by the Court of Appeal: *supra*, footnote 166, at p. 132.

[169] *Infra*, footnote 174.

[170] Lord Denning, M.R., and Waller, L.J.; Shaw, L.J., dissenting.

[171] *Supra*, footnote 166, at pp. 136-7.

[172] *Supra*, at p. 136.

[173] See *Musical Performers' Protection Ass'n, Ltd. v. British International Pictures, Ltd.* (1930), 46 T.L.R. 485 (K.B.), at p. 487, where McCardie, J., refused an injunction under the same statute, where the defendants had committed a less serious violation in failing to get a written consent before incorporating the performance in a motion picture: "If the plaintiff company are correct in their contention here, it will follow that they possess a powerful and menacing instrument of pressure against the defendants; they can impose what terms they will unless the defendants are prepared to face a heavy financial loss through being unable to let out the film."

[174] See Phillips, "Breach of Statutory Duty and Legislative Intent", 95 L.Q.R. 179 (1979), at p. 182, noting that when the bill was argued, one member "spoke passionately in favour of a civil remedy but failed to carry the day".

317   In a subsequent House of Lords decision,[175] Lord Diplock doubted the validity of the very wide proposition adopted by the majority of the Court of Appeal in the *Ex p. Island Records* case. The result could, he said, be justified "for entirely orthodox reasons. The Act was passed for the protection of a particular class of individuals, dramatic and musical performers; even the short title said so."[176] Lord Diplock expressly disagreed with the proposition: "that whenever a lawful business carried on by one individual in fact suffers damage as the consequence of a contravention by another individual of any statutory prohibition the former has a civil right of action against the latter for such damage."[177]

318   Lord Diplock also made it clear that the class of those suffering "special damage" was narrow and had to rest upon a public "right" rather than a mere "wrong":

> . . . it has first to be shown that the statute, having regard to its scope and language, does fall within that class of statutes which creates a legal right to be enjoyed by all of Her Majesty's subjects who wish to avail themselves of it. A mere prohibition upon members of the public generally from doing what it would otherwise be lawful for them to do is not enough.[178]

319   The distinction between a statute creating a right and one merely imposing a prohibition is not easy to define and seems to be but another way of asking the difficult question of whether private rights of action should be inferred from a statute creating an offence.

320   The *Lonrho* case was applied to the issue of "bootleg" recording in *R.C.A. Corp. v. Pollard*[179] where the plaintiff, a recording company with exclusive rights to the recordings of a well-known singer, sought to enjoin the defendant from "bootlegging" unauthorized recordings of that singer's performances. The claim was struck out on the basis that the recording companies were not within the class specially protected by the Act, and that the *Lonrho* case had overruled the wider proposition that an injunction can be sought to restrain any unlawful act which has the effect of diminishing the value of a contractual or property right.

321   The net result in England would appear to be that the performers themselves can still sue as being within the class specifically protected

---

[175] *Lonrho Ltd. v. Shell Petroleum Co. Ltd. (No. 2)*, [1982] A.C. 173 (H.L.).

[176] *Ibid.*, at p. 187.

[177] *Ibid.*, at p. 187.

[178] *Ibid.*, at p. 186.

[179] [1982] 3 W.L.R. 1007 (C.A.).

by the Act,[180] but that conduct prohibited by legislation cannot be enjoined by one with a merely contractual interest at stake.

322   If performers are able to sue as being those for whose benefit the statute was passed, it seems odd to deny the same right to the recording companies who, in effect, stand in the performer's shoes by reason of exclusive recording rights. The problem could be overcome by the simple procedural device of joining the performers as plaintiffs, as was done in the *Island Records* case. On the other hand, as pointed out above, the propriety of permitting even the performers to sue for injunctive relief appears dubious in light of the particular statutory context.

(6) Competitor suits

323   The special damage issue has often arisen in suits for injunctions brought by a competitor against a trade rival alleging breach of statute or failure to comply with licensing requirements. This question has hardly received the attention it deserves[181] and the authorities are divided. To the extent that the courts are prepared to grant injunctions to enforce statutory requirements, there is surely a case for saying that a competitor who is complying with the statute or regulatory scheme is not a "mere busybody" when he insists that his rival do the same.[182] Where compliance is burdensome or puts the one who obeys the law at a competitive disadvantage, that person has a genuine financial stake in seeing to it that his rival be required to comply as well. Surely nothing is more likely to lead to disrespect for the law than putting one citizen at a disadvantage because he obeys the law and then refusing him redress when he complains of his rival's breach.

324   The problem has arisen in several recent Canadian cases. In a Nova Scotia case,[183] the plaintiff sought an injunction and declaration

---

[180] Although it would appear that Lawton, L.J., felt that he was bound by the combined effect of *Ex p. Island Records* and *Lonrho* to hold that the statute did not confer a private right of action. To the same effect is *Shelley v. Cunane* (1983), 9 F.S.R. 390 (H.C.). In light of what Lord Diplock stated in *Lonrho*, quoted, *supra*, at footnote 176, it can hardly be doubted that the performer himself can sue.

[181] For a useful discussion, see Thio, *supra*, footnote 112, at pp. 195-200.

[182] *Cf. Institute of Patent Agents v. Lockwood*, [1894] A.C. 347 (H.L.), which appears to turn more on the issue of the appropriateness of injunctive relief at all than on standing.

[183] *Shore Disposal Ltd. v. Ed DeWolfe Trucking Ltd.* (1976), 72 D.L.R. (3d) 219 (N.S.S.C. App. Div.). See also *Rocca Group Ltd. v. Antigonish Optical Co. Ltd.* (1982), 131 D.L.R. (3d) 417 (N.S.S.C. App. Div.), refusing an injunction at the

to restrain a rival from violating public vehicle licensing legislation. At trial, injunctive relief was refused as the Attorney-General was not a party, but a declaration was granted. However, the Appeal Division reversed and held that not even the declaration should be awarded to the plaintiff as the licensing provisions were enacted in the public interest and were not intended to give the plaintiffs "any semi-monopolistic protection from competition in the business from other persons, licensed or unlicensed. The Act requires licensing . . . in the public interest and not for the interest or protection of the respondents or others required to be licensed."[184]

325   The fact that the enforcement of regulatory or other legal standards might restrain competition and impose additional costs on the public has been referred to in other cases.[185] It will hardly seem an acceptable answer to a law abider — especially when he merely seeks a declaration — that his insistence upon enforcement might merely allow him to charge a higher price by eliminating his illegal competitor.

---

suit of local merchants to restrain the building of a shopping centre without a proper building permit.

[184] *Shore Disposal Ltd., supra*, footnote 183, at p. 222, *per* MacKeigan, C.J.N.S.

[185] In *Law Society of Upper Canada v. Hood*, [1942] 4 D.L.R. 505, [1942] O.R. 611 sub nom. *Re Solicitors Act; Re Hood* (H.C.), Urquhart, J., enthusiastically enjoined the defendant from unauthorized practice as a solicitor, noting, at p. 509 D.L.R., pp. 615-16 O.R.: "I have practised . . . and I know that every year thousands of dollars worth of business is taken from the lawyers by real estate agents, notaries public, insurance agents and others doing the work that should be done by solicitors in the public interest." Compare, however, the comments of Schatz, J., refusing an injunction to restrain the unauthorized practice of accounting in *Public Accountants Council for Ontario v. Premier Trust Co.* (1963), 42 D.L.R. (2d) 411 at pp. 422-3, [1964] 1 O.R. 386 at pp. 397-8 (H.C.J.):

> . . . the plaintiff was established in order that there might be maintained an accountancy profession with high standards, so that the public would be properly served. This is for the benefit of the public and in the "public interest" — and not for the maintenance of this type of work as the private preserve of certain persons, and therefore, I do not consider a violation of the Act as an interference with any private rights.

In *Stockport District Waterworks Co. v. Corp. of Manchester* (1862), 9 Jur. N.S. 266 (Ch.), at p. 267, Westbury, L.C., refused a competitor standing to enjoin the defendant from exceeding its powers in drawing and selling water: "The plaintiffs, in point of fact, would, if they succeeded, have this consequence secured to them, that their own trade might possibly be benefited at the expense of their competitor. The people of Stockport might incur a very serious loss, because there would be a monopoly established in one company . . . ". See also *Pudsey Coal Gas Co. v. Corp. of Bradford* (1873), L.R. 15 Eq. 167; *Seafarer's Int'l Union of Canada v. Baltic Shipping Co.* (1975), 61 D.L.R. (3d) 530 (F.C.T.D.), where Walsh, J., refused to grant an interlocutory injunction restraining the defendants from transporting pas-

326   While standing has been refused in other Canadian cases,[186] there are also decisions favourable to the standing of competitors, although the issues have hardly been explored in depth. An Ontario court granted an interlocutory injunction to a cable television operator restraining a non-licensed rival from operating without a C.R.T.C. licence, in breach of the Broadcasting Act:

> . . . by operating without a licence the defendant . . . is interfering with the right of the plaintiffs to carry on their legitimate enterprises and they are suffering direct damage if the defendants or either of them have no right to operate without a CRTC licence.[187]

Similarly, the Manitoba Court of Appeal held that a competitor had standing to sue for a declaration and injunction restraining his rival from operating a transport facility in breach of an order of the provincial Highway Board on the grounds that "the applicants, who have a vital interest in the extent of [the respondent's] authority, because of the effect of competition . . . have the necessary status to invoke the Court's intervention."[188] In another Manitoba case, a licensed commercial airline successfully sued for an injunction to restrain the operations of unlicensed competition.[189]

---

sengers within Canada contrary to the Canada Shipping Act, s. 663, at the suit of the plaintiff union which asserted its members would lose employment opportunities, but also held that the action should not be struck out but allowed to go to trial.

[186] See also *Public Accountants Council for Ontario v. Premier Trust Co., supra*, footnote 185; *Inst. Chartered Accountants of Man. v. Bellamy*, [1926] 4 D.L.R. 230 (Man. K.B.), affd [1927] 3 D.L.R. 1071 (C.A.); *Moose Jaw Merchandisers v. Westport Enterprises Ltd.* (1971), 23 D.L.R. (3d) 21 (Sask. Q.B.). See also *Rothmans of Pall Mall Canada Ltd. v. M.N.R. (No. 1)*, [1976] 2 F.C. 500 at p. 510 (C.A.). There is also Australian authority refusing standing to competitors: *Californian Theatres Pty. Ltd. v. Hoyts County Theatres Ltd.* (1959), 59 S.R. (N.S.W.) 188 (S.C.); *Helicopter Utilities Pty. Ltd. v. Australian National Airline Com'n*, [1962] N.S.W.R. 747 (S.C.); *Grand Central Car Park Pty. Ltd. v. Tivoli Freeholders*, [1969] V.R. 62 (S.C.). See also *Beck v. Porter* (1980), 32 A.L.R. 428 (S.C.), denying an injunction in favour of one election candidate to restrain another candidate's violation of electoral law.

[187] *Terra Communications Ltd. v. Communicomp Data Ltd.* (1973), 41 D.L.R. (3d) 350 at p. 364, 1 O.R. (2d) 682 at p. 696 (H.C.J.), *per* Lerner, J.

[188] *Re Swan River — The Pas Transfer Ltd.* (1974), 51 D.L.R. (3d) 292 (Man. C.A.), at p. 302. See also *Re I. Peters Transport Ltd. and Motor Transport Board of Manitoba* (1981), 128 D.L.R. (3d) 529 (Man. C.A.), allowing a competitor to intervene in an appeal from a declaratory judgment as to the scope of a licence.

[189] *St. Andrews Airways Ltd. v. Anishenineo Piminagan Inc.* (1977), 80 D.L.R. (3d) 645 (Man. Q.B.). See also *Lambair Ltd. v. Aero Trades (Western) Ltd.* (1978), 87 D.L.R. (3d) 500 (Man. C.A.), leave to appeal to S.C.C. refused October 4, 1978; *New Brunswick Power Co. v. Maritime Transit Ltd.*, [1937] 4 D.L.R. 376 (N.B.S.C.), and *Toronto Transit Com'n v. Aqua Taxi Ltd.*, (1956), 6 D.L.R. (2d) 721, [1957] O.W.N. 65 (H.C.J.), granting injunctions to protect exclusive franchises.

327   A decision of the New Brunswick Appeal Division granted an injunction against an unlicensed rival to the holder of an exclusive licence to operate a bus service, and expressly rejected the argument that the Attorney-General needed to be joined as a party.[190] In another New Brunswick case,[191] an injunction was awarded at the suit of a trucking licence holder to restrain the activities of a non-licensed rival.

328   Many competitor suits have been brought with the Attorney-General's consent.[192] The leading case for the proposition that the Attorney-General's discretion is unassailable was one in which a competitor was the relator.[193] The defendant questioned the Attorney-General's reason for agreeing to lend his name, and the holding that the discretion could not be reviewed in fact allowed the action to go ahead. In another relator action, Sellers, L.J., observed that "[t]he matter becomes no more favourable when it is shown that by so defying the law the offender is reaping an advantage over his competitors who are complying with it."[194] It may be that the Attorney-General usually will consent to relator proceedings, but the number of reported cases in which the standing of a trade rival has been at issue suggests that this is not the case.

329   It is perhaps unnecessary to reiterate the special problems posed by claims for injunctions to enforce penal or regulatory offences. It is submitted that once the decision is made to abandon the traditional position and make injunctive relief available to enforce statutory prescriptions, then it seems incongruous to deny standing to a competitor on the basis that he lacks sufficient interest.

330   However, in some cases, licensing requirements are part of a complex regulatory scheme and the timing and methods of enforcement may require a sensitive balancing of interests by the agency charged with responsibility for the overall scheme.[195] In such cases it may be

---

[190] *Arseneau v. LeBlanc* (1952), 45 M.P.R. 173 (N.B.S.C. App. Div.).

[191] *S.M.T. (Eastern) Ltd. v. Ruch*, [1940] 1 D.L.R. 190 (N.B.S.C.).

[192] See, *e.g.*, *A.-G. v. Premier Line Ltd.*, [1932] 1 Ch. 303; *A.-G. v. Harris*, [1961] 1 Q.B. 74 (C.A.); *London County Council v. A.-G.*, [1902] A.C. 165 (H.L.); *A.-G. v. Niagara Falls International Bridge Co.* (1873), 20 Gr. 34.

[193] *London County Council v. A.-G.*, *supra*, footnote 192.

[194] *A.-G. v. Harris*, *supra*, footnote 192, at p. 86. See also *A.-G. v. Chaudry*, [1971] 3 All E.R. 938 (C.A.); *Stafford Borough Council v. Elkenford*, [1977] 2 All E.R. 519 (C.A.); *A.-G. v. Ely, Haddenham & Sutton Ry. Co.* (1869), L.R. 4 Ch. App. 194. Compare, however, *A.-G. v. Sheffield Gas Consumers Co.* (1853), 3 De G.M. & G. 304, 43 E.R. 119; *A.-G. v. Cambridge Consumers Gas Co.* (1868), L.R. 4 Ch. App. 71.

[195] *Infra*, §§344-348.

undesirable for the courts to pre-empt or ignore the decision of the agency with respect to enforcement, and a *mandamus* or injunction directed to the agency forcing it to consider or reconsider the matter may be preferable to the blunter solution of an injunction directed against the competitor.

5. Injunctions and Judicial Review

(1) Introduction

331   In Ontario,[196] British Columbia[197] and under the Federal Court Act,[198] the prerogative writs have been replaced by a statutory form of judicial review which assimilates the prerogative remedies with actions for declarations and injunctions. In those jurisdictions, reference may still be had to the jurisdiction formerly exercised with respect to each separate remedy, but a single form of statutory review makes the choice of one particular remedy or another insignificant.

332   However, it may still be of interest in those jurisdictions, and certainly of interest in other jurisdictions, briefly to consider the role played by injunctions in judicial review. It should be noted at the outset that injunctions may often provide a vehicle whereby an administrative or *quasi*-judicial order may be attacked collaterally. Where enforcement of a regulation, order or decision impinges upon some right of the plaintiff's, enforcement can be justified only if the administrative measure was validly made. Injunctions have often been granted to restrain the enforcement of invalid orders,[199] although the form the action takes is not judicial review but rather the protection of the particular right asserted by the plaintiff.

(2) Mandatory injunctions and mandamus

333   Where the plaintiff seeks to compel the performance of some posi-

---

[196] Judicial Review Procedure Act (Ont.).

[197] Judicial Review Procedure Act (B.C.).

[198] Under the Federal Court Act, separate proceedings, however, are normally required, as an injunction is ordinarily obtained in an action while the other remedies are obtained upon motion: *Re Dantex Woollen Co. Inc. and Minister of Industry, Trade and Commerce*, [1979] 2 F.C. 585, 100 D.L.R. (3d) 436 (T.D.), appeal quashed F.C. *loc. cit.* p. 598, D.L.R. *loc. cit.* p. 446*n* (C.A.).

[199] See, *e.g.*, *Gyle-Thompson v. Wall Street (Properties) Ltd.*, [1974] 1 W.L.R. 123 (Ch.); *Broadbent v. Rotherham Corp.*, [1917] 2 Ch. 31; *Greek Catholic Church v. McKinnon* (1916), 28 D.L.R. 509 (Alta. S.C.); *Hill v. Lethbridge Municipal District Council No. 25* (1955), 14 W.W.R. 577 (Alta. S.C.).

tive duty, there are, theoretically at least, three possible remedies: the prerogative writ of *mandamus*, the common law action for *mandamus*, or a mandatory injunction. The technical distinction and historical origins of these three remedies are clear,[200] but the lines of demarcation determining which is appropriate are hazy.[201] However, the question appears to give little cause for concern in practice. The common law action for *mandamus*, first made possible by the Common Law Procedure Act, 1854,[202] is now rarely employed.[203] It was confined to situations in which the plaintiff sought to enforce some private right,[204] and after the Judicature Acts, the principles upon which it was awarded were assimilated with those governing the award of mandatory injunctions.[205] Both are granted in an ordinary

---

[200] The origin and use of the common law action for *mandamus* are traced in *Rich v. Melancthon Board of Health* (1912), 2 D.L.R. 866 at pp. 868-71, 26 O.L.R. 48 at pp. 51-4 (Div. Ct.), *per* Middleton, J. See also *Glossop v. Heston and Isleworth Local Board* (1879), 12 Ch. D. 102 (C.A.).

[201] For a discussion of the distinction between the common law action for *mandamus* and the prerogative writ of *mandamus*, see de Smith, *Judicial Review of Administrative Action* (London, Stevens & Sons, 1959), at pp. 425-8.

[202] S. 68.

[203] It is described as "obsolete" in de Smith, *supra*, footnote 5, at p. 442. For examples see *Fotherby v. Metropolitan Ry. Co.* (1866), L.R. 2 C.P. 188 at p. 194 (requiring sheriff to summon jury to assess land for purpose of expropriation); *Young v. Erie & Huron Ry. Co.* (1896), 27 O.R. 530 (H.C.J.) (requiring construction of fences in compliance with statutory duty); *Graham & Strang v. Dominion Express Co.* (1920), 55 D.L.R. 39, 48 O.L.R. 83 (H.C.) (enforcing common law right to have common carrier accept goods for transportation). For a collection of cases, see Holmested & Gale, *Ontario Judicature Act and Rules of Practice*, vol. 1, s. 19, §§42-60. In *Re Morris and Morris* (1973), 42 D.L.R. (3d) 550 (Man. C.A.), leave to appeal to S.C.C. granted 51 D.L.R. (3d) 77*n*, the order sought was described as a *mandamus* but would appear to have been a mandatory injunction.

[204] The common law action of *mandamus* was not, however, available to enforce "the fulfilment of duties arising merely from a personal contract": *Benson v. Paull* (1856), 6 El. & Bl. 273 at p. 275, 119 E.R. 865, *per* Campbell, C.J. *Cf. Norris v. Irish Land Co.* (1857), 8 El. & Bl. 512, 120 E.R. 191; *Re Stratford & Huron Ry. Co. and Corp. of County of Perth* (1876), 38 U.C.Q.B. 112 at p. 158; *Grand Junction Ry. Co. v. Corp. of County of Peterborough* (1883), 8 S.C.R. 76 at pp. 122-4.

[205] *Rich v. Melancthon Board of Health, supra*, footnote 200, at p. 870 D.L.R., pp. 53-4 O.L.R., *per* Middleton, J.: "the great weight of modern authority is in favour of the view I have indicated, that the mandamus which may be awarded in an action is either in the nature of the old equitable mandatory injunction, or is merely ancillary to the enforcement of a legal right for which an action might be maintained at law." See also *Re Rowe and Harris*, [1928] 4 D.L.R. 951 at p. 953, 63 O.L.R. 163 at p. 166 (S.C. App. Div.), *per* Orde, J.A.: "The mandatory order is no more than a species of injunction"; *Davies v. Gas Light & Coke Co.*, [1909] 1 Ch. 708 (C.A.); *Cummings v. Corp. of Town of Dundas* (1907), 13 O.L.R. 384 at p. 395 (Div. Ct.); *City of Kingston v. Kingston, Portsmouth & Cataraqui Electric Ry. Co.* (1898), 25 O.A.R. 462 at p. 466; *The King v. Ottawa Electric Ry. Co.*, [1933] 1 D.L.R. 695, [1933] O.W.N. 219 (H.C.J.).

action, and there would appear to be no reason to distinguish them apart from their different historical origins. There would appear to be nothing common law *mandamus* can achieve which cannot also be achieved through one of the other remedies.

334   The extent of overlap between an injunction and a prerogative order of *mandamus* is less clear. As already noted, in some jurisdictions legislation assimilates the remedy of injunction along with prerogative writs so that either or both can be claimed in a single proceeding. In other jurisdictions, it will often be possible to sue for either remedy, although not in the same proceeding, since an injunction is usually awarded in an action while an application for a prerogative order is made by way of motion.

335   Mandatory injunctions have often been granted to enforce rights in the public law context. The English Court of Appeal awarded an injunction restraining the British Railways Board from discontinuing a service where it had failed to observe certain statutory procedures.[206] Similarly, injunctions have been granted restraining local education authorities from closing or ceasing to maintain schools where statutory procedures have not been followed,[207] or from failing to provide schooling on terms required by statute.[208]

336   However, an injunction will be granted only where standing requirements are met,[209] and although there seems to be no reason in principle to make the distinction, standing rules applying to injunctions appear to be narrower than those applicable to *mandamus*.[210] Certainly the prerogative writ of *mandamus* is the more usual remedy and there are, perhaps, several factors which explain this. Doubts regarding injunctions against the Crown or Crown servants[211] may have stifled the development of the mandatory injunction in the public law area. As well, the caution often expressed by the courts

---

[206] *Warwickshire County Council v. British Railways Board*, [1969] 1 W.L.R. 1117 (C.A.). See also *Birmingham & Midland Motor Omnibus Co. v. Worcestershire County Council*, [1967] 1 W.L.R. 409 (C.A.), restraining the closure of a road.

[207] *Bradbury v. Enfield London Borough Council*, [1967] 1 W.L.R. 1311 (C.A.); *Legg v. Inner London Education Authority*, [1972] 1 W.L.R. 1245 (Ch.); *Wilford v. County Council of West Riding of Yorkshire*, [1908] 1 K.B. 685 (restraining conversion of a school from one type to another). *Cf. Coney v. Choyce*, [1975] 1 W.L.R. 422 (Ch.); *Meade v. Haringey London Borough Council*, [1979] 1 W.L.R. 637 (C.A.); *Wood v. Ealing London Borough Council*, [1967] Ch. 364, refusing such relief on the merits.

[208] *Inkster v. Minitonka School District* (1912), 6 D.L.R. 57 (Man. K.B.).

[209] *Supra*, §290 *et seq.*

[210] See de Smith, *supra*, footnote 5, at pp. 550-3.

[211] *Infra*, §349 *et seq.*

when granting mandatory relief in the form of an injunction[212] has not been reflected to nearly the same extent where the plaintiff claims the prerogative remedy.

(3) Injunctions and prohibition

337   A prohibitive injunction could have the same effect as an order of prohibition, although the technical nature of the order would be quite different. A writ of prohibition issues to the inferior court in the name of the Sovereign and restrains it from pursuing certain action.[213] An injunction merely orders a party to the challenged proceedings to refrain from presenting or prosecuting his case.[214] The "common" injunction, forbidding a party from proceeding with his case in the courts of law, was once a familiar aspect of equitable jurisprudence and operated on this principle.[215]

338   Lord Denning has asserted that "the court has power to intervene by declaration and injunction in the case of statutory tribunals just as it has in domestic tribunals, and I do not think that we should admit of any doubt upon it."[216] While declarations are often granted in actions challenging the validity of decisions of inferior tribunals where *certiorari* might have been granted,[217] injunctions are rarely sought in place of the more usual prerogative writ of prohibition. However, this would appear to be a matter of habit rather than principle.

339   Shortly after the enactment of the Judicature Act, it was held that where the plaintiff had commenced an action restraining trespass and waste, alleging that improper notice had been given in land drainage proceedings, an injunction could issue in place of prohibition to restrain further proceedings before the magistrates.[218] Denying an injunction would require a separate proceeding, and Jessel, M.R., held that this was to be avoided:

> If I can grant a prohibition I can of course grant an injunction between the parties.

· · · · ·

---

[212] *Supra*, §50 *et seq.*; *Dowty Boulton Paul Ltd. v. Wolverhampton Corp.*, [1971] 2 All E.R. 277 (Ch.).

[213] See de Smith, *supra*, footnote 5, at pp. 590-1.

[214] *Infra*, §§446, 447.

[215] *Ibid.*

[216] *Barnard v. National Dock Labour Board*, [1953] 2 Q.B. 18 (C.A.), at p. 42.

[217] See de Smith, *supra*, footnote 5, Chapter 10.

[218] *Hedley v. Bates* (1880), 13 Ch. D. 498.

Now, if I have the power to grant prohibition in a particular case, it certainly is "just and convenient" to arrive at the same result by granting an injunction *inter partes*, instead of creating the great expense of granting a writ of prohibition against the magistrates.[219]

340 An injunction would be an attractive alternative, then, where the plaintiff joins his claim to have inferior proceedings stopped with a request for some other relief, such as damages, available only in an action. If an injunction is available in such a case, there seems no reason in principle why it should not always be available as an alternative to prohibition. In de Smith, it is argued that this is the case,[220] although in a later decision,[221] Jessel, M.R., did suggest that injunctions should not replace the remedy of prohibition. At one time, the Canadian courts appeared unwilling to grant injunctions in place of the prerogative writ of prohibition,[222] but the Saskatchewan Court of Appeal has quite properly held that a more liberal approach is to be preferred:

If a situation, for example, warrants the grant of an order for prohibition to restrain an act, it can hardly be unjust to grant an injunction to restrain the same act. From the standpoint of convenience and practicality, it is no less convenient or practical and, in many cases, may indeed be more convenient and practical. Injunctive relief, for example, obviates the need to observe the strict differentiation between judicial and *quasi*-judicial acts on one hand and administrative acts on the other.

The adoption, in this day, of the strict approach would signal an un-

---

[219] *Ibid.*, at p. 502.

[220] *Supra*, footnote 5, at pp. 471-3.

[221] *Stannard v. Vestry of St. Giles, Camberwell* (1882), 20 Ch. D. 190 (C.A.), at p. 197, *per* Jessel, M.R.: "It is a mere case of prohibition, and there is no reason for changing the mode of proceeding from prohibition to injunction where you are not compelled to decide the question on other grounds between the same parties". See also *Kerr v. Corp. of Preston* (1876), 6 Ch. D. 463, refusing to follow *Lord Auckland v. Westminster Local Board of Works* (1872), L.R. 7 Ch. App. 597, discussed, *infra*. Compare *Williams v. Deptford Urban District Council* (1924), 41 T.L.R. 47 at p. 48. See also *Land Com'r v. Pillai*, [1960] A.C. 854 (P.C.), at p. 882, suggesting that if *certiorari* is available, an injunction is inappropriate.

[222] *Hollinger Bus Lines Ltd. v. Ontario Labour Relations Board*, [1951] 4 D.L.R. 47, [1951] O.R. 562 (H.C.J.), affd [1952] 3 D.L.R. 162, [1952] O.R. 366 (C.A.), the effect of which has been superseded by legislation, *supra*, footnote 196. In *R. v. British Broadcasting Corp., ex p. Lavelle*, [1983] 1 W.L.R. 23 (Q.B.), it was held that domestic tribunals were not amenable to the prerogative writs but that declaration and injunctions were the appropriate remedies. See also *Johnson v. Hall* (1957), 10 D.L.R. (2d) 243 (B.C.S.C.); *Bimson v. Johnston* (1958), 12 D.L.R. (2d) 379, [1958] O.W.N. 217 (C.A.); *Kennedy v. Gillis* (1961), 30 D.L.R. (2d) 82, [1961] O.R. 878 (H.C.J.).

bending and blind adherence to tradition, labels and form, with little heed to the changing needs of society, to merit and substance.[223] Injunctions have in fact been awarded to restrain proceedings in several cases on the grounds of lack of jurisdiction,[224] and are regularly used in place of prohibition where the validity of proceedings before domestic tribunals is at issue.[225]

341   Injunctions may also be available to restrain purely administrative measures not susceptible to review by way of prerogative writ.[226] For example, injunctions are said to be available with respect to purely investigatory proceedings[227] for which *certiorari* or prohibition are often thought not to be available. The reported cases are inconclusive, as relief has almost invariably been refused on the merits.[228] However, as already noted, there is no doubt that an injunction is available to restrain the execution of an order vitiated by procedural or jurisdictional defect where its execution would thereby infringe the plaintiff's rights.[229]

---

[223] *City of Regina v. Regina City Policemen's Ass'n* (1982), 131 D.L.R. (3d) 496 (Sask. C.A.), at pp. 499-500, *per* Bayda, J.A.

[224] *Lord Auckland v. Westminster Local Board of Works, supra,* footnote 221; *St. James's Hall Ltd. v. London County Council* (1900), 83 L.T. 98 (C.A.). See also *Leeson v. General Council of Medical Education and Registration* (1889), 43 Ch. D. 366 (C.A.), and *Allinson v. General Council of Medical Education and Registration,* (1894) 1 Q.B. 750 (C.A.), where injunctions were refused on the merits; *Vancouver-Seattle Bus Lines Ltd. v. L.-G. in Council for Province of British Columbia* (1963), 42 D.L.R. (2d) 82 (B.C.S.C.) (refusing an injunction on the merits); *Community Health Services Ass'n (Saskatoon) Ltd. v. College of Physicians and Surgeons (Sask.)* (1966), 57 D.L.R. (2d) 71 (Sask. Q.B.).

[225] *Andrews v. Mitchell,* [1905] A.C. 78 (H.L.).

[226] *Freeman v. Farm Products Marketing Board* (1958), 15 D.L.R. (2d) 287, [1958] O.R. 349 (H.C.J.), restraining the defendant Board from exceeding its powers in purporting to limit voting rights of producers on a proposed marketing scheme.

[227] See, *e.g., R. v. Bates, ex p. Meaford General Hospital* (1970), 17 D.L.R. (3d) 641, [1971] 2 O.R. 305 (C.A.). It would appear that an injunction may be awarded to restrain inspectors appointed under legislation relating to companies: see *Maxwell v. Department of Trade and Industry,* [1974] Q.B. 523 (C.A.); *Norwest Holst Ltd. v. Secretary of State for Trade,* [1978] Ch. 201 (C.A.).

[228] *St. John v. Fraser,* [1935] S.C.R. 441, [1935] 3 D.L.R. 465; *Advance Glass & Mirror Co. v. A.-G. Can.,* [1950] 1 D.L.R. 488, [1949] O.W.N. 451 (H.C.J.); both seem to accept the appropriateness of an injunction if an excess of jurisdiction can be shown, but refuse relief on the merits. For other cases, see *Lane v. City of Toronto* (1904), 71 O.L.R. 423 (H.C.J.); *Chambers v. Winchester* (1907), 15 O.L.R. 316 (H.C.J.); *Calgary Power Ltd. v. Copithorne,* [1959] S.C.R. 24, 16 D.L.R. (2d) 241; *Guay v. Lafleur,* [1965] S.C.R. 12, 47 D.L.R. (2d) 226; *Meeson v. Etobicoke Board of Education* (1967), 61 D.L.R. (2d) 650, [1967] 1 O.R. 595 (C.A.). An injunction was granted in *B.C. Packers Ltd. v. Smith, MacDonald and A.-G. Can.,* [1961] O.R. 596 (H.C.J.), but see *Canadian Fishing Co. Ltd. v. Smith,* [1962] S.C.R. 294, 32 D.L.R. (2d) 641.

[229] *Supra,* §332. See also *Canadian Javelin Ltd. v. Sparling* (1978), 91 D.L.R. (3d) 64

342   The courts have resisted attempts to supersede the legitimate exercise of jurisdiction of inferior bodies through actions for injunctions alleging a threat to the plaintiff's property interests.[230] If a statute specifies a mode of procedure which may result in an order affecting the plaintiff's rights or property, so long as the inferior body acts within its jurisdiction and respects the rules of natural justice, obviously an injunction should be no more available than any other remedy for judicial review.

343   As noted in Chapter 5, injunctions are granted to restrain threatened vexatious proceedings which would constitute an abuse of process, and may, as well, be granted to restrain a party from taking or prosecuting proceedings in inferior tribunals on similar grounds.[231]

6. Administrative Boards and Injunctions

344   In many areas, injunctive relief from the courts may be inappropriate because jurisdiction has been specially assigned to an administrative board or tribunal. Often that assignment of jurisdiction will include the power to make restraining orders very similar to injunctions, although there are constitutional limits on the extent to which Parliament or a Legislature may assign jurisdiction to award injunctive relief proper.[232]

345   There can hardly be said to be any settled body of jurisprudence on the attitude of the courts when asked to grant injunctive relief in respect of a matter subject to some specific regulatory or administrative scheme. Adequate analysis of the issue would require extensive consideration of the relationship between administrative and judicial remedies. In general, however, it would appear that the courts have

---

(Fed. C.A.), leave to appeal to S.C.C. refused 24 N.R. 571*n*, assuming jurisdiction to restrain by injunction the unauthorized seizure and disclosure of documents in a Restrictive Trade Practices Commission inquiry.

[230] See, *e.g.*, *Merrick v. Liverpool Corp.*, [1910] 2 Ch. 449; *Grand Junction Waterworks Co. v. Hampton Urban District Council*, [1898] 2 Ch. 331. de Smith, *supra*, footnote 5, suggests at p. 473 that there may also be jurisdiction to restrain the institution or continuance of proceedings within the jurisdiction of the tribunal.

[231] *Infra*, §§480, 481. *Cf. McFetridge v. Nova Scotia Barristers' Society* (1981), 123 D.L.R. (3d) 475 (N.S.S.C. App. Div.), holding that an injunction to stay proceedings challenged by way of judicial review should be granted only in exceptional circumstances, where an adjournment has been refused and the consequences of not staying would be serious and irreversible.

[232] *Tomko v. N.S. Labour Relations Board*, [1977] 1 S.C.R. 112, 69 D.L.R. (3d) 250; *Reference re Residential Tenancies Act*, [1981] 1 S.C.R. 714, 123 D.L.R. (3d) 554; *cf. Reference re Proposed Legislation Concerning Leased Premises and Tenancy Agreements* (1978), 89 D.L.R. (3d) 460 (Alta. S.C. App. Div.) (improper to confer jurisdiction to order specific performance of tenancy agreement on board).

quite properly tended to avoid granting injunctions which would pre-empt the exercise of jurisdiction by a specialized board, tribunal or agency unless the administrative remedy will fail to meet the needs of the case. Thus, in some cases injunctions have been granted where necessary to protect legal rights which might otherwise be lost because of delay or inappropriateness of the administrative remedy.[233] On the other hand, deference has been shown by the courts to the specialized expertise and procedures of various administrative agencies, and where the interest the plaintiff seeks to protect falls squarely within that competence, and some non-judicial remedy is available to protect the right, the courts have tended to refuse injunctive relief.[234] In some cases, the courts have gone even farther, and denied interlocutory relief in circumstances where no provisional remedy was available from the board.[235]

346 Although addressed to the constitutional issue of the limits of a province's ability to confer jurisdiction on a labour board to issue cease and desist orders in relation to illegal work stoppages, the following comments of Laskin, C.J.C., indicate judicial recognition of the advantages of respect for the remedial authority of administrative agencies in certain circumstances:

> What is significant about the provision for a cease and desist order obtainable from the Board or, in the construction industry, from the special panel for that industry, is that it makes allowance for efforts at settlement before or after the making of an interim cease and desist order. The fluidity and the volatility of labour relations issues must be counted as weighing heavily with the Legislature in providing this al-

---

[233] See, *e.g.*, *Daily Mirror Newspapers Ltd. v. Gardner*, [1968] 2 Q.B. 762 (C.A.); *Brekkes Ltd. v. Cattel*, [1972] Ch. 105; *Stein v. City of Winnipeg* (1974), 48 D.L.R. (3d) 223 (Man. C.A.); *Hayward v. East London Waterworks Co.* (1884), 28 Ch. D. 138. As seen above, the fact that a statute provides for penalties on conviction in a summary jurisdiction court has not precluded the award of injunctive relief where standing requirements have been met.

[234] *Infra*, footnotes 235, 237-240; *City of Lethbridge v. Canadian Western Natural Gas, Light, Heat & Power Co., Ltd.*, [1923] S.C.R. 652, [1923] 4 D.L.R. 1055; *Jain v. North & West Vancouver Hospital Society* (1974), 43 D.L.R. (3d) 291 (B.C.S.C.) (interlocutory injunction refused where plaintiff failed to exhaust internal appeal procedures). Refusal to grant injunctive relief, at the suit of a competitor who complains that his rival has failed to comply with a regulatory requirement, is sometimes put on the basis that jurisdiction to prosecute has been specially assigned to the agency or to the summary conviction court where a penalty is provided for: see, *e.g.*, *Shore Disposal Ltd. v. Ed DeWolfe Trucking Ltd.* (1976), 72 D.L.R. (3d) 219 (N.S.S.C. App. Div.); *Rocca Group Ltd. v. Antigonish Optical Co. Ltd.* (1982), 131 D.L.R. (3d) 417 (N.S.S.C. App. Div.).

[235] *Stevenson v. Air Canada* (1982), 132 D.L.R. (3d) 406, 35 O.R. (2d) 68 (Div. Ct.), discussed, *infra*, §586.

ternative means of seeking an accommodation between employers and trade unions under the superintendence of the Board or its special division and with the assistance of the Department of Labour, an accommodation that puts to one side the alternative routes of prosecution and Court injunction. The policy considerations are evident, and in pursuit thereof the mechanism of a cease and desist order to restore the lawful *status quo ante* seems to me to be a rational way of dealing administratively with a rupture of peaceful labour relations.

The Labour Relations Board or the Construction Industry Panel does not approach the issue of a cease and desist order in the same way that a Court approaches the issue of an injunction. Unlike a Court, the Board or Panel makes its own investigation of the issues raised by a complaint and decides for itself on its own findings whether an interim order should issue; and it is required to do so irrespective of any balance of convenience once it is satisfied that there is an unlawful work stoppage. The Board or Panel is involved in continuous supervision directed to achieving a settlement, if it can, and this is something which ordinarily militates against the issue of an injunction by a Court.[236]

347   Another example is provided in a recent Ontario case[237] where the plaintiff, itself bidding for control of the target company, sought an interlocutory injunction to restrain the defendants from carrying out or facilitating a rival take-over bid. Both the plaintiff's and defendant's bids had been subject to the scrutiny of the Ontario Securities Commission. In refusing injunctive relief, Reid, J., made explicit reference to "the Court's reluctance to interfere with things the Court regards as lying within the proper ambit of the Securities Commission's responsibility and, of course, its supervisory power."[238] Reid, J., went on to explain the advantages of leaving the matter to be dealt with by the Commission:

It has a broad mandate to represent the interests of the public. In that way shareholders in a contest such as this are represented. It has extensive means to ensure that the provisions of the Act in relation to disclosure are complied with.

. . . . .

It seems to me that the Commission is better fitted by its jurisdiction, its nature and its expertise to maintain a watchdog type of supervision over the required level of disclosure in this kind of contest than is the Court. It is more flexible both in its ability to receive and deal with complaints and in the manner in which it can deal with com-

---

[236] *Tomko v. N.S. Labour Relations Board, supra*, footnote 232, at p. 257.

[237] *First City Financial Corp. Ltd. v. Genstar Corp.* (1981), 125 D.L.R. (3d) 303, 33 O.R. (2d) 631 (H.C.J.).

[238] *Ibid.*, at p. 314 D.L.R., p. 641 O.R.

plaints. If disclosure is insufficient in the opinion of the Commission, it is not caught in the "yes" or "no" situation that the Court is by reason of its nature and its jurisdiction. In the Court the application can result only in the issue of an injunction or the refusal to issue an injunction. The issue of an injunction would destroy the offer. The failure to issue an injunction could amount to permitting an offer to continue that is defective in terms of the *Securities Act*.

. . . . .

It is not open to the Judge on an application for an interlocutory injunction to suggest to a party that unless that party make further disclosure an order will issue. That is entirely contrary to the essential nature of an interlocutory application. The Court must act immediately. It cannot withhold action nor threaten to take action. An interlocutory application for an injunction is thus a win or lose proposition with no intermediate possibilities.[239]

348   In several cases,[240] injunctive relief has been refused where the plaintiff has already commenced proceedings before an administrative tribunal on the grounds that by so doing, he has elected that avenue of redress, and is disentitled to judicial relief, at least until he has exhausted the possibility of obtaining the administrative remedy.

7. Injunctions Against the Crown and Crown Servants

349   Suits for injunction against the Crown, government departments or Crown servants require consideration of the rules relating to governmental immunity.[241] In all Canadian jurisdictions, legislation now

---

[239] *Ibid.*, at pp. 315-8 D.L.R., pp. 643-5 O.R. See also the following passage from *Forefront Consolidated Explorations Ltd. v. Lumsden Building Corp. Inc.*, summarized in [1979] 1 A.C.W.S. 9 (Ont. H.C.J.), *per* Anderson, J.:

> Where sophisticated legislation of this type is in existence, together with a body skilled in its administration as is the Commission, courts have been careful to consider whether the interjection of traditional remedies was necessary or desirable. A wide degree of latitude in the exercise of jurisdiction has been accorded bodies such as the Commission. By parity of reasoning it seems to me that the court should in such circumstances be slow to intervene with a remedy which the legislation does not provide, and that a motion for interlocutory injunction, summary in its nature as in its result, is not the time for such intervention.

See also *Royal Trustco Ltd. v. Campeau Corp.* (1980), 31 O.R. (2d) 75 (H.C.J.), affd *loc. cit.* p. 130 (C.A.).

[240] *New Brunswick Telephone Co. Ltd. v. Relph* (1979), 107 D.L.R. (3d) 727 (N.B.C.A.); *Benincasa v. Ballentine* (1978), 7 C.P.C. 81 (Ont. H.C.J.); *Cummings v. Hydro-Electric Power Com'n of Ontario* (1965), 54 D.L.R. (2d) 583, [1966] 1 O.R. 605 (H.C.J.). An agreement to arbitrate has been held to preclude injunctive relief until the disputed provisions of a collective agreement have been interpreted by arbitration; *Re York University Faculty Ass'n and Board of Governors of York University* (1979), 106 D.L.R. (3d) 692, 27 O.R. (2d) 507 (Div. Ct.).

[241] See Hogg, *Liability of the Crown in Australia and New Zealand* (Melbourne, Law Book Co., 1971); Strayer, "Injunctions against Crown Officers", 42 Can. Bar Rev. 1 (1964).

puts the Crown, for the most part, on an equal footing with private litigants.[242] The procedure by way of petition of right has been abolished, and the Crown and Crown servants are subject to ordinary process. There remain, however, questions as to the availability of injunctive relief. All provinces now have legislation which governs the availability of injunctive relief against Crown and Crown servants,[243] but there is no such provision in the federal legislation. The position at common law is still important with respect to suits against the Crown in right of Canada where legislation makes no specific provision, and as will be seen, the provincial legislation can only be understood against the background of common law.

350 It is generally accepted that at common law an injunction cannot issue against the Crown itself.[244] Several reasons have been given for the inappropriateness of injunctive relief against the Crown. It has been said that as the court itself is an emanation of the Crown, it would be incongruous for the court to purport to control the Crown, and that no means could be found to enforce such an injunction.[245] However, in one Canadian case,[246] the Manitoba Court of Appeal departed from this doctrine and upheld an interlocutory injunction to

---

[242] Proceedings Against the Crown Act (Alta., Man., N.B., Nfld., N.S., Ont., Sask.); Crown Proceeding Act (B.C.); Crown Proceedings Act (P.E.I.); Crown Liability Act (Can.). There remain, of course, many differences where the Crown is a litigant. Suits against the federal Crown may be brought only in the Federal Court: Federal Court Act, s. 17; the Crown will usually not be required to give an undertaking on damages when awarded an interlocutory injunction: *supra*, §174; rights of discovery against the Crown are limited.

[243] *Infra*, footnote 268.

[244] *Grand Council of Crees (of Quebec) v. The Queen in right of Canada*, [1982] 1 F.C. 599, 124 D.L.R. (3d) 574 (C.A.); *The Queen v. The Lords Com'rs of Treasury* (1872), 7 Q.B. 387.

[245] *The Queen v. The Lords Com'rs of Treasury, supra*, footnote 244, at p. 394, *per* Cockburn, C.J. (*mandamus* case): "this Court cannot claim even in appearance to have any power to command the Crown; the thing is out of the question. Over the sovereign we can have no power." Declaratory orders incidentally affecting the Crown have long been made. See *Pawlett v. A.-G.* (1667), Hard. 465 at p. 469, 145 E.R. 550, (Ex.), *per* Baron Artyns: "the party ought in this case to be relieved against the King, because the King is the fountain and head of justice and equity; and it shall not be presumed, that he will be defective in either. And it would derogate from the King's honour to imagine, that what is equity against a common person, should not be equity against him."

[246] *Carlic v. The Queen and Minister of Manpower and Immigration* (1967), 65 D.L.R. (2d) 633 (Man. C.A.). The *Carlic* case was commented on by Lord Diplock in *Jaundoo v. A.-G. Guyana*, [1971] A.C. 972 (P.C.), at p. 985, where His Lordship approved granting the injunction against the Minister but added ". . . their Lordships do not accept as correct that the interim injunction granted in that case should have been expressed to be against both defendants instead of against the Minister to the exclusion of the Queen."

restrain the Crown and a Minister from executing a deportation order. The court held that as the Crown was not the main defendant, enforceability of the order could be assured by proceedings against the other defendants. In fact, it matters little whether the Crown itself may be properly enjoined. The Crown is an abstraction and works through individuals, and if those individuals can be controlled through injunctions, the Crown is thereby controlled.[247]

351   There is debate as to whether an injunction may issue against a Crown servant,[248] but despite this uncertainty, it is suggested that the Canadian cases support the award of injunctions against Ministers or servants of the Crown where their course of conduct cannot be justified in law. The basic principle which emerges is that an injunction will be granted to restrain a Crown servant from exceeding the lawful limits of his authority or from acting without any authority where his acts constitute a violation of the plaintiff's right.

352   The principle stated by the judicial committee of the Privy Council in *Nireaha Tamaki v. Baker* [249] is often taken as the leading statement on the point:

> It is unnecessary to multiply authorities for so plain a proposition, and one so necessary to the protection of the subject. Their Lordships hold that an aggrieved person may sue an officer of the Crown to restrain a threatened act purporting to be done in supposed pursuance of an Act of Parliament, but really outside the statutory authority.[250]

353   This principle has been reaffirmed on several occasions in Canada.[251] In *Rattenbury v. Land Settlement Board*,[252] a 1928 deci-

---

[247] See, *e.g., Jaundoo v. A.-G. Guyana, supra*, footnote 246, at p. 985, *per* Lord Diplock, suggesting that even if an injunction is not available against the Crown, the responsible Minister can be enjoined.

[248] The question is considered by Strayer, *supra*, footnote 241; Street, *Governmental Liability: A Comparative Study* (Cambridge, University Press, 1953), p. 140; Williams, *Crown Proceedings* (London, Stevens, 1948), p. 136. de Smith, *supra*, footnote 5, at p. 445, says the common law position was "uncertain".

[249] [1901] A.C. 561 (P.C.).

[250] *Ibid.*, at p. 576, *per* Lord Davey.

[251] Cases cited, *infra*, footnotes 252, 254 and 271; *Ontario Jockey Club v. Smith* (1922), 22 O.W.N. 373 (H.C.); *Re Lodge and Minister of Employment and Immigration*, [1979] 1 F.C. 775, 94 D.L.R. (3d) 326 (C.A.). For earlier statements of the principle see: *Rankin v. Huskisson* (1830), 4 Sim. 13, 58 E.R. 6; *Ellis v. Earl Grey* (1833), 6 Sim. 214, 48 E.R. 574. In *Re Gaglardi* (1961), 27 D.L.R. (2d) 281 (B.C.C.A.), a Minister of the Crown was held guilty of contempt where his department made a payment to a contractor restrained by injunction from receiving it. See also *Eastern Trust Co. v. Mackenzie, Mann & Co. Ltd.*, [1915] A.C. 750 (P.C.). *Cf. Jones v. Janke and Milledge* (1963), 38 D.L.R. (2d) 78 (B.C.S.C.) (achieving the same result by holding the Director, Veterans' Land Act, not to be a Crown servant).

[252] [1929] S.C.R. 52, [1929] 1 D.L.R. 242.

sion of the Supreme Court of Canada, the *Tamaki* case was cited and it was said "the doer of a wrongful act cannot escape liability by setting up the authority of the Crown"[253] and an injunction was granted. Forty years later in *National Harbours Board v. Langelier*,[254] an interlocutory injunction was granted against a Crown agent on the same principle. Speaking for the court, Martland, J., pointed out that the principle established by the *Tamaki* and *Rattenbury* cases demonstrated that it was "only when the Board is lawfully executing the powers entrusted to it by the Act that it is deemed to be a Crown agent."[255] Martland, J., went on to explain:

> If it [the Board] can be held liable civilly in damages for wrongs which it has itself committed or ordered, it is obvious that a person threatened with the commission of an unlawful act by a corporate Crown agent can seek the assistance of the Court to prevent the corporation from doing that which it is not authorized to do as a Crown agent. This is clearly the principle laid down in the *Tamaki* and the *Rattenbury* cases. . . . [T]here was always recourse in the common law Courts in respects of acts done, without legal justification, by an agent of the Crown, and the Board, on that principle, is liable if it commits itself, or orders or authorizes its servants to commit, an act done without legal justification. Equally, if it threatens to commit an act, without legal justification, a subject, whose legal rights are thereby threatened, has recourse to the Courts to restrain the commission of such act.[256]

354   On the other hand, it follows from this principle that injunctive relief will be refused where the government official is acting within the scope of his powers.[257] The question of determining whether acts are within or without a power or discretion conferred by statute is a difficult substantive law issue which will not be explored in a book on remedies.[258] It may be noted, however, that confusing language has

---

[253] *Ibid.*, at p. 64 S.C.R., p. 250 D.L.R., *per* Newcombe, J.

[254] (1968), 2 D.L.R. (3d) 81, [1969] S.C.R. 60 *sub nom. Conseil des Ports Nationaux v. Langelier.* See also *City of Jacques-Cartier v. City of Montreal* (1967), 66 D.L.R. (2d) 70 (Que. Q.B., Appeal Side).

[255] *National Harbours Board, supra,* at p. 91 D.L.R., p. 72 S.C.R.

[256] *Supra,* at pp. 92-3 D.L.R., pp. 73-5 S.C.R.

[257] *Re Lodge and Minister of Employment and Immigration, supra,* footnote 251; *A.-G. Ont. v. Toronto Junction Recreation Club* (1904), 8 O.L.R. 440 (H.C.J.); *Amalgamated Builders' Council v. McGregor* (1929), 36 O.W.N. 344 (H.C.); *Montreal & European Short Line Ry. Co. v. Stewart* (1887), 20 N.S.R. 115 (S.C.); *Melbourne v. McQuesten,* [1940] O.W.N. 311 (C.A.); *Johnson Woolen Mills Ltd. v. Southern Canada Power Co.,* [1945] Que. K.B. 134 (C.A.); *Hutton v. Secretary of State for War* (1926), 43 T.L.R. 106 (Ch.).

[258] See de Smith, *supra,* footnote 5.

often been used to describe the basic distinction between those acts which are properly supported by lawful authority and those which are not. It is sometimes said that an injunction will not be granted against a Crown servant in his "official" capacity, but only when he is acting in his "individual" capacity.[259] This, it is submitted, makes sense only if the former refers to acts which are *intra vires* while the latter refers to *ultra vires* acts. In other cases, a distinction is drawn between agents of the Crown, against which injunctive relief is said not to be available, and agents of the Legislature, against which injunctions are available.[260] These cases also, it is suggested, are best understood as reflecting the basic proposition that the courts will control *ultra vires* acts. If the official is described as an agent of the Legislature, this description suggests that he is performing a task the limits of which have been defined by legislation, and that, accordingly, he is subject to suit for an injunction if he transgresses the limits set out by the legislation or fails to comply with its requirements. On the other hand, the appellation "agent of the Crown" suggests the exercise of a discretionary power, the limits of which have not been exceeded.

355   Another line of cases in which injunctive relief has been denied concerns interference with the process of the Legislature. It has been held, for example, in two English cases[261] that an injunction will not be granted to restrain a Minister of the Crown from proceeding to have enacted regulatory schemes which, it is alleged, will be *ultra vires*. There is a consistent line of authority here that the courts should not interfere with the legislative process.[262] This is a wise rec-

---

[259] *Hutton v. Secretary of State for War, supra*, footnote 257; *Merricks v. Heathcoat-Amory and Minister of Agriculture, Fisheries and Food*, [1955] Ch. 567.

[260] *Minister of Finance of B.C. v. The King*, [1935] S.C.R. 278, [1935] 3 D.L.R. 316; *The Queen v. The Lords Com'rs of Treasury* (1872), 7 Q.B. 387; *Grand Council of the Crees (of Quebec) v. The Queen in right of Canada*, [1982] 1 F.C. 599, 124 D.L.R. (3d) 574 (C.A.); *Webster Industries v. The Queen* (1982), 141 D.L.R. (3d) 564 (F.C.T.D.).

[261] *Underhill v. Ministry of Food*, [1950] 1 All E.R. 591 (Ch.); *Merricks v. Heathcoat-Amory and Minister of Agriculture, Fisheries and Food, supra*, footnote 259.

[262] *Rediffusion (Hong Kong) Ltd. v. A.-G. Hong Kong*, [1970] A.C. 1136 (P.C.); *Bradlaugh v. Gossett* (1884), 12 Q.B.D. 271; *Chamberlist v. Collins* (1962), 34 D.L.R. (2d) 414 (B.C.C.A.); Sawer, "Injunction, Parliamentary Process, and the Restriction of Parliamentary Competence", 60 L.Q.R. 83 (1944); Cowen, "The Injunction and Parliamentary Process", 71 L.Q.R. 336 (1955); Note, 4 Sydney L. Rev. 105 (1962). There is some authority that an injunction may be awarded to restrain breach of an agreement not to promote or to oppose a private bill: *Bilston Corp. v. Wolverhampton Corp.*, [1942] Ch. 391, but even this has been doubted:

171

ognition of the disruptive effect on the formulation of policy which might result from pre-emptive injunctions issued prior to the formulation by Parliament or the Legislature of the legislation in its final form. Until the impugned measures have been enacted, and Parliament or the responsible body has finally declared what the law is to be, the courts will hold their hand and refuse to grant injunctions. However, as shown below,[263] in Canada and other federal jurisdictions[264] courts have had no hesitation in awarding injunctions to restrain the execution of unconstitutional legislation, once enacted.

356   All Canadian jurisdictions now have legislation which governs suits against the Crown.[265] The pattern for such enactment has been the 1947 English Act,[266] which formed the basis of a model Act proposed by the Conference of Commissioners on Uniformity of Legislation in Canada.[267] The following provision relating to injunctions against the Crown and Crown officers is found in virtually identical terms in all provincial statutes, but has been omitted from the federal Act:

> (1) Where in proceedings against the Crown any relief is sought that might, in proceedings between persons, be granted by way of injunction or specific performance, the court shall not, as against the Crown, grant an injunction or make an order for specific performance, but in lieu thereof may make an order declaratory of the rights of the parties.
>
> (2) The court shall not in any proceedings grant an injunction or make an order against a servant of the Crown if the effect of granting the injunction or making the order would be to give any relief against the Crown that could not have been obtained in proceedings against

---

Holdsworth, Note, 59 L.Q.R. 2 (1943); de Smith, *supra*, footnote 5, at p. 467: "it seems inconceivable that an injunction would now be awarded to restrain breach of such a contract." See also *Cummings v. Hydro-Electric Power Com'n of Ontario* (1965), 54 D.L.R. (2d) 583, [1966] 1 O.R. 605 (H.C.J.), refusing an injunction to restrain the defendant from applying to the provincial Cabinet for regulation changes which would alter a pension scheme in breach of a collective agreement; *Nelson and Fort Sheppard Ry. Co. v. Parker* (1897), 6 B.C.R. 1 (Full Ct.), refusing an injunction to restrain an application for a grant of Crown lands which could be invalid on the grounds that it cannot be assumed that the Crown would not do right.

[263] *Infra*, §362.

[264] See, *e.g., A.-G. N.S.W. v. Trethowan* (1931), 44 C.L.R. 394 (Aust. H.C.), affd 47 C.L.R. 97 (P.C.).

[265] *Supra*, footnote 242.

[266] Crown Proceedings Act, 1947, s. 21.

[267] Strayer, "Injunctions against Crown Officers", 42 Can. Bar Rev. 1 (1964), at p. 38.

the Crown, but in lieu thereof may make an order declaratory of the rights of the parties.[268]

357   The effect of these provisions is unclear, and there is surprisingly little authority interpreting them. The availability of declaratory relief against the Crown and Crown servants renders unimportant the question of whether a permanent injunction is available. Governments and government servants can be expected to obey declaratory orders, and there is no practical need for the coercive aspects of injunctive relief to ensure compliance. The real problem arises where interlocutory relief is sought.[269] It has been held that there is no such thing as an interim declaration,[270] and unless an interlocutory injunction is available, no immediate remedy to prevent or deter government wrongdoing will be possible.

358   The leading Canadian case is the decision of the Ontario Divisional Court in *MacLean v. Liquor Licence Board of Ontario*.[271] This

---

[268] Statutory references, *supra*, footnote 242: Alta., s. 17; B.C., s. 11; Man., s. 17; N.B., s. 14; Nfld., s. 17; N.S., s. 15; Ont., s. 18; Sask., s. 17, P.E.I., s. 15. The Federal Court Act provisions altering Crown immunity were expressly held not to abrogate the common law immunity of the Crown to injunctive relief in *Grand Council of Crees (of Quebec) v. The Queen in right of Canada, supra*, footnote 260.

[269] Most commentators support the view that interim relief should be available against Crown officers and agents: Williams, *supra*, footnote 248; Street, *supra*, footnote 248, at p. 142; Harris, "Interim Relief against the Crown", 5 Otago L. Rev. 92 (1981). Compare, however, Strayer, *supra*, footnote 267, at p. 42, and Barnes, "The Crown Proceedings Act, 1947", 26 Can. Bar Rev. 387 (1948). Note, however, that in Ontario, by virtue of the Judicial Review Procedure Act, where actions for injunction to review a statutory power of decisions are assimilated in an "application for judicial review", s. 4 permits the court to "make such interim order as it considers proper pending the final determination of the application." A similar provision is found in the British Columbia Judicial Review Procedure Act, s. 10. The English Law Commission, *Report on Remedies in Administrative Law*, Cmnd. 6407 (London, H.M.S.O., 1976), recommended that the court should be empowered "to declare the terms of an interim injunction which would have been granted between subjects" against the Crown. For discussion of this and similar proposals see Harris, *supra*.

[270] *International General Electric Co. of New York Ltd. v. Com'rs of Customs and Excise*, [1962] Ch. 784 (C.A.), at p. 790; *Meade v. Haringey London Borough Council*, [1979] 1 W.L.R. 637 (C.A.), at p. 648; *Inland Revenue Com'rs v. Rossminster Ltd.*, [1980] A.C. 952 at pp. 1000 and 1027; *Underhill v. Ministry of Food*, [1950] 1 All E.R. 591 (Ch.); *Canadian Industrial Gas & Oil Ltd. v. Government of Saskatchewan* (1974), 46 D.L.R. (3d) 314 (Sask. Q.B.); *Shaw v. The Queen in right of B.C.* (1982), 140 D.L.R. (3d) 178 (B.C.S.C.). *Amax Potash Ltd. v. Government of Saskatchewan*, [1977] 2 S.C.R. 576, 71 D.L.R. (3d) 1, assumes, without deciding, that an interlocutory declaration is not available, but states that an interim order for the preservation of assets might be made. *Cf. Ass'n of Calgary Electrical Contractors v. Electrical Union 254 etc.* (1963), 40 D.L.R. (2d) 907 (Alta. S.C.); *Harder v. N.Z. Tramways and Public Passenger Transport Authorities Employees Industrial Union of Workers*, [1977] 2 N.L.Z.R. 162 (S.C.).

[271] (1975), 61 D.L.R. (3d) 237, 9 O.R. (2d) 597 (Div. Ct.).

case suggests strongly that the Act does little more than codify the common law position which has just been outlined. In *MacLean*, the Divisional Court upheld an injunction granted against individual Board members and inspectors who had threatened to cancel or suspend liquor licences of premises in which the plaintiff entertainers were performing, on the basis that their performance was indecent or immoral. The court held that the Board had no power to determine the appropriateness of entertainment offered in licensed premises, and that the Board had unlawfully interfered with the contractual relationships between the plaintiffs and the owners of licensed premises in which they performed. It was also held that injunctive relief was not available against the Board because it was not a suable entity. However, the court held that although the Board was a Crown agent, the Proceedings Against the Crown Act did not preclude an injunction against the individual Board members on the basis that they had exceeded the limits of their authority. That statute preserves the common law doctrine of the Crown's immunity against injunctions, but, as the court said: "it surely cannot apply where a minor civil servant is officiously abusing his apparent powers."[272] Speaking for the court, Lerner, J., added:

> I am satisfied that an injunction to restrain the individual defendants from continuing the acts which have been complained of will not affect the Liquor Licence Board of Ontario in the performance of its statutory responsibilities and that s. 18(2) of the *Proceedings Against The Crown Act* [section precluding injunctions against Crown servants] is not applicable.[273]

359   It is submitted that the result reached in the *MacLean* case is supportable[274] and reflects a legitimate interpretation of the legisla-

---

[272] *Ibid.*, at p. 250 D.L.R., p. 610 O.R. *per* Lerner, J.

[273] *Ibid.*, at p. 253 D.L.R., p. 613 O.R.

[274] Hogg, *supra*, footnote 241, at p. 25, supports this view; see also *Harper v. Secretary of State for Home Department*, [1955] Ch. 238 (C.A.), at p. 254. In *Taal v. Saskatchewan Medical Care Ins. Com'n* (1962), 36 D.L.R. (2d) 568 (Sask. Q.B.), an interlocutory injunction restraining the implementation of an allegedly *ultra vires* scheme was refused because of a similar provision in the Saskatchewan Act. The courts are usually reluctant to grant interlocutory relief in such cases (*infra*, §362) and as well, the plaintiff failed to show irreparable harm. *Cf. Duplain v. Cameron (No. 2)* (1960), 26 D.L.R. (2d) 340 (Sask. Q.B.), holding that although the defendant officers, including the Chairman of the Saskatchewan Securities Commission, were "agents of the Legislature" rather than Crown servants, no injunction could be awarded in an action attacking the constitutionality of the Act because of s. 5(7) of the Proceedings Against the Crown Act, R.S.S. 1953, c. 79, which provided:

> No action shall be brought against any person for any act or thing heretofore

tion in light of the common law rules just discussed. Statutes curtailing rights of action in the courts are often given a narrow reading and interpreted not to preclude redress for unlawful acts, especially where the intended effect of the legislation is less than clear.

360   It has been suggested, however, that this provision should be given a more pervasive effect and in fact preclude any injunctive relief against Crown servants.[275] It is argued that the purpose of the provision is to afford the government complete freedom from any fear of judicial restraint in times of emergency, and to enable the government to override individual rights without fear of being stopped by an interlocutory injunction, and then press for retrospective legislation justifying its unlawful action later.[276] It is suggested that this argument should be rejected.[277] Such a legislative purpose is hardly borne out by the words of the statute. To achieve such an extraordinary result as to prohibit the court from restraining illegal acts simply on the grounds that the wrongdoer is a government officer would surely require clearer language. The parallel reference to specific performance suggests a more modest purpose.[278] It would be odd if

---

or hereafter done or omitted by him under the supposed authority of such statute . . . provided such action would not lie against him if the said statute . . . is or had been or may be within the jurisdiction of the Legislature enacting.

In *Amax Potash Ltd. v. Government of Saskatchewan, supra*, footnote 270, this section was held *ultra vires* to the extent that it barred recovery of taxes collected under a statute beyond the legislative competence of the province. In *Bridges Brothers Ltd. v. Forest Protection Ltd.* (1976), 72 D.L.R. (3d) 335 (Q.B.), at pp. 364-5, Stevenson, J., held that an independent contractor engaged by the Crown to spray forest areas with insecticide was entitled to the immunity in a nuisance action.

[275] Strayer, *supra*, footnote 241.

[276] Barnes, "The Crown Proceedings Act, 1947", 26 Can. Bar Rev. 387 (1948), at p. 395:

Section 21 [of the English Act corresponding to the section above] contains an important provision to the effect that no injunction or order for specific performance can be obtained against the Crown, but in lieu thereof the court may make an order declaratory of the rights of the parties. No doubt the principle underlying this provision is that in times of national emergency the Crown may be compelled to take, at the shortest possible notice and with the certainty that its operations will not be interrupted by the courts, measures which may be thought to infringe the rights or alleged rights of the subject. In such a case the appropriate course is for the Government of the day to ask Parliament to validate what it has done and no doubt Parliament will in those cases decide how far the acts of the Crown were justified in the circumstances. If Parliament approves of what has been done and ratifies it by retrospective legislation, it will also no doubt provide compensation for the persons aggrieved. The freedom of the Executive to meet a crisis by action of this kind would be fettered if it were open to the subject to obtain an interim injunction restraining the Crown from doing what it thought necessary in the public interest.

[277] The argument is considered in detail by Harris, *supra*, footnote 269.

[278] For a case dealing with this provision see *MacQuarrie v. A.-G. N.S.* (1972), 32

legislation designed to facilitate redress against the Crown and to put the Crown on the same basis as other litigants should be read so as to significantly curtail individual rights recognized prior to the legislation. The provision dealing with Crown servants may, it is submitted, be taken merely to restate the common law position and leave untrammelled the power of the courts to restrain illegal acts by State officials. The distinction between injunctions against the Crown and injunctions against Crown servants exceeding their powers has long been recognized. The subsection excludes injunctive relief only where the effect of the injunction against a Crown servant would be to give an injunction against the Crown. Injunctions against Crown servants exceeding their powers have never been considered to amount to injunctions against the Crown, and the legislation should be read in light of this basic distinction. In real cases of emergency, courts can almost inevitably be expected to exercise their discretion in deciding whether to award interlocutory injunctive relief so as to reflect public interest. As the British Columbia Law Reform Commission commented on this matter:[279] "If history proves anything, it is that during a crisis judicial compliance is to be feared more than judicial scrutiny."

361   Indeed, in many situations, problems will arise if no account is taken of the general public interest where interlocutory relief is sought.[280] In assessing the risk of harm to the defendant from an interlocutory injunction which might later be dissolved at trial, the courts may be expected to be conscious of the public interest.[281] Too ready availability of interlocutory relief against government and its

---

D.L.R. (3d) 603 (N.S.S.C.T.D.).

[279] Law Reform Commission of British Columbia, *Report on Civil Rights*, Part I: Legal Position of the Crown (Vancouver, 1972), p. 31. The Commission recommended against the inclusion of this provision in the British Columbia legislation, but the recommendation was not accepted: see Crown Proceedings Act, S.B.C. 1974, c. 24.

[280] Harris, *supra*, footnote 269, at p. 105. In *Inland Revenue Com'rs v. Rossminster Ltd.*, [1980] A.C. 952 (H.L.), conflicting views on the desirability of interim relief against the Crown were expressed at p. 1027 *per* Lord Scarman, and at pp. 1014-15 *per* Lord Diplock.

[281] *Barnard v. Walkem* (1880), 1 B.C.R. Pt. 1, 120 (S.C.); *Perusse v. School Com'rs of Municipality of St. Leonard de Port-Maurice* (1969), 11 D.L.R. (3d) 81 (Que. C.A.) (refusing an interlocutory injunction which would badly disrupt the functioning of schools during the academic year). See also *Edgett v. Taylor*, [1934] 1 D.L.R. 113 (B.C.C.A.). It has been suggested in England that an interlocutory injunction will be granted only with caution against a public authority: *Smith v. Inner London Education Authority*, [1978] 1 All E.R. 411 (C.A.); *Meade v. Haringey London Borough Council*, [1979] 1 W.L.R. 637 (C.A.).

agencies could disrupt the orderly functioning of government. This factor is amply reflected in the cases decided in the absence of legislation,[282] and there seems no need to fear that the reasoning of the *MacLean* case[283] would lead to an abuse of the power to grant injunctions.

362   Where a challenge is made to the constitutionality of legislation, it is clear that an injunction will lie to restrain a Minister or Crown servant from carrying into effect legislation which is shown to be *ultra vires*.[284] It has also been held that such an injunction may be made at the interlocutory stage where the plaintiff's case is particularly strong.[285] However, interlocutory relief in such circumstances is the exception rather than the rule, and the courts have sensibly paid heed to the fact that at the interlocutory stage they cannot fully explore the merits of the plaintiff's case. An injunction restraining implementation of legislation on the basis that it might be *ultra vires* could cause grave inconvenience to the public and the balance of risk of harm almost invariably favours denying interlocutory relief in such cases.[286]

---

[282] An injunction was granted, however, against the enforcement of a wartime requisition order held to be *ultra vires*: *Society of Love of Jesus v. Smart and Nicolls*, [1944] 2 D.L.R. 551 (B.C.S.C.).

[283] Passage quoted, *supra*, §358.

[284] *C.P.R. v. A.-G. Sask.*, [1951] 3 D.L.R. 362 (Sask. K.B.), revd in part [1951] 4 D.L.R. 21 (C.A.), vard [1952] 2 S.C.R. 231, [1952] 4 D.L.R. 11; *Home Oil Distributors Ltd. v. A.-G. B.C.*, [1939] 1 D.L.R. 573 (B.C.C.A.); *Société Asbestos Ltée v. Société Nationale de L'Amiante*, [1979] Que. C.A. 342 (C.A.). In *B.C. Power Corp. v. Royal Trust Co.*, [1962] S.C.R. 642 at pp. 644-5, 34 D.L.R. (2d) 196 at pp. 275-6, *per* Kerwin, C.J.C., a similar principle was recognized with respect to the Crown's amenability to a receivership order to test the validity of legislation on which the claim of Crown title rested:

> In a federal system, where legislative authority is divided, as are also the prerogatives of the Crown, as between the Dominion and the Provinces, it is my view that it is not open to the Crown, either in right of Canada or of a Province, to claim a Crown immunity based upon an interest in certain property, where its very interest in that property depends completely and solely on the validity of the legislation which it has itself passed, if there is a reasonable doubt as to whether such legislation is constitutionally valid. To permit it to do so would be to enable it, by the assertion of rights claimed under legislation which is beyond its powers, to achieve the same results as if the legislation were valid.

See also *Amax Potash Ltd. v. Government of Saskatchewan*, [1977] 2 S.C.R. 576, 71 D.L.R. (3d) 1.

[285] *Home Oil Distributors Ltd. v. A.-G. B.C.*, [1939] 1 D.L.R. 573 (B.C.C.A.); *Hammerstein v. B.C. Coast Vegetable Marketing Board* (1962), 37 D.L.R. (2d) 153 (B.C.C.A.) (injunction to restrain implementation of an impugned marketing scheme).

[286] *Morgenthaler et al. v. Ackroyd et al.* (1983), 20 A.C.W.S. (2d) 473 (Ont. H.C.J.);

363   Even if injunctions are available to restrain unlawful acts of government servants on the *ultra vires* theory, the net effect of the common law and statutory provisions which have been examined may
still leave some serious gaps. Ordinary breaches of contract, or torts
committed by a Crown agent within the pursuit of its defined powers
and objectives, give rise to problems. It is uncertain whether an injunction is available to restrain a Crown agent from committing a
tort or breach of contract within the sphere of its operations. In the
modern state where the government is involved in so many commercial activities, it is difficult to see why it should not be put on the
same footing as any other party for these purposes.

364   In *Baton Broadcasting Ltd. v. C.B.C.*,[287] the plaintiff sought an injunction to restrain the defendant, defined as a Crown agent by legislation, from using film which it had improperly obtained in violation
of the plaintiff's copyright. An interlocutory injunction was given
and explicit reference was made to the undesirability of putting the
Crown on a special footing:

> In cases where Crown agencies engage in business ventures in compe-
> tition with private interests and are guilty of acts therein which would
> be restrained by the Courts but for their character as Crown agents, it
> does not seem proper that they should be immune to the Court's juris-
> diction on the sole ground that they are Crown agents. In such cases,
> private rights are the subject of the litigation as distinguished from
> public rights which under the older cases was the matter in hand when
> immunity surrounding the Crown was set forth as a reason for the
> Court's lack of jurisdiction. In circumstances such as the present,
> Crown agencies are not *per se* exempt from judicial authority. The acts
> of the defendant corporation sought to be restrained herein are not in
> the area where a Minister of the Crown exercises a discretion for
> which he is responsible. There is nothing in the statute authorizing the
> defendant corporation to secure its programme in the method which

---

Campbell Motors Ltd. v. Gordon, [1946] 4 D.L.R. 36 (B.C.C.A.), at p. 48, *per* Sid-
ney Smith, J.A., refusing an interlocutory injunction to restrain execution of a challenged anti-inflation statute: "If this injunction were to stand there would be a risk
of confusion in the public mind which, in the general interest, should not without
good reason be authorized." *Cf. Ontario Jockey Club v. Smith* (1922), 22 O.W.N.
373 (H.C.), granting an injunction restraining a Minister and his official from taking steps to enforce a taxing statute impugned on constitutional grounds but, as a
condition of the injunction, requiring the plaintiff to pay the amount of the tax into
court to be held pending the final resolution of the action. *Cf.* also *Black v. Law Society of Alberta* (1983), 144 D.L.R. (3d) 439 (Alta. Q.B.), granting an interlocutory
injunction restraining implementation of a rule alleged to violate the Charter of
Rights and Freedoms, on the ground that there was a serious question to be tried.
[287] (1966), 56 D.L.R. (2d) 215, [1966] 2 O.R. 169 (H.C.J.).

its servants adopted in this case and which amounted to an unauthorized invasion of the plaintiff's rights.[288]

365   Although the case was decided under the federal legislation which contains no express exclusion of injunctive relief against the Crown, it may still be relevant where provincial legislation is involved. Under the federal Act, the plaintiff is required to give ninety days notice before commencing suit,[289] but in *Baton*, Grant, J., held that the notice provision did not apply to claims for an injunction.[290] Moreover, in reaching the conclusion that an injunction should be awarded, Grant, J., applied the *ultra vires* theory of the *Tamaki* and *Rattenbury* line of cases.[291]

366   Thus, it is quite possible that the *Baton* case would be followed in actions involving the Crown in right of a province where the legislation appears to limit the availability of injunctions, but where, as already noted, the *ultra vires* theory is still applied. However, in a recent Saskatchewan case,[292] it was held (without reference to *Baton*) that a receivership order which prevented Saskatchewan Telecommunications from cutting off services could not be made in the face of the legislation. A similar result was reached in New Zealand with respect to a threatened breach of contract.[293] Although the results reached in these cases may seem inevitable in light of the legislation, it is submitted that the result and reasoning of the *Baton* case is much to be preferred.

---

[288] *Ibid.*, at p. 220 D.L.R., p. 174 O.R., *per* Grant, J.

[289] Crown Liability Act, s. 10.

[290] Hughes, J., agreed on this point in refusing leave to appeal: *supra*, footnote 287, at p. 225 D.L.R., p. 180 O.R. See also *Hillyard v. City of St. John's* (1981), 26 C.P.C. 288 (Nfld. S.C.T.D.), holding that the notice provisions under the Newfoundland Proceedings Against the Crown Act do not apply to claims for injunctions.

[291] *Supra*, §§352, 353.

[292] *Royal Bank of Canada v. 238842 Alberta Ltd.* (1981), 129 D.L.R. (3d) 665 (Alta. Q.B.). See also *Banner Investments Ltd. v. Saskatchewan Telecommunications* (1977), 78 D.L.R. (3d) 127 (Sask. Q.B.); *Hamilton Hotel Co. Ltd. v. Saskatchewan Telecommunications* (1980), 114 D.L.R. (3d) 374 (Sask. Q.B.); *Toronto Dominion Bank v. Car-Tree Int'l Ltd.* (1967), 66 D.L.R. (2d) 552 (Sask. Q.B.).

[293] *Codelfa-Cogefar (N.Z.) Ltd. v. A.-G.* (unreported, N.Z.H.C., 1980), referred to in Harris, *supra*, footnote 269.

CHAPTER 4

INJUNCTIONS TO PROTECT PROPERTY

1. Introduction

367 Where the plaintiff complains of an interference with his property rights, injunctive relief is strongly favoured. This is especially so in the case of direct infringement in the nature of trespass.[1] It is also the case where the plaintiff's cause of action lies in nuisance,[2] although somewhat less categorically. The discretion in this area has crystallized to the point that, in practical terms, the conventional primacy of common law damages over equitable relief is reversed. Where property rights are concerned, it is almost that damages are presumed inadequate, and an injunction to restrain continuation of the wrong is the usual remedy.[3] However, as always with equity, this must be understood to be a principle rather than a rule, and as will be seen, many factors are taken into account.

---

[1] Discussed, *infra*, §425 *et seq.*

[2] *Infra*, §372 *et seq.*

[3] See *Pride of Derby and Derbyshire Angling Ass'n v. British Celanese Ltd.*, [1953] Ch. 149 (C.A.), at p. 181, *per* Evershed, M.R.: "if A proves that his proprietary rights are being wrongfully interfered with by B, and that B intends to continue his wrong, then A is prima facie entitled to an injunction, and he will be deprived of that remedy only if special circumstances exist". See also *Shelfer v. City of London Electric Lighting Co.*, [1895] 1 Ch. 287 (C.A.), discussed, *infra*, §§373-375; *McKinnon Industries v. Walker*, [1951] 3 D.L.R. 577 (P.C.), at p. 581, *per* Lord Simonds: "special circumstances may occur in which the remedy of damages will adequately compensate a plaintiff for the loss he has suffered and may in the future suffer. But it is for the wrongdoer to satisfy the Court that such special circumstances exist."

180

368   The reason for the primacy of injunctive relief is that an injunction more accurately reflects the substantive definition of property than does a damages award. It is the very essence of the concept of property that the owner should not be deprived without his consent. An injunction brings to bear coercive powers to vindicate that right. Compensatory damages for a continuous and wrongful interference with a property interest offers only limited protection in that the plaintiff is, in effect, deprived of his property without his consent at an objectively determined price. Special justification is required for damages rather than an injunction if the principle of autonomous control over property is to be preserved. A damages award rather than an injunction permits the defendant to carry on interfering with the plaintiff's property. Even if the plaintiff would have "sold" his right to be free from the interference, denial of an injunction constitutes a denial of an attribute of ownership. Compensation to the plaintiff for the interference is fixed by the court in the form of damages, rather than by the plaintiff in the form of a bargained-for price. Damages will be assessed on an objective basis, measured by the market value of the decrease in the value of the plaintiff's property, and any peculiar or personal value which the plaintiff puts on his property will not ordinarily be reflected in such an award.[4]

369   Until the middle of the 19th century, an injunction was more than just a preferred remedy in the case of continuing wrongs. It was only after the passage of Lord Cairns' Act[5] in 1858 that either equity or common law could award prospective damages. Common law damages were for past injury only,[6] and chancery could not award damages at all. Thus, until chancery was given the power to award damages in lieu of an injunction in 1858, the only remedy available in either court for anticipated injury was an injunction. Refusing an injunction condemned the plaintiff to an endless series of common law actions for past damages. In light of this restricted remedial choice, it is not difficult to see why injunctions were strongly favoured. Not only did injunctive relief coincide with the more traditional view of property rights, if the court wanted to resolve the dispute once and for all, it was the only remedy available.[7]

---

[4] Waddams, *The Law of Damages* (1983), §§239-256.

[5] Chancery Amendment Act, 1858 (U.K.).

[6] See, *e.g.*, *Bathishill v. Reed* (1856), 25 L.J.C.P. 290 at p. 292, *per* Jervis, C.J.

[7] Note, however, that in trespass cases, injunctions were often not available until the plaintiff had established his right at law: *infra*, §431. Similarly, in nuisance cases,

370   The courts retain the power conferred in 1858 to award "equitable" damages, in the present context, damages in substitution for an
injunction.[8] The quantum of such damages may be calculated to
reflect the diminution in market value of the plaintiff's property
caused by the defendant's wrong.[9] The defendant is permitted to
continue his wrongful conduct, but must pay the price, objectively
determined by the court, to compensate the plaintiff for what
amounts to a partial expropriation of his property.[10]

371   Thus, the modern court has three remedial choices where the
plaintiff establishes a wrongful and continuing interference with his
property. The court can refuse equitable relief altogether, and
merely award common law damages for past wrong; it can refuse an
injunction but award damages, so as to permit the activity to continue but require the defendant to compensate the plaintiff for the
market value decrease his property suffers by being saddled with the
interference; or it can award an injunction. Many cases will call for a
combination of these remedies, and as will be seen,[11] the third possibility has several variations: an injunction can be suspended, partial,
or conditional, and these variations are frequently employed when
property rights are at issue.

2. Nuisance

(1) Traditional rule

372   In nuisance cases, once the plaintiff has made out his substantive

---

chancery was reluctant to interfere before the legal right had been established:
A.-G. v. Cleaver (1811), 18 Ves. Jun. 211, 34 E.R. 297.

[8] See Waddams, *supra*, footnote 4, §86, and, *supra*, §§19-22.

[9] There appears to be doubt as to whether a successor in title to the plaintiff is bound
by such an award, although in principle, it is submitted that, as the damages paid by
the defendant reflect market value loss to the plaintiff, no subsequent action should
be permitted. See, *infra*, §§518, 519, dealing with injunction cases. Compare
Gallant v. MacDonald (1970), 3 N.S.R. (2d) 137 (S.C.); *Dempsey v. J.E.S. Developments Ltd.* (1976), 15 N.S.R. (2d) 448 (S.C.T.D.), both holding that, as a condition of obtaining equitable damages to reflect market value diminution caused by a
building encroachment, the plaintiff should be required to release its interest to the
defendant.

[10] See, *e.g.*, *Rombough v. Crestbrook Timber Ltd.* (1966), 57 D.L.R. (2d) 49
(B.C.C.A.), at p. 59, *per* Maclean, J.A.: "where the Court does see fit to award
damages in lieu of a complete injunction for nuisance, the Court is permitting the
continuing of a nuisance on payment of once-and-for-all damages", and at p. 68,
per Bull, J.A.: "What the Court is doing, where such damages are awarded in lieu
of an injunction, is making the defendant pay for a licence to commit the wrong by
in effect legalizing his act."

[11] *Infra*, §§391-397.

right, the ordinary remedy is an injunction. This is especially so in England where the courts have traditionally refused to entertain any notion of balancing burden and benefit.[12] Thus, even where the advantage an injunction would confer on the plaintiff is slight compared to the burden it would impose on the defendant, injunctions are still awarded, and the English courts have refused to consider the hardship an injunction would inflict upon third parties or the public at large.[13] Although the substantive law of nuisance may have been significantly altered in the mid-19th century to accommodate industrial expansion,[14] the English courts have remained faithful throughout to traditional principles at the remedial level once the substantive wrong was found.[15]

373   The circumstances in which a court is justified in awarding damages rather than an injunction were identified in *Shelfer v. City of London Electric Lighting Co.*,[16] a decision of the Court of Appeal in

---

[12] See Ogus and Richardson, "Economics and the Environment: A Study of Private Nuisance", 36 Camb. L.J. 284 (1977); Tromans, "Nuisance — Prevention or Payment?", 41 Camb. L.J. 87 (1982); cases cited, *infra*, footnote 13.

[13] *Broadbent v. Imperial Gas Co.* (1857), 7 De G. M. & G. 436 at p. 462, 44 E.R. 170, *per* Cranworth, L.C.:

> I cannot enter into any question of how far it might be convenient for the public that the gas manufacture should go on. That might be a good ground for the Legislature to declare that the company might make gas if they indemnified the Plaintiff; but, unless the company had such a right, I think the present is not a case in which this Court can go into the question of convenience or inconvenience.

A.-G. v. Birmingham Council (1858), 4 K. & J. 528 at pp. 539-40, 70 E.R. 220, *per* Sir Page Wood, V.-C.: "it is a matter of almost absolute indifference whether the decision will affect a population of 25,000, or a single individual carrying on a manufactory for his own benefit". *Cf.* de Smith, *Judicial Review of Administrative Action*, 4th ed. by Evans (London, Stevens & Sons Ltd., 1980), p. 444, footnote 96: "It would be unjustifiable for a court to adopt such an extreme position now". *Trinidad Asphalt Co. v. Ambard*, [1899] A.C. 594 (P.C.), at pp. 602-3: "Whatever the result may be, rights of property must be respected, even when they conflict, or seem to conflict with the interests of the community." See also *Pride of Derby and Derbyshire Angling Ass'n v. British Celanese Ltd.*, [1953] Ch. 149 (C.A.); *Pennington v. Brinsop Hall Coal Co.* (1877), 5 Ch. D. 769 (loss to plaintiff estimated at £100, cost of closing defendants' undertaking £190,000 and loss of 500 jobs); *Wood v. Conway Corp.*, [1914] 2 Ch. 47; *Halsey v. Esso Petroleum Co. Ltd.*, [1961] 2 All E.R. 145 (Q.B.). See also *Allen v. Gulf Oil Refining Ltd.*, [1981] 1 All E.R. 353 (H.L.), and comment by Jolowicz, 40 Camb. L.J. 226 (1981).

[14] Horwitz, *The Transformation of American Law* (1977); Nedelsky, Chapter 8 in *Essays in the History of Canadian Law*, Flaherty, ed. (Toronto, University of Toronto Press, 1981).

[15] The actual impact of nuisance injunctions as a means of protecting the environment is said to have been minimal; see Brenner "Nuisance Law and the Industrial Revolution", 3 J. of Leg. Stud. 403 (1974).

[16] [1895] 1 Ch. 287 (C.A.).

1895. The formulation set out by A.L. Smith, L.J., is almost invariably referred to:

> In my opinion, it may be stated as a good working rule that—
>
> (1.) If the injury to the plaintiff's legal rights is small,
> (2.) And is one which is capable of being estimated in money,
> (3.) And is one which can be adequately compensated by a small money payment,
> (4.) And the case is one in which it would be oppressive to the defendant to grant an injunction:—
>
> then damages in substitution for an injunction may be given.[17]

374   Although *Shelfer* stands for the proposition that an injunction is the preferred remedy, implicit in this formulation is the notion that, in certain cases, it is appropriate to balance the burden an injunction imposes on the defendant against the benefit it confers on the plaintiff. However, the statement is vague: what is a "small" injury, "capable of being estimated in money" and "adequately compensated by a small money payment"? If "small" is taken to mean small absolutely, then an injunction will rarely be refused. On the other hand, if "small" is related to the cost imposed upon the defendant, then the test is a much more flexible one allowing the court considerable latitude. Similarly, the court can always try to estimate appropriate monetary compensation for intangible injuries. The issue is a relative one: when are the risks and costs associated with money awards sufficiently high to justify an injunction? It is fairly clear from the *Shelfer* case itself and from subsequent English cases that, except in two areas,[18] the English courts refuse to engage in balancing costs and benefits, and presume that injury to property calls for injunctive relief.[19]

375   In *Shelfer*, the plaintiff had a twenty-year lease on the house he occupied, and sued to restrain noise and vibrations caused by engines and generators recently installed by the defendant. Clearly, an injunction would impose costs on the defendant out of all proportion to the loss suffered by the plaintiff in such a case. The defendant's "sunk" costs would be lost. Assuming the plaintiff could be persuaded to sell his rights to enforce the injunction, the price the plaintiff could demand would still approach the cost to the defendant of moving its installations. None the less, an injunction was granted.[20]

---

[17] *Ibid.*, at pp. 322-3.
[18] *Infra*, §§376-378.
[19] *Cf. Miller v. Jackson*, [1977] Q.B. 966 (C.A.), discussed, *infra*, §387.
[20] It was, however, suspended for a considerable period: [1895] 2 Ch. 389 (C.A.). See further, *infra*, §§391-396, on the question of suspension.

376   The English courts have consistently favoured injunctive relief over damages in similar cases, although not without exception in cases of "trifling" injuries.[21] Several cases involve rights to light.[22] Here, the English courts have been much more flexible. Although the substantive right theoretically takes the same shape and definition, even English courts have refused to grant injunctive relief where the actual interference with the plaintiff's enjoyment appeared inconsequential, especially where it appeared that the plaintiff was merely using that right to "extort" money from the defendant.[23] Thus, explicit reference has been made to the possibility of post-judgment bargaining, seen in this context as a ground for refusing injunctive relief.

377   The use of the word "extortion" in this context is perhaps unduly emotive, if not positively misleading.[24] It suggests the assertion of an

---

[21] *A.-G. v. Sheffield Gas Consumers Co.* (1853), 3 De G. M. & G. 304, 43 E.R. 119; *Duke of Grafton v. Hilliard* (1735), 4 De G. & SM. 326, 64 E.R. 853; *Swaine v. Great Northern Ry.* (1864), 4 De G. J. & S. 211, 46 E.R. 899; *Cooke v. Forbes* (1867), L.R. 5 Eq. 166; *Harrison v. Southwark & Vauxhall Water Co.*, [1891] 2 Ch. 409.

[22] See especially *Isenberg v. East India House Estate Co. Ltd.* (1863), 3 De G. J. & S. 263, 46 E.R. 637; *Colls v. Home & Colonial Stores, Ltd.*, [1904] A.C. 179 (H.L.).

[23] In *Isenberg, supra*, footnote 22, at p. 273, Westbury, L.C., said:

To what end, then, should I exercise a jurisdiction which in such a case as this would simply be mischievous to the Defendants, without being attended with corresponding benefit to the Plaintiff, unless, indeed, I could approve of the Plaintiff taking advantage of the mischief and loss that the Defendants would have to sustain, in order to aggravate his claim for pecuniary compensation.

This is a case in which the benefit of the recent statute giving power to this Court to assess and ascertain damages is peculiarly felt; and I hold it, therefore, to be the duty of the Court in such a case as the present not, by granting a mandatory injunction, to deliver over the Defendants to the Plaintiff bound hand and foot, in order to be made subject to any extortionate demand that he may by possibility make, but to substitute for such mandatory injunction an inquiry before itself, in order to ascertain the measure of damage that has been actually sustained.

In *Colls, supra*, footnote 22, at p. 193, Lord Macnaghten stated:

It is quite true that a man ought not to be compelled to part with his property against his will, or to have the value of his property diminished, without an Act of Parliament. On the other hand, the Court ought to be very careful not to allow an action for the protection of ancient lights to be used as a means of extorting money. Often a person who is engaged in a large building scheme has to pay money right and left in order to avoid litigation, which will put him to even greater expense by delaying his proceedings. As far as my own experience goes, there is quite as much oppression on the part of those who invoke the assistance of the Court to protect some ancient lights, which they have never before considered of any great value, as there is on the part of those who are improving the neighbourhood by the erection of buildings that must necessarily to some extent interfere with the light of adjoining premises.

[24] See especially Thompson, "Injunction Negotiations: An Economic, Moral, and Legal Analysis", 27 Stanford L. Rev. 1563 (1975).

illegal threat to extract a money payment. A property owner who merely stands by his rights, and refuses to overlook an infringement unless mollified by a money payment, is plainly not exerting any illegal threat. Indeed, in other contexts, the courts have explicitly recognized the likelihood of post-judgment bargaining, and seen injunctive relief as an appropriate remedy to guarantee that the plaintiff is able to bargain from a position of strength.[25] In such cases, injunctions vindicate the plaintiff's right to exploit the value of his veto over the use of his property, and to prevent the defendant from circumventing the bargaining process.

378   Another exception to the invariable award of injunctive relief can be seen in cases involving mandatory injunctions.[26] There, the propriety of balancing the burdens and benefits of an injunction has the sanction of the House of Lords,[27] especially where the defendant has acted reasonably rather than in deliberate disregard of his neighbour's rights. It is often suggested that because mandatory relief requires a positive course of action it is more costly, but a prohibitive injunction often imposes even greater costs. Injunctions which restrain nuisance-creating activities often require entire factories to be shut down, or substantial and expensive alterations to existing practices to be undertaken.[28] Once it is accepted, in principle, that it is appropriate to take into account the costs an injunction would impose, it seems difficult to justify distinguishing between mandatory and prohibitive forms of injunctive relief. In virtually all nuisance cases, the practical effect of a prohibitive injunction enjoining a nuisance will be to require the defendant to take positive steps to abate the nuisance. The costs associated with altering industrial processes or moving a nuisance-creating installation will very often greatly exceed the sort of costs which the House of Lords had in mind when it approved the balance of burden and benefit in mandatory injunction cases. The validity of the distinction between the costs imposed by mandatory injunctions and those imposed by prohibitive injunctions is surely questionable.

(2) Balance of burden and benefit

379   The Canadian courts[29] routinely cite the English cases, but in fact,

---

[25] *Infra*, §427; *supra*, §§17, 18.
[26] *Supra*, §50 *et seq.*
[27] *Redland Bricks Ltd. v. Morris*, [1970] A.C. 652 (H.L.), discussed, *supra*, §60.
[28] *Infra*, §§385, 386 and 393.
[29] Canadian cases are discussed, *infra*, §380 *et seq.* For a good review, see McLaren,

the Canadian practice has been more flexible than the English. In Canada, as in England, *Shelfer* is inevitably cited as setting out the guiding principle, but there is a distinct line of Canadian cases which holds that it is appropriate in deciding whether to afford injunctive relief to weigh the hardship an order will cause the defendant, and the economic and social impact it might have upon the community.

380   One of the leading cases, *Canada Paper Co. v. Brown*,[30] a decision of the Supreme Court of Canada, illustrates the ambivalent Canadian approach. The plaintiff complained of sulphate fumes emanating from the defendant's pulp and paper works. These fumes seriously interfered with the enjoyment of the plaintiff's expensive home built on land which had been owned by his family for over 100 years. The defendant's plant was an important local industry employing many people. There was clearly a nuisance, and the Supreme Court held that the plaintiff was entitled to an injunction. The opinions, however, indicate widely different judicial approaches. Idington, J.'s judgment is a forceful statement of the need to defend individual rights against sacrifice to the general welfare of society. He refused to consider the possibility that the plaintiff's property rights should be compromised in order to enhance the general prosperity of the community. The fact that the invasion of the plaintiff's rights would suit "the grasping tendencies of some and incidentally the needs or desires of the majority in any community"[31] could not, in Idington, J.'s view, justify depriving the plaintiff of his injunction in the absence of specific statutory authority to expropriate. His judgment concluded as follows:

> . . . as long as we keep in view the essential merits of the remedy in the way of protecting the rights of property and preventing them from being invaded by mere autocratic assertions of what will be more conducive to the prosperity of the local community by disregarding such rights, we will not go far astray in taking as our guide the reasoning of any jurisprudence which recognizes the identical aim of protecting people in their rights of property when employing their remedy of perpetual injunction.[32]

381   Duff, J., on the other hand, held a more qualified view of the remedial protection to be afforded, and defended the balancing approach which would take into account the burdens an injunction

---

"The Common Law Nuisance Actions and the Environmental Battle — Well-Tempered Swords or Broken Reeds?", 10 Osgoode Hall L.J. 505 (1972).

[30] (1921), 63 S.C.R. 243, 66 D.L.R. 287.

[31] *Ibid.*, at p. 248 S.C.R., p. 289 D.L.R.

[32] *Ibid.*, at p. 250 S.C.R., p. 291 D.L.R.

would impose. The test he formulated was dramatically different:

> An injunction will not be granted where, having regard to all the circumstances, to grant it would be unjust; and the disparity between the advantage to the plaintiff to be gained by the granting of that remedy and the inconvenience and disadvantage which the defendant and others would suffer in consequence thereof may be a sufficient ground for refusing it.[33]

382   Denying an injunction and awarding damages would not, according to Duff, J., be tantamount to expropriation. It would merely apply "the limitations and restrictions which the law imposes in relation to the pursuit of this particular form of remedy in order to prevent it becoming an instrument of injustice and oppression".[34]

383   Duff, J., agreed, however, that an injunction should be granted in the case at bar, as he thought that "the cessation of the [defendant's] . . . operations would be neither the necessary nor the probable result of that relief ".[35]

384   *Canada Paper* thus illustrates two very different judicial approaches, and is cited on both sides of the debate — both for the proposition that an injunction follows automatically, and to support the assertion that the remedy depends in part on the balance of burden and benefit. However, Idington, J.'s view appears to be the prevailing one, and once a nuisance is found, the Canadian courts will usually award an injunction. In a subsequent Supreme Court of Canada decision[36] involving another pulp and paper mill, this one polluting a river to the annoyance of the plaintiff cottage owners, fishermen and tourist camp operators, it was said: "Pollution has been shown to exist, damages would not be a complete and adequate remedy, and the Court's discretion should not be exercised against the 'current of authority which is of many years' standing'."[37] The court repeated the familiar concern that damages could lead to "an abuse . . . by legalizing the commission of torts by any defendant who was able and willing to pay damages".[38] A long list of Canadian cases can be cited in support of this view,[39] including cases in which injunctions

---

[33] *Ibid.*, at p. 252 S.C.R., p. 292 D.L.R.

[34] *Ibid.*, at p. 253 S.C.R., p. 292 D.L.R.

[35] *Ibid.*, at p. 252 S.C.R., p. 292 D.L.R.

[36] *K.V.P. Co. Ltd. v. McKie*, [1949] S.C.R. 698, [1949] 4 D.L.R. 497.

[37] *Ibid.*, at p. 703 S.C.R., p. 501 D.L.R., *per* Kerwin, J.

[38] *Ibid.*, at p. 702 S.C.R., pp. 500-1 D.L.R., *per* Kerwin, J. Note, however, that the Supreme Court suspended operation of the injunction for six months, and the injunction was dissolved by legislation: An Act respecting The K.V.P. Company Limited, S.O. 1950, c. 33, discussed, *infra*, §402.

[39] *McKenzie v. Kayler* (1905), 1 W.L.R. 290 (Man. K.B.) (plaintiff month-to-month

have been awarded which imposed significant costs on municipalities and public authorities.[40]

385   However, there is a distinct line of cases which has adopted the balancing of burden and benefit analysis suggested by Duff, J., in the *Canada Paper* case, and often found in American cases.[41] The Canadian courts have often made explicit reference to the disproportionate hardship an injunction would cause, either to the defendant or the public at large.[42] Thus, despite apparent adherence to the power-

---

tenant, injunction awarded against defendant's livery stables); *Gauthier v. Naneff* (1970), 14 D.L.R. (3d) 513 at p. 519, [1971] 1 O.R. 97 at p. 103 (H.C.J.), *per* Dunlap, L.J.S.C.: "It is trite law that economic necessities of the defendants are irrelevant"; *Patton v. Pioneer Navigation & Sand Co.* (1906), 16 Man. R. 435 (K.B.), at p. 436, *per* MacDonald, J.: "Inconvenience to the public cannot be set up as against private rights"; *Atwell v. Knights* (1967), 61 D.L.R. (2d) 108, [1967] 1 O.R. 419 (H.C.J.); *Walker v. McKinnon Industries*, [1949] 4 D.L.R. 739, [1949] O.R. 549 (H.C.J.), affd [1950] 3 D.L.R. 159, [1950] O.W.N. 309 (C.A.), affd [1951] 3 D.L.R. 577 (P.C.); *Rolston v. Lapa Cadillac Gold Mines*, [1950] O.R. 103 (H.C.J.); *Russell Transport Ltd. v. Ontario Malleable Iron Co.*, [1952] 4 D.L.R. 719, [1952] O.R. 621 (H.C.J.); *Epstein v. Reymes*, [1973] S.C.R. 85, 29 D.L.R. (3d) 1; *Caplin v. Gill* (1977), 84 D.L.R. (3d) 765 (B.C.S.C.); *Corp. of City of North Vancouver v. North Shore Land Co.*, [1973] 6 W.W.R. 295 (B.C.S.C.)

[40] *Groat v. City of Edmonton*, [1928] S.C.R. 522 at p. 534, [1928] 3 D.L.R. 725 at p. 732, *per* Rinfret, J.: "But, whatever the consequences, and much as the result may cause inconvenience, the principle must be upheld that, unless Parliament otherwise decrees, 'public works must be so executed as not to interfere with private rights of individuals'." *Stephens v. Village of Richmond Hill*, [1955] 4 D.L.R. 572, [1955] O.R. 806 (H.C.J.), affd 1 D.L.R. (2d) 569, [1956] O.R. 88 (C.A.); *Plater v. Collingwood* (1967), 65 D.L.R. (2d) 492, [1968] 1 O.R. 81 (H.C.J.); *River Park Enterprises Ltd. v. Fort St. John* (1967), 62 D.L.R. (2d) 519 (B.C.S.C.); *Weber v. Town of Berlin* (1904), 8 O.L.R. 302 (H.C.J.); *B.C. Pea Growers Ltd. v. City of Portage La Prairie* (1963), 43 D.L.R. (2d) 713 (Man. Q.B.), affd 49 D.L.R. (2d) 91 (C.A.), affd [1966] S.C.R. 150, 54 D.L.R. (2d) 503.

[41] See, *e.g.*, *Boomer v. Atlantic Cement Co.*, 257 N.E. 2d 870 (N.Y.C.A., 1970); Thompson, *supra*, footnote 24; Keeton and Morris, "Notes on 'Balancing the Equities' ", 18 Tex. L. Rev. 412 (1940); McClintock, "Discretion to Deny Injunction Against Trespass and Nuisance", 12 Minn. L. Rev. 565 (1928). Tromans, *supra*, footnote 12, argues in favour of "balancing the equities" in nuisance cases.

[42] See cases cited, *infra*, footnotes 43-47. See also *Taylor v. Mullen Coal Co.* (1915), 21 D.L.R. 841 at pp. 841-2, 7 O.W.N. 764 (H.C.), affd D.L.R. *loc. cit.* p. 845*n*, 8 O.W.N. 445 (S.C. App. Div.), *per* Lennox, J.:

I should be careful, on the one hand, that industrial enterprise and the company's business is not unnecessarily obstructed, and, on the other, that the reasonable comfort and enjoyment, quiet and happiness, of the plaintiffs' homes are not unlawfully or wantonly sacrificed or set at naught.

Huston v. Lloyd Refineries Ltd., [1937] O.W.N. 53 (H.C.J.), at p. 56, *per* Greene, J. (affd on appeal but unreported, referred to in *Rombough v. Crestbrook Timber Ltd.* (1966), 57 D.L.R. (2d) 49 at p. 58) (granting a limited injunction): "It would not be proper to grant an absolute injunction which would destroy an investment of half a million dollars where adequate relief might be granted by awarding damful rhetoric of the 19th century English cases, the Canadian courts have not been constrained by a narrowly defined remedial choice. In *Chadwick v. City of Toronto*,[43] noise from a municipal pumping station was found to constitute a nuisance, but an injunction was refused on the ground that water was required for municipal purposes, and a damages award in substitution was preferable. The factual similarity between *Chadwick* and *Shelfer* is striking, and the different choice of remedy illustrates the difference between the Canadian and English approaches. Similarly, in *Black v. Canadian Copper Co.*,[44] it was said that, in certain cases, a plaintiff should not be allowed "so to assert his individual rights as to inflict a substantial injury upon the whole community . . . . The Court ought not to destroy the mining industry—nickel is of great value to the world—even if a few farms are damaged or destroyed; but in all such cases compensation, liberally estimated, ought to be awarded."[45]

386   In another case,[46] the Ontario Court of Appeal refused an injunction to restrain a nuisance where the effect would have been to destroy a local industry and throw a large number of people out of work, on the ground that there was "greatest disparity between the advantage to the plaintiff to be gained by the granting of an injunction and the inconvenience and disadvantage which the defendant and others would suffer in consequence".[47]

---

ages." See also *Morris v. Dominion Foundries & Steel*, [1947] 2 D.L.R. 840, [1947] O.W.N. 413 (H.C.J.), where explicit attention was paid to the cost to the defendant of having to move; *Mendez v. Palazzi* (1976), 68 D.L.R. (3d) 582, 12 O.R. (2d) 270 (Co. Ct.), where an injunction against encroaching tree roots was refused on the grounds that an injunction would be "oppressive" (*cf. McCombe v. Read*, [1955] 2 Q.B. 429); *Rombough v. Crestbrook Timber Ltd.* (1966), 57 D.L.R. (2d) 49 (B.C.C.A.); *Lockwood v. Brentwood Park Investments Ltd.* (1970), 10 D.L.R. (3d) 143 (N.S.S.C. App. Div.) (refusing an injunction restraining interference with owner's right to a free and undiminished flow of water); *Bridges Brothers Ltd. v. Forest Protection Ltd.* (1976), 72 D.L.R. (3d) 335 (N.B.S.C.). The approach taken in these cases is strongly supported by Read, "Equity and Public Wrongs", 11 Can. Bar Rev. 73 (1933), but resisted by McLaren, *supra*, footnote 29. Tromans, *supra*, footnote 12, at p. 99, commenting on the Canadian cases, states that despite the strict view taken in some cases, "on reading the Canadian cases, one is left with an impression of freshness and flexibility lacking in this country [England]".

[43] (1914), 32 O.L.R. 111 (S.C. App. Div.). *Cf. Hopkin v. Hamilton Electric Light & Cataract Power Co.* (1901), 2 O.L.R. 240 (H.C.J.), affd 4 O.L.R. 258 (C.A.), discussed further, *infra*, footnote 85.

[44] (1917), 12 O.W.N. 243 (H.C.), affd 17 O.W.N. 399 (Div. Ct.).

[45] *Ibid.*, at p. 244.

[46] *Bottom v. Ontario Leaf Tobacco Co. Ltd.*, [1935] 2 D.L.R. 699, [1935] O.R. 205 (C.A.).

[47] *Ibid.*, at p. 704 D.L.R., p. 210 O.R., *per* Macdonell, J.A., applying the dictum of

387   More recently, English courts have also vacillated on the automatic right to injunctive relief. In *Miller v. Jackson*,[48] the plaintiff
complained of cricket balls hit into her garden from the ground adjacent to her house. The cricket ground had been there long before the
surrounding and adjacent area was developed for housing. The village clearly derived great benefit from the cricket ground, and the
plaintiff had "come to the nuisance". On traditional principles, however, neither community benefit[49] nor "first come"[50] govern. Still,
Mrs. Miller did not get her injunction, and the opinions of the three
members of the Court of Appeal indicate an interesting range of
opinion. Lord Denning, M.R., would have found no liability at all,
placing special emphasis on the community interest and attaching
perhaps unorthodox significance to the fact that the cricket ground
was there first. Geoffrey Lane, L.J., took a traditional view, and
held that the cricket balls hit into the garden did constitute an unreasonable interference with the plaintiff's enjoyment, constituted a
nuisance, and should be enjoined. Cumming-Bruce, L.J., took a
middle position. He agreed that nuisance had been proved, but
openly applied a balance of interest approach. Taking into account
the interest of the defending cricketers and the inhabitants of the
community as a whole, an injunction would inflict an unreasonable

---

Duff, J., *supra*, §381, from *Canada Paper v. Brown*. In *Bottom*, Riddell, J.A., said
at p. 700 D.L.R., pp. 206-7 O.R.: "The public good can never be absent from the
mind of the Court when dealing with a matter of discretion." Both *Chadwick* and
Black were decided by Middleton, J. He wavered from the views expressed in those
cases both before: *Appleby v. Erie Tobacco Co.* (1910), 22 O.L.R. 533 (Div. Ct.);
and after, when he had been elevated to the Court of Appeal: *Duchman v. Oak-
land Dairy Co. Ltd.*, [1929] 1 D.L.R. 9, 63 O.L.R. 111 (S.C. App. Div.). In
Duchman, at p. 10 D.L.R., p. 127 O.L.R., *per* Riddell, J.A., there was disagree-
ment as to whether the Canadian practice varied from the English: "our Courts
have apparently been more liberal in applying Lord Cairns' Act than the Courts of
England"; *cf.* at p. 17 D.L.R., p. 134 O.L.R., *per* Middleton, J.A.:

> It has been suggested that our Courts are more free than the English Courts in
> substituting damages for an injunction. I do not agree with this proposition. Both
> in England and in this country there was a period of time in which the Courts had
> no settled policy . . . Each Judge did that which was right in his own eyes without
> recognizing any guiding principle, but as the law has come to be settled, the prin-
> ciple crystallized in the *Shelfer* case gradually emerged, and this has been ac-
> cepted everywhere as a sound guiding principle, and I think it should not be
> departed from.

[48] [1977] Q.B. 966 (C.A.).
[49] *Supra*, footnote 13.
[50] *Sturges v. Bridgman* (1879), 11 Ch. D. 852 (C.A.).

burden and, accordingly, he held that compensatory damages would be more appropriate.[51]

388 This range of views, expressed in a single case, is indicative of the difficulty of the remedial problems posed by nuisance cases, especially where the plaintiff has "come to the nuisance".[52]

389 A subsequent Court of Appeal decision suggests something of an English retrenchment. In *Kennaway v. Thompson*,[53] the plaintiff complained of noise produced by the defendant's speedboat club. The trial judge had refused an injunction and awarded damages, partly on the grounds of the public interest, as the club's activities were well attended. The defendants relied on *Miller v. Jackson*, but the Court of Appeal held that "there is nothing in *Miller v. Jackson* . . . binding on us, which qualifies what was decided in *Shelfer's* case",[54] and expressly refused to allow the public interest to prevail over the private interest.[55]

390 The result is that, while injunctive relief remains the preferred remedy in nuisance cases, it is not inevitable. Even in England, the courts have recognized a category of "trifling" injury where injunctions will be refused,[56] and the principle of balancing burden and benefit has been expressly adopted in nuisance cases where the plaintiff seeks mandatory relief.[57] In Canada, the practice is more flexible, and the same balancing principle has been applied in prohibitive injunction cases as well.

---

[51] Several Canadian cases have dealt with similar problems, although there has been less emphasis on community interest, and injunctions have usually been given. See *Segal v. Derrick Golf & Winter Club* (1977), 76 D.L.R. (3d) 746 (Alta. S.C.T.D.) (restraining the nuisance of golf balls being hit into plaintiff's garden); *Pardy v. Hiscock, Rose, Tulk and Burin Peninsula Integrated School Board* (1977), 17 Nfld. & P.E.I.R. 71 (Nfld. S.C.T.D.); *Cooke v. Town of Lockeport* (1969), 3 D.L.R. (3d) 155 (N.S.S.C.T.D.) (contempt application), 7 N.S.R. (2d) 191 (S.C.T.D.) (restraining nuisance of balls being struck on to plaintiff's property); *Savoie v. Breau* (1973), 8 N.B.R. (2d) 512 (S.C.Q.B.) (restraining playing of baseball altogether). In *Segal v. Derrick Golf & Winter Club*, *supra*, at p. 750, Belzil, J., quoted with approval the decision of Anderson, J., in *Lester-Travers v. City of Frankston*, [1970] V.R. 2 at p. 10: "it would be contrary to one's sense of justice, as well as inconsistent with the law, that the plaintiff's rights should be subordinated to the leisurely pursuits of sportsmen".

[52] For a discussion of the "coming to the nuisance" problem from an economic perspective, see Wittman, "First Come, First Served: An Economic Analysis of Coming to the Nuisance", 9 J. of Leg. Stud. 557 (1980).

[53] [1981] Q.B. 88 (C.A.).

[54] *Ibid.*, at p. 93, *per* Lawton, L.J.

[55] The Court did, however, substantially limit the scope of the injunction: see, *infra*, §395.

[56] *Supra*, §376.

[57] *Supra*, §378.

(3) Suspended injunctions

391   Another important technique employed by the courts, which also reflects a balancing approach, relates to the actual form the injunction can take. It has become common practice in nuisance cases for the court carefully to mould the order to soften the impact which would result from an absolute prohibition.

392   Several techniques are used. The most common is to stay the operation of the injunction, sometimes over an extended period, to give the defendant an opportunity to find some way of abating the nuisance.[58] Often such stays are coupled with leave to the defendant to apply for an extension if reasonable progress is being made.[59]

393   By ordering a stay, the courts often take away with one hand what they have just given with the other. *Stollmeyer v. Trinidad Lake Petroleum Co., Ltd.*,[60] a decision of the Privy Council, is often cited for the proposition that an injunction must follow a finding of nuisance, even where the hardship to the defendant is greatly in excess of the benefit to the plaintiff. Lord Sumner held that the defendants "cannot excuse or defend their wrong by showing how disproportionate is the loss which they will suffer", yet he went on to point out that these "considerations may be relevant to the form of the remedy, especially to the time and opportunities which should be given them for finding some way out of their difficulty".[61] In the result, it was held that only a declaration should issue forthwith, and that the plaintiff should have leave to apply for an injunction after two years. In a related proceeding,[62] while insisting that the "grant of an injunction is

---

[58] *K.V.P. Co. Ltd. v. McKie*, [1949] S.C.R. 698, [1949] 4 D.L.R. 497; *Plater v. Collingwood* (1967), 65 D.L.R. (2d) 492, [1968] 1 O.R. 81 (H.C.J.); *McKinnon Industries v. Walker*, [1951] 3 D.L.R. 577 (P.C.); *Stephens v. Village of Richmond Hill*, [1955] 4 D.L.R. 572, [1955] O.R. 806 (H.C.J.), affd 1 D.L.R. (2d) 569, [1956] O.R. 88 (C.A.); *Appleby v. Erie Tobacco Co.* (1910), 22 O.L.R. 533 (Div. Ct.); *Pride of Derby and Derbyshire Angling Ass'n v. British Celanese Ltd.*, [1953] Ch. 149 (C.A.); *Halsey v. Esso Petroleum Co. Ltd.*, [1961] 2 All E.R. 145 (Q.B.); *Manchester Corp. v. Farnworth*, [1930] A.C. 171 (H.L.). For a thorough review of the English practice, see Ogus and Richardson, *supra*, footnote 12.

[59] See, *e.g.*, *Taylor v. Mullen Coal·Co.* (1915), 21 D.L.R. 841, 7 O.W.N. 764 (H.C.), affd D.L.R. *loc. cit.* p. 845n, 8 O.W.N. 445 (S.C. App. Div.); *Stevenson v. Colvin* (1918), 13 O.W.N. 426 (H.C.); *Francklyn v. People's Heat & Light Co.* (1899), 32 N.S.R. 44 (C.A.); *Brown v. Town of Morden*, [1958] 12 D.L.R. (2d) 576 (Man. Q.B.); *River Park Enterprises Ltd. v. Fort St. John* (1967), 62 D.L.R. (2d) 519 (B.C.S.C.); *Canada Paper Co. v. Brown* (1921), 63 S.C.R. 243 at p. 258, 66 D.L.R. 287 at p. 296, *per* Anglin, J.

[60] [1918] A.C. 485 (P.C.).

[61] *Ibid.*, at p. 494.

[62] *Stollmeyer v. Petroleum Development Co., Ltd.*, [1918] A.C. 498 (P.C.).

the proper remedy for a violation of right according to a current of authority, which is of many years' standing and is practically unbroken",[63] Lord Sumner observed that the "loss to the respondents would be out of all proportion to the appellant's gain",[64] and suspended the injunction for two years with leave to apply for a further extension.

394   The suspension of the injunction may be made conditional upon the payment of damages for harm suffered during the period of suspension.[65] As the effect of suspending the injunction is to saddle the plaintiff with what has been held to be a wrongful interference, a strong argument can be made that payment of damages should be an ordinary term of a suspension. On the other hand, it has been suggested that refusing compensation may be legitimate in certain cases as a way of forcing the plaintiff to bear some of the costs of an injunction,[66] analogous to the compensated injunction, discussed below.[67] Conditional injunctions of this kind offer a variety of flexible solutions which may help to achieve the sensitive balancing of interests often involved in these cases.[68]

(4) Defining levels of harm

395   Injunctions may be limited to restraining certain levels of activity or certain types of interference. While in earlier cases orders were framed very generally, simply prohibiting the defendant from behaving so as to cause a nuisance to the plaintiff,[69] it is becoming more common for the order to provide specific guidance, and to avoid lan-

---

[63] *Stollmeyer, supra*, footnote 62, at p. 499, a passage applied in *K.V.P. Co. Ltd. v. McKie*, [1949] S.C.R. 698, [1949] 4 D.L.R. 497, discussed, *supra*, §384.

[64] *Stollmeyer, supra*, at p. 500.

[65] In *Stollmeyer, supra*, footnote 60, the defendant undertook to pay damages, and the suspension was ordered on that basis. For Canadian examples, see *Vancouver Waterfront Ltd. v. Vancouver Harbour Com'rs*, [1936] 1 D.L.R. 461 (B.C.C.A.); *River Park Enterprises Ltd. v. Fort St. John* (1967), 62 D.L.R. (2d) 519 (B.C.S.C.).

[66] See Ogus and Richardson, *supra*, footnote 12.

[67] *Infra*, §397.

[68] See, *e.g.*, *Crane v. Crane* (1976), 14 Nfld. & P.E.I.R. 231 (Nfld. S.C.T.D.) (varying an interlocutory injunction to permit defendant to grow and harvest crops on disputed land); *Culp and Hart v. Township of East York* (1956), 6 D.L.R. (2d) 417, [1956] O.R. 983 (H.C.J.), affd 9 D.L.R. (2d) 749, [1957] O.W.N. 515 (C.A.) (mandatory injunction to remove traffic signal suspended, and to be dissolved if requisite approval obtained within period of suspension); *Belleville v. Moxam*, [1953] 4 D.L.R. 151, [1953] O.W.N. 567 (H.C.J.) (construction commenced on faith of building permit later held to be void; injunction granted on condition municipality bears expenses incurred by defendant until action commenced).

[69] *Supra*, §40.

guage which effectively amounts to outright prohibition of the activity complained of.[70] In most cases, the problem is not seen as one of eliminating the interference but rather limiting it to a more tolerable level. A good example is provided by the decision of the English Court of Appeal in *Kennaway v. Thompson*.[71] While insisting on injunctive relief rather than damages, the court made a complex and detailed order which did not prevent the defendants from conducting their speedboat races, but limited the type and frequency of such events. Between the extremes of finding no wrong at all and awarding an injunction which would completely stop whatever it is the defendant is doing, there is a wide range. In an area where the substantive definition of rights is so flexible and relative, it would be unfortunate to impose black and white remedial choices, and the courts have properly exploited the flexibility of partial or qualified injunctions.

396   It is submitted that where the situation has crystallized and the court has sufficient information at the trial, the practice of issuing relatively specific orders of this type offers distinct advantages. They allow the court to adopt a more refined and precise approach to the balancing of competing property interests. They assist the defendant in telling him precisely what he can do, and avoid causing unnecessary caution on his part, which may often be prompted by a vague order in general terms. In addition, specific orders avoid postponing the decision as to important details to the more awkward procedural form of a contempt application.[72]

(5) Compensated injunction

397   Another device, which so far has remained mostly theoretical, is the compensated injunction.[73] Under such an order, the plaintiff is given an injunction, but only on the condition that he compensate

---

[70] See, *e.g.*, *Walker v. Pioneer Construction* (1975), 56 D.L.R. (3d) 677, 8 O.R. (2d) 35 (H.C.J.); *Rombough v. Crestbrook Timber Ltd.* (1966), 57 D.L.R. (2d) 49 (B.C.C.A.); *Huston v. Lloyd Refineries Ltd.*, [1937] O.W.N. 53 (H.C.J.), affd on appeal but unreported, referred to in *Rombough v. Crestbrook Timber, supra*, at p. 58; *Turtle v. City of Toronto* (1924), 56 O.L.R. 252 (S.C. App. Div.), at p. 274, *per* Masten, J.A.: "[the court] will lean against obstructing by its order the operations of a public service corporation if that corporation is *bona fide* endeavouring to perform its statutory functions in a fair and reasonable manner".

[71] [1981] Q.B. 88 (C.A.).

[72] *Supra*, §39.

[73] The leading, if not only, example of this device is provided by *Spur Industries, Inc. v. Del E. Webb Development Co.*, 494 P. 2d 700 (Ariz. S.C., 1972). See further, *infra*, §416.

the defendant for all or part of the costs the injunction imposes. Such an order may seem appropriate where the plaintiff is entitled to be free of the defendant's nuisance-creating activity, but it seems harsh or unfair to impose upon the defendant all of the costs of abating or removing the nuisance.[74]

(6) Conclusion

398   The choice the courts must make between injunction and damages, or as to the appropriate form of injunction, raises difficult issues. As mentioned at the outset, injunctive relief reflects the very essence of a property right: the owner is not to be deprived of his right or suffer interference with it except when he consents or, if his property right is to be sold, at his own price. While a damages award does recognize the existence of a right, it does deny these essential attributes of a property right. Making the availability of injunctive relief contingent upon the outcome of a balance of burden against benefit appears, then, to permit the form of remedy to qualify the nature of the substantive right. The balancing approach may be criticized as permitting an illegitimate sacrifice of individual rights to the general social welfare. It deprives an individual of his right to property merely because the enjoyment of that right has become inconvenient to society at large, or because someone else can make more efficient use of it.

399   The conflicting principle which favours balancing reflects a concern for efficiency and general social welfare, and accepts those values as legitimate goals to be pursued by courts in making remedial choices.

400   These issues go beyond the study of remedies and to the heart of political and ethical theory, and range much wider than the scope of this book. However, within the context of a discussion of remedial issues, there are several points which can be made.

401   The first is that the principle of social necessity overriding individual property rights, especially where compensation is provided, is in fact well accepted. Probably no theory of property rights would go so far as to deny the proposition that social need and the general social welfare may, in certain circumstances, justify overriding rights of private property. At some point, a limit to the acceptable level of net social cost caused by adherence to an absolute definition of property rights is reached, and at that point, compulsory acquisition with com-

---

[74] Rabin, "Nuisance Law: Rethinking Fundamental Assumptions", 63 Va. L. Rev. 1299 (1977), favours this form of remedy.

pensation is justified. There can be debate upon when that point is reached, but few, if any, would deny the principle. Once the principle is accepted, then the question becomes an institutional one: is only the Legislature competent to define that point, or is the principle one which may be legitimately applied in the process of adjudication? As the cases which have been discussed show, there are two distinct and virtually irreconcilable theories. The English approach, and that taken by most Canadian courts, is to deny any power to allow efficiency or general welfare to govern. However, this absolute position has not been followed in many other Canadian judgments, and is certainly contradicted by cases dealing with mandatory injunctions.

402 In Ontario, a series of important riparian cases illustrate the play between the courts and the Legislature, and how legislative action may be provoked where the court finds itself unable to consider the general community interest.[75] At trial in the *K. V. P.* case already discussed,[76] McRuer, C.J.H.C., held that an agreement between the defendant company and the province apparently permitting the discharge in question provided no defence. The pulp and paper mill was virtually the sole employer in the community, and while an appeal to the Supreme Court of Canada was pending, the Ontario Legislature amended the Lakes and Rivers Improvement Act,[77] which allowed the court to balance community interest, to include expressly discharge of chemical waste from pulp and paper mills. The Supreme Court of Canada held, however, that it had to dispose of the case on the basis of the law as it existed at the time the Court of Appeal had heard the appeal, and the injunction was upheld. The Legislature acted again, this time expressly dissolving the injunction which the courts had granted.[78]

403 Shortly thereafter, a similar problem occurred when injunctions were granted against two municipalities prohibiting the pollution of rivers by sewage disposal. In the first case, *Stephens v. Village of Richmond Hill*,[79] Stewart, J., explicitly rejected the notion of balanc-

---

[75] See Anisman, "Water Pollution Control in Ontario", 5 Ottawa L. Rev. 342 (1972), at pp. 373-9.

[76] *Supra*, §384.

[77] Lakes and Rivers Improvement Act, S.O. 1949, c. 48, s. 6; R.S.O. 1980, c. 229, s. 39.

[78] *Supra*, footnote 38.

[79] [1955] 4 D.L.R. 572, [1955] O.R. 806 (H.C.J.), affd 1 D.L.R. (2d) 569, [1956] O.R. 88 (C.A.).

ing interests: "it is not for the judiciary to permit the doctrine of utilitarianism to be used as a make-weight in the scales of justice. In civil matters, the function of the Court is to determine rights between parties. . . . It is the duty of the state (and of statesmen) to seek the greatest good for the greatest number."[80] The Legislature acted again and dissolved the injunctions.[81] These cases led to the establishment of the Ontario Water Resources Commission,[82] and to the implementation of an elaborate administrative mechanism to cope with the problems of water pollution. There have been few, if any, reported Ontario riparian cases since. There is little doubt that the rigid refusal of the courts to consider community needs and their refusal to consider more flexible solutions in riparian cases led to the effective demise of the common law action in this type of case and to its replacement by an administrative scheme. Because the effects of pollution are widespread and require consideration not only of community, social and economic interests but also of detailed technical problems, an administrative solution is perhaps to be expected.[83] However, nuisance cases will still come before the courts, and the Ontario experience suggests that where the courts ignore the social consequences of their orders, alternative solutions will be found to accommodate a broader range of interests than is possible in an adversarial proceeding between particular parties.

404   Apart from institutional constraints many factors favour injunctions. One point, implicit in the case-law, is that there are social costs associated with departing from an order which fully vindicates a property right. This occurs where the award appears to permit the defendant to circumvent the ordinary bargaining process.[84] If damages rather than injunctions are routinely awarded on an objectively

---

[80] [1955] 4 D.L.R. at pp. 578-9, [1955] O.R. at pp. 812-13.

[81] Public Health Act, S.O. 1956, c. 71, s. 6(23). See also s. 6(22), overriding the injunction granted in *Burgess v. Woodstock*, [1955] 4 D.L.R. 615, [1955] O.R. 814 (H.C.J.).

[82] Ontario Water Resources Commission Act, S.O. 1956, c. 62; R.S.O. 1980, c. 361. See Anisman, *supra*, footnote 75.

[83] See also Environmental Protection Act (Ont.). The legal techniques available to control pollution are discussed in Lucas, "Legal Techniques for Pollution Control: The Role of the Public", 6 U.B.C. L. Rev. 167 (1971); Anisman, *supra*, footnote 75; Landis, "Legal Controls of Pollution in the Great Lakes Basin", 48 Can. Bar Rev. 66 (1970); Elder, "Environmental Protection through the Common Law", 12 Western Ont. L. Rev. 107 (1973); Juergensmeyer, "Common Law Remedies and Protection of the Environment", 6 U.B.C. L. Rev. 215 (1971).

[84] Michelman, "Property, Utility and Fairness: Comments on the Ethical Foundations of 'Just Compensation' Law", 80 Harv. L. Rev. 1165 (1967).

measured market value scale, potential defendants, who know that their proposed activity will interfere with neighbours, will have less incentive to resolve the problem of conflicting use outside the court-room.[85] An injunction which operates harshly on one defendant may seem justified if it will deter others from failing to heed the interests of their neighbours at the outset. As the courts have often said, damages in substitution for an injunction should not be used to license wrongdoing.[86] If the defendant knows he can do no worse than an objectively measured market value assessment, he will avoid the ordinary bargaining process where he can hardly do any better, and may do a whole lot worse. This would make damage awards a particularly objectionable form of expropriation. The defendant would have to give no notice, satisfy no predetermined standard of public necessity or need, and the plaintiff would only receive compensation by undertaking costly litigation. This suggests that even the pursuit of the goal of minimizing net social costs may lead to the award of injunctions if consideration is given to the message an order would give to potential defendants. It also suggests that consideration of the deliberateness of the defendant's conduct, a matter often referred to in the cases,[87] is important. If the defendant has harmed the plaintiff inadvertently, then there is less need to impose a harsh or costly order, which would have less deterrent force for others.

405   Another point favouring injunctions relates to the unlikelihood of the defendant having to compensate all those affected. This factor is undoubtedly one which underlies the resort to legislative schemes designed to control air and water pollution. The common law depends upon the initiative of the injured party to litigate and, as a practical matter, these law suits are bound to be rare. If the harmful effect of his activity is suffered by a large number of people, all of whom suffer relatively small losses, under present law the chances of the defendant ever having to compensate are remote. In some cases, an

---

[85] This point appears to have been implicitly accepted in *Hopkin v. Hamilton Electric Light & Cataract Power Co.* (1901), 2 O.L.R. 240 (H.C.J.), affd 4 O.L.R. 258 (C.A.). The facts were similar to *Shelfer*, and in awarding an injunction, Street, J., said, at p. 247: "To ask a railway company to buy all the land within the limits of the nuisance they cause by smoke, fire, and vibration would be prohibitive, but the same considerations do not apply to the case of isolated works such as these." On appeal, Moss, J.A., stated, at p. 261: "it is not shewn to be impossible that land might be acquired in such a situation and of such an extent as to enable the works to be operated without being a nuisance to adjoining land".

[86] *Shelfer v. City of London Electric Lighting Co.*, [1895] 1 Ch. 287 (C.A.), at pp. 315-16, *per* Lindley, L.J.

[87] *Supra*, §§59-62.

individual plaintiff who suffers a small loss and does sue may merely represent a larger number of injured parties. Under existing rules, class actions are not available as a procedural device to enable damage claims of this variety to be grouped.[88] An injunction in favour of an individual plaintiff who has suffered a small loss may be justified as a means of protecting the many absent parties who are also injured. Even if class actions are made available, injunctions may offer certain advantages if administrative and judicial costs are taken into account. Costs of notification and the task of assessing a large number of individual claims, even if on a global basis, are avoided through an injunction.

406   A third argument in favour of injunctive relief relates to distinguishing the short from the long term. A decision based upon what appears to be socially beneficial or efficient between the immediate parties may fail to take into account the interests of future generations.[89] Environmentalists argue that these issues are much more complex than simply resolving the dispute between immediate parties.[90] A tough order against the defendant which appears to impose costs on him disproportionate to the benefit accruing to the plaintiff may be justified, even from an efficiency point of view, if the long-term effects of the defendant's activity are taken into account. While the primary task of the courts is to resolve the dispute presented by the immediate parties, it is not uncommon for the courts to take third party interests into account when making remedial choices.[91] Explicit reference to the long-term effects of pollution has been made in the case-law,[92] and it would appear to be an important factor. Where the nuisance consists of an activity producing pollution which will have certain long-term effects, the courts almost invariably award injunctions despite disproportionate short-term costs. As noted, riparian owners in particular are routinely awarded injunc-

---

[88] *Preston v. Hilton* (1920), 55 D.L.R. 647, 48 O.L.R. 172 (H.C.); *Turtle v. City of Toronto* (1924), 56 O.L.R. 252 (S.C. App. Div.). Compare, however, the class action regime proposed by the Ontario Law Reform Commission, *Report on Class Actions* (1982).

[89] See Calabresi and Melamed, *infra*, footnote 101, at p. 1124; Michelman, *supra*, footnote 84, at p. 684; McLaren, *supra*, footnote 29, at p. 556.

[90] See esp. McLaren, *supra*, footnote 29.

[91] Cases cited, *supra*, §§385-388.

[92] *Pride of Derby and Derbyshire Angling Ass'n v. British Celanese Ltd.*, [1953] Ch. 149 (C.A.), at p. 192, *per* Denning, L.J.: "The power of the courts to issue an injunction for nuisance has proved itself to be the best method so far devised of securing the cleanliness of our rivers". See also *K.V.P. Co. Ltd. v. McKie, supra*, §384.

tions despite trivial personal monetary loss.[93] Most cases involving an award of damages over an injunction involve non-physical annoyances which interfere with the plaintiff's enjoyment of his property, but which have no apparent long-term effects.[94] It is difficult to distinguish these cases on the basis of the extent of harm suffered by the individual plaintiffs, whereas consideration of the longer-term harmful impact on society of the defendant's activity does provide a rationale.

407   There are, however, important considerations which will often favour a damages award over an injunction. In some cases, the value of the objectively measured interest, which the plaintiff seeks to protect, may be so minimal compared with the social cost of respecting that interest to the full, that injunctive relief is inappropriate. It is argued below[95] that this situation may be encountered even in trespass cases; if the case can be made out there, the same argument applies, *a fortiori*, to nuisance.

408   A closely related point fastens upon the relationship between substantive and remedial law in the nuisance area. In a sense, a theory of absolute property rights can hardly be applied in nuisance cases.[96] The very definition of rights conferred by the substantive law of nuisance negates any absolute view. Substantive rights are determined by the relative concepts of reasonableness and local standards. The law of nuisance attempts to reconcile competing property interests. The defendant's conduct is not wrongful *per se*; the exploitation and enjoyment of his own property becomes actionable only when it interferes with the plaintiff's reasonable enjoyment. The problem is one of balancing the plaintiff's right to enjoy his property in the way he wishes against the right of the defendant to exploit his own property to suit his own purposes. It is hardly surprising that the balanc-

---

[93] See esp. the *K.V.P.* case, discussed, *supra*, §384.

[94] *Epstein v. Reymes*, [1973] S.C.R. 85 at p. 95, 29 D.L.R. (3d) 1 at p. 8, *per* Laskin, J., makes it clear, however, that injunctions are often appropriate in such cases: "The absence of physical injury or property damage does not affect the right to an injunction where there is conduct, not merely temporary, which materially interferes with the comfort and enjoyment of living in the locality." See also *La-Ko Enterprises Ltd. v. Van Wart* (1981), 124 D.L.R. (3d) 553 (N.B.C.A.); *Walker v. Pioneer Construction* (1975), 56 D.L.R. (3d) 677, 8 O.R. (2d) 35 (H.C.J.); *Kennaway v. Thompson*, [1981] Q.B. 88 (C.A.).

[95] *Infra*, §430.

[96] See Horwitz, *supra*, footnote 14, at p. 31, discussing the shift from the concept of absolute dominion to conflicting use: "because this [absolute] conception of ownership necessarily circumscribed the rights of others to develop their land, it was, in fact, incompatible with a commitment to absolute dominion".

ing of rights and interests which is such an integral part of the substantive law of nuisance, should be continued to the point where the court must make a choice of remedies. Indeed, it would be regrettable to force all cases into an inflexible and inevitable choice of injunction as the only appropriate remedy. Even from the point of view of protecting individual property rights, it may be preferable to maintain remedial flexibility. The definition of substantive rights is not fixed with precision, and if the court assumes that it must grant an injunction, it will surely be less willing to find a nuisance in the first place. In that situation, the plaintiff receives no remedy at all. If the remedial choice is more flexible, and the consequences of finding liability less drastic, the courts will be more willing to find liability in the first place.[97] Thus, it is suggested, flexible remedial choice and the possibility that damages rather than an injunction might be awarded is not only consistent with, but may in fact enhance, the protection of individual property rights. Indeed, there are several Canadian cases in which damages have been awarded on facts which barely amount to actionable nuisance.[98] One wonders whether the more flexible choice between damages and injunctions in Canada did not make the court more willing to find a nuisance in the first place.[99]

409   The conclusion is, then, that there is much to be said for what at first appears to be the inconsistent Canadian position. Injunctions will ordinarily be awarded in nuisance cases, especially where the harmful effects are widespread or permanent, but damages can be substituted where an injunction would impose costs clearly disproportionate to the benefits it confers.

3. Economic Analysis

410   Economists have turned their attention to the question of remedial choice in nuisance cases, and while lawyers may find the analysis unfamiliar, there is benefit to be derived from seeing legal problems subjected to the analytic techniques of another discipline.

---

[97] Ellickson, "Alternatives to Zoning: Covenants, Nuisance Rules, and Fines as Land Use Controls" 40 U. of Chi. L. Rev. 681 (1973), at p. 720; Rabin, *supra*, footnote 74, at p. 1346.

[98] *Nestor v. Hayes Wheel Co.* (1924), 26 O.W.N. 129 (H.C.); *Ramsay v. Barnes* (1913), 5 O.W.N. 322 (H.C.); *Belisle v. Canadian Cottons Ltd.*, [1952] O.W.N. 114 (H.C.J.); *Pope v. Peate* (1904), 7 O.L.R. 207 (H.C.J.); *Morris v. Dominion Foundries & Steel*, [1947] 2 D.L.R. 840, [1947] O.W.N. 413 (H.C.J.).

[99] Nedelsky, *supra*, footnote 14, suggests that the Canadian courts are more willing to find a nuisance than are the English. Tromans, *supra*, footnote 12, argues that the converse has occurred in England, *i.e.*, courts have refused to find a nuisance because to do so would require that an injunction be awarded.

411   The starting point of economic analysis in this area is the so-called Coase theorem[100] which contains a valuable insight into the relationship between legal rights and efficiency. Ordinarily, property rights can be bought and sold. The thrust of the Coase theorem is that whatever initial assignment of rights is made by the law, economic forces will operate so that the person who most values the right will acquire it in the end. Thus, market forces will tend to produce the most efficient allocation of resources whether or not the law gives a right to use that resource to the party who can put it to the most efficient use. Such a result is said to be "efficient" in that it maximizes net social wealth: the gain to the party acquiring the right exceeds the loss to the party giving it up.[101] The theory assumes that both parties conduct themselves so as to maximize their own wealth, and on that hypothesis, transactions will occur until the gains from trading are exhausted. Thus, while the legal approach is to determine who is in the "right", economic forces will "correct" judicial decisions which produce inefficient results. In the context of nuisance disputes, the focus of economic analysis is "whether the gain from preventing the harm is greater than the loss which would be suffered elsewhere as a result of stopping the action which produces the harm".[102]

412   The analysis suggested by the Coase theorem may be illustrated by the following example. Assume a factory which creates a nuisance and derives a $100,000 benefit from increased production directly attributable to the nuisance-creating activity. The home-owner beside the factory is bothered by the nuisance, but would be prepared to put up with it if paid $80,000. Thus, it can be said that the value to the home-owner of being free of the nuisance is $80,000. The efficient allocation of resources would be to permit the factory to go on polluting, because it is worth $20,000 more to the factory to pollute than it is to the home-owner to breathe clean air. That allocation of the resource will in fact occur, according to the Coase theorem, whether the law says that the home-owner has the right to be free of pollution or whether the factory has the right to pollute. Even if the home-

---

[100] Coase, "The Problem of Social Cost", 3 J. of Law and Econ. 1 (1960).

[101] There are a variety of definitions of efficiency used in this context. The definition used in the most influential article, Calabresi and Melamed, "Property Rules, Liability Rules and Inalienability: One View of the Cathedral", 85 Harv. L. Rev. 1089 (1972), at p. 1094, is the following: "[that] allocation of resources which could not be improved in the sense that a further change would not so improve the condition of those who gained by it that they could compensate those who lost from it and still be better off than before".

[102] Coase, *supra*, footnote 100, at p. 27.

owner gets an injunction against the factory, the factory will be willing to pay him up to $100,000 in exchange for his right to enforce the injunction. If the figures are reversed, and freedom from nuisance is worth more to the home-owner than creating the nuisance is worth to the factory, then even if the home-owner has no legal right to stop the nuisance, he will pay the factory up to $100,000 to stop, as he would still be better off by the equivalent of $20,000 to be free of the nuisance.

413   If the Coase theorem told the whole story, the law could ignore the goal of efficiency as a consideration in resolving disputes. The problem of social costs would be solved by economic forces whatever goals the law sought to pursue in the initial assignment of rights and determination of appropriate remedies.[103] Clearly, however, as Coase himself pointed out,[104] the theory is based upon the usually unrealistic assumption of perfect market conditions. In this blissful economic state, transactions occur without cost. In the real world, where there usually are costs in striking bargains, those costs must be taken into account in the overall calculation of social gains and losses. When there are costs associated with transactions, a bargain which would otherwise benefit both parties will not be struck if the gains from the bargain do not exceed the costs of reaching the bargain.

414   While economists do not appear to have derived a settled definition of "transaction costs",[105] the economic analysis of law literature identifies certain sources relevant to the nuisance problem.[106] Numerous parties in the same interest are said to produce "holdout" and "freerider" problems. Thus, where pollution would be worth $100,000 to the factory in increased production, and the 100 residents affected value freedom from pollution at $800 each, the efficient allocation of resources would be to allow the factory to continue polluting, as it values pollution by $20,000 more than the residents value being free of pollution. However, assuming an initial inefficient assignment is made to the 100 residents, some of them will try to get a share of the full $100,000 that the factory derives from

---

[103] See Weinrib, "Utilitarianism, Economics, and Legal Theory", 30 U. of T. L.J. 307 (1980), esp. at p. 328: "What seems to follow from Coase's demonstration is not that the initial distribution is irrelevant to legal theory, but that it is the *only* relevant issue, since it is the only issue which can be affected by the operation of the judicial process."

[104] *Supra*, footnote 100.

[105] See Veljanovski, "The Economic Approach to Law: A Critical Introduction", 7 Br. J. of Law and Society 158 (1980).

[106] See especially Calabresi and Melamed, *supra*, footnote 101.

pollution, and will conceal their true valuation and "hold out" for more than \$800. The factory will incur costs in discovering their true valuation and bargaining with them. If the amount it takes to buy them out together with the cost of the transaction exceeds \$100,000, then the transaction will not occur, although, *ex hypothesi*, a bargain would be efficient. Conversely, if the factory is given the entitlement and the figures are reversed, and each of the 100 residents values clean air at \$1,000 and pollution is worth \$80,000 to the factory, "freeriders" will refuse to disclose their true valuation, hoping that the \$80,000 will be made up by others. In either case, strategic behaviour may generate prohibitive transaction costs, and the "market" will fail to produce the efficient outcome.

415 At this point, there is an important shift in economic analysis. In the absence of transaction costs, the law can ignore efficiency, and pursue whatever goals seem appropriate. However, in the real world of high transaction costs, the legal system cannot rely on the market to correct "errors" — from the efficiency point of view — in the initial assignment of rights. Economic analysis becomes prescriptive and suggests that if the goal of efficiency is to be pursued, the law must consciously develop a strategy aimed at achieving that goal.

416 The starting point is the identification of three levels of protection and four remedial possibilities.[107] While this categorization was adopted to facilitate the development of the economic model, it is also usefully employed in more traditional legal analysis, and has influenced recent thinking on remedies, as is evident from other parts of this book. The three levels of protection or types of "entitlement"[108] are:

(1) a property rule, that is: "someone who wishes to remove the entitlement from its holder must buy it from him in a voluntary transaction in which the value of the entitlement is agreed upon by the seller";

(2) a liability rule allowing the defendant to "destroy the initial entitlement if he is willing to pay an objectively determined value for it";

---

[107] See the Calabresi-Melamed article, *supra*, footnote 101, developing the analysis first undertaken by Michelman, "Pollution as a Tort: A Non-Accidental Perspective on Calabresi's *Costs*", 80 Yale L.J. 647 (1971). Needless to say, not all economists agree with the Calabresi-Melamed approach: see, *e.g.*, Burrows, "Nuisance, Legal Rules and Decentralized Decisions: a Different View of the Cathedral Crypt", Chapter 6 in *The Economic Approach to Law*, Burrows and Veljanovski, eds (London, Butterworths, 1981).

[108] Calabresi and Melamed, *supra*, footnote 101, at p. 1092.

(3) inalienability, that is, "that its transfer is not permitted between a willing buyer and a willing seller".

The four remedial[109] possibilities are as follows:

(1) An injunction. The polluter is restrained and the plaintiff is fully protected. In this situation, the plaintiff is said to be given a property-type protection in that his right to be free of pollution can only be taken away from him if he chooses to sell, and then it must be paid for at an agreed price.

(2) Damages. The polluter is liable but the plaintiff is merely compensated. The polluter may go on polluting and the effect of the order is to "buy out" the plaintiff at an objective and judicially determined price rather than at a price agreed to by the plaintiff and the defendant. The plaintiff is given a liability-type of protection only.

(3) No liability. This choice may be described as a property-type protection in favour of the polluter. He is permitted to go on polluting and can be stopped only if the plaintiff buys him out at an agreed price. This third choice is the reverse of the first.

(4) Compensated injunction. This final remedial choice is one which has many attractions but which has been rarely employed.[110] The property owner is protected by an injunction, but only on the condition that he buy out the polluter at a judicially determined price, usually fixed to compensate the polluter for relocation expenses and the loss of sunk costs. This is the reverse of the second possibility, and may be said to make the property owner "liable" for the cost of removing the source of the harm.

417   As indicated above, in the absence of transaction costs, an efficient allocation will occur as a result of post-judgment bargaining, even if the court opts for an apparently inefficient result by granting or refusing an injunction, and thereby imposes burdens on the loser out of

---

[109] In this context, 'remedial' is more broadly defined than elsewhere in the book. The economist obviously is concerned with the question of substantive liability as well as with that of the selection of the appropriate remedy once the substantive right is found.

[110] The only example appears to be *Spur Industries, Inc. v. Del E. Webb Development Co.*, 494 P. 2d 700 (Ariz. S.C., 1972). *Cf.* Rabin, "Nuisance Law: Rethinking Fundamental Assumptions", 63 Va. L. Rev. 1299 (1977), favouring increased use of this possibility. Where a plaintiff obtains an interlocutory injunction, he must pay the price through his undertaking in damages should he fail at trial, *supra*, §§173-178, and this may be seen as analogous to the "compensated injunction". See also, *supra*, §397, where the defendant is required to pay damages as a condition of having an injunction suspended.

proportion with the benefit derived by the winner. Where, however, there are transaction costs which would preclude such a bargain, a court motivated solely to attain the efficient result must pursue a conscious strategy to that end.

418   Assuming that there are high transaction costs, and that the choice of remedy is to be governed solely by the goal of efficiency, economic analysis is said to yield the following result.[111] If the court is certain that one party can avoid or reduce the cost of the conflicting property use more cheaply than the other, then a "property" rule is called for, which assigns the entitlement to the latter so as to induce the former to adopt cost-minimizing precautions (injunction in favour of the polluted, no liability on polluter, as appropriate). Because the court is certain that one party is the least cost avoider, there is no need to incur the judicial and administrative costs inherent in a liability rule which requires assessment of the value of the nuisance.

419   Where there is doubt as to which party is the least cost avoider (and this is likely to be so in most pollution cases), a property rule should be avoided. If the court is wrong in its guess, transaction costs will prevent the market from correcting the error. What the court must do here is construct a hypothetical market, and through a damages award, determine objectively the valuation which would have been made had there been no market failure. Almost invariably, this means imposing liability on the polluter, and awarding damages in compensation.[112] So long as the amount of damages is an accurate reflection of the injury caused, efficiency will be satisfied. The damages award, taking the place of the market transaction which circumstances prevent, will put the conflict to the efficiency test: can the polluter's enterprise pay damages and still operate profitably, or does the value to the property owners (objectively measured) exceed the value in production gained by polluting? Theoretically, a similar result can be obtained from the fourth possible choice, that of a compensated injunction. Making the affected party pay the costs that an injunction imposes upon the polluter weighs the relative values of the parties in a similar way.

---

[111] Calabresi and Melamed, *supra*, footnote 101.

[112] *Cf.* Polinsky, "Resolving Nuisance Disputes: The Simple Economics of Injunctive and Damage Remedies", 32 Stanford L. Rev. 1075 (1980), suggesting that efficiency does not unambiguously favour either damages or injunctions. Polinsky's analysis examines combined remedies, where injunctions limit harmful activities to intermediate levels and damages are given for harm actually suffered. The analysis is based, however, on the assumption of a single victim, and Polinsky seems to accept that damages may be favoured where there are many victims.

420   Thus, in terms of actual results, the economic model outlined here
would probably produce more damage awards than does the existing
case-law.[113] Economic analysis avoids injunctions which cannot, as a
practical matter, be bargained around. Many nuisance cases involve
harmful effects on a large number of parties, and thus market failure
due to high transaction costs suggests damages as the effective remedy. Assuming high transaction costs, an injunction will be awarded
against a polluter only where he is clearly the least cost avoider. This
is a much narrower range of case than presented by the case-law.
Plaintiffs who are least cost avoiders would also be disfavoured by
economic analysis: if the court determines that the value of pollution
exceeds the value of being pollution free, the plaintiff would be denied relief altogether and the polluter would have the "remedy" of
no liability.

421   Clearly, there are substantial objections and major difficulties in
the way of implementing this economic model as the sole standard
for the resolution of nuisance disputes.[114] The law tends to focus on
righting past wrongs and preventing future wrongs, whereas the
economist's concern is to provide the appropriate structure of incen-
tives to encourage the efficient allocation of resources. While the
pursuit of efficiency is also an important legal goal, it is a pursuit
qualified by the concept of rights which may not be superseded
merely because the general social welfare would be advanced. To
take perhaps the most obvious example emerging from the foregoing
discussion, a concept of rights renders inconceivable a result whereby
the plaintiff is told by the court that he has lost because he is clearly
the least cost avoider, or even that he is being denied an injunction
and being judicially expropriated for an objectively measured
amount because transaction costs are high. Taken to its logical conclusion and if fully implemented as a legal principle, efficiency analysis would appear to make expropriation legislation unnecessary.[115] It
would provide justification for allocating and altering property rights
solely on the basis of efficiency. The jurisprudential limit upon the
value of efficiency is not a subject within the scope of this book;

---

[113] Ellickson, *supra*, footnote 97, at p. 740, argues for damages in all cases except
where there has been a fundamental infringement: "A trade-off must be made between the value of individual autonomy and the possible efficiency and liberty gains
from fewer restrictions or interaction."

[114] Ogus and Richardson, *supra*, footnote 12.

[115] See Calabresi, *supra*, footnote 101.

suffice it to say that it is rarely suggested that justice can be defined in terms of efficiency alone.[116]

422   The economic model is also based on certain assumptions which cause difficulty if the model is to be used as a means of resolving concrete problems. The most important from the legal perspective is first, that the motive for all behaviour can be explained as a desire to maximize wealth, and second, that the existing distribution of wealth must be taken as a given. Few will accept that human behaviour can be entirely or adequately explained, for legal purposes, on the basis of the theory of wealth maximization.[117] The other important point is the fact that the differences in wealth and ability to bargain render efficiency analysis much less precise than it first appears to be. The ability and willingness to pay is clearly affected by wealth, and hence, for every different distribution of wealth, there is a different efficient outcome.[118] Since efficiency analysis is determined in part by the respective wealth of the parties, it surely follows that efficiency alone is unlikely to produce a result which can be described as just, once distributive issues are taken into account.[119]

423   Economists do not, in fact, believe that all people always behave in a rational, economic and wealth-maximizing way, or that the existing distribution of wealth must not be tampered with. These assump-

---

[116] For an attempt, see Posner, "Utilitarianism, Economics, and Legal Theory", 8 J. of Leg. Stud. 103 (1979). Compare Weinrib, *supra*, footnote 103; Fletcher, "Fairness and Utility in Tort Theory", 85 Harv. L. Rev. 537 (1972). The modesty of the claim made by Calabresi and Melamed for their approach is worth recalling. It is suggested rather obscurely by the title to their article, explained in footnote 2: "it should be emphasized that this article concerns only one possible way of looking at and analyzing legal problems . . . this article is meant to be only *one* of Monet's paintings of the Cathedral at Rouen. To understand the Cathedral one must see all of them." See also the concluding paragraphs, at pp. 1127-8, admitting the shortcomings of model-building, but pointing out the "compensating advantages" of relationships perceived because of the more precise categories.

[117] Ogus & Richardson, "The Role of Private Law in the Protection of Pollution Victims", 40 Rabels Zeitshrift für ausländisches und interlationales Privatrecht 449 (1976), at p. 471, are particularly scathing about the unrealistic economic assumption of ordinary behaviour:

The economists' rational man is wise, articulate, uninhibited, resourceful and knowledgeable. It does not require a sophisticated sociological survey or profound psychological penetration to realize the patent falsity of generalizing from this prototype. . . . The idea of a Hounslow householder walking into Heathrow Airport with his Post Office Savings book ready to strike a bargain over Concorde is risible.

[118] Burrows and Veljanovski, "Introduction", *The Economic Approach to Law*, *supra*, footnote 107, at p. 12: "for each different distribution of income, there is a different socially efficient outcome". Calabresi and Melamed, *supra*, footnote 101, at pp. 1095-6.

[119] Rawls, *A Theory of Justice* (Oxford, Oxford University Press, 1972), at pp. 67-72.

tions are merely devices to make possible the construction of theoretical models which will reveal certain patterns or relationships which might not otherwise be seen.[120] The analysis is at a general and abstract level; it is not intended to solve particular problems. The lawyer's immediate objection to such assumptions derives from the legal need to develop theories and rules which allow him to solve each particular problem. A general theory which rests on such assumptions cannot be relied upon for this purpose.

424   At the same time, however, these criticisms are not a reason for totally rejecting economic analysis, but rather suggest that it must be viewed critically and employed cautiously. Some of the leading exponents of economic analysis are explicit about the shortcomings of the formal analytic model-building approach.[121] Similarly, lawyers should be conscious of the advantages of an analysis which does tend to highlight or identify certain relationships and general theoretical points which might otherwise not be apparent. Economic analysis of the pollution problem provides no panacea; neither is it an exercise that the law should ignore. From the earlier discussion of the case-law, it does seem clear that the goal of efficiency plays an important part in the resolution of nuisance disputes, including the selection of the appropriate remedy. To the extent economists can help improve analysis already undertaken, that contribution should be welcomed. In particular, the perception that greater explicit attention should be paid to the fact that market forces will operate in some cases to alter the legal result is an important one. The degree to which consideration of post-judgment bargaining helps explain and elucidate the significance of legal results suggests that courts and lawyers can benefit from taking economic analysis into account.

4. Trespass

425   Where there is a direct interference with the plaintiff's property constituting a trespass, the rule favouring injunctive relief is even stronger than in the nuisance cases. Especially where the trespass is deliberate and continuing, it is ordinarily difficult to justify the denial of a prohibitive injunction. A damages award in such circumstances does amount to an expropriation without legislative sanction.[122] The

---

[120] Calabresi and Melamed, *supra*, footnote 101, at p. 1128; Burrows and Veljanovski, *supra*, footnote 118, at pp. 14-15.

[121] Calabresi and Melamed, *supra*, footnote 101, especially the passages quoted, *supra*, footnote 116.

[122] See, *e.g.*, *Krehl v. Burrell* (1878), 7 Ch. D. 551.

courts have expressly condoned injunctive relief, even where the balance of convenience is overwhelmingly in favour of the defendant.[123] In trespass, there has been less concern than in nuisance with the problem of "extortion".[124] Even if the plaintiff is merely holding out for the highest possible price, and suffers no out-of-pocket loss because of the trespass, the courts have awarded injunctions.[125] Such orders may be said to vindicate the plaintiff's right to exploit his property for whatever it is worth to the defendant, and prevent the defendant from circumventing the bargaining process.[126]

426 Yet even here, there may well be limits to the granting of injunctive relief, and the present state of the law is by no means entirely settled. The difficult cases involve temporary interferences. In *Woollerton & Wilson Ltd. v. Richard Costain Ltd.*,[127] the plaintiff sued for an injunction to enjoin the defendant from permitting the jib of a crane to swing over the plaintiff's premises. This caused no harm or apprehension of injury to the plaintiff and, as Stamp, J., put it,[128] "something more than £250 which the defendants have offered would have been required to induce [the plaintiffs] to change their mind" and permit the crane to swing overhead. Clearly, as the construction was well in progress, an injunction would have worked a severe hardship on the defendants. Stamp, J., held that, because the plaintiffs had made out a case of trespass, they were entitled to an injunction but that, in the circumstances, it was appropriate to suspend the order until the defendants had the proper opportunity to finish the job. He emphasized that the defendants got themselves into the position of being "held up to ransom, not by any flagrant disregard of the plaintiff's proprietary rights but by inadvertence".[129]

427 While denial of the injunction claim at the interlocutory stage would not preclude the plaintiff from proceeding with a claim for damages, Stamp, J., assumed that no damages would be recoverable

[123] See cases cited, *infra*, §427; *Stocker v. Planet Building Society* (1879), 27 W.R. 877 (C.A.).
[124] *Supra*, §§376, 377.
[125] *Cooper v. Crabtree* (1882), 20 Ch. D. 589 (C.A.), at pp. 592-3, *per* Jessel, M.R.; *Goodson v. Richardson* (1873), L.R. 9 Ch. 221. Proof of damage is not required; see, *e.g.*, *Long v. Roberts* (1965), 55 D.L.R. (2d) 195, [1966] 1 O.R. 771 (H.C.J.).
[126] *Goodson v. Richardson, supra*, footnote 125; *Eardley v. Granville* (1876), 3 Ch. D. 826 at p. 832, *per* Jessel, M.R.; Sharpe and Waddams, "Damages for Lost Opportunity to Bargain", 2 Ox. J.L.S. 290 (1982).
[127] [1970] 1 W.L.R. 411 (Ch.).
[128] *Ibid.*, at p. 413.
[129] *Ibid.*, at p. 416.

as the plaintiff suffered no loss. This, it is submitted, is doubtful. The plaintiff should be given some remedy for the loss of opportunity to bargain for whatever his property right was worth.[130] As the defendant had apparently not acted in deliberate disregard of the plaintiff's right, a damages award seems preferable to an injunction in the circumstances. However, a recent Newfoundland case[131] posed the same problem, and the court granted an injunction. Goodridge, J., held that, despite the "tremendous inconvenience" to the defendant and the public, an injunction was called for: "Under our system of law, property rights are sacrosanct. For that reason, the rules that generally apply to injunctions do not always apply in cases as this. The balance of convenience and other matters may have to take second place to the sacrosanctity of property rights in matters of trespass."[132] Faced with a similar problem, an Australian court also came to the conclusion that an injunction must be awarded,[133] and the result in *Woollerton* has been questioned by the English Court of Appeal.[134]

428   In another English case,[135] the defendant was under compulsion of a municipal order to repair his building, but could not do so without gaining access to the plaintiff's property. An injunction was awarded to the plaintiff who steadfastly refused his permission. Although the defendant was caught between both "the Scylla of the dangerous building and . . . the Charybdis of trespassing upon the plaintiff's land",[136] the court held it had no choice but to award injunctive relief to the plaintiff. A possible distinguishing factor between this case and *Woollerton* was that here the defendant knew all along that he was acting against the wishes and rights of the plaintiff, and was deliberately violating a property right he knew the plaintiff intended to assert. Still, even in this sort of case, it is submitted that there is much to be said for refusing an injunction and ordering monetary

---

[130] Sharpe and Waddams, *supra*, footnote 126.

[131] *Lewvest Ltd. v. Scotia Towers Ltd.* (1981), 126 D.L.R. (3d) 239 (Nfld. S.C.T.D.).

[132] *Ibid.*, at p. 240.

[133] *Graham v. K.D. Morris & Sons Pty. Ltd.*, [1974] Qd. R. 1.

[134] *Charrington v. Simons & Co. Ltd.*, [1971] 2 All E.R. 588 (C.A.), at p. 592, *per* Russell, L.J. The substantive law question of trespass to air space is discussed in *Bernstein v. Skyviews & General Ltd.*, [1977] 2 All E.R. 902 (Q.B.); *Re The Queen in right of Manitoba and Air Canada* (1978), 86 D.L.R. (3d) 631 (Man. C.A.), affd [1980] 2 S.C.R. 303, 111 D.L.R. (3d) 513.

[135] *John Trenberth Ltd. v. National Westminster Bank Ltd.* (1979), 39 P. & C.R. 104 (Ch.).

[136] *Ibid.*, at p. 106, *per* Walton, J.

compensation to the plaintiff. It is certainly not entirely without precedent. In an early Manitoba decision,[137] where a similar problem arose, an injunction was refused on the grounds that the injury was trifling and temporary. Galt, J., said as follows:

> . . . where an adjoining land owner is desirous of erecting a building upon his property, it is inevitable that to a certain extent the workmen will frequently and almost of necessity do acts which in the strict eye of the law are legal trespasses upon the adjoining owner; but in such cases one would have supposed that people . . . would apply their reason, common sense and ordinary forbearance, rather than go to law over trifles.[138]

429   Even Jessel, M.R., a stalwart champion of property rights, suggested in one decision[139] that no injunction should be awarded where a neighbour is merely erecting scaffolding temporarily to effect some necessary repair.[140]

430   While such cases technically amount to trespass, it might be preferable, if only from the remedial point of view, to employ the analysis used in nuisance cases. Trespass involves an invasion by one with no entitlement into the property of another. Viewed broadly, the cases under consideration may be seen to involve the exercise of conflicting property rights rather than unilateral invasion or appropriation. Where there is no question of permanent appropriation of property, nor serious inconvenience or harm which could not be compensated in damages, it is not at all obvious that the absolute autonomy of an owner should inevitably be vindicated over the reason-

[137] *Bertram v. Builders' Ass'n of North Winnipeg* (1915), 23 D.L.R. 534 (Man. K.B.). See also *Douglas v. Bullen* (1912), 3 D.L.R. 898, 22 O.W.R. 837 (H.C.), and 12 D.L.R. 652, 24 O.W.R. 890 (H.C.).

[138] *Bertram, supra*, footnote 137, at pp. 539-40.

[139] *Leader v. Moody* (1875), L.R. 20 Eq. 145 at p. 153.

[140] *Cash & Carry Cleaners Ltd. v. Delmas* (1973), 44 D.L.R. (3d) 315 (N.B.S.C. App. Div.), appears somewhat ambivalent. Knowing the plaintiff would object, the defendant went ahead with repair work which interfered with the plaintiff's access. The court upheld an award of exemplary damages on the grounds that the defendant had acted high handedly. The court also reluctantly upheld an injunction restraining parking on the plaintiff's property; see at p. 317, *per* Hughes, C.J.N.B.:

> Where a trespass is trifling and causes no appreciable injury to the plaintiff a Court will not grant injunctive relief. Where, however, a plaintiff's rights in property are violated and threatened the plaintiff as a general proposition is entitled to protection of rights by injunction if that appears to be necessary.

> While I reluctantly uphold the permanent injunction restraining trespass of the plaintiff's property by the parking of vehicles I do so only because of the absence of any other satisfactory remedy for dealing with petty trespasses, such as is found in some of the other Provinces.

able needs of his neighbour. It should not be forgotten that refusing an injunction does not deny the right altogether. It is a less extreme curtailment of property rights than is the defence of necessity which, to some extent, the law does recognize,[141] and which provides a parallel. The necessity defence amounts to a similar recognition that there must come a point at which an unreasonably antisocial insistence upon the assertion of a property right does not deserve the protection of the law.[142]

431   Oddly enough, the use of injunctions to restrain trespass is a relatively recent development, and injunctions were formerly granted only to prevent acts of destruction.[143] The common law courts jealously guarded their right to resolve disputes as to title, and common law jury trials would have been subverted had injunctions been routinely available.[144] It was accepted that, where the defendant's conduct was going to destroy or cause serious and irreparable harm to the plaintiff's property, an injunction could be awarded, and the courts drew a distinction between "naked" and "destructive" trespasses.[145] Shortly before the Judicature Act, it was said that: "the tendency of the Court is *not* to grant an injunction, unless there are special circumstances, but to leave the plaintiff to his remedy at law,

---

[141] See Bohlen, "Incomplete Privilege to Inflict Intentional Invasions of Interests of Property and Personality", 39 Harv. L. Rev. 307 (1925); *Dwyer v. Staunton*, [1947] 4 D.L.R. 393 (Alta. Dist. Ct.); *Burmah Oil Co. v. Lord Advocate*, [1965] A.C. 75 (H.L.). "Squatters", however, have been expelled, even where housing is in short supply: *The King v. Trudel*, [1947] 2 D.L.R. 238, [1947] O.W.N. 175 (H.C.J.); *Southwark London Borough Council v. Williams*, [1971] Ch. 734 (C.A.).

[142] The problem is considered and reform proposals presented in the English Law Commission, *Rights of Access to Neighbouring Land*, Working Paper No. 78 (London, H.M.S.O., 1980).

[143] *Lowndes v. Bettle* (1864), 33 L.J. Ch. 451 at p. 457, *per* Kindersley, V.-C.; *A.-G. v. McLaughlin* (1849), 1 Gr. 34 (C.A.), *per* Blake, C., expressing some dissatisfaction with the rules. *Cf. Coulson v. White* (1743), 3 Atk. 21, 26 E.R. 816 (Ch.), where Hardwicke, L.C., suggested equity would intervene where the trespass was a permanent one. For a good discussion of the development of the power of equity to grant injunctions in trespass cases, see *A.-G. v. Ryan* (1887), 5 Man. R. 81 (Q.B.), *per* Killam, J. See also *McLaren v. Caldwell* (1880), 5 O.A.R. 363; *Hamilton v. Brown* (1866), 6 N.S.R. 260 (S.C.); *Creighton v. Jenkins* (1884), 17 N.S.R. 352 (C.A.).

[144] See, *e.g.*, *Godard v. Godard* (1910), 4 N.B. Eq. 268 at p. 269, *per* Barker, C.J.:
   But if the Court were to interfere in this present case, there is no case of trespass where this Court might not as well be asked to act, and the result would be that all such cases might be transferred here instead of remaining in the other branch of the Court where they properly belong.

[145] Cases cited, *supra*, footnote 143.

though where the acts tend to the destruction of the estate, the Court will grant it".[146]

432   The jurisdictional impediment was of course removed,[147] but there is still perhaps something left of the former reluctance to interfere where an act of trespass would apparently cause no injury to the plaintiff. In *Behrens v. Richards*,[148] the plaintiffs purchased a large tract of coastal lands, and sued for an injunction to restrain the defendants, local inhabitants and fishermen, from trespassing by walking along paths on his property. No physical damage was caused to the plaintiff's property by the trespass, nor was there any interference with the plaintiff's use and enjoyment. Buckley, J., rejected the defence that the paths were public rights of way, but also refused to grant an injunction. He was clearly anxious to have the parties to this "petty contest" come to terms, as it was "a matter for the application of reason, common sense and ordinary forbearance, not for an injunction".[149] Buckley, J., went on to indicate the basis for his refusal to grant injunctive relief, namely, that the protection of property rights was in some sense contingent upon their reasonable exercise: "The existing security of the tenure of land in this country is largely maintained by the fact that the owners of the land behave reasonably in the matter of its enjoyment."[150]

433   *Behrens v. Richards* is by no means an isolated example of the courts refusing to grant an injunction to vindicate property rights, even where the trespass is deliberate. A municipal corporation which owned the foreshore was refused an injunction to restrain a preacher from holding religious services there, although the court did grant a declaration that his activity, which was regularly practised, constituted a trespass.[151] In another case,[152] a father was refused an injunction to restrain his shiftless adult son from occupying his house, and in yet another,[153] a decision of the English Court of Appeal, Jessel, M.R., found a trespass to be of a temporary and trivial nature, and refused to grant an injunction on the grounds that "I should be

---

[146] *Lowndes v. Bettle* (1864), 33 L.J. Ch. 451 at p. 457, *per* Kindersley, V.-C.

[147] The Court of Chancery was empowered to determine matters of title by the Chancery Regulation Act, 1862 (U.K.), s. 1 ("Sir John Rolt's Act").

[148] [1905] 2 Ch. 614.

[149] *Ibid.*, at p. 619.

[150] *Ibid.*, at p. 622.

[151] *Llandudno Urban District Council v. Woods*, [1899] 2 Ch. 705.

[152] *Waterhouse v. Waterhouse* (1905), 94 L.T.R. 133 (Ch.). *Cf. Stevens v. Stevens* (1907), 24 T.L.R. 20 (K.B.).

[153] *Leader v. Moody* (1875), L.R. 20 Eq. 145.

inflicting a great injury on the Defendants, and should be giving no benefit to the Plaintiff ".[154] In all of these cases, the courts have identified overriding concerns which might be taken to qualify the extent to which property rights ought to be protected.[155] Rather than qualifying the property right itself, they have chosen to alter the nature of the remedy attached to that right. Although theoretically less pure, this solution is perhaps more satisfactory than altering the substantive law which would, as with nuisance, leave the plaintiff without any remedy at all. Damages can still be awarded to vindicate the plaintiff's interest. Damages may even be measured on the basis of a bargain which might reasonably have been struck.[156] This subtlety of remedial choice introduces an important element of flexibility which permits the courts to vindicate rights, but at the same time control their socially harmful exploitation.

434   Where the trespass is inadvertent, it is easier to make out a case for damages rather than an injunction. Building encroachment cases do not inevitably result in injunctions where they have occurred because of a *bona fide* mistake.[157] Although an injunction would be

---

[154] *Ibid.*, at p. 154. In *Walker v. Westington* (1912), 6 D.L.R. 858, 23 O.W.R. 110 (H.C.), an injunction was refused where the trespass was trivial. See also *Fielden v. Cox* (1906), 22 T.L.R. 411 (Ch.).

[155] A number of cases involve allegedly defective expropriation proceedings. In *Holmested v. Canadian Northern Ry.* (1915), 22 D.L.R. 55 (Sask. S.C.), an injunction was granted restraining an entry until title was acquired. *Cf.*, however, *Stannard v. Vestry of St. Giles, Camberwell* (1882), 20 Ch. D. 190 (C.A.), holding that the matter should be remitted to the magistrates to be dealt with under the statute; *Sandon Water Works & Light Co. v. Byron N. White Co.* (1904), 35 S.C.R. 309, and *Smith v. Public Parks Board of Portage La Prairie* (1905), 15 Man. R. 249 (K.B.), staying an injunction until proper expropriation proceedings had been taken. In *Copithorne v. Calgary Power Ltd.* (1955), 17 W.W.R. 105 (Alta. S.C. App. Div.), an interlocutory injunction was refused, on the grounds that the plaintiff had not clearly established his case, and an injunction would cause serious damage and inconvenience to the citizens of Calgary. For subsequent proceedings see 5 D.L.R. (2d) 588 (Alta. S.C.T.D.), 10 D.L.R. (2d) 161 (App. Div.), 16 D.L.R. (2d) 241 (S.C.C.).

[156] See Sharpe and Waddams, *supra*, footnote 126.

[157] See Keeton and Morris, "Notes on 'Balancing the Equities' ", 18 Tex. L. Rev. 412 (1940), for a good account of the arguments; *Armstrong v. Sheppard & Short Ltd.*, [1959] 2 Q.B. 384 (C.A.); *Mayfair Property Co. v. Johnston*, [1894] 1 Ch. 508 (refusing an injunction on the basis that the party claiming an injunction could remove the encroachment himself, and awarding damages measured by the cost of removal); *Buyserd v. Baylay* (1963), 40 D.L.R. (2d) 983 (B.C.S.C.). See also *Delorme v. Cusson* (1897), 28 S.C.R. 66, a case decided under the Quebec Civil Code, refusing an injunction to demolish an encroaching building, but ordering payment of a reasonable indemnity. In *Dempsey v. J.E.S. Developments Ltd.* (1976), 15 N.S.R. (2d) 448 (S.C.T.D.), the court held that despite deliberateness on the defendant's

granted to restrain an encroachment before it actually took place, and even to require the destruction of a structure where the defendant has acted deliberately,[158] the waste involved in dismantling and rebuilding an existing structure, which has inadvertently been built upon the plaintiff's land, has led the courts to deny mandatory injunctive relief. In a decision of the British Columbia Court of Appeal,[159] a mandatory injunction requiring the defendant to remove fill which it had deposited on the plaintiff's land was suspended for two years on condition that the defendants pay a monthly rental until removal. In a 19th century case,[160] an English court refused to restrain an inadvertent underground trespass committed by the defendant municipality laying pipes for its water works, on the grounds that it would be pointless to force the defendants to bear the costs of removing the pipes, and the plaintiff was awarded compensatory damages in the amount the defendant had offered when the trespass was discovered. The importance of the public interest was also recognized in another 19th century case[161] where a railway had, through a *bona fide* mistake, occupied the plaintiff's land. The court denied an injunction on the grounds that it would "stop the opening of the railway without giving any benefit to the Plaintiff, except, perhaps, the

---

part, a mandatory injunction should be refused and punitive damages awarded. See also *Mayo v. Hefferton* (1972), 3 Nfld. & P.E.I.R. 236 (Nfld. S.C.), and *Luedee v. Nova Construction Co. Ltd.* (1973), 4 Nfld. & P.E.I.R. 361 (Nfld. S.C.), both awarding punitive damages. *Cf. Gallant v. MacDonald* (1970), 3 N.S.R. (2d) 137 (S.C.), granting a mandatory injunction to remove an encroachment despite inadvertence. In some jurisdictions, legislation confers jurisdiction on the court to allow a party to retain land, built on through *bona fide* mistakes as to ownership, upon payment of appropriate compensation. See, *e.g.*, Conveyancing and Law of Property Act, Ont., s. 37(1); *Gay v. Wierzbicki* (1967), 63 D.L.R. (2d) 88, [1967] 2 O.R. 211 (C.A.).

[158] *Kelsen v. Imperial Tobacco Co.*, [1957] 2 Q.B. 334; *Andrews v. Abertillery Urban District Council*, [1911] 2 Ch. 398 (C.A.); *Pearen v. Rural Municipality of Indian Head No. 156 and Horsman* (1964), 45 D.L.R. (2d) 301 (Sask. Q.B.).

[159] *Vancouver Waterfront Ltd. v. Vancouver Harbour Com'rs*, [1936] 1 D.L.R. 461 (B.C.C.A.). *Cf. District of North Saanich v. Murray* (1974), 40 D.L.R. (3d) 270 (B.C.S.C.), granting a mandatory injunction for the removal of a wharf, and staying the order for six months.

[160] *Riley v. Halifax Corporation* (1907), 97 L.T.R. 278 (H.C.J.). *Cf. Schweder v. Worthing Gas Light & Coke Co.*, [1912] 1 Ch. 83, where the defendant's pipes interfered with an underground passage actually used by the plaintiff. A mandatory injunction requiring the abatement of the trespass was granted.

[161] *Wood v. Charing Cross Ry. Co.* (1863), 33 Beav. 290, 55 E.R. 379.

means of enhancing the price to be paid to him, and that [it would] be causing an inconvenience to the company and an injury to the public".[162]

5. Other Forms of Property

435   The problems which have been discussed in this chapter have involved real property. Injunctions are also routinely granted to protect other types of property interests. The difficult issue of balancing defendants' and plaintiffs' interests which arise in the real property cases typically involve conflicting property rights rather than the outright appropriation of the plaintiff's property. Outside the realm of real property, claims of competing property uses are rare, and more often the issue is a substantive one, namely, does the plaintiff have a property right at all? If that question is answered affirmatively, and if a real threat or actual invasion by the plaintiff is proved, an injunction will ordinarily follow as of right.

436   In the industrial property area, injunctions are a familiar remedy.[163] The difficult issues tend to arise at the interlocutory stage when the court must assess the likelihood of irreparable harm and weigh the relative risks of granting or withholding relief pending trial. These issues arising on interlocutory injunction applications have been considered in Chapter 2.

---

[162] *Ibid.*, at p. 295, *per* Romilly, M.R.

[163] See Fox, *Canadian Law of Copyright and Industrial Designs*, 2nd ed. (Toronto, Carswell Co. Ltd., 1967), at pp. 637-46; Fox, *Canadian Law of Trade Marks and Unfair Competition*, 3rd ed. (Toronto, Carswell Co. Ltd., 1972), at pp. 455-63; *Terrell on the Law of Patents*, 13th ed. by Adlous, Young, Watson and Thorley (London, Sweet and Maxwell, 1982), at pp. 419-26.

CHAPTER 5

INJUNCTIONS TO PROTECT NON-PROPRIETARY RIGHTS

1. Introduction

437   This chapter deals with the use of injunctions in the protection and enforcement of certain personal, non-proprietary claims. It used to be said that an injunction would only be granted to protect a property interest. This has for a long time been completely discredited.[1] It is now clear that injunctions will be granted to protect interests which are not ordinarily described as proprietary in nature. Cases dealing with the enforcement of the criminal law have been examined in Chapter 2. Chapter 9 examines the use of injunctions in the contractual setting, and this chapter deals with a number of diverse areas in which personal, non-proprietary rights are enforced by injunction.

438   Although the notion that injunctive relief may only be had to protect property interests has been rejected, as will be apparent from the preceding chapter dealing with the enforcement of property rights by injunction, describing an injunction as conferring a property-type protection is often useful analytically.

439   Just as the owner of property can refuse to sell, so can the holder of an injunction insist that the course of action prescribed by the injunction be followed. If there is to be a "sale", an injunction means that the defendant will have to buy in a voluntary exchange the

---

[1] The property theory is discussed and criticized by Spry, *The Principles of Equitable Remedies*, 2nd ed. (London, Sweet & Maxwell Ltd., 1980), pp. 315-20, 578-82.

plaintiff's right just as if the plaintiff were selling his own property. Other forms of remedial protection, damages or declaration, differ. A declaration merely states the legal position, and damages involves an objective and necessarily circumscribed inquiry into the plaintiff's loss. As indicated in Chapter 4, this basic difference between specific relief and damages renders the former particularly appropriate where property rights are involved. The remedial protection corresponds to the definition of a substantive property right. While the position that injunctive relief is restricted to situations where property rights are at stake has been departed from, that does not mean that the courts have gone so far as to say injunctive relief is invariably available to prevent a threatened wrong. Rather, it is submitted, the courts look carefully at the interest involved and assess whether the nature of the protection extended by specific relief is appropriate.

2. Defamation Actions

440   The jurisdiction to award injunctions in defamation actions emerged only late in the 19th century.[2] While such injunctions have often been awarded, the courts have been extremely cautious in this area, and have formulated relatively strict rules which govern the discretion. Most cases arise at the interlocutory stage. The risk that the proposed publication will defame and perhaps cause serious damage to the plaintiff must be balanced against the risk that an injunction will unjustifiably restrain publication. If the issue were simply one between the parties, in most cases an injunction would issue. Only rarely would the defendant have an interest in immediate publication sufficient to warrant the risk of harm to the plaintiff. However, in these cases the courts have looked beyond the interests of the immediate parties. There is a significant public interest in the free and uncensored circulation of information and the important principle of

---

[2] Defamation actions were regarded as criminal, and hence not the subject for equitable relief: *St. James Evening Post Case* (1742), 2 Atk. 469, 26 E.R. 683 (Ch.); *Gee v. Pritchard* (1818), 2 Swans. 402, 36 E.R. 670 (Ch.). Another factor was the disinclination of equity to grant injunctions except where property rights were concerned. The jury-trial requirement and freedom of the press concern, also played an important role. For discussion of the early cases, see Pound, "Equitable Relief against Defamation and Injuries to Personality", 29 Harv. L. Rev. 640 (1916). The jurisdictional obstacle was overcome by the Common Law Procedure Act, 1854 (U.K.), which conferred jurisdiction upon the common law courts to grant injunctions, later held to include the power to award injunctions in defamation cases: *Bonnard v. Perryman*, [1891] 2 Ch. 269 (C.A.); *Quartz Hill Consolidated Gold Mining Co. v. Beall* (1882), 20 Ch. D. 501 (C.A.); *cf. Prudential Ass'ce Co. v. Knott* (1875), L.R. 10 Ch. 142.

freedom of the press to be safeguarded.[3] In view of "the importance of leaving free speech unfettered",[4] it has been considered preferable to subject the plaintiff to the risk of harm and perhaps inadequate monetary compensation than to risk stifling freedom of expression.

441   Another factor often referred to by the courts is the need to respect jury trial requirements.[5] An interlocutory injunction would, as a practical matter, pre-empt the statutorily prescribed role of the jury as fact finder. It has been said that freedom of the press is of greater concern than respect for the jury,[6] but it appears that both concerns are closely related. The press is not free to publish material which is actually found to be defamatory,[7] but a matter can only be known to be defamatory after trial. Once it is determined that the defendant's words are actionable, there is little hesitation in granting an injunction.[8] However, virtually all of the cases arise at the interlocutory stage where the judge can usually only speculate whether the plaintiff will succeed, and freedom of the press would be substantially impaired if publication were restrained on the ground that the judge thought a jury might give a verdict for the plaintiff.

---

[3] A passage from *Blackstone, Commentaries on the Laws of England*, 16th ed., vol. 4 (London, Butterworth & Son, 1825), p. 15, has been cited both in English and American cases on this point: "[certain] libels are punished by the English Law . . . the *liberty of the press*, properly understood, is by no means infringed or violated. The liberty of the press . . . consists in laying no *previous* restraints upon publications, and not in freedom from censure for criminal matter when published." See also Martin, "Interlocutory Injunctions in Libel Actions", 20 U.W.O.L. Rev. 129 (1982). The freedom of expression protection now contained in the Charter of Rights and Freedoms, s. 2(*b*), undoubtedly fortifies this traditional view.

[4] *Bonnard v. Perryman, supra*, footnote 2, at p. 284, *per* Coleridge, C.J.

[5] See, *e.g.*, Judicature Act, Ont., s. 57, requiring actions for libel or slander to be tried by a jury unless the parties waive such a trial.

[6] *Fraser v. Evans*, [1969] 1 Q.B. 349 (C.A.), at p. 360, *per* Lord Denning, M.R.; *Bestobell Paints Ltd. v. Bigg*, [1975] F.S.R. 421 at p. 430, *per* Oliver, J.

[7] *Gatley on Libel and Slander*, 8th ed. by P. Lewis (London, Sweet & Maxwell, 1981), p. 566; *Thomas v. Williams* (1880), 14 Ch. D. 864; *Thorley's Cattle Food Co. v. Massam* (1880), 14 Ch. D. 763 (C.A.); *Hayward & Co. v. Hayward & Sons* (1886), 34 Ch. D. 198; *Kerr v. Gandy* (1886), 3 T.L.R. 75.

[8] *Ibid.* See also *Safeway Stores Ltd. v. Harris*, [1948] 4 D.L.R. 187 (Man. C.A); *cf.* however *Watson & Sons v. Daily Record (Glasgow), Ltd.*, [1907] 1 K.B. 853 (C.A.), refusing leave to serve a writ *ex juris* claiming an injunction; at p. 860, *per* Cozens-Hardy, L.J.: "there is no reported instance in which an injunction has been granted against a newspaper, even when heavy damages have been recovered. And it is doubtful whether an injunction has ever been seriously applied for after verdict." *Cf.* also *Salomons v. Knight*, [1891] 2 Ch. 294 (C.A.), refusing the plaintiff an interlocutory injunction in a second action, although the plaintiff had been unable to collect damages awarded in the first action and the defendant was repeating the same statements. Given the plaintiff's plight, the result is, to say the least, difficult to justify.

442	The well-established rule is that an interlocutory injunction will not be granted where the defendant indicates his intention to justify the statements complained of, unless the plaintiff is able to satisfy the court at the interlocutory stage that the words are both clearly defamatory and impossible to justify.[9] Unless the plaintiff can demonstrate that the verdict of a jury accepting the truth of the statements made by the defendant would necessarily be set aside on appeal as perverse, no injunction will be granted. A similar rule applies to other defences as well, so that the defendant will not be forced to plead justification to resist the plaintiff's claim for an injunction. Thus, where the defendant does not plead justification, but relies on privilege,[10] fair comment,[11] consent,[12] argues that the statement is not defamatory,[13] or presumably relies on any other defence,[14] an interlocutory injunction will not be granted where the material discloses a case to go to the jury. In addition, the plaintiff must, of course, show a likelihood of repetition.[15]

443	It might be argued in certain cases that the effect of a defamatory statement would be disastrous for a particular plaintiff, and that the issue is not one of significant public interest, so that the balance of convenience favours an order even where the defendant asserts a defence. However, it seems clear that the rule is unaffected by the *American Cyanamid* case[16] and that the balance of convenience is not a factor.[17] The primary concern is quite properly seen to be to avoid

---

[9] *Canada Metal Co. Ltd. v. C.B.C.* (1975), 55 D.L.R. (3d) 42n, 7 O.R. (2d) 261n (Div. Ct.); *Bonnard v. Perryman, supra,* footnote 2; *Quartz Hill Consolidated Gold Mining Co. v. Beall, supra,* footnote 2; *William Coulson & Sons v. James Coulson & Co.* (1887), 3 T.L.R. 846 (C.A.); *Rapp v. McClelland & Stewart* (1981), 128 D.L.R. (3d) 650, 34 O.R. (2d) 452 (H.C.J.); *Gagnon v. France-Film Co.,* [1952] 3 D.L.R. 753 (Que. S.C.), leave to appeal refused [1952] Que. P.R. 241; *Stocker v. McElhinney (No. 2)* (1961), 79 W.N. (N.S.W.) 541 (S.C.).

[10] *Bryanston Finance v. De Vries,* [1975] Q.B. 703 (C.A.); *Quartz Hill Consolidated Gold Mining Co. v. Beall, supra,* footnote 2; *Harakas v. Baltic Mercantile Shipping Exchange Ltd.,* [1982] 2 All E.R. 701 (C.A.).

[11] *Fraser v. Evans,* [1969] 1 Q.B. 349 (C.A.).

[12] *Monson v. Tussauds,* [1894] 1 Q.B. 671 (C.A.).

[13] *Sim v. H.J. Heinz Co. Ltd.,* [1959] 1 All E.R. 547 (C.A.).

[14] As where the character of the plaintiff is in issue: *Bonnard v. Perryman,* [1891] 2 Ch. 269 (C.A.), at pp. 284-5.

[15] *Quartz Hill Consolidated Gold Mining Co. v. Beall* (1882), 20 Ch. D. 501 (C.A.), at pp. 508-9; *London Motor Cab Proprietors' Ass'n v. Twentieth Century Press* (1917), 34 T.L.R. 68; *New Musical Express, Ltd. v. Cardfont Publishers, Ltd.,* [1956] R.P.C. 211; *Pryce & Son v. Pioneer Press* (1925), 42 T.L.R. 29.

[16] *American Cyanamid Co. v. Ethicon Ltd.,* [1975] A.C. 396 (H.L.), discussed, *supra,* Chapter 2.

[17] *Rapp v. McClelland & Stewart, supra,* footnote 9; *Woodward v. Hutchins,* [1977] 1

prior restraint on publication which might fetter freedom of the press.

444 Despite the cautious approach the courts have taken and the restrictive rules which have been formulated, there are many cases in which injunctions have been granted to restrain publication pending trial.[18] Interlocutory injunctions have been granted in cases where the defendant offers no substantive defence to the plaintiff's claim, or where the court can determine on the basis of the material then before it that no defence could possibly be made out.[19]

445 Indeed, there is even authority for granting such an injunction on an *ex parte* basis. In an Ontario case,[20] an *ex parte* injunction was dissolved when the defendant filed material indicating his intention to plead and defend on the basis of justification. However, in setting aside the *ex parte* order, R.E. Holland, J., expressly noted that he did not intend any criticism of the *ex parte* order as it had been properly granted on the basis of the material then before the judge.[21] In some cases, even the limited delay involved when an *ex parte* injunction is granted may be extremely significant. In the Ontario case, it was only after several months and lengthy interlocutory appeals that the defendant was able to have the *ex parte* order discharged. Consistency with the established principles on which the courts have acted requires that *ex parte* relief should be granted only in the most

---

W.L.R. 760 (C.A.); *Bestobell Paints Ltd. v. Bigg*, [1975] F.S.R. 421; *Lennon v. News Group Newspapers, Ltd.*, [1978] F.S.R. 573 (C.A.); *cf. Hubbard v. Pitt*, [1976] Q.B. 142 (C.A.), applying the *Cyanamid* test in a picketing case although the injunction would operate "incidentally to prevent the publication of an alleged libel in a particular place."

[18] *Church of Scientology of B.C. v. Radio NW Ltd.* (1974), 46 D.L.R. (3d) 459 (B.C.C.A.); *Canadian Tire Corp. Ltd. v. Desmond* (1972), 24 D.L.R. (3d) 642, [1972] 2 O.R. 60 (H.C.J.); *Quirk v. Dudley* (1902), 4 O.L.R. 532 (H.C.J.); *Collard v. Marshall*, [1892] 1 Ch. 571; *Dallas v. Felek*, [1934] O.W.N. 247 (C.A.); *Wolfenden v. Giles* (1892), 2 B.C.R. 279 (Div. Ct.); *Hermann Loog v. Bean* (1884), 26 Ch. D. 306 (C.A.). See also *F. W. Woolworth Co. Ltd. v. Retail Food & Drug Clerks Union, Local 518* (1961), 30 D.L.R. (2d) 377 (B.C.S.C.), enjoining picketing in a lawful strike which conveyed false information.

[19] If an order is to be made, the court must be able to specify precisely what the defendant is restrained from publishing, and injunctions to restrain libellous statements generally will be refused: *Natural Resources v. Saturday Night* (1910), 16 O.W.R. 927 (H.C.J.); *Liverpool Household Stores Ass'n v. Smith* (1887), 37 Ch. D. 170 (C.A.).

[20] *Canada Metal Co. Ltd. v. C.B.C.* (1974), 44 D.L.R. (3d) 329, 3 O.R. (2d) 1 (H.C.J.), affd 55 D.L.R. (3d) 42n, 7 O.R. (2d) 261n (Div. Ct.). For the subsequent contempt proceedings, see *sub nom. (No. 2)* (1974), 48 D.L.R. (3d) 641, 4 O.R. (2d) 585 (H.C.J.), affd 65 D.L.R. (3d) 231, 11 O.R. (2d) 167 (C.A.). See also *Fraser v. Evans*, *supra*, footnote 11, where an *ex parte* injunction was granted.

[21] 44 D.L.R. (3d) 329 at p. 351, 3 O.R. (2d) 1 at p. 23 (H.C.J.).

exceptional cases, and that when granted, the contested hearing should take place in as short a time as possible. It may well be that the constitutional guarantee of freedom of expression[22] will fortify the established policy which rejects prior restraints and thereby render *ex parte* injunctions restraining publication a thing of the past.

446	Although the established practice strongly favours defendants, it may often be awkward to have to make out a defence at such an early stage in the action. The facts supporting the defence must be sworn to, and while hearsay evidence is permitted, sources for the defendant's belief should be disclosed.[23] This may, for example, effectively force the defendant's hand at a very early stage on the sensitive matter of journalist's sources of information, although, it would seem, the courts have not been unduly stringent in the detail required.[24]

447	There is a marked contrast between the firm policy against prior restraint expressed at these injunction cases, and the relatively uncertain nature of the common law of contempt of court.[25] The uncertain definition of the law of contempt will often mean that once an action has been commenced the defendant will only publish with trepidation. By its very vagueness, the law of contempt may effectively constitute a prior restraint.[26] It is clear that a so-called "gagging" writ, issued solely for the purpose of stifling comment, will not have its intended effect.[27] On the other hand, if the court is satisfied that the action is genuine, comments which would tend to prejudice the trial will amount to a contempt. In a British Columbia case,[28] a plain-

[22] *Supra*, footnote 3.
[23] *Canada Metal Co. Ltd. v. C.B.C.* (1975), 55 D.L.R. (3d) 42n, 7 O.R. (2d) 261n (Div. Ct.); *Bonnard v. Perryman, supra*, footnote 14; *Cullen v. Stanley*, [1926] Ir. R. 73.
[24] See esp. *Bonnard v. Perryman, supra*, footnote 14, and *Cullen v. Stanley, supra*, footnote 23, where scant, if any, grounds for belief were given.
[25] For discussion see Robertson, *Courts and the Media* (Scarborough, Butterworths, 1981); Miller, *Contempt of Court* (London, Elek Books Ltd., 1976); Borrie and Lowe, *The Law of Contempt* (London, Butterworths, 1973). The matter is now governed by legislation in the United Kingdom: Contempt of Court Act, 1981. In Canada, the rules of contempt now must be read in light of the Charter of Rights and Freedoms, s. 2(*b*).
[26] In *A.-G. v. B.B.C.*, [1981] A.C. 303 (H.L.), at p. 312, Lord Denning, M.R., remarked in the Court of Appeal: "It would seem strange to me that a party who could not get an interim injunction restraining a libel could all the same get . . . an interim injunction restraining a contempt of court."
[27] *Thompson v. Times Newspapers, Ltd.*, [1969] 3 All E.R. 648 (C.A.), at p. 651, *per* Salmon, L.J.; *Wallersteiner v. Moir*, [1974] 1 W.L.R. 991 (C.A.), at p. 1005; *A.-G. v. Times Newspapers Ltd.*, [1974] A.C. 273 (H.L.), at p. 301.
[28] *Campbell v. Sun Printing & Publishing Co.*, [1921] 2 W.W.R. 987 (B.C.S.C.).

tiff was granted an interlocutory injunction to restrain repetition of an alleged libel pending trial on the basis, not that the libel *per se* should be restrained, but "for the purpose of preventing the defendants from publishing any matter which might prejudice him in obtaining a fair trial before an impartial jury."[29] Detailed consideration of contempt for comment on matters *sub judice* is beyond the scope of this book. It is worth noting, however, that although there is a clear policy expressed in the injunction cases against prior restraint, the uncertainties of contempt law may have a distinctly chilling effect on publication.

448   In some cases of trade libel, special damage must be proved to make out the cause of action.[30] It has been held that in such cases, a plaintiff will be denied an injunction unless he proves special damage: "obviously . . . it would be necessary to shew that there was an actionable wrong well laid. . . . [T]he plaintiff would not be entitled to an injunction, any more than he would be entitled to maintain an action unless he established all that was necessary to make out that a tort had been committed".[31] It is possible to read the cases on this point as laying down a strict rule precluding injunctive relief for apprehended damage prior to any damage actually having been sustained.[32] However, it is submitted that a preferable reading avoids such a serious departure from the ordinary availability of *quia timet* relief. In the reported cases applying this rule, the allegedly actionable statements have been made and no actual damage has been shown. The purpose of the rule of substantive law requiring such damage is presumably to deny relief for puffery or other similar statements, frequently made in the commercial context, which are untrue but harmless. To grant an injunction there would truly be to provide a remedy although there had been no wrong. On the other hand, where it is clear that a false statement would cause damage, the case is quite different.[33] An injunction would not subvert the substantive law rule, but would merely provide a plaintiff with a more certain and satisfactory remedy than would damages.

---

[29] *Ibid.*, at p. 989, *per* Macdonald, J. *Cf. Bellitti v. C.B.C.* (1973), 44 D.L.R. (3d) 407, 2 O.R. (2d) 232 (H.C.J.).

[30] *Cf.* Libel and Slander Act, Ont., s. 19.

[31] *White v. Mellin*, [1895] A.C. 154 (H.L.), at pp. 163-4, *per* Lord Herschell, L.C.

[32] This is the interpretation suggested by *Dunlop Pneumatic Tyre Co. Ltd. v. Maison Talbot* (1904), 20 T.L.R. 579 (C.A.); *Lyne v. Nicholls* (1906), 23 T.L.R. 86; *Royal Baking Powder Co. v. Wright Crossley & Co.* (1900), 18 R.P.C. 95 (H.L.).

[33] See *British Ry. Traffic & Electric Co. v. C.R.C. Co.*, [1922] 2 K.B. 260 at p. 273, *per* McCardie, J. *Cf. Thomas v. Williams* (1880), 14 Ch. D. 864.

3. Breach of Confidence

449   Injunctions are frequently awarded to protect against a wrongful
disclosure or use of confidential information.[34] The breach of confidence principle embraces cases emerging from a variety of settings,
ranging from trade secrecy to matrimonial communications, which
give rise to a variety of issues on injunction applications. The cause
of action for breach of confidence has been variously described as
resting on property,[35] tort,[36] fiduciary duty,[37] and a general obligation
of good faith.[38] Discussion of the substantive law issue is beyond the
scope of this book, but a number of issues do arise at the remedial
level when an injunction is sought.

450   Injunctive relief for breach of confidence has been particularly important in the industrial and commercial context where information
as to trade secrets, industrial processes, and customers is at stake. In
these cases, the plaintiff typically seeks to prevent the defendant
from reaping an illegitimate advantage, and there is little hesitation
on the part of the courts in granting an injunction to prevent such
wrongful gains.[39] Information of this type is commercially exploita-
ble, and an injunction effectively forces the defendant either to refrain from using it altogether, or to pay the plaintiff's price for
permission to use it.[40] The remedial principle here corresponds to
that applied in cases dealing with more conventional forms of industrial property, namely, copyright, patents, and trade marks. Ordinarily, an injunction will be granted at trial, although damages in lieu of
an injunction may also reflect the full commercial value of the in-

---

[34] The injunction is described in the U.K. Law Commission, "Breach of Confidence",
Working Paper 58 (London, H.M.S.O., 1974), at p. 31, as the "principal remedy"
for breach of confidence.

[35] Neave and Weinberg, "The Nature and Function of Equities", 6 U. of Tas. L. Rev.
24, 115 (1978), at pp. 115-30; Ricketson, "Confidential Information — A New Proprietary Interest?", 11 Melb. U.L. Rev. 223 (Part I), and p. 289 (Part II) (1977).

[36] North, "Breach of Confidence: Is There a New Tort?", 12 J.S.P.T.L. 149 (1972).

[37] Hammond, "Is Breach of Confidence Properly Analysed in Fiduciary Terms?", 25
McGill L.J. 244 (1979).

[38] *Fraser v. Evans*, [1969] 1 Q.B. 349 (C.A.), at p. 361, *per* Denning, M.R. See also
Jones, "Restitution of Benefits Obtained in Breach of Another's Confidence", 86
L.Q.R. 463 (1970).

[39] See, *e.g.*, *Tenatronics Ltd. v. Hauf* (1971), 23 D.L.R. (3d) 60, [1972] 1 O.R. 329
(H.C.J.). *Cf. Woodward v. Hutchins*, [1977] 1 W.L.R. 760 (C.A.); *Lennon v. News
Group Newspapers, Ltd.*, [1978] F.S.R. 573 (C.A.), refusing injunctive relief in favour of pop stars on the grounds that having sought publicity and profit from re-
vealing their private lives, equity would not enjoin further invasion.

[40] *Cf.*, *supra*, §439.

formation appropriated by the defendant.[41] Interlocutory applications are more likely to produce difficulties, but because the essence of the action is to restrain disclosure, the plaintiff will often have a strong case for interlocutory injunctive relief. In certain cases, disclosure of secret information may effectively destroy the right the plaintiff seeks to protect. In other cases, however, where the gist of the action lies in the unauthorized use of an idea or process, or where the plaintiff's interest will not be impaired by further disclosure, the balance of convenience pending trial may favour limited protection, whereby the injunction is refused, but the defendant is required to keep an account of profits pending trial.[42]

451   In other contexts, the breach of confidence action more closely resembles a claim for defamation, or violation of the plaintiff's privacy. The plaintiff sues to avoid the embarrassment or humiliation of having private personal matters revealed. In such cases, the defendant will often be seeking to exploit the commercial possibilities of such revelations, but the plaintiff's motivation in suing to prevent disclosure is plainly not the desire to protect his commercial interests. Again, the difficult issues arise at the interlocutory stage before the substantive issues have been fully resolved. Viewing the matter as one simply between the immediate parties, the plaintiff's case for injunctive relief is particularly strong. Damages for humiliation and embarrassment are difficult to measure, and prevention in this area is clearly much preferable to cure from the plaintiff's point of view. If the injunction is not granted at the interlocutory stage, the confidential material will be revealed. This may be tantamount to destroying the right altogether. At the very least, the court will be faced with a very difficult issue as to damage measurement. However, as with defamation cases, the issue cannot always properly be seen as involving only the immediate parties. Often there is a public interest in freedom of information and freedom of the press to be considered. So far, in breach of confidence cases, the courts have been less willing to

---

[41] See, *e.g.*, *Seager v. Copydex Ltd. (No. 2)*, [1969] 1 W.L.R. 809 (C.A.); Waddams, *The Law of Damages* (1983), §631-638, 957.

[42] *Potters-Ballotini, Ltd. v. Weston-Baker*, [1977] R.P.C. 202 (C.A.), refusing an interlocutory injunction where the substantive issue was in doubt and where a substantial investment in constructing a new plant was already committed by the defendants. See also *Bostitch Inc. v. McGarry & Cole, Ltd.*, [1964] R.P.C. 173. In some cases, where the potential market for a product is limited, the plaintiff may lose goodwill as well as profits on particular sales, and thus render unsatisfactory a result which permits the defendant to carry on, keeping an account until trial: *Collins (Engineers) Ltd. v. Roberts & Co., Ltd.*, [1965] R.P.C. 429.

consider the general public interest in having free access to information and injunctions have been granted more readily than in defamation cases. Lord Denning, however, has sought to enunciate a
general doctrine of prior restraint which would apply in defamation,
breach of confidence, contempt, and other areas as well where an injunction is sought to stifle comment on matters of public interest.[43]
The defamation cases have already been examined,[44] and reference is
made below to the contempt cases.[45]

452   In *Hubbard v. Vosper*,[46] an interlocutory injunction was sought to
restrain publication of *The Mind Benders*, a highly critical account of
the cult of Scientology, on the grounds of breach of copyright and
breach of confidence. The defendant, a former member of the sect,
pleaded the defence of "public interest" to the breach of confidence
claim, and fair dealing to the breach of copyright allegation. The
Court of Appeal set aside an interlocutory injunction, and Lord
Denning's reasons concluded as follows:

> These defences are such that he should be permitted to go ahead with
> the publication. If what he says is true, it is only right that the dangers of
> this cult should be exposed. We never restrain a defendant in a libel ac-
> tion who says he is going to justify. So in copyright action, we ought not
> to restrain a defendant who has a reasonable defence of fair dealing.
> Nor in an action for breach of confidence, if the defendant has a reason-
> able defence of public interest. The reason is because the defendant, if
> he is right, is entitled to publish it: and the law will not intervene to sup-
> press freedom of speech except when it is abused.[47]

453   While this suggests that breach of confidence cases should be dealt
with on the same footing as defamation cases, the extent to which
English courts are prepared to uphold a general doctrine against
prior restraint in breach of confidence has been thrown into doubt by
the more recent decision in *Schering Chemicals v. Falkman Ltd.*[48]
There, the plaintiff, a drug company, sought to restrain the broadcast on television of a film which examined an allegation that one of
its products was responsible for harmful effects upon unborn children. Information for the film had been supplied in breach of confidence by one of the defendants, whom the plaintiff had actually

---

[43] *Infra*, §453.
[44] *Supra*, §§440-448.
[45] *Infra*, §491.
[46] [1972] 2 Q.B. 84 (C.A.).
[47] *Ibid.*, at pp. 96-7.
[48] [1981] 2 All E.R. 321 (C.A.).

hired for advice on how to put its view across more effectively to counter the bad publicity it had been receiving as a result of these allegations. The Court of Appeal held, by a majority, that an injunction should issue. Lord Denning, dissenting, would have refused the injunction on the grounds of "prior restraint":

> Freedom of the press is of fundamental importance in our society. It covers not only the right of the press to impart information of general interest or concern, but also the right of the public to receive it. It is not to be restricted on the ground of breach of confidence unless there is a "pressing social need" for such restraint. In order to warrant a restraint, there must be a social need for protecting the confidence sufficiently pressing to outweigh the public interest in freedom of the press.
>
> . . . . .
>
> . . . in our present case, the *public* interest in the drug . . . and its effects far outweighs the *private* interest of the makers in preventing discussion of it.[49]

Templeman, L.J., however, differed:

> It has been suggested that an injunction restraining breach of confidentiality should only be granted in circumstances in which the right to preserve confidentiality is so important that it takes priority over freedom of the press. If this means that the court should consider the consequences to the public of withholding or granting an injunction, then I fully agree . . . It is important in the present case that, if the injunction is withheld, the court will enable a trusted adviser to make money out of his dealing in confidential information. These consequences must be weighed against the argument that, if an injunction is granted, the public will be deprived of information.[50]

454   However, Templeman, L.J., did not consider that an injunction would prevent information as to the drug reaching the public. It would only prevent the defendant himself from acting as the source and inspiration of any publication in breach of his duty of confidence. In fact, Lord Denning's view was based, in part, on the point that much of the information was already in the public domain. The other member of the majority, Shaw, L.J., merely expressed the view that breach of the confidence would result in irreparable harm to the plaintiff.

455   It appears doubtful that the nearly absolute prohibition of prior restraint applied in defamation cases is applicable in the context of breach of confidence. There are several factors which suggest that it should be easier to justify interlocutory relief where the plaintiff sues

---

[49] *Ibid.*, at p. 334.

[50] *Ibid.*, at p. 347.

to prevent a breach of confidence. It will usually be less difficult to predict the result in a breach of confidence action at the interlocutory stage. There is no need to protect the defendant's right to have the factual issues tried by a jury, as such actions are almost invariably tried by judge alone. More important, these actions are less likely to turn on the ability of the defendants to prove the truth or falsehood of certain facts, and more likely to turn upon the legal implications to be drawn from the relationship between the parties. In a defamation case, the plaintiff can only complain if what is said about him is defamatory and false. In a breach of confidence case, the plaintiff has the right to restrain any comment at all. The truth or falsehood of the information to be disclosed is not at issue and the fear of prior restraint and imposing an unjustifiable gag is much less a factor. Moreover, as Lord Denning has put it, breach of confidence cases involve two fundamental rights; freedom of the press must be reconciled with the right of privacy.[51] The very definition of the right involved in breach of confidence suggests that such cases ought to have a higher claim to injunctive protection than does the right not to be defamed. Confidential information is explicitly not for publication, and by recognizing the existence of a confidential relationship, the law clearly places the plaintiff's right to keep information secret above any interest the public may have in knowing that information. Once the information is disclosed, that interest is destroyed, and damages to reflect the degree of hurt involved in having one's private affairs broadcast are much less satisfactory than an injunction preventing publication in the first place.[52] A damages award cannot make secret again matters divulged in breach of confidence.

---

[51] *Ibid.*, at p. 333.

[52] The U.K. Law Commission, Report No. 110, "Breach of Confidence", Cmnd. 8388 (London, H.M.S.O., 1981), at p. 154, argues that defamation and breach of confidence cases should be treated differently:

In a defamation case, if an interlocutory injunction is not granted and nevertheless the defences put forward ultimately fail, the plaintiff will have the satisfaction of the vindication of his good name in court as well as an award of damages. In a breach of confidence case, on the other hand, if the plaintiff is refused an interlocutory injunction but succeeds at the trial, there may be no way, comparable to the vindication of the plaintiff's good name in a defamation case, by which he can undo the harm caused by the disclosure of the information which he is seeking to protect and for which, where the information is of a personal character, damages may not be an adequate compensation.

For an unusual illustration of this point, see *Foster v. Mountford & Rigby Ltd.* (1976), 14 Aust. L.R. 71 (S.C.N.T.), where it was alleged that revelation of aboriginal tribal secrets to women, children and the uninitiated would undermine the social and religious stability of an entire community.

4. Membership in Unions and Unincorporated Associations

456   One area in which the theory that injunctions should only be granted to protect property rights has had an impact is that of the protection of interests in unincorporated associations and clubs. These cases deal with rights of membership in bodies ranging from purely social clubs to large and economically powerful trade unions.

457   In the case of clubs, it has been held that an injunction should not be granted to restrain expulsion or to protect rights of membership unless the plaintiff can point to some infringement of his property interests.[53] Thus, a distinction has been drawn between clubs in which members hold a personal stake in club property, so that in the event of dissolution they would share in the proceeds,[54] and proprietary clubs where the property is vested in some individual and members merely pay a subscription.[55] In the former case, injunctive relief can be obtained to protect membership rights, whereas in the latter, in many cases, the member has been left to his action in damages for breach of contract.[56]

458   The property theory is obviously deficient as an analytic tool in these cases. Members of social clubs suing for injunctions to restrain their wrongful expulsion, rarely, if ever, are seeking to protect their contingent and ephemeral property interest in the club's assets. Rather, it is the desire to avoid "a humiliation, and indignity, akin to violation of privacy and akin to defamation".[57] Serious issues arise as to whether an injunction is the most appropriate remedy to vindicate such rights, but those issues are hardly elucidated by an analysis which turns on the presence or absence of property rights.

459   In the case of trade unions, injunctive relief for wrongful expulsion was at one time refused on the grounds that the expelled member had no property interest in his union membership.[58] However, in

---

[53] *Baird v. Wells* (1890), 44 Ch. D. 661; *Rowe v. Hewitt* (1906), 12 O.L.R. 13 (Div. Ct.).

[54] *Ibid.*; *Rigby v. Connol* (1880), 14 Ch. D. 482.

[55] The distinction is explained and criticized as a basis of decision in Chafee, "The Internal Affairs of Associations not for Profit", 43 Harv. L.R. 993 (1930).

[56] See, *e.g.*, *Young v. Ladies' Imperial Club, Ltd.*, [1920] 2 K.B. 523 (C.A.), granting a declaration that the plaintiff was still a member, awarding a farthing damages, but refusing an injunction because the club was not proprietary.

[57] Pound, *supra*, footnote 2, at p. 677. See, *e.g.*, *Fisher v. Keane* (1878), 11 Ch. D. 353 at p. 363, *per* Jessell, M.R., stating that expulsion could ". . . blast a man's reputation for ever — perhaps to ruin his prospects for life." But in *Baird v. Wells* (1890), 44 Ch. D. 661 at p. 677, Stirling, J., rejected the contention that damages were insufficient to repair the damage to "character and position in society".

[58] *Rigby v. Connol, supra*, footnote 54.

union cases and in cases involving trade and other professional associations, there is clearly an economic interest at stake which may not
properly fall under the rubric of "property", and yet may be more
valuable and more worthy of protection than a formal right contingent on dissolution of the association.

460   Gradually, the courts have moved from the strict property theory,
and injunctive relief is now more freely granted in this class of case.[59]
This has developed in two ways. First, the courts have taken a
broader view of what constitutes property in this context. The right
to trade and right to work have been seen as worthy of injunctive
protection.[60] Many trade and professional associations confer upon
members a distinct economic advantage by excluding others from
some particular work or trade. In such cases, injunctive relief is
available to protect a member's right not to be removed from the
association unless it acts in good faith, and according to its own constitution and rules as well as the rules of natural justice.[61] The courts
have explicitly abandoned the need to find property before interven-
ing, and have justified injunctive relief as being necessary to protect
the individual's right to trade or work. Even where loss of membership does not mean loss of job, the courts have accepted that the status of membership may significantly affect the plaintiff in his work or
trade, and have afforded injunctive relief accordingly.[62]

---

[59] Stone, "Wrongful Expulsion from Trade Unions: Judicial Intervention at Anglo-
American Law", 34 Can. Bar Rev. 1111 (1956); *Bimson v. Johnston* (1957), 10
D.L.R. (2d) 11, [1957] O.R. 519 (H.C.J.), affd 12 D.L.R. (2d) 379, [1958] O.W.N.
217 (C.A.); *Lee v. Showmen's Guild of Great Britain*, [1952] 2 Q.B. 329 (C.A.).
See also *Vancouver Real Estate Board v. Moscrop Realty Ltd.*, [1961] S.C.R. 418,
28 D.L.R. (2d) 85; *Labelle v. Ottawa Real Estate Board* (1977), 78 D.L.R. (3d)
558, 16 O.R. (2d) 502 (H.C.J.), granting relief in the case of trade associations.

[60] See *Nagle v. Feilden*, [1966] 2 Q.B. 633 (C.A.), at p. 646, *per* Denning, M.R.:
"The true ground of jurisdiction in all these cases is a man's right to work . . . a
man's right to work at his trade or profession is just as important to him as, perhaps
more important than, his rights of property. Just as the courts will intervene to protect his rights of property, they will also intervene to protect his right to work." See
also *Abbott v. Sullivan*, [1952] 1 K.B. 189 (C.A.), at p. 216, *per* Morris, L.J.

[61] See *Dawkins v. Androbus* (1881), 17 Ch. D. 615 (C.A.). In some cases, however,
the courts have refused to interfere with the discretion of the association official:
Cassel v. Inglis, [1916] 2 Ch. 211, dealing with re-election to a Stock Exchange.

[62] *Lawlor v. Union of Post Office Workers*, [1965] Ch. 712 at p. 734, *per* Ungoed-
Thomas, J.:

> . . . loss of membership of the union does not mean loss of job, so that the disad-
> vantage to the plaintiffs is not of a financial character. But the disadvantage is
> more than merely social. The expulsion does affect the expelled member in his
> work. It affects his standing with and relation to other members . . . Trade
> unions, to their honour, also develop strong ties of loyalty amongst their mem-

461   Secondly, the courts have found that the rules of the union or association constitute a contract between the members governing their
relationship.[63] Breach of the rules involves an actionable breach of
contract, and if the association has acted unfairly, a contractual obligation to follow rules of natural justice can readily be implied. While
there appear to be no modern cases involving purely social clubs, it is
quite possible that this theory, which evolved in the context of trade
unions, might now be used. It has been said that the presence or absence of a property right now only goes to the form of remedy,[64] and
it is quite likely that a modern court would take the next step and not
deny injunctive relief solely on the grounds that no property interest
is infringed.

462   However, the contract theory, like that of property, is artificial.
Indeed, in one decision of the English Court of Appeal, it was described as a fiction.[65] In that case, a contract could not possibly have
been found — the plaintiff was wrongfully denied admission to a
jockey club which had monopolized the racing industry — and yet injunctive relief was given. In another case, the High Court of Australia refused to apply the contract theory and denied an injunction to a
plaintiff who alleged that he had been wrongfully excluded from a
political party on the basis that the members of the party could not
have intended to create a legal and, therefore, justiciable
relationship.[66]

463   It is suggested that the real concern in all these cases is whether judicial intervention into personal relationships in the form of the coercive remedy of injunction can be justified in principle. The theory
based upon the technical niceties of the member's property or contractual rights may often conceal the real concern of the court: does
the plaintiff's interest in membership have sufficient weight and im-

---

bers, and loss of membership, particularly amongst members of standing like
some of the plaintiffs, strikes deep, and not the less so because it may not strike
at the pocket.

[63] *White v. Kuzyck*, [1951] A.C. 585, [1951] 3 D.L.R. 641 (P.C.); *cf. Tunney v.
Orchard*, [1955] 3 D.L.R. 15 (Man. C.A.), at p. 41, *per* Tritschler, J.: "the Judges
found it possible to move from property to contract to meet the exigencies of the
times. The step from contract to *status* is not more revolutionary . . . In my opinion
the destruction of plaintiff's Union *status* was a tort."
This decision was upheld, but the contract theory was reasserted: *Orchard v.
Tunney*, [1957] S.C.R. 436, 8 D.L.R. (2d) 273.

[64] *Lee v. Showmen's Guild of Great Britain, supra*, footnote 59, at p. 342, *per* Denning, L.J.

[65] *Nagle v. Feilden, supra*, footnote 60, at pp. 646, 653.

[66] *Cameron v. Hogan* (1934), 51 C.L.R. 358 (Aust. H.C.).

portance to justify risks of friction inherent in coercing the group to accept him back into their midst? The issue bears some similarity to that found with respect to the specific enforcement of contracts of personal service.[67] In the case of unions, trade or professional associations, formed primarily for economic rather than social reasons, this personal element is bound to be minimal, and even where it does exist, it should rarely, if ever, prevail over the individual's right in asserting his right to trade. Such associations may well have close personal ties, but their purpose is to promote the economic interests of their members. When one member is wrongfully denied those advantages, the purpose of the group is not frustrated by injunctive intervention. Different considerations may well apply to social or political clubs where social, moral, political, or intellectual cohesion is of the essence. Once lost, it may be difficult to replace, and coercive judicial remedies may often be misplaced. In these cases, even where some form of judicial intervention is legally justified, less drastic remedies such as a declaration or damages may be more appropriate. The plaintiff's true concern is usually vindication of honour or reputation, and a declaration or award of damages to show that he has been wronged may satisfy his interest but at the same time avoid the undesirable effects of a coercive order forcing the parties back

---

[67] *Infra*, §§577-586. In *Rigby v. Connol* (1880), 14 Ch. D. 482 at p. 487, a trade union case, Jessel, M.R., made specific reference to this factor:

> . . . the Courts . . . have never dreamt of enforcing agreements strictly personal in their nature, whether they are agreements of hiring and service, being the common relation of master and servant, or whether they are agreements for the purpose of pleasure, or for the purpose of scientific pursuits, or for the purpose of charity or philanthropy—in such cases no Court of Justice can interfere so long as there is no property the right to which is taken away from the person complaining.

It is interesting to compare Jessel, M.R.'s eagerness to grant injunctive relief in *Fisher v. Keane, supra*, footnote 57, where membership in a social club was at stake and the real issue the plaintiff's reputation, with his refusal to grant relief in *Rigby v. Connol, supra*, which involved a trade union, where he could find no property right at stake, but where the economic consequences might well have been more severe for the plaintiff than in *Fisher*. The language of the judges who decided the "club" cases indicates that they were not strangers to such institutions: see, *e.g.*, *Dawkins v. Antrobus, supra*, footnote 61, at p. 629, *per* James, L.J.: "Perhaps I am going further than I ought . . . but . . . I can conceive nothing more injurious to the character and interests of a club than one member of a club sending through the post an open envelope with those charges upon it"; and at p. 637, *per* Cotton, L.J.: "I cannot accede to the suggestion in a matter like this, that members of a club, or any body of gentlemen, will support their committee at the expense of truth and honesty."

into an unwilling relationship which may well be inconsistent with the very essence of the association or club.[68]

464   Injunctions may also be awarded to require officers and other members of unincorporated associations and unions to adhere to the constitution and rules of the organization.[69] Several cases deal with the election of officers,[70] where the courts have referred to their common law jurisdiction to superintend the conduct of political elections, and held that they also have jurisdiction to intervene in non-political elections.[71]

5. Injunctions to Protect Shareholders' Rights

465   Corporate shareholders are often entitled to injunctive relief to protect their interests. The complex rules determining when a shareholder may bring a personal action *against* the company to protect his own rights as a shareholder and when a derivative suit may be brought *on behalf* of the company in respect of a wrong done to it are obviously beyond the scope of this book.[72] The present discussion is, however, concerned with the former class of case, and it is very often there that injunctive relief will be appropriate. Again, the complex substantive issues raised in these cases are beyond the scope of a book on remedies, but some remedial issues may be considered.

466   In many instances, the shareholder's action for an injunction will assert a statutory right. Perhaps the most common cases are those where shareholders seek to restrain *ultra vires* acts on the part of the company. Often, in the past, such suits were brought by the Attorney-General,[73] but it is also clear that a shareholder may sue to

---

[68] *Cf.* Pound, *supra*, footnote 2, at p. 679, who argued that the wrongdoers should be put to the choice of receiving the expelled member back or dissolving the club: "It is not necessary to order the defendants to associate with the plaintiff. If they desire to abandon or to dissolve the club, they may be left free to do so. But they might be enjoined from wrongfully and maliciously excluding the plaintiff so long as they keep it up." Another consideration raised by Chafee, *supra*, footnote 55, at p. 1013, is that damages may penalize innocent members of the club, whereas an injunction avoids pecuniary payment.

[69] *McMillin v. Yandell* (1971), 22 D.L.R. (3d) 398, [1972] 1 O.R. 146 (H.C.J.) (injunction to restrain merger of union with another in breach of union constitution).

[70] *Howard v. Parrinton* (1971), 21 D.L.R. (3d) 395, [1971] 3 O.R. 659 (H.C.J.); *Brodie v. Bevan* (1921), 38 T.L.R. 172; *Watson v. Smith*, [1941] 2 All E.R. 725 (Ch.); *Leigh v. National Union of Railwaymen*, [1970] Ch. 326; *Davidson v. Grange* (1854), 4 Gr. 377; *Tully v. Farrell* (1876), 23 Gr. 49.

[71] See *Howard v. Parrinton*, *supra*, footnote 70, at p. 400 D.L.R., p. 664 O.R., referring to *Re South Waterloo Provincial Election; Mercer v. Homuth* (1924), 55 O.L.R. 245 (S.C. App. Div.), at p. 247.

[72] See *Gower's Principles of Modern Company Law*, 4th ed. (London, Stevens & Sons, 1979), pp. 653-6, for a discussion of the member's personal action.

[73] See, *e.g.*, *A.-G. ex rel. Warwickshire County Council v. London & North Western Ry. Co.*, [1900] 1 Q.B. 78 (C.A.); *supra*, §253.

prevent a corporation in which he holds an interest from exceeding its powers.[74] Other statutory rights which have been enforced by injunction include the right to inspect books or the register of members.[75] In other cases, the shareholder may seek to enjoin an act which violates the company's internal constitution. Injunctions may be awarded to restrain the irregular calling or conducting of shareholders' meetings,[76] interference with shareholders' voting rights,[77] or other personal rights conferred by the articles or by-laws.[78] Often, the action will be more obviously proprietary in nature, as where the shareholders seek to restrain: payment of dividends except in accordance with the company's constitution,[79] the unauthorized issue of shares,[80] directors from issuing shares to maintain their own control,[81] the illegal or oppressive forfeiture of shares, alteration of the company's internal structure or otherwise conducting the affairs of the company so as to constitute a fraud on minority shareholders.[82]

467   In most cases, either an injunction or a declaration will be the only appropriate remedy. It would be difficult to imagine an award of damages in respect of an *ultra vires* act.[83] Whether the illegitimate activity results in gain or loss to the company, the shareholders' rights to sue for an injunction is unaffected.[84] It has been held that the

---

[74] *Colman v. Eastern Counties Ry. Co.* (1846), 10 Beav. 1, 50 E.R. 481; *Simpson v. Westminster Palace Hotel Co.* (1860), 8 H.L.C. 712 at p. 717, 11 E.R. 608; *Hoole v. Great Western Ry. Co.* (1867), L.R. 3 Ch. 262; *Hare v. London & North-Western Ry. Co.* (1861), 30 L.J. Ch. 817; Gower, *supra*, footnote 72, at p. 653: "Thus, it is clear that an action to restrain the company from acting *ultra vires* may be brought by any member as plaintiff in his own right against the company as a defendant."

[75] *Holland v. Dickson* (1888), 37 Ch. D. 669; *Mutter v. Eastern & Midlands Ry. Co.* (1888), 38 Ch. D. 92 (C.A.); *Lemon v. Austin Friars Investment Trust,* [1926] 1 Ch. 1 (C.A.).

[76] *Charter Oil Co. Ltd. v. Beaumont* (1967), 65 D.L.R. (2d) 112 (B.C.C.A); *Harben v. Phillips* (1882), 23 Ch. D. 14 (C.A.).

[77] *Pender v. Lushington* (1877), 6 Ch. D. 70.

[78] *Baillie v. Oriental Telephone & Electric Co.*, [1915] 1 Ch. 503 (C.A.).

[79] *Sturge v. Eastern Union Ry. Co.* (1855), 7 De G.M. & G. 158, 44 E.R. 62 (Ch.).

[80] *Mosely v. Koffyfontein Mines, Ltd.*, [1911] 1 Ch. 73 (C.A.), affd [1911] A.C. 409 (H.L.).

[81] *Bernard v. Valentini* (1978), 83 D.L.R. (3d) 440, 18 O.R. (2d) 656 (H.C.J.).

[82] *Brown v. Can-Erin Mines Ltd.* (1960), 25 D.L.R. (2d) 250, [1961] O.R. 9 (H.C.J.); *Beauchamp v. Conterants Sanitaires C.S. Inc.* (1979), 7 B.L.R. 200 (Que. S.C.); *cf. Pylypchuk and Ewachniuk v. Dell Hotel Ltd.* (1958), 15 D.L.R. (2d) 589 (B.C.S.C.), where no fraud was established. See also Canada Business Corporations Act, s. 234, specifically empowering the court to grant an injunction in case of oppression.

[83] Gower, *supra*, footnote 72, at p. 656.

[84] *Colman v. Eastern Counties Ry. Co.*, *supra*, footnote 74.

court will not inquire into the motives of a shareholder who seeks an injunction to protect his rights. Injunctions have been granted even where it was suggested that the plaintiff's reason for suing was not so much to protect his own genuine interest in having his rights respected, but to give some advantage to a rival or competing company.[85]

468   Cases involving corporate reorganizations,[86] take-over bids,[87] and proxy solicitations,[88] raise difficult problems because they usually must be dealt with very quickly on an interlocutory application where it may be difficult to deal adequately with the complex legal issues raised.[89] The issue of whether the court should leave the matter to be dealt with by a Securities Commission is examined elsewhere.[90] An interlocutory injunction in favour of one faction puts that group in an extremely powerful bargaining position. In one recent Ontario case,[91] minority shareholders alleged that the majority were not respecting statutory provisions in a proposed amalgamation whereby shares owned by the minority would be converted into non-voting preference shares, redeemable by the amalgamated corporation. It was held that as the plaintiffs had an arguable case, and that although, in the end, "whatever happens the major issue is money",[92] the plaintiffs were entitled not to be deprived of their shares without their consent. The court felt that damages would be difficult to fix because of the complexity of the inter-company transactions involved,

---

[85] *Pender v. Lushington, supra,* footnote 77; *Mutter v. Eastern & Midlands Ry. Co., supra,* footnote 75. Such an interest may, however, preclude him from suing on behalf of other shareholders: *Forrest v. Manchester, Sheffield & Lincolnshire Ry. Co.* (1861), 4 De G.F. & J. 126, 45 E.R. 1131 (Ch.).

[86] *Infra,* footnotes 91-93.

[87] *Re Calgary Power Ltd. and Atco Ltd.* (1980), 115 D.L.R. (3d) 625 (Alta. Q.B.); *Royal Trustco Ltd. v. Campeau Corp.* (1980), 118 D.L.R. (3d) 207, 31 O.R. (2d) 75 (H.C.J.), affd D.L.R. *loc. cit.* p. 271, O.R. *loc. cit.* p. 130 (C.A.) (injunction refused on merits).

[88] *Infra,* footnote 89.

[89] See *Brown v. Duby* (1980), 111 D.L.R. (3d) 418, 28 O.R. (2d) 745 (H.C.J.), refusing an interlocutory injunction to restrain an improper proxy solicitation on the grounds that it would appear to favour unduly one side; *Babic v. Milinkovic* (1972), 25 D.L.R. (3d) 752 (B.C.C.A.), at p. 753, *per* McFarlane, J.A., refusing to enjoin an alleged breach of a shareholders' voting argument and "allowing these shareholders, right or wrong, at a properly constituted meeting to elect the directors of their choice. If, following the trial, a different result should be found to exist, it can be corrected". See also *Schiowitz v. I.O.S. Ltd.* (1971), 23 D.L.R. (3d) 102 (N.B.S.C. App. Div.).

[90] *Supra,* §347.

[91] *Carlton Realty Co. Ltd. v. Maple Leaf Mills* (1978), 93 D.L.R. (3d) 106, 22 O.R. (2d) 198 (H.C.J.).

[92] *Ibid.,* at p. 206, *per* Steele, J.

and an interlocutory injunction was granted. Similar results have been recorded in other cases.[93]

469   Such cases clearly call for the most careful sifting of the merits, even though the matter arises at the interlocutory stage. The result of refusing an injunction will be to permit the corporate restructuring to occur without any chance of injunctive relief later. The effect of granting the injunction will almost always be either to end any real prospect of the reorganization occurring, quite possibly to the detriment of the majority shareholders who may be in the right, or to force the majority to buy out the minority at whatever price the minority can bargain for. There is nothing wrong with that position if the minority shareholders have a sound case, but surely they should not be put in that position merely on the basis of an arguable case, or on showing nothing more than that there is a substantial issue to be tried.[94]

470   In those jurisdictions which provide for judicial scrutiny of the terms of the proposed reorganization schemes before it becomes effective, the courts may be expected to be much less willing to afford injunctive relief at the interlocutory stage.[95] Similarly, the existence of a statutory appraisal remedy provides an attractive alternative in many cases.[96]

471   The position of directors of corporations who sue for injunctions to restrain their removal or exclusion from meetings or functions[97] is complicated by the fact that they owe duties of a personal nature not ordinarily susceptible to specific relief. Injunctions have been refused where the plaintiff director sues the company and it is clear that the company and majority of shareholders do not wish to have the plaintiff managing the company's affairs.[98] The courts have seen such cases as specific performance of a personal contract: "it would be

---

[93] *Alexander v. Westeel-Rosco* (1978), 93 D.L.R. (3d) 116, 22 O.R. (2d) 211 (H.C.J.); *Ruskin v. Canada All-News Radio Ltd.* (1979), 7 B.L.R. 142 (Ont. H.C.J.); *cf. Stevens v. Home Oil Co. Ltd.* (1980), 123 D.L.R. (3d) 297 (Alta. Q.B.), denying an interlocutory injunction on the grounds that the amalgamation could not be effective without the court's approval under the Alberta legislation, and that minority interest will be protected at that stage.

[94] *Supra*, §§154-161.

[95] See *Stevens v. Home Oil Co. Ltd.*, *supra*, footnote 93.

[96] See, *e.g.*, the Canada Business Corporations Act, 1974-75-76, ss. 184 and 234.

[97] For a good discussion of this problem, see Pennington, *Company Law*, 4th ed. (1979), pp. 508-10.

[98] *Harben v. Phillips* (1882), 23 Ch. D. 14 (C.A.); *Bainbridge v. Smith* (1889), 41 Ch. D. 462 (C.A.); *cf. Munster v. Cammell Co.* (1882), 21 Ch. D. 183.

contrary to the principles on which this Court acts to grant specific performance of this contract by compelling this company to take this gentleman as managing director, although he was qualified so to act, when they do not desire him to act as such."[99] However, fellow directors have been enjoined from interfering with the exercise of the plaintiff's functions on the theory that the court is protecting the plaintiff's status conferred by the company by-laws, and not indirectly specifically enforcing the contract.[100] Similarly, it has been said that a director may be entitled to an injunction where he is seeking to protect some property right, such as shares he owns, or even his right to remuneration.[101]

6. Injunctions to Restrain Inducing Breach of Contract

472   It is well established that an injunction may be granted to restrain the defendant from inducing breach of contract.[102] There has been virtually no discussion in the cases of the appropriateness of injunctive relief. It might be asked why an injunction should be granted to restrain inducing the breach of a contract when the contract itself is one for which specific performance would not be granted. If the plaintiff's right on the primary obligation is insufficient to call for the award of specific relief, how can it be that one who interferes with that right is automatically restrained?

473   One obvious point is that the refusal to award specific performance in many cases turns upon considerations which do not at all apply as against the third party who induces breach. The best example is contracts involving personal service which are not enforced by specific performance. The reason for refusing specific relief is the avoidance of involuntary servitude,[103] but that consideration does not apply where relief is sought against one who induces breach. A more general point is that the extent of the liability of one who induces breach may extend far beyond that of the party who actually commits the breach. It has been said, for example, that damages for inducing

---

[99] *Bainbridge v. Smith, supra,* footnote 98, at p. 474, *per* Cotton, L.J.
[100] *Pulbrook v. Richmond Consolidated Mining Co.* (1878), 9 Ch. D. 610.
[101] *Hayes v. Bristol Plant Hire Ltd.,* [1957] 1 All E.R. 685 (Ch.).
[102] *Glamorgan Coal Co. v. South Wales Miners' Federation,* [1903] 2 K.B. 545 (C.A.); *J. T. Stratford & Son Ltd. v. Lindley,* [1965] A.C. 269 (C.A.); *Emerald Construction Co. Ltd. v. Lowthian,* [1966] 1 All E.R. 1013 (C.A.); *Torquay Hotel Co. Ltd. v. Cousins,* [1969] 1 All E.R. 522 (C.A.); *Midland Cold Storage Ltd. v. Steer,* [1972] 3 All E.R. 941 (Ch.); *Fokuhl v. Raymond,* [1949] 4 D.L.R. 145, [1949] O.R. 704 (C.A.); *Body v. Murdock,* [1954] 4 D.L.R. 326, [1954] O.W.N. 515 (C.A.).
[103] *Infra,* §579.

breach may well exceed damages allowable for the breach itself.[104] Someone who fails to pay a debt on time may cause the collapse of the creditor's business, but usually he will not be liable for more than the amount of the debt.[105] On the other hand, the party who induced the debtor not to pay with intent to injure the creditor will be liable for more extensive damages.[106] The measure of remedial protection afforded to the plaintiff's interest in being free from interference with his contractual relations is wider than the protection afforded to the contract itself, and thus specific relief is almost certainly available in the former case, while it is only exceptionally available in the latter. Injunctions to restrain inducing breach of contract may be seen as one aspect of the protection of the right to trade which, in its various manifestations, has long been seen as an appropriate matter for specific relief.[107]

474   A similar but perhaps more controversial principle emerges from *De Mattos v. Gibson*[108] and *Lord Strathcona S.S. Co. v. Dominion Coal Co., Ltd.*[109] Those cases indicate that a person who proposes to deal with property in such a way as knowingly to bring about a breach of contract affecting that property may be restrained by injunction.[110] This overlaps to some extent the restraining of the tort of interference with contractual rights.[111] The plaintiff's contractual interest is sufficient to justify injunctive relief against interference by a third party, although he has no property interest enforceable by specific performance against the other contracting party.

7. Family Law

475   Injunctions are often granted in family law cases, restraining one spouse from molesting, harassing or annoying the other spouse or children, or excluding one spouse from the matrimonial home.[112] In

---

[104] *Lumley v. Gye* (1853), 2 El. & Bl. 216, 118 E.R. 749 (K.B.).

[105] Waddams, *supra*, footnote 41, §836. There are, however, some cases where greater liability has been imposed: see Waddams, §§831-836.

[106] *Lumley v. Gye, supra*, footnote 104, at pp. 230, 234.

[107] *Supra*, §460. For further examples, see *Daily Mirror Newspapers Ltd. v. Gardner*, [1968] 2 Q.B. 762 (C.A.). See also Waddams, §§561-565, discussing the damages awarded for inducing breach of contract.

[108] (1859), 4 De G. & J. 276, 45 E.R. 108 (Ch.).

[109] [1926] A.C. 108, [1926] 1 D.L.R. 873 (P.C.).

[110] These cases are also discussed, *infra*, §§676, 677.

[111] *Infra*, §677.

[112] See, *e.g.*, Cretney, *Principles of Family Law*, 3rd ed. (London, Sweet & Maxwell, 1979), pp. 181-97; Pelling and Purdie, *Matrimonial and Domestic Injunctions* (London, Butterworths, 1982).

several Canadian jurisdictions, legislation[113] has supplemented the ordinary jurisdiction to award an injunction with a statutory remedy.[114] In the absence of legislation, courts were cautious in this area, especially where the effect was to force one spouse to vacate the matrimonial home.[115] However, even prior to legislation, such injunctions were often granted, and quite clearly the interest protected was of a non-proprietary nature. The courts held that if necessary, a spouse could be excluded from the matrimonial home in which he held some proprietary interest, if that were necessary to protect the personal right of the other spouse to remain, to prevent the hardship of living in an impossible situation, or to ensure that the remaining spouse is not prevented or discouraged from obtaining justice in a pending matrimonial proceeding.[116]

8. Injunctions to Restrain Litigation

476   A substantial portion of the law of injunctions, before the Judicature Acts, dealt with the "common injunction" — injunctions to stay proceedings in the common law courts.[117] This was one of the principal devices used by Chancery to see that equitable doctrines were implemented. On the theory that the injunction operates *in personam*,

---

[113] See, *e.g.*, Family Law Reform Act (Ont.), which allows the court (including the provincial Family Court) to restrain one spouse "from molesting, annoying or harassing" the other, or the children (s. 34), and to grant exclusive possession of the matrimonial home, notwithstanding ownership (s. 45). There are constitutional issues where jurisdiction to make such an order is vested in a provincial court: see *Reference Re Section 6 of the Family Relations Act* (1980), 116 D.L.R. (3d) 221 (B.C.C.A.), vard [1982] 1 S.C.R. 62, 131 D.L.R. (3d) 257; *cf. Re Kleinsteuber and Kleinsteuber* (1980), 113 D.L.R. (3d) 192, 29 O.R. (2d) 358 (Prov. Ct. Fam. Div.). For cases interpreting s. 34, see *Sniderman v. Sniderman* (1981), 25 R.F.L. (2d) 319 (H.C.J.); *Re Layton and Layton* (1982), 134 D.L.R. (3d) 570, 37 O.R. (2d) 201 (H.C.J.). Section 745 of the Criminal Code, empowering the court to make a binding-over order, is often used in domestic proceedings. In England, see Domestic Violence and Matrimonial Proceedings Act, 1976. It has been held that an injunction against assault can be awarded even in the absence of legislation: *Egan v. Egan*, [1975] Ch. 218.

[114] An injunction to protect property rights in favour of one spouse may be made even where statutory criteria are not met: see, *e.g.*, *Gundy v. Gundy*, [1981] 6 W.W.R. 355 (Sask. Q.B.).

[115] *Duggan v. Duggan* (1965), 51 D.L.R. (2d) 576, [1965] 2 O.R. 651 (H.C.J.); *Montgomery v. Montgomery*, [1965] P. 46.

[116] *Donoghue v. Donoghue* (1973), 11 R.F.L. 305 (Ont. S.C.); *Iachetta v. Iachetta* (1973), 11 R.F.L. 309 (H.C.J.); *Hersog v. Hersog*, [1975] R.F.L. 138 (B.C.S.C.); *Jones v. Jones*, [1971] 2 All E.R. 737 (C.A.); *Bassett v. Bassett*, [1975] Fam. 76 (C.A.). For a detailed review of the English practice, see Pelling and Purdie, *supra*, footnote 112.

[117] See Eden, *The Law of Injunctions* (1821).

such injunctions were not deemed to interfere with the common law courts *per se*, but seen as a device whereby a party to a common law suit could be forced to respect the principles of equity.[118] Fusion of law and equity and the establishment of a single Supreme Court meant that equitable pleas could be heard in all suits, and equitable procedures such as discovery were always available. In those cases where it is still appropriate for the court to exercise its discretionary powers to control unfairness or inequitable conduct not covered by a specific rule or statutory procedure, the statutory remedy of a stay[119] has replaced the pre-Judicature Act "common injunction".

477   There remain, however, a narrow range of cases in which injunctions to restrain proceedings may be ordered. The theory upon which such jurisdiction is exercised remains the same as before the Judicature Act. In issuing the injunction, the court is not, in theory, purporting to control the inferior or foreign court, but rather exercising *in personam* control over the litigants.

478   The Judicature Act replaced injunctions to restrain the prosecution of suits pending in the high court with the stay,[120] but this has been held not to preclude the court from awarding an injunction to restrain the institution of proceedings threatened but not yet commenced.[121] An injunction forbidding a party from commencing a proceeding is one aspect of the court's jurisdiction to control abuses of its process.[122] The most frequently encountered cases are those involving threatened corporate winding-up proceedings. If it can be shown that such proceedings are bound to fail, and are threatened in bad faith to put unfair pressure upon the company, an injunction to restrain instituting such proceedings will issue.[123] A winding-up petition in such circumstances has been deemed productive of irreparable harm to the company and innocent shareholders,[124] and injunctive relief therefore becomes appropriate. These injunctions are necessarily heard at the interlocutory stage. Because they effectively

---

[118] *Ibid.*

[119] See, *e.g.*, Judicature Act, Ont., s. 18.6.

[120] *Supra*, footnote 119.

[121] *Besant v. Wood* (1879), 12 Ch. D. 605.

[122] *Mann v. Goldstein*, [1968] 1 W.L.R. 1091 (Ch.), at pp. 1093-4, *per* Ungoed-Thomas, J.; *Re A. Co.*, [1894] 2 Ch. 349.

[123] *Supra*, footnotes 121 and 122; *Cadiz Waterworks Co. v. Barnett* (1874), L.R. 19 Eq. 182; *Cercle Restaurant Castiglione Co. v. Lavery* (1881), 18 Ch. D. 555; *Charles Forte Investments Ltd. v. Amanda*, [1964] Ch. 240 (C.A.); *Bryanston Finance Ltd. v. De Vries (No. 2)*, [1976] Ch. 63 (C.A.).

[124] See *Charles Forte Investments Ltd. v. Amanda*, *supra*, footnote 123.

determine the right in question, that is, whether the defendant is entitled to proceed or not, the balance of convenience test clearly is not the appropriate one.[125] The jurisdiction is exercised on the same principles as those governing the applications to stay an action *in limine*, and is one only "to be exercised with great circumspection".[126] A prospective litigant is not lightly to be deprived of access to the courts, whatever his motive, and it is only where the plaintiff can show that the proceedings would constitute an abuse that injunctive relief is available.

479   Most of the reported cases deal with winding-up proceedings, but those cases are undoubtedly an instance of a general jurisdiction to restrain threatened proceedings which will constitute an abuse. There have been instances of restraining threatened matrimonial litigation,[127] and restraining an action to force a creditor to sue in a debenture holder's action.[128] As well, there is power to restrain threatened patent proceedings which are groundless and which would injure the prospective defendant in his trade.[129]

(1) Proceedings in inferior courts

480   The usual remedy to restrain an inferior court from exceeding its jurisdiction is prohibition,[130] and while the remedy of an injunction could achieve the same result, the courts have been reluctant to use it in this way.[131] However, there are cases in which a litigant may be entitled to have proceedings restrained which do not involve an excess of jurisdiction, in which case the injunction will be the appropriate remedy. The usual situation is where proceedings before an inferior court or tribunal raise the same issue as has been raised in an action pending in the High Court. Here the High Court may act on the traditional equitable principle, now enshrined in the Judicature Act, to avoid a multiplicity of proceedings, and to protect the plaintiff from the vexation of two proceedings where one will do.[132]

---

[125] *Bryanston Finance Ltd. v. De Vries (No. 2)*, *supra*, footnote 123.

[126] *Bryanston Finance Ltd. v. De Vries (No. 2)*, *supra*, at p. 78, *per* Buckley, L.J.

[127] *Besant v. Wood*, *supra*, footnote 121; *Hart v. Hart* (1881), 18 Ch. D. 670 (specific performance of agreement to compromise suit).

[128] *Re Maidstone Palace of Varieties Ltd.*, [1909] 2 Ch. 283.

[129] *Mentmore Manufacturing Co. v. Formete (Sterling) Area, Ltd.*, [1954] 72 R.P.C. 12, affd *loc. cit.* p. 157 (C.A.); Fox, *The Canadian Law and Practice Relating to Letters Patent for Invention*, 4th ed. (Toronto, Carswell Co. Ltd., 1969), pp. 529-39. In England, the power is codified in statute: Patents Act 1949, s. 65.

[130] Prohibition and injunctions in public law are discussed, *supra*, §§337-343.

[131] *Johns v. Chatalos*, [1973] 1 W.L.R. 1437 (Ch.).

[132] *Hedley v. Bates* (1880), 13 Ch. D. 498; *The "Teresa"* (1894), 71 L.T. 342; *Re Con-*

481   If no action is pending in the High Court, it will be rare for an injunction to be granted,[133] and while the courts have stated that there is jurisdiction to enjoin litigants before inferior tribunals, they have properly been reluctant to exercise that jurisdiction.[134] However, on principle, it would seem that if the plaintiff can show that the inferior proceedings are abusive or vexatious, he should be granted the protection of an injunction.

(2) Arbitrations

482   Injunctions are available in certain situations to restrain a party from proceeding with an arbitration.[135] If the arbitrator or board is a statutory one, that is, a person or board to whom parties must resort by statute, the inherent supervisory powers of the High Court may be resorted to and judicial review had through *certiorari* or prohibition.[136] However, these remedies are not available with respect to purely consensual arbitrations, and it is in those cases where resort is most likely to be had to injunctive relief.

483   Injunctions restraining arbitration proceedings have been awarded in two types of case. First, it is well established that where the validity of the agreement to arbitrate itself is impeached, or where the obligation to arbitrate has been discharged by breach, an injunction will be granted to restrain a party from proceeding with the arbitration.[137] Secondly, where a named arbitrator has become disqualified, usually through bias, an injunction will be granted to restrain a party from proceeding before him.[138] The rationale for granting an injunction in these cases has been recently described by Lord Diplock in the

---

nolly Bros. Ltd., [1911] 1 Ch. 731 (C.A.). This extends to criminal proceedings as well: *Thames Launches Ltd. v. Trinity House Corp.*, [1961] Ch. 197; *cf. Saull v. Browne* (1874), L.R. 10 Ch. 64. See also *Shawn v. Robertson* (1964), 46 D.L.R. (2d) 363, [1964] 2 O.R. 696 (H.C.J.), refusing to strike out an action for an injunction alleging *mala fides* in the election to proceed by way of indictment rather than summarily in a tax prosecution.

[133] *Stannard v. Vestry of St. Giles, Camberwell* (1882), 20 Ch. D. 190 (C.A.).

[134] See, *e.g.*, *Re Original Hartlepool Collieries Co.* (1882), 51 L.J. Ch. 508; *Murcutt v. Murcutt*, [1952] P. 266.

[135] The converse, a stay of a court action to enforce an arbitration clause, may be seen as a form of specific performance of an agreement to arbitrate rather than litigate disputes.

[136] *Howe Sound Co. v. Int'l Union of Mine, Mill & Smelter Workers*, [1962] S.C.R. 318, 33 D.L.R. (3d) 1; *R. v. National Joint Council for Craft of Dental Technicians*, [1953] 1 Q.B. 704; *Re Civic Employees' Union No. 43 and Municipality of Metropolitan Toronto* (1962), 34 D.L.R. (2d) 711, [1962] O.R. 970 (C.A.).

[137] *Kitts v. Moore*, [1895] 1 Q.B. 253 (C.A.).

[138] *Beddow v. Beddow* (1878), 9 Ch. D. 89; *Malmesbury Ry. Co. v. Budd* (1876), 2 Ch. D. 113.

Bremer Vulkan case as being the protection of the plaintiff's legal right "to prevent his being harassed by the making of a purported award against him which on the face of it will be enforceable against him in England and many foreign countires, thus forcing him to incur the costs of resisting its enforcement."[139]

484   However, the correctness of the decision of the House of Lords in that case is highly controversial. The issue was whether an injunction should be granted to restrain long-delayed proceedings for want of prosecution where the plaintiff applying for the injunction had taken no steps in the arbitration itself to prompt his opponent into action. By a three to two majority, the House of Lords adopted a restrictive view. Speaking for the majority, Lord Diplock held that no legal right of the plaintiff had been infringed. Delay itself did not give rise to the infringement of a right, and the plaintiff's failure to prompt action by the arbitrator to prevent the delay disentitled him from asserting that there had been termination of the agreement to arbitrate by breach. As Lord Diplock put it: "Respondents in private arbitrations are not entitled to let sleeping dogs lie and then complain that they did not bark."[140]

485   The minority, Lord Fraser of Tullybelton and Lord Scarman, would have upheld the injunction on the grounds that the plaintiff's legal right to have a fair hearing had been infringed by the delay, a right which could be supported either by implying a contractual term or by reference to the principles of natural justice. It is difficult to discern a clear difference between the analysis of the minority and majority in that Lord Diplock's formulation of what constituted the infringement of a legal right was a broad one encompassing harassment.[141] Presumably, the difference lies in the fact that, according to Lord Diplock, mere delay did not vitiate the arbitration and it would remain enforceable, whereas bias or repudiation by breach would render the arbitration itself unenforceable even if proceeded with. Thus, Lord Diplock's judgment purports to stand on the simple proposition that an injunction will only issue to protect some recognized legal right. The remedy of injunction should not be used to create new substantive rights.[142]

486   In a subsequent decision of the Court of Appeal,[143] an injunction was granted on the ground of inordinate delay despite the *Bremer*

---

[139] *Bremer Vulkan Schiffbau und Maschinenfabrik v. South India Shipping Corp. Ltd.*, [1981] A.C. 909 (H.L.), at p. 981.

[140] *Ibid.*, at p. 988.

[141] *Ibid.*, at p. 981.

[142] *Supra*, §§112-117.

[143] *Andre et Compagnie S.A. v. Marine Transocean Ltd.*, [1981] Q.B. 694 (C.A.).

Vulkan decision. In that case, Lord Denning, M.R., noted that Lord Diplock's judgment had taken those experienced in arbitrations by surprise.[144] It meant that cases could be revived after years of inactivity unless the respondent had made efforts to move the arbitration along, something completely out of keeping with established practice. A later decision of the House of Lords[145] refused to reconsider *Bremer Vulkan*, partially on the grounds of the particular need for certainty in commercial cases. However, Lord Diplock approved the result reached in the Court of Appeal decision, just referred to, on the basis that it was open to the court to find that the arbitration agreement had been terminated by abandonment.[146] In *Bremer Vulkan* itself, Lord Diplock appeared prepared to accept that an injunction could be granted to restrain a party who had committed a repudiatory breach from proceeding with the arbitration.[147]

487   It is submitted that should the issue arise in Canada, the preferable course would be to follow the view taken by the minority in *Bremer Vulkan* and to avoid the necessarily technical and complex analysis of whether conduct amounts to repudiatory breach or abandonment, and rest the decision squarely on the plaintiff's right to have a fair hearing which is infringed by extensive delay.

(3) Injunctions to restrain foreign suits

488   Injunctions have also been employed as a remedy where there is a dispute between the parties as to where a suit should be litigated.[148] Where the party applying for relief wishes to prevent proceedings within the jurisdiction and force his opponent to litigate elsewhere, the appropriate procedure is to apply for a stay.[149] Where, however, the applicant wishes to restrain foreign proceedings so as to compel his opponent to litigate within the jurisdiction, the appropriate remedy is an injunction. Again, the theory is that the court is not purporting to control a foreign tribunal, but merely exercising personal jurisdiction over the litigants.[150]

---

[144] *Ibid.*, at p. 701.

[145] *Paal Wilson & Co. A/S v. Partenreederei Hannah Blumenthal*, [1982] 3 W.L.R. 1149 (H.L.).

[146] *Ibid.*, at p. 1167.

[147] *Bremer Vulkan, supra*, footnote 139, at p. 982.

[148] See Castel, *Canadian Conflict of Laws*, vol. 1 (Toronto, Butterworths, 1975), at pp. 308-9; *Dicey and Morris on the Conflict of Laws*, 10th ed. by J.H.C. Morris (London, Stevens & Sons Ltd., 1980), at pp. 247 *et seq.*

[149] *Supra*, §476.

[150] *Supra*, §476.

489 The principles in this area have recently undergone extensive review in a series of decisions by the House of Lords.[151] Formerly, the courts required the applicant to show something akin to abuse of process or vexatiousness in the proceeding sought to be stopped, but now the principle is much more akin to *forum non conveniens*.

490 It has been held by the House of Lords that the same principles apply whether the applicant is asking that domestic proceedings be stayed, or for an injunction to restrain foreign proceedings.[152] The party applying must show, in the context of an injunction to restrain foreign proceedings:

> (a) that the English court is a forum to whose jurisdiction they are amenable in which justice can be done at substantially less inconvenience and expense; *and* (b) the injunction must not deprive the plaintiff of a legitimate personal or juridical advantage which would be available to him if he invoked the [foreign] jurisdiction.[153]

(4) Restraining comment on pending proceedings

491 An injunction may be granted to restrain comment on pending proceedings where such comment would be contemptuous. Although the courts are very hesitant to restrain allegedly defamatory material,[154] the practice with respect to comment on matters *sub judice* is quite different.[155] It is clearly established that in addition to its power to commit for contempt, the court may act preventively and restrain comment by injunction.[156] The application for an injunction may be brought either by the litigant affected,[157] or by the Attorney-General suing in the public interest.[158]

---

[151] The *"Atlantic Star"*, [1974] A.C. 436 (H.L.); *MacShannon v. Rockware Glass Ltd.*, [1978] A.C. 795 (H.L.); *Castanho v. Brown & Root (U.K.) Ltd.*, [1981] A.C. 557 (H.L.).

[152] *Castanho v. Brown & Root (U.K.) Ltd.*, *supra*, footnote 151.

[153] *Castanho v. Brown & Root (U.K.) Ltd.*, *supra*, at p. 575, *per* Lord Scarman.

[154] *Supra*, §§440-448.

[155] *Campbell v. Sun Printing & Publishing Co.*, [1921] 2 W.W.R. 987 (B.C.S.C.).

[156] *Kitcat v. Sharp* (1882), 52 L.J. Ch. 134; *J. & P. Coats v. Chadwick*, [1894] 1 Ch. 347; *Coleman v. West Hartlepool Harbour & Ry. Co.* (1860), 2 L.T. 766; *Mackett v. Com'rs of Herne Bay* (1876), 24 W.R. 845 (Ch.); *Bowden v. Russell* (1877), 46 L.J. Ch. 414; *Guilding v. Morel Brothers, Cobbett & Sons (Ltd.)* (1888), 4 T.L.R. 198.

[157] *Ibid.*

[158] See, *e.g.*, *A.-G. v. Times Newspapers Ltd.*, [1974] A.C. 273 (H.L.). But compare the comments of Lord Denning, M.R., in the Court of Appeal and Lord Edmund-Davies in the House of Lords, in *A.-G. v. B.B.C.*, [1981] A.C. 303 (H.L.), at pp. 311 and 346, stating that such an injunction should not be granted to the Attorney-General "except in a clear case where there would manifestly be a contempt of court for the publication to take place".

CHAPTER 6

ENFORCEMENT

1. Introduction

492   A fundamental characteristic of specific relief is that non-compliance with the court's order carries the possible sanction of imprisonment. Once a party has obtained a specific equitable remedy,[1] coercive powers will be brought to bear to ensure that the order is obeyed. Enforcement proceedings have two quite distinct aspects. First is the desire to obtain compliance with the court's order. In this sense, coercive measures are employed not to punish, but to force the defendant to act as he should. This first aspect is often described as "civil contempt". The matter is seen as one strictly between the parties, and the task of the court is to respond to the plaintiff's request that the defendant be required to conduct himself according to the requirements of the decree.

493   However, there is also a second aspect to enforcement proceedings which has a distinctly punitive aspect. Here, the significance of disobedience ceases to be simply a matter between the parties. The court itself is concerned to vindicate its process and authority. From

---

[1] An undertaking in lieu of injunction may also be enforced through the contempt power: see, *e.g.*, *Biba Ltd. v. Stratford Investments Ltd.*, [1972] 3 All E.R. 1041 (Ch.). *Cf. Northwest Territories Public Service Ass'n v. Com'r of Northwest Territories* (1979), 107 D.L.R. (3d) 458 (N.W.T.C.A.), construing such an undertaking on a contempt application.

248

that viewpoint, the focus becomes punitive, and steps are taken against the defendant, not to ensure that he complies, but to demonstrate publicly that violation of the court's order will not be tolerated. When motivated by these concerns, the penalty imposed will be measured so as to mark the court's disapproval of the defendant's conduct, and so as to deter others from flouting the law. Cases in this second category are described as cases of "criminal contempt".

2. Criminal and Civil Contempt

494   At one time much emphasis was placed upon the distinction between civil and criminal contempt. The leading Canadian case[2] dealt with a protracted labour dispute.[3] The parties to the action had actually settled their differences, and the court itself had instituted contempt proceedings[4] because there had been a flagrant and well-publicized breach of an injunction. The Supreme Court of Canada adopted a textbook definition of criminal contempts as being those "which tend to bring the administration of justice into scorn, . . . In other words, where contempt involves a *public* injury or offence . . .".[5] Civil contempt, on the other hand, consists in simply "disregarding . . . or in not doing something ordered to be done in a cause".[6] The court held that in the case of a criminal contempt, which it found to be present in the case before it, a punitive sentence is called for, whereas in civil matters "the requirements of the situation from the standpoint of enforcement of the rights of the opposite party constitute the criterion upon which the court acts".[7]

495   While the principles underlying the treatment of the two varieties of contempt differ markedly, the distinction is a fluid and flexible one. Violation of the same order can lead to one or another form of contempt depending upon the degree of publicity the breach has attracted, and the extent of contumacy demonstrated by the defendant. Thus, it has been accurately observed in an English text that the formal distinction between the two types of contempt is relatively

---

[2] *Poje v. A.-G. B.C.*, [1953] 1 S.C.R. 516, [1953] 2 D.L.R. 785.

[3] For the background and criticism of the case, see Carrothers, *The Labour Injunction in British Columbia* (Toronto, CCH Canadian, 1956), at pp. 11-23.

[4] This point is discussed further, *infra*, §524.

[5] Oswald, *Contempt of Court*, 3rd ed. by Robertson (London, Butterworth & Co., 1910), at p. 36.

[6] *Poje v. A.-G. B.C.*, *supra*, footnote 2, at p. 522 S.C.R., p. 792 D.L.R., *per* Kellock, J.

[7] *Poje, supra*, at p. 517 S.C.R., p. 787 D.L.R.

unimportant and that what matters is "whether the response of the court is predominantly punitive or coercive in the particular circumstances of the case".[8]

(1) Criminal contempt

496   Cases of criminal contempt are difficult to deal with. They often arise from situations highly charged with emotion and politics. Several of the leading cases have involved trade union activity where the defendants have decided to put trade union interests and principles ahead of the obligation to obey the law, and their actions have attracted widespread public attention.[9] The issue here is clearly not one of ensuring enforcement, but rather of imposing punishment for past transgressions and trying to deter others. The courts have dealt severely with those who publicly and deliberately disobey orders by imposing heavy fines or substantial periods of imprisonment, insisting that everyone must be subject to law.[10]

497   In sentencing those found to be guilty of criminal contempt, it has been said that deterrence is the "primary objective",[11] and that retribution or revenge are much less important. All the same, the sentence does allow the court "to publicize its legitimate and vital authority"[12] and the fact of an apology will be influential. Thus, while retribution and revenge may not be the most accurate descriptions, there is clearly an element of vindication of judicial authority which goes beyond simple deterrence.

---

[8] Miller, *Contempt of Court* (London, Elek Books Ltd., 1976), at p. 10. See also Borrie and Lowe, *The Law of Contempt* (London, Butterworths, 1973), at p. 371: "these distinctions have been steadily eroded so that now the point has virtually been reached where the issue of classification is of academic importance only". The same authors quote *Jennison v. Baker*, [1972] 2 Q.B. 52 (C.A.), at p. 61, *per* Salmon, L.J.: "Contempts have sometimes been classified as criminal and civil contempts. I think that, at any rate today, this is an unhelpful and almost meaningless classification".

[9] For a survey of English cases arising under the now repealed national Industrial Relations Act, 1971, see Miller, *supra*, footnote 8, at pp. 236-42.

[10] See cases cited, *infra*, footnotes 13-16, and *A.-G. Que. v. Charbonneau* (1972), 40 D.L.R. (3d) 64 (C.A.), leave to appeal to S.C.C. refused [1973] S.C.R. x; *Foothills Provincial General Hospital Board v. Broad* (1975), 57 D.L.R. (3d) 758 (Alta. S.C.T.D.).

[11] *Re Tilco Plastics Ltd. v. Skurjat* (1966), 57 D.L.R. (2d) 596 at p. 629, [1966] 2 O.R. 547 at p. 580 (H.C.J.), *per* Gale, C.J.H.C., affd 61 D.L.R. (2d) 664n, [1967] 1 O.R. 609n (C.A.), leave to appeal to S.C.C. refused [1966] S.C.R. vii, D.L.R. *loc. cit.*, O.R. *loc. cit.* See also *R. v. United Fishermen & Allied Workers' (No. 2)*, [1968] 2 C.C.C. 361 (B.C.C.A.), at p. 363, *per* Davey, C.J.B.C., leave to appeal to S.C.C. refused [1968] 2 S.C.R. 255, 67 D.L.R. (2d) 644; *R. v. Neale* (1967), 60 D.L.R. (2d) 619 (B.C.C.A.).

[12] *Re Tilco Plastics Ltd.*, *supra*, footnote 11, at p. 629 D.L.R., p. 580 O.R.

498   Where the defendant has committed a past breach of an injunction but has complied by the time the contempt application is heard, only a punitive approach justifies the imposition of any penalty beyond payment of the plaintiff's costs.[13] No coercive order could be called for from the point of view of requiring compliance. In an Ontario case[14] involving the use of French in separate schools, Masten, J., refused to consider that subsequent compliance wholly purged or excused an earlier contempt:

> If in Courts of law repentance condoned offence, offenders would multiply. On any other basis our Courts of Justice would soon lose their hold upon public respect, and the maintenance of law and order would be rendered impossible. I am of opinion that the jurisdiction to entertain the motion now pending is not ousted by the cessation on the part of the respondents from the act complained of.[15]

Fear of disobedience of court orders leading to mob rule has been a familiar theme of cases where the actions of the defendant have been public and defiant.[16]

499   On the other hand, if the court views the matter as one of coercing compliance, and the defendant continues in his refusal to comply, an order of indefinite imprisonment, to terminate only when the court is

---

[13] *Cf. A.-G. v. N.B. Power Co.* (1944), 17 M.P.R. 326 (N.B.S.C. App. Div.), at p. 336, *per* Grimmer, J.: "To permit this to go unchallenged, would permit a serious fraud as we have stated, to be perpetrated upon the Court, and the offending parties to escape punishment, which cannot be permitted"; but where the court refused to order any penalty other than payment of costs.

[14] *McDonald v. Lancaster Separate School Trustees* (1916), 29 D.L.R. 731, 35 O.L.R. 614 (S.C. App. Div.).

[15] *Ibid.*, at p. 739 D.L.R., pp. 622-3 O.R.

[16] *Re Tilco Plastics Ltd. v. Skurjat, supra*, footnote 11, at p. 625 D.L.R., p. 576 O.R., *per* Gale, C.J.H.C.: "a public deprecation of the authority of the Court and of the administration of justice"; *R. v. United Fishermen & Allied Workers' Union (No. 2), supra*, footnote 11, at p. 363, *per* Davey, C.J.B.C.:

> No society can allow its judicial institutions, . . . to be so defied. If disobedience to Court orders is tolerated in the field of labour disputes, the effect will be cumulative and progressive, spilling over into other areas of society, until mob rule supplants the rule of law, and personal and property rights, including the important rights of trade-unions, cease to be protected.

See also *Iron Ore Co. of Canada v. United Steel Workers of America, Local 5795* (1979), 20 Nfld. & P.E.I.R. 27 (Nfld. C.A.), at p. 35, *per* Furlong, C.J.N., leave to appeal to S.C.C. refused 28 N.R. 339 *sub nom. Forfar v. Iron Ore Co. of Canada*: "it clearly tends to interfere with the due administration of justice and goes far beyond the preservation of any private rights"; *B.C. Telephone Co. v. Telecommunications Workers Union* (1981), 121 D.L.R. (3d) 326 (B.C.S.C.), at p. 336, *per* McKenzie, J.: "Unless the authority of the Courts is respected then violence and counter-violence will drive out order and freedom under the law. The law of the jungle will prevail."

satisfied that compliance will come about, may be justified on a civil basis. Indefinite imprisonment, potentially more painful to the defendant, cannot be justified from a criminal point of view.[17]

500 Many cases, of course, involve elements of both civil and criminal contempt. Even where the court views the matter as being primarily civil, and has enforcing compliance as its main objective, a punitive and deterrent motive often lies behind the sanction chosen.[18] Thus, for example, in a recent Ontario case[19] involving a county court judge's personal contempt of a matrimonial property injunction, the court held that although its primary concern was to enforce compliance, it could not let the matter pass without imposing a penalty of a fine, costs on a solicitor-and-client basis, and requiring an apology as well.

(2) Civil contempt

501 Generally speaking, where the element of public defiance is absent, the matter is regarded primarily as coercive rather than punitive.[20] Once compliance is assured the court only need concern itself with the question of costs.[21] Even where the court commits a contemner to prison, the object is to secure compliance, and he will be released and relieved from the consequences of his contempt by doing or assuring that which he previously neglected or refused to do.[22] While in a criminal contempt case the defendant will have to serve the fixed period of imprisonment designed to punish and deter,[23] in civil cases, where fixed terms are usually (although not

---

[17] *A.-G. v. James*, [1962] 2 Q.B. 637.

[18] *Buck Stove Co. v. Guelph Foundry Co.* (1905), 6 O.W.R. 116 at p. 120, *per* Anglin, J.:

> But the breach of an injunction concerns the Court as well as the parties in whose favour such injunction has issued. The contempt of the Court involved in disobedience to its mandate is not at all necessarily purged when the culprit has satisfied the requirements, however exacting, of the other party litigant.

See also *Snowball Co. v. Sullivan* (1913), 14 D.L.R. 528 (N.B.S.C.).

[19] *Re Sheppard and Sheppard* (1975), 62 D.L.R. (3d) 35, 10 O.R. (2d) 19 (H.C.J.), affd 67 D.L.R. (3d) 592, 12 O.R. (2d) 4 (C.A.).

[20] *Re Bolton and County of Wentworth* (1911), 23 O.L.R. 390 (H.C.J.), at p. 395, *per* Middleton, J.; *Loughead v. Thompson and McDonald* (1928), 26 O.W.N. 139 (H.C.), revd in part on other grounds 36 O.W.N. 84 (S.C. App. Div.); *Real Cake Coke Co. v. Robinson* (1915), 8 O.W.N. 568 (H.C.), affd 9 O.W.N. 127 (S.C. App. Div.); *Watson v. Jackson* (1915), 8 O.W.N. 410 (S.C. App. Div.).

[21] *Broom v. Godwin* (1910), 2 O.W.N. 321 (H.C.J.), affd *loc. cit.* p. 566 (Div. Ct.).

[22] *Re Labour Relations Board for Saskatchewan and Daschuk Construction Ltd.*, [1976] 5 W.W.R. 562 (Sask. C.A.).

[23] *A.-G. v. James*, [1962] 2 Q.B. 637.

inevitably)[24] employed, the defendant can apply for discharge before the term of the committal has come to an end.[25]

3. Sanctions for Contempt

502 In most cases of civil contempt, the object of compliance will be achieved by making an order for imprisonment or the payment of a fine, but suspending its operation for a stated period to give the defendant a second chance to comply.[26]

503 It is quite clear that the courts regard committal as an exceptional matter, and as a sanction of last resort.[27] There is, of course, the power to impose an indefinite term of imprisonment so that the contemner will be released only upon complying with the order or satisfying the court that he will do so.[28] Before making such an order, however, the court should be satisfied that there is a reasonable prospect that the defendant will comply.[29] Even the most stubborn or unreasonable defendant will not be held in prison for ever.[30]

504 In modern times, it would seem that committals of an indefinite term are not frequently used in Canada,[31] and there is much to be said for avoiding them. As pointed out by the Phillimore Committee Report which recommended their abolition,[32] the court may impose successive terms of imprisonment to coerce performance[33] without

---

[24] *Infra*, §504.

[25] *Yager v. Musa*, [1961] 2 Q.B. 214 (C.A.); *Vaughan v. Vaughan*, [1973] 3 All E.R. 449 (C.A.).

[26] *Brennan v. Myers* (1977), 26 N.S.R. (2d) 131 (S.C.T.D.); *Gamble v. Howland* (1852), 3 Gr. 281; *Shields v. Shields* (1923), 23 O.W.N. 531 (H.C.); *Latchford v. Chartrand* (1918), 15 O.W.N. 168 (H.C.); *Alley v. Duchemin* (1880), 2 P.E.I.R. 360 (Ch.).

[27] *Re Bolton and County of Wentworth, supra*, footnote 20; *Leaseconcept Ltd. v. French* (1976), 1 C.P.C. 160 (Ont. H.C.J.); *Danchevsky v. Danchevsky*, [1974] 3 All E.R. 934 (C.A.); *Ansah v. Ansah*, [1977] Fam. 138 (C.A.), at p. 144, *per* Ormrod, L.J.: "Committal orders are remedies of last resort; in family cases they should be the very last resort." In *Re W. (B) (An Infant)*, [1969] 2 Ch. 50 (C.A.), a suspended sentence had been imposed. The injunction was broken again, and the Court of Appeal substituted a fine for the term of the suspended sentence.

[28] *Glazer v. Union Contractors Ltd. and Thornton* (1960), 26 D.L.R. (2d) 349 (B.C.C.A.).

[29] *Danchevsky v. Danchevsky, supra*, footnote 27, at p. 937, *per* Lord Denning, M.R.

[30] *Re Davies* (1888), 21 Q.B.D. 236 at p. 238.

[31] In England, however, *sine die* committals were said to be the normal practice in the *Report of the Committee on Contempt of Court* (Phillimore Committee Report), Cmnd. 5794 (London H.M.S.O., 1974), §172. For modern Canadian examples, see *Glazer, supra*, footnote 28; *Re Fernandez* (1976), 26 R.F.L. 255 (B.C.S.C.).

[32] *Supra*, footnote 31.

[33] See, *e.g.*, *Yager v. Musa, supra*, footnote 25.

the risk of "the appearance of a climb-down"[34] in the case of an obstinate defendant who will not comply and who must eventually be released in any event.

505   A variety of sanctions are available, details of which will vary depending on the particular provisions of provincial statutes and rules of court. Generally, the court can order imprisonment, fine, or sequestration of property. Imprisonment can follow either committal or attachment proceedings. The difference between committal and attachment is that imprisonment follows directly upon an order of committal whereas an attachment order merely requires the defendant to come before the court and explain his contempt.[35] If his explanation proves wanting and he remains recalcitrant, imprisonment will follow. At one time, a great deal of emphasis was placed on the difference between these two proceedings.[36] Committal was the appropriate procedure where the defendant had failed to comply with a prohibitive injunction, while attachment was appropriate where he had not done something which he had been ordered to do.[37] In modern practice, apart from technical formalities which must be observed, there is little difference between the two. The courts regularly suspend the operation of committal orders to give the contemner an opportunity to comply. From the reported cases at least, it would appear that a party is rarely, if ever, sent directly to prison unless he is obviously bent on defying the authority of the court. As an attachment order will not issue unless the plaintiff makes out at least a *prima facie* case of contempt, and as the defendant must be notified of the application for an attachment order, in the end there is very little real difference between the two proceedings.[38]

506   Sequestration of property is the usual sanction against a corporate body which is in contempt, but it may also be used against individuals.[39] A writ of sequestration allows for the seizure of the con-

---

[34] Phillimore Committee Report, *supra*, footnote 31, §172.

[35] *Link v. Thompson* (1917), 40 O.L.R. 222 (H.C.).

[36] *Chatham Harvester Co. v. Campbell* (1888), 12 P.R. (Ont.) 666; *Mattock v. Mattock*, [1937] 3 W.W.R. 317 (B.C.S.C.); *R. v. Kuhtey* (1944), Nfld. R. 296 (S.C.).

[37] *Golden Gate Mining Co. v. Granite Creek Mining Co.* (1896), 5 B.C.R. 145 (Full Court); *Link v. Thompson, supra*, footnote 35.

[38] See *Iron Ore Co. of Canada v. United Steel Workers of America, Local 5795* (1979), 20 Nfld. & P.E.I.R. 27 (Nfld. C.A.), *per* Gushue, J.A., leave to appeal to S.C.C. refused 28 N.R. 339 *sub nom. Forfar v. Iron Ore Co. of Canada*; *A.-G. Can. v. Redli* (1958), 13 D.L.R. (2d) 572 (B.C.C.A.), at p. 576, *per* Davey, J.A.

[39] Borrie and Lowe, *supra*, footnote 8, at p. 349; *Leaseconcept Ltd. v. French, supra*,

temner's property until he purges his contempt.[40] The order may permit the seizure of all or only part of the contemner's property. Its effect is not to confiscate the property but to deprive the contemner of its enjoyment until he has complied.[41] Thus, it is primarily a sanction designed to coerce performance, although it may be employed in the punitive sense to ensure the collection of a fine imposed for a contempt, and may also be applied to enforce the discharge of an equitable obligation to pay money.[42]

4. Liability

(1) Degree of diligence required

507   It is often said that both the spirit and the letter of an injunction must be obeyed, and that a party must make all reasonable efforts to see that it is obeyed.[43] Much will depend upon the clarity and specificity of the original order. This has been a factor in nuisance cases where the courts have often made very general and vague orders that the defendant conduct himself so as not to cause a nuisance to the plaintiff.[44] If the defendant's abatement efforts do not satisfy the

---

footnote 27. *Cf. Twinriver Timber Ltd. v. Int'l Woodworkers of America, Local No. 1-71* (1970), 14 D.L.R. (3d) 704 (B.C.C.A.), holding that the British Columbia Supreme Court Rules permit sequestration only against a corporation.

[40] See *Australian Consolidated Press Ltd. v. Morgan* (1965), 39 A.L.J.R. 32 (H.C.), at p. 40, quoted in Borrie and Lowe, *supra*, footnote 8, at p. 343, for a general description of the effect of a writ of sequestration.

[41] Borrie and Lowe, *supra*, footnote 8.

[42] Borrie and Lowe, *supra*, footnote 8.

[43] *Taylor v. Mullen Coal Co.* (1916), 10 O.W.N. 149 (H.C.), *per* Lennox, J.: "It was not enough for the company to do all it could to avoid a nuisance; it must so work its plant as not to continue the nuisance enjoined; or else not carry on its operations at that place at all." See also *Davis v. Barlow* (1911), 18 W.L.R. 239 (Man. K.B.); *Glazer v. Union Contractors Ltd. and Thornton* (1960), 26 D.L.R. (2d) 349 (B.C.C.A.); *Bickford v. Welland Ry.* (1870), 17 Gr. 484. *Cf. Downey v. Burney* (1914), 6 O.W.N. 174 (H.C.), finding a contempt for a technical breach, holding that the "letter as well as the spirit" must be observed. In *Dominion Bridge Co. Ltd. v. Int'l Ass'n of Bridge, Structural & Ornamental Ironworkers* (1959), 20 D.L.R. (2d) 621 (B.C.C.A.), at p. 624, DesBrisay, C.J.B.C., stated: "Appellants were obliged to comply in good faith with the mandatory order, but they were not obliged to do so gracefully, and a reluctant compliance was in itself no contempt."
An order forbidding a strike is not violated where work stoppages occur because of other matters not related to labour relations and not intended to gain an advantage over management: *MacMillan Bloedel (Alberni) Ltd. v. Swanson* (1972), 26 D.L.R. (3d) 641 (B.C.S.C.); *Crown Zellerbach Canada Ltd. v. Annand* (1972), 27 D.L.R. (3d) 129 (B.C.S.C.). *Cf. The Queen v. Perry*, [1982] 1 F.C. 719, 128 D.L.R. (3d) 347 (T.D.), revd 133 D.L.R. (3d) 703 (C.A.), leave to appeal to S.C.C. refused 43 N.R. 444n.

[44] *Supra*, §40.

plaintiff, the matter will have to be resolved on a contempt application. If the defendant has made some genuine effort to abate, the contempt hearing amounts, in effect, to a new trial on the issue of nuisance in light of the changes which have been made since the trial.[45] The reported cases suggest that so long as some effort has been made,[46] the penalty will rarely, if ever, be more than a fine.[47] In an Ontario case[48] where the court felt that the defendant had "taken chances", a writ of sequestration was ordered, but stayed for one week to give the defendant a chance to put matters right. The matter has been seen as one of working out a mode of compliance which will satisfy the plaintiff's interests rather than punishing for past transgression. The order of the court is not being flouted in such situations and the details of the rather vague initial injunction have to be worked out gradually as the court judges the adequacy of the steps taken by the defendant. If those steps are found wanting, the ordinary course is to give the defendant yet another chance to put the matter right.

508   In the case of *Mareva* injunctions, which often put third parties at risk, the courts appear willing to adopt a lenient approach. In the first place, the plaintiff has to indemnify such a party for expenses incurred in compliance. Moreover, it was said in one case that:

> Carelessness or even recklessness on the part of the banks ought not in my opinion to make them liable for contempt unless it can be shown that there was indifference to such a degree that was contumacious. A *Mareva* injunction is granted for the benefit of an individual litigant and it seems to me to be undesirable that those who are not immediate parties should be in danger of being held in contempt of court unless they can be shown to have been contumacious.[49]

509   Obviously, vague orders present difficulties and prolong the litiga-

---

[45] See especially *A.-G. B.C. ex rel. Eaton v. Haney Speedways Ltd.* (1963), 41 D.L.R. (2d) 85 (B.C.S.C.).

[46] The public interest has also been considered: *Leahy v. North Sydney* (1906), 1 E.L.R. 431 (N.S.S.C.), at p. 432, *per* Russell, J., refusing a contempt application where a municipality had acted in good faith: "I do not think that I am bound to make an order which will paralyze every industry in North Sydney and Sydney Mines and make life intolerable to every inhabitant."

[47] *Macievich v. Anderson*, [1952] 4 D.L.R. 507 (Man. C.A.); *Cook v. Town of Lockeport* (1971), 7 N.S.R. (2d) 191 (S.C.T.D.).

[48] *Browne v. Britnell & Co.* (1924), 27 O.W.N. 232 (H.C.). See also *Harding v. Liprovitch* (1929), 35 O.W.N. 361 (H.C.), where there had been "some effort" to comply, and a fine rather than committal was imposed.

[49] *Z Ltd. v. A-Z*, [1982] 2 W.L.R. 288 (C.A.), at p. 305, *per* Eveleigh, L.J: See also, *supra*, §§227-229.

tion and should be avoided if possible. It has been held in some contexts that contempt is inappropriate and will not be found where the
original order was lacking in definition.[50]

(2) Intention and deliberateness

510   To constitute contempt, the act or omission which contravenes the
injunction must have been intentional, but not necessarily deliberately contumacious. It is well established that "it is no answer to say
that the act was not contumacious in the sense that, in doing it, there
was not direct intention to disobey the order".[51] The requirement of
intention excludes only "casual or accidental"[52] acts. In other words,
the party seeking a finding of contempt must prove no more than that
the defendant intentionally did the forbidden act or consciously omitted to do what was required.[53] This reasoning has been employed especially in cases where the defence asserts that intention to contra-
vene the order has not been proved beyond a reasonable doubt. In a

---

[50] See *Sonoco Ltd. v. Local 433, etc.* (1970), 13 D.L.R. (3d) 617 (B.C.C.A.), at p.
621, per Davey, C.J.B.C.: "persons enjoined ought to be able to tell from the order
what they may not do without having to decide whether they are acting lawfully or
not." See also *Re Swan River-The Pas Transfer Ltd.* (1974), 51 D.L.R. (3d) 292
(Man. C.A.); *Re Distillery, Brewery, Winery, Soft Drink & Allied Workers' Union
604 and B.C. Distillery Co. Ltd.* (1975), 57 D.L.R. (3d) 752 (B.C.S.C.); *Re United
Steelworkers of America, Local No. 663 and Anaconda (Canada) Ltd.* (1969), 3
D.L.R. (3d) 577 (B.C.S.C.) (involving labour board orders, but holding that the
standard for court orders applies); *Iberian Trust, Ltd. v. Founders Trust & Investment Co. Ltd.*, [1932] 2 K.B. 87; *P. A. Thomas & Co. v. Mould*, [1968] 1 All E.R.
963 (Q.B.), at p. 967, per O'Connor, J., refusing to find the defendant in contempt
of an interlocutory injunction protecting the plaintiffs "know how": "the court has
granted the injunction in the terms prayed by the plaintiffs. That is the plaintiffs'
own doing . . . where parties seek to invoke the power of the court to commit people to prison and deprive them of their liberty, there has got to be quite clear certainty about it."
[51] *Stancomb v. Trowbridge Urban District Council*, [1910] 2 Ch. 190 at p. 194, per
Warrington, J.; applied in *Heatons Transport (St. Helens) Ltd. v. Transport & General Worker's Union*, [1973] A.C. 15 (H.L.), at pp. 108-9, per Lord Wilberforce; *Re
Sheppard and Sheppard* (1976), 67 D.L.R. (3d) 592 at p. 595, 12 O.R. (2d) 4 at p. 8
(C.A.); *Browne v. Britnell & Co.* (1924), 27 O.W.N. 232 (H.C.); *McDonald v.
Lancaster Separate School Trustees* (1916), 29 D.L.R. 731 at p. 741, 35 O.L.R. 614
at p. 625 (S.C. App. Div.), per Masten, J.
[52] *Ibid.*
[53] Some cases, however, would seem to go so far as to deny a mistake of fact defence:
see *Davis v. Barlow, supra*, footnote 43; *Harding v. Tingey* (1864), 12 W.R. 684
(Ch.), both holding a party in contempt who asserted a belief in facts which, if true,
would render him innocent. *Cf. Ex p. Langley* (1879), 13 Ch. D. 110 (C.A.). See
also *MacMillan Bloedell (Alberni) Ltd. v. Swanson* (1972), 26 D.L.R. (3d) 641
(B.C.S.C.), holding that where pressure to join in a strike is demonstrated, proof
that an individal member was absent from work does not establish that individual's
agreement to refuse to work.

leading Ontario case,[54] counsel for the defendant in a matrimonial proceeding argued that the order was truncated and ambiguous and that there was doubt as to whether the breach had been deliberate. The Court of Appeal answered that it was enough to prove the doing of the act, and upheld the contempt conviction although it agreed that a deliberate intention to disobey the order had not been established. Thus, the defendant cannot excuse himself by his own carelessness in failing to inform himself as to the precise requirements of the order.[55]

511   However, it is also clear that the presence or absence of a contumacious intent is a factor which strongly influences the court in fixing the penalty.[56] As penalties range from the payment of costs of the application, to heavy fines and lengthy imprisonment, the question of contumacious intent remains an important one.

512   The courts have dealt leniently where the party acted in a *bona fide* belief that his conduct did not constitute contempt.[57] The usual sanction in such cases is the payment of costs of the contempt application, usually coupled with a finding of contempt, but sometimes not.[58] Thus, although it is no excuse[59] that the contemner acted on legal advice that his proposed course of conduct was lawful,[60] payment of costs is the usual penalty in such cases. Similarly, where an act which technically amounts to a contempt can be described as an error of judgment rather than an attempt to flout or disregard the order of the court,[61] payment of costs is the usual sanction.[62] It would appear

---

[54] *Re Sheppard and Sheppard* (1975), 62 D.L.R. (3d) 35, 10 O.R. (2d) 19 (H.C.J.), affd 67 D.L.R. (3d) 592, 12 O.R. (2d) 4 (C.A.).

[55] See also *Re Witten* (1887), 4 T.L.R. 36 (Ch.), at p. 37, *per* Kay, J.

[56] An apology is also a relevant factor which may mitigate the penalty: see, *e.g.*, *Foothills Provincial General Hospital Board v. Broad* (1975), 57 D.L.R. (3d) 758 (Alta. S.C.T.D.); *Re. A.-G. N.S. and Miles* (1970), 15 D.L.R. (3d) 189 (N.S.S.C.T.D.).

[57] *Infra*, footnotes 58-62.

[58] See *Hardie v. Lavery* (1887), 5 Man. R. 134 (Q.B.).

[59] Cf. *Dennis v. Saanich* (1961), 29 D.L.R. (2d) 644 (B.C.S.C.) (municipality acted deliberately but in ignorance that expropriation proceedings were defective; no contempt); *Ex p. Baird; Re Steadman* (1890), 29 N.B.R. 200 (S.C.) (county court judge proceeded with election recount in *bona fide* belief that Supreme Court injunction void; contempt found but no penalty). *Cf., infra*, footnote 66.

[60] *Sayre v. Harris* (1879), 18 N.B.R. 677 (C.A.); *Re Mileage Conference Group of Tyre Manufacturers' Conference, Ltd.'s Agreement*, [1966] 2 All E.R. 849 (R.P.C.), at p. 862; *Canada Metal Co. Ltd. v. C.B.C. (No. 2)* (1974), 48 D.L.R. (3d) 641 at p. 659, 4 O.R. (2d) 585 at p. 605 (H.C.J.), affd 65 D.L.R. (3d) 231, 11 O.R. (2d) 167 (C.A.).

[61] *Ex p. Baird; Re Steadman* (1890), 29 N.B.R. 200 (S.C.); *Casey v. Kansas* (1913), 4

that a higher degree of intention is required to make a non-party liable for contempt. Eveleigh, L.J., has said, in the context of a *Mareva* injunction, that a non-party, particularly a bank, will be liable for contempt only "when he knows that what he is doing is a breach of the terms of that injunction".[63] The equitable and pragmatic spirit which motivates decisions in this area is well illustrated by one Ontario case[64] where the court accepted the defence of entrapment where decoys had been used by the plaintiff. The court held that "however such methods may be regarded in criminal law"[65] they were not to be encouraged or countenanced in a court of equity.

513   It is well established that a contempt application is not answered by the assertion that the injunction was erroneously granted or even that it was void.[66] The proper course is to move against the injunction or to appeal and the court will not permit the original order to be attacked collaterally in contempt proceedings. Again, however, courts have considered the wisdom or validity of the initial decree in determining the appropriate sanction.[67]

(3) Vicarious liability

514   It has been held that principles of vicarious liability are applicable

O.W.N. 1581 (H.C.); *Prentiss v. Brennan* (1850), 1 Gr. 428 (C.A.); *Tilden Rent-A-Car Co. v. Rollins* (1966), 57 W.W.R. 309 (Sask. Q.B.); *Bickford v. Welland Ry.* (1870), 17 Gr. 484.

[62] *Dunn v. Board of Education* (1904), 7 O.L.R. 451 (H.C.J.).

[63] *Z Ltd. v. A.-Z., supra,* footnote 49, at p. 302.

[64] *Canadian Foundry Co. v. Emmett* (1903), 2 O.W.R. 1102.

[65] *Ibid.,* at p. 1102, *per* Boyd, C.

[66] *Eastern Trust Co. v. MacKenzie, Mann & Co.,* [1915] A.C. 750, 22 D.L.R. 410 (P.C.); *Canadian Transport (U.K.) Ltd. v. Alsbury,* [1953] 1 D.L.R. 385 (B.C.C.A.), affd [1953] S.C.R. 516, [1953] 2 D.L.R. 785 *sub nom. Poje v. A-G. B.C.; R. v. Hunchuk; R. v. Andres* (1956), 20 W.W.R. 446 (B.C.C.A.); *Allen v. Edinburgh Life Ass'ce Co.* (1879), 26 Gr. 192; *Dunn v. Board of Education* (1904), 7 O.L.R. 451 (H.C.J.). *Cf. McLeod v. Noble* (1897), 28 O.R. 528 (Div. Ct.), at p. 548, *per* Boyd, C., where the court refused to hold a county court judge in contempt for conducting an election recount contrary to an injunction on the grounds that the injunction was a nullity: "Before contempt arises for disobedience to an order, it must be as to a matter which is legally and jurisdictionally *coram curia,* that is, the tribunal must be competent and must act within its jurisdiction."
See also Miller, *supra,* footnote 8, at p. 254, suggesting that "it is open to argument" whether public policy requires that an order be obeyed where there is "an irregularity of substance, or a lack of jurisdiction to make the order".

[67] See *Dunn v. Board of Education* (1904), 7 O.L.R. 451 (H.C.J.), quoting and applying *Drewry v. Thacker* (1819), 3 Swans. 529 at p. 546, 36 E.R. 963, *per* Lord Eldon: "On an application against persons guilty of a breach of it [the order], the Court would forget its duty, if it did not give to them the benefit of the fact that the order ought not to have been made."

in determining whether a corporate entity is liable for the acts of its employees committed within the course of employment.[68] It would appear that the principle of corporate criminal liability requiring that fault be demonstrated on the part of the directing mind and will of the corporation need not be established, and that it is sufficient to show that the employee or agent violating the injunction was acting within the course of his employment.[69] This imposes a stricter test of liability on corporations and, it is submitted, is more readily applied to civil cases where the matter is one of enforcing compliance, and where it is entirely appropriate to hold the corporation to account. However, in cases of criminal contempt, it is not clear why principles which cast a wider net of liability than the ordinary rules of criminal law should be applied.

515   Alternatively, even where the company itself is a named party, it has been held appropriate to hold its officers liable for contempt and to impose measures upon them personally either to coerce performance or simply to punish, so long as the officer had it within his power to act or to refrain from acting as required by the injunction.[70]

---

[68] *Upholsterers Int'l Union v. Harkin & Struck Furniture Ltd.* (1965), 48 D.L.R. (2d) 248 (B.C.C.A.), imposing liability on the company although the employee had ignored instructions given by the president; *Davis v. Barlow* (1911), 18 W.L.R. 239 (Man. K.B.), at p. 243, *per* Mathers, C.J.K.B.: "if they employ officials who will violate their rules and disobey an order of this Court, they must take the consequences".

[69] *Heatons Transport (St. Helens) Ltd. v. Transport & General Workers' Union*, [1973] A.C. 15 (H.L.), at pp. 99 and 109, holding a trade union liable in contempt for acts of its agents so long as they were acting within the scope of their authority, and apparently rejecting the criminal law "directing mind and will" test established in *Tesco Supermarket Ltd. v. Nattrass*, [1972] A.C. 153 (H.L.). *Cf. Re New Brunswick Electric Power Com'n and Local Union No. 1733 etc.* (1976), 73 D.L.R. (3d) 94 (N.B.S.C. App. Div.), leave to appeal to S.C.C. refused 13 N.R. 534*n*, holding that complicity of union officials could be inferred from concerted strike action and that there was no evidence that the officials took steps to bring the forbidden activity to an end.

[70] *Glazer v. Union Contractors Ltd. and Thornton* (1960), 26 D.L.R. (2d) 349 (B.C.C.A.); *Taylor v. Mullen Coal Co.* (1916), 10 O.W.N. 149 (H.C.J.); *Re Bolton and County of Wentworth* (1911), 23 O.L.R. 390 (H.C.J.); *Mackell v. Ottawa Separate School Trustees* (1917), 12 O.W.N. 265 (H.C.); *Battle Creek Toasted Corn Flake Co. v. Kellogg Toasted Corn Flake Co.* (1924), 55 O.L.R. 127 (S.C. App. Div.); *Phonographic Performance Ltd. v. Amusement Caterers (Peckham) Ltd.*, [1964] Ch. 195. *Cf. Canada Metal Co. Ltd. v. C.B.C. (No. 2)* (1974), 48 D.L.R. (3d) 641 at pp. 660-1, 4 O.R. (2d) 585 at pp. 604-5 (H.C.J.), affd 65 D.L.R. (3d) 231, 11 O.R. (2d) 167 (C.A.):

The violation of the injunction may give rise in some cases to a presumption that the director or officer did or failed to do something that caused the breach, and may put that officer or director on his defence. Where, however, it is clear on the

The more usual sanction, however, in the case of a corporation, is fine or sequestration.[71]

(4) Non-parties

516   An injunction, like any other order of the court, only binds the actual parties to the suit.[72] However, injunctions are often made enjoining not only defendants, but also officers, members and servants, and, on some occasions, any person having notice of the order. The power to enforce such an order has been doubted,[73] but in a recent decision of the Supreme Court of Canada,[74] Estey, J., held that while more precise language might be preferred, the use of looser language was not invalidating, and could be justified "for the good reason that it makes the impact and sense of the order clear to all those likely to be affected thereby".[75] Estey, J., undoubtedly had in mind the well-established rule that a non-party may be held in contempt where he is involved in violation of the injunction, "not because he is bound by the injunction by being a party to the cause, but because he is conducting himself so as to obstruct the course of justice".[76] It has been expressly held unnecessary to include the wider language to require

evidence that the director or officer did all he could to ensure that the injunction would be abided by and, where the breach occurred without fault on the part of the director or officer, then I am unable to see how that director or officer can be punished for contempt of Court.

[71] *Browne v. Britnell & Co.* (1924), 27 O.W.N. 232 (H.C.).

[72] *Toronto-Dominion Bank v. Car-Tree Int'l Ltd.* (1967), 66 D.L.R. (2d) 552 (Sask. Q.B.); *Iveson v. Harris* (1802), 7 Ves. Jun. 251 at p. 257, 32 E.R. 102, *per* Eldon, L.C.: "you cannot have an injunction except against a party to the suit".

[73] *Marengo v. Daily Sketch & Sunday Graphic Ltd.*, [1948] 1 All E.R. 406; *C.P.R. Co. v. Brady* (1960), 26 D.L.R. (2d) 104 (B.C.S.C.), at p. 114, *per* Collins, J. (pointing out that such orders have been confirmed on appeal without any comment on the point); *Evergreen Press Ltd. v. Vancouver Typographical Union Local 226* (1959), 18 D.L.R. (2d) 401 (B.C.S.C.); *Mitchell Bros. Truck Lines v. General Truck Drivers' & Helpers' Union Local 31* (1974), 57 D.L.R. (3d) 540 (B.C.S.C.); *Griffin Steel Foundries Ltd. v. Canadian Ass'n of Industrial, Mechanical & Allied Workers* (1977), 80 D.L.R. (3d) 634 (Man. C.A.). *Cf.*, however, *Bartle & Gibson Co. Ltd. v. Retail, Wholesale & Department Store Union, Local 580* (1971), 18 D.L.R. (3d) 232 (B.C.C.A.), at p. 238.

[74] *Int'l Longshoremen's Ass'n, Local 273 v. Maritime Employers' Ass'n*, [1979] 1 S.C.R. 120, 89 D.L.R. (3d) 289.

[75] *Ibid.*, at p. 144 S.C.R., p. 307 D.L.R.

[76] *Seaward v. Patterson*, [1897] 1 Ch. 545 (C.A.), at p. 555, *per* Lindley, L.J. See also *Re Tilco Plastics Ltd. v. Skurjat* (1966), 57 D.L.R. (2d) 596, [1966] 2 O.R. 547 (H.C.J.), affd 61 D.L.R. (2d) 664n, [1967] 1 O.R. 609n (C.A.), leave to appeal to S.C.C. refused [1966] S.C.R. vii, D.L.R. *loc. cit*, O.R. *loc. cit.*; *Catkey Construction Ltd. v. Moran* (1969), 8 D.L.R. (3d) 413, [1970] 1 O.R. 355 (H.C.J.); *Cities Service Oil Co. Ltd. v. Menard* (1960), 24 D.L.R. (2d) 495 (Ont. H.C.J.).

that non-parties abide by the injunction in this sense.[77] The fundamental principle is that of public respect for court orders and the rationale has been explained as follows: "All members of the public
are bound to obey Court orders in the sense that they must not deliberately act in defiance of them or aid others to do so. If it were otherwise, it would be a simple matter for the actual parties involved in
the granting of a court order to enlist the aid of others and to thereby
circumvent the order."[78]

517   Canadian courts have often enforced injunctions against non-parties, particularly in the context of labour disputes. On occasion, the
practice of holding non-parties to the order may have been taken too
far.[79] In an Ontario case,[80] the Court of Appeal held that "one who
knows of an injunction order forbidding anyone doing a specified
act, and himself acts 'in contravention of the injunction' can be committed 'for his contempt in intermeddling with these matters' ".[81] It
cannot be objected that the net of liability is cast too wide where the
plaintiff is able to show that the non-party has deliberately agreed to
flout the order at the instigation of the defendant.[82] However, the
court must be cautious not to hold in contempt a party who acts independently of the defendant, and who may exercise a right distinct
from that of the defendant. Such a person has not yet had his day in
court and should not be bound by an order made in an action to
which he was not a party. In labour cases, the courts are often prepared to find, from the very fact that the activity in question is repeated by others belonging to the same trade union, that an
inference of aiding and abetting can be drawn.

518   One important issue which is the subject of conflicting authority is
the binding effect of an injunction on successors in title. In *Ruthig v.
Stuart Bros. Ltd.*,[83] the Ontario Court of Appeal held that although
an injunction acts *in personam*, it will bind subsequent purchasers of

---

[77] *Re Tilco Plastics Ltd. v. Skurjat*, *supra*, footnote 76; *Canada Metal Co. Ltd. v.
C.B.C. (No. 2)*, *supra*, footnote 60.

[78] *Re Tilco Plastics Ltd. v. Skurjat*, *supra*, footnote 76, at p. 618 D.L.R., p. 569 O.R.

[79] For examples outside the labour area, see *Davis v. Barlow* (1910), 15 W.L.R. 49
(Man. K.B.); *Hynes v. Fisher* (1883), 4 O.R. 78 (H.C.J.); *Crooks v. Crooks* (1849),
1 Gr. 57.

[80] *Bassell's Lunch Ltd. v. Kick*, [1936] 4 D.L.R. 106, [1936] O.R. 445 (C.A.).

[81] *Ibid.*, at p. 110 D.L.R., p. 456 O.R., *per* Riddell, J.A., quoting *Wellesley v.
Mornington* (1848), 11 Beav. 180, 50 E.R. 785, which dealt with the liability of the
defendant's agent.

[82] *Supra*, §516.

[83] (1923), 53 O.L.R. 558 (S.C. App. Div.).

property who acquired title with knowledge of an injunction affecting such property. Thus, the plaintiff was entitled to enforce an injunction restraining an interference with the flow of water in a river against a party who had purchased the defendant's property with knowledge of the injunction. The court held that whether the purchaser should be regarded as being liable for breach of the injunction itself, or whether its liability was for contempt of the court's process, the injunction could be enforced against him. The contrary result would mean, the court pointed out, that the plaintiff could "be driven to sue perpetually . . . in a new action successive perpetrators of the same wrong who are privies in title to the party originally restrained".[84] The court recognized the problem posed by the notion of an injunction acting *in personam* but reasoned by analogy to the principle of *lis pendens* — that the defendant cannot defeat the plaintiff by conveying property which is the subject of a suit — and held that the defendant could not be better off once the suit had been taken to judgment.

519   It is submitted that this view is preferable to that expressed in the decision of the English Court of Appeal in *A.-G. v. Birmingham, Tame, and Rea Drainage Board*,[85] where Jessel, M.R., said:

> If they have sold the property to somebody else, there is no injunction against the new owner, and nobody ever heard in such a case of the new owner or purchaser of land being liable to the former decree. If he continues the nuisance or commits a fresh nuisance, you can bring an action against him, and that is all; he has nothing to do with the former proceedings, and I cannot see any ground whatever for supposing that he can be bound by that decree: nor, I believe, was such a thing ever heard of before.[86]

520   Certainly, there should be little doubt that any sort of deliberate attempt, through change of ownership, to evade the effects of an injunction, would be unsuccessful. Similar problems have arisen involving successors in office or changes in corporate structure.[87] In a

---

[84] *Ibid.*, at p. 564, *per* Logie, J.

[85] (1881), 17 Ch. D. 685 (C.A.).

[86] *Ibid.*, at p. 692. This analysis is, however, supported by Miller, *supra*, footnote 8, at p. 253. It was also assumed to be correct in *Godfrey v. Good Rich Refining Co. Ltd.*, [1940] 2 D.L.R. 164, [1940] O.R. 190 (C.A.), where the plaintiff brought a second nuisance action, having succeeded one year earlier against the previous owner.

[87] In *Macievich v. Anderson*, [1952] 4 D.L.R. 507 (Man. C.A.), it was held that the defendant did not escape the reach of an injunction restraining a nuisance by having incorporated his undertaking.

19th century English case,[88] it was held that successor trustees of a friendly society were in contempt of an order enjoining their predecessors from distributing certain funds. The court found that the change in membership was a ruse to avoid the breach of the order. On the other hand, where a *bona fide* change in membership or corporate structure occurs for other reasons, the new entity may not be bound by the injunction.[89]

5. Procedure

521   The precise details of procedure upon contempt and enforcement applications will, of course, vary from province to province, depending upon the relevant statutes and rules of court. In principle, the court regards contempt proceedings as involving the liberty of the subject and affords important procedural protections to the person accused. It would appear that whether the matter is treated as one of civil or criminal contempt, these protections will obtain. Thus, it has been held that proof of the alleged offence must be on the criminal standard beyond a reasonable doubt.[90] Similarly, the party accused has the right to remain silent in the face of the accusation,[91] although, it must be said, inferences of guilt have been drawn from such silence.[92] The courts have scrupulously ensured that notice requirements have been observed and that sufficient details of the alleged contempt have been given to enable the defendant to defend his conduct.[93]

---

[88] *Avery v. Andrews* (1882), 51 L.J. Ch. 414.

[89] *Bosch v. Simms Manufacturing Co. Ltd.* (1909), 25 T.L.R. 419 (Ch.), refusing to hold in contempt a new company which had been reorganized, *bona fide*, and not for the purpose of avoiding an injunction against soliciting certain customers.

[90] *Re Sheppard and Sheppard* (1975), 62 D.L.R. (3d) 35, 10 O.R. (2d) 19 (H.C.J.), affd 67 D.L.R. (3d) 592, 12 O.R. (2d) 4 (C.A.); *Re Bramblevale Ltd.*, [1970] Ch. 128 (C.A.), at p. 137; *Tilden Rent-A-Car Co. v. Rollins* (1966), 57 W.W.R. 309 (Sask. Q.B.); *Imperial Oil Co. Ltd. v. Tanguay*, [1971] Que. C.A. 109.

[91] *MacNeil v. MacNeil* (1975), 67 D.L.R. (3d) 114 (N.S.S.C. App. Div.), holding that where the defendant does file on an affidavit he is subject to cross-examination; *Comet Products U.K. Ltd. v. Hawkex Plastics Ltd.*, [1971] 2 Q.B. 67 (C.A.), at pp. 73-4, *per* Lord Denning, M.R., and also holding that the court has a discretion to limit cross-examination on an affidavit filed by the defendant where the contempt application arose from an interlocutory injunction, and where the proposed cross-examination would cover broad issues in the action.

[92] See, *e.g.*, *Re New Brunswick Electric Power Com'n and Local Union No. 1733 etc.* (1976), 73 D.L.R. (3d) 94 (N.B.S.C. App. Div.), leave to appeal to S.C.C. refused 13 N.R. 534n. *Cf.*, however, *Canada Metal Co. Ltd. v. C.B.C. (No. 2)* (1975), 59 D.L.R. (3d) 430, 8 O.R. 375 (C.A.), reversing an order denying a successful defendant costs because he failed to give evidence.

[93] *Re Sheppard and Sheppard*, *supra*, footnote 90; *Re Retail, Wholesale and Department Store Union, Local 955 etc.* (1973), 38 D.L.R. (3d) 419 (Sask.Q.B.).

522   *Ex parte* committals are rare[94] and may be precluded in some jurisdictions where rules of court require personal service of the application to commit in all cases. They are used in England in family
cases involving children and their removal from the jurisdiction
where the practice is to bring the contemner before the judge as soon
as possible to enable him to make representations.[95]

(1) Role of Attorney-General

523   Contempt proceedings are ordinarily launched by the opposite
party in the suit. However, it is clear that the parties themselves do
not have absolute control over these proceedings, and that even
where the dispute has been settled, and the plaintiff is satisfied with
the defendant's performance, the public interest may require that
contempt proceedings be taken.[96] Ordinarily, the Attorney-General
will be the party to take proceedings either upon motion,[97] or by
launching a prosecution under the Criminal Code.[98] Proceedings
taken under the Criminal Code involve the full paraphernalia of the
trial of an indictable offence, including the right to elect trial by
judge and jury. Since such cases are seen as criminal in the sense that
they are taken to punish rather than coerce compliance,[99] it is difficult to see why proceedings under the Code should not be the ordinary course. However, this does not seem to be the case, and it
would appear that the usual practice is to proceed by way of motion.

(2) Court initiated proceedings

524   It has been held that the court itself is entitled to take
proceedings,[100] Obviously, there are dangers involved in descending

---

[94] For a recent example, see *Warwick Corp. v. Russell*, [1964] 2 All E.R. 337 (Ch.).

[95] The Phillimore Committee Report, *supra*, footnote 31, noted that *ex parte* committal orders were important in family law matters where the respondent was about to
remove a child from the jurisdiction in violation of an order.

[96] *Supra*, §494.

[97] *Re Tilco Plastics Ltd. v. Skurjat* (1966), 57 D.L.R. (2d) 596, [1966] 2 O.R. 547
(H.C.J.), affd 61 D.L.R. (2d) 664*n*, [1967] O.R. 609*n* (C.A.), leave to appeal to
S.C.C. refused, [1966] S.C.R. vii, D.L.R. *loc. cit.*, O.R. *loc. cit.*; *Nissho (Canada)
Ltd. v. Int'l Longshoremen's & Warehousemen's Union* (1965), 54 D.L.R. (2d) 758,
(B.C.S.C.); *Re A.-G. N.S. and Miles* (1970), 15 D.L.R. (3d) 189 (N.S.S.C.T.D.).

[98] S. 116. See *R. v. Clement*, [1981] 2 S.C.R. 468 at p. 478, 127 D.L.R. (3d) 419 at p.
427. This procedure is available so long as no statute or regulation expressly provides for punishment or penalty.

[99] Although in *R. v. Clement, supra*, footnote 98, it was said that the distinction between civil and criminal contempt was not relevant in determining the availability
of the procedure under the Criminal Code.

[100] *Foothills Provincial General Hospital Board v. Broad* (1975), 57 D.L.R. (3d) 758

into the arena and becoming both accuser and judge. The rationale for permitting the court to act is that the parties themselves may be timid or unmotivated to act in cases where the public interest requires that steps be taken.[101] In such cases, however, it would seem preferable that the matter be referred to the Attorney-General for his consideration,[102] especially in light of the usually highly charged emotional and political aura which surrounds such cases.

(Alta. S.C.T.D.); *Churchman v. Joint Shop Stewards' Committee of Workers of Port of London*, [1972] 3 All E.R. 603 (C.A.); *Con-Mech (Engineers) Ltd. v. Amalgamated Union of Engineering Workers*, [1973] I.C.R. 620; *R. v. United Fishermen and Allied Workers' Union* (1967), 63 D.L.R. (2d) 356 (B.C.C.A.).

[101] The practice is supported by Miller, *supra*, footnote 8, at pp. 13-14; Phillimore Committee Report, *supra*, footnote 31, §171.

[102] This is suggested in *Iron Ore Co. of Canada v. United Steel Workers of America, Local 5795* (1979), 20 Nfld. & P.E.I.R. 27 (Nfld. C.A.), at p. 45, leave to appeal to S.C.C. refused 28 N.R. 339 *sub nom. Forfar v. Iron Ore Co. of Canada*.

PART II

SPECIFIC PERFORMANCE

CHAPTER 7

GENERAL PRINCIPLES

1. Introduction[1]

525   The framework of rules determining the availability of specific performance has been shaped largely by historical factors. The common law courts ordered actual performance of the defaulting party's obligation in a very narrow range of cases.[2] As Fry put it, "the same

---

[1] Parts of this chapter first appeared in Sharpe, "Specific Relief for Contract Breach", Chapter 5 in *Studies in Contract Law*, Reiter and Swan, eds (Toronto, Butterworths, 1980).

[2] See Fry, *Specific Performance of Contracts*, 6th ed. by Northcote (London, Stevens, 1921), pp. 4-20. The prerogative writ of *mandamus* could be issued by the common law courts to compel the performance of a public duty which arose from a private contract. It was expressly held that this power did not extend to contracts not involving public duties: *Norris v. Irish Land Co.* (1857), 8 El. & Bl. 512, 120 E.R. 191; *Benson v. Paull* (1856), 6 El. & Bl. 273, 119 E.R. 865. The common law courts could also order delivery of a chattel in detinue in certain cases where the vendor failed to deliver upon payment which in practice, if not in theory, amounted to specific performance. The old writ of covenant described in Blackstone,

spirit of commerce which led to the enforcement of contracts, also brought in the notion that money is an equivalent of everything",[3] and as a practical matter, common law remedies were virtually confined to damages. The courts of chancery, however, provided an alternative to the money remedies in the form of specific performance and injunction. But equity was only a gloss on the common law[4] and could relieve only cautiously against certain of its strictures and inadequacies. Hence, history determined that the presumptive remedy was that of the common law and that equity could extend its special form of relief only where the common law remedy was inadequate. The adequacy of damages test remains the primary one in determining the availability of specific relief, and will be examined in this chapter.[5]

526   Also to be examined in this chapter is the second major qualification on the granting of specific performance shaped by history, namely, the problem of supervision.[6] In the struggle between the courts of law and equity, chancery perceived that its authority could be undermined by rendering orders which could not be enforced. Orders involving complex or extended performance were seen to expose the courts to the risk that even imprisonment for contempt of the recalcitrant defendant might not achieve the objective of having the contract performed, and hence there developed a "prejudice for historic reasons against affirmative decrees in cases calling for more than a single simple act".[7]

527   In Chapter 10, attention will be directed to the discretionary defences which come into play to defeat a claim which has otherwise met the criteria for specific relief. These represent the third qualification on the availability of specific performance. The discretionary nature of specific relief allowed the courts to consider matters and defences of particular concern to equity. Much of the modern law on mistake, misrepresentation and unconscionability was developed by chancery. Specific performance was often refused on these grounds,

---

Commentaries on the Laws of England, 16th ed., vol. 3 (London, Butterworth & Son, 1825), at pp. 156-7, amounted to a form of specific performance which was available with respect to agreements for conveyance of land.

[3] Fry, *supra*, footnote 2, at pp. 4-5.

[4] Maitland, *Equity, A Course of Lectures*, 2nd ed. by Brunyate (Cambridge, Harvard University Press, 1936), pp. 16-22.

[5] *Infra*, §§529-557.

[6] *Infra*, §§558-576.

[7] Pound, "The Progress of the Law, 1918-1919, Equity", 33 Harv. L. Rev. 420 (1920), p. 435.

although as noted in Chapter 10 it will now be much rarer for the court to fasten on a discretionary matter of this sort which falls short of providing a general defence to the enforcement of the contract, but which is seen to render specific relief inappropriate.

528 While specific relief for breach of contract continues to bear these distinctive marks of history, it will be argued that the courts are now moving away from the strictures formerly imposed on chancery. The courts are abandoning the more rigid 19th century approach in favour of one which calls for a more thorough and sensitive review of the interests of the contracting parties and the techniques available to protect those interests.[8] Without ignoring or abandoning the lessons of history, it is surely now appropriate for the courts to develop a modern rationale for specific relief. It is against this background that the rules relating to specific relief for breach of contract are examined, and an attempt made to isolate and identify the advantages and disadvantages of specific relief as a remedy.

2. Inadequacy of Damages

(1) Advantages of specific performance

529 It has often been said that the general goal of contract remedies is so far as possible to put the plaintiff in the position he would have been in had the contract been performed.[9] There are two methods whereby this goal may be achieved. The first is to award the injured party compensatory damages. The second is to order the defaulting party specifically to perform its obligation. The existing regime of remedial law strongly favours the first option of damages and awards

---

[8] See, *e.g.*, *Beswick v. Beswick*, [1968] A.C. 58 (H.L.), at p. 91, *per* Lord Pearce, quoting with approval *Coulls v. Bagot's Executor and Trustee Co. Ltd.* (1967), 119 C.L.R. 460 (Aust. H.C.), at p. 503, *per* Windeyer, J.:

> There is no reason to-day for limiting by particular categories, rather than by general principle, the cases in which orders for specific performance will be made. The days are long past when the common law courts looked with jealousy upon what they thought was a usurpation by the Chancery court of their jurisdiction.

This theme in the substantive context is developed at length in Waddams, *The Law of Contracts* (Toronto, Canada Law Book Ltd., 1977). Particular reference is made to remedial flexibility at p. 421.

[9] See Waddams, The Law of Damages (1983), §§537, 538. The classic statement of this principle is that of Parke, B., in *Robinson v. Harman* (1848), 1 Ex. 850 at p. 855, 154 E.R. 363: "The rule of the common law is, that where a party sustains a loss by reason of a breach of contract, he is, so far as money can do it, to be placed in the same situation, with respect to damages, as if the contract had been performed."

specific performance only in exceptional cases. Yet in many cases, specific relief may seem to be the only sure way to put the plaintiff in the position he would have been in had the contract been performed. Obviously, specific relief will not always achieve this end. The time of anticipated performance has usually passed by the date of trial, and circumstances may well be such that the plaintiff will want no more than damages. However, where a practical choice between damages and specific performance remains, the latter has certain distinct advantages. The assessment of damages the innocent party has suffered can be a difficult, expensive and time-consuming task. Specific performance has the advantage of avoiding the problems and costs the parties and the judicial system must incur if damages are to be assessed. Perhaps more significant is the very real element of risk that the translation into money terms of the effect of the breach on the plaintiff may be inaccurate. Some cases will present more risk than others, but it cannot be denied that the element of risk of error is virtually swept away if the court is able to make an order of specific performance. The innocent party receives the very thing he bargained for rather than a monetary estimate of its worth to him. If the matter were to be viewed from the perspective of protecting the innocent party, it might even be argued that the very fact that the plaintiff is seeking specific performance indicates that damages will be inadequate to him.[10] If an adequate substitute were available, and if damages would make the plaintiff whole for any loss caused by the defendant's breach, few plaintiffs would proceed with an action for specific performance. Willing performance from another will ordinarily be much preferable to grudging performance from one who has refused until forced to perform by order of the court.

530   Arguments for greater availability of specific performance are often heard,[11] and in light of the moral force behind the proposition that promises solemnly made ought to be performed to the full, it is at first blush surprising that specific performance remains a secondary remedy. However, one still hears the often quoted phrase, "the Court gives specific performance instead of damages, only when it can by that means do more perfect and complete justice".[12] "More

---

[10] See Schwartz, "The Case for Specific Performance", 89 Yale L.J. 271 (1979).

[11] For two recent examples, see Schwartz, *supra*, footnote 10; Linzer, "On the Amorality of Contract Remedies — Efficiency, Equity, and the Second *Restatement*", 81 Columbia L. Rev. 111 (1981). *Cf.* Yorio, "In Defence of Money Damages for Breach of Contract", 82 Columbia L. Rev. 1365 (1982), responding to these arguments.

[12] *Wilson v. Northampton & Banbury Junction Ry. Co.* (1874), 9 Ch. App. 279 at p.

perfect and complete justice" must mean more than satisfying the plaintiff's expectation and putting him in the position he would have been in had the contract been performed. If that were the only concern, surely specific performance would be available for the asking. The issues are, however, more complex, and "more perfect and complete justice" will only be achieved if the full implications to the defendant as well as to the plaintiff of granting specific performance are taken into account.

(2) Burden of specific performance

531   An understanding of the notion of inadequacy of damages requires some consideration of the policies of the law of contract damages. Detailed consideration of this is to be found in the companion volume to this book, but reference may be made here to some of the basic points. The first principle is that damages are to be measured by the plaintiff's expectation interest rather than just costs incurred in reliance on the contract, or by restitution of benefits he has conferred.[13] At the same time, however, it is observed that a fundamental problem in the law of damages is the need to balance the desire to afford complete protection against the consequences of breach with the practical need to impose reasonable limits on recovery in the interests of convenience and commercial efficacy.[14] While the law does have as its objective putting the plaintiff in the position he would have been in had the contract been performed, there are principles which effectively limit the plaintiff's damage recovery. Indeed, the very existence of rules to define the quantification of damages arising from the breach points to the fact that it is often inappropriate to compensate the plaintiff for certain losses.

532   Discussion of specific remedies here, and the discussion of damages in the companion volume, suggests that the goals and policies of contract remedies are not entirely captured by the concept of putting the plaintiff in the position he would have been in. The law of damages contains rules which limit the extent of the plaintiff's recovery[15] and similarly, in awarding specific performance, careful consideration is given to the cost or burden the remedy imposes upon the defendant. The basic goal is to protect the plaintiff's expectation

---

284, *per* Selborne, L.C.

[13] Waddams, *supra*, footnote 9, §§536-549.

[14] *Ibid.*, §203.

[15] *Ibid.*, §§1051-1278, discussing limiting principles of certainty, remoteness and mitigation.

interest and to put him in the position he would have been in, but at the same time to avoid remedial measures which are unduly burdensome to the defendant. It is suggested, in the discussion which follows, that the notion of inadequacy of damages as a criterion for specific performance is best understood as reflecting that basic aim, namely, limiting the cost or burden of breach so far as possible in a manner consistent with the protection of the plaintiff's reasonable expectation. The plaintiff's expectation is to be protected, but the burden a remedy imposes on the defendant deserves careful consideration. While specific performance will provide greater assurance that the plaintiff's expectation is protected, as seen from the discussion following, this greater assurance will often be bought at a price of imposing burdens on the defendant avoidable through damage awards.

(3) Mitigation and commercial efficacy

533   The most important limiting principle in the law of damages, which would be undercut by the more general availability of specific relief, is that of mitigation and early crystallization of the plaintiff's loss.[16] As soon after breach as is reasonably practicable the plaintiff is expected to procure alternate performance in mitigation. Offering specific relief is inconsistent with limiting the plaintiff to avoidable losses. If the plaintiff is entitled to specific relief, he cannot be faulted for failing to take immediate steps to reduce the impact of the breach. It would be inconsistent on the one hand to allow or encourage the plaintiff to insist upon performance by the defendant, but on the other hand to insist that he take immediate steps to mitigate his loss. So long as the plaintiff proceeds expeditiously with his suit, and so long as his claim for specific relief has some real substance, even his alternative damages claim should not be diminished in the event that he ultimately fails to obtain specific performance.[17]

534   It could be argued, however, that the prospect of a specific performance decree does not necessarily mean that efforts will not be made to avoid losses incurred after breach.[18] The effect of a damages

---

[16] *Ibid.*, §§65-110 and 1194-1253.

[17] *Asamera Oil Corp. Ltd. v. Sea Oil & General Corp.*, [1979] 1 S.C.R. 633 at p. 668, 89 D.L.R. (3d) 1 at p. 26, *per* Estey, J.:

> Before a plaintiff can rely on a claim to specific performance so as to insulate himself from the consequences of failing to procure alternate property in mitigation of his losses, some fair, real, and substantial justification for his claim to performance must be found. Otherwise its effect will be to cast upon the defendant all the risk of aggravated loss by reason of delay in bringing the issue to trial.

[18] *Cf., infra*, footnote 23.

award is to place the burden of avoiding such losses on the plaintiff. A presumptive granting of specific relief would, in effect, shift that burden to the party in breach. If the breaching party wanted to reduce avoidable losses, it would be to his advantage to go to the innocent party and strike some sort of bargain to effect mitigation. Such an approach does have its attractions. Why should the mitigation burden not be placed on the guilty rather than on the innocent? Yet this solution surely increases the net costs of effecting mitigation. Securing alternate arrangements in substitution for performance must be geared to the needs of the innocent party. Usually it will be easier and less burdensome for him to see that his own needs are satisfied than it would be for the defendant to do so.[19] The innocent party can recover, as part of his damages award, compensation for his mitigation efforts. As the defendant will have to compensate the plaintiff for the cost of obtaining alternate performance in mitigation, there will remain an incentive for him to assist the plaintiff if he is in fact in a position to find alternate performance for the plaintiff more cheaply than the plaintiff himself.

535   The mitigation rules and the general concern for what might be called commercial efficacy facilitate and encourage commercial activity.[20] The common law has wisely imposed limitations on the responsibility of the party in breach. This has been described as a "marked solicitude for men who do not keep their promises".[21] Upon analysis, however, it would seem that the attitude stems, not from a blind eye to dishonesty, but from a desire to encourage the maximization of profit and commercial activity in an open-market economy. So long as the plaintiff's expectation interest is protected, there is no reason to impose more burdensome remedial measures which might inhibit such activity.

---

[19] See, *infra*, §630, where this point is discussed in relation to contracts for the sale of land; Yorio, *supra*, footnote 11, at p. 1384. *Cf.*, however, Schwartz, *supra*, footnote 10, arguing that the defaulting party will often be in a better position to mitigate.

[20] See, *e.g.*, Farnsworth, "Legal Remedies for Breach of Contract", 70 Columbia L. Rev. 1145 (1970).

[21] Farnsworth, *supra*, footnote 20, at p. 1216. This is reflected in Holmes' often cited statement ("The Path of the Law", 10 Harv. L. Rev. 457 (1897), at p. 462): "The duty to keep a contract at common law means a prediction that you must pay damages if you do not keep it, — and nothing else."

See also Simpson, *A History of the Common Law of Contract: The Rise of the Action of Assumpsit* (Oxford, Clarendon Press, 1975), at p. 597: "the common law in effect gave to the promisor an option to perform his contract or pay damages, which option equity denied".

(4) Theory of efficient breach

536 The limiting aspects of contract remedies and the desire to protect the plaintiff's expectation as cheaply as possible is sometimes described as the theory of efficient breach.[22] Where the innocent party's expectation interest can be fully protected by a damages award, damages are to be preferred on this theory. The innocent party is protected, and at the same time the party in breach is able to pursue a more profitable or desirable venture. A rule which forced the latter to perform in such circumstances, it is argued by some, would needlessly waste an opportunity for profit.[23]

537 Granting the plaintiff specific performance in such cases will often go farther than achieving the goal of putting the plaintiff in the position he would have been in had the contract been performed, and may well impose on the defendant a substantial cost or burden which might otherwise be avoided. The point to be made here turns upon the distinction between the plaintiff's and the defendant's relative costs and advantages of contract breach. By putting the plaintiff in

---

[22] There is now considerable literature on this subject. See Barton, "The Economic Basis for Damages for Breach of Contract", 1 J. of Leg. Stud. 277 (1972); Birmingham, "Breach of Contract, Damage Measures, and Economic Efficiency", 24 Rutgers L. Rev. 273 (1970); Clarkson, Miller and Muris, "Liquidated Damages v. Penalties: Sense or Nonsense?", [1978] Wisc. L. Rev. 351; Posner, *Economic Analysis of Law*, 2nd ed. (Toronto, Little, Brown & Co., 1977), p. 88 *et seq.*; Goetz and Scott, "Liquidated Damages, Penalties and the Just Compensation Principle: Some Notes on an Enforcement Model and a Theory of Efficient Breach", 77 Columbia L. Rev. 554 (1977); Kronman, "Specific Performance", 45 U. of Chi. L. Rev. 351 (1978); Schwartz, *supra*, footnote 10; Linzer, *supra*, footnote 11; Macneil, "Efficient Breach of Contract: Circles in the Sky", 68 Va. L. Rev. 947 (1982); Yorio, *supra*, footnote 11.

[23] See especially Posner, *supra*, footnote 22, at pp. 89-90:

. . . in some cases a party would be tempted to breach the contract simply because his profit from breach would exceed his expected profit from completion of the contract. If his profit from breach would also exceed the expected profit to the other party from completion of the contract, and if damages are limited to loss of expected profit, there will be an incentive to commit a breach. There should be. The opportunity cost of completion to the breaching party is the profit that he would make from a breach, and if it is greater than his profit from completion, then completion will involve a loss to him. If that loss is greater than the gain to the other party from completion, breach would be value-maximizing and should be encouraged. And because the victim of the breach is made whole for his loss, he is indifferent; hence encouraging breaches in these circumstances will not deter people from entering into contracts in the future.

Cf., however, Schwartz, *supra*, footnote 10, and Macneil, *supra*, footnote 22, arguing that absent transaction costs, an "efficient breach" will still occur even if specific performance is the presumed remedy as the only difference will be distributive, *i.e.*, the breaching party will be forced to share some of the profit from breach with the innocent party. This point is discussed, *supra*, §534.

the position he would have been in we mean to ensure that he receives the value to him of the defendant's performance. Where the defendant defaults, it may be assumed that he has done so to gain an advantage or to avoid some hardship in performance. Fulfilling his obligation to the plaintiff may have become a losing proposition. A more attractive and more profitable arrangement with another party may be available. The plaintiff's loss arising on breach is not always a mirror image of the advantage the defendant gains by failing to perform. The accepted view is that contract remedies are not designed to punish the contract breaker, and the proper measure for contract damages is compensation for the plaintiff's loss rather than lifting the benefits of breach from the defendant.[24] As it was put in a recent English case, "[t]he question is not one of making the defendant disgorge what he has saved by committing the wrong, but one of compensating the plaintiff. . . . [I]t by no means necessarily follows that what the defendant has saved the plaintiff has lost".[25]

538   Where the cost of performance to the defendant exceeds the value of performance to the plaintiff, specific performance will tend to produce either one of two possibilities. If the plaintiff insists on having the decree carried out, there will be waste in the form of performance by the defendant at a cost to him which exceeds the value of the benefit to the plaintiff. The second possibility is settlement of the dispute by the parties either before trial under threat of a specific performance decree or after trial and judgment. Here, it is likely that the plaintiff will be over-compensated in the sense that he will recover more from the settlement or post-judgment bargain than is represented by the value he placed on performance before breach. As a practical matter, it may be expected that the threat of specific performance will not invariably mean that the defendant will be required actually to perform his obligation. He would often seek relief by "buying out" the plaintiff's right to enforce performance.[26] In such circumstances, a specific decree in favour of the plaintiff would put him in a bargaining position vis-à-vis the defendant whereby the measure of what he will receive will be the value to the defendant of

---

[24] Waddams, *supra* footnote 9, §§969-974; *Asamera Oil Corp. Ltd. v. Sea Oil & General Corp.*, *supra*, footnote 17, at p. 672 S.C.R., p. 30 D.L.R., *per* Estey, J.: "It seems to me that the motives or unjust enrichment of the defendant on breach are generally of no concern in the assessment of contractual damages."

[25] *Tito v. Waddell (No. 2)*, [1977] Ch. 106 at p. 332, *per* Megarry, V.-C.

[26] See Harris, Ogus and Phillips, "Contract Remedies and the Consumer Surplus", 95 L.Q. Rev. 581 (1979); Kronman, *supra*, footnote 22. The impact of post-judgment bargaining with respect to injunctions is discussed, *supra*, §§15-18.

being released from performance. If the plaintiff bargains effectively, the amount he will set as his price will exceed the value to him of performance and will approach the cost to the defendant to complete.[27]

539   If the defendant has a more profitable option to pursue, specific performance will allow the plaintiff to bargain for a share of the profit to be made from breach. This may seem attractive in that the gain from apparent wrongdoing is lifted. However it would also go against the grain of the basic damages rule that the plaintiff's loss rather than the defendant's gain is the appropriate measure. It could, of course, be argued that that rule is wrong, but if one were to accept that the law of damages was in need of change, that change should be brought about directly. Making specific performance readily available would have a limited and even haphazard effect. Specific performance is often inappropriate simply because of temporal considerations. Other factors as well as adequacy of damages determine its availability. As a practical matter, whatever say the rules governing its availability, specific performance will be feasible in a relatively narrow range of cases. The argument that the defendant should be required to share with the plaintiff the profit he has made from breach has not been accepted. Even if it were, making specific performance generally available would be an ineffective and inappropriate way to bring about that objective.

540   It is suggested, then, that one of the primary policies of remedial rules in the contractual setting is limiting the burden of breach upon the defendant, so long as the plaintiff's expectation interest is protected. This results in the avoidance of waste and the maximization of profit and commercial activity. Expectation damage awards rather than enforced performance allow the defendant to buy peace at an objectively defined and limited price which is just enough to cover the ordinary commercial interests of the innocent party. Damages allow sour commercial relationships to be severed, the price to be paid and the past to be forgotten.

541   Limiting the costs of breach in the interest of commercial efficacy serves not just to protect the interest of defendants, but is in the interest of all other purchasers or consumers of like goods or services. The price of any good or service will reflect the cost of satisfying a court-imposed remedy in the event of breach. If added remedial costs are imposed, ultimately the defendant will have to pass those costs on to his consumers. Surely consumers would rather not pay

---

[27] Posner, *supra*, footnote 22, at pp. 96-7.

more for the assurance that one particular remedy will be available, when for less they can still have the assurance that their expectation interest will be protected through damages.[28]

(5) Expectation damages inadequate

542   However, where ordinary damages will not meet the goal of protecting the plaintiff's expectation, the added cost of specific performance becomes worth incurring. The assumptions which lie behind expectation damages as an adequate level of protection are that the injured party is in the position of a commercial trader, motivated to enter the contract with the aim of maximizing profit, and that the subject-matter of the bargain is a fungible good or service for which there is readily available alternate performance. The notion of "inadequacy of damages" as a rationale for specific performance reflects the desire to avoid the harshness which would result from the application of the ordinary rules where these assumptions are not met. Where expectation damages fail to reflect the interest of the plaintiff, specific relief ensures that the plaintiff gets exactly what he bargained for, and whatever the nature of his interest in performance, it is protected. This will usually increase the cost of breach imposed upon the defendant, and the court's task should be to weigh the disadvantage of increasing the defendant's burden against the advantage of affording more complete protection to the plaintiff's expectation. One can, then, accept the force of the argument that policies underlying contract damage rules properly reflect the need to limit the remedial burden imposed on the defendant, and at the same time contemplate the award of specific performance in a variety of situations without contravening or undercutting those policies.

543   The development of the law, as already noted, was shaped by historical factors which have, perhaps, been more explicitly stated as grounds for decision than the need to balance protection of the plaintiff's expectation against the cost or burden imposed upon the defendant. However the courts are becoming less willing to justify decisions in terms of historical categories, and more willing explicitly to recognize and state underlying principles.[29] It seems clear that the courts are now determined to pay less heed to the language of the dual court system which was abolished over 100 years ago, and to consider the relative advantages and disadvantages of damages and

---

[28] Rea, "Nonpecuniary Loss and Breach of Contract", 11 J. of Leg. Stud. 35 (1982).

[29] *Supra*, footnote 8, and, *infra*, §§565-568.

specific relief. The analysis here suggests that this will not, and should not, involve any categorical shift in the availability of specific relief, but that there may be reason to reconsider the award of specific performance in some cases where it is now available,[30] and at the same time, that it may be the appropriate remedy in other cases formerly thought to be excluded.[31]

544   What is required is a careful consideration of the plaintiff's interest in performance, and to distinguish, for example, cases where the plaintiff seeks specific relief merely to avoid mitigation or crystallization rules from cases where the plaintiff has a demonstrated need or interest in the very item he bargained for which is difficult to satisfy through substitutes. The variety and complexity of contractual interests preclude categorical conclusions, and it is suggested that a careful weighing of those interests in light of remedial policies is called for.

(6) Uniqueness

545   Where the subject-matter of the contract is "unique", a strong case can be made for specific performance. The more unusual the subject-matter of the contract, the more difficult it becomes to assess the plaintiff's loss. The special treatment accorded land,[32] rare artifacts and family heirlooms[33] is familiar in this regard.

546   An award of damages presumes that the plaintiff's expectation can be protected by a money award which will permit him to acquire substitute performance. If the item he has bargained for is unique, then there is no exact substitute. The lack of an available substitute produces two problems. First, it makes the purely monetary loss caused by the defendant's breach very difficult to measure. There are no comparable sales to which reference may be made in order to establish an objective estimate of the value of the promised item or performance. Secondly, even if an objective value of some sort can be found, the effect of denying specific performance and granting damages is to force the plaintiff to settle for some inexact substitute. The plaintiff may, however, have attached to the particular item he bargained for a value, sometimes called the "consumer surplus",[34]

---

[30] See, e.g., infra, §§614-633, discussing contracts for the sale of land.

[31] See, e.g., infra, §§651-663, discussing long-term supply contracts.

[32] Infra, §§612-634 where, however, the automatic remedy of specific performance is criticized.

[33] Infra, §644.

[34] See Harris, Ogus and Phillips, supra, footnote 26, for a useful discussion of this

which is not reflected by objective measurement. In such a case, the value of the item to the plaintiff exceeds the market value (even if it can be established), and it is difficult to justify forcing the plaintiff to accept only the lesser objective value.[35] It might be argued that money relief could also be awarded to compensate the plaintiff for this loss above the market value, but because of its subjective nature, that extra value is extremely difficult to assess. However, if no account is taken of this aspect of the plaintiff's interest in performance, his expectation will not be protected, and one of the basic aims of contract remedies will not be fulfilled. By requiring performance of the defendant's obligation *in specie*, the court can avoid the expensive and time-consuming task of translating the effect of the breach into money terms, and more importantly, avoid the risk of inaccurate assessment and thereby achieve a virtual guarantee of remedial adequacy in favour of the plaintiff.

547   The more unusual the subject-matter of the contract, the stronger the argument for specific relief becomes. Chapter 8 considers the concept of uniqueness in the case of contracts of sale. Land is almost invariably presumed unique, while chattels are presumed fungible unless the contrary is shown. In the case of land or rare objects, the subject-matter of the defendant's performance is intrinsically unique. Whatever the time, place or circumstances of the bargain, it is considered that the matter promised would almost inevitably, by its very nature, demonstrate the qualities of uniqueness calling for specific performance.

(7) Negative covenants

548   Another category of case in which damages are presumptively considered inadequate is that of negative covenants. These cases are examined in detail in Chapter 9 where it is seen that the plaintiff will rarely be denied specific relief to enforce a negative covenant. This is

---

concept and the appropriate remedial response. For an economic analysis of the concept of "uniqueness" and the uncertainty of assessing damages, see Kronman, *supra*, footnote 22. Kronman, at p. 362, argues that the "uniqueness" test is economically sound:

> In asserting that the subject matter of a particular contract is unique and has no established market value, a court is really saying that it cannot obtain, at reasonable cost, enough information about substitutes to permit it to calculate an award of money damages without imposing an unacceptably high risk of undercompensation on the injured promisee. Conceived in this way, the uniqueness test seems economically sound.

[35] See, *supra*, §§15-18 and 368, where the same point is discussed in relation to injunctions.

partly because such orders are easily enforced and relatively unobtrusive in so far as the defendant is concerned, but also turns on the difficulty of assessing damages. Where a positive obligation is broken, the plaintiff is deprived of something the value of which can be measured. Where the defendant does something that he has promised not to do, the impact of his wrongful act is much more difficult to measure in money terms. It is considered preferable to stop the defendant from doing what he promised not to do rather than to try to estimate the loss.

549   The issue of inadequacy of damages was formerly determined for the most part simply by asking whether the plaintiff's case fell into one of these categories. However, such a blunt statement cannot explain the practice of the courts, and in the succeeding pages, many other particular instances appropriate for specific relief are identified.[36] The courts are increasingly less willing to be bound by narrow categories, and are looking to the more general principle that specific performance should be available if damages are inadequate.[37]

(8) Insolvency

550   Damages often can be readily assessed but not so easily collected. If the defendant is unable to pay a damages award, then however accurate the assessment of the plaintiff's loss may have been, the remedy of damages can hardly be described as adequate. There is surprisingly little authority on whether the defendant's insolvency will make damages "inadequate" so as to justify specific relief.[38] Fry was categorical in his dismissal of the proposition that the defendant's insolvency could justify specific performance: "this principle . . . if it were admitted, would give the Court jurisdiction by way of specific performance in all cases of contract, whether for the sale of chattels or of any other nature, which is certainly not the law of the Court".[39] Spry, however, is equally categorical the other way: "it appears to be clear that a significant risk that a legal remedy such as damages will be ineffective, on the grounds of the insolvency of the

---

[36] See, e.g., infra, §660.

[37] Supra, footnote 8, and infra, §§565-568.

[38] The plaintiff's insolvency need not bar specific relief absent hardship to the defendant: see Dyster v. Randall & Sons, [1926] 1 Ch. 932.

[39] Supra, footnote 2, at p. 30, arguing against the suggestion made in Doloret v. Rothschild (1824), 1 Sim. & St. 590 at p. 598, 57 E.R. 233, per Leach, V.-C., that insolvency does provide a basis for specific performance.

defendant or otherwise, will itself justify the conclusion that it is inadequate".[40]

551   It has been noted that injunctions have been granted on the basis of the defendant's insolvency,[41] and indeed the only case Spry cites on the point is one involving an injunction against a trespass[42] where, it is argued below, different considerations apply.[43] The cases provide no clear authority. Often one finds statements confirming the award of specific performance, already justifiable on other grounds, on the basis of the defendant's insolvency and similarly, where specific relief is refused, it is sometimes said that as the defendant is solvent, there will be no problem in collecting damages.[44] These dicta hardly provide authority for granting the remedy on the ground of insolvency alone. The difficulty with allowing the defendant's insolvency by itself to constitute the ground for specific performance is that very often the effect of the decree will be to confer an unfair preference over other creditors.[45] Specific performance would, in theory, be available to all creditors, and yet the very fact of the defendant's insolvency would preclude the effective enforcement of all decrees. It is much preferable in such a case to have the defendant's assets distributed fairly among the creditors under the appropriate bankruptcy or insolvency legislation. This is not to say, however, that if the plaintiff's interest is otherwise specifically enforceable, he should not be granted a decree. If the plaintiff has a proprietary interest in some good, then of course the defendant's insolvency provides all the more reason for granting a specific performance decree to enforce his *in specie* claim.[46] Prior proprietary claims should be recognized, but the fact of insolvency itself should not be used to confer a proprietary claim in the form of a specific performance decree.

552   Injunctions, including cases where injunctions are sought to en-

---

[40] *The Principles of Equitable Remedies*, 2nd ed. (London, Sweet & Maxwell, 1980), p. 64.

[41] *Supra*, §23.

[42] *Hodgson v. Duce* (1856), 2 Jur. N.S. 1014.

[43] *Infra*, §552.

[44] See, *e.g.*, *Dobell v. Cowichan Copper Co. Ltd. (N.P.L.)* (1967), 65 D.L.R. (2d) 440 (B.C.S.C.); *Bell v. Milner* (1956), 3 D.L.R. (2d) 202 (B.C.S.C); *Canada Starch Co. Ltd. v. St. Lawrence Starch Co. Ltd.*, [1935] O.W.N. 412 (H.C.J.).

[45] For discussion of the point, see Horack, "Insolvency and Specific Performance", 31 Harv. L. Rev. 702 (1917-18); McClintock, "Adequacy of Ineffective Remedy at Law", 16 Minn. L. Rev. 233 (1932).

[46] See *Tailby v. Official Receiver* (1888), 13 App. Cas. 523. See also, *infra*, §§638, 639.

force negative covenants, fall into a different category. A prohibitive injunction will not result in the transfer from the defendant to the plaintiff of assets or property otherwise available for distribution among creditors. Moreover, it is hard to imagine an injunction being granted solely because of the defendant's insolvency. Usually the plaintiff will have some claim to injunctive relief which will be strengthened by the defendant's inability to pay damages.

553   Often, moreover, specific performance may properly be awarded without conferring any priority on the ground that damages are inadequate because of the defendant's insolvency. Corbin argues[47] that the court should never order specific performance where performance if voluntarily made would constitute an illegitimate preference, but points out that in many cases of insolvency specific performance could be granted without this effect. The plaintiff may be the defendant's only creditor, and clearly no preference problems arise in that situation. The contract may remain bilateral, in the sense that a mutual exchange will be effected through specific performance. This would not result in a net diminution of the value of the assets possessed by the defendant, and thus there is no reason not to protect the plaintiff. In some cases, damages may represent a greater loss than actual performance. For example, failure of the defendant to deliver some necessary item may result in colossal consequential damages for which he would be liable. In such a case, specific performance would have the effect of preserving assets for distribution and should be granted.

554   Another situation in which specific performance may be granted in the context of insolvency is where execution of an agreement to give security is sought. In such cases, specific performance is given "not necessarily because of insolvency, but rather because of the possibility of it".[48]

(9) Avoiding multiplicity of suits

555   Where confining the plaintiff to damages will require him to bring a succession of suits, the remedy in damages may be considered inadequate and provide a basis for specific relief.[49] Equity acts "to prevent the trouble and expense of a multiplicity of actions"[50] in such

---

[47] *Corbin on Contracts*, vol. 5A (St. Paul, West Publishing Co., 1964), §1156.

[48] Horack, *supra*, footnote 45, at p. 714.

[49] See also, *supra*, §§24, 25.

[50] *Beswick v. Beswick*, [1968] A.C. 58 (H.L.), at p. 97, *per* Lord Upjohn.

cases. Avoiding a succession of suits is more often encountered as a justification for injunctive relief where it is often preferable to stop the wrongful conduct entirely rather than to put the plaintiff to the expense and inconvenience of suing, in theory on a daily basis, for each cause of action that accrues.[51]

556   In the case of specific performance, the best example of the application of this principle is found in the enforcement of annuity contracts. The leading modern case is *Beswick v. Beswick*[52] where Lord Upjohn cited with approval an Irish case[53] decided in 1841 in which it was said that to force the plaintiff to sue for damages once and for all "would be compelling her to accept a certain sum, a sum to be ascertained by the conjecture of a jury as to what was the value of the annuity".[54]

557   It is perhaps questionable that the same reasoning should be applied today in cases of annuities, for which there is an established market. It will be recalled that in the *Beswick* case, the problem was that the recipient of the annuity was not a party to the contract and specific performance was found to be the only way to enforce the defendant's obligation. In the ordinary case between immediate parties, the plaintiff can purchase another annuity contract in the market, and it is likely that a modern court in such a case would award damages rather than specific performance.

3. Supervision

(1) Introduction

558   Where performance of the defendant's obligation would require a complex series of acts or the maintenance of an ongoing relationship, the remedy of specific performance will ordinarily be refused. The reason usually given is that the court will not make an order which would require it to watch over and supervise performance.[55] Thus, in

---

[51] *Supra*, §24.

[52] *Supra*, footnote 50.

[53] *Swift v. Swift* (1841), 3 Ir. Eq. R. 267.

[54] *Ibid.*, at p. 276, *per* Lord Plunket, L.C.

[55] Fry, *supra*, footnote 2, at pp. 46-7, puts the principle in characteristically definite language: "it is a recognized rule that the Court will not decree specific performance of a contract, the execution of which would require watching over and supervision by the Court". See also *Blackett v. Bates* (1865), 1 Ch. App. 117; *Powell Duffryn Steam Coal Co. v. Taff Vale Ry. Co.* (1874), 9 Ch. App. 331 at p. 335, *per* James, L.J.: "Where what is required is not merely to restrain a party from doing an act of wrong, but to obligate him to do some continuous act involving labour and

a leading case[56] where specific performance was sought of a land-lord's obligation to employ a porter to provide certain services for tenants, Lord Esher, M.R., refused the remedy on the grounds that

> . . . it is . . . a long-continuing contract, to be performed from day to day, and under which the circumstances of non-performance might vary from day to day. I apprehend, therefore, that the execution of it would require that constant superintendence by the Court, which the Court in such cases has always declined to give.[57]

559   The supervision concern has already been examined in the context of injunctions.[58] There it was observed that while there is a preference for orders which do not require subsequent litigation to test the adequacy of the defendant's compliance, such orders will be made where justice requires. Similarly, with specific performance, there has never been an absolute refusal to award the remedy in cases which might require supervision where the plaintiff is able to demonstrate sufficient need for it. In fact, the principle is a flexible one.

(2) Contract partly performed

560   An important exception to the usual reluctance to make a specific performance order where a complex or lengthy performance would

---

care, the Court has never found its way to do this by injunction." *Pollard v. Clayton* (1855), 1 K. & J. 462, 69 E.R. 540; *Fothergill v. Rowland* (1873), L.R. 17 Eq. 132. Similar statements have been made in Canadian cases; see, *e.g.*, *City of Kingston v. Kingston, Portsmouth & Cataraqui Electric Ry.* (1898), 25 O.A.R. 462 at p. 466, *per* Moss, J.A., refusing specific performance of an agreement to operate a street railway:

> It is, in substance, an action to compel the performance in specie by the defendants of an agreement amounting to a covenant on their part to do certain acts continuous in their nature and extending over a period of thirty-six years from the present year. These are continuous duties involving personal labour and care of a particular kind; and if the Court should direct their performance in specie it would have to assume their superintendence in order to enforce obedience to its judgment.
>
> The obvious inconvenience, not to say impossibility, of imposing upon the Court any such task is a sufficient reason for holding that this relief should not be accorded.

Cf. however, *City of Hamilton v. Hamilton Street Ry. Co. (No. 2)* (1905), 10 O.L.R. 594 (C.A.), affd 39 S.C.R. 673, where a similar agreement was enforced. This case is discussed, *supra*, §32.

[56] *Ryan v. Mutual Tontine Westminster Chambers Ass'n*, [1893] 1 Ch. 116 (C.A.), discussed further, *infra*, §815. See also *Barnes v. City of London Real Property Co.*, [1918] 2 Ch. 18 at pp. 38-9.

[57] *Ryan v. Mutual Tontine*, *supra*, footnote 56, at p. 123.

[58] *Supra*, §§26-49.

be required is made in cases where a plaintiff has already performed his side of the bargain, and sues to enforce the defendant's obligation. Here especially, problems of supervision are superseded where specific performance is needed to provide an adequate remedy.

561 There are many examples of this type of case.[59] In a 19th century English case,[60] the plaintiff agreed to construct a railway line which was to be worked by the defendant railway. The line was built, and the defendants took possession, but the defendants failed to use the line as promised. While the court recognized that ordinarily orders requiring supervision over such a lengthy period would not be made — the term of the agreement was 999 years — it held that different principles applied where the plaintiff's obligation had been fully executed. The defendant was in possession of the benefits of the plaintiff's performance, and the court held it to be within its power to see to it that the defendant used the line as had been agreed.

562 Perhaps the best-known example of the court making orders possibly requiring extensive supervision because the agreement has been partially executed are building cases where the defendant has acquired the plaintiff's land on a promise of constructing some work upon it for the plaintiff's benefit, but has failed to carry out the construction. The courts have refused to let supervision concerns defeat the plaintiff's rights. In one case,[61] the defendant had refused to meet his obligation to construct a wharf for the plaintiff's use, having obtained as part of the bargain the land which was to be the site of the wharf. James, V.-C., said as follows:

> It would be monstrous if the company, having got the whole benefit of the agreement, could turn round and say, "This is a sort of thing which the Court finds a difficulty in doing, and will not do." Rather than allow such a gross piece of dishonesty to go unredressed the Court would struggle with any amount of difficulties in order to perform the agreement.[62]

563 There are many similar cases,[63] and by the early 20th century the

---

[59] In addition to cases cited, *infra*, footnotes 60-69, see *Ledyard v. McLean* (1863), 10 Gr. 139; *McManus v. Cooke* (1887), 35 Ch. D. 681.

[60] *Wolverhampton & Walsall Ry. Co. v. London & North-Western Ry. Co.* (1873), L.R. 16 Eq. 433.

[61] *Wilson v. Furness Ry. Co.* (1869), L.R. 9 Eq. 28.

[62] *Ibid.*, at p. 33.

[63] *Sanderson v. Cockermouth & Workington Ry. Co.* (1849), 11 Beav. 497, 50 E.R. 909; *Lytton v. Great Northern Ry. Co.* (1856), 2 K. & J. 394, 69 E.R. 836; *Price v. Corp. of Penzance* (1845), 4 Hare 506, 67 E.R. 748; *Greene v. West Cheshire Ry.*

award of specific performance in such cases was described as an exception to the rule, expressed by Romer, L.J., in the following often quoted formulation:

> . . . a plaintiff must establish three things. The first is that the building work, of which he seeks to enforce the performance, is defined by the contract; that is to say, that the particulars of the work are so far definitely ascertained that the Court can sufficiently see what is the exact nature of the work of which it is asked to order the performance. The second is that the plaintiff has a substantial interest in having the contract performed, which is of such a nature that he cannot adequately be compensated for breach of the contract by damages. The third is that the defendant has by the contract obtained possession of land on which the work is contracted to be done.[64]

564　　Stating the principle as an exception to the rule may put the matter too narrowly.[65] In a later case it was said that Romer, L.J.'s formulation ought not to be taken as being exhaustive "so as to prevent [the trial judge] granting specific performance if [he] think[s] it right to do so".[66] Specific performance has been awarded in similar cases although the work was not to be performed upon land acquired by the defendant as part of the agreement.[67] Moreover, the courts have said that in cases of part performance, they will struggle to give the plaintiff his remedy, even if description of the construction to be performed is in language which otherwise would be considered too vague to allow for the remedy.[68] An Ontario case, *Tanenbaum v.*

Co. (1871), L.R. 13 Eq. 44; *Fortescue v. Lostwithiel & Fowey Ry. Co.*, [1894] 3 Ch. 621; *Ryan v. Lockhart* (1872), 14 N.B.R. 127 (S.C.). A similar rule provided for specific performance of contracts to build on leased land, on the grounds that the security the landlord lost if the building was not erected could not otherwise be remedied; *City of London v. Nash* (1747), 1 Ves. Sen. 12, 27 E.R. 859; *Cubitt v. Smith* (1864), 11 L.T. 298; *Molyneux v. Richard*, [1906] 1 Ch. 34.

[64] *Wolverhampton Corp. v. Emmons*, [1901] 1 Q.B. 515 (C.A.), at p. 525.

[65] See Spry, *supra*, footnote 40, at pp. 107-9.

[66] *Carpenters Estates Ltd. v. Davies*, [1940] 1 Ch. 160 at p. 165, *per* Farwell, J. See also *Thomas v. Harper* (1935), 36 S.R. (N.S.W.) 142.

[67] *Greene v. West Cheshire Ry. Co.*, *supra*, footnote 63.

[68] *Hart v. Hart* (1881), 18 Ch. D. 670 at p. 685, *per* Kay, J.:

> . . . although there may be considerable vagueness in the terms, and although it may be such an agreement as the Court would hesitate to decree specific performance of, if there had not been part performance, yet when there has been part performance the Court is bound to struggle against the difficulty arising from the vagueness.

See also *Molyneux v. Richard*, *supra*, footnote 63, at p. 42, *per* Kekewich, J., holding that an agreement to build dwellings "similar to" other dwellings nearby was sufficiently defined: "It cannot have been intended [by the Court of Appeal in the *Wolverhampton* case, *supra*, footnote 64] that 'clearly specified' should mean leav-

W.J. Bell Paper Co.,[69] puts the practice on a more general basis. There, the defendant had acquired a parcel of land from the plaintiff, and had promised to construct a roadway over the acquired parcel to provide the plaintiff with access to a parcel he retained. Gale, J., granted specific performance of the defendant's obligation to construct the road, and adopting a passage from *Williston on Contracts*,[70] stated:

> The basis of equity's disinclination to enforce building contracts specifically is the difficulty of enforcing a decree without an expenditure of effort disproportionate to the value of the result. But where the inadequacy of damages is great, and the difficulties not extreme, specific performance will be granted and the tendency in modern times has been increasingly towards granting relief, where under the particular circumstances of the case damages are not an adequate remedy.[71]

(3) Modern trend

565   This statement reflects what is becoming an increasing tendency to play down supervision problems and a willingness to decree specific performance of long-term or complex obligations which do involve the risk of future supervision. Cases involving long-term supply arrangements are discussed below.[72] Megarry, V.-C., has said that while "it was at one time said that an order for the specific performance of the contract would not be made if there would be difficulty in the court supervising its execution . . . [t]he real question is whether there is a sufficient definition of what has to be done in order to comply with the order of the court."[73]

566   Similarly, in *Beswick v. Beswick*,[74] the House of Lords held that an agreement to be performed over time and hence requiring supervision ought to be specifically enforced if no other adequate remedy could be found: "It is argued that the court should be deterred from making the order because there will be technical difficulties in enforcing it. In my opinion, the court should not lightly be deterred by

---

ing no room for doubt." In some cases, the court was prepared to deal with the case in stages to overcome problems of definition; see *Price v. Corp. of Penzance, supra*, footnote 63, and the injunction cases, discussed, *supra*, §§33-38.

[69] (1956), 4 D.L.R. (2d) 177, [1956] O.R. 278 (H.C.J.).

[70] Rev. ed., vol. 5 (New York, Baker, Voorhis & Co., 1937), at pp. 3976-7. This same passage appears in the most recent edition (3rd ed., vol. 11, 1968), at pp. 762-3.

[71] *Supra*, footnote 69, at p. 204 D.L.R., p. 307 O.R.

[72] *Infra*, §660.

[73] *Tito v. Waddell (No. 2)*, [1977] Ch. 106, at pp. 321-2.

[74] [1968] A.C. 58 (H.L.).

567 such a consideration from making an order which justice requires."[75]

Again, to quote Megarry, J., in another case:

> Of course, a requirement for the continuous performance of service has the disadvantage that repeated breaches may engender repeated applications to the court for enforcement. But so may many injunctions; and the prospects of repetition, although an important consideration, ought not to be allowed to negative a right. As is so often the case in equity, the matter is one of the balance of advantage and disadvantage in relation to the particular obligations in question; and the fact that the balance will usually lie on one side does not turn this probability into a rule.[76]

(4) Basis for concern over supervision

568 It may be concluded that the tendency to refuse specific performance in cases involving supervision has never been absolute, and is now becoming much less pronounced.[77] It is, then, particularly appropriate to consider the question of supervision as a matter of principle and to examine the factors which ought to be taken into account. The precise reason for equity's concern in this area requires careful analysis. There appear to be several aspects to it. First, from an historical perspective, the reluctance of chancery to grant specific performance in cases which might involve supervision of a series of acts perhaps stemmed from the genuine fear that an order which might not be enforced would jeopardize the dignity of the court.[78] It may be that this fear, although originally fed by the rivalry of the

---

[75] *Ibid.*, at p. 91, *per* Lord Pearce.

[76] *C.H. Giles & Co. v. Morris*, [1972] 1 W.L.R. 307 (Ch.), at p. 318, a passage quoted with approval in *Price v. Strange*, [1978] Ch. 337 (C.A.), at pp. 359-60.

[77] In several cases, the courts have ordered defendants to make "best efforts" to obtain planning or building approvals: *Dynamic Transport Ltd. v. O.K. Detailing Ltd.*, [1978] 2 S.C.R. 1072, 85 D.L.R. (3d) 19; *Steiner v. E.H.D. Investments Ltd.* (1977), 78 D.L.R. (3d) 449 (Alta. S.C. App. Div.), leave to appeal to S.C.C. refused November 21, 1977; *Ludlow v. Beattie* (1978), 87 D.L.R. (3d) 561, 20 O.R. (2d) 363 (H.C.J.). See also *Jeune v. Queens Cross Properties Ltd.*, [1974] 1 Ch. 97 (specific enforcement of landlord's obligation to repair); *Bennison Lane Enterprises Ltd. v. W. Krause Logging Ltd.*, [1977] 6 W.W.R. 93 (B.C.S.C.), at p. 96, *per* Lander, L.J.S.C.:
> . . . counsel for the defendant queried how the court could ensure such an order would be carried out. The simple reply is that the court need not ensure or oversee it — it cannot. The defendant and plaintiffs have been working together prior in time; they know what is the reality of the situation in the forest. The court relies on honourable men to use reason and to apply common sense and the interference that exists will cease.

[78] See Pound, "The Progress of the Law, 1918-1919, Equity", 33 Harv. L. Rev. 420 (1920), at p. 425.

pre-Judicature Act dual court system, retains some validity. The court should try to avoid issuing orders which are unlikely to be effective. Part of the judge's task is to fashion a remedy which will achieve a practical result. To the extent the court fails to ensure that its pronouncement of the rights of the parties is given concrete effect, there is a risk that respect for the judicial process might diminish.[79] Hence, in the words of a modern text, "Equity's view is that of a wise parent dealing with his children; it is best not to issue orders unless you can be absolutely sure of effecting compliance."[80]

569 On the other hand, the difficulty of ensuring compliance reflected by this thinking can easily be overstated. Casting the problem in terms of supervision is perhaps apt to mislead. The court itself does not supervise the defendant's performance by maintaining an active interest in the case simply because it has made a specific performance decree. The plaintiff is the one who will monitor the adequacy of the defendant's performance, and the court will only be involved where the plaintiff considers that the defendant has failed to comply, and that his failure merits a contempt application. It is not at all clear that the dignity of the court suffers in the unlikely event that resort must be had to imprisonment for contemptuous refusal to comply with the positive decree. The availability of a remedy to which the innocent party is otherwise entitled is surely not to be determined by the suspected extent of the recalcitrance of the party in breach. Courts have never refused to make damage awards because the judgment may not be collectable, and it may well be the case that a greater threat to the integrity of a judicial system is posed by the granting of an unenforceable damages award in that sanctions for non-compliance are much less severe.

570 So long as the obligation is sufficiently defined,[81] enforcement machinery can be made available to ensure compliance.[82] In light of

---

[79] *Re Morris and Morris* (1973), 42 D.L.R. (3d) 550 (Man. C.A.), p. 569, *per* Guy, J.A., refusing to make an order requiring the defendant to satisfy a contractual obligation to obtain a Jewish bill of divorcement:

> It is true, in the instant case, that Mr. Morris could be fined or imprisoned for contempt if he failed to appear before the rabbinical court. That would not accomplish the performance of the so-called contract. That would simply be a matter of a superior Court in Canada demeaning both itself and the administration of justice by delivering with great solemnity a judgment that nobody can enforce.

[80] Hanbury and Maudsley, *Modern Equity*, 11th ed. by Maudsley and Martin (London, Stevens & Sons, 1981), at p. 54.

[81] *Infra*, §576.

[82] This was recognized in the construction cases discussed, *supra*, §§560-564. See *e.g.*,

modern regulatory experience in an age of closely enforced building, safety and industrial standards, difficulty of enforcement is an unconvincing reason for refusing specific performance. The point has already been examined in the context of injunctions where it was suggested that too little had been made of the cases in which the courts had seen fit to enforce complex obligations.[83] It is suggested that the real concern here is the implication of relitigation and the expenditure of judicial resources which may be involved in obtaining enforcement rather than any question as to the court's ability to ensure the performance of obligations if it decides to make a specific decree.[84]

571   From this perspective, the supervision concern differs from other criteria determining the availability of specific relief. It is based, not upon the weighing of relative advantage and disadvantage to the parties, but rather on the weighing of the advantage of doing justice by granting specific relief against the general cost to society of having justice administered. By way of contrast to specific relief, damage awards do hold certain advantages. A money judgment is final, and enforcement is left to the administrative rather than the judicial machinery of the court. The cost of enforcement is largely borne by the parties. A decree for specific performance does involve a substantially higher risk that further judicial resources will be required. The more complex or extended the performance, the more likely further proceedings will be needed to ascertain whether the defendant has complied with his obligations. This fear of extended and complex litigation and the need for repeated requests for judicial intervention may be seen as a legitimate concern. The cost to society of providing the resources necessary to implement specific performance decrees is properly considered by the court when weighing the advantages the specific relief might otherwise offer.

572   On the other hand, calculation of the increased cost incurred by ordering specific performance is extremely difficult. While the courts have assumed that specific performance is more "costly" from this

---

Storer v. Great Western Ry. Co. (1842), 2 Y. & C.C.C. 48 at p. 53, 63 E.R. 21, *per* Knight Bruce, V.-C.:
> . . . the Plaintiff has a right to specific performance, and it is competent to this Court to say that the work shall be properly done. . . . There is no difficulty in enforcing such a decree. The Court has to order the thing to be done, and then it is a question capable of solution whether the order has been obeyed.

[83] *Supra,* §§29-38.

[84] See Kronman, *supra,* footnote 22, who discusses but does not entirely accept the point.

point of view, others have argued that these difficulties are exaggerated.[85] Specific performance does avoid the time and cost in litigation of having damages assessed, and this saving might well balance to some extent the loss occasioned by securing performance in certain cases. Moreover, as noted in the discussion of supervision relating to injunctions, there are many other situations in which the courts do undertake an ongoing role in the regulation of management of the litigant's affairs.[86] Most litigation is much more complex now than it was years ago when these principles were first formulated. Lengthy trials are the rule and the burden a specific decree would impose on the court is now relatively much less significant than it was in the past.

573 Still, the problem posed by the suspected additional cost of specific performance to society at large is a difficult one. In formulating rules to govern the availability of specific relief, the courts have given it little explicit attention. It is fundamentally different in nature from the normal judicial task which involves choosing a remedy which meets the particular interests of the parties. To say to the party that although enforcement could be assured, and would provide a more satisfactory remedy, it will not be made because it is too expensive to society is surely harsh. On the other hand, there must be a limit to the resources which can be devoted to achieving justice between particular parties in a private dispute.[87]

---

[85] The possibility that making all promises specifically enforceable or allowing parties to stipulate performance might reduce the involvement of courts, and thereby save on judicial resources, is raised by Kronman, *supra*, footnote 22, at pp. 373-74. The calculus, according to Kronman, is a complex one, and requires consideration of the following factors:

> (1) the frequency of litigation under both rules; (2) the administrative cost of resolving litigated disputes under both rules; (3) the portion of the administrative costs involved in dispute resolution borne by the parties and the portion borne by society under both rules; (4) the likelihood and cost, under each rule, of pretrial settlement; and (5) special institutional costs, such as the potential loss in court prestige that results from non-compliance with a direct order to perform, and the cost of invoking the court's contempt powers.

See also Schwartz, *supra*, footnote 10, at p. 294, note 67, stating that even if such decrees involve more work, greater efficiency might be achieved "because the prospect of these decrees might induce more parties to settle or perform because judges might expand output".

[86] *Supra*, §48.

[87] Schwartz, *supra*, footnote 10, at p. 294, argues that the cost of supervision might effectively be shifted to the parties by appointing special masters, to be "used to fashion decrees as well as to supervise performance". The cost of such masters would be borne by the parties, and could be imposed on the party in breach so as to

574   Another important aspect of specifically enforcing contracts involving long-term relationships does, however, relate to the balancing of interest between the parties. The consideration here is the
desire to avoid forcing a contractual relationship which has gone
sour. Specific performance of a contract requiring performance over
time will force an unwilling defendant back into his relationship with
the plaintiff. Friction between the parties is likely, and satisfactory
performance of the promised obligation may be extracted only with
difficulty. It may often be better to avoid remedial intervention
which may unduly force the relationship. This concern has been especially strong in the context of personal service contracts.[88]

575   Again, however, it is suggested that care should be taken not to
give undue weight to this factor. It is necessary to consider whether
specific relief is being refused to protect the plaintiff or the defendant. It will be rare, it is submitted, for the court to know more than
the plaintiff about the likelihood of being able to compel satisfactory
performance. If the plaintiff is prepared to accept the risk of grudging compliance from the defendant or even the defendant's outright
refusal to obey, it should not be for the court to decline the remedy
to which the plaintiff is otherwise entitled, unless it is considered that
an order would entail undue expenditure of judicial resources. The
defendant's interest may, however, often deserve protection. Where
the contract involves a long-term relationship, a specific performance
decree may well become an instrument for oppression. The possibility for post-judgment bargaining has already been considered,[89] and
clearly cases which involve complex or long-term performance may
often pose problems of that type. Courts have guarded against granting specific relief where to do so will permit the plaintiff to extract a
payment from the defendant which is measured not by the plaintiff's
own loss, but by the extent of the inconvenience or difficulty the
specific decree imposes upon the defendant.[90]

576   Another point to consider is the question of uncertainty or vagueness. Where the nature of required performance is ill-defined, specific performance may cause difficulty.[91] First, if the plaintiff complains

---

   give the innocent party the complete protection of specific performance at no additional cost.

[88] Discussed in greater detail, *infra*, §§577-586.

[89] *Supra*, §§538, 539.

[90] *Supra*, §§537-539.

[91] See, *e.g.*, *South Wales Ry. Co. v. Wythes* (1854), 5 De G.M. & G. 880, 43 E.R.
   1112; *Greenhill v. Isle of Wight (Newport Junction) Ry. Co.* (1871), 19 W.R. 345

that the defendant has failed to comply with the decree, it may be a difficult matter to assess the adequacy of the performance which has been rendered. Secondly, it is sometimes said that the decree for performance of such an obligation may operate harshly on the defendant in that he would not know what he has to do to avoid a finding of contempt.[92] Often it will be easier and more practicable to measure damages than to require performance where details of the defendant's obligation are vague. For example, damages can readily be assessed where the defendant breaks his contract to build a house of a certain value on leased land. It would be quite another matter, however, to force the defendant to build a house of such value without construction details.[93] To the extent there is difficulty in assessing damages in such cases, it is perhaps preferable to the greater problems uncertainty causes if the obligation is put in the form of a specific decree. Thus, in assessing the wisdom of ordering specific performance, the court will want to examine not only the nature of the obligation, but also the extent of its definition, and the extent to which it tells the defendant precisely what it is he must do, and hence allow for accurate judgment of the adequacy of his performance.

(Ch.); *Brace v. Wehnert* (1858), 25 Beav. 348 at p. 351, 53 E.R. 670, *per* Romilly, M.R.: "An agreement for building a house of a certain value is not one which this Court will direct to be specifically performed. The Court would have great difficulty in determining whether its decree had or had not been performed, and it might lead to much litigation"; *Wilson v. Northampton & Banbury Junction Ry. Co.* (1874), 9 Ch. App. 279 at p. 284, *per* Selborne, L.C.:

. . . the Court gives specific performance instead of damages, only when it can by that means do more perfect and complete justice. An agreement, which is not so specific in its terms or in its nature as to make it certain that better justice will be done by attempting specifically to perform it than by leaving the parties to their remedy in damages, is not one which the Court will specifically perform.

See also *Joseph v. National Magazine Co. Ltd.*, [1959] Ch. 14 (court not prepared to supervise defendant's editing of plaintiff's article, but prepared to award damages for defendant's failure to publish). Compare *Hepburn v. Leather* (1884), 50 L.T. 660, granting specific performance of a contract to build a wall where the work was well defined.

[92] *Redland Bricks Ltd. v. Morris*, [1970] A.C. 652 (H.L.) (mandatory injunction case discussed, *supra*, §§42-44 and 60); *Mosely v. Virgin* (1796), 3 Ves. Jun. 184 at p. 185, 30 E.R. 959, *per* Loughborough, L.C.:

. . . if the transaction and agreement is in its nature defined, perhaps there would not be much difficulty to decree specific performance: but if it is loose and undefined, and it is not expressed distinctly what the building is, so that the Court could describe it as a subject for the report of the Master, the jurisdiction could not apply.

[93] *Brace v. Wehnert, supra*, footnote 91. *Cf.*, *supra*, footnotes 63, 68.

4. Contracts of Personal Service

577   There has always been a strong reluctance to grant specific performance of contracts of personal service. Such contracts are characterized by their personal and non-delegable nature. Very often the continuation of the contract entails the continuation of a personal relationship which the courts can neither require nor enforce. Although the refusal of specific relief in such cases is amply supported by authority,[94] it has recently been judicially described as a "strong reluctance rather than a rule",[95] and arguments in favour of the greater availability of specific relief in such cases are often heard.[96] It is, then, of interest to consider the reasons for the attitude courts have taken as there are now exceptional cases in which specific relief may be justified,[97] and the possibility that over the long run the courts may become more flexible. Admittedly, the issue will arise in relatively few cases as most contracts of employment are subject to termination on reasonable notice by either party so that relatively few employers or employees have an interest in seeking specific performance.

578   Several reasons have been given to explain the refusal of the courts to grant specific performance of contracts of personal service. The supervision argument may be dealt with first. The concern here ordinarily relates to the performance of the employee's obligations and

---

[94] See, *e.g., Red Deer College v. Michaels*, [1976] 2 S.C.R. 324 at pp. 342-4, 57 D.L.R. (3d) 386 at pp. 399-400, *per* Laskin, C.J.C.; *McWhirter v. Governors of University of Alberta (No. 2)* (1977), 80 D.L.R. (3d) 609 (Alta. S.C.), revd on other grounds 103 D.L.R. (3d) 255 (C.A.), leave to appeal to S.C.C. refused *loc. cit.* p. 255*n*; *Kapp v. B.C. Lions Football Club* (1967), 64 D.L.R. (2d) 426 (B.C.S.C.); *Ross v. C.N.R.*, [1928] 2 D.L.R. 880 (Man. C.A.); *Field v. C.N.R.*, [1934] 3 D.L.R. 383 (N.S.C.A.); *Southern Foundries (1926) Ltd. v. Shirlaw*, [1940] A.C. 701 (H.L.), at p. 723, *per* Lord Wright: "No one, individual or company, can be compelled against his or their will, to employ a man, though, if the contract is broken, damages will have to be paid."

[95] *C.H. Giles & Co. v. Morris*, [1972] 1 W.L.R. 307 (Ch.), at p. 318, *per* Megarry, J.

[96] See Brown, "Contract Remedies in a Planned Economy: Labour Arbitration Leads the Way", Chapter 4 in *Studies in Contract Law, supra*, footnote 1; Cohen, "The Relationship of Contractual Remedies to Political and Social Status: A Preliminary Inquiry", 32 U. of T. L.J. 31 (1982); Kyer, "A Case Study in Party Stipulation of Remedy: The N.H.L. Standard Player's Contract", 39 U. of T. Fac. of Law Rev. 1 (1981); Whitehill, "Enforceability of Professional Sports Contracts — What's the Harm in it?", 35 Southwestern L.J. 803 (1981); Parks, "Equitable Relief in Contracts Involving Personal Services", 66 U. of Pa. L. Rev. 251 (1918).

[97] See *Hill v. Parsons & Co.*, [1972] Ch. 305 (C.A.), discussed, *infra*, §585. See also *C.H. Giles & Co. v. Morris, supra*, footnote 95; *Price v. Strange*, [1978] Ch. 337 (C.A.), at pp. 359-60; *Bell v. Milner* (1956), 3 D.L.R. (2d) 202 (B.C.S.C.), discussed, *infra*, footnote 112.

arises where the employer sues. It was well expressed by Megarry, J., who, while not choosing to characterize the problem as involving "the difficulties of constant superintendence by the court", did explain the point in the following amusing terms:

> The reasons why the court is reluctant to decree specific performance of a contract for personal services (and I would regard it as a strong reluctance rather than a rule) are, I think, more complex and more firmly bottomed on human nature. If a singer contracts to sing, there could no doubt be proceedings for committal if, ordered to sing, the singer remained obstinately dumb. But if instead the singer sang flat, or sharp, or too fast, or too slowly, or too loudly, or too quietly, or resorted to a dozen of the manifestations of temperament traditionally associated with some singers, the threat of committal would reveal itself as a most unsatisfactory weapon: for who could say whether the imperfections of performance were natural or self-induced? To make an order with such possibilites of evasion would be vain: and so the order will not be made. However, not all contracts of personal service or for the continuous performance of services are as dependent as this on matters of opinion and judgment, nor do all such contracts involve the same degree of the daily impact of person upon person.[98]

579   Obligations of an artistic, sophisticated or highly specialized nature may be difficult to supervise because judgment of the adequacy of performance of an unwilling defendant would be difficult. On the other hand, it could be argued that performers of this kind may often be sufficiently motivated by their own pride and desire to maintain their reputation.[99] Another point is that in such situations, the plaintiff will be more aware than the judge of the temperament of the defendant and of the chances of enforced performance being adequate by the plaintiff's standard. Moreover, as Megarry, J., observed, not all employment contracts involve delicate assessment of performance on the basis of opinion or judgment, nor do they invariably impose a close personal relationship. Many, if not most, modern employment arrangements involve performance of well-defined tasks of an impersonal nature, and this surely diminishes the strength of the supervision argument. History shows that the court could enforce such a contract if it wanted to. In the 19th century, employment contracts were indeed enforced under master-and-servant legislation which imposed criminal penalties for breach.[100] A more powerful argument against the enforcement of employment contracts at the suit of the

---

[98] *Supra*, footnote 95, at p. 318.
[99] See Kyer, *supra*, footnote 96, at p. 27.
[100] See Cohen, *supra*, footnote 96, at pp. 68-9.

employer is that granting specific performance would be tantamount to a form of slavery.[101] The moral argument that promises should be kept gives way to another, deemed to be of greater force, namely, that an individual should not be allowed to sell himself into a situation which amounts to involuntary servitude. However difficult it may be to assess damages, it is surely preferable to limit the plaintiff to damages than to force the defendant to continue his employment on pain of contempt and imprisonment.

580   The closest the courts have come to awarding specific performance of personal service contracts at the suit of the employer is through the *Lumley v. Wagner* injunction.[102] There, it was held that the court could grant an injunction to restrain a famous opera singer from breaking her promise not to sing for anyone else, while at the same time the court acknowledged its inability to grant specific performance of her promise to perform for the plaintiff. The line of cases following *Lumley v. Wagner* is considered in detail in Chapter 9, where it is argued that there is a valid distinction between granting specific performance of a personal service contract and enforcing the negative terms of such contracts where the employer has a legitimate interest in their enforcement apart from the pressure enforcement puts on the plaintiff to perform his positive obligations.

581   The Supreme Court of Canada has expressly upheld an injunction prohibiting a strike "engaged in in direct violation of the terms of a collective agreement binding on the striking employees and in breach of the express provisions of the [Provincial Labour Relations] Act",[103] thereby ordering the defendants to return to work. In so holding, the court accepted the proposition that an ageement for hiring and service constituting the common relation of master and servant will not be specifically enforced, but added:

> There is a real difference between saying to one individual that he must go on working for another individual and saying to a group bound by a collective agreement that they must not take concerted ac-

---

[101] See *Millican v. Sulivan* (1888), 4 T.L.R. 203 (C.A.); *De Francesco v. Barnum* (1890), 45 Ch. D. 430 at p. 438, *per* Fry, L.J.:
> . . . I should be very unwilling to extend decisions the effect of which is to compel persons who are not desirous of maintaining continuous personal relations with one another to continue those personal relations. . . . I think the Courts are bound to be jealous, lest they should turn contracts of service into contracts of slavery.

[102] Discussed in detail, *infra*, §§689-698.

[103] *Int'l Brotherhood of Electrical Workers v. Winnipeg Builders Exchange*, [1967] S.C.R. 628 at p. 640, 65 D.L.R. (2d) 242 at p. 251.

tion to break this contract and to disobey the statute law of the province. . . . to hold otherwise would be to render illusory the protection afforded to the parties by a collective agreement and by the statute.[104]

582 Where the employee rather than the employer sues, the considerations are different and, it is suggested, there seems more reason to doubt the wisdom of invariably refusing specific relief. Normally, the employer's obligation will not require constant supervision. The concern here is usually expressed in terms of the trust and confidence owed by an employee to his employer.[105] If specific performance were granted in favour of the employee, the element of trust and confidence necessary to the healthy maintenance of the relationship would be absent, and accordingly, the employer should be protected from having the relationship forced upon him.

583 Again it is suggested that the force of the trust and confidence concern will depend very much upon the nature of the employee's obligation. If the employee's task is clearly defined, relatively impersonal, and allows for a readily measurable performance, it is surely difficult to justify the refusal of specific performance on this ground alone. The experience gained in the field of labour arbitration strongly suggests that the courts have been unnecessarily cautious in this context.[106] There, reinstatement is a routinely available

---

[104] *Ibid.*, at pp. 640-1 S.C.R., p. 251 D.L.R., *per* Cartwright, J. See also *McLaughlin v. Westward Shipping Ltd.* (1959), 21 D.L.R. (2d) 770 (B.C.S.C.); *W.C. Wells Construction Co. Ltd. v. Sloney* (1968), 69 D.L.R. (2d) 685 (Sask. Q.B.); *Winnipeg Builders Exchange v. Operative Plasterers and Cement Masons Int'l Ass'n* (1964), 48 D.L.R. (2d) 173 (Man. C.A.); *Prince Albert Pulp Co. Ltd. v. Davidson* (1970), 14 D.L.R. (3d) 509 (Sask. C.A.). *Cf. Brady v. Heinekey and Black Ball Ferries Ltd.* (1960), 24 D.L.R. (2d) 737 (B.C.C.A.), and *Board of Broadview School Unit No. 18 of Saskatchewan v. Saskatchewan Teachers' Federation* (1972), 32 D.L.R. (3d) 33 (Sask.C.A.), both refusing injunctions on the merits.

[105] See, *e.g., Pickering v. Bishop of Ely* (1843), 2 Y. & C.C.C. 249 at p. 267, 63 E.R. 109, refusing an injunction to restrain the defendant from interfering with the plaintiff's exercise of office as receiver of profits and rents from lands of the bishopric, which order would have amounted to specific performance, *per* Knight Bruce, V.-C.:

To force upon [the defendant] . . . a person however estimable, however professionally eminent, who is objectionable to him, or in whom he does not happen to confide, would, if legal, be surely hard; and sitting in a Court of Equity, I do not feel any inclination to do it.

See also *Page One Records Ltd. v. Britton*, [1968] 1 W.L.R. 157 (Ch.); *Red Deer College v. Michaels, supra,* footnote 94. See also *Chappell v. Times Newspapers*, [1975] 1 W.L.R. 482 (C.A.), at p. 506, *per* Geoffrey Lane, L.J.: " . . . if one party has no faith in the honesty or integrity or the loyalty of the other, to force him to serve or to employ that other is a plain recipe for disaster."

[106] Brown, *supra*, footnote 96.

remedy. Similarly, employees who hold positions under statutory authority are often entitled to reinstatement where there has been a failure to observe appropriate procedures leading to their dismissal.[107] Human rights legislation often provides for reinstatement of employees unfairly dismissed in violation of non-discrimination standards.[108] It would not appear that reinstatement in these cases creates unusual difficulties. Moreover, legislation typically provides that arbitration awards are to be enforced by the court in the event of non-compliance.[109] Thus, to this extent the courts already are engaged in the enforcement of such orders. Even if difficulties are encountered, the issue is whether the employee's interest in having his contractual rights fully protected is sufficiently strong to justify risking those difficulties. It has been argued that the status of employment may often mean more to the employee than can properly be reflected by a damages award.[110] If that argument is accepted, it is suggested that so long as the task or service to be performed is of the character just described, protection of the plaintiff's employment status may be achieved without necessarily forcing the parties into a debilitating and frictional relationship.

584 Where the plaintiff seeking specific performance would be required to perform services of a highly specialized or personal nature, there may be more reason for concern. If the employment relationship requires close personal contact between employer and employee, the difficulties of enforced performance are obvious. Indeed, before the full development of the mass production economy of the 20th century, most employment contracts were probably of a more personal nature, and from an historical point of view, the traditional refusal to grant specific performance is readily understood.

585 The admittedly unusual case of *Hill v. Parsons & Co.*[111] indicates a

---

[107] See, *e.g.*, *Vine v. National Dock Labour Board*, [1957] A.C. 488 (H.L.), at p. 500; *Ridge v. Baldwin*, [1964] A.C. 40 (H.L.); *Placsko v. Board of Humboldt School Unit No. 47 of Sask.* (1971), 18 D.L.R. (3d) 374 (Sask. Q.B.), affd 22 D.L.R. (3d) 663 (C.A.); *Re Wright and Public Service Staff Relations Board*, [1973] F.C. 765, 40 D.L.R. (3d) 698 (C.A.); Napier, "Injunctions to Stop Dismissals", 133 New L.J. 68 (1983). *Cf. Francis v. Municipal Councillors of Kuala Lumpur*, [1962] 3 All E.R. 633 (P.C.).

[108] See, *e.g.*, Saskatchewan Human Rights Code, s. 31(7)(*b*).

[109] Such an order was upheld in *Zeller's (Western) Ltd. v. Retail, Wholesale & Department Store Union*, [1975]·1 S.C.R. 376, 40 D.L.R. (3d) 761. *Cf. Rankin v. National Harbours Board* (1979), 99 D.L.R. (3d) 631 (B.C.S.C.), vard 127 D.L.R. (3d) 714 (C.A.), where damages were awarded for failure to comply with an arbitrator's reinstatement award.

[110] Cohen, *supra*, footnote 96; Beatty, "Labour is Not a Commodity", Chapter 9 in *Studies in Contract Law, supra*, footnote 1.

[111] [1972] Ch. 305 (C.A.). *Hill v. Parsons* has been described as "unusual if not

judicial willingness to look beyond the black letter rules. There, the English Court of Appeal granted an injunction against an employer to prevent the dismissal of an employee, on the grounds that the employee's interest in pension and retirement benefits could not be adequately compensated through a damages award, and because the employer's motive for dismissal was pressure from the closed-shop trade union which the plaintiff refused to join. The element of trust and confidence between the plaintiff and defendant appeared unimpaired, and although the court undoubtedly ran the risk of strife between the employer and the trade union, its decision does indicate a willingness to look behind the stated rule against specific relief, and to the very nature of the relationship to see whether the rationale behind the rule would be met by its application.[112]

586 It may well be that the Canadian courts are less willing to risk the disruption such an injunction might cause to labour-management relationships in order to ensure an individual an appropriate remedy. In three recent cases,[113] Canadian courts have refused injunctive relief at the suit of an employee who challenged the legality of mandatory age retirement. In each case, the applicant had brought proceedings before the Canadian Human Rights Commission, and sought interlocutory injunctive relief to protect his right to be reinstated in the event the Commission should find in his favour. One judge was willing to adopt the reasoning of *Hill v. Parsons*, on the grounds that damages could not compensate the plaintiff for the lost sense of purpose or fulfilment he would derive from the exercise of his profession.[114] However, this holding was reversed on appeal where the Ontario Divisional Court[115] followed an earlier British Columbia decision[116] in finding on the facts that substantial damages had

---

unique" in subsequent English cases: see *Chappell v. Times Newspapers, supra,* footnote 105, at p. 503, *per* Stephenson, L.J., citing *Sanders v. Ernest A. Neale Ltd.*, [1974] I.C.R. 565 at p. 571, *per* Donaldson, J.

[112] See also *Bell v. Milner* (1956), 3 D.L.R. (2d) 202 (B.C.S.C.), restraining a trustee for bondholders from discharging a manager in the face of an express agreement not to discharge him except under certain conditions, on the grounds that the plaintiff might otherwise be left with a hollow claim for damages, and also because he had personally guaranteed the company's indebtedness and stood to lose more than his job if the company failed.

[113] *Stevenson v. Air Canada* (1982), 132 D.L.R. (3d) 406, 35 O.R. (2d) 68 (Div. Ct.); *Chambers v. Canadian Pacific Air Ltd.* (1981), 128 D.L.R. (3d) 673 (B.C.S.C.); *Lamont v. Air Canada* (1981), 126 D.L.R. (3d) 266, 34 O.R. (2d) 195 (H.C.J.).

[114] *Stevenson v. Air Canada* (1981), 126 D.L.R. (3d) 242 (Ont. H.C.J.), *per* Henry, J.

[115] *Stevenson, supra,* footnote 113.

[116] *Chambers v. Canadian Pacific Air Ltd., supra,* footnote 113.

not been suffered. The court went on to point out that granting the injunction would frustrate the expectations of younger pilots and possibly lead to the filing of innumerable grievances.[117] An important aspect of the refusal of injunctive relief was, however, the determination that, as the matter was within the jurisdiction of the Canadian Human Rights Commission, no relief was available from the courts and, accordingly, it may still be the case that the Canadian courts will apply the reasoning of *Hill v. Parsons* where a case is entirely within their competence.

5. Party Stipulation

(1) Introduction

587   Contracts often purport to specify the remedy available upon breach. There are many varieties of remedy clauses.[118] Parties may attempt to increase the burden of breach by a penalty clause so as to coerce performance. Frequently, an attempt is made to pre-estimate damages, and the remedy clause provides for payment of that liquidated amount in the event of breach. Perhaps less common are the clauses to be discussed here, those providing for either specific performance or injunction. In general, the courts have zealously guarded the question of remedy as their own preserve. A fundamental question is posed, namely, to what extent may the parties ensure the protection of certain interests which they fear the standard legal and equitable doctrines will fail to recognize?

588   The treatment afforded remedy stipulation clauses by the courts comprises an important and difficult body of case-law. Detailed con-

---

[117] *Stevenson, supra,* footnote 113, at p. 414 D.L.R., p. 76 O.R., *per* Osler, J.

[118] The impact of liquidated damages clauses upon damages is discussed by Waddams, *supra,* footnote 9, §§916-949. For a general discussion, see Brownsword, " 'Remedy-Stipulation' in the English Law of Contract—Freedom or Paternalism?", 9 Ottawa L. Rev. 95 (1977); Macneil, "Power of Contract and Agreed Remedies", 47 Cornell L.Q. 495 (1962); McDowell, "Party Autonomy in Contract Remedies" 57 Boston Univ. L. Rev. 429 (1977); Clarkson, Miller and Muris, "Liquidated Damages v. Penalties: Sense or Nonsense?", [1978] Wisc. L. Rev. 351; Goetz and Scott, "Liquidated Damages, Penalties and the Just Compensation Principle: Some Notes on an Enforcement Model and a Theory of Efficient Breach", 77 Columbia L. Rev. 554 (1977). In addition to clauses specifying liquidated damages or specific relief, many contractual terms may amount to remedy stipulation, *e.g.*, a provision that a certain term is a contractual condition so as to give rise to the promisee's election to treat the contract as at an end; arbitration clauses; choice of forum or choice of law clauses in inter-jurisdictional contracts; provisions for rejection or other remedies in the context of sale of goods; repossession or other remedies in security instruments.

sideration of liquidated damages and penalty clauses is found in the companion volume.[119] The wary judicial attitude to allowing parties to stipulate remedies may be seen in some cases as an unjustifiable restriction on the freedom of contracting parties to arrange their affairs as they see fit. In other cases, it may be justified as the imposition of an external standard deemed necessary by the courts to achieve justice. Very often, the motivation appears to be to prevent unconscionable dealing or unfairness in arriving at such a clause.[120] Other explanations have also been suggested. It has been argued that contractual remedies should be limited to a principle of just compensation,[121] and that the parties should be denied a power to impose sanctions which go beyond the protection of reliance, expectation, or restitutionary interests.[122] It has also been suggested that the refusal to enforce penalty clauses can be supported on economic efficiency grounds[123] but, on the other hand, economic analysis has also been used to support upholding specific performance clauses.[124]

589 It is difficult to see how any of the theories mentioned could be taken to justify the court in ignoring a clause stipulating a specific remedy. Unless the circumstances have changed so that the burden of actual performance is significantly greater than contemplated at the time of contracting, it can hardly be unconscionable to require performance of the very thing that was promised. The principle of just compensation or any possible limited power of contract available to the parties is not violated. As indicated, efficiency analysis tends to support respecting party stipulation of specific performance.[125] Yet it is sometimes suggested that such clauses should be regarded with considerable suspicion. The argument is usually expressed in terms of discretion. Since the equitable remedies are discretionary by their nature, it is said that the parties lack the power to impose them as a

[119] Waddams, *supra*, footnote 9, §§916-949.
[120] *Ibid.*
[121] See *Restatement of the Law Second: Contracts* (St. Paul, American Law Institute Publishers, 1981), §356.
[122] See especially Macneil, *supra*, footnote 118.
[123] See Clarkson, Miller and Muris, *supra*, footnote 118.
[124] See Kronman, *supra*, footnote 22, and Goetz and Scott, *supra*, footnote 118. *Cf.* Clarkson, Miller and Muris, *supra*, footnote 118, suggesting that efficiency analysis indicates that penalty clauses should be enforced only where the opportunity to induce breach is not present so that there is no incentive on the part of the promisee to get the advantage of the penalty by inducing the promisor to breach his contract. It is inconsistent to induce breach and get performance. Thus, this analysis would presumably also support the enforcement of a specific performance clause.
[125] *Supra*, §588.

remedial solution.[126] This, however, hardly provides a rationale. Discretion is not completely open-ended and its exercise is defined by certain standards and even rules. Discretion does not necessarily exclude party choice as an important, perhaps even governing, factor, and certainly does not mean that careful examination as to the weight to be attached to party stipulation is not called for.

590　　　There is, of course, a long tradition in the courts of equity of ignoring such clauses in related contexts. The early and well-established doctrine permitting the court to relieve from forfeiture of penalties and other such clauses provides an example.[127]

(2) Liquidated damage clauses and specific relief

591　　　The effect of a liquidated damages clause on a plaintiff's right to either specific performance or an injunction has been raised in a number of cases.[128] The principle which emerges is that a clause specifying the amount of damages to be paid upon breach will preclude the innocent party from obtaining an equitable remedy otherwise available only where the contract can be said to impose an obligation on the part of the defendant which can be satisfied either by performance or by payment of the stipulated sum. It is rare for the court to find that the damages clause was intended to give the defendant a choice between performing or paying the stipulated amount, and hence in most cases, specific relief will be granted despite the liquidated damages clause.

592　　　In an English case, *Howard v. Hopkyns*,[129] Hardwicke, L.C., rejected the argument that a provision requiring a breaching party to

---

[126] See, for example, Brownsword, *supra*, footnote 118, who dismisses the possibility of party stipulation of equitable remedies with the following sentence in a footnote (note 18): "Since the equitable remedies lie at the courts' discretion, it is difficult to see remedy-stipulation having any impact here."

[127] See Fry, *supra*, footnote 2, at pp. 65-74.

[128] *Infra*, footnotes 129-133. See also Spry, *supra*, footnote 40, at pp. 68-70; Fry, *supra*, footnote 2, at p. 65:

> The question always is, What is the contract? Is it that one certain act shall be done, with a sum annexed, whether by way of penalty or damages, to secure the performance of this very act? or is it that one of two things shall be done at the election of the party who has to perform the contract, namely, the performance of the act or the payment of the sum of money? If the former, the fact of the penal or other like sum being annexed will not prevent the Court's enforcing performance of the very act, and thus carrying into execution the intention of the parties: if the latter, the contract is satisfied by the payment of a sum of money, and there is no ground for proceeding against the party having the election to compel the performance of the other alternative.

[129] (1742), 2 Atk. 371, 26 E.R. 624.

pay £100 in an agreement of purchase and sale of an estate should deprive the innocent party of his right to specific performance:

> As to the defence of the stipulated sum, I cannot take this, to let off either party when they please, but is no more than the common case of a penalty . . .
>
> In all these cases where penalties are inserted in a case of non-performance, this has never been held to release the parties from their agreement, but they must perform it notwithstanding.[130]

This principle has been applied in several specific performance cases.[131]

593   More recently, in *Elsley v. J.G. Collins Ins. Agencies Ltd.*,[132] the Supreme Court of Canada held that a plaintiff was not to be deprived of an injunction to restrain breach of a negative covenant simply because the agreement provided for a stipulated sum in the event of breach: "Thus, even where there is a provision for liquidated damages, the plaintiff may elect instead to ask for an injunction to prevent breach. . . . if the plaintiff is entitled to an injunction, the defendant cannot deprive him of this remedy by paying damages".[133]

---

[130] *Ibid.*

[131] In another early English case, *Crutchley v. Jerningham* (1817), 2 Mer. 502 at p. 506, 35 E.R. 1032, Lord Eldon stated that a "purchaser has no right to say that he will put an end to the agreement, forfeiting his deposit". In *Long v. Bowring* (1864), 33 Beav. 585, 55 E.R. 496, it was held in a case of an agreement for the sale of an underlease of property that a liquidated damages clause did not deprive the plaintiff of his right to specific performance. Romilly, M.R., at pp. 588-9, explained the point as follows:

> There is no contract on their part that they will accept [the liquidated sum of £1,000], nor is there anything which prevents their insisting on having specific performance of the contract. All that is fixed by this clause is, that if they bring an action for damages the amount to be recovered is £1000, and neither more nor less.

[132] [1978] 2 S.C.R. 916, 83 D.L.R. (3d) 1.

[133] *Ibid.*, at pp. 929-30 S.C.R., p. 10 D.L.R. For other cases dealing with injunctions and liquidated damage clauses, see *National Provincial Bank of England v. Marshall* (1888), 40 Ch. D. 112 (C.A.); *Mills v. Gill*, [1952] 3 D.L.R. 27, [1952] O.R. 257 (H.C.J.); *Deacon v. Crehan*, [1925] 4 D.L.R. 664, 57 O.L.R. 597 (H.C.); *Toronto Dairy Co. v. Gowans* (1879), 26 Gr. 290; *Mossop v. Mason* (1869), 16 Gr. 302, affd 18 Gr. 453. *Cf. Vancouver Island Milk Producers' Ass'n v. Alexander* (1922), 30 B.C.R. 524 (C.A.), and *B.C. Poultry Ass'n v. Allanson* [1922], 2 W.W.R. 831 (B.C.S.C.), holding to the contrary. In the *Elsley* case, at p. 938 S.C.R., pp. 15-16 D.L.R., Dickson, J., later summarized the position with respect to the plaintiff's right as between liquidated damages and injunctions in the following language:

> 1.   Where a fixed sum is stipulated as and for liquidated damages upon a breach, the covenantee must elect with respect to that breach between these liquidated damages and an injunction.

(3) Party stipulation for specific relief

594   There is, however, relatively little authority on the weight the courts are prepared to give contractual terms expressly stipulating specific relief. While such clauses appear to be relatively common in the case of personal service contracts providing for injunctive relief for breach of non-competition clauses,[134] the use of such clauses in other commercial contracts appears infrequent.

595   One of the few cases in England or Canada dealing with such a clause in fact arose from the personal service contract. In *Warner Bros. Pictures, Inc. v. Nelson*,[135] where the plaintiff's claim for an injunction to prevent a famous movie actress from breaching her agreement not to work for another company was supported by a clause specifying injunctive relief as appropriate, Branson, J., held as follows:

> I think it is not inappropriate to refer to the fact that, in the contract between the parties, . . . there is a formal admission by the defendant that her services, being "of a special, unique, extraordinary and intellectual character" gives them a particular value "the loss of which cannot be reasonably or adequately compensated in damages" and that a breach may "cost the producer great and irreparable injury and damage," and the artiste expressly agrees that the producer shall be entitled to the remedy of injunction. Of course, parties cannot contract themselves out of the law; but it assists, at all events, on the question of evidence as to the applicability of an injunction in the present case, to find the parties formally recognizing that in cases of this kind injunction is a more appropriate remedy than damages.[136]

---

2.   If he elects to take the liquidated damages stipulated he may recover that sum irrespective of his actual loss.

3.   Where the stipulated sum is a penalty he may only recover such damages as he can prove, but the amount recoverable may not exceed the sum stipulated.

4.   If he elects to take an injunction and not the liquidated sum stipulated, he may recover damages in equity for the actual loss sustained up to the date of the injunction or, if tardy, up to the date upon which he should have sought the injunction, but in either case, not exceeding the amount stipulated as payable upon a breach.

5.   Where a liquidated damages sum is stipulated as payable for each and every breach, the covenantee may recover this sum in respect of distinct breaches which have occurred and he may also be granted an injunction to restrain future breaches.

These propositions are commented on in Waddams, *supra*, footnote 9, §§937-940.

[134] See Finlayson "Personal Service Contracts", in *Law Society of Upper Canada Special Lectures on Current Problems in the Law of Contracts*, 1975, 355.

[135] [1937] 1 K.B. 209.

[136] *Ibid.*, at pp. 220-1.

596 This suggests that the agreement will be relevant, although perhaps not determinative in the assessment of the nature of the
plaintiff's interest in obtaining actual performance rather than damages. The court, however, maintains an overriding discretion to refuse the remedy.[137]

597 Even this authority may not be particularly persuasive when it
comes to a clause which calls for specific performance. As seen in
Chapter 9, the courts almost invariably enforce express negative covenants by injunction and an express negative covenant may be seen
as a form of stipulated remedy even without specific reference to injunction as the desired remedy.[138] There appear to be no cases dealing with the treatment to be given a clause specifying specific performance where enforcement of a positive obligation is sought.

(4) A suggested rationale

598 An approach that might facilitate analysis here is to consider two
categories. In the first, the nature of the plaintiff's interest is such as
to entitle him to specific performance, but because that interest is for
some reason difficult to establish or because the plaintiff wishes to be
sure that it is accepted and admitted by the defendant, the agreement
sets out the reasons for the inadequacy of damages so that in case of
breach, the agreement can be referred to as evidence to establish the
plaintiff's case for specific performance. In this type of case, it is difficult to see why the court should not pay careful attention to the
agreement. There is a strong parallel here to the rule relating to the
enforcement of liquidated damage clauses. Where the clause represents a reasonable and genuine attempt to estimate actual damages
and it is fairly bargained, such a clause will be enforced.[139] Difficulty
and cost of proof of damages is thereby avoided, resulting in saving
not only to the parties but also to the judicial system, the benefits of
which have long been recognized.[140] While liquidated damage clauses

---

[137] The leading American case, *Stokes v. Moore*, 77 So. 2d 331 (Alabama S.C., 1955),
at p. 335, also deals with the breach of a covenant not to compete, and expresses a
similar philosophy:

> We do not wish to express the view that an agreement for the issuance of an in-
> junction, if and when a stipulated state of facts arises in the future, is binding on
> the court to that extent. Such an agreement would serve to oust the inherent ju-
> risdiction of the court to determine whether an injunction is appropriate when
> applied for and to require its issuance even though to do so would be contrary to
> the opinion of the court.

[138] *Infra*, §670.

[139] Waddams, *supra*, footnote 9, §§916-949.

[140] See *Kemble v. Farren* (1829), 6 Bing. 141 at p. 148, 130 E.R. 1234, *per* Tindal, C.J.:

must be distinguished from penalties, which are not enforced, it is difficult to see stipulation of specific performance as constituting a penalty. It is surely a contradiction to suggest that performance of the very obligation promised is punitive in nature. The essence of a penalty is that a greater burden is imposed in the event of breach so as to coerce performance. Unless the agreement failed to allocate the risk of events now making performance more burdensome, even where performance has become very costly, stipulation of specific performance in the agreement should be taken into account. Although in the absence of stipulation for specific performance the court might have decided to award damages, where the parties have clearly and fairly bargained for specific performance there is a strong argument against unravelling the contract. Although specific performance is more "costly" in the sense already discussed, a stipulated remedy clause indicates that the plaintiff has paid for the added protection of specific performance and should, therefore, receive it.

599   In the second category, however, upholding a stipulated remedy clause is more difficult to justify. The best example is a contract of personal services. It is, surely, inconceivable that the courts would or should grant specific performance in favour of an employer simply because the employee has agreed to such a term.[141] Similarly, where a contract would involve extensive supervision by the court, it is unlikely that a clause providing for an equitable remedy will be effective.

600   As seen above,[142] the rationale to the supervision concern appears to be that specific performance decrees are thought to involve a greater expenditure of judicial effort and use more court time and facilities. If parties are free to stipulate such remedies with some assurance that they will be awarded, an unjustifiable shift of cost from the parties to society as a whole could result.[143]

"such an agreement fixes that which is almost impossible to be accurately ascertained; and in all cases, it saves the expense and difficulty of bringing witnesses to that point".

[141] Note, however, that in *Warner Bros. v. Nelson, supra,* footnote 135, where the clause was treated as being of evidentiary value, the result reached has been criticized as in effect granting specific performance of an employment contract: *infra,* §693.

[142] *Supra,* §§570-573.

[143] On the other hand, some commentators, especially Kronman, *supra,* footnote 22, suggest that freer availability of specific performance might actually limit the frequency of contract litigation. It may well be that a rule of practice which explicitly paid close heed to party choice of remedy in the contract would remove an element of uncertainty, and hence reduce the incidence of litigation.

601   Thus, in both categories, factors external to the parties are likely to be seen to be of sufficient importance to prevent permitting the parties to govern the remedial choice. In the first, the public policy against involuntary servitude prevents a court from allowing a party to bind himself indefinitely to a contract of personal service. In the second, the fear is that specific performance might impose unjustifiable costs on the courts and society at large.

602   This suggests that what is called for is maintaining a discretion to refuse the remedy, although specified by the parties, where its grant could violate the policy against involuntary servitude or impose an unreasonable burden on the courts.

603   Apart from these external considerations of individual liberty and unjustifiable increased judicial costs, where a freely bargained contract provides for specific performance, and the contract has allocated the risk of the event making performance undesirable to the defendant, it is submitted that the stipulated remedy clause should be enforced. As indicated above, the reason for such a clause may simply be to ensure that proof of inadequacy of damages can be had or had cheaply.[144]

604   It does appear that the category of special interests is expanding, that specific performance is becoming more flexible. Some heed has been paid to clauses stipulating specific remedies, and as the courts themselves become more willing to grant specific performance, it would not be surprising to see an increasing tendency to accept party stipulation.[145]

6. Mutuality

605   The principle of mutuality has two versions, one affirmative and the other negative. As will be seen, there is considerable doubt as to the actual significance of mutuality as a factor governing the availa-

---

[144] *Supra*, §598. There are other possibilities as well. See Clarkson, Miller and Muris, *supra*, footnote 118, at p. 367, referring to reasons for liquidated damage clauses: the plaintiff may have an interest which traditional damage rules will not protect; the contract may involve a new firm for which a guarantee of performance is necessary; the parties' perception of risks or their risk preferences may differ, as may their ability to adjust to unforeseen occurrences.

[145] *Cf.* McDowell, *supra*, footnote 118, at p. 448, who concludes as follows with respect to stipulated specific performance:

Modern equity decisions reflect this more liberal attitude toward specific enforcement of contracts when the needs of corporate enterprise so require. As a result, resort to contractual provisions governing granting of the remedy has been largely unnecessary.

bility of specific performance. For purposes of introduction, however, the two versions of the principle may be identified as follows. The affirmative version is that if the remedy of specific performance would be available to one party in the event of breach, then reciprocity requires that it be made available to the other party as well. The negative is that if specific performance would not have been available to one side to compel performance, then it should on that account be denied to the other.

606   Corbin demonstrated convincingly that the affirmative and negative versions could not simultaneously be correct:

> The two rules have seldom been set side by side; and it has not often been observed that in the form stated they are inconsistent and incapable of application. Each of the two rules appears to be applicable to every case falling within the other; and in each of them it appears to be assumed that the availability of the remedy with respect to one party can be determined independently of its availability to the other. In applying rule (1), if the plaintiff is a person who could have obtained specific enforcement, by rule (2) the defendant would not have been denied the remedy; the result of this would always seem to be that rule (1) itself would have no application. In applying rule (2), if the plaintiff would not be entitled to specific enforcement, by rule (1) the defendant, also, could not have obtained it; and the result would seem to be that rule (2) would have no application. Thus, the two rules are reduced to an appearance of absurdity: A can get specific performance, and therefore B can also. But B cannot get specific performance, and therefore A cannot. By applying the two rules together, it is made to appear that both A and B can get specific enforcement, and at the same time that neither A nor B can get specific enforcement, as a remedy against the other. This absurdity has generally been prevented from appearing, because the courts have never attempted to apply the two rules at the same time, and also because these two rules have seldom been stated together for comparison.[146]

607   Here, it is proposed to consider the force of the affirmative version. The extent to which the negative version affords a defence to specific performance will be considered in Chapter 10.[147]

608   The primary example of the application of affirmative mutuality is the remedial treatment afforded the vendor of real property.[148] Although in most cases the vendor will be unable to demonstrate inadequacy of damages,[149] it is usually upon the affirmative principle of mutuality that the award of specific relief is justified.[150] Because the

---

[146] *Supra*, footnote 47, §1178.
[147] *Infra*, §§745-759.
[148] *Infra*, §§627.
[149] *Infra*, §621-626.
[150] *Infra*, §627.

purchaser could have obtained specific performance, a corresponding right is said to arise in favour of the vendor.

609　While affirmative mutuality has also been employed with respect to other contracts,[151] and while modest versions of the affirmative principle have received support from respectable sources,[152] it is submitted that it is difficult to see any force in an argument based upon reciprocity of remedy. The existence of a special interest in performance on the part of one party to the contract of the sort sufficient to justify specific relief, bears no necessary relationship to the interest in performance possessed by the other. The rationale for specific performance is based upon the existence of some interest of the plaintiff that will not adequately be protected by damages. The fact of one party's entitlement to specific performance surely says little or nothing about the remedial interest of the other.

610　It would seem that the basis of the mutuality rule may rest on the dual court system which existed over 100 years ago. One reason for allowing the vendor of real property specific performance before the fusion of law and equity was that the award of common law damages was the province of the jury, and until the mid-19th century, the jury was relatively uncontrolled.[153] Contracts were perhaps regarded with a more scrupulous eye by the courts of equity than the courts of law,[154] and there was perhaps more concern for mutuality of jurisdiction than mutuality of remedy.[155] The mutuality principle merely asserted equity's jurisdiction over all aspects of the contract, as it might well have been harsh to permit one party access to the courts of equity, but to deny it to the other. Obviously, this reason has long since been removed. Moreover, even in pre-Judicature Act times, there

---

[151] See, *e.g.*, *Kenney v. Wexham* (1822), 6 Madd. 355, 56 E.R. 1126 (sale of annuity). See also the dicta in *Beswick v. Beswick*, [1968] A.C. 58 (H.L.), at p. 89, *per* Lord Pearce, and *Hounslow London Borough Council v. Twickenham Garden Developments Ltd.*, [1971] Ch. 233 at p. 256, *per* Megarry, J.

[152] See Durfee, "Mutuality in Specific Performance", 20 Mich. L. Rev. 289 (1922), at pp. 290-1. The *Restatement of the Law of Contracts* (St. Paul, American Law Institute Publishers, 1932), §372(2), stated that the availability of specific performance to one party was not a sufficient reason by itself to make the remedy available to the other, but could be weighed in the balance in doubtful cases. This provision has been dropped from the *Restatement of the Law Second: Contracts, supra*, footnote 121.

[153] See, *e.g.*, *Lewis v. Lord Lechmere* (1722), 10 Mod. 503, 88 E.R. 828, discussing the unreliability of the jury as a reason for affording the same remedy to both sides.

[154] *Infra*, Chapter 10.

[155] See *Clifford v. Turrell* (1841), 1 Y. & C.C.C. 138 at p. 150, 62 E.R. 826. See also, *infra*, §§755-757, discussing the same point in relation to negative mutuality.

were a large number of cases in which specific relief was available to one side and not the other,[156] and the scope accorded affirmative mutuality is hardly as wide as some dicta in the early cases would suggest.

611   Still, it might be argued that there is something in the mutuality principle. Remedial choice will often affect the bearing of post-breach risks, and hence, it may seem appropriate to examine the extent to which the innocent party was at risk in order to assess the nature of the risk to be assigned to the party in breach. For example, the purchaser of real property, when granted specific performance, is thereby given the full benefit of any increase in price accruing after the breach and up to the point of judgment. This might seem to suggest that the vendor should also have specific performance so that the

---

[156] Ames, "Mutuality in Specific Performance" in *Lectures on Legal History* (Cambridge, Harvard University Press, 1913), at pp. 370-1, gives the following list of exceptions:

(1) A bilateral contract between a fiduciary and his principal is often enforced in favour of the principal, although not enforceable against him.

(2) A similar contract procured by the fraud or misrepresentation of one of the parties may be enforced against him, although not by him.

(3) In England, one who, after making a voluntary settlement, has entered into a contract to sell the settled property, may be compelled to convey, although he cannot force the buyer to accept a conveyance.

(4) A vendor, whose inability to make a perfect title debars him from obtaining a decree against the buyer, may in many cases be forced by the buyer to convey with compensation.

(5) Notwithstanding the opinions of Lord Redesdale and Chancellor Kent to the contrary, a party to a bilateral contract, who has signed a memorandum of it, may be compelled to perform it specifically, although he could not maintain a bill against the other party who had not signed such a memorandum.

(6) A contract between an infant and an adult may be enforced against the adult after the infant comes of age, although no decree could be made against the plaintiff.

(7) A plaintiff who has performed his part of the contract, although he could not have been compelled in equity to do so, may enforce specific performance by the defendant.

(8) One who has contracted to sell land not owned by him, and who, therefore, could not be cast in a decree, may, in many cases, by acquiring title before the time fixed for conveyance, compel the execution of the contract by the buyer.

. . . But a rule so overloaded with exceptions is fairly open to . . . severe criticism . . .

See also cases such as *James Jones & Sons Ltd. v. Earl of Tankerville*, [1909] 2 Ch. 440, and *Gervais v. Edwards* (1842), 2 Dr. & War. 80, 59 R.R. 647, granting an injunction to restrain a defendant from preventing the plaintiff from entry to cut timber despite the contention that the defendant could not have compelled performance of the plaintiff's obligation to cut the timber, on the grounds that the defendant was fully protected upon payment by the plaintiff.

risk of decline in value is imposed upon the purchaser along with the benefit of potential increase. However, this confuses mutuality of remedy with mutuality of obligation. It is submitted that the vendor's interest can adequately and fully be protected by a damages award,[157] including later assessment of damages if that seems appropriate.[158] If specific performance is denied to the vendor, this merely means that he is expected to mitigate, and if compensated for mitigation costs and given the difference between the contract and the sale price, he is fully protected. His only interest is in getting the price promised. It is argued below[159] that there seems good reason to require the vendor to mitigate the loss even where the purchaser is in breach, on the ground that he will usually be in a much better position to do so. It is submitted, accordingly, that although reciprocity of remedy has an attractive ring, and has the support of respectable pre-Judicature Act authority, it is not now a meaningful objective, and should be reconsidered. In modern cases, it is rarely employed except to support the claim of the vendor of real estate for specific performance, other aspects of which are discussed elsewhere in this book.[160]

---

[157] *Infra*, §§621-623.
[158] Waddams, *supra*, footnote 9, §§675-677.
[159] *Infra*, §630.
[160] *Infra*, §621-634.

CHAPTER 8

CONTRACTS OF SALE

1. Contracts for the Sale of Land

612   The remedy of specific performance is almost invariably granted when sought to enforce contracts for the purchase and sale of land. Discussion of the issues arising here will be facilitated by dealing in turn with the purchaser's and vendor's rights to specific performance.

(1) Specific performance in favour of the purchaser

613   The rationale for specific performance in favour of the purchaser is usually put in terms of the inadequacy of damages.[1] It is often said

---

[1] See, *e.g., Flint v. Corby* (1853), 4 Gr. 45 at p. 52, *per* Esten, V.-C.:

> The specific performance of an agreement respecting land, is enforced because the court intends in every particular instance that the estate, which forms the subject matter of the contract, possesses a peculiar value for the purchaser, and that pecuniary damages will furnish no adequate equivalent for the loss of his bargain. In this case the peculiar value, which attracts the jurisdiction of the court, is implied and needs not be proved.

See also *Adderley v. Dixon* (1824), 1 Sim. & St. 607 at p. 610, 57 E.R. 239, *per* Leach, V.-C.: "a Court of Equity decrees performance of a contract for land, not because of the real nature of the land, but because damages at law, which must be calculated upon the general money value of land, may not be a complete remedy to the purchaser, to whom the land may have a peculiar and special value"; *Buxton v. Lister* (1746), 3 Atk. 383 at p. 384, 26 E.R. 1020: "As to the cases of contracts for purchase of lands, or things that relate to realties, those are of a permanent nature, and if a person agrees to purchase them, it is on a particular liking to the land, and is quite a different thing from matters in the way of trade." The concept of inadequacy of damages is discussed above, §§529-557. More recently, Cohen, "The Rel-that no two parcels of land can be identical, and that therefore damages must be inadequate.[2] The purchaser is entitled to get the very parcel he bargained for and not to be forced to take an inexact substitute.

614   For the most part, inquiry in individual cases into the plaintiff's interest in the particular parcel of land in question has been foreclosed. Inadequacy of damages has been presumed simply because land was at issue. However, formulating the criterion for the remedy in terms of inadequacy of damages invites inquiry, and in a few recent cases, purchasers have been refused specific performance and awarded damages where the courts were able to conclude that the nature of the plaintiff's interest in acquiring the land was such that it could adequately be protected by a damages award.[3] It may be that Canadian

---

ationship of Contractual Remedies to Political and Social Status: A Preliminary Inquiry", 32 U. of T. L.J. 31 (1982), at p. 54, has put forth an attractive argument to the effect that the virtually automatic right to specific performance can be explained historically on the basis that land represented not only wealth but political and legal identity and authority as well as social status: "[contracts for the sale of land] were in reality political, legal, and social acts of extraordinary significance."

[2] Story, *Equity Jurisprudence*, 12th ed., vol. 1 (Boston, Little, Brown, 1877), §746:

The locality, character, vicinage, soil, easements or accommodation of the land generally, may give it a peculiar and special value in the eyes of the purchaser; so that it cannot be replaced by other land of the same precise value, but not having the same precise local conveniences or accommodations; and therefore, a compensation in damages would not be adequate relief.

See also *Scott v. Alvarez*, [1895] 2 Ch. 603 (C.A.), at p. 615, *per* Rigby, L.J.: "the foundation of the doctrine of specific performance was this, that land has quite a character of its own"; *Cud v. Rutter* (1719), 1 P. Wms. 570 at p. 571, 24 E.R. 521, *per* Parker, L.C.: "It is true, one parcel of land may vary from, and be more commodious, pleasant, or convenient than another parcel."

[3] *Heron Bay Investments Ltd. v. Peel-Elder Developments Ltd.* (1976), 2 C.P.C. 338 (Ont. H.C.J.), at p. 339, *per* Weatherston, J., refusing a certificate of *lis pendens*:

The remedy of specific performance is one that is peculiar to real estate transactions and is based on the fact that real estate is regarded as unique and of particular importance to the purchaser . . . That reasoning does not apply when land is purchased merely as an investment . . . True it may be a uniquely good investment, but it was not being purchased by the plaintiffs for their own use but only to develop and resell at a profit. Obviously, any loss of profits can be compensated for in damages.

Chaulk v. Fairview Construction Ltd. (1977), 14 Nfld. & P.E.I.R. 13 (Nfld. C.A.), at p. 21, *per* Gushue, J.A.:

There was nothing whatever unique or irreplaceable about the houses and lots bargained for. They were merely subdivision lots with houses, all of the same general design, built on them, which the respondent was purchasing for investment or re-sale purposes only. . . . It would be quite different if we were dealing with a house or houses which were of a particular architectural design, or were situated in a particularly desirable location, but this was certainly not the case.

McNabb v. Smith (1981), 124 D.L.R. (3d) 547 (B.C.S.C.), affd 132 D.L.R. (3d)

courts are prepared to consider the advantages and disadvantages of
the remedy of specific performance in particular cases rather than
grant it automatically simply because land is involved, although there
is strong authority that specific performance is almost always to be
granted.[4]

615   From the purchaser's point of view, it is usually the case that land
has the quality of uniqueness which renders damages less appropriate
than specific performance. The concept of uniqueness has already
been examined.[5] A truly unique item poses problems for damage assessment because substitutes are not available and there is no market
to establish value. Moreover, an imperfect substitute may not supply
to the purchaser the same qualities and satisfactions. Even if market
value could be determined, the purchaser may honestly place on the

---

523*n* (B.C.C.A.); *306793 Ontario Ltd. v. Rimes* (1979), 100 D.L.R. (3d) 350 at p.
352, 25 O.R. (2d) 79 at pp. 80-1 (C.A.), leave to appeal to S.C.C. refused December 3, 1979, *per* MacKinnon, A.C.J.O.: "There was no issue raised before us
whether, given the fact that the land was vacant land sold by one developer to another for future development, the plaintiff would have been entitled to specific performance of the contract due to some unique qualities in the land"; *Prittie v.
Laughton* (1902), 1 O.W.R. 185 (Div. Ct.), at p. 187, *per* Meredith, J.:

> The lots, apparently about 20 in number, were to be sold for $100 altogether, an
> average of $5 each. They were bought to sell again for the purpose of speculation
> only. They were tax title lots in Toronto Junction. No one can doubt the feasibil-
> ity of going into the market, and being able to buy abundantly of such lots. . . . It
> is not a case in which damages will not "afford a complete remedy" . . . Here
> damages will completely compensate.

See also *Loan Investment Corp. of Australasia v. Bonner*, [1970] N.Z.L.R. 724
(P.C.), at p. 735, *per* Lord Pearson, refusing specific performance of a transaction
which would also have forced the defendant to lend money unsecured, where the
property was bought not for the purchaser's own use "but for selling, letting, mort-
gaging and perhaps developing".

[4] *Kloepfer Wholesale Hardware & Automotive Co. Ltd. v. Roy*, [1952] 2 S.C.R. 465
at p. 472, [1952] 3 D.L.R. 705 at p. 708, *per* Kerwin, J.: "as to the suggestion that
damages would be sufficient because it is contended that the plaintiff [purchaser]
desired to use the property as an investment, it is sufficient to say that generally
speaking, specific performance applies to agreements for the sale of lands as a matter of course." See also *Bashir v. Koper* (1983), 40 O.R. (2d) 758 (C.A.); *Roberto
v. Bumb*, [1943] 2 D.L.R. 613 at p. 621, [1943] O.R. 299 at p. 311 (C.A.), *per* Laid-
law, J.A.; *Dennis v. Evans* (1972), 23 D.L.R. (3d) 625, [1972] 1 O.R. 585 (H.C.J.),
affd 27 D.L.R. (3d) 680*n*, [1972] 3 O.R. 228*n* (C.A.); *Regent's Canal Co. v. Ware*
(1857), 23 Beav. 575, 53 E.R. 226; *Pianta v. National Finance & Trustees Ltd.*
(1964), 38 A.L.J.R. 232 (Aust. H.C.), at p. 233, *per* Barwick, C.J., referring to the
"faint" effort to argue that as the plaintiff was a land developer, damages would be
adequate: "But in my opinion this proposition is without foundation in law, even if
the respondent had had no other business than that of subdividing and selling land
and had made a decision to subdivide and sell the subject land."

[5] *Supra*, §§545-547. See also, *infra*, §§644-648.

item he bargained for a value of a purely personal kind, the "consumer surplus",[6] which the market price will not reflect.

616   The extent to which the uniqueness criterion fits contracts for land will vary from case to case. Most purchasers who intend to occupy and use the land will have selected a particular parcel because it meets their own needs and subjective desires. A potential house purchaser will usually examine many properties and make a selection on the basis of a combination of price, location, design, and many other purely individual factors which will usually make it very difficult to find another house which exhibits all of those same features. Although the court may be able, through evidence, to place a market value on the house the purchaser has selected, damages will not necessarily enable him to purchase or obtain an exact substitute. But it will sometimes be the case that a substitute parcel would supply the same amenities and satisfactions, even for the purchaser who intends to occupy the parcel. This has been suggested of large tracts of prairie farm land.[7] The same might be said of certain modern condominium or subdivision residences, or plots in commercial industrial estates where there are row upon row of identical models or parcels in almost identical locations.[8]

617   Where the purchaser's interest is investment or resale,[9] the proposition that a substitute could not be found and that therefore damages are inadequate appears even more dubious. Take first the case of the purchaser who intends to use the property as an income-producing asset. Plainly, such a purchaser has no subjective attachment to the particular parcel. He may, however, argue that his own judgment as to the income-producing qualities of this parcel makes it unique for his purposes. He may fear, if awarded damages and in effect forced back into the market to acquire another parcel in another location, that the substitute will not offer the same income-producing qualities as the land he first bargained for. In other words, because no two pieces of land are identical, the purchaser's argument is that he should not be forced to accept the objective judgment of the court as to value. Unless it can be fairly said that the income-producing po-

---

[6] *Supra*, §546.

[7] Jones, "Specific Performance of Contracts for the Conveyance of Real Estate", 22 Kentucky L.J. 143 (1933), at p. 144; Hume, "Specific Performance of Contracts to Convey Land", 21 Kentucky L.J. 348 (1933), at p. 350.

[8] See Brun, Comment, 43 U. of Cin. L. Rev. 935 (1974).

[9] For a detailed discussion of this, see Brenner, "Specific Performance of Contracts for the Sale of Land Purchased for Resale or Investment", 24 McGill L.J. 513 (1978). This article provides a good collection of Commonwealth and American authorities on the point.

tential of a given parcel of land is unusually difficult to assess, then this argument should be rejected. There is almost inevitably some risk of error in damage assessment, and when that risk becomes significant, specific performance is called for. However, it is not clear that the risks of error inherent in establishing land values for investment purposes are severe.[10]

618   Similar considerations arise where the purchaser is a speculator acquiring the property for profit on a resale. Land is a fungible good to such a purchaser,[11] and the arguments which have been considered elsewhere in this book as to the relative advantages and disadvantages of specific performance and damages apply.[12] Again, such a purchaser may argue that since land is so especially difficult to value objectively, he should not be forced to accept the assessment of others. On the other hand, granting specific performance to such a purchaser will often allow him, at the expense of the vendor, a risk-free period of speculation between the date of the breach and the date of the trial. There seems to be no reason why a speculator in real estate should not be subject to the same principle of mitigation as the speculator in any other commodity.

619   Another argument, however, has been made in favour of the speculator's right to specific performance which turns on the rights of third parties.[13] Often, the plaintiff who intends to resell will already have done so by the time his own action is tried. Often the sub-purchaser will be one for whom the land does have a particular value. Denying specific performance to the speculator has the effect of denying the remedy to the sub-purchaser who would otherwise be entitled to a decree. However, some courts have taken the factor of resale quite the other way, and held that because the plaintiff, the original purchaser, has already resold, damages can be more readily calculated.[14] Perhaps insufficient attention has been given to the

---

[10] *Cf.* Brenner, *supra*, footnote 9, who argues that damages are inadequate for the investor.

[11] See the cases cited, *supra*, footnote 3, but *cf.* cases cited, *supra*, footnote 4.

[12] *Supra*, especially §§536-541.

[13] Brenner, *supra*, footnote 9.

[14] *Chaulk v. Fairview Construction Ltd.* (1977), 14 Nfld. & P.E.I.R. 13 (Nfld. C.A.), at p. 21, *per* Gushue, J.A.: "It is therefore obvious that damages do afford an adequate remedy to Chaulk, and that these damages should be capable of assessment, with very little difficulty". In *Armstrong and Armstrong v. Graham*, [1947] 3 D.L.R. 59, [1947] O.W.N. 295 (H.C.J.), the plaintiffs had taken possession prior to conveyance. They resold, but lost the sale when the defendant refused to convey. Specific performance was granted along with damages for the lost resale. For

rights of sub-purchasers in this context. The answer may be to allow the joinder of the sub-purchaser as a party affected in any suit brought by the original purchaser in which the subsale is pleaded as a reason for a specific performance, so that the sub-purchaser's rights and interest can fully be taken into account. Granting specific performance where the speculator has resold would not undercut the mitigation argument and at the same time would satisfy the interests of the third party.

620 One disadvantage of assessing the adequacy of damages according to the circumstances of each particular case is that an element of uncertainty is introduced. The rule which prevailed until recently, was to presume the inadequacy of damages in the case of land, and while this presumption may seem inappropriate in particular cases, it may perhaps be justified on the ground that it is usually apt and that it provides a more or less clear and definite rule. It may be felt that it is important for both parties to know what form of remedy is available, not only to avoid the cost of litigation, but also to enable the purchaser to know whether he ought to buy a substitute, and to enable the vendor to know whether he can resell. On the other hand, the equitable origin of specific performance has meant that discretion has been its hallmark. Certainty is not the only legal value worth pursuing in the remedial context, and perhaps the courts are appropriately confident that identifiable principles of sufficient clarity underlie these recent decisions which question the traditional presumption.

(2) Specific performance in favour of the vendor

621 While the vendor's right to specific performance[15] is well supported by the authorities,[16] it is not at all clear in principle that the vendor's interest invariably merits the protection of specific relief. Oddly enough, there has been less discussion in recent cases of the propriety of awarding specific performance in favour of the vendor. However, discussion of inadequacy of damages in the cases dealing with purchasers just discussed[17] is bound to prompt a similar debate

---

discussion of the American cases where the problem has arisen more frequently, see Brenner, *supra*, footnote 9.

[15] The vendor's right to specific performance of an executory contract is, of course, to be distinguished from the vendor's action for the price after completion, which is an action in debt and not a claim for a remedy for a breach of contract. See Waddams, *The Law of Damages* (1983), §§792, 793 and 1226-1252. The discussion here assumes a binding executory agreement to buy and sell and that the purchaser refuses to complete the transaction.

[16] *Infra*, footnotes 18, 20, 22.

[17] *Supra*, §§614-620.

as to the vendor's right, especially as the vendor's case for specific performance appears to be much weaker.

622　　Three arguments are usually advanced in support of the vendor's right to specific performance. The first is that although the vendor's specific performance claim is merely one for money, damages would be inadequate on the grounds that he will get only the difference between the contract price and market value, whereas under a specific performance decree, the vendor gets the entire price immediately. As it was put in an old case, "damages would not place him in the same situation as if the contract had been performed, for in that case he would have entirely got rid of his land, and he would have in his pocket the net sum for which he had agreed to sell it . . .".[18]

623　　This argument might seem to hark back to a period when the market in real estate was more constrained, and when it was more difficult to find a buyer for land. In fact, a damages award with interest[19] can readily reflect any loss the vendor has sustained by being kept out of his money. The need for immediate judgment for the entire price is not regarded as sufficient reason to justify specific performance in other sale cases, and it is difficult to see why there should be a special rule in the case of land.

624　　However, there is perhaps a more serious concern here with respect to damage assessment. If the vendor is desperate enough to undertake the expense of the specific performance action and has been unable to sell the property in the time leading up to trial, this ordinarily will provide a strong indication that the property is not readily saleable. The very fact that the vendor has trouble finding another purchaser indicates that assessment of the market value of the land necessary to measure damages may be difficult. Where the plaintiff has agreed to purchase at an inflated price, specific performance assures the vendor of complete recovery. On the other hand, where the court is required to assess damages, there may be a natural inclination to play down evidence of low present value in the face of the plaintiff's agreement to pay more and effectively reduce the vendor's recovery.[20]

625　　Against this must be weighed the argument in favour of

---

[18] *Eastern Counties Ry. Co. v. Hawkes* (1855), 5 H.L.C. 331 at p. 360, 10 E.R. 928, *per* Lord Campbell. See also Brun, *supra*, footnote 8, for a more modern statement of the argument.

[19] Waddams, *supra*, footnote 15 §§825-915.

[20] The uncertainty of having damages assessed by the jury was formerly a strong factor: *Lewis v. Lord Lechmere* (1722), 10 Mod. 503, 88 E.R. 828.

mitigation.[21] If specific performance is presumptively available, the vendor will not be penalized for failing to mitigate, and can sit on his right to specific performance. A rule which made specific performance available to the vendor of land only if he could demonstrate the inadequacy of damages would have the desirable effect of forcing the vendor to make serious mitigation efforts, and yet at the same time still permit the court to award specific performance where problems of assessment were sufficiently difficult.

626   On the whole, the proposition that damages in favour of the vendor are inadequate seems dubious and the vendor's right to specific performance is usually based on other grounds.

627   More frequently, one finds the vendor's right to specific performance justified on the basis of mutuality:[22] "In every case justice requires that the purchaser should be entitled to specific performance, for as to him no amount of damage would necessarily be an adequate compensation; and there must be reciprocity of remedy between vendor and purchaser." The various meanings attributed to the mutuality principle are discussed elsewhere in this book.[23] Here, the argument is based on the affirmative version which is to the effect that the availability of specific relief to the opposite party, the purchaser, provides justification for its award against him as well. This argument has been considered in greater detail above,[24] and it has been argued that in modern terms, there is little if anything in principle to support it. Admittedly, there is ample authority in the case-law to support the black letter proposition that mutuality requires that specific performance be made available to the vendor as well as the purchaser.[25] However, for the reasons already given, it is submitted that a modern court should seek more satisfactory grounds upon which to base the vendor's claim.

628   The third argument, like the second, turns on the fact that specific

---

[21] *Supra*, §§533-535.

[22] *Eastern Counties Ry. Co. v. Hawkes, supra*, footnote 18; *Walker v. Eastern Counties Ry. Co.* (1848), 6 Hare 594 at p. 602, 67 E.R. 1300; *Turner v. Bladin* (1951), 82 C.L.R. 463 (Aust. H.C.). *Cf.* Ames, "Mutuality in Specific Performance" in *Lectures on Legal History* (Cambridge, Mass., Harvard University Press, 1913), at p. 380:

> In truth the vendor's right to specific enforcement has nothing to do with any question of mutuality. The vendor, from the time of the bargain, holds the legal title as security for the payment of the purchase money, and his bill is like a mortgagee's bill for payment and foreclosure of the equity of redemption.

[23] *Supra*, §§606-611, *infra*, §§745-759.

[24] *Supra*, §§606-611.

[25] *Supra*, footnote 22.

performance is available to the purchaser, and is related to the principle of equitable conversion. Equity deems done what ought to have been done, and accordingly, the equitable title to the property passes upon the formulation of the final agreement, even before the vendor's claim has crystallized as a debt.[26] The equitable doctrine developed primarily in relation to the devolution of property where either party died pending completion.[27] As the availability of specific performance is often used to determine whether conversion has occurred,[28] it would be circular to say that conversion determines the availability of specific performance. Even so, one might express the rationale for specific performance under this head as being the need for a point of finality in the transaction to facilitate dealing with the property in the interim between agreement and closing. If it is convenient to say that property has passed to the purchaser for other purposes, it is perhaps unwise to distinguish the situation where the purchaser fails to fulfil his final and formal obligation to complete the transaction.

629   However, the apparent simplicity and convenience achieved through the doctrine of conversion is misleading. Courts are not prepared to consider that property has passed for all purposes or that the transaction is finalized at the point of agreement.[29] It has been

---

[26] *Hillingdon Estates Co. v. Stonefield Estates Ltd.*, [1952] Ch. 627 at pp. 631-2, *per* Vaisey, J.:

> . . . when there is a contract by A to sell land to B at a certain price, B becomes the owner in equity of the land, subject, of course, to his obligation to perform his part of the contract by paying the purchase-money . . . [The vendor] has, it is true, the legal estate in the land, but, for many purposes, from the moment the contract is entered into he holds it as trustee for B, the purchaser. True, he has certain rights in the land remaining, but all those rights are conditioned and limited by the circumstance that they are all referable to his right to recover and receive the purchase-money. His interest in the land when he has entered into a contract for sale is not an interest in land; it is an interest in personal estate, in a sum of money . . .

See generally, Pettit, "Conversion Under a Contract for the Sale of Land", 24 Conveyancer and Property Lawyer 47 (1960).

[27] See Pettit, *supra*, footnote 26; Langdell, "Equitable Conversion", 18 Harv. L. Rev. 1, 83, 245 (1904-5).

[28] It is often said that in a contract for sale, there is only conversion if specific performance is available: *Holroyd v. Marshall* (1862), 10 H.L.C. 191 at pp. 209-10, 11 E.R. 999, *per* Westbury, L.C.; *Howard v. Miller*, [1915] A.C. 318 at p. 326, 22 D.L.R. 75 at pp. 79-80, *per* Lord Parker of Waddington. However, conversion has been found where specific performance was not available to both parties: see Pettit, *supra*, footnote 26, citing *Hudson v. Cook* (1872), L.R. 13 Eq. 417; *Rose v. Watson* (1864), 10 H.L.C. 672, 11 E.R. 1187; *Gordon Hill Trust v. Segall*, [1941] 2 All E.R. 379 (C.A.), and arguing that the availability of specific performance does not determine the issue whether there has been conversion.

[29] It is possible in some estate cases to have conversion with respect to the purchaser

held appropriate to require the vendor to bear certain risks.[30] Other values apart from finality must be considered and weighed against the apparent simplicity of taking the transaction as completed.

630 It is submitted that from the remedial point of view, especially in relation to mitigation, there may be definite advantages to a rule which requires the vendor to prove inadequacy of damages. The very fact that the plaintiff has refused to complete the transaction suggests strongly that he does not want the property and that if forced by a specific performance decree to take it, he will resell. Thus, the real choice here is whether the vendor or the purchaser should be forced to sell in mitigation. It is argued elsewhere in the book[31] that as a general matter, it is preferable to impose that obligation on the plaintiff even though he is the innocent party. In the case of real property where the purchaser has broken the contract, especially where the vendor retains possession, the vendor will ordinarily be in a much better position to dispose of the property. He will already have established a procedure for selling the property and engaged an agent, and will know the possibilities for sale. Money will compensate him for the extra time and effort required. On the other hand, forcing the unwilling purchaser to take up the property will often cause him considerable inconvenience and expense which would be avoided through a damages award in favour of the vendor. The purchaser will have some knowledge of the market, but that knowledge will relate to his own particular needs and desires rather than to the various uses or prospects for the subject property. He will have entered the market as a buyer, not a seller, and will inevitably incur costs in becoming a seller which the vendor would avoid.

631 It is submitted, then, that although the prospect of having a point of finality to transactions is attractive, it is obtained at a substantial price. The courts have been unwilling to pay that price in other instances, and it is submitted, neither should the price of added mitigation costs be invariably incurred in cases involving land.

632 Another argument, not discussed in the cases, may offer some support to the vendor's right to specific performance in the case of house purchases. Very often, the completion of one house purchase depends upon completion of another since many purchasers are unable

---

where it would not be applied if the vendor's estate were being administered: Pettit, *supra*, footnote 26, at pp. 55-6.

[30] See Reiter, "Real Estate — Agreement of Purchase and Sale — Downzoning before Closing: How Frustrating?", 56 Can. Bar Rev. 98 (1978).

[31] *Supra*, §534.

to finance the purchase of their new house unless they have the proceeds from their old one. If one purchase and sale arrangement collapses, others can follow. The virtually automatic availability of specific performance provides some assurance that the full sale price will be forthcoming to finance the purchase. In many jurisdictions, specific performance decrees can be obtained quickly in such cases, and the very threat of an action may well prevent a purchaser from backing out, thereby preventing the collapse of a whole chain of transactions.

633   On the whole, however, it is suggested that the vendor's case for specific performance is ordinarily much weaker than that of the purchaser. It is submitted that should the courts be prepared to reconsider the virtually automatic award of specific performance of contracts for the purchase and sale of real estate, the vendor's right will be found to be somewhat wanting.

Restriction of vendor's remedies in Alberta and Saskatchewan

634   Legislation in Alberta and Saskatchewan restricts the vendor's remedy in damages on default.[32] In both provinces, the vendor's rights are limited to recovery of the land sold and cancellation of the agreement. It has been held that the legislation precludes a vendor from suing a defaulting purchaser for the difference between the contract price and the amount recovered on a subsequent sale.[33] Although the legislation was presumably intended to protect purchasers upon default, it must surely enhance the vendor's claim to some other remedy, either specific performance or an action in debt for the price. If, indeed, damages for loss of bargain cannot be recovered against the defaulting purchaser, then surely specific performance must be available.[34] If it is not, the defaulting purchaser would be completely immune. Accordingly, in Alberta and Saskatchewan, the

---

[32] Law of Property Act, Alta., s. 41; Limitation of Civil Rights Act, Sask., s. 2(1).

[33] *Clift v. Tonnellier* (1983), 144 D.L.R. (3d) 188 (Sask. Q.B.). *Cf. Luscombe v. Mashinter* (1978), 84 D.L.R. (3d) 203 (Alta. Dist. Ct.), and *Bell v. Robutka* (1964), 48 D.L.R. (2d) 755 (Alta. Dist. Ct.), affd 55 D.L.R. (2d) 436 (Alta. S.C. App. Div.), permitting the recovery of expenses made on the land at the expense of the defaulting purchaser. The legislation has also been given a narrow reading when raised as a defence to an action on a covenant contained in a collateral mortgage or security: *Krook v. Yewchuk*, [1962] S.C.R. 535, 34 D.L.R. (2d) 676; *Ross and Ross v. Haines* (1966), 55 D.L.R. (2d) 511 (Alta. S.C. App. Div.); *Kleiman v. Bazin* (1970), 10 D.L.R. (3d) 384 (Sask. C.A.). See also *Sigurdson v. Farrow* (1981), 121 D.L.R. (3d) 183 (Alta. Q.B.), holding the Alberta Act inapplicable on conflict of law principles.

[34] The Alberta Act clearly contemplates an action for specific performance: s. 41(2).

argument that the vendor's right to specific performance should be reconsidered can have no application so long as legislation of this kind is held to remove the vendor's right to damages.

2. Contracts for the Sale of Goods

(1) Introduction

635   While specific performance is the presumptive remedy for breach of contracts for the sale of land, damages is the usual remedy for breach of contracts for the sale of goods. Land is presumed unique; goods are presumed fungible. There are other important differences which will be considered in this chapter. Sale of goods law is governed by statute, and there is a provision dealing with specific performance. Sale of goods cases may also involve more complex questions of enforcement. A contract for the sale of land involves a single act of transfer, but many sale of goods cases involve long-term arrangements which may give rise to questions of supervision.

(2) The Sale of Goods Act

636   Sale of goods legislation in each common law province contains the following provision with respect to specific performance:

> In an action for breach of contract to deliver specific or ascertained goods, the court may, if it thinks fit, direct that the contract be performed specifically, without giving the defendant the option of retaining the goods on payment of damages, and may impose such terms and conditions as to damages, payment of the price, and otherwise, as to the court seems just.[35]

637   The phrase "specific goods" is defined in the Act as "goods identified and agreed upon at the time the contract of sale is made".[36] There is no statutory definition of "ascertained". It would appear to mean identification of the goods at some time later, after the contract has been made, either in accordance with the contract, or in some

---

[35] Sale of Goods Act, Ont., s. 50. The same, or virtually same, provision is found in all Canadian common law jurisdictions: Alta., s. 52; B.C., s. 55; Man., s. 53; N.B., s. 49; Nfld., s. 53; N.W.T., s. 50; N.S., s. 52; P.E.I., s. 52; Sask., s. 51; Yukon, s. 50. For discussion of the interpretation of this provision, see Ontario Law Reform Commission, *Report on Sale of Goods*, vol. 2 (Ministry of the Attorney-General, 1979), at pp. 436-40.

[36] Alta., s. 1(*m*); B.C., s. 1; Man., s. 2(1)(*n*); Ont., s. 1(*m*); N.B., s. 1(1); Nfld., s. 2(*m*); N.W.T., s. 2(*m*); P.E.I., s. 1(*n*); Sask., s. 2(1)(*s*); Yukon, s. 2(1); N.S., s. 1(*n*). The phrase "specific or ascertained" also determines passage of title: see, *e.g.*, Sale of Goods Act, Ont., ss. 17, 18(1), 19, Rules 1, 2, 3, and the availability of the defence of frustration where goods perish: ss. 7, 8.

other way.[37] What is not clear from the statute itself is the degree of specificity or individual identification of the goods required by the phrase "specific or ascertained". The leading case on the point is the decision of the English Court of Appeal in *Re Wait*.[38] Wait had purchased 1,000 tons of wheat for future delivery and prior to shipment, had resold 500 tons. Wait issued an invoice and was paid by the sub-purchaser before the wheat arrived and before the 500 tons had been appropriated from the shipment of 1,000 tons. Before receipt of the wheat, Wait became bankrupt. The sub-purchaser sued for specific performance, repayment of purchase price, or a declaration of its beneficial interest in the wheat. It was argued that the identification of 500 tons of wheat out of a parcel twice that size to be shipped at a definite time, by definite shippers, and on a definite vessel, identified the wheat with sufficient specificity to justify a specific performance decree.[39] However, the majority of the Court of Appeal held otherwise, and reversed an order for specific performance on the grounds that the goods were not identified or agreed upon within the meaning of the Act at the date of contract, nor at any subsequent time.[40]

638   On its facts, the result in *Re Wait* is understandable. A buyer who had paid for goods on the faith of an invoice was denied any priority

---

[37] *Re Wait*, [1927] 1 Ch. 606 (C.A.), at p. 630, *per* Atkin, L.J.: "'Ascertained' probably means identified in accordance with the agreement after the time a contract of sale is made"; *Thames Sack & Bag Co. Ltd. v. Knowles & Co. Ltd.* (1918), 88 L.J.K.B. 585 at p. 588, *per* Sankey, J.: " 'ascertained' means that the individuality of the goods must in some way be found out, and when it is, then the goods have been ascertained." Both cases were applied in *Re Western Canada Pulpwood Co. Ltd.*, [1930] 1 D.L.R. 652 (Man. C.A.).

[38] *Supra*, footnote 37.

[39] There was some support for this proposition in the case-law: see *Hoare v. Dresser* (1859), 7 H.L.C. 290 at p. 317, 11 E.R. 116; *Holroyd v. Marshall* (1862), 10 H.L.C. 191 at p. 209, 11 E.R. 999. See also the comment by Sir Frederick Pollock, 43 L.Q.R. 293 (1927), describing the result reached by the majority as being "as inconvenient to many merchants as it is surprising to the Equity Bar". However, a similar result had been reached in *Thames Sack & Bag Co. Ltd. v. Knowles & Co. Ltd.*, *supra*, footnote 37, where specific performance of ten items to be taken from a lot of forty-five was refused.

[40] There are several cases dealing with "specific or ascertained" in the context of ascertaining whether property has passed, where it has also been held that until a selection of the part of a larger whole has been made, the goods are not "ascertained": *Ross v. Hurteau* (1890), 18 S.C.R. 713; *Haverson v. Smith* (1906), 16 Man. R. 204 (C.A.); *Zaiser v. Jesske* (1918), 43 D.L.R. 223 (Sask. C.A.); *Lee v. Culp* (1904), 8 O.L.R. 210 (Div. Ct.). *Cf. McGregor v. Whalen* (1914), 20 D.L.R. 489, 31 O.L.R. 543 (S.C. App. Div.), holding (for the purpose of determining whether property had passed) that a contract covering all the timber on a lot was for ascertained chattels, if not at the time of the contract, then immediately upon severance.

over other creditors in the vendor's bankruptcy. It is clear that the majority of the court was concerned with the "far-reaching effects upon commercial transactions",[41] and was strongly influenced by the fact that a specific performance decree declared in the circumstances of an insolvency would seriously affect the reliability of usual financing arrangements and would, as Atkin, L.J., stated, "throw the business world into confusion, for credit would be seriously restricted".[42]

639   On the other hand, it is regrettable that this reasoning should apply to restrict the availability of specific performance generally. Had the commodity been not wheat but some other item in short supply, essential to the plaintiff, and had the plaintiff sued for specific performance, not to gain priority in a bankruptcy, but because he genuinely needed the commodity he had bargained for, it is difficult on principle to see why he should be denied the remedy.[43] Yet if *Re Wait* is to be followed generally, that would be the result. As Professor Treitel has observed, "the main obstacle in the way of a rational development of this branch of the law"[44] has been that the courts have not always focused on the particular interest the plaintiff is seeking to advance, and distinguished cases where there is a genuine desire for the item bargained for, from those cases where the plaintiff is simply trying to obtain priority in a bankruptcy or avoid ordinary mitigation requirements.[45] Oddly enough, however, it would appear that where the "specific or ascertained" requirement is satisfied, the courts have, if anything, been more generous in granting specific performance in bankruptcy cases, sometimes apparently ignoring the uniqueness requirement altogether.[46]

---

[41] *Re Wait, supra*, footnote 37, at p. 625, *per* Atkin, L.J.

[42] *Re Wait, supra*, at p. 640, *per* Atkin, L.J. See also, *supra*, §§550-554.

[43] *Infra*, §§649, 650. ·

[44] "Specific Performance in the Sale of Goods", [1966] Jo. of Bus. Law 211 at pp. 211-12. As Professor Treitel points out at pp. 216-18, the provision may be traced back to the Mercantile Law Amendment Act, 1856, s. 2, which was intended to bring English law more into line with Scots law by enlarging the jurisdiction to award specific performance. However, in Scots law, the right to the equivalent of specific performance was expressly barred in the case of insolvency. Unfortunately, a like provision was not carried forward with the English Act.

[45] See Treitel, *supra*, footnote 44, at pp. 218-21. In Ontario, the purchaser may evade the ordinary requirements by seeking replevin in certain cases: *Report on Sale of Goods, supra*, footnote 35, at p. 439.

[46] See *Bear Creek Lumber Co. v. Edmonton Lumber Co.*, [1930] 3 D.L.R. 406 (Alta. S.C.); *George Eddy Co. Ltd. v. Corey*, [1951] 4 D.L.R. 90 (N.B.S.C. App. Div.); *Fraser v. Sam Kee* (1916), 9 W.W.R. 1281 (B.C. Co. Ct.); Hanbury, *Modern Equity*, 5th ed. (London, Stevens & Sons Ltd., 1949), at p. 608: "[The section]

640   It is unclear whether the line of reasoning followed in *Re Wait* excludes future goods from the ambit of the Act. Arguably, a contract
for the sale of goods to be produced in the future would be for specific or ascertained goods if nothing remained to be done to identify or
earmark the goods once they were produced or once they came into
the seller's possession. Thus, a contract for "the next crop to be
grown on your land" or "the next million cars to come off your as-
sembly line"[47] might be taken to identify sufficiently the subject-matter to bring the case within the Act. The cases have dealt with the issue once the goods have been produced. In an Alberta case, for
example, it was held that as soon as lumber was cut, it had been ascertained for the purposes of specific performance of a contract for
the entire output of a sawmill.[48] In a New Brunswick case,[49] it was
held that where the defendant had contracted to sell the plaintiff "all
the mill cut" of spruce and pine lumber over a three-month period,
approximately 1,500,000 board feet, the lumber was ascertained as
soon as it was sawn, although some culling had to be done.

641   The significance of how "specific or ascertained" is defined is
heightened by the second branch of *Re Wait* which suggests that the
Sale of Goods Act is exhaustive in defining the circumstances in
which specific performance is available, and that there is no discretion outside the Act to award specific performance for contracts for
the sale of goods. In *Re Wait*, Atkin, L.J., said as follows:

> Speaking generally, Courts of equity did not decree specific perfor-
> mance in contracts for the sale of commodities which could be ordinarily
> obtained in the market where damages were a sufficient remedy. Possi-
> bly the statutory remedy was intended to be available even in those
> cases. But the Code appears to have this effect, that in contracts for the
> sale of goods the only remedy by way of specific performance is the stat-
> utory remedy, and it follows that as the goods were neither specific nor
> ascertained the remedy of specific performance was not open to the
> creditors.[50]

642   Despite the tentative way in which this proposition was put, it has

gives to the court a general power which older equity had tended to confine to the
case of chattels of especial beauty or rarity." *Cf.* the current edition, 11th ed. by
Maudsley and Martin (1981), at p. 51: "It was intended to broaden the scope of the
remedy of specific performance in connection with the purchase of chattels, but less
use has been made of it than might have been expected."

[47] Treitel, *supra*, footnote 44, at p. 218.
[48] *Bear Creek Lumber Co. v. Edmonton Lumber Co., supra*, footnote 46.
[49] *George Eddy Co. Ltd. v. Corey, supra*, footnote 46.
[50] *Re Wait, supra*, footnote 37.

been followed, and is often thought to decide the matter.[51] However, the authorities on this point are perhaps not altogether settled. It is clear that the Act deals only with the buyer's right to specific performance. Thus, the buyer may obtain an injunction restraining the breach of a contract of sale where appropriate in circumstances not covered by the Act.[52] In addition, while the Act deals with the vendor's right to sue for the price, the vendor's right to specific performance is not touched, and it has been suggested that the courts retain the discretion to make a specific performance award in the vendor's favour notwithstanding.[53] Thus, the Act hardly provides a comprehensive code of the availability of specific relief with respect to the sale of goods. It might be argued, then, that the Act should not be given a restrictive reading, but that it should be read as leaving intact whatever discretion existed before its enactment. It was enacted with the intention of expanding the circumstances in which specific performance is available, and it would be ironic if legislation designed to expand the availability of a remedy in fact had the effect of restricting it.[54]

643   More recent cases suggest that the courts may be prepared to de-

---

[51] See, *e.g., Humboldt Flour Mills Co. Ltd. v. Boscher* (1974), 50 D.L.R. (3d) 477 (Sask. Q.B.).

[52] *Infra*, §§681-688.

[53] *Shell-Mex Ltd. v. Elton Cop Dyeing Co. Ltd.* (1928), 34 Com. Cas. 39 at p. 46; *Elliott v. Pierson*, [1948] 1 All E.R. 939 (Ch.), at p. 942. Ordinarily, of course, the seller will simply sue for the price after property has passed.

[54] The Ontario Law Reform Commission in its *Report on Sale of Goods, supra*, footnote 35, at pp. 443-4, considered the issue of specific performance and recommended that the discretionary character of the remedy be retained but that s. 50 of the Sale of Goods Act be revised removing the reference to "specific or ascertained goods":

> We recommend that the provision in the revised Act comparable to section 50 of the existing Ontario Act should not be confined to contracts for the delivery of "specific or ascertained goods", but should read as follows:
>
>> In an action against the seller for breach of contract to deliver promised goods, whether or not the goods existed or were identified at the time of the contract, the court may direct that the contract be performed specifically and may impose such terms and conditions as to damages, payment of the price, and otherwise, as seem just to the court.
>
> It will be observed that the important difference between the existing and the recommended section, is that the recommended section omits any requirement that the goods must be in existence or identified to the contract at the time of the contract. As is true of the present section, the recommended section imposes no restrictions on the court's discretion, whether by reference to "unique goods" or otherwise. This should allow ample scope for the development of the remedy of specific performance in the light of changing circumstances and new perceptions about the adequacy of damages.

part from *Re Wait* on this point. In *Sky Petroleum v. V.I.P. Petroleum*,[55] an interlocutory injunction was granted, the court acknowledging that it amounted to specific performance for the contract to supply petroleum notwithstanding the fact that petroleum was neither specific nor ascertained. Similarly, in a Canadian case, specific performance of a contract to supply chicken offal for a five-year period was granted.[56] It is submitted that a restrictive reading is not required by the Act itself, and is certainly undesirable in principle. A Canadian court could properly restrict *Re Wait* to the insolvency situation where it produces an appropriate result. In other cases where the plaintiff demonstrates an interest otherwise worthy of specific relief, but where he cannot satisfy the requirements of the Act, the remedy should be granted on the basis that there remains a discretion to award specific relief outside the confines of the legislation.

(3) Uniqueness

644   Damages are the presumptive remedy for breach of contract for the sale of chattels. Where ordinary, readily available chattels are concerned, a damages award reflecting any difference in price will permit the innocent party to obtain substitute performance in the market.[57] However, it has long been recognized that damages may be inadequate to protect the innocent party's interest in certain cases where market loss does not accurately reflect the loss the plaintiff has actually suffered. This interest has been given a variety of labels. It was once referred to as *pretium affectionis*,[58] and identified especially with family artifacts, or rare artistic or ceremonial objects. The economist's label, "consumer surplus" is now gaining currency.[59] What-

---

[55] [1974] 1 W.L.R. 576 (Ch.).

[56] *Marquest Industries Ltd. v. Willows Poultry Farms Ltd.* (1967), 63 D.L.R. (2d) 753 (B.C.S.C.), revd on other grounds 1 D.L.R. (3d) 513 (B.C.C.A.).

[57] *Adderley v. Dixon* (1824), 1 Sim. & St. 607 at p. 610, 57 E.R. 239, *per* Leach, V.-C.:

> So a Court of Equity will not, generally, decree performance of a contract for the sale of stock or goods, not because of their personal nature, but because damages at law, calculated upon the market price of the stock or goods, are as complete a remedy to the purchaser as the delivery of the stock or goods contracted for; inasmuch as, with the damages, he may purchase the same quantity of the like stock of goods.

Cf., however, the bankruptcy cases referred to, *supra*, footnote 46.

[58] *Nutbrown v. Thornton* (1804), 10 Ves. Jun. 159, 32 E.R. 805, *per* Eldon, L.C., explaining the result in *Pusey v. Pusey* (1684), 1 Vern. 273, 23 E.R. 465.

[59] Harris, Ogus and Phillips, "Contract Remedies and the Consumer Surplus", 95 L.Q.R. 581 (1979). These concepts are also discussed, *supra*, §§545-547.

ever label is used, the concept is essentially the same: the value of the item in question to the plaintiff is not aptly measured by market value because the plaintiff attaches to it some special subjective or emotional value which exceeds its market value.

645　　It has been said on occasion that the intended effect of the Sale of Goods Act provision dealing with specific performance was to remove the equitable restriction limiting the remedy to unique goods, and to permit specific performance so long as the goods are specific or ascertained.[60] There are, however, few if any cases granting specific performance where the plaintiff was not able to demonstrate some particular interest, which would not be met by a damages award, in having the contract performed *in specie* and the traditional discretion has, for the most part, been retained.[61]

646　　The case-law provides many examples of the application of the uniqueness principle. Specific performance or specific restitution orders have been granted with respect to paintings,[62] antiques,[63] ceremonial ornaments, dresses, decorations and papers,[64] family heirlooms,[65] an "Adam" door,[66] and rare china jars.[67]

647　　It would appear that the courts look not only at the nature of the object itself, but also to the plaintiff's interest in it. In one case,[68] an antique dealer was denied specific relief in respect of a set of Hepplewhite chairs which were to form part of his "usual trade stock". In another, a painter was denied specific relief in respect of one of his own paintings on the grounds that he himself had set a price on it which he was prepared to accept in exchange.[69] Presumably, however, even a commercial dealer would be entitled to specific performance where the object was so unusual as to make accurate estimation of its value difficult.

648　　In some cases, items which are ordinarily available may not be so

---

[60] *Supra*, footnote 46.

[61] See, however, the cases cited, *supra*, footnote 46.

[62] *Lowther v. Lowther* (1806), 13 Ves. Jun. 95, 33 E.R. 230.

[63] *Somerset v. Cookson* (1735), 3 P. Wms. 390, 24 E.R. 1114.

[64] *Fells v. Read* (1796), 3 Ves. Jun. 70, 30 E.R. 899; *Lloyd v. Loaring* (1802), 6 Ves. Jun. 773, 31 E.R. 1302.

[65] *Pusey v. Pusey, supra*, footnote 58.

[66] *Phillips v. Lamdin*, [1949] 2 K.B. 33.

[67] *Falcke v. Gray* (1859), 4 Drew. 651 at p. 658, 62 E.R. 250 (specific performance refused on other grounds).

[68] *Cohen v. Roche*, [1927] 1 K.B. 169 at p. 179, *per* McCardie, J.

[69] *Dowling v. Betjemann* (1862), 2 J. & H. 544, 70 E.R. 1175.

because of some disruption in the market, and here too, specific relief has been granted. Specific performance of a Cadillac automobile was awarded in a British Columbia case in 1945 because another could not be had.[70] Similarly, specific relief has been granted with respect to contracts for the supply of such items as sawlogs and petroleum where the items were essential to the plaintiff, and where the market failed to provide either alternate supplies or substitutes.[71]

(4) Commercial cases

649   The courts have held certain purely commercial chattels to be unique and therefore properly the subject of a specific performance decree.[72] In *Behnke v. Bede Shipping Co.*,[73] a ship was found to qualify as being of "peculiar and practically unique value to the plaintiff" because of her cheapness, the fact that the quality of her engines and boilers would qualify her for immediate registration in Germany, the purchaser's place of operation, and the fact that the plaintiff required her for immediate use.[74] Similarly, the High Court of Australia upheld a decree for specific performance of a licensed taxi-cab on the grounds that the number of licences was restricted and "because of the extent to which the price represents the value of the licence, and because of the essentiality to the purchasers' calling of the chattel and the licence annexed thereto, we should treat the contract as within the scope of the remedy of specific performance."[75]

---

[70] *Simmons & McBride Ltd. v. Kirkpatrick*, [1945] 4 D.L.R. 134 (B.C.S.C.).

[71] *Infra*, §650.

[72] *Supra*, §648. See also *Lingen v. Simpson* (1824), 1 Sim. & St. 600, 57 E.R. 236 (pattern books); *Thorn v. Com'rs of Public Works* (1863), 32 Beav. 490, 55 E.R. 192 (building stone from old Westminster Bridge). Formerly, the courts may have been more generous. In *Buxton v. Lister* (1746), 3 Atk. 383 at p. 385, 26 E.R. 1020, Lord Hardwicke suggested the following two cases as appropriate for specific relief:

> A man may contract for the purchase of a great quantity of timber, as a ship carpenter, by reason of the vicinity of the timber, and this on the part of the buyer.

> On the part of the seller, suppose a man wants to clear his land, in order to turn it to a particular sort of husbandry, there nothing can answer the justice of the case, but the performance of the contract in *specie*.

Cf. *Pearne v. Lisle* (1749), Amb. 75 at p. 77, 27 E.R. 47, *per* Hardwicke, L.C., refusing specific relief with respect to slaves in Antigua: "As to the merits, a specific delivery of the Negroes is prayed; but that is not necessary, others are as good . . .".

[73] [1927] 1 K.B. 649.

[74] Specific relief has often been granted in respect of contracts for sale of ships: *Claringbould v. Curtis* (1852), 21 L.J. Ch. 541; *Batthyany v. Bouch* (1881), 50 L.J.Q.B. 421; *Hart v. Herwig* (1873), 8 Ch. App. 860.

[75] *Dougan v. Ley* (1946), 71 C.L.R. 142 (Aust. H.C.), at p. 151, *per* Dixon, J.

650   In certain cases, usually ordinary items become essential to the plaintiff and otherwise unavailable. In such cases, the courts have granted specific performance. In an early English case, the plaintiff was granted specific relief in respect of a number of coal wagons essential to his trade and not readily available on the market.[76] In another, the court granted an order of specific restitution of items of farming stock-in-trade, by themselves ordinary chattels, recognizing the importance of the chattels together as a farming unit.[77] In a New Brunswick case,[78] an order for specific performance of a large quantity of lumber was upheld on appeal where the lumber was of exceptional quality, although it was apparently to be used only for ordinary building purposes. In several early Ontario cases,[79] specific relief was granted in respect of contracts for the sale of sawlogs to mill owners. There was nothing unique or special about the sawlogs themselves. However, they could be conveyed by river only at certain seasons, and were then in short supply as each mill owner had entered contracts to guarantee his own supply. If the supply arrangements were disrupted, it was not feasible, as a practical matter, to secure an alternate supply during that season. The result was that the mill would go idle. The rationale for specific relief in favour of the mill owner was well expressed by Blake, C., as follows:

> To deprive the plaintiff of this property, would not be to subject him to the loss of its mere value as raw material, but it would be to deprive him of all the profit derivable from the manufacture, leaving his invested capital, in the meantime, unproductive. Were we to refuse the assistance of this Court, we should enable the defendants to inflict an injury, which, if it admit at all of any satisfactory measurement of the amount of damages, would be, most certainly, very inadequately compensated by the verdict of a jury. And yet, from the nature of such property, and the manner in which it is necessarily brought to market, it is peculiarly liable to the species of depredation complained of by the plaintiff in this case. Now, did we decline to interpose for the plaintiff's protection, in relation to such property, and under such circumstances, we should, in my opinion, not only limit the jurisdiction of the Court most injuriously,

---

[76] *North v. Great Northern Ry. Co.* (1860), 2 Giff. 64 at p. 69, 66 E.R. 28, *per* Stuart, V.-C.: "It cannot be pretended that the plaintiff could have got, on a sudden, fifty-four other coal waggons fit for his business as readily and promptly as he could have purchased fifty-four tons of coal or fifty-four bushels of wheat."

[77] *Nutbrown v. Thornton* (1804), 10 Ves. Jun. 159, 32 E.R. 805.

[78] *George Eddy Co. Ltd. v. Corey*, [1951] 4 D.L.R. 90 (N.B.S.C. App. Div.).

[79] See *Fuller v. Richmond* (1850), 2 Gr. 24 (interlocutory injunction), 4 Gr. 657 (trial); *Farwell v. Wallbridge* (1851), 2 Gr. 332 (specific delivery of logs wrongfully taken); *Stevenson v. Clarke* (1854), 4 Gr. 540; *Flint v. Corby* (1853), 4 Gr. 45.

as regards suitors, but in a way warranted neither by principle nor authority.[80]

(5) Long-term supply contracts

651   The cases just examined have assumed a single, simple transaction involving the purchase and sale of some good. Often, contractual arrangements are more complex and provide for longer-term supply and purchase of goods.

652   These contracts may take a variety of forms. The most obvious is a straightforward agreement to take a given quantity of some commodity by instalments over a stated period of time. In other cases, the quantity may not be fixed except in terms of the producer's output or the purchaser's requirements. A supplier may agree to sell his entire output, thereby limiting his right to sell to anyone else.[81] Similarly, a purchaser may agree to purchase all his requirements of a certain item, thereby forgoing the right to purchase elsewhere.[82] Such arrangements are often coupled with exclusive agency or franchise arrangements which govern the marketing of the goods supplied.

653   There are many commercial reasons for such arrangements.[83] A buyer may require a guaranteed source of supply of some commodity or ingredient essential to his endeavour. He may wish to protect himself against price fluctuations over time, and to avoid having to buy huge quantities of the goods now which would have to be stored until needed. A supplier may find such arrangements reduce his selling costs and provide him with an assured market which will facilitate

---

[80] *Farwell v. Wallbridge, supra*, footnote 79, at p. 340. *Cf. Société des Industries Metallurgiques S.A. v. Bronx Engineering Co.*, [1975] 1 Lloyd's Rep. 465 (C.A.), refusing an interlocutory injunction to restrain the sale pending trial of a suit for specific performance of a contract to supply a sophisticated machine which had taken nine months to manufacture. Substitutes were available from other suppliers, but only on special order and only after nine to twelve months delay. The court held that while the machine was not an "ordinary article of commerce", it lacked the "unique quality" necessary to award specific relief, and held that the plaintiff could be compensated in damages for any loss suffered by additional delay. The case may perhaps be partly explained on the grounds that the defendant had raised a substantive defence, and as the interlocutory injunction would not only have prevented it from making a profitable sale to a third party, but also caused heavy storage charges, the balance of convenience favoured the defendant.

[81] See, *infra*, §§681-688.

[82] *Ibid.*

[83] The following discussion is adopted from Heydon, *The Restraint of Trade Doctrine* (London, Butterworths, 1971), at p. 205 *et seq.* For discussion of substantive law issues arising in such contracts, see Howard, "The Requirements and the Outputs Contracts", 2 U. of Tasmania L. Rev. 446 (1967); Adams, "Consideration for Requirements Contracts", 94 L.Q.R. 73 (1978).

long-term investment planning. Exclusive supply arrangements may be prompted by a group of producers wishing to reduce costs and gain bargaining strength against powerful purchasers. Exclusive dealer arrangements may allow the producer to reduce sales and advertising costs through an assured channel of distribution which can also offer post-sales service, and at the same time, the dealer benefits from being the only marketing agent of the product within a given area.

654   It is often said that specific performance of long-term commodity contracts will be refused for two reasons. The first has just been examined. Such contracts involve ordinary fungible and unascertained chattels for which specific performance is not ordinarily available.[84] Secondly, specifically enforcing such agreements would involve supervision problems which the courts have wished to avoid.[85] However, such statements are misleading. In fact, the courts often grant specific relief with respect to such arrangements. In the case of negative covenants — agreements not to purchase other than from the plaintiff — injunctions are regularly awarded.[86] The use of injunctions in this area is more conveniently dealt with in the next chapter. Here, however, it is proposed to examine generally the case for and against specific relief with respect to long-term supply contracts.

655   In light of the reasons and motivations for these contracts, it would seem doubtful that damages will always provide a satisfactory remedy. One of the prime effects of a long-term supply contract is to allocate the risk of market fluctuation over the life of the contract. The supplier bears the risk of increase in market prices and enjoys profit if the price declines. With respect to many commodities the market will provide alternate long-term supply sources, and the price of buying equivalent protection against market fluctuation by entering another long-term contract should be readily ascertainable. In such a case,[87] damages will be an adequate remedy, and indeed preferable to specific performance on the grounds that the plaintiff gets what he bargained for, and the need to force compliance against an unwilling defendant is avoided.[88] On the other hand, where an alternate long-

---

[84] *Supra*, §644.

[85] *Pollard v. Clayton* (1855), 1 K. & J. 462, 69 E.R. 540; *Fothergill v. Rowland* (1873), L.R. 17 Eq. 132; *Dominion Coal Co. v. Dominion Iron & Steel Co.*, [1909] A.C. 293 (P.C.).

[86] *Infra*, §§681-688.

[87] See, *e.g., Olds Products Co. v. Montana Mustard Seed Co.* (1973), 37 D.L.R. (3d) 625 (Sask. Q.B.).

[88] This point is developed in greater detail, *supra*, §§538-541.

term contract cannot be made, it would be very difficult for the court to predict accurately market patterns so as to be in a position to measure the plaintiff's loss. Hence, the traditional assertion that damages are adequate in this context is, it is submitted, well founded only on the assumption that another long-term supplier is available. If there is not, and the plaintiff will be forced to cover on a spot basis over the contract period, then accurate estimation of damages must surely be very difficult. The very fact that no other supplier is prepared to enter a similar long-term contract suggests that no one else in the market has the information necessary to speculate on the future price of the commodity in question, and this means that it will be very difficult for the court to make that assessment.

656   In the case of a requirements contract where the plaintiff agrees to take only what he needs rather than a fixed quantity, the very nature of the contract indicates that the plaintiff does not know the precise quantity which will be required during the contract, and hence damage assessment must be largely speculative. Indeed, in these cases, specific relief is ordinarily available by way of injunction.[89] However, a contract not to sell a commodity except to the plaintiff will often not be enforced by injunction,[90] and similar measurement problems occur.

657   The arguments against the proposition that damages are adequate seem more convincing,[91] and have the support of authority. In an early case, specific performance of an agreement for the sale of a quantity of iron to be delivered in instalments over a number of years was granted on the grounds "that the profit upon the contract, being to depend upon future events, cannot be correctly estimated in damages where the calculation must proceed upon conjecture".[92] In an analogous case, where the amount to be paid by way of annuity depended in part upon the quantity of product manufactured by the defendant, the House of Lords granted specific performance.[93] The

---

[89] *Infra*, §§681-684.

[90] *Infra*, §§686, 687.

[91] Treitel, *supra*, footnote 44, concludes at p. 224: "Thus it seems that specific relief should not be excluded in these cases on the grounds that damages are an adequate remedy", but notes that there are other arguments against specific relief, including supervision. See also Waddams, *supra*, footnote 15, §§610-638 for discussion of problems of assessment relating to loss of goodwill and business interruption.

[92] *Adderley v. Dixon* (1824), 1 Sim. & St. 607 at p. 611, 57 E.R. 239, *per* Leach, V.-C., explaining the decisions in *Taylor v. Neville*, cited in *Buxton v. Lister* (1746), 3 Atk. 383, 26 E.R. 1020.

[93] *Ball v. Coggs* (1710), 1 Brown 140, 1 E.R. 471.

same point was made by a Nova Scotia judge in *Dominion Iron & Steel Co. v. Dominion Coal Co.*, which involved a long-term contract for the supply of coal: "Of what possible value could be any opinion given to-day as to the probable price of coal fifty years from this date? If ever there was a case in which it could be said that the remedy at law by way of damages must be inadequate, surely it is such a case as the present."[94] However, the decision to award specific performance was reversed by the Judicial Committee of the Privy Council which merely said that "this is not a contract of which, on the authorities cited, specific performance would be decreed".[95]

658 A possible answer to the plaintiff who complains that damages cannot accurately be assessed is to say that he must either take the risk of inaccurate assessment before the term of the contract has elapsed or, if he wants the assurance of an entirely accurate damages award, wait until the end of the contract period when exact measurement will be possible. However, this answer is surely unsatisfactory. The legal system generally does not favour remedial solutions which require the postponement of litigation,[96] and from the practical point of view, the financial peril in which the plaintiff may find himself may well make such an option unrealistic, especially if the contract extends over a long period of time. Thus, where the plaintiff has entered a long-term supply arrangement for the purpose of protecting himself against fluctuations in price, there would seem to be many cases in which damages may be extremely difficult to assess.

659 The other important aspect of long-term supply arrangements which may render damage awards less than satisfactory relates to the guarantee of the source of supply. Here, the courts have been more sympathetic. The plaintiff's business or industrial activity may be dependent upon a guaranteed source of supply. If so, his reason for entering the contract extends beyond the desire to cover the risk of price fluctuation, and includes the need to ensure that he will have a steady supply of the commodity or item in question. Such a plaintiff may have more at stake than could be reflected in a damages award, as his entire business may be dependent upon the continuation of performance by the defendant. Again, if an alternate source of supply is available, there is no need and probably no desire on the plaintiff's part to resort to specific performance. On the other hand,

---

[94] (1908), 43 N.S.R. 77 (S.C.), at p. 143, *per* Russell, J.

[95] [1909] A.C. 293 (P.C.), at p. 311, *per* Lord Atkinson.

[96] See Waddams, *supra*, footnote 15, §§65-110.

if alternate arrangements are not available, it can surely be argued that the chattel or item in question, although ordinary in one sense, when coupled with the element of guaranteed supply over a lengthy period, is sufficiently unique so as to justify the award of specific relief.

660　　　Recently, in an English case,[97] an interim injunction was granted in favour of a service station operator to restrain a breach pending trial of a gasoline supply agreement, notwithstanding the court's acceptance of the well-known doctrine that specific performance will be refused where the contract involved non-specific and non-ascertained chattels, on the grounds that the rationale behind the rule that damages would be sufficient was lacking. The court recognized that the plaintiff's survival in business depended upon a guaranteed supply and that this interest could not be met through an ordinary damages award in the circumstances. A similar order was made by the British Columbia Supreme Court involving the repudiation of an automobile dealer's franchise agreement on the grounds that the plaintiff's business would be severely disrupted.[98] Anderson, J., held that "a 'dealer franchise agreement' is not a mere contract for the sale of goods. It possesses many unique factors and creates goodwill which is effectively destroyed by termination of the agreement. Damages for breach of this agreement would be extremely difficult to ascertain and would not afford adequate compensation."[99] In another British Columbia case,[100] specific performance of a contract whereby the defendant had agreed to sell the plaintiff chicken offal at a fixed price over a five-year period was awarded. Interim relief has been granted in both Manitoba[101] and Ontario[102] restraining the breach of exclusive agency agreements, effectively forcing defendants to continue supplying plaintiffs, on the grounds that the plaintiff's business would be severely disrupted. In the Ontario case, the court noted that "damages in this case would not be an adequate

---

[97] *Sky Petroleum v. V.I.P. Petroleum*, [1974] 1 W.L.R. 576 (Ch.).

[98] *Baxter Motors Ltd. v. American Motors (Canada) Ltd.* (1973), 40 D.L.R. (3d) 450 (B.C.S.C.).

[99] *Ibid.*, at p. 457.

[100] *Marquest Industries Ltd. v. Willows Poultry Farms Ltd.* (1967), 63 D.L.R. (2d) 753 (B.C.S.C.), revd on other grounds 1 D.L.R. (3d) 513 (B.C.C.A.).

[101] *North West Beverages Ltd. v. Pepsi-Cola (Canada) Ltd.* (1971), 20 D.L.R. (3d) 341 (Man. Q.B.).

[102] *Pasen v. Dominion Herb Distributors Inc.* (1968), 67 D.L.R. (2d) 405, [1968] 1 O.R. 688 (H.C.J.), affd 69 D.L.R. (2d) 651, [1968] 2 O.R. 516 (C.A.). Cf. *Paxton v. Spira* (1965), 54 D.L.R. (2d) 627 (B.C.S.C.), discussed, *infra*, §702.

remedy. In a commercial enterprise such as the plaintiff's, the dealerships which have been built up, always with considerable effort, and the servicing of their accounts are important in the conduct of a business."[103] On similar reasoning, the English Court of Appeal[104] granted an interlocutory injunction restraining breach of a sole distributorship agreement, emphasizing the difficulty of damage assessment in such cases.[105] American courts have long been willing to specifically enforce long-term supply contracts.[106] In the next chapter, cases dealing with injunctive relief for breach of negative covenants are examined. There, it is seen that the courts regularly specifically enforce contracts where the defendant has entered an exclusive sup-

---

[103] *Ibid.*, at p. 409, *per* Wilson, J.

[104] *Evans Marshall & Co. Ltd. v. Bertola S.A.*, [1973] 1 W.L.R. 349 (C.A.).

[105] See also *Montana Mustard Seed Co. Inc. v. Continental Grain Co. (Canada) Ltd. (No. 2)* (1974), 42 D.L.R. (3d) 624 (Sask. C.A.), granting an injunction pending an appeal from the refusal of an interlocutory injunction to restrain breach of a seed supply contract, at pp. 626-7, *per* Maguire, J.A.: "It was not seriously argued that assuming Montana's success on the appeal, it could be fully compensated in damages. Substantial disruption of trade relationships and obligations would be most difficult to estimate in damages and could have far-reaching effect on the present and future business of Montana."

[106] As long ago as 1920, Pound, "The Progress of the Law: Equity", 33 Harv. L. Rev. 420 (1920), at p. 430, when comparing the American and English treatment of instalment contracts, was able to say:

> . . . the American courts have taken a less mechanical and more enlightened view, looking to the circumstances of each particular case to see whether the legal remedy is or is not substantially adequate and not trying to lay down a hard and fast rule that all instalment contracts are or are not specifically enforceable simply because they call for performance in the future.

This experience is now bolstered by a provision in the Uniform Commercial Code which permits the court to decree specific performance "where the goods are unique or in other proper circumstances": s. 2-716(1). The official comment to this paragraph says as follows:

> In view of this Article's emphasis on the commercial feasibility of replacement, a new concept of what are "unique" goods is introduced under this section. Specific performance is no longer limited to goods which are already specific or ascertained at the time of contracting. The test of uniqueness under this section must be made in terms of the total situation which characterizes the contract. Output and requirements contracts involving a particular or peculiarly available source or market present today the typical commercial specific performance situation, as contrasted with contracts for the sale of heirlooms or priceless works of art which were usually involved in the older cases. However, uniqueness is not the sole basis of the remedy under this section for the relief may also be granted "in other proper circumstances" and inability to cover is strong evidence of "other proper circumstances".

See further "Specific Performance and Long Term Supply Contracts: An Application of U.C.C. §2-716", 30 Arkansas L. Rev. 65 (1976); Van Hecke, "Changing Emphasis in Specific Performance", 40 North Carolina L. Rev. 1 (1961); and Note, "Specific Performance: A Liberalization of Equity Standards", 49 Iowa L. Rev. 1290 (1964).

ply agreement whereby he undertakes not to buy a given commodity from anyone except the plaintiff.[107] Although the obligation enforced by the court is cast in negative terms, it is argued that very often the practical effect of such an injunction is to grant specific performance in a positive sense.[108] Thus, it is submitted that many of the injunction cases can perhaps be added here as instances of the court's willingness to grant specific relief of positive aspects of long-term supply agreements where it is clear that the plaintiff's interest in performance would not adequately be protected by a damages award.

661   On the other hand, there are risks involved in the specific performance of such contracts. The problem of possible over-compensation, discussed above,[109] may be particularly acute in cases involving an ongoing relationship between the parties. If there is an alternate source of supply, the plaintiff can be completely protected by a damages award making up any difference in price, and the defendant is left free to follow alternate pursuits. A specific performance decree will force the defendant to carry on a relationship or some activity which for his own reasons he wishes to stop. As noted above, the result will either be waste, in the form of actual performance at a cost to the defendant which exceeds the value to the plaintiff, or a "buy out" by the defendant of the plaintiff's right to insist upon performance.[110] The amount such a defendant will pay to the plaintiff in order to be released from the burden of a specific performance decree will be related to his own situation rather than that of the plaintiff. That amount does not necessarily bear any relationship to the extent of the plaintiff's interest or loss. Unless the plaintiff is able to demonstrate a special interest in having the contract performed, such as those described above, then it is difficult to see any justification for benefiting him to the extent of the defendant's difficulty rather than merely to the extent of his loss.

662   A related concern is that of supervision. It is argued above that the courts have unnecessarily stressed the supervision concern and that compliance with decrees requiring ongoing performance could, as a practical matter, be assured in many situations.[111] On the other hand, there would appear to be a cost involved in enforcing such decrees, a cost which is borne by society at large rather than the parties to the

---

[107] *Infra*, §§681-684.
[108] *Infra*, §§679 and 685.
[109] *Supra*, §§537-539.
[110] *Ibid*.
[111] *Supra*, §§569, 570 and 575.

particular dispute.[112] Accordingly, one of the factors to be assessed by the court is the potential cost of the future judicial involvement in the dispute, which would be avoided through a damages award. The court is, in effect, called upon to make a careful assessment of whether the risk of incurring this cost is justified by the particular need of the plaintiff for the added and more certain protection of specific relief.

663 The variety of potential interests involved in such contracts makes a uniformly applicable remedial solution inappropriate. While it is probably the case that the courts have been unnecessarily cautious in withholding specific performance in this area, there has never been a flat refusal to grant the remedy, and recent cases suggest a greater sensitivity to the diversity of interests and the need for careful analysis of the interests at stake to enable the court to determine whether those interests will be adequately protected by a damages award. To justify the refusal of specific relief, it is submitted that the court should satisfy itself either that damages are truly an adequate remedy, or that the costs and difficulties of specific performance are so great as to outweigh the advantages of giving a more adequate remedy to the plaintiff. With respect to the adequacy of damages, it must be assumed that there is a readily available substitute and that the plaintiff's only interest is to be made whole for any difference in price.[113] Such an assumption perhaps holds, as a practical matter, in most supply or requirements contracts. However, as noted, in the absence of alternate sources of supply, damage assessment will be difficult. In other cases, the plaintiff may have interests beyond the protection against fluctuation in price, which will not be protected unless an order for specific performance is made.

3. Contracts for the Sale of Shares

664 Specific performance is often awarded to enforce contracts for the purchase and sale of shares in corporations. Here, the courts have been much more willing to grant the remedy than is the case with respect to contracts for the purchase and sale of other items, apart from real property. If consistency is to be maintained, specific relief should not be granted unless damages are inadequate. However, as has been noted,[114] "inadequacy of damages" is a most elastic con-

---

[112] *Supra*, §§570-573.

[113] *Supra*, §§542-544.

[114] *Supra*, §§529-549.

cept, and in the case of contracts for the purchase and sale of shares, courts have been prepared to stretch it in favour of specific relief.

665   Where the shares are not publicly traded, obvious valuation problems arise. Presumably, reasonably accurate estimates of value could be made, but the cost might often be excessive, and is readily avoidable through a specific performance decree.[115] Although alternate investments could be found, shares in one company are not the equivalent of shares in another, and even though the plaintiff's interest is purely financial, the courts have consistently awarded specific performance in such cases.[116] Indeed, specific performance has been awarded even with respect to very small companies, where personal co-operation between shareholders as investors is involved.[117]

666   Where, however, the shares are traded on the market, valuation can be had readily, and unless the plaintiff has some special interest there would seem to be no reason to depart from the normal remedy of damages. Indeed, a damages award which effectively crystallizes the effect of breach at an early point offers distinct advantages over specific performance here as the value of shares is often fluctuating.[118] A specific performance decree might often permit the plaintiff to speculate at the defendant's expense, something normally discouraged.[119] There is good authority to the effect that specific performance should not be awarded where there is a market in the shares,[120] but not all cases have followed this, and specific relief has

---

[115] *Connor v. MacCulloch* (1974), 18 N.S.R. (2d) 404 (S.C.).

[116] *Eansor v. Eansor*, [1946] S.C.R. 54, [1946] 2 D.L.R. 781; *McGregor v. Curry* (1914), 20 D.L.R. 706, 31 O.L.R. 261 (S.C. App. Div.), affd 25 D.L.R. 771 (P.C.); *Helwig v. Siemon* (1916), 10 O.W.N. 296 (Div. Ct.); *Gilbert v. Barron* (1958), 13 D.L.R. (2d) 262, [1958] O.W.N. 98 (H.C.J.). In *Duncuft v. Albrecht* (1841), 12 Sim. 189 at p. 199, 59 E.R. 1104, Shadwell, V.-C., distinguished shares from government stocks which produced a fixed return, where specific performance is not available:

> . . . in my opinion, there is not any sort of analogy between a quantity of 3 per cents. or any other stock of that description (which is always to be had by any person who chooses to apply for it in the market), and a certain number of railway shares of a particular description; which railway shares are limited in number, and which, as has been observed, are not always to be had in the market.

[117] See, *e.g., Reardon v. Franklin* (1917), 35 D.L.R. 380 (N.S.S.C.), affd 55 S.C.R. 613, 39 D.L.R. 176, where the shares were required to qualify the plaintiff as a director; *Poole v. Middleton* (1861), 29 Beav. 646, 54 E.R. 778, granting specific performance to a purchaser although the vendor could not get the consent of the directors required by a joint stock company's deed of settlement. See also *New Brunswick & Co. v. Muggeridge* (1859), 4 Drew. 686, 62 E.R. 263, where the analogy to a partnership is discussed.

[118] Waddams, *supra*, footnote 15, §§65-110, especially §110.

[119] *Supra*, §§94 and 533-535.

[120] *Re Schwabacher* (1908), 98 L.T. 127 (Ch.), at p. 128, *per* Parker, J.: "when shares

been awarded even with respect to publicly traded shares.[121]

667   Even where the market provides ready valuation of individual shares, specific relief may be called for if market value does not accurately reflect the plaintiff's interest in the contract. The clearest example is where the plaintiff's shares represent a controlling block in the company.[122] Whether completion of the contract would give the plaintiff majority or *de facto* control,[123] the value of such shares will exceed the value of their number times the market price of individual shares. However, fixing that extra value may be extremely difficult and expensive. In such a case, specific performance is called for. Sometimes, however, the issue may be more complex than a straightforward agreement to buy a controlling block.[124] The plaintiff may own a substantial block and be buying a few more shares to take his holdings to the point of control. If other shares are available in the market, specific performance would seem unnecessary, but if they are not, he should be given specific performance. Another problem arises where control is being acquired through several contracts for smaller amounts. Denying specific performance of one contract suggests that it would be denied in any individual case, but at some point, that would operate unfairly against the plaintiff. Thus, it is suggested that specific performance should be available where its denial in an individual case potentially threatens the plaintiff's scheme for acquiring control.

---

are dealt in largely on the market, and anyone can go and buy them as appears to be the fact in this case — there is no reason why they should not be in the same position as Government Stock"; *Asamera Oil Corp. Ltd. v. Sea Oil & General Corp.*, [1979] 1 S.C.R. 633 at pp. 644-5, 89 D.L.R. (3d) 1 at p. 8, *per* Estey, J.; *Cud v. Rutter* (1719), 1 P. Wms. 570 at p. 571, 24 E.R. 521, *per* Parker, L.C., refusing specific performance with respect to South-Sea stock: "a court of equity ought not to execute any of these contracts, but to leave them to law, where the party is to recover damages, and with the money may if he pleases buy the quantity of stock agreed to be transferred to him; for there can be no difference between one man's stock and another's." See also *Cappur v. Harris* (1723), Bunb. 135, 145 E.R. 623.

[121] *W.C. Pitfield & Co. Ltd. v. Jomac Gold Syndicate Ltd.*, [1938] 3 D.L.R. 158, [1938] O.R. 427 (C.A.). See also *Re Overend, Gurney, & Co.* (1867), L.R. 5 Eq. 193; *Paine v. Hutchinson* (1868), 3 Ch. App. 388; *Shepherd v. Gillespie* (1867), L.R. 5 Eq. 293, affd 3 Ch. App. 764, specifically enforcing share sale contracts in the context of liquidation proceedings.

[122] *Dobell v. Cowichan Copper Co. Ltd. (N.P.L.)* (1967), 65 D.L.R. (2d) 440 (B.C.S.C.); Note, "Specific Performance of Contracts for a Controlling Interest in a Corporation", 49 Harv. L. Rev. 122 (1935); *Asamera Oil Corp. Ltd. v. Sea Oil & General Corp., supra,* footnote 120.

[123] *Dobell v. Cowichan Copper Co. Ltd. (N.P.L.), supra,* footnote 122.

[124] Note, "Specific Performance of Contracts for a Controlling Interest in a Corporation", *supra,* footnote 122.

668   Specific performance has been awarded to vendors of shares as
well as to purchasers.[125] Many of the arguments for and against the
vendor's right to specific performance made in the context of land
contracts[126] could also be made here and will not be repeated. In addition to those considerations, certain other points may be made. In
several cases in which the vendor has succeeded, the shares were
subject to calls for further contributions to the company and this may
well have made for valuation problems.[127] It has been held that an
employer's agreement to buy back shares sold to an employee may
be specifically enforced,[128] again perhaps because of valuation problems. Many cases have involved the company itself as vendor, and it
may well be that specific performance was essential where other buy-
ers could not be found readily, and where immediate cash was required to launch the enterprise.[129] In a Canadian case,[130] specific performance in the vendor's favour was held appropriate, although the
shares were freely traded on the market, on the grounds that the
agreement involved such a large block of shares that the market price
would be depressed if they were dumped on the market. Presumably, a damages award could reflect any loss caused by a depression
in the price of the shares, but there may have been longer-term effects more difficult to assess.

---

[125] *David v. Dow* (1916), 27 D.L.R. 689 (Alta. C.A.); *Canada Life Ass'ce Co. v. Peel
General Manufacturing Co.* (1879), 26 Gr. 477.

[126] *Supra*, §§621-634.

[127] *New Brunswick & Co. v. Muggeridge, supra*, footnote 117; *Cheale v. Kenward*
(1858), 27 L.J. Ch. 784.

[128] *MacDonald v. Soulis*, [1925] 2 D.L.R. 926 (N.S.S.C.).

[129] See, *e.g.*, *Odessa Tramways Co. v. Mendel* (1878), 8 Ch. D. 235 (C.A.), at p. 248,
per Thesiger, L.J.

[130] *McDougall Segur Exploration Co. of Canada Ltd. v. Solloway Mills & Co. Ltd.*,
[1931] 2 W.W.R. 516 (Alta. S.C.).

CHAPTER 9

INJUNCTIONS TO RESTRAIN BREACH OF CONTRACT

1. Introduction

669 In many cases, injunctive relief will be appropriate as the specific remedy for breach of contract. Where a party has by contract undertaken not to do something, specific performance of that obligation is achieved by enjoining its breach. Where specific performance is sought of a positive obligation, the plaintiff must establish that the ordinary remedy of damages would be inadequate. In the case of negative obligations, however, the courts have more readily granted injunctive relief. Reference is almost invariably made to the dictum of Lord Cairns, L.C., in *Doherty v. Allman*:

> If parties, for valuable consideration, with their eyes open, contract that a particular thing shall not be done, all that a Court of Equity has to do is to say, by way of injunction, that which the parties have already said by way of covenant, that the thing shall not be done; and in such case the injunction does nothing more than give the sanction of the process of the Court to that which already is the contract between the parties. It is not then a question of the balance of convenience or inconvenience, or of the amount of damage or of injury—it is the specific performance, by the Court, of that negative bargain which the parties have made, with their eyes open, between themselves.[1]

670 Stated in such absolute terms, the doctrine that an injunction will always be available may be misleading,[2] but if taken as a statement of general principle, it accurately reflects the attitude of the courts to

---

[1] (1878), 3 App. Cas. 709 (H.L.), at p. 720.

[2] *Infra*, §§671, 672. *Cf.* also the more cautious dictum of Blackburn, J., in *Doherty*, *supra*, footnote 1, at p. 730: "Even where there have been negative words, circumstances may change, so that though the covenant still remains it would not be reasonable that it should be enforced."

contractual obligations which are negative in character. Even where the obligation extends over a period of time, the court does not concern itself with problems of enforcement. Ordinarily it is easier to ensure that a party has refrained from doing something than it is to ensure that some act of positive performance is carried out satisfactorily. Similarly, the cost of compliance to the party enjoined is less likely to prove disproportionate to the value of the benefit conferred on the plaintiff than in other injunction cases, because the defendant has unequivocally and voluntarily accepted the obligation.[3] The courts have sometimes said that in the case of an express negative covenant, it is unnecessary for the plaintiff to establish any damage at all.[4] This appears not so much to depart from the principle that the plaintiff must show irreparable harm as to be an instance where the courts are prepared to respect what is analogous to a stipulated remedy clause.[5] In one old case,[6] where the court granted an injunction restraining violation of a covenant not to keep a school, the court responded to the argument that the plaintiff had failed to show irreparable harm as follows: "But a person who stipulates that her neighbour shall not keep a school stipulates that she shall be relieved from all anxiety arising from a school being kept; and the feeling of anxiety is damage."

671   Notwithstanding the seeming inflexibility of the *Doherty v. Allman* principle, there are, however, many cases in which injunctions have been refused when sought to enforce negative contractual obligations.[7] These cases have usually arisen where the injunction is sought after the completion of work or building in violation of a neg-

---

[3] See *Thomas Borthwick & Sons (Australasia) Ltd. v. South Otago Freezing Co.*, [1978] 1 N.Z.L.R. 538 (C.A.), at p. 547, *per* Cooke, J.:

As we see it, the main significance of an express negative covenant . . . is twofold. It enables the court readily to define what the defendant may be enjoined from doing; and it emphasises that the defendant has unequivocally accepted this obligation, thus tending to make it more difficult for him to set up hardship.

[4] *Dickenson v. Grand Junction Canal Co.* (1852), 15 Beav. 260 at p. 271, 51 E.R. 538, *per* Romilly, M.R.: "It is for them to judge whether the agreement shall be preserved, so far as they are concerned, in its integrity, or whether they shall permit it to be violated"; *Elliston v. Reacher*, [1908] 2 Ch. 374, affd *loc. cit.* p. 665 (C.A.); *A.-G. v. Comox Logging Co.*, [1955] 2 D.L.R. 211 (B.C.S.C.); *Munnion v. Winch*, [1938] 4 D.L.R. 656 (Man. C.A.); *Dobell v. Cowichan Copper Co. Ltd. (N.P.L.)* (1967), 65 D.L.R. (2d) 440 (B.C.S.C.).

[5] *Supra*, §§594-604.

[6] *Kemp v. Sober* (1851), 1 Sim. (N.S.) 517 at p. 520, 61 E.R. 200, *per* Cranworth, V.-C. See also *Manners v. Johnson* (1875), 1 Ch. D. 673.

[7] See *Servicemaster Industries Inc. v. Servicemaster of Victoria Ltd.* (1979), 101 D.L.R. (3d) 376 (B.C.S.C.), refusing an injunction on the grounds of delay.

ative obligation, and mandatory relief is required to put matters right,[8] or where the breach is a trivial one.[9] Here, there may be a disproportion of burden to benefit.[10] In one case, where the defendant had installed a window in defiance of a covenant not to alter the exterior of his house, but where the plaintiff was unable to prove any diminution in market value of his property, the court refused an injunction on the grounds that,[11] "if the granting of a mandatory order would inflict damage upon the defendant out of all proportion to the relief which the plaintiff ought to obtain, the Court will . . . refuse it". In a more recent English case,[12] Megarry, J., held that there were important differences between prohibitory and mandatory injunctions to enforce negative obligations: "whereas a prohibitory injunction merely requires abstention from acting, a mandatory injunction requires the taking of positive steps, and may (as in the present case) require the dismantling or destruction of something already erected or constructed". Megarry, J., referred to the statement of Astbury, J., quoted above, as one "to which the books, I think, have not given due attention".[13]

672   For rather different reasons, neither does the *Doherty v. Allman* principle apply with the same force to interlocutory injunctions.[14] There, the court does not have the advantage of a full review of the facts and law, and the validity or enforceability of the covenant may not be upheld at trial. The ordinary criteria determining the availability of interlocutory injunctions apply,[15] and a plaintiff who sues

---

[8] *Leader v. Moody* (1875), L.R. 20 Eq. 145; *Bowes v. Law* (1870), L.R. 9 Eq. 636. The principles governing mandatory injunctions are discussed, *supra*, §§50-65.

[9] *Harrison v. Good* (1871), L.R. 11 Eq. 338 at p. 352, *per* Bacon, V.-C.:

> . . . we all know that, although the Court of Chancery interferes, when it thinks it right, by way of injunction to prevent the violation of a covenant, yet, if the violation is so slight, formal, and unsubstantial that the Plaintiff can have no ground in conscience to complain of it, the Court will not grant an injunction.

See also *Denison v. Carrousel Farms Ltd* (1982), 138 D.L.R. (3d) 381, 38 O.R. (2d) 52 (C.A.), granting an injunction, but resting the decision on the grounds that the harm was substantial, and that the hardship to the defendant did not outweigh the benefit to the plaintiff.

[10] *Supra*, §558.

[11] *Sharp v. Harrison*, [1922] 1 Ch. 502 at p. 515, *per* Astbury, J.

[12] *Shepherd Homes Ltd. v. Sandham*, [1971] Ch. 340 at p. 348.

[13] *Ibid.*, at p. 350.

[14] *Texaco Ltd. v. Mulberry Filling Station Ltd.*, [1972] 1 W.L.R. 814 (Ch.), at pp. 830-1, *per* Ungoed-Thomas, J.; *Crampton and Brown v. Robertson*, [1977] 6 W.W.R. 99 (B.C.S.C.); *Heinke and Blaeberry River Timber Co. v. Canadian Credit Men's Trust Ass'n Ltd.* (1956), 4 D.L.R. (2d) 298 (B.C.S.C.).

[15] *Supra*, Chapter 2.

upon an express negative covenant will not be awarded interlocutory injunctive relief automatically.

2. Distinguishing Positive and Negative Obligations

673   Rigid adherence to a formal distinction between positive and negative obligations would produce awkward results. It is possible to phrase a positive obligation in negative terms by excluding everything but the positive act which the contracting party has undertaken to perform. This point was made by Lindley, L.J., in *Whitwood Chemical Co. v. Hardman*:

> Now every agreement to do a particular thing in one sense involves a negative. It involves the negative of doing that which is inconsistent with the thing you are to do. If I agree with a man to be at a certain place at a certain time. I impliedly agree that I will not be anywhere else at the same time, and so on *ad infinitum*; but it does not at all follow that, because a person has agreed to do a particular thing, he is, therefore, to be restrained from doing everything else which is inconsistent with it. The Court has never gone that length, and I do not suppose that it ever will.[16]

674   In applying the *Doherty v. Allman* principle then, the courts are to be governed by the substance of the obligation and not the form.[17] Thus, an undertaking not to terminate the plaintiff's employment, although phrased in negative terms, in fact expresses a substantively positive obligation. In making such a contract, the defendant has agreed to continue employing the plaintiff, and the obligation is negative in form only and an injunction will be refused.[18] One of the leading cases on this point, *Fothergill v. Rowland*,[19] involved an

---

[16] [1891] 2 Ch. 416 (C.A.), at p. 426.

[17] *Wolverhampton & Walsall Ry. Co. v. London & North-Western Ry. Co.* (1873), L.R. 16 Eq. 433 at p. 440, *per* Selborne, L.C.:

> I can only say, that I should think it was the safer and the better rule, if it should eventually be adopted by this Court, to look in all such cases to the substance and not to the form. If the substance of the agreement is such that it would be violated by doing the thing sought to be prevented, then the question will arise, whether this is the Court to come to for a remedy. If it is, I cannot think that ought to depend on the use of a negative rather than an affirmative form of expression. If, on the other hand, the substance of the thing is such, that the remedy ought to be sought elsewhere, then I do not think that the forum ought to be changed by the use of a negative rather than an affirmative.

[18] *Davis v. Foreman*, [1894] 3 Ch. 654; *Kirchner & Co. v. Gruban*, [1909] 1 Ch. 413. *Cf. Crisp v. Holden* (1910), 54 Sol. Jo. 784, granting an interlocutory injunction restraining the dismissal of a school teacher, on the grounds that a notice of termination had been given without authority.

[19] (1873), L.R. 17 Eq. 132. A similar case is *Pollard v. Clayton* (1855), 1 K. & J. 462, 69 E.R. 540.

agreement by the defendant to sell all of the coal mined from a specified seam in a colliery for a five-year period. The court held that it would not grant specific performance of the contract had the obligation been put in positive terms, because the commodity was readily available and damages afforded adequate protection to the plaintiff. Because specific performance would not have been available, the court refused to grant an injunction restraining the defendant from selling his coal to anyone else, as this amounted to achieving "the same thing by a roundabout method".[20]

675 Similarly, the fact that an obligation is expressed in positive terms will not deter the courts from granting injunctive relief on the *Doherty v. Allman* principle, if that obligation is in substance negative.[21] Thus, an agreement to purchase all of the defendant's requirements of a certain commodity, although phrased in positive language, has been treated as negative in substance.[22] In such an agreement, the essence of the obligation is not that any particular quantity will be purchased, or even that the defendant will purchase any at all, but rather that, if he does purchase any of the commodity in question, he will buy from the plaintiff.[23]

676 A related doctrine is that expressed by the Privy Council in *Lord Strathcona Steamship Co. Ltd. v. Dominion Coal Co. Ltd.*[24] There, it

---

[20] *Fothergill, supra*, footnote 19, at p. 140, *per* Jessel, M.R. For other examples of refusal to grant an injunction which would amount to specific performance, see *London, Chatham & Dover Ry. Co. Ltd. v. Spiers & Pond, Ltd.* (1916), 32 T.L.R. 493 (injunction against closing a hotel refused); *Prosperity Ltd. v. Lloyds Bank* (1923), 39 T.L.R. 372 (injunction against closing bank account refused); *Hooper v. Brodrick* (1840), 11 Sim. 47, 59 E.R. 791 (injunction against closing inn refused). *Cf.* however, *infra*, §§681-688, and *Le Blanch v. Granger* (1866), 35 Beav. 187, 55 E.R. 866.

[21] *Manchester Ship Canal Co. v. Manchester Racecourse Co.*, [1901] 2 Ch. 37 (C.A.) (right of "first refusal"). See also *Snider v. McKelvey* (1900), 27 O.A.R. 339, and *National Provincial Bank of England v. Marshall* (1888), 40 Ch. D. 112 (C.A.), holding that an agreement to pay a stated sum if the defendant did compete with the plaintiff was properly the subject of an injunction. For an unusual example, see *Bradley v. McClure* (1908), 18 O.L.R. 503 (Div. Ct.), holding that an agreement to lease farm land for pasture purposes permits the defendant to cut hay, but not to sell it, since by feeding it to animals on the farm, the pasture could still benefit from the manure. *Cf. City of Hamilton v. Hamilton Street Ry. Co. (No. 2)* (1905), 10 O.L.R. 594 (C.A.), affd 39 S.C.R. 673 (discussed, *supra*, §32), granting an injunction which restrained the defendant from operating its railway other than in a manner consistent with its agreement; *Mortimer v. Beckett*, [1920] 1 Ch. 571, refusing to imply a negative term from a "sole" agency agreement.

[22] *Metropolitan Electric Supply Co. Ltd. v. Ginder*, [1901] 2 Ch. 799. This case and others like it are discussed in greater detail, *infra*, §§681-688.

[23] See also *Erskine MacDonald Ltd. v. Eyles*, [1921] 1 Ch. 631, enforcing an exclusive publishing contract for future novels by way of injunction.

[24] [1926] A.C. 108, [1926] 1 D.L.R. 873 (P.C.).

was held that there could be implied a negative obligation, enforceable by injunction, not to use a ship which had been chartered in a manner inconsistent with that charter. An injunction was granted restraining a purchaser who had notice of the charter from defeating the rights of the charterer. The Privy Council adopted and applied the reasoning of Knight Bruce, L.J., in *De Mattos v. Gibson*:

> Why should it [the court] not prevent the commission or continuance of a breach of such a contract, when, its subject being valuable, as for instance a trading ship or some costly machine, the original owner and possessor, or a person claiming under him, with notice and standing in his right, having the physical control of the chattel, is diverting it from the agreed object, that object being of importance to the other? A system of laws in which such a power does not exist must surely be very defective. I repeat that, in my opinion, the power does exist here.[25]

677   In *Lord Strathcona*, Lord Shaw, giving the opinion of the Board, said that it did not matter that the court could not enforce specific performance; it could proceed "if there is expressed or clearly implied a negative stipulation".[26] The reasoning in the *Lord Strathcona* and *De Mattos* cases would appear to be contradicted by that in the *Whitwood* case referred to above,[27] as here the court appears to be saying that, although it could not specifically enforce a positive obligation, it can issue an injunction restraining the defendant from doing everything else which is inconsistent with that obligation. However, the particular context of those cases must be remembered, and it is submitted that, from the remedial point of view,[28] the results are defensible. Although the plaintiff has no proprietary interest, en-

---

[25] (1859), 4 De G. & J. 276 at p. 283, 45 E.R. 108.

[26] *Supra*, footnote 24, at p. 125 A.C., p. 884 D.L.R.

[27] *Supra*, §673.

[28] These cases also raise difficult issues of substantive law as to the extent to which third parties can be bound by restrictions imposed on the use of chattels for the benefit of the plaintiff: see *McGruther v. Pitcher*, [1904] 2 Ch. 306 (C.A.); *Barker v. Stickney*, [1919] 1 K.B. 121 (C.A.), refusing to follow *De Mattos*; and *Greenhalgh v. Mallard*, [1943] 2 All E.R. 234 (C.A.); *Port Line Ltd. v. Ben Line Steamers Ltd.*, [1958] 2 Q.B. 146, refusing to follow *Lord Strathcona*. Cf. however *Swiss Bank Corp. v. Lloyds Bank*, [1979] 1 Ch. 548, vard [1982] A.C. at p. 587 (C.A.) affd *loc. cit.* p. 584 (H.L.); *Trudel v. Clairol Inc. of Canada*, [1975] 2 S.C.R. 236, 54 D.L.R. (3d) 399; *Manchester Ship Canal Co. v. Manchester Racecourse Co.*, *supra*, footnote 21. There has been considerable discussion recently of the substantive law problems raised by these cases: see Cohen-Grabelsky, "Interference with Contractual Relations and Equitable Doctrines", 45 Mod. L. Rev. 241 (1982); Tettenborn, "Covenants, Privity of Contract, and the Purchaser of Personal Property", 41 Camb. L.J. 58 (1982); Gardner, "The Proprietary Effect of Contractual Obligations under *Tulk v. Moxhay* and *De Mattos v. Gibson*", 98 L.Q.R. 279 (1982).

forceable by specific performance, in the property in question, the courts will not permit another to deal with that property in such a way as knowingly to bring about a breach of contract affecting it. While the doctrine may not coincide exactly with the tort of inducing breach of contract, the rationale here is a similar one.[29] Hence, the *Lord Strathcona* and *De Mattos* cases do not permit the court to imply negative obligation so as to achieve specific performance in a backhanded way, but represent one aspect of the power of the courts to grant injunctions to protect parties from having their contractual rights interfered with by others.

678   The strength of the distinction between negative and positive obligations would appear to rest both on the nature of the burden imposed and upon the ease of enforcement. The essence of a negative obligation in this context is that the defendant is restrained from doing one particular and specific act or activity. The argument in favour of specific relief is that, by forbidding the defendant from doing that act, he is free to do anything else, and the obligation is both readily enforceable and relatively unburdensome because of his agreement. The essence of enforcing a positive obligation is to require the defendant to undertake a certain specific course of action. Whether the court is asked to do this by a specific performance decree requiring that act to be carried out, or by way of an injunction restraining the defendant generally from doing anything else which is inconsistent with that obligation should not matter. The important point is that a certain positive course of action is required, and principles governing the availability of specific performance should not be circumvented on the basis of formal wording of the obligation or of the order the court is asked to make.

679   Viewed in a broader light, however, it might be argued that the courts have placed too much weight on the supposed difference between positive and negative obligations. In many cases, excluding the defendant from doing an act will amount in practical terms to an order requiring him to take some positive course of action. If that positive course of action is one for which the courts would not award specific performance, then injunctive relief should also be avoided. The range of cases in which excluding the defendant from doing an act will, in practical terms, force him to perform an obligation the

---

[29] *Cf. Swiss Bank Corp. v. Lloyds Bank, supra,* footnote 28, at pp. 570-5, *per* Browne-Wilkinson, J.; Treitel, "Limited Interest in Chattels", 21 Mod. L. Rev. 433 (1958); Cohen-Grabelsky, *supra,* footnote 28; Tettenborn, *supra,* footnote 28.

court would not specifically enforce is perhaps much wider than the courts have admitted. In the discussion of the enforcement of long-term supply contracts which follows,[30] it will be seen that injunctions have often been granted notwithstanding the fact that they must have amounted, in practical terms, virtually to an order of specific performance, and in some cases the courts have even admitted this.[31] While the justification for an injunction has turned on the distinction between negative and positive obligations, it is submitted that this strong line of authority enforcing negative long-term supply agreements might now be taken as implicitly recognizing that specific relief of such arrangements may often be appropriate. Admittedly, there is a difference between enjoining the defendant from purchasing a commodity from anyone but the plaintiff and forcing him to take a fixed quantity. He can still choose to buy nothing at all, an option not available if a specific performance decree is made. Still, in many of the cases, it will be seen that the court must have known that the practical effect would be to force the defendant to buy from the plaintiff, and perhaps these authorities may now be used to justify the extension of specific relief by modern courts more prepared to recognize different interests as meriting protection.

680   Another point relates to the supervision concern. It is not entirely accurate to say that enforcing a negative promise by injunction does not give rise to enforcement problems. Often, the obligation extends over a lengthy period, and while the definition of what is to be done or not done may be clear, the court is certainly leaving itself open to the possibility of subsequent enforcement proceedings.[32] In addition,

---

[30] *Infra*, §§681-688.

[31] In *Thomas Borthwick & Sons (Australasia) Ltd. v. South Otago Freezing Co.*, [1978] 1 N.Z.L.R. 538 (C.A.), at p. 548, *per* Cooke, J., an injunction restraining the defendant from handling anyone else's stock was upheld, the court accepting that the order amounts to "specific performance in a roundabout way: that the injunction means that [the defendants] could use its works to fulfil the contract or not at all". See also *George Eddy Co. Ltd. v. Corey*, [1951] 4 D.L.R. 90 (N.B.S.C. App. Div.); *Bennison Lane Enterprises Ltd. v. W. Krause Logging Ltd.*, [1977] 6 W.W.R. 93 (B.C.S.C.).

[32] See, *e.g.*, *Nimmons v. Gilbert* (1907), 6 W.L.R. 531 (N.W.T.), enjoining breach of an agreement not to employ more than ten men in a group; *Transcontinental Ry. Com'rs v. G.T.P. Ry.* (1912), 4 O.W.N. 495 (H.C.), enjoining breach of an agreement not to remove equipment from a building site for a stated period. *Cf. Hill v. Fraser* (1914), 18 D.L.R. 1 (Alta. S.C.), refusing an injunction against removal of goods from leased premises at the suit of the landlord to protect his rights of distress, on the grounds that the order would call for supervision of the defendant's business; and *Altman v. Royal Aquarium Society* (1876), 3 Ch. D. 228, where positive action would have been required as a result of the injunction.

injunctions enforcing exclusive purchase agreements are always coupled with the condition that the plaintiffs supply a reasonable quantity and quality of goods at a reasonable price.[33] This leaves room for debate as to the adequacy of performance which may extend over a lengthy period, but has not stopped the courts from granting such injunctions. It is submitted that the decisions are not to be criticized on this account, but rather taken in a positive sense as indicating the willingness of the courts to grant specific relief in a broader range of cases than is usually admitted.

3. Long-term Supply Contracts

681   Despite the disinclination to order specific performance of agreements for the purchase of ordinary commodities,[34] agreements not to purchase fungible goods over extended periods from anyone but the plaintiff are regularly enforced by injunction. The courts have distinguished these cases from those where the plaintiff seeks specific performance of a positive obligation to supply such goods, or even those where the defendant has promised not to sell his goods to anyone but the plaintiff, on the grounds that injunctive relief should be awarded on the *Doherty v. Allman*[35] principle where the obligation is negative in substance.

682   The case-law provides many examples. Service station operators often enter exclusive supply contracts with petroleum companies, and in cases where the operator attempts to purchase products covered by the agreement from someone other than the plaintiff, injunctions have been granted.[36] Similarly, in England, publicans enter "tied house" agreements, and these are regularly enforced by injunction.[37]

---

[33] See, *e.g.*, *Metropolitan Electric Supply Co. Ltd. v. Ginder*, [1901] 2 Ch. 799 at p. 812, *per* Buckley, J.:

> I must reserve liberty to the defendant to apply, by which I mean this—that if at any time the plaintiffs are not prepared to supply the energy which he wants, or if they supply an energy which is not an efficient supply such as they are bound to give by the Act of Parliament, then I think he ought to be at liberty to apply to be relieved from the operation of the injunction.

[34] *Supra*, §§644-650.

[35] *Supra*, §669.

[36] *Cities Service Oil Co. v. Pauley*, [1931] O.R. 685 (H.C.); *McColl Bros. v. Avery* (1928), 34 O.W.N. 275 (Div. Ct.); *British American Oil Co. v. Hey*, [1941] 4 D.L.R. 725, [1941] O.W.N. 397 (H.C.J.); *Foley v. Classique Coaches Ltd.*, [1934] 2 K.B. 1 (C.A.).

[37] *Clegg v. Hands* (1890), 44 Ch. D. 503 (C.A.); *Courage & Co. v. Carpenter*, [1910] 1 Ch. 262; *Catt v. Tourle* (1869), 4 Ch. App. 654. See also *Servais Bouchard v. Prince's Hall Restaurant* (1904), 20 T.L.R. 574 (C.A.).

683   Three early western Canadian cases[38] dealing with "ready prints", partially printed newspapers containing general material and advertising to be completed with local material by local newspapers, provide an interesting illustration of the application of this principle. The arrangements were that the supplier of ready prints sold his product to local newspapers at a reduced price, sometimes below cost, the newspaper undertaking not to purchase ready prints from anyone else. The supplier's revenue depended on advertising for which he needed firm circulation figures. While it is unlikely that the courts would have enforced the positive agreement by the defendant to take a fixed number of ready prints over an extended period, enforcing the negative covenant did provide the supplier with some, albeit more limited, guarantee of a firm circulation.[39] At the same time, the burden of the negative obligation was perhaps less onerous than a positive decree would have been. By enforcement of the negative obligation, the local paper was not bound to continue purchasing ready prints should the nature of its operations change.

684   The leading English case, *Metropolitan Electric Supply Co. Ltd. v. Ginder*,[40] dealt with a contract whereby the defendant had undertaken to purchase all his electricity requirements from the plaintiff. It was mentioned in argument that in exchange for this obligation the defendant had been given a reduced price for his electricity. The court made it clear that the obligation was in substance negative and that, by enforcing it, the court was not requiring the defendant to take any energy at all from the plaintiff. He could use gas or some other form of energy if he liked, but if he chose to use electricity, he had to take it from the plaintiff. There was no discussion of the plaintiff's interest in the case, but it is likely that some form of established distribution network was essential to its enterprise.

685   As indicated above,[41] it can be argued that too much is made here

---

[38] *Winnipeg Saturday Post Ltd. v. Couzens* (1911), 19 W.L.R. 25 (Man. K.B.); *Toronto Type Foundry Co. v. Leach*, [1920] 2 W.W.R. 18 (Sask. K.B.); *Toronto Type Foundry Co. v. Juckes*, [1920] 2 W.W.R. 22 (Sask. K.B.).

[39] See also *Berliner Gramophone Co. v. Scythes* (1916), 31 D.L.R. 789 (Sask. S.C.), at pp. 792-3, *per* Lamont, J., enjoining a retailer from breaching an undertaking to sell only the plaintiffs' machines where the plaintiffs had advertised the defendants' shop: "The restriction imposed . . . is, to my mind, a very reasonable one, and one calculated to secure to the plaintiffs the benefits resulting from the advertising done by them."

[40] *Supra*, footnote 33. For a similar Canadian case, *Power Com'n of St. John v. New System Laundry Ltd.*, [1928] 2 D.L.R. 661 (N.B.S.C. App. Div.), reversing on other grounds the granting of an injunction at trial.

[41] *Supra*, §§679, 680.

of the distinction between negative and positive covenants, and it may well be that the practice of granting injunctions to restrain breach of negative commitments, which is so well established, might be used by a modern court to justify the cautious extension of specific relief in appropriate cases even where the obligation is a positive one. As seen in the preceding chapter, the courts have never absolutely refused specific performance of long-term supply contracts, and indeed, more recent cases suggest an increasing willingness to make it available.

686   By way of contrast, agreements whereby the defendant undertakes to sell all his output of a certain commodity have not usually been enforced by way of injunction. The leading case of *Fothergill v. Rowland*[42] has already been noted, and the same result has been reached in other cases,[43] including a decision of the Supreme Court of Canada.[44] The rationale here is that such agreements amount in substance to a positive obligation to sell a fungible commodity, and the court should not indirectly make a positive order it would not be prepared to make if asked to do so directly. However, a similar argument could be made with respect to the exclusive supply agreements just discussed. Where the commodity is a necessary one to the purchaser, just as the purchaser who, as a practical matter, requires the given commodity is forced to buy, so might a vendor whose business it is to supply commodities be forced to sell to one particular client. Perhaps a more satisfactory rationale for *Fothergill v. Rowland* is simply that there was no indication that damages would not have provided adequate protection to the plaintiff's interest, as the commodity, coal, was freely available, and the defendant could be forced to make up any difference in price the breach had cost the plaintiff.

687   The practice with respect to output contracts, however, has not been uniform. While most cases refuse to grant injunctive relief in such circumstances, there have been exceptions. In an early Ontario

---

[42] (1873), L.R. 17 Eq. 132.

[43] *Vancouver Island Milk Producers' Ass'n v. Alexander* (1922), 30 B.C.R. 524 (C.A.); *B.C. Poultry Ass'n v. Allanson*, [1922] 2 W.W.R. 831 (B.C.S.C.); *Kelowna Growers' Exchange v. De Caqueray* (1922), 70 D.L.R. 865 (B.C.S.C.); *Pakenham Upper Fruit Co. Ltd. v. Crosby* (1924), 35 C.L.R. 386 (Aust. H.C.); *Wood v. Corrigan* (1928), 28 S.R. (N.S.W.) 492 (S.C.). Cf. *Manitoba Wheat Pool v. Tracey*, [1931] 2 D.L.R. 805 (Man. C.A.), where an injunction was granted to protect a marketing scheme, but partly on the basis that a specific performance and injunction clause in the agreement had been included in the Act to Incorporate Manitoba Co-operative Wheat Producers, Limited, S.M. 1925, c. 112, s. 4(3).

[44] *Kidston v. Stirling & Pitcairn* (1920), 61 S.C.R. 193.

case,[45] an agreement by salt manufacturers to market their products through a trade association survived an attack as an illegal restraint on trade, and breach by one of the parties to the arrangement, who sought to sell his salt elsewhere, was restrained.[46] The New Brunswick Court of Appeal upheld an injunction restraining the defendant sawmill operator from selling part of his lumber elsewhere, the defendant having agreed to sell and deliver to the plaintiff "all the mill cut" of a certain grade of timber over a stated period.[47] In a 19th century English case, *Donnell v. Bennett*,[48] the defendant had agreed to sell his entire output of fish offal over a two-year period, whereby the plaintiff had gained a substantial monopoly of fish refuse, important in the manufacture of fertilizer. With some reluctance, Fry, J., granted an injunction, the stated reason being that the contract was negative. At first, the result seems to turn on the form of words used by the parties, and it is hard to reconcile with the other cases already discussed. However, the injunction can be justified on the grounds that the interest of the plaintiff in having the monopoly was sufficient to justify injunctive relief, and not readily measurable in damages.

688   Agreements such as those which have been discussed are subject to the restraint of trade doctrine, and will not be enforced at all unless the restrictions are justifiable as reasonable in the interests of both parties and the public.[49] The restraint must go no further than to afford adequate protection to the party it favours. However, exclusive supply contracts of several years duration have been upheld, and the courts have recognized the legitimate need for "maintaining a stable system of distribution throughout the country so as to enable

---

[45] *Ontario Salt Co. v. Merchants Salt Co.* (1871), 18 Gr. 540 and 551. See also *Cass v. Couture; Cass v. McCutcheon* (1903), 14 Man. R. 458 (K.B.), where Killam, C.J., was prepared to grant an injunction restraining breach of an entire output contract, but refused because the wrong party had sued. See also *Dietrichsen v. Cabburn* (1846), 2 Ph. 52, 41 E.R. 861, restraining breach of an agreement not to sell a product at a lower price than that offered to the plaintiff.

[46] *Cf. Construction Labour Relations Ass'n of B.C. v. Atlas Installations Ltd.* (1970), 16 D.L.R. (3d) 415 (B.C.S.C.), denying an injunction to restrain a company, which had agreed to bargain collectively only through an employer's trade association, from entering a collective agreement on its own behalf.

[47] *George Eddy Co. Ltd. v. Corey*, [1951] 4 D.L.R. 90 (N.B.S.C. App. Div.).

[48] (1883), 22 Ch. D. 835.

[49] *Stephens v. Gulf Oil Canada Ltd.* (1975), 65 D.L.R. (3d) 193, 11 O.R. (2d) 129 (C.A.); *Esso Petroleum Co. Ltd. v. Harper's Garage (Stourport) Ltd.*, [1968] A.C. 269. For a detailed discussion of the operation of the restraint of trade doctrine in this type of case, see Heydon, *The Restraint of Trade Doctrine* (London, Butterworths, 1971).

[the plaintiff's] business to be run efficiently and economically".[50]

4. The Lumley v. Wagner Injunction

689   Some contracts entail both negative and positive obligations. An issue which has proved difficult to resolve is the extent to which breaches of a negative promise can be restrained where specific performance of the coextensive positive obligation would be inappropriate. As already noted, an injunction will ordinarily be granted to enjoin the breach of a negative obligation. However, to the extent that enforcement of the negative obligation will have the effect of forcing the plaintiff to perform his positive obligation, the rule which would deny specific performance if asked for directly is circumvented. Some balance must be struck between these competing values.

690   Most cases in this area involve contracts of personal service or employment, where the defendant has agreed not only that he will perform certain work for the plaintiff, but also that he will not engage his services elsewhere during the term of the agreement. The leading case is *Lumley v. Wagner*.[51] In that well-known case, the Chancellor, Lord St. Leonards, enjoined a famous opera singer from breaking her promise not to sing for anyone else but the plaintiff theatre operator, all the while acknowledging that he had no power to require her to live up to her coextensive positive contract to perform for the plaintiff.

691   Enforcement of the negative obligation not to sing elsewhere plainly did not, in itself, give rise to the same problems as specific performance.[52] The defendant was not forced to sing, and there would be no problem of enforcement or assessing the adequacy of performance. Moreover, although this aspect is not discussed in the decision itself, the plaintiff had an interest to protect in having the exclusivity clause enforced specifically, which was quite distinct from his interest in having the defendant perform at his own theatre. If she were to sing at a rival theatre in competition with the plaintiff, as a star performer she would attract customers away from the plaintiff, and the loss the plaintiff would thereby suffer would be difficult to measure. It would be next to impossible to determine how many customers had been lost because of her breach of the negative obliga-

---

[50] *Esso Petroleum Co. Ltd. v. Harper's Garage (Stourport) Ltd.*, *supra*, footnote 49, at p. 302, *per* Lord Reid.

[51] (1852), 21 L.J. Ch. 898.

[52] Specific performance of personal service contracts is discussed, *supra*, §§577-586.

tion. On this ground, the result in *Lumley v. Wagner* is readily defensible. The contract had distinct aspects, and the negative term was, in itself, worthy of injunctive protection.

692   The concern with the result, however, is that being precluded from singing for anyone else, the plaintiff could well have been indirectly forced to live up to her positive obligation. Indeed, in that case, the Chancellor went so far as to say:

> I cannot compel her to perform, of course; that is a jurisdiction that the Court does not possess, and it is very proper that it should not possess that jurisdiction; but what cause of complaint is it that I should prevent her from doing an act which may compel her to do what she ought to do?—though that is not the object the Court has in view; for the Court cannot indirectly do a thing, and I disclaim doing a thing indirectly which I cannot do directly.[53]

693   It is this aspect of the decision which has been criticized.[54] Because of the pressure upon the defendant to perform the covenant the court could not directly enforce, *Lumley v. Wagner* has been adversely commented upon and described in a decision of the English Court of Appeal, *Whitwood Chemical Co. v. Hardman* as "an anomaly which it would be very dangerous to extend".[55] However, in *Whitwood*, the injunction sought plainly would have amounted to nothing more than a roundabout specific performance decree. The defendant had been engaged for a fixed period to manage the affairs of the plaintiff's company, and had agreed to "give the whole of his time to the company's business". The plaintiff argued that this should be read as a negative obligation and that an injunction should therefore be granted, but the English Court of Appeal disagreed.[56]

---

[53] *Lumley v. Wagner*, *supra*, footnote 51, at p. 902.

[54] See Heydon, *supra*, footnote 49, at pp. 64-71; Stevens, "Involuntary Servitude and Injunction", 6 Cornell L.Q. 235 (1921). *Corbin on Contracts*, vol. 5A (St. Paul, West Publishing Co., 1964), at p. 410, however, supports *Lumley v. Wagner*, and argues that, so long as the negative covenant is by itself worthy of enforcement: "There is no reason why the court should not avoid difficulties of enforcing an affirmative decree by using an injunction and then rely on the self-interest of the defendant to cause him to perform his affirmative promises."

[55] [1891] 2 Ch. 416 (C.A.), at pp. 427-8, *per* Lindley, L.J. See also *Macdonald v. Casein Ltd.* (1917), 35 D.L.R. 443 (B.C.C.A.), at pp. 444-5, *per* Macdonald, C.J.A.: "The tendency of the Courts now appears to be not to follow *Lumley v. Wagner* . . . and the line of cases founded on that decision, unless there be in the particular case an express negative stipulation."

[56] See also *Chapman v. Westerby*, [1913] W.N. 277 (Ch.), at p. 278, *per* Warrington, J., refusing an injunction with respect to a "whole time and attention" clause: "[There must be a stipulation] requiring the contracting party not to do some par-

The result, it is submitted, can be fully reconciled with *Lumley v. Wagner* on the basis that the defendant's services were not unique, and the plaintiff would have suffered no competitive disadvantage of the sort present in *Lumley v. Wagner*. The suit for an injunction was nothing more than an attempt to have the contract of employment specifically enforced.

694   Although often criticized, *Lumley v. Wagner* has been frequently followed,[57] and injunctions precluding the violation of such exclusivity clauses during the term of the contract have frequently been granted, even in cases where the plaintiff had no interest having the negative obligation performed beyond putting pressure on the defendant to perform his positive contract.[58]

695   It could be argued that the tendency such injunctions have to enforce the positive obligation is justifiable on the basis that there is a very real difference between forced idleness and forced service. Quite apart from the question of supervision, there is a strong moral and policy argument against forcing someone to work for an extended period against his will.[59] That argument does not apply where he is restrained from engaging in an activity from which he has undertaken to abstain. While this argument would not apply where the injunction presented the defendant with a choice between starvation or living up to his promise to work, it conceivably could be made in cases where the range of activity excluded would not preclude the defendant from earning a livelihood. In *Warner Brothers Pictures Inc. v. Nelson*,[60] a famous movie actress was prohibited from occupying herself with any other movie studio in violation of her promise to perform only for the plaintiff. Although the court agreed that no injunction would be granted "if the effect of so doing would be to drive the defendant either to starvation or to specific performance of the positive covenants",[61] it held that as she was "a person of intelligence, capacity and means, [and therefore] able to employ herself both usefully and remuneratively in other spheres of activity, though not as remuneratively as in her special line", the injunction could be

---

ticular act on which the Court can put its finger." Another similar case is *Heine Bros. (Aust.) Pty. Ltd. v. Forrest*, [1963] V.R. 383.

[57] For a review, now somewhat out of date, of the English and American cases, see Tannenbaum, "Enforcement of Personal Service Contracts in the Entertainment Industry", 42 Cal. L. Rev. 18 (1954).

[58] *Infra*, §698.

[59] *Supra*, §579.

[60] [1937] 1 K.B. 209.

[61] *Ibid.*, at p. 216.

given notwithstanding the temptation it might cause her to perform the positive aspect of her contract.[62]

696   Thus, while there is ample authority for the proposition that no injunction will be granted where the practical result is to grant specific performance by presenting the defendant with the choice between starvation and working for the plaintiff,[63] in cases such as *Lumley v. Wagner* and *Warner Brothers v. Nelson*, injunctive relief will still be available. In the case of such highly skilled performers, the injunction may amount to a means of enticing performance of the positive obligation without actually making an order amounting to a decree of involuntary servitude.

697   The point against such an approach turns not so much upon the appropriateness of the injunction as a remedy as on the common law restraint of trade doctrine which has a robust distrust of such fetters. It has been said in some cases, including the *Nelson* case,[64] that the restraint of trade doctrine has no application where it is sought to restrain the defendant from violating his contractual obligations during the term of his employment. On the other hand, even these cases have refused to grant injunctions against competition for longer than a period reasonably necessary to protect the plaintiff's interest, and indeed, the reasoning of restraint of trade cases has been applied to some extent in identifying the sort of interest the court will deem fit to protect by way of injunction.[65] Moreover, the better view is that the doctrine does apply during the term of the contract.[66] In the lead-

---

[62] *Ibid.*, at p. 219. See also *Warner Brothers Pictures Inc. v. Ingolia*, [1965] N.S.W.R. 988 (S.C.). *Cf.* however, *Page One Records Ltd. v. Britton*, [1968] 1 W.L.R. 157 (Ch.), refusing an injunction to restrain the dismissal of the exclusive manager of a pop group on the grounds, *inter alia*, that the group could not perform as a pop group without a manager and hence, the injunction would amount to specific enforcement of a contract of personal service.

[63] See *Chapman v. Westerby, supra*, footnote 56; *Capitol Records — EMI of Canada Ltd. v. Gosewich* (1977), 80 D.L.R. (3d) 737, 17 O.R. (2d) 501 (H.C.J.). In *Rely-A-Bell Burglar & Fire Alarm Co., Ltd. v. Eisler*, [1926] Ch. 609, Russell, J., rejected as unrealistic the argument that the defendant, an ordinary employee, could mitigate the effect of an injunction by starting his own business.

[64] *Supra*, footnote 60, at p. 214; *Rely-A-Bell Burglar & Fire Alarm Co. Ltd. v. Eisler, supra*, footnote 63.

[65] See, *e.g.*, *Rely-A-Bell Burglar & Fire Alarm Co. Ltd. v. Eisler, supra*, footnote 63, holding that the doctrine does not apply during the term of the contract, but narrowing the injunction to what is reasonably necessary to protect the plaintiff's interest. In *Warner Brothers Pictures Inc. v. Nelson, supra*, footnote 60, the term of the injunction was also limited.

[66] Heydon, *supra*, footnote 49, at pp. 60-61. See also *Petrofina (Gt. Britain) Ltd. v. Martin*, [1966] 1 Ch. 146 (C.A.).

ing Canadian case, *Detroit Football Co. v. Dublinski*,[67] it was held that such obligations are subject to the reasonableness requirements of the restraint of trade doctrine. That case holds that the restriction will not be enforced by injunction at all unless the plaintiff demonstrates an interest in enforcement distinct from requiring the plaintiff to fulfil his positive obligation, and that will only be enforced to the extent reasonably necessary to protect such distinct interest. The case involved a professional football player who had undertaken to play exclusively for a team in the American National Football League. In breach of his contract, so the plaintiff alleged, he had engaged to play for a team in the Canadian Football League. McRuer, C.J.H.C., held that the term could not be enforced in the circumstances since there was no element of competition between the two clubs or leagues.[68] The case restated the rationale for enforcing such obligations by expressly excluding the propriety of any attempt to put pressure on the defendant to perform the positive side of his obligation, and holding that, unless the plaintiff is able to show some interest to protect beyond putting pressure on the defendant to perform positively, equitable relief will be refused. The remedy is given, in other words, not for the loss the plaintiff suffers from deprivation of the defendant's services, but for the disadvantages to which he has been put by virtue of the defendant's employment elsewhere.

698   Clearly, both *Lumley v. Wagner* and *Warner Brothers Pictures Inc. v. Nelson* can be explained on a similar basis. However, not all the cases can. There are several English decisions in which the courts have adopted a more literal approach, and enjoined an employee of ordinary skill engaged to perform ordinary tasks from violating an exclusivity clause. In one case, the court expressly rejected restricting the *Lumley v. Wagner* doctrine situations where the defendant was possessed of unusual skills.[69] In two others,[70] injunctions were

---

[67](1956), 4 D.L.R. (2d) 688, [1956] O.R. 744 (H.C.J.), vard 7 D.L.R. (2d) 9, [1957] O.R. 58 (C.A.).

[68] *Cf. Radford v. Campbell* (1890), 6 T.L.R. 488 (C.A.), *per* Ester, M.R., refusing an injunction where the defendant footballer was going to play for a rival team: "Ought the solemn machinery of the Court in granting an injunction to be invoked in order to satisfy their [the plaintiffs'] pride in winning their matches?" *Cf.* also *Pitre v. L'Association Athlétique d'Amateurs Nationale* (1910), 20 Que. K.B. 41, dealing with a Quebec statutory provision in such a case.

[69] *Lanner v. Palace Theatre (Ltd.)* (1893), 9 T.L.R. 162 (Ch.), at p. 163, *per* Chitty, J. See also *William Robinson & Co. Ltd. v. Heuer*, [1898] 2 Ch. 451 (C.A.). *Cf. Ehrman v. Bartholomew*, [1898] 1 Ch. 671.

[70] *Marco Productions Ltd. v. Pagola*, [1945] K.B. 111; *Grimston v. Cuningham*, [1894] 1 Q.B. 125.

granted restraining theatre performers from violating exclusivity clauses where there could have been no question at all — in one case the court said so explicitly—[71] of any detriment to the plaintiff from having the defendant perform in another theatre, apart from the loss he would suffer from not having the performer in his own theatre. In light of *Dublinski*,[72] it is doubtful that these cases would now be followed in Canada.

5. Restrictive Covenants

699   Injunctions to enforce restrictive covenants are routinely granted on the general principle that a negative covenant calls for injunctive relief. Where an injunction is sought after a contract of employment has terminated or after the sale of a business, there is no problem as to the indirect enforcement of a positive obligation. Such cases do, however, require examination of the restraint of trade doctrine, a matter of substantive law beyond the scope of this book.[73]

700   One issue which has arisen is whether the contract of employment has been terminated in cases where the exclusivity clause runs only during the term. If the defendant can show that his contract has been terminated, he may be able to argue that the negative term was not intended to apply after termination, and that he is free to do as he pleases.[74] However, in a recent case, it has been held that an employee cannot free himself from an otherwise enforceable obligation by unilateral termination.[75]

6. Exclusive Agent Agreements

701   In certain cases, the party seeking enforcement of an exclusivity clause is more in the position of an employee than of an employer.

---

[71] *Marco Productions Ltd. v. Pagola, supra*, footnote 70, at p. 113, *per* Hallett, J.: "Nobody can suppose that the audience that would go to the Oxford Theatre to see the defendants would be diverted to Manchester to see them."

[72] *Supra*, footnote 67.

[73] See Heydon, *supra*, footnote 49, for discussion of its application in this context.

[74] *Gerlach-Barklow Co. v. MacPherson*, [1928] 3 W.W.R. 150 (Man. K.B.); *Ehrman v. Bartholomew, supra*, footnote 69. Cf. *William Robinson & Co. Ltd. v. Heuer, supra*, footnote 69.

[75] *Thomas Marshall (Exports) Ltd. v. Guinle*, [1979] Ch. 227 at p. 243, *per* Megarry, V.-C.:

   . . . why should the court's inability to make a servant work for his employer mean that as soon as the servant refuses to do so the court is forthwith disabled from restraining him from committing any breach, however flagrant, of his other obligations during the period of his contract? I would wholly reject the doctrine of automatic determination, whether in its wide form or in its narrowed version.

Where the obligations are of a confidential or fiduciary nature, not surprisingly, injunctive relief has been refused. Exclusive agents of boxers[76] and pop groups[77] have been denied injunctive relief where their performers were determined to employ other managers.[78]

702   Injunctions have also been refused in two British Columbia cases[79] where it was sought to protect exclusive sales agency agreements, the stated reason being that to enforce such agreements would amount to an enforcement of personal service contracts. These decisions, it is submitted, are not entirely satisfactory, and could perhaps be distinguished where the plaintiff is able to show that the arrangement is not one calling for close personal or fiduciary ties, but rather one designed to protect his legitimate interest in establishing and protecting a sales network for a particular product. The result reached in an Ontario case[80] is perhaps more satisfactory. There, an exclusive agreement relating to the right to manufacture and sell certain products was protected by injunction, the court recognizing that in "a commercial enterprise such as the plaintiff's, the dealerships which have been built up, always with considerable effort, . . . are important in the conduct of a business".[81]

703   Similarly, in *Evans Marshall & Co. Ltd. v. Bertola S.A.*,[82] the English Court of Appeal granted an interlocutory injunction restraining the breach of a sole distributorship agreement. The court rejected the argument that enforcing the contract encountered the problems of enforcing a contract for personal services:

> This is a commercial agreement between trading companies that can be implemented to the profit of both parties, if each conforms with its express and implied terms. As in a great many commercial contracts consultation between the parties as to implementation is desirable; but that does not necessarily turn them into joint ventures. But in any event, the fact that some degree of mutual co-operation or confidence is needed does not preclude the court from granting negative injunc-

---

[76] *Mortimer v. Beckett*, [1920] 1 Ch. 571.

[77] *Page One Records Ltd. v. Britton*, [1968] 1 W.L.R. 157 (Ch.).

[78] *Cf. Harrigan v. Brown*, [1967] 1 N.S.W.R. 342 (S.C.), holding that such an agreement could be enforced by injunction, but dismissing the claim on other grounds.

[79] *Macdonald v. Casein Ltd.* (1917), 35 D.L.R. 443 (B.C.C.A.); *Paxton v. Spira* (1965), 54 D.L.R. (2d) 627 (B.C.S.C.). See also *Atlas Steels (Australia) Pty. Ltd. v. Atlas Steels Ltd.* (1948), 49 S.R. (N.S.W.) 157 (S.C.).

[80] *Pasen v. Dominion Herb Distributors Inc.* (1968), 67 D.L.R. (2d) 405, [1968] 1 O.R. 688 (H.C.J.), affd 69 D.L.R. (2d) 651, [1968] 2 O.R. 516 (C.A.).

[81] *Ibid.*, at p. 409 D.L.R., p. 692 O.R., *per* Wilson, J.

[82] [1973] 1 W.L.R. 349 (C.A.).

tions designed to encourage the party in breach to perform his part.[83]

The Court also emphasized the difficulties of damage assessment in such cases, a factor which strongly favours injunctive relief:

> The courts have repeatedly recognised that there can be claims under contracts in which, as here, it is unjust to confine a plaintiff to his damages for their breach. Great difficulty in estimating these damages is one factor that can be and has been taken into account. Another factor is the creation of certain areas of damage which cannot be taken into monetary account in a common law action for breach of contract: loss of goodwill and trade reputation are examples.
>
> .   .   .   .   .
>
> In the instant case . . . an attempt is being made which, if unjustified would deprive the plaintiffs of the benefit of having built up a name for Bertola sherry with the aid of expending the best part of half a million pounds for that purpose in a dozen years.[84]

---

[83] *Ibid.*, at p. 379.
[84] *Ibid.*, at p. 380 and 382.

CHAPTER 10

DISCRETIONARY DEFENCES

1. Introduction

704   This chapter examines certain discretionary factors which may bar specific relief, otherwise available, but leave the plaintiff's right to damages intact. In this area, it is especially important to keep historical factors in proper perspective. The courts of equity were perhaps more protective than courts of law in cases of unconscionable dealing. It was primarily on the chancery side that relief against mistake, misrepresentation, fraud, and unfairness was developed. Because specific relief was formerly available only in the courts of equity, the special equitable treatment afforded the matters under discussion here became associated with that particular form of remedy. In many cases, equity would grant rescission, thereby precluding any action in the law courts, but in other cases, equity would go no further than to refuse specific relief. It was then for the plaintiff to sue in the courts of law if he wished, and for the courts of law to decide whether, or to what extent, the contract would be enforced. Obviously, this is not what happens today. There is one court, administering both law and equity, which must decide in one suit whether the contract is enforceable at all and if it is enforceable, what is the appropriate remedy. It is still possible to distinguish equitable from legal doctrines, and

365

analysis in historical categories may facilitate exposition of their development and operation.[1] On the other hand, the phenomenon of
two separate bodies of doctrine has tended to obscure general principles, and it can be misleading, after well over 100 years, to discuss
the two strands of development as if they had never been entwined.[2]

705   In this book, an effort has been made to distinguish questions of
remedial choice from issues of substantive law, and to exclude, so far
as possible, detailed discussion of the latter. In this chapter, the focus
on the issues of mistake, misrepresentation, unfairness, and hardship, will be deliberately narrow. A contract which is "valid at law",
but "liable to be set aside in equity" is, so far as the parties to it are
concerned, not an enforceable contract.[3] The issues of contract formation and enforceability are matters of substantive law, and detailed discussion of mistake, misrepresentation, and unconscionability fall outside the scope of a book on remedies which assumes an
enforceable obligation giving rise to remedial choice as a starting
point.

706   Here, it is proposed to examine these discretionary defences to the
extent that they go to the issue of remedy selection.[4] In other words,
it is proposed to consider cases where a valid and enforceable contract has been broken, or breach is threatened, and the choice between damages and specific relief turns on an element of mistake,
misrepresentation, unfairness, or hardship.[5] Plainly, this is a narrow

---

[1] See, *e.g.*, Treitel, *The Law of Contract*, 5th ed. (London, Stevens & Sons Ltd., 1979), pp. 222-38, for a comprehensive analysis of the legal and equitable doctrines relating to mistake.

[2] See *United Scientific Holdings Ltd. v. Burnley Borough Council*, [1978] A.C. 904 (H.L.).

[3] See Waddams, *The Law of Contracts* (Toronto, Canada Law Book Ltd., 1977), pp. 211-12 and pp. 324-5. Traditional analysis distinguishes between contracts which are "void" and those which are "voidable": see *Solle v. Butcher*, [1950] 1 K.B. 671 (C.A.). It has been convincingly argued that this distinction is neither necessary nor helpful: Swan, "The Allocation of Risk in the Analysis of Mistake and Frustration" in *Studies in Contract Law*, Reiter and Swan, eds. (Toronto, Butterworths, 1980), pp. 191-2.

[4] The choice is even more refined. In some cases, the plaintiff will be granted equit-able relief, but denied costs because of a discretionary factor not grave enough to warrant denial of the remedy: *Greenhalgh v. Brindley*, [1901] 2 Ch. 324.

[5] For a statement of the traditional position, see *Mortlock v. Buller* (1804), 10 Ves. Jun. 292 at p. 308, 32 E.R. 857, *per* Eldon, L.C.:

> . . . the distinction is always laid down, that there are many cases, in which the party has obtained a right to sue upon the contract at Law, and under such cir-cumstances, that his conscience cannot be affected here, so as to deprive him of that remedy; and yet, on the other hand the Court, declaring, he ought to be at

compass. The discretionary factor must be disturbing enough to deny a remedy otherwise available, but not so bad as to deny enforceability altogether.[6]

707   It will make no sense merely to deny specific relief, giving the plaintiff his remedy in damages, unless there is a discrepancy in the respective burdens imposed. If the amount of the damage award would be the same as the cost of satisfying a specific performance decree, the court will achieve nothing by refusing the latter but granting the former. In the cases which follow, the defendant is almost invariably trying to avoid the enforcement of an improvident bargain. Allowing a discretionary defence to specific performance will be pointless if, in its next breath, the court awards damages without taking the same factor into account. For example, if A has agreed to sell land worth $2,000 to B for $1,000, refusing specific performance to B, but at the same time leaving B's right to damages intact, leaves A liable for $1,000. Taking only monetary value into account, A is no better off having succeeded in avoiding a specific performance decree, the net cost of which would have been $1,000. However, other factors may make the distinction meaningful. A may place some subjective value on the land not reflected by the market.[7] In that case, in light of his non-commercial interest, A would rather pay $1,000 in damages than give up the land for $2,000. Another possibility is that

---

liberty to proceed at Law, will not actively interpose to aid him, and specifically perform the contract.

Harris v. Robinson (1892), 21 S.C.R. 390 at p. 397, *per* Strong, J.: "It is not sufficient to entitle a party seeking this peculiar relief to show what would be sufficient to entitle him to recover in a court of law, namely, that a contract existed".

[6] Comment, "Equitable Contract Remedies — Denial of Both Specific Performance and Rescission", 32 Mich. L. Rev. 518 (1934), at p. 525 (quoted in Waddams, *supra*, footnote 3, at p. 325): "If the chancellor's conscience rebels at the thought of specifically enforcing so hard a bargain, why is it so easily appeased by a dismissal of the bill, which opens the door to the imposition of heavy damages at law?" See also Chafee, *Some Problems of Equity* (Ann Arbor, University of Michigan Law School, 1950), p. 28: "Why should the same judges be very moral in a specific performance suit and brutally mathematical in a damage suit?" and at p. 102: "If injunctions and specific performance ought sometimes to be refused in situations where damages are granted, this distinction is due to the nature of these specific remedies and not to the existence of different levels of morality inside the judicial system."

[7] It might be asked why A would have sold for $1,000 if he valued the property at even more than $2,000. *Ex hypothesi*, however, A has bargained under some mistake, because of some misrepresentation or has otherwise been taken advantage of. For an example, see *Manser v. Back* (1848), 6 Hare 443, 67 E.R. 1239, refusing specific performance where, by mistake, a right of way over the property sold was not reserved. For discussion of "non-commercial" interest, see, *supra*, §§546, 547.

the market value of the land may in fact have increased from the date of breach, and the same discretionary factor which precluded B from getting specific performance may also be seen to preclude assessment later than the breach date.[8] Thus, A would be better off paying breach date damages than surrendering the property now increased in value.

708   Thus, the analysis turns on the assumption that specific relief is more burdensome to the defendant than a damages award, and that the discretionary factor makes it unjust to give the plaintiff, and impose on the defendant, the full measure of specific relief, but not unjust to award damages.

709   It is worth noting here that at the time these discretionary defences were developed, before the fusion of law and equity, the significance of denying specific relief but allowing the plaintiff to pursue his remedy at law was often quite significant. The dismissal of the bill for specific performance, with costs, represented a considerable expense to the plaintiff. Many must have been unwilling to then bear the expense of a proceeding in the law courts. More importantly, until well into the 19th century, juries had a wide discretion in the matter of damages. Whatever the stricter common law rules of contract may have said, the plaintiff whose case shocked the chancellor's conscience would rarely have fared much better in front of a jury.[9] Indeed, here the common law was possibly more flexible than equity, and by taking hardship or unconscionability into account, the jury could moderate the damage award.[10] The point is well explained in a mid-19th century Ontario case by Blake, C.:

> Where the contract is hard or unconscionable, the jurisdiction [to award specific performance] is sparingly exercised; because the equitable remedy, from its nature, is incapable of modification according to the circumstances of the case. In decreeing specific performance equity secures to the plaintiff the utmost benefit derivable from the agree-

---

[8] See the cases dealing with delay, *infra*, §§93-94.

[9] *Infra*, footnotes 10 and 11; Comment, 32 Mich. L. Rev. 518 (1934); see also Chafee, *supra*, footnote 6, at p. 27: "After all, jurymen are sometimes just as sensitive as an equity judge to the unconscionable behaviour of a plaintiff." It would seem, however, that common law actions were sometimes prosecuted: see, *infra*, footnote 16.

[10] As pointed out by Comment, 32 Mich. L. Rev. 518 (1934), other techniques were used to control resort to damages: see, *e.g.*, *Savage v. Taylor* (1736), Cases t. Talb. 234, 25 E.R. 753, offering the plaintiff compensation for improvement if he delivered up the contract rather than sue at law; *Day v. Newman* (1788), 2 Cox. 77, 30 E.R. 36, offering to dismiss a cross bill for rescission with costs if the plaintiff would forgo his right to sue at law.

ment. Whereas in the ordinary mode of procedure juries have power to apportion the damages according to the justice of the case. In cases of that kind, therefore, as more complete justice may be done by the ordinary tribunals, the foundation of the jurisdiction fails.[11]

710   Now that juries are seldom used, and when used are closely controlled, there is surely much less scope for finding contracts the proper subjects of damage awards but not specific relief on such grounds.[12] Moreover, as the principles of equity and law coalesce, and relief for mistake, misrepresentation, and unconscionability develop along more general lines, more and more cases will be the subject of complete relief, and fewer and fewer found properly the subject of the more limited form of relief described in this chapter.[13] It is worth noting that in refusing specific relief, the courts often use the language of the early cases and speak as if the plaintiff's right to damages was unaffected, but then decline to make any award.[14]

2. Mistake

711   The law relating to mistake in contract is a complex and controversial area of substantive law which falls outside the scope of this book.[15] Here, it is proposed to examine those cases where an element of mistake goes to the question of remedy rather than enforceability: in other words, to consider those cases where mistake bars the remedy of specific performance or injunction, but does not go to the validity of the contract itself so as to preclude recovery for damages.[16]

---

[11] *Paul v. Blackwood* (1852), 3 Gr. 394 at p. 411 (dissenting, but appeal allowed (1854), 4 Gr. 550).

[12] Comment, 32 Mich. L. Rev. 518 (1934), at pp. 525-6, suggesting that whereas damage rules rather than jury discretion now govern ". . . can it not be argued that modern courts of equity are proceeding on the wrong assumption in leaving the parties to their damage remedies, which now may be almost as harsh as specific execution of the contract?"

[13] For consideration of mistake, misrepresentation and unconscionability and an analysis of the development along these lines, see, Waddams, *supra*, footnote 3, at pp. 189-340.

[14] See, *e.g.*, *McCorkell v. McFarlane*, [1952] O.W.N. 653 (H.C.J.), where the court refused specific performance on grounds of hardship and unfairness, and then disbelieved the plaintiff's evidence on damages. See also *Holliday v. Lockwood*, [1917] 2 Ch. 47, upholding the contract, but refusing specific performance, and finding the plaintiff had failed to prove damages; *Thompson v. B.A. Oil Co.* (1956), 7 D.L.R. (2d) 116 (B.C.S.C.), is a similar case.

[15] See Waddams, *supra*, footnote 3, at pp. 189-241: Swan, *supra*, footnote 3.

[16] See *Wood v. Scarth* (1855), 2 K. & J. 33, 69 E.R. 682 (specific performance refused because of mistake in omitting to include a premium in the written contract); *Wood*

712   The principles to be applied have never been put into sharp focus
by the cases. Dicta from early cases suggest a generous equitable discretion to relieve against mistake.[17] Equity, it was said, acted on the
principle that "it is against conscience for a man to take advantage of
the plain mistake of another, or, at least, that a Court of Equity will
not assist him in doing so."[18]

713   There are many pre-Judicature Act cases in which mistake was
held to be a defence to specific performance.[19] On the facts disclosed
in many of them, it would be surprising if a modern court did not refuse to enforce the contract altogether, but some suggest a more lenient approach. With respect to remedy selection, the post-Judicature
Act courts developed rather more precise formulations which take
into account the dual and often conflicting goals of upholding the
sanctity of contract, but at the same time avoid unreasonably harsh
results.

714   The leading case is *Tamplin v. James*[20] where the plaintiff agreed
at an auction to buy a property he "had known . . . from a boy". Unfortunately, the defendant relied on his mistaken understanding of
the property limits, and made no reference to the survey which was
available, and which indicated that a garden he thought to be part of
the parcel was not included. The vendor sued for specific performance, and the defendant resisted, unsuccessfully, on the ground of
his mistake. At trial, the court found no reason to doubt the defendant's assertion that he had been honestly mistaken, and it also accepted the proposition that specific performance would not be
decreed against the defendant who entered a contract under a mistake "where injustice would be done to him were performance to be
enforced".[21] However, the court went on to define in general terms
when it would consider that enforcement would constitute injustice.

---

v. Scarth (1858), 1 F. & F. 293, 175 E.R. 733 (same agreement successfully sued on
at law); *Douglas v. Baynes*, [1908] A.C. 477 (P.C.); *Malins v. Freeman* (1837), 2
Keen. 25, 48 E.R. 537; *Webster v. Cecil* (1861), 30 Beav. 62, 54 E.R. 812.

[17] See, *e.g.*, *Malins v. Freeman* (1837), 2 Keen. 25, 48 E.R. 537; *Webster v. Cecil*
(1861), 30 Beav. 62, 54 E.R. 812; *Stephenson v. Clinch* (1884), 24 N.B.R. 189
(S.C.).

[18] *Manser v. Back* (1848), 6 Hare 443 at p. 448, 67 E.R. 1239, *per* Wigram, V.-C.

[19] See, *e.g.*, cases cited, *supra*, footnote 17; *Twining v. Morrice* (1788), 2 Bro. C.C.
326, 29 E.R. 182; *Swaisland v. Dearsley* (1861), 29 Beav. 430, 54 E.R. 694; *Moxey
v. Bigwood* (1862), 4 De G.F. & J. 351, 45 E.R. 1219; *Denny v. Hancock* (1870), 6
Ch. App. 1; *Earley v. McGill* (1864), 11 Gr. 75; *Mason v. Armitage* (1806), 13 Ves.
Jun. 25, 33 E.R. 204; *Day v. Wells* (1861), 30 Beav. 220, 54 E.R. 872.

[20] (1880), 15 Ch. D. 215 (C.A.).

[21] *Ibid.*, at p. 217.

Mistake by itself was not enough. Baggallay, L.J. (sitting as a trial judge), considered that such a rule would open the door to perjury; if mistake by itself were grounds to refuse performance, "the performance of a contract could rarely be enforced upon an unwilling party who was also unscrupulous."[22] On appeal, the order for specific performance was upheld. The court said that "if a man makes a mistake of this kind without any reasonable excuse he ought to be held to his bargain",[23] and that a mistake, not contributed to by the plaintiff, would constitute grounds for refusal of specific performance only where "a hardship amounting to injustice would have been inflicted"[24] upon the defendant by holding him to his bargain.

715   In preference to the more generous language of the early cases, modern courts[25] have followed the analysis of *Tamplin v. James.* While there are several cases in which mistake has provided a defence to specific performance,[26] modern cases in which specific per-

---

[22] *Ibid.*, at p. 218.

[23] *Ibid.*, at p. 221, *per* James, L.J.

[24] *Ibid.* Hardship as a separate ground for refusing specific performance is discussed, *infra*, §§735-740. For examples of "hardship" arising from mistake, see *Mortlock v. Buller* (1804), 10 Ves. Jun. 292, 32 E.R. 857 (agent's neglect, property sold at substantial undervalue); *Twining v. Morrice, supra*, footnote 19 (irregularity in bidding at auction because of inadvertence of vendor's solicitor); *Day v. Wells, supra*, footnote 19 (auctioneer mistaken in instructions, property sold under value); *Wedgwood v. Adams* (1843), 6 Beav. 600, 49 E.R. 958 (written agreement would have made trustees personally liable); *Watson v. Marston* (1853), 4 De G.M. & G. 230, 43 E.R. 495 (written agreement providing for sale under power of sale, vendor intending to sell under foreclosure). Mistake may produce a substantial discrepancy without hardship: see *Goddard v. Jeffreys* (1881), 51 L.J. Ch. 57, where the mistake represented an additional £800 on a purchase price of £1,230, but the court held that the bargain was still a good one and ordered specific performance.

[25] *Stewart v. Kennedy* (1890), 15 App. Cas. 75 (H.L.), at p. 105; *Hobbs v. Esquimalt & Nanaimo R. Co.* (1899), 29 S.C.R. 450; *Milestone v. City of Moose Jaw* (1908), 8 W.L.R. 901 (Sask. K.B.); *Van Praagh v. Everidge*, [1902] 2 Ch. 266, revd on other grounds [1903] 1 Ch. 434 (C.A.); *Slee v. Warke* (1949), 86 C.L.R. 271 (Aust. H.C.); *Miller v. Dahl* (1894), 9 Man. R. 444 (Q.B.); *Freeman v. Kaltio* (1963), 39 D.L.R. (2d) 496 (B.C.S.C.); *Goddard v. Jeffreys, supra*, footnote 24; *Burtini v. Sovilj* (1975), 61 D.L.R. (3d) 505 (B.C.S.C.).

[26] See, *e.g.*, *Omnium Securities Co. v. Richardson* (1884), 7 O.R. 182 (H.C.J.) (mistake as to terms of payment); *Drummond Mines Co. v. Fernholm* (1906), 8 O.W.R. 864 (Div. Ct.) (mistake as to lands included in contract); *Thompson v. B.A. Oil Co.* (1956), 7 D.L.R. (2d) 116 (B.C.S.C.) (clerical error giving plaintiff right to conveyance earlier than contemplated); *Fraser v. Pugsley* (1920), 37 T.L.R. 87 (Ch.) (liquor licence for six rather than seven days). *Cf. Powell v. Smith* (1872), L.R. 14 Eq. 85 (specific performance ordered where defendant mistaken as to effect of terms of lease); *Freeman v. Kaltio, supra*, footnote 25 (granting specific performance despite defendant's mistake as to borrowing arrangements).

formance is refused on the ground of mistake, but where damages are at the same time awarded, are rare.[27]

716   It is also to be noted that the defences of mistake, misrepresentation and hardship merge to some extent. To avoid specific performance, the defendant must show some element of fault on the part of the plaintiff that hints at misrepresentation, or must show that he would suffer extreme hardship. The precise nature of the fault or hardship has never been defined, and it is often difficult to place these cases into categories.

717   An example is *Hope v. Walter*[28] where the vendors, trustees for sale, sued to enforce the sale at an auction of an investment property in which the tenant was found to be keeping a brothel. The vendors had no knowledge of this, nor of course, did the purchaser. Specific performance was refused on the grounds that although both parties were perfectly innocent of any misconduct, the mistake as to the present use of the property would produce a hardship. "It would be little short of a scandal, to my mind, if the Court, having the power of refusing the extraordinary remedy of specific performance, were to thrust down the throat of an innocent buyer the obligation of becoming the landlord of a brothel".[29] At the same time, however, the court refused rescission, and suggested that if the plaintiff could prove damages he would recover. The burden of a specific performance decree could have been significant — the court observed that the defendant might face criminal liability as well as the possible obloquy of being the owner of a brothel. Thus, specific enforcement would have been more burdensome than a damages award as the defendant would have suffered more than the financial consequences of a bad bargain had he been forced to complete.

718   In some cases of mistake, it may be inappropriate to deny specific

---

[27] One such case is *Beyfus v. Lodge*, [1925] Ch. 350, a vendor's action for specific performance of an agreement to sell a leasehold interest under which the purchaser assumed certain obligations to repair. Quite innocently, but quite mistakenly, the plaintiff represented that no notices had been served by the lessor; in fact, notices requiring repairs had been served, and on learning this, the purchaser refused to complete. Russell, J., at p. 358, held that specific performance should be refused — "the vendors having concealed a material fact which it was their duty to disclose" — but that the mere omission to state a material fact did not vitiate the contract at law and the purchaser should lose his deposit for failure to complete. This would appear to be a generous view of the facts in the vendor's favour, and arguably, the case was one for rescission. *Dell v. Beasley*, [1959] N.Z.L.R. 89 (S.C.), would also seem to have been a case for rescission: *cf. Alessio v. Jovica* (1973), 42 D.L.R. (3d) 242 (Alta. S.C. App. Div.), where rescission was granted on similar facts.

[28] [1900] 1 Ch. 257 (C.A.).

[29] *Ibid.*, at p. 258, *per* Lindley, M.R.

relief outright, but also unjust not to take the defendant's mistake into account. An important technique, which may be used in such cases and which is discussed below,[30] is to put the plaintiff to an election between having specific performance refused altogether, or having the contract performed on the basis of the defendant's understanding. Another, also discussed below,[31] is the award of specific performance with compensation. Although not formally linked with mistake, it does provide relief in certain cases for the plaintiff who is getting less in performance than he expected.

719   It would be wrong to exaggerate the scope of relief from specific performance on the ground of mistake. The tendency has been for the remedial and substantive doctrines to coalesce. In specific performance cases, it has been noted that while the early 19th century cases suggest a wider ground for relief, the cases following *Tamplin v. James*[32] and the Judicature Acts have narrowed the grounds. A parallel, but widening, basis for relief for mistake may be traced in the substantive law of contract.[33] Thus, the gap between the two is narrower than it was, and almost certainly will continue to narrow. Still, there may well be cases where the refusal of specific relief provides an alternative middle ground and offers an important element of remedial flexibility.

3. Misrepresentation

720   Misrepresentation by a plaintiff as to some relevant matter will provide a basis for the refusal of specific performance.[34] Here again, it is especially difficult to distinguish grounds for rescission from circumstances which will merely form the basis for successful defence to specific performance. The power to rescind contracts for innocent misrepresentations, even where the plaintiff had the means, using reasonable diligence, to ascertain the truth, is well established.[35] This covers a wide area[36] and leaves little, if any, scope for cases where

---

[30] *Infra*, §§821, 822.

[31] *Infra*, §§793-806.

[32] (1880), 15 Ch. D. 215 (C.A.).

[33] See Waddams, *supra*, footnote 3, at pp. 189-241; Swan, *supra*, footnote 3.

[34] See, *e.g.*, *Halliday v. Roy* (1914), 7 O.W.N. 546 (H.C.); *Labelle v. Bernier* (1911), 2 O.W.N. 634 (H.C.J.); *Walmsley v. Griffith* (1884), 10 O.A.R. 327, appeal quashed 13 S.C.R. 434; *Davis v. Moranis and Smith*, [1949] 4 D.L.R. 433, [1949] O.W.N. 638 (C.A.).

[35] *Redgrave v. Hurd* (1881), 20 Ch. D. 1 (C.A.).

[36] See Waddams, *supra*, footnote 3, at p. 251; *Alessio v. Jovica, supra*, footnote 27; *F. & B. Transport Ltd. v. White Truck Sales Manitoba Ltd.* (1965), 49 D.L.R. (2d) 670 (Man. C.A.).

both specific performance and rescission will be refused and damages awarded. However, it has often been said that a less serious misrepresentation will afford a defence to a specific performance action, than is required to support a claim for rescission.[37] It is often difficult to distinguish misrepresentation from mistake in this context. As has been noted,[38] an important factor in mistake cases is any element of fault on the part of the plaintiff. If mistake is to be distinguished from misrepresentation, such fault must, in theory at least, fall short of outright misrepresentation. A little further along the spectrum spanning mistake and misrepresentation, one finds misrepresentation sufficient to defeat specific performance, but not enough to warrant rescission.

721   Specific performance has also been refused where the plaintiff has used subtle tactics to induce bargains which bordered on misrepresentation, but which perhaps fell short of what would be needed to persuade a court to set aside the agreement. Here, a passage from a mid-19th century case is often quoted. "But a single word, or (I may add) a nod or a wink, or a shake of the head, or a smile from the purchaser intended to induce the vendor to believe the existence of a non-existing fact, which might influence the price of the subject to be sold, would be sufficient ground for a Court of Equity to refuse a decree for a specific performance . . .".[39]

722   Thus, lack of candour amounting to, or even bordering on, concealment may afford a defence to specific performance.[40] It has also been held that misrepresentation as to some collateral point will afford a defence to specific performance, but not grounds for rescis-

---

[37] *Cadman v. Horner* (1810), 18 Ves. Jun. 10, 34 E.R. 221; *Re Terry and White's Contract* (1886), 32 Ch. D. 14 (C.A.), at p. 29, *per* Lindley, L.J.: "it is well known that a less serious misleading is sufficient to enable a purchaser to resist specific performance than is required to enable him to rescind the contract"; *Lamare v. Dixon* (1873), L.R. 6 H.L. 414 at p. 428, *per* Lord Cairns; *Dell v. Beasley, supra*, footnote 27.

[38] *Supra*, §§714-716.

[39] *Walters v. Morgan* (1861), 3 De G.F. & J. 718 at p. 724, 45 E.R. 1056, *per* Westbury, L.J.; *Irish v. McKenzie* (1907), 6 W.L.R. 209 (Man. K.B.). The same dictum has, however, also been applied in rescission cases: *Aspden v. Moore* (1914), 5 O.W.N. 971 (H.C.).

[40] *Summers v. Cocks* (1927), 40 C.L.R. 321 (Aust. H.C.) (vendor wanting in candour with respect to liquor licence problems); *Mason v. Armitage* (1806), 13 Ves. Jun. 25, 33 E.R. 204 (irregular conduct at auction producing unsatisfactory price); *Falcke v. Gray* (1859), 4 Drew. 651, 62 E.R. 250 (plaintiff knowing that vendor relying on erroneous estimate of value provided by third party); *Phillips v. Homfray* (1871), 6 Ch. App. 770 (plaintiff concealing appropriation of coal from the defendant's mine prior to contract).

sion, where enforcing the contract would, on account of the misrepresentation, cause hardship.[41]

723   In spite all of this, the doctrine of *caveat emptor* applies even in equity,[42] and specific performance is often granted in favour of a plaintiff who failed to disclose some relevant fact, provided there was nothing in the circumstances to impose a duty on the plaintiff to disclose it.[43]

724   It has also been held that where the right to rescind has been lost because of delay or waiver, the plaintiff's misconduct in inducing the contract may still be relevant in deciding whether specific performance should be granted.[44] In an Ontario case[45] involving misrepresentation, specific performance was refused, but rescission was also refused on the grounds of waiver, and an inquiry into damages was ordered.

725   It is suggested that it is difficult to justify fine distinctions between misrepresentation which allows the innocent party to avoid the contract, and misrepresentation which merely affects the right to specific performance. While the courts continue to use the language of the 19th century, it must be recognized that modern cases in which both specific performance and rescission have been refused are very rare.

4. Unfairness and Hardship

(1) Introduction

726   Although often closely related, the principles underlying the doctrines of unfairness and hardship as grounds for refusal of specific performance may be distinguished to facilitate analysis.[46] Unfairness may be taken to refer to misconduct of the plaintiff in procuring the

---

[41] *Holliday v. Lockwood*, [1917] 2 Ch. 47.

[42] *Haywood v. Cope* (1858), 25 Beav. 140, 53 E.R. 589; *Allen v. Richardson* (1879), 13 Ch. D. 524; *Morley v. Clavering* (1860), 29 Beav. 84 at p. 86, 54 E.R. 558 *per* Romilly, M.R.: "It is not the duty of the vendor to say to the purchaser, 'You will not be able under these covenants to effect your object;' it is for the purchaser to ascertain for himself whether what he purchases will answer his purpose."

[43] *Turner v. Green*, [1895] 2 Ch. 205; *Dyster v. Randall & Sons*, [1926] Ch. 932. *Cf. Greenhalgh v. Brindley*, [1901] 2 Ch. 324, granting specific performance but refusing costs because of non-disclosure.

[44] See, *e.g.*, *Shaw v. Masson*, [1923] S.C.R. 187 at p. 200, *per* Anglin, J.: "fraud is a personal bar to specific performance which may be set up by a defendant not entitled to rescission".

[45] *Panzer v. Zeifman* (1978), 88 D.L.R. (3d) 131 (Ont. C.A.).

[46] The distinction used here is that suggested by Spry, *Equitable Remedies*, 2nd ed. (London, Sweet & Maxwell, 1980), p. 177.

bargain in the form of overreaching, sharp dealing, or taking advantage of a weaker party. Hardship may be taken to refer to any case in which the consequences to the defendant of enforcement would require him to bear an unreasonably or unexpectedly heavy burden.

727   To attempt to state specific rules here would be impossible and the result would be positively misleading. Although the courts have insisted that the discretion to refuse specific performance is not arbitrary or capricious,[47] the principles upon which they have acted have been very general.[48] The judges have expressly refused to be tied down to specific categories or rules, and have insisted upon the right to take into account a wide range of factors, looking closely to the circumstances of each individual case, and measuring the case for equitable relief against a standard of conscientious behaviour. This area is properly seen as a branch of the law of unconscionability where gradually, basic underlying principles are being evolved, disparate strands of authority intertwined, and various gaps filled in.[49] The specific performance cases in which unfairness and hardship play a part often also involve elements of mistake or misrepresentation, and provide further examples of the difficulty in adopting rigid categories to explain the various matters discussed in this chapter.

728   Unfairness or hardship will often lead to rescission of the contract. The courts are acting on the same principle, namely, that interven-

---

[47] *Walters v. Morgan* (1861), 3 De G.F. & J. 718 at pp. 721-2, 45 E.R. 1056, *per* Campbell, L.C.: "It was quite unnecessary to argue that an Equity Judge has not an unlimited discretion as to decreeing or refusing to decree the specific performance of an agreement. He is bound by rules which his predecessors have laid down, founded on justice and expediency"; *Lamare v. Dixon* (1873), L.R. 6 H.L. 414 at p. 423, *per* Lord Chelmsford: the discretion is "not an arbitrary or capricious discretion, but one to be governed as far as possible by fixed rules and principles"; *White v. Damon* (1802), 7 Ves. Jun. 30 at p. 35, 32 E.R. 13, *per* Eldon, L.C.: "giving a specific performance is a matter of discretion: but that is not an arbitrary, capricious, discretion. It must be regulated upon grounds, that will make it judicial."

[48] *Wedgwood v. Adams* (1843), 6 Beav. 600 at p. 605, 49 E.R. 958, *per* Langdale, M.R.:

> . . . the Court exercises a discretion, in cases of specific performance, and directs a specific performance unless it should be what is called highly unreasonable to do so. What is more or less reasonable, is not a thing that you can define, it must depend on the circumstances of each particular case. The Court, therefore, must always have regard to the circumstances . . . knowing . . . that if it abstains from [awarding specific performance], a measure of damages may be found and awarded in another Court.

Blomley v. Ryan (1956), 99 C.L.R. 362 (Aust. H.C.), at p. 401, per Fullagar, J.: "when we look for the principle on which equity did grant relief in such cases, we find as so often in equity, only very wide general expressions to guide us."

[49] See Waddams, *supra*, footnote 3, at pp. 266-340.

tion is called for "whenever it appears that one of the parties was incapable of adequately protecting his interests and the other has made some immoderate gain at his expense."[50] There are many cases, mostly before but some after the Judicature Acts, where both specific performance and rescission have been refused.[51] While the courts have insisted that there is a dividing line between the criteria for specific performance and rescission, it is an exceptionally difficult one to draw. All that can be said is that everything must be seen as a matter of degree, that the courts have not been willing to circumscribe their wide discretion by precise rules, and that careful scrutiny will be given to the particular circumstances of each case.

(2) Unfairness

729   Justice has always required that the courts be vigilant in the protection of perceptibly weaker parties. No list could be exhaustive, but it has been said that the category of disadvantage includes: "poverty or need of any kind, sickness, age, sex, infirmity of body or mind, drunkenness, illiteracy, or lack of education, lack of assistance or explanation where assistance or explanation is necessary".[52]

730   More must be shown than weakness alone. The condition of weakness must have had the effect of putting the party affected at some significant disadvantage, usually permitting the other party to exploit the weakness and reach a bargain which, from the weaker party's point of view, is improvident.[53]

731   Where advantage is taken of a special relationship involving fiduci-

---

[50] Crawford, Comment, 44 Can. Bar Rev. 142 (1966), at p. 143; *Morrison v. Coast Finance Ltd.* (1965), 55 D.L.R. (2d) 710 (B.C.C.A.). See Sheridan, *Fraud in Equity: A Study in English and Irish Law* (London, Sir Isaac Pitman & Sons Ltd., 1957), p. 71 *et seq.*, for discussion of setting aside agreements on grounds of inequality or unconscionability.

[51] *Mortlock v. Buller* (1804), 10 Ves. Jun. 292, 32 E.R. 857; *Vivers v. Tuck* (1863), 1 Moo. P.C. (N.S.) 516, 15 E.R. 794; *Cooke v. Clayworth* (1811), 18 Ves. Jun. 12, 34 E.R. 222; *Gough v. Bench* (1884), 6 O.R. 699 (H.C.J.); *McColl-Frontenac Oil Co. v. Saulnier & Saulnier*, [1949] 3 D.L.R. 208 (N.B.S.C. App. Div.), leave to appeal to S.C.C. refused D.L.R. *loc. cit.* p. 777; *Conlan v. Murray*, [1958] N.I. 17 (C.A.), at p. 25, *per* Black, L.J. citing Kerr, *The Law of Fraud and Mistake*, 7th ed. by McDonnell and Monroe (London, Sweet & Maxwell, 1952), p. 268: "When the aid of the Court is sought by way of specific performance of a contract the principles of ethics have a more extensive sway than when a contract is sought to be rescinded"; *Blomley v. Ryan, supra*, footnote 48 (although there the agreement was set aside); *infra*, footnotes 60 and 62.

[52] *Blomley v. Ryan, supra*, footnote 48, at p. 405, *per* Fullagar, J. Surely sex would not now be included.

[53] *O'Neil v. Arnew* (1976), 78 D.L.R. (3d) 671, 16 O.R. (2d) 549 (H.C.J.).

ary obligations, the transaction is almost inevitably set aside, although it is perhaps conceivable that a court might uphold the transaction and refuse only specific performance in the event of a minor or technical breach of such an obligation.

732   Most unfairness cases involve a combination of factors involving sharp dealing by one party combined with an element of mistake and the other side being in some way subject to imposition.[54] The courts attempt to strike a balance between freedom of contract on the one hand, and the prevention of unconscionable advantage being taken on the other. It was explained by a British Columbia judge as follows:

> Now not every man who knowingly buys a property for less than it is worth is to be penalized. Trade and commerce survive by the application of this idea and to buy in the anticipation of a profit on resale is perfectly respectable.
>
> What must be controlled is the victimization of the ignorant by the knowing through the application of undue influence.[55]

733   In one case,[56] the New Brunswick Court of Appeal refused specific performance where the plaintiff had snapped at a bargain at a considerable undervalue, the defendant being advanced in age, illiterate, lacking in advice, and unaware of the true value. Similarly, in an Ontario case,[57] specific performance was refused where the plaintiff was innocent of any fraud, misrepresentation, or intentional unfairness, but had snapped at a somewhat undervalued offer made by an elderly defendant with impaired eyesight, although the court held it

---

[54] Useful discussions of unfairness are found in *Buckley v. Irwin*, [1960] N.I. 98 (Ch.), and *Blomley v. Ryan*, *supra*, footnote 48. In addition to the cases cited, *infra*, §733, see *Hawkins v. Price*, [1947] Ch. 645; *Walters v. Morgan* (1861), 3 De G.F. & J. 718, 45 E.R. 1056; *Vivers v. Tuck* (1863), 1 Moo. P.C. (N.S.) 516 at pp. 526-7, 15 E.R. 794, *per* Knight Bruce, L.J.:

> It is not the habit of a Court of Equity to decree the specific performance of an agreement more favourable to the Plaintiff than to the Defendant, involving hardship upon the Defendant and damage to his property, if he entered into it without advice or assistance, and there be reasonable ground for doubting whether he entered into it with a knowledge and understanding of its nature and its consequences.

[55] *Hnatuk v. Chretian* (1960), 31 W.W.R. 130 (B.C.S.C.), at p. 132, *per* Wilson, J.

[56] *Huttges v. Verner* (1975), 64 D.L.R. (3d) 374 (N.B.S.C. App. Div.); see also *McColl-Frontenac Oil Co. v. Saulnier & Saulnier*, *supra*, footnote 51 (inadequate price, lessor ill and lacking advice prevailed upon by plaintiff lessee).

[57] *McCorkell v. McFarlane*, [1952] O.W.N. 653 (H.C.J.). *Cf. McLaughlin v. Mallory* (1915), 9 O.W.N. 325 (H.C.), at p. 326, *per* Masten, J., affd 10 O.W.N. 47 (S.C. App. Div.): "a contract genuinely made shall not lightly be disregarded"; *O'Neil v. Arnew* (1976), 78 D.L.R. (3d) 671, 16 O.R. (2d) 549 (H.C.J.).

would have awarded damages had any been proved. Similarly, in a British Columbia decision,[58] specific performance was refused where the plaintiff, the assignee of a mechanics' lienholder's claim, was a sophisticated party who put pressure on the illiterate and ignorant defendants, and "represented to them the helplessness of their position in terms that were not justified".[59] Surely, however, in such a case, rescission would have been awarded if asked for. In a decision of the Saskatchewan Court of Appeal,[60] both specific performance and damages were refused in the case of an agreement for the sale of farm property at a grossly inadequate price, made by a senile defendant who had no independent advice.

734   Although the possibility of damages is often mentioned, there is no indication in the modern cases of damages actually having been awarded. In cases where specific performance is refused on grounds of unfairness, it is highly unlikely that the contract will be enforced in any way, even though some modern courts still insist on using the language of the pre-Judicature Act era.

(3) Hardship

735   The concept of hardship, like the others in this area, is difficult to define. Relief ought not to be granted to a party simply because the bargain proves to be more onerous or less advantageous than he expected. One of the functions of contract is to allocate risks of future change, and reliance on contract as a planning device could be destroyed if ordinarily available remedies were denied simply on the ground that a risk turned out for the worst for the defendant.[61]

736   Equally, however, it has been recognized that in some cases the burden of enforcing the contract is so unexpected or unreasonable as to be unjust, and that relief against hardship may be given without denying reasonable expectations and thereby subverting the fundamental goals of contract. Here also, the courts have stated that there is a middle ground of upholding the contract but denying specific performance,[62] although again, as the principle of unconscionability

---

[58] *Hnatuk v. Chretian* (1960), 31 W.W.R. 130 (B.C.S.C.).

[59] *Ibid.*, at p. 131, *per* Wilson, J.

[60] *Knupp v. Bell* (1968), 67 D.L.R. (2d) 256 (Sask. C.A.).

[61] *McDonell v. McDonell* (1874), 21 Gr. 342 at p. 345, *per* Blake, V.-C.:

　　. . . the utmost caution must be exercised in distinguishing between a case where an actual misunderstanding or misapprehension did exist, and one where the defendant, simply rueing his bargain, seeks to prevent a decree for the performance of the contract being pronounced against him.

[62] *Day v. Newman* (1788), 2 Cox. 77, 30 E.R. 36; *Re Scott and Alvarez's Contract,*

has become more generally accepted, cases which make this distinction are becoming rarer. Once again, the principles are general and fluid, and difficult to describe with precision.

737   As with unfairness, hardship cases usually involve a combination of other discretionary factors which have already been examined. As seen from the discussion of mistake,[63] hardship is often an important ingredient in determining whether specific performance should be denied where the defendant has bargained under some misapprehension. Similarly, with misrepresentation, the courts have often used the language of hardship to describe the plight of the defendant and thereby justify denial of equitable relief.[64] The general point is that where some element of mistake or misrepresentation, not otherwise sufficient to justify complete relief, would produce unexpected or unreasonable burdens on the defendant, specific performance may be denied. There have, however, been cases where specific performance has been denied on the grounds of hardship not produced by misrepresentation, mistake or unfairness.[65] One of the best examples is *Webb v. Direct London & Portsmouth Ry. Co.*[66] where the promoters of the defendant agreed to purchase land owned by the plaintiff for the purpose of constructing a railway, and in return, the plaintiff waived his objection to a bill pending before Parliament to incorporate the company, and as well released any claim for consequential damage to property he retained. The bill was passed, the contract ratified by the defendant, but after several years, the railway was abandoned. The plaintiff's bill for specific performance was dismissed on the ground that to enforce the contract would be "making the machinery of this Court instrumental in doing injustice instead of justice".[67] Although the damages awarded by a modern court would undoubtedly reflect the difference between present market value and the price the defendant had agreed to pay, the result might still be justified on the basis that it would have been more costly to force the defendant to take up the property and resell it, than to require the

---

[1895] 2 Ch. 603 (C.A.) (purchaser agreeing not to object to title, vendor unable to give marketable title, specific performance in vendor's favour refused, but purchaser's claim for return of deposit also refused).

[63] *Supra*, §716.

[64] See, *e.g.*, *Holliday v. Lockwood*, [1917] 2 Ch. 47.

[65] *Ukrainian Greek Orthodox Church v. Independent Bnay Abraham etc. Ass'n* (1959), 20 D.L.R. (2d) 363 (Man. C.A.).

[66] (1852), 1 De G.M. & G. 521, 42 E.R. 654.

[67] *Ibid.*, at p. 529, *per* Cranworth, L.J.

plaintiff to sell in mitigation and recover from the defendant the difference in price.[68]

738　A similar case is an early Ontario decision, *Blackwood v. Paul*,[69] where the defendant had agreed to purchase land from the plaintiff at a price greatly in excess of market value to buy relief from claims for flooding. The land was used as a mill pond, and the defendant's mill had burned down. Specific performance at the suit of the plaintiff was refused, and the court was plainly troubled at the prospect of enforcing a contract which had been procured by the plaintiff under the threat of a nuisance action. While the plaintiff was said to be free to pursue an action at law, the court doubted whether a common law jury would award the full difference in value.[70]

739　It is sometimes said that in assessing hardship, the situation must be examined as of the date of contract.[71] This is potentially misleading, and in fact, in several cases, events occurring after the date of the contract have been taken into account.[72] It is perhaps more accurate to say that a party will not be relieved against a speculation which has gone wrong. Where the parties have by contract allocated certain risks, if specific performance is otherwise available it should not be refused simply because the risk has materialized adversely to the defendant.[73] Thus, for example, in one case dealing with a mining lease, specific performance was resisted on the ground that the mine was useless and that the rent would be paid for nothing, but Romilly, M.R., rejected the defence and granted specific performance: "[The mines] have turned out ill, but the consequence of that is not, in my opinion, that the Defendant can reject the contract, any more than

---

[68] This point is developed more fully, *supra*, §707.

[69] (1854), 4 Gr. 550.

[70] See passage quoted, *supra*, §709.

[71] *Matthews v. McVeigh*, [1954] 2 D.L.R. 338, [1954] O.R. 278 (C.A.); *Stewart v. Ambrosina* (1975), 63 D.L.R. (3d) 595, 10 O.R. (2d) 483 (H.C.J.), affd 78 D.L.R. (3d) 125, 16 O.R. (2d) 221 (C.A.). See also *Rawn v. Anderson* (1923), 24 O.W.N. 521 (H.C.), granting specific performance where the hardship plea was based on post-breach actions by the defendant, at p. 523, *per* Rose, J.: "It did not arise out of the contract or any act of the vendor, but solely from the fact that the plaintiff, placing an erroneous construction upon the contract . . . acted upon the assumption that he . . . was free from the obligations . . . ".

[72] *Mitz v. Wiseman* (1971), 22 D.L.R. (3d) 513, [1972] 1 O.R. 189 (H.C.J.); *City of London v. Nash* (1747), 1 Ves. Sen. 12, 27 E.R. 859; *Blackwood v. Paul* (1854), 4 Gr. 550; *Hill v. Buffalo & Lake Huron Ry. Co.* (1864), 10 Gr. 506.

[73] *Webb and Reeves v. Dipenta*, [1925] S.C.R. 565, [1925] 1 D.L.R. 216; *Jefferys v. Fairs* (1876), 4 Ch. D. 448; *City of London v. Richmond* (1701), 2 Vern. 421 at p. 423, 23 E.R. 870: "As a beneficial bargain will be decreed in equity; so if it happens to be a losing bargain, for the same reason it ought to be decreed."

the Plaintiff could have rejected it, or have demanded higher terms, if the seams had turned out profitable."[74]

740   A point not to be overlooked is that hardship cases may often call for consideration of the plaintiff's interests as well. An unexpectedly harsh result on the defendant's side may well be matched by hardship to the plaintiff if specific performance is refused. A balance has to be struck between these competing interests.[75] In a recent Ontario case[76] dealing with residential property, the vendor pleaded hardship based on unfortunate personal circumstances combined with a dramatic increase in the value of real estate. The court pointed out, however, that the increase in value equally affected the purchaser as refusal of specific relief constituted a hardship to him, and the defence was rejected.

(4) Inadequacy of consideration

741   Inadequacy of consideration is often a factor in these cases. It has often been said that mere inadequacy of consideration will not justify the refusal of specific performance,[77] unless it is such as to shock the conscience.[78] Plainly, the courts will no more scrutinize the wisdom of bargains in actions for specific performance than where other remedies are sought. Often, however, inadequacy of consideration will be a determining factor where some other discretionary defence is advanced. An argument that unfair advantage has been taken of a weaker party will seldom succeed in the absence of inadequacy.[79] Also, the court is bound to be much more sympathetic in mistake or

---

[74] *Haywood v. Cope* (1858), 25 Beav. 140 at p. 149, 53 E.R. 589.

[75] *Shaw v. Thackray* (1853), 1 Sm. & Giff. 537, 65 E.R. 235.

[76] *Stewart v. Ambrosina, supra*, footnote 71.

[77] *Webb and Reeves v. Dipenta, supra*, footnote 73, at p. 574 S.C.R., p. 224 D.L.R., *per* Rinfret, J.; *Naylor v. Winch* (1824), 1 Sim. & St. 555 at p. 565, 57 E.R. 219, *per* Leach, V.-C.: "Where is [the Court] to find a scale for determining the true measure of adequacy?"

[78] *Coles v. Trecothick* (1804), 9 Ves. Jun. 234 at p. 246, 32 E.R. 592, *per* Eldon, L.C.; *Abbott v. Sworder* (1852), 4 De G. & Sm. 448 at p. 461, 64 E.R. 907, *per* Lord St. Leonards, L.C.; *Bower v. Cooper* (1843), 2 Hare 408 at p. 411, 67 E.R. 168, *per* Wigram, V.-C., noting that earlier cases were more generous than the "modern rule of treating inadequacy of price in contracts for the purchase of interests in possession as nothing more than an ingredient in evidence". *Cf. Falcke v. Gray* (1859), 4 Drew. 651 at p. 664, 62 E.R. 250, citing *Day v. Newman* (1788), 2 Cox. 77, 30 E.R. 36; *White v. Damon* (1800), 7 Ves. Jun. 30, 32 E.R. 13 (where the very proposition is doubted).

[79] *Wiltshire v. Marshall* (1866), 14 L.T. 396 (Ch.), at p. 397, *per* Page Wood V.-C.: "[inadequacy of consideration will be] . . . an important ingredient in considering whether a person did exercise any degree of judgment in making a contract, or whether there is a degree of unfairness in accepting the contract".

misrepresentation cases where the defendant can show a disparity between contract and market value which is to his disadvantage.

Contracts under seal

742   It has frequently been said that specific performance is not available with respect to contracts which are "voluntary, or where no consideration emanates from the party seeking performance, even though they may have the legal consideration of a seal".[80] The courts of equity did not treat consideration on a different basis than that developed by the courts of law, and hence, the only category in which a distinction is drawn for remedial purposes is that of contracts under seal, which may certainly give rise to a remedy in damages. It is suggested that in modern times, the proposition that specific performance will not be granted where the consideration requirement is satisfied by seal is dubious.[81] In principle, there appears to be no reason to draw distinctions between legal and equitable remedies here. The seal provides a formal and often convenient way of ensuring enforceability, and it is difficult to see why the law should exclude one remedy, otherwise available. Once again, the only reason would appear to be the differences which formerly existed between law and equity, which have been eradicated now for well over 100 years.

743   While the doctrine has been repeated in cases arising after the Judicature Acts,[82] it has also been held that where the contract recites no consideration and is based upon a seal, it is possible to prove that actual consideration was given, and specific performance can then be made.[83] In most cases, it is likely that some form of consideration can be found to support the promise.

744   More important, in a recent English case,[84] specific performance was decreed of an option agreement where the consideration had been a purely nominal payment of £1. The defendant sought to withdraw the option he had granted the plaintiff, but the plaintiff exercised the option and sued for specific performance. The court held that the option created an equitable interest in land, enforceable by

---

[80] Fry, *Specific Performance*, 6th ed. by Northcote (London, Stevens, 1921), at p. 53; Spry, *supra*, footnote 46, at p. 55; *Jefferys v. Jefferys* (1841), Cr. & Ph. 138, 41 E.R. 443; *Savereux v. Tourangeau* (1908), 16 O.L.R. 600 (Div. Ct.); *Riches v. Burns* (1924), 27 O.W.N. 203 (H.C.).

[81] Waddams, *supra*, footnote 3, at p. 116.

[82] *Supra*, footnote 80.

[83] *Riches v. Burns, supra*, footnote 80.

[84] *Mountford v. Scott*, [1974] 1 All E.R. 248 (Ch.).

specific performance: "It is only necessary, as I see it, that the option should have been validly created. It is not the function of equity to protect only those equitable interests which have been created for valuable consideration."[85] If the courts are prepared to grant specific performance in a case such as this where the consideration is nominal, as it is submitted they should, then there seems no reason why a similar result should not be reached where the contract is supported by seal.

(5) Plaintiff's performance unsecured — want of mutuality

745   Another aspect of hardship arises where the plaintiff has yet to perform his side of the contract when he sues to enforce the defendant's obligation. If the plaintiff's performance cannot be assured by the court, the defendant may be dealt with harshly if forced to perform. This problem is usually described as want of mutuality. Mutuality has already been considered in Chapter 7,[86] where it was noted that there are two versions of the mutuality principle. The affirmative principle is that the availability of specific performance to one party provides a reason for making the remedy available to the other, although it has been argued that the reasons offered to support this principle are not convincing.[87] Here, it is proposed to examine negative mutuality which, although superficially similar to the affirmative version, is in fact quite different.

746   Although the rule of negative mutuality has often been stated rather crudely as apparently requiring that specific relief itself be available to both parties to the contract,[88] the best known and ac-

---

[85] *Ibid.*, at p. 255, *per* Brightman, J.

[86] *Supra*, §§605-611.

[87] *Ibid.*

[88] The most notable example being Fry, *supra*, footnote 80, at p. 219:

A contract to be specifically enforced by the Court must, as a general rule, be mutual — that is to say, such that it might, at the time it was entered into, have been enforced by either of the parties against the other of them. When, therefore, whether from personal incapacity to contract, or the nature of the contract, or any other cause, the contract is incapable of being enforced against one party, that party is, generally, incapable of enforcing it against the other, though its execution in the latter way might in itself be free from the difficulty of attending its execution in the former.

See also Snell, *Principles of Equity*, 27th ed. by Megarry and Baker (London, Sweet & Maxwell Ltd., 1973), pp. 582-3: "As a rule, the court will not grant specific performance at the suit of one party when it could not do so at the suit of the other." *Cf.* Keeton and Sheridan, *Equity*, 2nd ed. (Milton, Oxon., Professional, 1976), p. 373: "it is doubtful whether [the mutuality rule] serves any useful purpose."

cepted statement of the principle is that offered by Ames in his classic article: "Equity will not compel specific performance by a defendant if, after performance, the common-law remedy of damages would be his sole security for the performance of the plaintiff's side of the contract."[89]

747   Thus, according to the negative rule, the plaintiff will not be granted specific enforcement if the defendant cannot be ensured that the plaintiff himself will perform his side of the contract. The negative principle comes into play in situations where the plaintiff is entitled to sue before having performed his side of the bargain.[90]

748   This aspect of mutuality is conveniently discussed in this chapter as it is a discretionary defence to specific performance,[91] and is really one variety of the general argument based upon hardship. The defendant's plea is that forcing him to perform his side without assurance that the plaintiff will render performance in return, places the defendant in a situation so disadvantageous as to warrant withholding specific performance.

749   It is now clear that the time to assess the situation for this purpose is at the date of judgment rather than the date the contract was entered into.[92] Thus, although at the time of contracting, the nature of the plaintiff's obligation was such that specific relief would have been withheld, that provides no reason to refuse specific performance if performance by the plaintiff has in fact been rendered by the time of judgment.

---

[89] Ames, "Mutuality in Specific Performance", *Lectures on Legal History* (Cambridge, Mass., Harvard University Press, 1913), at p. 371. See *Price v. Strange*, [1978] Ch. 337 (C.A.); Treitel, *supra*, footnote 1, at p. 689; Hanbury and Maudsley, *Modern Equity*, 11th ed. by Maudsley and Martin (London, Stevens & Sons, 1981) p. 50; Spry, *supra*, footnote 46, at p. 83.

[90] Sometimes the refusal to award specific performance for contracts to lend money is put on this basis: see *Loan Investment Corp. of Australasia v. Bonner*, [1970] N.Z.L.R. 724 (P.C.), at p. 375, *per* Lord Pearson:

There is an obvious objection in principle to granting specific performance of an unsecured loan. It would have a one-sided operation, creating a position of inequality. The borrower obtains immediately the whole advantage of the contract to him, namely the loan itself — a sum of money placed completely at his disposal. The lender on the other hand has to wait and hope for the payment of interest from time to time and for the eventual repayment of the capital.

Cf. cases where it is possible to sever an ongoing obligation into parts so as to justify the grant of specific performance for those parts already performed: *Wilkinson v. Clements* (1872), 8 Ch. App. 96; *Lowther v. Heaver* (1889), 41 Ch. D. 248 (C.A.).

[91] *Price v. Strange*, *supra*, footnote 89.

[92] *Price v. Strange*, *supra*, footnote 89; *Emerald Resources Ltd. v. Sterling Oil Proper-*

750   While the mutuality rule is based upon hardship to the defendant, it is important to note that the rule itself causes hardship to the plaintiff. Although otherwise entitled to specific relief, the mutuality argument is that he should be deprived of the remedy because of the concern that he might not render his promised performance to the defendant. It might be argued that that is precisely the position the defendant himself bargained for. The problem of mutuality occurs only where the defendant's obligation to perform is not conditional on the plaintiff's performance, but arises immediately. By enforcing the contract specifically, the court is doing nothing more than requiring the defendant to do what he undertook, namely, render performance and risk non-performance on the part of the plaintiff. As an early American commentator said: "Why should the court being able to make the delinquent defendant live up to his obligations, hesitate to do so, because they would place him in a position in which he has expressly agreed to place himself?"[93] This suggests that the mutuality doctrine is hardly one to be encouraged, and that the emphasis should be on finding ways to secure the plaintiff's performance so that specific relief may be granted, avoiding hardship to the defendant, rather than denying specific performance altogether.

751   Indeed, an argument against even securing performance follows from what has just been said. The defendant has undertaken to perform his side while risking non-performance by the plaintiff. The effect of securing the plaintiff's performance is to alter the agreement to the benefit of the defaulting party, and the net effect is to increase the value conferred upon him to the detriment of the innocent party.[94]

752   On the other hand, the situation after litigation will often be very different than before. When a transaction has gone sour and the plaintiff has been forced to litigate, his willingness to render full and adequate performance may well have been dampened. There will often be good reason to take steps to ensure that the plaintiff will perform: as another American commentator put it: "The defendant is not an outlaw who has forfeited all claim to justice."[95] Moreover, the

---

ties *Management Ltd.* (1969), 3 D.L.R. (3d) 630 (Alta. S.C. App. Div.), at p. 647; *Westman v. Macdonald*, [1941] 4 D.L.R. 793 (B.C.S.C.).

[93] Lewis, "The Present Status of the Defence of Want of Mutuality in Specific Performance", 51 American Law Register (O.S.) 591 (1903), at p. 629, quoted in Durfee, "Mutuality in Specific Performance", 20 Mich. L. Rev. 289 at p. 306. See also Schwartz, "The Case for Specific Performance", 87 Yale L.J. 271 (1979), at pp. 301-2.

[94] See Schwartz, *supra*, footnote 93, at pp. 301-5.

[95] Durfee, *supra*, footnote 93, at p. 307.

cost to the plaintiff of assuring performance is insubstantial. It may well be the case that had he offered security at the time of contracting, he might have been able to obtain the defendant's promise more cheaply, but having entered the bargain, and assuming his good faith and willingness to carry out his obligation, it will now cost him nothing to give security. Unless it be assumed that defendants will default in unsecured transactions in order to obtain security, surely an unlikely hypothesis, then the element of redistribution to the defendant to the detriment of the plaintiff is slight, and a price well worth paying in order to secure the position of the defendant where the court perceives a serious risk of non-performance.

753   A familiar application of the negative mutuality rule occurs where the plaintiff is an infant. In the leading case of *Flight v. Bolland*, specific performance in favour of an infant was refused: "No case of a bill filed by an infant for the specific performance of a contract made by him has been found in the books. It is not disputed, that it is a general principle of courts of equity to interpose only where the remedy is mutual."[96] The rationale here is presumably that the court had no method whereby it could guarantee performance of the infant's obligation in favour of the defendant, and thus had the court awarded specific performance, it would have required the defendant to complete with no assurance that the performance would be mutual.[97]

754   Another common class of case in which relief has been denied on grounds of want of mutuality is one in which the defendant has promised to convey real estate in exchange for personal services.[98] In such

---

[96](1828), 4 Russ. 298 at p. 301, 38 E.R. 817, *per* Leach, M.R. See also *Lumley v. Ravenscroft*, [1895] 1 Q.B. 683 (C.A.).

[97]In *Gretzky v. Ontario Minor Hockey Ass'n* (1975), 64 D.L.R. (3d) 467, 10 O.R. (2d) 759 (H.C.J.), at p. 469 D.L.R., p. 761 O.R., Southey, J., refused an injunction to restrain the defendant from interfering with the plaintiff playing for a certain hockey team, *inter alia*, on the following grounds:

> If there are contracts between the [plaintiffs] and the [defendant], they are voidable because of the ages of the boys and are not enforceable against the boys. There is no mutuality of rights and obligations as between the boys and the associations and I do not think that the Court should grant an interim injunction, which is an equitable relief, to enforce a contract at the suit of a party who can avoid the contract.

[98]See, *e.g.*, *Cooke and Cooke v. Gay and Morse* (1956), 4 D.L.R. (2d) 146 (N.S.S.C.), at p. 147, *per* Doull, J.: "this is not the kind of an agreement which a Court of equity will enforce by a decree of specific performance. The agreement is one which involves future personal services which the Court cannot supervise and will consequently refuse to decree performance against the other party." See also

cases, it has been held that as the court cannot and will not specifically enforce contracts of personal services, there can be no guarantee that the defendant will receive the promised benefit, and hence, specific performance of the defendant's obligation to convey should be refused.

755   It is submitted that once again, historical factors ought to be kept in perspective. A modern court may often be able to satisfy itself that the defendant will be adequately protected through monetary compensation rather than specific performance. While the pre-Judicature Act cases enthusiastically support the idea of mutuality of remedy, it is clear that at least part of the problem was produced by the hazards of the dual court system. Chancery was not prepared to saddle the defendant with the risk of another suit at law. In one case it was said that "nothing can be left to depend upon chance, the Court must itself execute the whole contract."[99] In another case, a plaintiff who had agreed to construct a railway line in exchange for shares in a company was refused specific relief on the grounds that "this Court should have complete control", and that should the plaintiffs fail to carry out their obligation, the court " . . . could not place the parties in the position in which both sides intended that they should be; and I should be driven to leave the Defendants, when they came here to complain of such failure, to their remedy at law."[100] Similarly, in a case where the consideration to be given by the plaintiff was personal service for a period of two years after the defendant had performed, specific performance was again refused: "[The Plaintiff] now seeks to compel the Defendants to form the company, and then they would

---

Rushton v. McPherson, [1939] 4 D.L.R. 781 (N.B.S.C.); *Garnett v. Armstrong* (1977), 83 D.L.R. (3d) 717 (N.B.S.C. App. Div.). The latter case refused specific performance although the plaintiff had fully performed at the date of trial, and hence, the result seems wrong in light of the cases cited, *supra*, footnote 92.

[99] *Gervais v. Edwards* (1842), 2 Dr. & War. 80 at p. 83, *per* Lord St. Leonards (quoted in *Stocker v. Wedderburn* (1857), 3 K. & J. 393 at p. 406, 69 E.R. 1162). It is noteworthy, however, that Lord St. Leonards limited the principle somewhat as follows:

> Thus a contract for sale of timber can be specifically executed, although the timber is to be cut down at a future time or at intervals, and the money to be paid by instalments. It is a certain contract, and the manner of dealing with the thing sold, by future cuttings, is no objection to a specific performance. The one man sells the timber, and the other pays for it the price contracted for.

[100] *Peto v. Brighton, Uckfield & Tunbridge Wells Ry. Co.* (1863), 1 H. & M. 468 at pp. 483, 489, 71 E.R. 205, *per* Page Wood, V.-C. See also *Blackett v. Bates* (1865), 1 Ch. App. 117.

be left to their remedy against him at law if he should fail in his part of the agreement."[101]

756   The concern expressed in these cases is clearly that it would be unfair to the defendant to force him to perform without some immediate assurance from the same court that the plaintiff would also perform.

757   Failing this assurance, a decree against the defendant could have seemed very unfair as the defendant would have been faced with the expense and inconvenience of an entirely new set of proceedings in the law courts. Hence, formulating the rule in terms of availability of equitable remedies is perfectly understandable for that period. It is, however, more difficult to justify now that a single court dispenses both law and equity. It may well have been that when the court was restricted to giving equitable relief, the defendant could be assured of his side of the bargain only where an equitable remedy was equally available to him. Surely, such a concern is now irrelevant where monetary compensation would provide the defendant with appropriate protection.

758   This suggests that negative mutuality should operate only where the court concludes that specific relief would impose an unjustifiable risk that the plaintiff will not perform, and that no remedial technique, whether at origin equitable or legal, can be employed to protect the defendant. In fact, the cases would seem to support this proposition in what they do, if not in what they say. Thus, the well-known reformulation of the negative mutuality principle of Professor Ames, quoted above,[102] may require some modification, not only in principle, but also to adequately explain the way the courts have dealt with the problem.[103] Rather than deny specific performance outright, courts have devised many techniques to ensure performance by the plaintiff. A recent English Court of Appeal decision suggests that specific performance may "perhaps" be ordered where "damages would be an adequate remedy to the defendant for any default on the plaintiff's part."[104] The negative covenant cases[105] pro-

---

[101] *Stocker v. Wedderburn, supra,* footnote 99, at p. 407, *per* Page Wood, V.-C.

[102] *Supra,* §746.

[103] See Durfee, *supra,* footnote 93; Cook, "The Present Status of the 'Lack of Mutuality' Rule", 36 Yale L.J. 897 (1927), for criticism of the Ames formulation.

[104] *Price v. Strange,* [1978] Ch. 337 (C.A.), at p. 368, *per* Buckley, L.J.; see also *James Jones & Sons Ltd. v. Earl of Tankerville,* [1909] 2 Ch. 440; *Dougan v. Ley* (1946), 71 C.L.R. 142 (Aust. H.C.), at p. 155, *per* Williams, J.: "[the plaintiffs] have offered by their statement of claim to do everything that is necessary to complete the contract. There was, therefore, no want of mutuality from the date the suit was brought".

[105] *Supra,* Chapter 9.

vide a good example of this. There, very often, the courts have granted specific relief to one side, although it is not available to the other, and damages are the only remedy available.[106] At the same time, the courts have not left the defendant totally unprotected, but have often expressly extended to the defendant the right to apply for dissolution of the injunction should performance by the plaintiff not be forthcoming.[107] In a recent English case,[108] specific performance of an agreement to transfer shares was resisted on the grounds that the agreed price, based upon future corporate earnings, could only be calculated several months after the transaction, and that the defendant should not be required to give up his shares without adequate security. The court approved an order whereby the shares were transferred, but held by the plaintiff's solicitors until payment had been made. A similar solution was suggested in a Supreme Court of Canada case[109] involving an agreement to exchange land in Saskatchewan for land in Iowa. The court rejected the want of mutuality plea, and held that if necessary to protect the defendant, it would order that the conveyance of the Saskatchewan lands be held by an officer of the court until the Iowa property had been properly transferred in exchange.[110]

759   It is submitted, therefore, that the negative principle of mutuality should be used sparingly to justify depriving a plaintiff otherwise entitled to specific relief on the grounds that his performance is not ensured. In most cases, any risk of hardship or oppression to the defendant can be met by moulding the decree in a way so as to secure the concurrent or future performance of the plaintiff to the satisfaction of the court.

---

[106] This was decided as early as 1846: see *Dietrichsen v. Cabburn* (1846), 2 Ph. 52 at p. 57, 41 E.R. 861, *per* Cottenham, L.C.: "The equitable jurisdiction to restrain by injunction an act which the Defendant by contract or duty was bound to abstain from cannot be confined to cases in which the Court has jurisdiction over the acts of the Plaintiff."

[107] For a good example see *Metropolitan Electric Supply Co. Ltd. v. Ginder*, [1901] 2 Ch. 799 at p. 812, *per* Buckley, J., where the court granted an injunction restraining the defendant from violating his agreement to take the whole of the electric energy required for his premises from the plaintiff for a stated period, but provided that "if at any time the plaintiffs are not prepared to supply the energy which he [the defendant] wants, or if they supply an energy which is not a sufficient supply such as they are bound to give by the Act of Parliament, then I think he ought to be at liberty to apply to be relieved from the operation of the injunction."

[108] *Langen & Wind Ltd. v. Bell*, [1972] 1 Ch. 685.

[109] *Jones v. Tucker* (1916), 53 S.C.R. 431, 30 D.L.R. 228.

[110] See also *Nives v. Nives* (1880), 15 Ch. D. 649, declaring a lien to give security in a

5. The Plaintiff in Breach

760   An important aspect of the plaintiff's conduct to be examined is whether he has fulfilled his own contractual obligation. This is sometimes referred to as a matter relating to the court's discretion,[111] but it is doubtful whether there is really any distinction here between situations in which the plaintiff will be denied specific relief on account of his own breach, and cases where the effect of breach is to discharge further obligations, thereby defeating his right to damages.

761   The courts have distinguished between "trivial" breaches which will not defeat the plaintiff's right to specific relief, and breaches of essential terms which will.[112] While the language of discretion is often used in specific performance cases, suggesting a more pervasive power to deny specific performance, the legal and equitable principles are clearly parallel, and it is submitted, virtually indistinguishable. Lord Denning has referred to the common approach of law and equity here,[113] and in a 19th century Privy Council decision, it was said as follows:

> The meaning of the maxim in Chancery that he who seeks equity must do equity, is not clear, because equity has not been clearly defined. The maxim, as their Lordships understand it, includes the rule at law which in all suits upon contracts, either for specific performance or for damages, guides to discriminate whether an alleged breach of the duty of the Plaintiff under the contract is a bar to the suit.
>
> The rule has been expressed in various forms, the substance of it, as regards the present purpose, is, that such breach is a bar when it goes to the whole of the consideration for the promise sued on; but when it amounts only to a partial failure of such consideration, it is no bar to the suit: the Defendant being entitled to recover in a cross action compensation for such failure, if it should be proved to exist.[114]

---

vendor's suit for specific performance of a contract which called for payment by instalments.

[111] See, *e.g.*, *Lamare v. Dixon* (1873), L.R. 6 H.L. 414; *Pearson v. Arcadia Stores Guyra (No. 1)* (1935), 53 C.L.R. 571 at pp. 585-6.

[112] For examples of cases where specific relief was granted despite a "trivial" breach, see, *e.g.*, *Dyster v. Randall & Sons*, [1926] Ch. 932 at p. 942, *per* Lawrence, J.; *Besant v. Wood* (1879), 12 Ch. D. 605 at pp. 627-8, *per* Jessel, M.R.; *Western v. MacDermott* (1866), 2 Ch. App. 72; *Hooper v. Bromet* (1903), 89 L.T. 37. On the other hand, for example, wrongful dismissal of an employee may, depending on the contract, discharge the employee's obligation to respect non-competition covenants: *Telegraph Despatch & Intelligence Co. v. McLean* (1873), 8 Ch. App. 658; *General Billposting Co. v. Atkinson*, [1909] A.C. 118 (H.L.); *Measures Brothers Ltd. v. Measures*, [1910] 2 Ch. 248 (C.A.).

[113] *Chappell v. Times Newspapers Ltd.*, [1975] 1 W.L.R. 482 (C.A.), at p. 502. See also Beale, *Remedies for Breach of Contract*, (London, Sweet & Maxwell, 1980) p. 139.

[114] *Oxford v. Provand* (1868), L.R. 2 P.C. 135 at p. 156, *per* Sir William Erle.

762   Thus, it is suggested that the effect of the plaintiff's breach is not so much a matter affecting choice of remedy, as one which goes to the very substance of the defendant's obligation to perform. The maxim "he who comes to equity must come with clean hands" has been discussed in the context of injunctions,[115] and it was pointed out that it is best understood as a catch-all phrase encompassing discretionary factors which are better considered in more precise terms. Similarly, in contract cases, the want of equity relied upon must have an immediate and necessary relation to the equity sued for[116] and thus, unless the plaintiff's breach is such as to discharge the defendant's obligation to perform, it should not provide grounds for refusing specific performance.

763   It is the case, however, that formerly, a party in breach of some minor obligation was more likely to get specific performance than damages. Courts of equity were more willing to look at the substance and not merely the letter of the contract, than were the courts of law, and to the extent that there was any difference, equity favoured the plaintiff in breach.[117] For example, prior to the Judicature Act, it was often possible for a plaintiff in breach of a provision as to time for completion, to succeed in equity and obtain specific relief where the common law courts would have refused his action for damages. The tendency was for the courts of law to presume time provisions to be of the essence, but for the courts of equity to so regard them only if specific provision to that effect was made in the contract. Equity, influenced by the doctrine that mortgagors should be relieved from the harsh consequences of late payment, would not refuse relief despite the plaintiff's failure to comply with the time clause "unless the express words of the contract, the nature of its subject matter or the surrounding circumstances made it inequitable not to treat the failure of one party to comply exactly with the stipulation as relieving the other party from the duty to perform his obligations under the contract."[118]

764   As a result of the Judicature Acts and the fusion of law and equity, stipulations in contracts as to time or otherwise which would not have been considered to be of the essence in equity, are to be similarly interpreted in all actions.[119] It has been held by the House of

---

[115] *Supra*, §110.

[116] *Ibid.*

[117] See Fry, *supra*, footnote 80 at p. 440. The early cases are also discussed in *United Scientific Holdings Ltd. v. Burnley Borough Council*, [1978] A.C. 904 (H.L.).

[118] *Ibid.*, at p. 927, *per* Lord Diplock.

[119] See, *e.g.*, Mercantile Law Amendment Act, Ont., s. 15:

Lords that this provision means that whether the relief or remedy sought may have been formerly classified as legal or equitable, the equitable doctrine prevails.[120]

6. Plaintiff's Readiness and Willingness

765   A matter related to the effect of breach by the plaintiff is the principle that the plaintiff must plead and prove that he is ready and willing to fulfil his own contractual obligations.[121] This applies with respect to continuing and future obligations of the plaintiff which are interdependent, and to be performed concurrently with obligations of the defendant which the plaintiff seeks to enforce.[122] Although this principle is usually associated with equitable relief, there is a parallel common law rule and both principles have been described by Lord Denning, M.R., as follows: "It has long been settled both at common law and in equity that in a contract where each has to do his part concurrently with the other, then if one party seeks relief, he must be ready and willing to do his part in it."[123]

766   If the plaintiff has put it beyond his power to carry out his own obligation by past breaches, or if his conduct after the defendant's breach indicates an unwillingness or inability to perform, then specific performance will be refused.[124] The principle is that the defendant should not be forced to perform without getting the promised ex-

---

Stipulations in contracts as to time or otherwise that would not, before the coming into force of *The Ontario Judicature Act, 1881*, have been deemed to be or to have become of the essence of such contracts in a court of equity shall receive in all courts the same construction and effect as they would prior to the coming into force of that Act have received in equity.

Law of Property Act, 1925 U.K., s. 41:

Stipulations in a contract, as to time or otherwise, which according to rules of equity are not deemed to be or to have become of the essence of the contract, are also construed and have effect at law in accordance with the same rules.

[120] *United Scientific Holdings Ltd. v. Burnley Borough Council*, *supra*, footnote 117. *Cf*. Spry, *supra*, footnote 46, at p. 205.

[121] See also, *infra*, §779 regarding the plaintiff's obligation to make formal tender. The phrase "ready and willing" is also often used in the context of delay by the plaintiff in presenting his claim, a matter discussed, *supra*, §§92-97.

[122] *Australian Hardwoods Pty. Ltd. v. Com'r for Railways*, [1961] 1 W.L.R. 425 (P.C.), at pp. 432-3, *per* Lord Radcliffe:

. . . where the agreement is one which involves continuing or future acts to be performed by the plaintiff, he must fail unless he can show that he is ready and willing on his part to carry out those obligations, which are, in fact, part of the consideration for the undertaking of the defendant that the plaintiff seeks to have enforced.

[123] *Chappell v. Times Newspapers Ltd.*, *supra*, footnote 113.

[124] See, *e.g.*, *Sutherland v. Westhaver* (1906), 39 N.S.R. 52 (S.C.).

change, and is similar to want of mutuality, discussed above.[125] The "ready and willing" rule will normally be applied where the exchange is simultaneous (as in the case of most contracts of sale) while the mutuality concern ordinarily comes into play where the defendant is required, by the contract, to perform before receiving the return performance by the plaintiff.

7. Impossibility

767   If it is no longer possible for the defendant to perform his promise, specific relief is obviously excluded. It would be a mockery of justice to make an order, enforceable through contempt proceedings and indefinite imprisonment, which could not be complied with.[126] The most common class of case in which performance is said to be impossible is one in which the defendant has resold to a *bona fide* third party whose rights are unaffected by the plaintiff's prior interest.[127] The matter is not so much one of impossibility as the observance of the substantive rules of property which protect innocent third parties in this situation.

768   It has also been held that performance must be not only physically possible but also lawfully competent. An early Irish case is often quoted on this point where it was said that a party seeking specific performance must show that "he does not call upon the other party to do an act which he is not lawfully competent to do; for if he does, a consequence is produced that quite passes by the object of the court in exercising the jurisdiction, which is to do more complete justice."[128]

769   In a recent English case, the Court of Appeal refused specific performance of an agreement to sublet premises where the defendant did not have the right to enter the sublease, and would expose himself to forfeiture under his own lease.[129] Similarly, an order to pull

---

[125] *Supra*, §§745-759.

[126] See, *e.g.*, *Seawell v. Webster* (1859), 29 L.J. Ch. 71 at p. 73, *per* Kindersley, V.-C.: "Put the extreme case of a vendor burning a title-deed: the Court could not make a decree that he should deliver it up, and be imprisoned if he does not."

[127] See, *e.g.*, *Ferguson v. Wilson* (1866), 2 Ch. App. 77; *Leftley v. Moffat*, [1925] 3 D.L.R. 825, 57 O.L.R. 260 (H.C.); *McRae v. Sutherland* (1919), 16 O.W.N. 289 (H.C.). Where the subsequent purchaser is, in equity, bound by the prior sale, specific performance will, of course, be awarded: *MacIntyre v. Commerce Capital Mortgage Corp.* (1981), 34 O.R. (2d) 104 (H.C.J.); *Kirilenko v. Lavoie* (1981), 127 D.L.R. (3d) 15 (Sask. Q.B.), affd 141 D.L.R. (3d) 573 (C.A.); *Carmichael v. Bank of Montreal* (1972), 25 D.L.R. (3d) 570 (Man. Q.B.).

[128] *Harnett v. Yeilding* (1805), 2 Sch. & Lef. 549 at p. 554, 9 R.R. 98, *per* Lord Redesdale, L.C. of Ireland.

[129] *Warmington v. Miller*, [1973] Q.B. 877 (C.A.).

down a wall, built in contravention of a restrictive covenant, was refused where a statutory authority had determined that the wall should remain.[130] However, specific performance decrees requiring the defendant to use his best efforts to obtain regulatory or planning approval are now common.[131]

8. Uncertainty

770   Vagueness in the definition of contractual obligation may cause problems for specific performance. The question of supervision has been considered in Chapter 7, and there it was observed that clarity of the definition of the defendant's obligation is a factor which influences the availability of specific performance.[132] However, the word "uncertainty" is also sometimes used in the context of contract formation, but there, common law and equitable rules must be the same. Again, when specific relief is sought courts sometimes use the language of equitable discretion to explain their refusal of relief.[133] Except in so far as problems of supervision may be involved, it seems clear that there is not a higher standard of certainty where specific performance is sought than where the action is for damages.

771   However, as noted in the discussion of supervision,[134] there may be cases where want of definition of the obligation will render specific performance less appropriate than damages, as in the case of a contract to build a house to a certain value without specifications as to precisely how the house is to be designed and built.

9. Election

772   The plaintiff's right to specific relief may be lost where his own

---

[130] *Seawell v. Webster* (1859), 29 L.J. Ch. 71.

[131] See Chapter 7, footnote 77.

[132] *Supra*, §576.

[133] See, *e.g.*, *Foster v. Wheeler* (1888), 38 Ch. D. 130 (C.A.); *Roman Hotels v. Desrochers Hotels* (1976), 69 D.L.R. (3d) 126 (Sask. C.A.), at p. 143; *South Wales Ry. Co. v. Wythes* (1854), 5 De G.M. & G. 880, 43 E.R. 1112; *Campbell v. Barc* (1916), 31 D.L.R. 475 (Man. C.A.).

[134] *Supra*, §576. See also *Waring & Gillow Ltd. v. Thompson* (1912), 29 T.L.R. 154 (C.A.), at p. 155, *per* Buckley, L.J., disagreeing with the proposition set forth in Fry, *supra*, footnote 80, at p. 179 *et seq.*, that less certainty was required for damages than for specific performance, except according to Buckley, L.J., in the following "very limited sense":

> There were some agreements as to rights to be enjoyed in which there was no question as to what the right was whose enjoyment was the subject of the contract, but in which the mode of enjoyment had not been so identified as that a Court could order specific performance.

post-breach conduct makes the remedy inappropriate. Delay in asserting his claim is perhaps the most common example of such conduct, and has been examined under a separate heading.[135] The issue to be examined here is election: in this context, the plaintiff's manifestation of a choice of remedy other than specific relief, which makes it unjust to allow him later to change his mind and claim specific relief.

773   The issue of election, as it is meant here, arises when the promisee is faced with a breach on the part of the promisor in circumstances which allow, physically and temporally, for the continuing possibility of performance. Usually, this will arise as a result of an anticipatory breach where the promisor repudiates his contractual obligation prior to the date on which performance is required.[136] A breach of a contractual condition or a breach "going to the root of the contract", in other words, a breach by the promisor of sufficient gravity so as to excuse the promisee from any further obligation to perform, will also produce this situation.[137]

774   Faced with a breach of such a nature, the promisee may either insist upon the promisor's performance notwithstanding, or decide to sue for damages. In certain cases, the promisee may also have the option of claiming restitution of benefits already conferred.[138] The nature of the innocent[139] party's obligation to make and manifest his choice, and the consequences which flow from such choice, are the subject of a rather technical and at times obscure body of case-law.

775   It has been held that if the promisee asks the promisor for restitution of benefits conferred, usually the return of his deposit, he has made an election for that relief, the contractual obligation of the promisor is at an end, and specific performance is no longer available to the promisee.[140] It has been said that even an unanswered request for restitution will preclude the promisee from later opting for some other remedy: the election has been made by the request itself and

---

[135] *Supra*, §82 *et seq.*

[136] See, *e.g.*, Waddams, *supra*, footnote 3, at pp. 384-93.

[137] Waddams, *supra*, at pp. 363-4.

[138] See Albery, "Mr. Cyprian Williams' Great Heresy", 91 L.Q.R. 337 (1975).

[139] Where a party repudiates a contract and the repudiation is accepted the repudiating party cannot retract and sue for specific performance: *Hetherington v. Roberts* (1959), 18 D.L.R. (2d) 39 (Alta. S.C. App. Div.).

[140] *Macnaughton v. Stone*, [1950] 1 D.L.R. 330, [1949] O.R. 853 (H.C.J.); *McDougall v. Allen* (1922), 65 D.L.R. 320 (N.S.S.C.). *Cf. Cull v. Heritage Mills Development Ltd.* (1974), 49 D.L.R. (3d) 521 at pp. 531-2, 5 O.R. (2d) 102 at pp. 112-13 (H.C.J.), holding that such a demand does not bar an action in damages.

can be set up as a defence by the promisor even though he has not acted upon it.[141] The propriety of holding the promisee to an election which has not caused detrimental reliance on the part of the promisor is discussed below.[142]

776   Where the promisee decides to claim damages, he is said to "accept the breach".[143] His election is to treat the contract as having been broken at the point of breach and in effect, to discharge the promisor from any further contractual obligation other than to pay damages.[144]

777   The accepted position is that subsequent insistence upon specific performance is inconsistent with the acceptance of the promisor's breach. The effect of acceptance, or the assertion of a damages claim, is to discharge both parties from further performance, and hence, specific performance is no longer possible.[145] Again, the issue of the validity of this rule in the absence of detrimental reliance is examined below.

778   Sloppiness of language has often led to what has aptly been called

---

[141] See, *e.g.*, *Macnaughton v. Stone*, *supra*, footnote 140, at p. 336 D.L.R., p. 859 O.R., *per* McRuer, C.J.H.C.:

> The request for the return of the deposit is not consistent with an intention to treat the contract as valid and subsisting and to bring an action for specific performance if the contract was not performed according to the terms thereof. The plaintiff, having elected to treat the contract as at an end by demanding the return of the deposit, could not by himself revive it when the deposit was not returned. It is just as true that it takes two to revive the contract as it is that it takes two to rescind one.

[142] *Infra* §§784-790.

[143] Cheshire and Fifoot, *The Law of Contract*, 9th ed. by Furmston (London, Butterworths, 1976), pp. 573-4 states the rules as follows:

> Where A and B are parties to an executory contract and A indicates that he is no longer able or willing to perform his outstanding obligations, he in effect makes an offer to B that the contract shall be discharged. Therefore B is presented with an option. He may either refuse or accept the offer. More precisely, he may either affirm the contract by treating it as still in force, or on the other hand he may treat it as finally and conclusively discharged.

[144] The measurement of damages in case of anticipatory breach is discussed in Waddams, *The Law of Damages* (1983), §§1226-1252.

[145] Thus, in *Johnson v. Agnew*, [1980] A.C. 367 (H.L.), at p. 392, Lord Wilberforce put forth as an "uncontroversial" proposition of law, the following:

> . . . if the vendor treats the purchaser as having repudiated the contract and accepts the repudiation, he cannot thereafter seek specific performance. This follows from the fact that, the purchaser having repudiated the contract and his repudiation having been accepted, both parties are discharged from further performance.

See also *Saunders v. Multi Builders Ltd. and Haywood* (1981), 30 B.C.L.R. 236 (S.C.).

"a fertile source of confusion" at this point.[146] Because the effect of his choice is to discharge both parties from further performance, courts have sometimes referred to the promisee's action in opting for damages as rescinding the contract. There is, however, a basic difference between rescinding a contract, which in law treats it as if it had never come into existence, and accepting repudiatory breach, which merely discharges the promisor from further performance but still obliges him to pay damages.[147] Usually the intention of the promisee is clear, but occasionally the courts have reached unexpected and inappropriate results because of ambiguity and imprecision of language.[148]

779　　The other option is to insist upon further performance. This usually involves suing for specific performance, but a similar issue arises where the innocent party is able to perform his side of the contract without further co-operation from the repudiating party other than payment.[149] The effect of suing for specific performance is to keep the contract alive. The obligation to perform remains for both parties,[150] and certain important implications follow. The promisee must remain ready, willing and able to complete his side of the contract. If the repudiation was less than clear, he must ordinarily demonstrate his desire and ability to complete the transaction on the date fixed for completion through tender, although it now seems well accepted that the innocent party need not tender where the refusal to perform is clear and tender would be useless.[151] If the innocent party does choose to keep the contract alive, he must take care not to put himself in breach by failing to meet his own obligations. In the often-quoted language of Asquith, L.J.: "An unaccepted repudiation is a thing writ in water and of no value to anybody: it confers no legal rights of any sort or kind."[152] The risk the promisee takes in keeping

---

[146] *Johnson v. Agnew, supra,* footnote 145, at p. 392.

[147] *Johnson v. Agnew, supra,* at p. 393.

[148] See Weir, "Remedies with Respect to Contracts of Purchase and Sale" in *Law Society of Upper Canada Special Lectures,* 1960, 427 at pp. 430-2.

[149] See *White & Carter (Councils) Ltd. v. McGregor,* [1962] A.C. 413 (H.L.), and discussion in Waddams, *The Law of Damages* (1983), §§1229-1252.

[150] *Goldenberg v. Lieberman,* [1951] O.W.N. 405 (H.C.J.), at p. 406, *per* McRuer, C.J.H.C. *Cf.* however, *Lyew v. 418658 Ontario Ltd.* (1982), 134 D.L.R. (3d) 384n, 35 O.R. (2d) 241 (C.A.) setting aside a specific performance judgment in favour of a defendant who had withdrawn his defence and moved for judgment on the basis that the plaintiff had sued for specific performance and thereby kept the contract alive for his benefit as well.

[151] *Kloepfer Wholesale Hardware & Auto Co. Ltd. v. Roy,* [1952] 2 S.C.R. 465, [1952] 3 D.L.R. 705.

[152] *Howard v. Pickford Tool Co.,* [1951] 1 K.B. 417 (C.A.), at p. 421. See also

the contract alive, although usually slight, is that he keeps the contact alive for both parties,[153] and if subsequent events arise which excuse the defendant from performing, the defendant will be excused despite his earlier breach. This point is dramatically illustrated by the case of *Avery v. Bowden*.[154] There the plaintiff, faced with a repudiatory breach of a charter-party, sued for specific performance. Despite the defendant's clear and inexcusable repudiation, the plaintiff failed in his action because the subsequent outbreak of war extended a contractual defence upon which the defendant was able to rely since the plaintiff's specific performance claim kept the contract alive.[155] Similarly, the innocent party who decides to pursue performance must himself be careful to avoid committing an act which will put him in breach of the sort to excuse performance by the defendant, as the contract is said to be alive for all purposes.[156]

780 A related point, and a potential source of confusion, is the view sometimes expressed that a party who disregards a repudiation cannot later recover damages on account of the breach. Because the breach has not been "accepted" the contract remains alive and unbroken.[157] In certain circumstances failure to act on the repudiation within a reasonable time may preclude the promisee from relying on it to establish his action later.[158] However, it is inaccurate to state that the breach must be accepted. The innocent party may adopt an equivocal position and keep his options open by suing for specific performance and claiming damages in the alternative, and postpone his election until judgment.

Heyman v. Darwins Ltd., [1942] A.C. 356 (H.L.), at p. 361, *per* Viscount Simon, L.C.: "repudiation by one party standing alone does not terminate the contract. It takes two to end it, by repudiation, on the one side, and acceptance of the repudiation, on the other"; *Decro-Wall Int'l S.A. v. Practitioners in Marketing Ltd.*, [1971] 2 All E.R. 216 (C.A.).

[153] *Frost v. Knight* (1872), L.R. 7 Ex. 111.

[154] (1855), 5 El. & Bl. 714, 119 E.R. 647.

[155] External circumstances arising after the date of breach which would excuse performance may also affect the calculation of damages: see *The Mihalis Angelos*, [1971] 1 Q.B. 164 (C.A.).

[156] See, for example, *Dalrymple v. Scott* (1892), 19 O.A.R. 477, dismissing a damages claim where the plaintiff had refused to accept a repudiatory breach on the part of a defendant to deliver a certain commodity, but had himself failed to provide the particulars as to place and date of delivery as required by the contract. In *Dunlop v. Bolster* (1912), 6 D.L.R. 468 (Alta. S.C.), it was said that where the purchaser defaults, and the vendor claims the instalment of purchase price then due, the purchaser may assert a claim for specific performance.

[157] See Cheshire and Fifoot, *supra*, footnote 143, at p. 573.

[158] See McRae, "Repudiation of Contracts in Canadian Law", 56 Can. Bar Rev. 233 (1978).

> The plaintiff, in effect, is saying: "I don't accept your repudiation of the contract but am willing to perform my part of the contract and insist upon your performing your part — but if I cannot successfully insist on your performing your part, I will accept the repudiation and ask for damages."[159]

781   The assertion of a claim for specific performance does not, then, amount to making an election in the sense of taking an irretrievable step. Rather, the plaintiff keeps the contract alive, preserving his right to insist upon performance, but also maintaining the possibility of later asserting his alternative claim in damages. So long as the contract is kept alive by an absence of elective behaviour on the part of the plaintiff, and so long as the defendant maintains his refusal to perform, in the absence of circumstances which would excuse performance on the part of the defendant, the remedial choice between damages and specific performance is open up to the point of judgment.

782   The prudent course for a plaintiff seeking specific performance and wishing to maintain the damages option is to claim both remedies in the alternative. In *Dobson v. Winton & Robbins Ltd.*,[160] the Supreme Court of Canada approved of an equivocal pleading. On the other hand, it would seem that even where only specific performance is claimed, the court can still award damages if specific performance is refused.[161]

783   It has been held that the plaintiff's option may extend even beyond judgment in certain circumstances and that the plaintiff may elect damages even after judgment for specific performance.[162] The point was dealt with recently by the House of Lords in *Johnson v. Agnew*.[163] There the defendant purchasers had failed to comply with a specific performance decree, and as the plaintiff vendor was in arrears, mortgagees realized upon their security, leaving a deficiency. The House of Lords upheld the plaintiff's right to insist upon damages although the judgment for specific performance had been taken out: "if an order for specific performance is sought and is made, the contract remains in effect and is not merged in the judgment for spe-

---

[159] *McKenna v. Richey*, [1950] V.L.R. 360 at p. 372, *per* O'Bryan, J., a passage quoted and approved in *Johnson v. Agnew*, [1980] A.C. 367 (H.L.), at p. 397.

[160] [1959] S.C.R. 775, 20 D.L.R. (2d) 164.

[161] *Tamplin v. James* (1880), 15 Ch. D. 215 (C.A.). *Cf. Mines Ltd. v. Woodworth*, [1941] 4 D.L.R. 101 (B.C.C.A.), affd [1942] 1 D.L.R. 135 (S.C.C.).

[162] *Widrig v. Strazer*, [1964] S.C.R. 376, 44 D.L.R. (2d) 1.

[163] [1980] A.C. 367 (H.L.).

cific performance.''[164] In such circumstances, where the order is not complied with, to assert his rights the plaintiff will have to come back to the court and ask either for enforcement of the order, or request that the specific performance decree be dissolved so as to put an end to the contract and entitle him to damages. The decision in *Johnson v. Agnew* recognizes a discretion in the court not to dissolve such a decree where to do so would be unjust.[165] Thus, such relief may be denied where performance has become a losing proposition for the plaintiff, as it would be harsh to impose the risk of post-judgment fluctuation in value upon the defendant. In an Ontario case,[166] the court refused the plaintiff's application to rescind a judgment for specific performance ordering the defendant to transfer certain shares at the contract price, where after judgment, the price changed dramatically so as to make the contract very favourable to the defendant.

784   As noted above, it is usual to state the rules relating to election in rather strict and inflexible language, and to say that the plaintiff will be barred from pursuing a claim for specific relief once he has made an election to take some other remedy, even though there has been no detrimental reliance on the part of the defendant. Perhaps there is reason to reconsider this position.

785   The word "election" suggests the selection of one of two mutually exclusive alternatives.[167] The language of offer and acceptance, often used to describe the plaintiff's choice when faced with a breach, carries with it the connotation of the creation of a distinctive legal relationship in circumstances where the need for certainty and finality is sufficiently strong to preclude any revocation and alteration of the initial choice. One might question, however, whether these concepts are particularly apt in the remedial context.

786   With respect to election, Lord Atkin observed in an analogous context,[168] "it is essential to bear in mind the distinction between choosing one of two alternative remedies, and choosing one of two inconsistent rights."[169] The need for certainty and finality in the for-

---

[164] *Ibid.*, at p. 393.

[165] *Ibid.*, at p. 399.

[166] *Gray v. Holton Securities*, [1953] 1 D.L.R. 100, [1952] O.R. 793 (H.C.J.). See also *Leckie v. Marshall* (1912), 4 D.L.R. 94, 22 O.W.R. 870 (C.A.).

[167] See, *e.g.*, *Scarf v. Jardine* (1882), 7 App. Cas. 345 (H.L.), at p. 360; *Osmack v. Stan Reynolds Auto Sales Ltd.*, [1976] 2 W.W.R. 576n (S.C.C.) (affg [1974] 1 W.W.R. 408 (Alta. S.C. App. Div)).

[168] *United Australia Ltd. v. Barclay's Bank*, [1941] A.C. 1 (H.L.), at p. 29.

[169] *Cf.* the use of "election" in cases involving inconsistent rights: *Scarf v. Jardine*, *supra*, footnote 167, at p. 360, *per* Lord Blackburn:

mation of contractual relationships is not paralleled in the context of remedial choice. The law offers various means for redressing a wrong, and the plaintiff is entitled to a choice. He should not be permitted to alter that choice where to do so would put the defendant in a worse position than he would have been in had the altered choice been made first. However, it is difficult to see why an initial option for one means of redress should preclude later altering the choice for another in the absence of material detriment suffered by the defendant because of the change in position. If, as Lord Wilberforce has observed, "Election, though the subject of much learning and refinement, is in the end a doctrine based on simple considerations of common sense and equity,"[170] surely the flexibility of estoppel is preferable to the rigidity of election and offer and acceptance.[171]

787   The issue becomes whether, in the remedial context, it is enough that the other party *may* have been led to alter his position, or whether it must be shown that he *did* alter his position in reliance. While the language of text writers and cases suggests that any initial choice of remedy is final, some element of detrimental reliance can usually be found in the cases taken to establish this rule. In *McDougall v. Allen*,[172] the Nova Scotia Court of Appeal held that a simple demand by the purchaser for the return of his deposit prevented him from claiming specific performance, but on the facts, it is clear that the vendor had relied on the purchaser's demand and resold the property to an innocent third party shortly thereafter. In the leading Ontario case, *Macnaughton v. Stone*,[173] the plaintiff was prevented from asserting a specific performance claim after making a re-

---

... where a man has an option to choose one or other of two inconsistent things, when once he has made his election it cannot be retracted, it is final and cannot be altered. . . . When once there has been an election to do one of the two things you cannot retract it and do the other thing; the election once made is finally made.

[170] *Johnson v. Agnew, supra*, footnote 159, at p. 398. It must be pointed out, however, that Lord Wilberforce did say the following in the next sentence: "It is easy to see that a party who has chosen to put an end to a contract by accepting the other party's repudiation cannot afterwards seek specific performance. This is simply because the contract has gone — what is dead is dead."

[171] Estoppel would seem clearly to be the basis for the election rule. As it was put in an early English case, *Ward v. Day* (1863), 4 B. & S. 337 at p. 352, 122 E.R. 486, *per* Crompton, J: "if a man, having an option, by some solemn act declares his determination and election he cannot afterwards recede from it; and the reason of this is, that the other party may have been led by this expression communicated to him to alter his position."

[172] (1922), 65 D.L.R. 320 (N.S.S.C.).

[173] [1950] 1 D.L.R. 330, [1949] O.R. 853 (H.C.J.).

quest for the return of his deposit, which was refused. However, the plaintiff was a solicitor and had a serious conflict of interest in that he was acting for the vendor in the same transaction. McRuer, C.J.H.C., held that having failed to advise the vendor to return the deposit so as to be relieved of further obligation, he could not take advantage of his own default.

788   The decision of the Manitoba Court of Appeal in *O'Kelly v. Downie*[174] provides further support for a more flexible approach. There, the defendant defaulted, and by error, the plaintiff's solicitor delivered a statement of claim insisting on specific performance. The defendants tendered performance, and argued that the plaintiff was in breach. The court rejected the defendant's contention, and refused to hold the plaintiff to the mistake of his solicitor, stating:[175] "The defendant has not been induced to change his position because of this misstatement."

789   Moreover, before the Judicature Acts the plaintiff was by no means refused equitable relief because he had earlier put forth a damages claim. Indeed, specific performance could be awarded even after a common law action had been commenced. To prevent multiplicity of suits and possible double recovery, the practice was to issue an injunction on the motion of the defendant restraining the suit at law which had the effect of requiring the plaintiff to elect.[176] The practice of granting an equitable remedy despite the plaintiff's action at law may perhaps be explained by the fact that at one time, a separate action at law was required to decide the strictly legal issues.[177] This, however, should not obscure the fact that the courts saw it possible to give equitable relief in certain cases even where the

---

[174] (1914), 17 D.L.R. 395 (Man. C.A.).

[175] *Ibid.*, at p. 396, *per* Howell, C.J.M. *Cf. Lyew v. 418658 Ontario Ltd.* (1982), 134 D.L.R. (3d) 384n (Ont. C.A.).

[176] See Story, *Equity Jurisprudence*, 12th ed., vol. 1 (Boston, Little, Brown, 1877), pp. 74-5: "Courts of equity will not only award an injunction to stay proceedings at law, but they will also, where the party is proceeding at law and in equity for the same matter at the same time, compel him to make an election of the suit, in which he will proceed, and will stay the proceedings in the other court." See also Spry, *supra*, footnote 46, at pp. 208-12; *Fennings v. Humphery* (1841), 4 Beav. 1, 49 E.R. 237; *Fox v. Scard* (1863), 33 Beav. 327, 55 E.R. 394. In *Greene v. West Cheshire Ry. Co.* (1871), L.R. 13 Eq. 44, it was held that the fact of unsuccessful negotiations for monetary compensation did not defeat the plaintiff's right to specific performance.

[177] See *Fox v. Scard, supra,* footnote 175.

plaintiff had indicated initially that damages rather than performance was being sought.[178]

790   Thus, it is suggested that the matter is perhaps not entirely clear-cut. It is quite possible that a court would not hold a plaintiff to an initial indication of which remedy he selects in the absence of detrimental reliance on the part of the defendant.[179] Analysis based upon detrimental reliance would permit flexibility of choice on the part of the plaintiff, and prevent undue consequences from a hasty, ill-advised, or unfortunate initial choice, while still protecting the defendant in cases where actual harm to him occurred because of the change of selection by the plaintiff. Although the rules appear to be somewhat rigid and inflexible, and to some extent create a potential trap for the unwary, there is also a good chance that the courts would reach an acceptable result where no reliance had been placed on an inadvertent or ill-advised initial choice of remedy.

10. Other Discretionary Defences

791   The principles governing the discretionary defences of delay,[180] "clean hands"[181] and "he who seeks equity must do equity"[182] have

---

[178] An analogous principle is that at common law, it was held that a demand for payment for goods delivered to the plaintiff did not necessarily preclude an action in conversion: *Valpy v. Sanders* (1848), 5 C.B. 886, 136 E.R. 1128.

[179] Corbin, *Contracts* (St. Paul, West Publishing Co., 1964), §1220, p. 461. Corbin's statement of the principle reads as follows:

. . . where a party injured by a breach definitely manifests a choice of a remedy that is actually available to him, in the place of some other alternative remedy, such a manifestation will bar an action for the latter remedy, provided that the party against whom the remedy is asked makes a substantial change in position in reliance on the manifestation of intention before notice of its retraction

Similarly, the election principles set out in the Restatement (Second) are based upon a detrimental reliance analysis:

§381(1) When the alternative remedies of damages and restitution are available to a party injured by a breach, his manifested choice of one of them by bringing suit or otherwise, followed by a material change of position by the other party in reliance thereon, is a bar to the other alternative remedy.

(2) The bringing of an action for one of these remedies is a bar to the alternative one unless the plaintiff shows reasonable ground for making the change of remedy.

§382 The bringing of a suit either for specific performance or for compensation in money is not such an election of the remedy sued for as to operate as a bar to a later suit or to an amendment asking for the other remedy with respect to the same breach; but a material change of position by the defendant in reasonable reliance upon the plaintiff's first choice of remedy may operate as such a bar.

§383 If one of the remedies for breach of contract is not in fact available to the plaintiff, a mistaken effort made in good faith to obtain it is not a bar to a suit for a different remedy.

[180] *Supra*, §§82-102.

[181] *Supra*, §§103-109.

[182] *Supra* §110.

been discussed in Chapter 1, in the part of this book dealing with injunctions. This earlier discussion encompasses the application of these defences to specific performance.

CHAPTER 11

PARTIAL, MODIFIED AND CONDITIONAL
PERFORMANCE

1. Introduction

792   This chapter examines a variety of situations in which specific relief is granted, but where the performance decreed varies in some way from the literal terms of the agreement between the parties, or is made subject to terms or conditions imposed by the court. If some form of specific relief is called for, but performance exactly as promised is not possible, or would lead to unexpected or unjust results because of circumstances existing at the time the court is called upon to decide, the techniques described here may be important to enable the court to meet those exigencies. The central theme is that while the court's order may depart from the literal terms of the contract, at the same time, the decree may be moulded in an effort properly to reflect the reasonable expectations of the parties.

2. Specific Performance with Compensation

793   In many cases, although one party is unable to perform his promise to the full, it may seem unjust or inappropriate to refuse enforcement of the contract. At the same time, enforcement without taking into account the deficiency in performance would also be unjust. Specific performance with compensation provides a middle ground between the outright grant or refusal of specific relief in such cases. Almost invariably, these cases arise in the context of contracts for the sale of land where there is a defect in the vendor's title or a deficiency in the land he is actually able to convey.

794   The appropriateness of ordering specific performance with compensation will depend upon whether the vendor is seeking or resisting the remedy. It is one thing for the purchaser to say that notwithstanding the vendor's inability to convey exactly what was promised, he will take all that the vendor has to offer with compensation for the deficiency. It is quite another for the vendor to insist that the purchaser be forced to take all that he has to offer, even with compensation for the deficiency. Obviously, the court will be more prepared to order performance with compensation in the former case than in the latter. In either case, the task of the court is to arrive at a solution which protects and fosters the reasonable expectations of the parties.

(1) Purchaser suing for specific performance with compensation

795   Where the purchaser sues for specific performance with compensation for deficiency in the vendor's performance, the statement of Eldon, L.C., in 1804 is often referred to:

> . . . if a man, having partial interests in an estate, chooses to enter into a contract, representing it, and agreeing to sell it, as his own, it is not competent to him afterwards to say, though he has valuable interests, he has not the entirety; and therefore the purchaser shall not have the benefit of his contract. For the purpose of this jurisdiction, the person contracting under those circumstances, is bound by the assertion in his contract; and, if the vendee chooses to take as much as he can have, he has a right to that, and to an abatement; and the Court will not hear the objection by the vendor, that the purchaser cannot have the whole.[1]

All else being equal, this expresses the principle which the courts have followed consistently. The purchaser is entitled to a conveyance of whatever the vendor has[2] with appropriate compensation.[3] The ef-

---

[1] *Mortlock v. Buller* (1804), 10 Ves. Jun. 292 at pp. 315-16, 32 E.R. 857.

[2] *Infra*, footnotes 6-7.

[3] A rateable reduction is often appropriate. See also *Topfell Ltd. v. Galley Properties Ltd.*, [1979] 1 W.L.R. 446 (Ch.), at p. 451, *per* Templeman, J.: "[The reduction in price should be based on the] sort of price that he [the purchaser] might have been willing to pay or the hypothetical reasonable purchaser might have been willing to pay with full knowledge." See also *Re Chifferiel* (1888), 40 Ch. D. 45, holding that the appropriate measure of compensation where a road on a subject property did not meet contract specifications was the difference in market value rather than the actual cost of repairing the road. It has been held that where the defect is not one readily valued, relief should be refused: *Rudd v. Lascelles*, [1900] 1 Ch. 815 (undisclosed restrictive covenant), but it is rare for relief to be refused on this ground, and usually the courts have said that they must do their best to value the defect or deficiency: see, *e.g.*, *Barnes v. Wood* (1869), L.R. 8 Eq. 424. For a detailed discus-

fect of the rule is usually to give the purchaser a choice where the vendor is unable to convey that which he has promised.[4] Ordinarily, the plaintiff will be able to have rescission, to treat the vendor's failure as a breach giving rise to an action in damages,[5] or to take whatever it is that the vendor has at a reduced price. The rule has been acted upon many times both in the case of title defects[6] and in the case of deficiency in the quantity or quality of land being conveyed.[7]

796   This basic principle, however, must be read as subject to certain other important considerations. In the first place, reference must be made to the actual agreement between the parties, and as will be seen later, terms in agreements of purchase and sale often curtail the purchaser's right to have specific performance with compensation.[8]

797   More basically, the power to order specific performance with compensation must be exercised in a manner consistent with its underlying principle. The task of the court is to decide whether reasonable expectations will be fostered or frustrated by a specific performance decree with compensation. This will often involve the difficult issues of construing the agreement and the intention of the parties. If, in

---

sion of the assessment of compensation, see Harpum, "Specific Performance with Compensation as a Purchaser's Remedy — A Study in Contract and Equity", 40 Camb. L.J. 47 (1981), at p. 76 et seq. In Grant v. Dawkins, [1973] 1 W.L.R. 1406 (Ch.), where liabilities exceeded the price, the purchaser was given not only abatement of the price but damages as well.

[4] The vendor's right to specific performance with an abatement is discussed, infra, §§800-806.

[5] Although the rule in Bain v. Fothergill (1874), L.R. 7 H.L. 158, appears to have been superseded in Canada: A.V.G. Management Science Ltd. v. Barwell Developments Ltd., [1979] 2 S.C.R. 43, 92 D.L.R. (3d) 289, the agreement itself may limit or exclude recovery of expectation damages: see Waddams, The Law of Damages (1983), §188, thereby possibly making specific performance with compensation more attractive. However, the agreement may also preclude this possibility as well: see, infra, §§807-810.

[6] Kennedy v. Spence (1911), 24 O.L.R. 535 (H.C.J.); Barnes v. Wood (1869), L.R. 8 Eq. 424; Burrow v. Scammell (1881), 19 Ch. D. 175; Re Jackson and Haden's Contract, [1906] 1 Ch. 412 (C.A.); Hurley v. Roy (1921), 64 D.L.R. 375, 50 O.L.R. 281 (S.C. App. Div.); Re Des Reaux and Setchfield's Contract, [1926] Ch. 178. Specific performance with abatement of price has also been ordered where there is more than one vendor and it transpires that one has no interest: Basma v. Weekes, [1950] A.C. 441 (P.C.); Horrocks v. Rigby (1878), 9 Ch. D. 180. Contra, Lumley v. Ravenscroft, [1895] 1 Q.B. 683 (C.A.).

[7] Butler v. Purcell (1956), 2 D.L.R. (2d) 317 (N.S.S.C.); Rodgers v. Fisher (1911), 20 O.W.R. 196 (H.C.J.); McKenzie v. Hesketh (1877), 7 Ch. D. 675; Silvert v. Carlson (1914), 17 D.L.R. 714 (Man. K.B.); Bowes v. Vaux (1918), 43 O.L.R. 521 (H.C.); Lavine v. Independent Builders Ltd., [1932] 4 D.L.R. 569, [1932] O.R. 669 (C.A.); Levy and Levy v. Rodewalt (1959), 18 D.L.R. (2d) 77 (Alta. S.C. App. Div.); Ruskowsky v. Palechek (1978), 87 D.L.R. (3d) 243 (Alta. S.C.T.D.).

[8] Infra, §§807-810.

fact, the bargain can fairly be construed as the purchaser having agreed to take all that the defendant had for the stated price, it would work a hardship on the defendant to reduce that price. Thus, in one case, the purchaser was refused compensation on the grounds that he knew of the deficiency when he entered into the contract and had no expectation that the deficiency could be made up.[9] Compensation has been refused where the price was calculated with reference to matters not specifically related to the deficiency or defect,[10] or even where giving compensation would distort the agreement and make it unduly favourable to the plaintiff.[11] It has also been held that where forcing the vendor to sell at a reduced price would cause a hardship, the purchaser's action should be dismissed.[12] In other cases of substantial discrepancy between what was promised and what the vendor could actually convey, the entire agreement has been held vitiated by the error.[13] It has sometimes been said that the purchaser's knowledge of a deficiency will not affect his right to relief,[14] but it would also seem that where the plaintiff has not really been misled by a written term which proves inaccurate, and would in fact get what he really bargained for, no compensation will be awarded.[15]

798   Another important qualification is that the deficiency or defect must relate to a contractual term, and not merely to some matter

---

[9] *Bullen v. Wilkinson* (1912), 2 D.L.R. 190, 21 O.W.R. 427 (C.A.). Similarly, specific performance with compensation will be refused where the purchaser knows that the vendor is acting in a representative capacity requiring consent for the sale: *A. Harvey Hacker Builders Ltd. v. Akerfeldt* (1964), 48 D.L.R. (2d) 119, [1965] 1 O.R. 369 (H.C.J.), affd 50 D.L.R. (2d) 130n, [1965] 2 O.R. 182n (C.A.), or where the purchaser knows that the vendor has only a partial interest, and that he purports to sell no more: *Castle v. Wilkinson* (1870), L.R. 5 Ch. 534.

[10] *Rudd v. Lascelles, supra*, footnote 3.

[11] *Schlote v. Richardson*, [1951] 2 D.L.R. 233, [1951] O.R. 58 (H.C.J.); *Osborne v. Farmers' & Mechanics' Building Society* (1855), 5 Gr. 326; *Bullen v. Wilkinson, supra*, footnote 9.

[12] *Earl of Durham v. Legard* (1865), 34 Beav. 611, 55 E.R. 771; *Osborne v. Farmers' & Mechanics' Building Society, supra*, footnote 11; *Martens v. Burden* (1974), 45 D.L.R. (3d) 123 (Alta. S.C.T.D.). Hardship to third parties has also been considered a relevant factor: *Thomas v. Dering* (1837), 1 Keen 729, 48 E.R. 488; *Kaunas v. Smyth* (1976), 75 D.L.R. (3d) 368, 15 O.R. (2d) 237 (H.C.J.).

[13] *Earl of Durham v. Legard, supra*, footnote 12; *Hyrski v. Smith* (1969), 5 D.L.R. (3d) 385, [1969] 2 O.R. 360 (H.C.J.).

[14] *Whittemore v. Whittemore* (1869), L.R. 8 Eq. 603 at p. 605, *per* Malins, V.-C.: "I am firmly persuaded that the purchaser would have given exactly the same price for the property if those words had been omitted; but as they have been put in I must treat them as part of the contract"; *Watson v. Burton*, [1957] 1 W.L.R. 19 (Ch.), at p. 25; but *cf. Hopcroft v. Hopcroft* (1897), 76 L.T.R. 341.

[15] *Bullen v. Wilkinson, supra*, footnote 9.

which induced the contract. Here, the relationship between deficient performance and misrepresentation becomes important. As seen from Lord Eldon's statement of the basic rule quoted above,[16] compensation is based to some extent on the vendor's representation of title. Having represented his ability to convey, he should not be heard to resist the claim for whatever he has at a reduced price. However, cases in which compensation is appropriate differ from misrepresentation cases. In compensation cases, the vendor is unable to fulfil promised performance, whereas misrepresentation ordinarily refers to misleading statements inducing the contract. According to a much criticized line of authority, there can be no recovery of damages for innocent misrepresentation.[17] In the absence of deceit, the plaintiff who complains of misrepresentation inducing the contract is in the somewhat anomalous position of having to choose between rescission and no relief at all.[18] The courts have been concerned lest the rule precluding damages for innocent misrepresentation be short-circuited by permitting the plaintiff to have specific performance with compensation. Accordingly, the rule which precludes damages for innocent misrepresentation has been held also to preclude specific performance with an abatement of price unless the plaintiff is able to show that the misrepresentation in question was not merely an inducement, but that it is an actual term of the contract which the defendant cannot fulfil.[19]

799   Another important qualification to the right to specific performance with compensation is that the compensation is not ordinarily available after the contract has been completed.[20] In a formal sense, this follows from the fact that relief by way of compensation or

---

[16] *Supra*, §795.

[17] *Heilbut, Symons & Co. v. Buckleton*, [1913] A.C. 30 (H.L.). For discussion of the point, see Waddams, *The Law of Contracts* (Toronto, Canada Law Book Ltd., 1977), pp. 242-65.

[18] See Waddams, *supra*, footnote 17, at p. 254.

[19] *Rutherford v. Acton-Adams*, [1915] A.C. 866 (P.C.); *Whitney v. MacLean*, [1932] 1 W.W.R. 417 (Alta. S.C. App. Div.); *Gilchester Properties, Ltd. v. Gomm*, [1948] 1 All E.R. 493 (Ch.); *Clayton v. Leech* (1889), 41 Ch. D. 103 (C.A.).

[20] *Allen v. Richardson* (1879), 13 Ch. D. 524 at p. 537, *per* Malins, V.-C.: ". . . you must, if you are wise, be wise in time"; *Di Cenzo Construction Co. Ltd. v. Glassco* (1978), 90 D.L.R. (3d) 127, 21 O.R. (2d) 186 (C.A.). In *De Clerval v. Jones* (1908), 8 W.L.R. 300 (Alta. S.C.T.D.), the vendor was given the option of paying compensation or having the sale rescinded. Compensation may be available after completion if a compensation clause so provides: *Palmer v. Johnson* (1884), 13 Q.B.D. 351 (C.A.); *Schlote v. Richardson, supra*, footnote 11; *Bartlet v. Delaney* (1913), 17 D.L.R. 500, 29 O.L.R. 426 (S.C. App. Div.); *McCall v. Faithorne* (1863), 10 Gr. 324.

abatement is ancillary to specific performance, but the real point in restricting relief here relates perhaps less to the technical aspect of specific performance being inappropriate, and more to the desire to preserve finality in completed transactions.

(2) Vendor suing for specific performance with compensation

800   Where a vendor who is unable to perform exactly as he promised sues for specific performance with compensation, an order in his favour is more difficult to justify than if the purchaser had sued. The vendor's case rests upon a different principle, namely, that the courts should not insist unduly upon literal performance. As was said in one case, "[i]n exercising its jurisdiction over specific performance Court of Equity looks at the substance and not merely at the letter of the contract".[21] In other words, if the reasonable expectation of the purchaser would not be frustrated by a decree forcing him to take less than promised, but with compensation, then relief in favour of the vendor can be justified.

801   The case invariably referred to here is *Flight v. Booth*,[22] which clearly casts the test in terms of protecting reasonable expectations:

> . . . where the misdescription, although not proceeding from fraud, is in a material and substantial point, so far affecting the subject-matter of the contract that it may reasonably be supposed, that, but for such misdescription, the purchaser might never have entered into the contract at all, in such case the contract is avoided altogether . . . . Under such a state of facts, the purchaser may be considered as not having purchased the thing which was really the subject of the sale.[23]

802   Though cast in subjective terms, clearly the test is an objective one.[24] The purchaser will only defend the case where he is prepared to say that he would not have contracted at all had he known of the defect. However, an objective standard is applied, and where the court is satisfied that a reasonable purchaser would have taken the

---

[21] *Rutherford v. Acton-Adams, supra,* footnote 19, at p. 869, *per* Viscount Haldane.

[22] (1834), 1 Bing. (N.C.) 370, 131 E.R. 1160. Although the case is always applied in the specific performance context, it was a decision at law in which the purchaser sued for the return of his deposit. For examples of specific performance cases, see *Foster v. Goodacre* (1917), 34 D.L.R. 42 (B.C.C.A.); *Martin v. Kellogg,* [1932] 2 D.L.R. 496, [1932] O.R. 274 (S.C.), affd [1932] 4 D.L.R. 617, 41 O.W.N. 356 (C.A.); *Re Marchment Co. Ltd. and Midanik,* [1947] O.W.N. 363 (H.C.J.); *Re Hughes and Macaulay* (1969), 10 D.L.R. (3d) 86 (B.C.S.C.), affd 14 D.L.R. (3d) 110 *sub nom. Hughes v. Lukuvka* (C.A.).

[23] *Flight v. Booth, supra,* footnote 22, at p. 377, *per* Tindal, C.J.

[24] *Hamilton v. Munro* (1951), 51 S.R. (N.S.W.) 250.

property at a reduced price, an order in the vendor's favour will be made.

803   Where the property is subject to restrictions which might affect the plaintiff's use, specific performance has been refused.[25] In *Flight v. Booth*,[26] it was held that where leasehold property in a commercial area was subject to much wider restrictions as to use than specified in the contract, it could not be said that the purchaser would have wanted the property, even at a reduced price.[27] Similarly, a purchaser will not be required to take an unmarketable title.[28] On the other hand, where a deficiency in area or other defect in the property would not materially affect the plaintiff's intended use, but would reduce its market value, specific performance with compensation has been awarded.[29]

804   It has been suggested that if the vendor has been guilty of misrepresentation, he will not be granted relief.[30] However, not all the cases can be explained on that basis,[31] and it has also been suggested that the vendor's knowledge of the defect will not bar specific performance with compensation in his favour.[32] It would appear that the courts merely try to resolve whether the discrepancy, however produced, is so great as to preclude relief.

805   Orders have been made in some cases where the discrepancy has been quite substantial,[33] and any attempt to explain the cases purely in terms of raw numbers or percentages would be inappropriate.[34]

---

[25] It has been held that relief may be refused even where the defect or deficiency does not affect actual market value: *Lee v. Rayson*, [1917] 1 Ch. 613.

[26] *Supra*, footnote 22.

[27] In *Cato v. Thompson* (1882), 9 Q.B.D. 616 (C.A.), the same result was reached, but on the basis that the market-value effect of such a clause could not be determined.

[28] *Pryke v. Waddingham* (1852), 10 Hare 1, 68 E.R. 813; *Danby v. Stewart* (1979), 97 D.L.R. (3d) 734, 23 O.R. (2d) 449 (H.C.J.). There must, however, be a "reasonable, decent possibility of litigation": *Logan v. Stein*, [1958] O.W.N. 343 (C.A.).

[29] *Re Contract between Fawcett and Holmes* (1889), 42 Ch. D. 150 (C.A.); *Shepherd v. Croft*, [1911] 1 Ch. 521; *Re Belcham and Gawley's Contract*, [1930] 1 Ch. 56; *Powell v. Elliot* (1875), L.R. 10 Ch. 424.

[30] *Rutherford v. Acton-Adams*, [1915] A.C. 866 (P.C.), at p. 870, *per* Viscount Haldane.

[31] See, *e.g.*, *Powell v. Elliot*, *supra*, footnote 29.

[32] *Shepherd v. Croft*, *supra*, footnote 29; *Re Belcham and Gawley's Contract*, *supra*, footnote 29.

[33] *Powell v. Elliot*, *supra*, footnote 29 (reduction of £52,020 off purchase price of £365,000); *Shepherd v. Croft*, *supra*, footnote 29 (reduction of £600 off purchase price of £9,000); *Re Contract between Fawcett and Holmes*, *supra*, footnote 29 (1,033 sq. yds rather than 1,372 sq. yds conveyed).

[34] See, *e.g.*, *Boyko v. Wakal* (1974), 48 D.L.R. (3d) 607 (Man. Q.B.).

Not surprisingly, there have been judicial statements cautioning against too broad an application of the principle lest the courts become involved in making a new contract for the parties.[35] Discussion in these terms is misleading. What the court attempts to do is to discern the true nature of the contract, identify the expectations it gives rise to, and make remedial decisions which will foster those expectations rather than frustrate them.

806   Where the deficiency or defect is one that the vendor might be expected to repair, the court can require him to make reasonable efforts to that end before ordering specific performance with compensation.[36] As will be seen from the discussion which follows,[37] even where contractual terms purport to exonerate the vendor from making such efforts, the courts will not allow such terms to be used arbitrarily.

(3) Contractual terms relating to compensation

807   The authority of the court to order specific performance with compensation may, of course, be affected by specific provisions in the agreement itself.

808   Where the agreement expressly provides for compensation to be made in the case of deficiency, it might be expected that the courts would be more willing to grant specific performance with compensation at the suit of the vendor.[38] However, in practice, the presence or absence of such a clause appears to make very little difference. In the leading case of *Flight v. Booth*,[39] discussed above, there was such a

---

[35] *Halsey v. Grant* (1806), 13 Ves. Jun. 73 at p. 76, 33 E.R. 222, *per* Lord Erskine, L.C.:

> If a Court of Equity can compel a party to perform a contract, that is substantially different from that, which he entered into, and proceed upon the principle of compensation, as it has compelled him to execute a contract substantially different, and substantially less than that, from which he stipulated, without some very distinct limitation of such a jurisdiction, having all the precision of law, the rights of mankind under contracts must be extremely uncertain.

However, as pointed out by *Bowes v. Vaux* (1918), 43 O.L.R. 521 (H.C.), where the purchaser successfully sued to recover his deposit where he had refused to complete because of a deficiency, the vendor may be able to sue for specific performance on the altered contract, but not for common law damages.

[36] *Duggan v. Franco-Belgian Investment Co.* (1920), 51 D.L.R. 602 (Alta. S.C.).

[37] *Infra*, §§807-810.

[38] *Rudd v. Lascelles*, [1900] 1 Ch. 815 at p. 818, *per* Farwell, J.: "Cases where there is such a provision do not present so much difficulty because compensation is part of the bargain."

[39] (1834), 1 Bing. (N.C.) 370, 131 E.R. 1160.

clause, and yet the reasoning in that case has been applied where no such clause was present.[40] The result is that a compensation clause would appear to confirm the jurisdiction the court already has, but to add very little one way or the other.

809   However, where the agreement specifically excludes compensation for defects or deficiencies, it will be more difficult for the court to justify specific performance in favour of the vendor. It has been held that no compensation can be awarded to the purchaser in the face of such a clause.[41] The choice, then, will be between specific performance with no compensation, or refusal of specific performance altogether.[42] Thus, it will be harder for the vendor, giving less than he promised, to justify a specific performance decree, as compensation for the defect is precluded.[43] Where compensation for defects or deficiencies is excluded, a purchaser is much less likely to seek specific performance, although presumably if he does, and is prepared to take the vendor's interest without compensation, there should be no difficulty in granting a decree in his favour.

810   Often, however, agreements of purchase and sale contain so-called annulment clauses. The effect of such a clause is to permit the vendor to return the deposit and treat the agreement as at an end if he is unwilling or unable to remove any title[44] objection insisted upon by the purchaser.[45] Where the agreement provides for the right of the vendor to annul the contract in the case of any title defect which he cannot repair, the very purpose of the clause presumably is to prevent the purchaser from forcing the vendor to convey what he has with compensation. Unless the vendor chooses not to rescind, the effect of the contractual term is to preclude the court from forcing an objectively determined bargain on the vendor, and the clause provides the vendor with an escape from the agreement so that he can, in ef-

---

[40] *Shepherd v. Croft*, [1911] 1 Ch. 521.

[41] *Jacobs v. Revell*, [1900] 2 Ch. 858.

[42] The purchaser will still be able to have the agreement rescinded if there is a material defect, even if there is a clause precluding annulment and compensation for defects: *Puckett and Smith's Contract*, [1902] 2 Ch. 258 (C.A.); *Lee v. Rayson*, [1917] 1 Ch. 613.

[43] *Rudd v. Lascelles, supra*, footnote 38; *Watson v. Burton*, [1957] 1 W.L.R. 19 (Ch.), also holding that the vendor cannot "waive" such a clause.

[44] This will depend upon the precise wording of the clause. In *Farantos Development Ltd. v. Canada Permanent Trust Co.* (1975), 56 D.L.R. (3d) 481, 7 O.R. (2d) 721 (H.C.J.), matters of conveyancing were distinguished from matters of title, and the vendor was held not to be entitled to rescind.

[45] *Louch v. Pape Avenue Land Co. Ltd.*, [1928] S.C.R. 518, [1928] 3 D.L.R. 620; *Ashburner v. Sewell*, [1891] 3 Ch. 405.

fect, decide for himself whether or not he wants to renegotiate.[46] However, the courts will not permit such a clause to be abused by the vendor, and relief by way of specific performance with some protection in the purchaser's favour other than compensation is not altogether precluded. As was put in one case, the provision "was not intended to make the contract one which the vendor can repudiate at his sweet will".[47] In the leading Canadian case,[48] the Supreme Court of Canada held that a vendor could not rely on such a clause where "his attempted rescission was arbitrary and capricious and there was complete and deliberate failure on his part to do what an ordinarily prudent man having regard to his contractual obligations would have done".[49] There, the vendor pleaded that he could not convey free of his wife's inchoate dower right. The court awarded specific performance with a portion of the purchase price to be paid into court as security against the wife's claim.[50]

3. Piecemeal Performance

811   Often, a contract will call for the performance of several obligations, some of which are the appropriate subject of specific relief, and some of which are not. Contracts of this variety pose problems for specific relief. Cases in which the obligation of the defendant is the appropriate subject of specific relief, while that of the plaintiff is not, have been examined in the preceding chapter.[51] The present discussion is concerned with cases where the plaintiff seeks specific relief in circumstances where only part of the defendant's promise is the appropriate subject of a decree for specific relief. Here, sweeping dicta to the effect that "when the Court cannot compel specific performance of the contract as a whole, it will not interfere to compel specific performance of part of a contract"[52] are entirely misleading.

---

[46] Compare Waddams, *supra*, footnote 5, §183, pointing out that vendors will ordinarily be unaware of title defects and that restricting purchasers' remedies for such defects may be justifiable.

[47] *Hurley v. Roy* (1921), 64 D.L.R. 375 at p. 377, 50 O.L.R. 281 at p. 285 (S.C. App. Div.), *per* Middleton, J. See also *Mason v. Freedman*, [1958] S.C.R. 483, 14 D.L.R. (2d) 529.

[48] *Mason v. Freedman, supra*, footnote 47.

[49] *Mason v. Freedman, supra*, at p. 488 S.C.R., p. 534 D.L.R., *per* Judson, J.

[50] This is discussed further, *infra*, §824.

[51] *Supra*, §§745-759.

[52] *Ryan v. Mutual Tontine Westminster Chambers Ass'n*, [1893] 1 Ch. 116 (C.A.), at p. 123, *per* Esher, M.R. See also *Merchants' Trading Co. v. Banner* (1871), L.R. 12 Eq. 18 at p. 23, *per* Romilly, M.R.; *Ford v. Stuart* (1852), 15 Beav. 493 at p. 501, 51 E.R. 629, *per* Romilly, M.R.: "no matter is more fully settled in this Court than

There are, in fact, many situations in which specific relief will be granted in respect of only part of a contract, and where the court will in effect order piecemeal performance. The essential criterion here is again that the remedy selected should foster rather than frustrate the reasonable expectations of the parties. In certain cases, specific relief in respect of part of the contract may distort what was intended, and will on that account be refused. In other cases, specific relief of one aspect of the agreement may safely be ordered notwithstanding the inappropriateness of specific relief for other aspects.

812   In dealing with this problem, the courts have said that if the portion of the defendant's obligation which is appropriate for specific relief can be seen as independent of, and severable and separate from that portion of the obligation which cannot, then specific relief can be ordered.[53] In dealing with the issue of severability or independence, mechanical formulations are bound to produce awkward results. It is submitted that the cases do reflect an effort on the part of the courts to identify the true intentions and expectations of the parties, and to measure the impact of specific relief for part of the contract against those interests.[54] This is a difficult exercise as the contract rarely states what is to happen if only part of it can be performed, and it requires careful examination of the overall purpose of the contract.

813   In a leading 19th century case,[55] the defendant had agreed to lease a wharf to the plaintiff, and to be employed on the wharf by the plaintiff for the period of the lease. The defendant defaulted, and the plaintiff sought specific performance of the lease only, realizing that specific performance of the contract of employment would not be granted. The court refused specific performance, holding that the agreement was "one entire contract" with "correlative" and dependent obligations. The court found that the purpose of the agreement including the term as to employment was to allow the defendant to maintain a connection with the business carried on at the wharf, and thereby be able to resume it himself at the end of the lease. That purpose, the court found, would have been frustrated by specific perfor-

---

that a contract cannot be specifically performed in part; it must be wholly performed, or not at all . . .".

[53] *Infra*, footnotes 56, 57, 59 and 62.

[54] *Wilkinson v. Clements* (1872), L.R. 8 Ch. 96 at p. 111, *per* Mellish, L.J.: "the Court ought to carry out the agreement according to what it sees is really the intention and object of the parties in making it".

[55] *Ogden v. Fossick* (1862), 4 De G.F. & J. 426, 45 E.R. 1249.

mance of the agreement to lease by itself. By way of contrast, in another 19th century case,[56] the court was prepared to award specific performance of an agreement to purchase a patent, although it could not award specific performance of another part of the agreement, to form a company to exploit the patent. The result can be justified, as the plaintiff's interest in having the company set up could be reflected in a damages award, and the defendant could not complain that the agreement was distorted by specific performance of one of its terms. In another case,[57] specific performance of an agreement to lease property was awarded although the contract provided that the defendant should have to take up the lease only when he had completed the construction of a house on the property. The court held that he could not "aver his own wrong as a reason why the lease should not be taken before the house is built"[58] and that damages could be awarded to reflect the loss the plaintiff suffered from his failure to build.

814   In many other cases, the courts have found one or more terms of a contract properly the subject of an order of specific relief although other terms are not.[59] Perhaps the best examples of this are the cases involving negative covenants. As already noted, injunctions are granted regularly to enjoin certain employees from violating an exclusivity clause, although the court will not specifically enforce the positive aspects of the same employment contract.[60] An important consideration in these cases is the extent to which enforcing the negative covenant amounts in practical terms to indirectly enforcing the positive. It has been argued, however, that injunctions in such cases are available only where the plaintiff has some legitimate interest in having the negative covenant performed distinct from any desire to have the positive term performed.[61] If this limiting rationale is applied, then it can fairly be said that the negative obligation is, for remedial purposes, severable from the positive. Specifically enforc-

---

[56] *Elmore v. Pirrie* (1887), 57 L.T.R. 333.

[57] *Soames v. Edge* (1860), Johns. 669, 70 E.R. 588.

[58] *Ibid.*, at p. 674, *per* Page Wood, V.-C.

[59] *Odessa Tramways Co. v. Mendel* (1877), 8 Ch. D. 235 (C.A.); *Wilkinson v. Clements, supra*, footnote 54; *Rigby v. Great Western Ry. Co.* (1846), 15 L.J. Ch. 266; *Lewin v. Guest* (1826), 1 Russ. 325, 38 E.R. 126; *infra*, footnote 62. *Cf. Brett v. East India and London Shipping Co. (Ltd.)* (1864), 2 H. & M. 404, 71 E.R. 520; *Treadgold v. Rost* (1912), 7 D.L.R. 741 (Yukon Terr. Ct.); *Stocker v. Wedderburn* (1857), 3 K. & J. 393, 69 E.R. 1162.

[60] *Supra*, §§689-696.

[61] *Supra*, §§697, 698.

ing the negative aspect does not distort the intended effect of the agreement, but merely recognizes that the plaintiff's interest in enforcing the negative term is best reflected by an injunction, whatever remedy might be available for breach of the positive.

815   In some cases, the defendant could hardly be prejudiced by the plaintiff's desire to take an order for less than full performance for one aspect of the agreement, and to rely on damages for the other. In a 19th century railway case,[62] the court granted specific performance of the defendant's obligation to construct a siding, but held that it could not grant specific relief of its obligation to keep the siding in repair as that would involve extended supervision. Thus, the plaintiff was entitled to have the siding installed, but would have to look to a damages award in the event of non-repair. On the other hand, in the well-known case of *Ryan v. Mutual Tontine Westminster Chambers Ass'n*,[63] the court refused specific performance to appoint a resident porter on the grounds that the defendant's obligation to supply a porter could not fairly be broken down into an obligation to appoint one and an obligation to see that the services were provided. The result seems unduly paternalistic. If the plaintiff was prepared to accept a limited order only requiring the appointment of the porter, and then rely on his right to damages in the event of unsatisfactory performance, there hardly seems to be any hardship to the defendant.

816   An issue related to severability arises where the plaintiff is in breach of some obligation owed to the defendant, but sues to enforce the defendant's obligation to him. If the covenants are independent, in other words, if the defendant can fairly be said to have contemplated that the plaintiff should have the advantage of one aspect of the agreement whether or not the plaintiff has performed his own obligation, specific relief may be ordered.[64] The maxim "he who seeks equity must do equity", does not allow the court in such cases to impose terms on the plaintiff which would alter this aspect of the agreement.[65] Any conditions imposed must relate to the very obligation the plaintiff seeks to enforce.

817   However, where the plaintiff is in breach of an obligation which is interdependent with the one he sues to enforce, his right to specific

---

[62] *Lytton v. Great Northern Ry. Co.* (1856), 2 K. & J. 394, 69 E.R. 836.

[63] [1893] 1 Ch. 116 (C.A.).

[64] *Peck and Coleman v. Powell* (1884), 11 S.C.R. 494; *Gibson v. Goldsmid* (1854), 5 De G.M. & G. 757, 43 E.R. 1064.

[65] *Supra*, §110.

performance may be affected.[66] Of course not all breaches by the plaintiff will deprive him of his right to specific relief. This is illustrated by the principle that courts will not insist on literal performance, but will rather look to the substance, as in the case of the vendor's right to specific performance with compensation.[67]

818 The distinction between "trivial" breaches, which will not defeat the plaintiff's right to specific performance, and breaches of "essential" terms seems identical to that drawn to identify breaches which are so fundamental as to discharge the defendant from further obligations to perform.[68] Although the courts traditionally use the language of discretion, the test is that of the substantive law of contract which determines whether one party's breach has discharged the other from his contractual obligations. If the plaintiff is asking the court to force the defendant to perform where the defendant has not and will not receive the substance of the exchange he bargained for, specific performance or for that matter any other remedy, is obviously inappropriate. Assimilation of the doctrine of discharge by breach and the effect on the plaintiff's right to specific performance is in keeping with the more general and desirable drift towards assimilation of legal and equitable principles.[69]

4. Modified and Conditional Performance

819 In ordering specific relief, the courts will often impose terms or conditions which alter the letter but not the spirit of the agreement, where the situation makes it inappropriate to grant a straightforward and unqualified order.[70]

820 The need for such terms or conditions may spring from a variety of sources. One important area, examined in the preceding chapter,[71] is usually described as want of mutuality. It was seen that the courts have concerned themselves with the plight of the defendant who is called upon to perform his obligation before the plaintiff has performed his, and that a variety of techniques have been evolved to secure the defendant's position.[72]

---

[66] *Supra*, §§760-764.
[67] *Supra*, §§800, 801.
[68] *Supra*, §§760-762.
[69] *Supra*, §§764-771.
[70] See *Davis v. Hone* (1805), 2 Sch. & Lef. 341 at p. 348, 9 R.R. 89, *per* Lord Redesdale: "This Court will execute the covenant, according to a conscientious modification of it, to do justice as far as circumstances will permit."
[71] *Supra*, §§745-759.
[72] *Supra*, §758.

821   As discussed in the preceding chapter, an element of mistake or misrepresentation which does not vitiate the contract altogether may sometimes give rise to a defence to specific performance.[73] A remedial technique which may be used in many cases, and which adds an element of flexibility here, is granting specific performance conditionally so as to give the plaintiff the choice between having specific performance refused, or granted on the basis of the plaintiff's acceptance of the terms as understood by the defendant.[74] This may often provide an attractive possibility, as it achieves a balance between the plaintiff's interest in having specific performance and the defendant's interest in not having to shoulder a burden unexpectedly greater because of mistake or misrepresentation.[75]

822   In one case,[76] where plans had not revealed clearly that the plaintiff vendor retained a small block of land adjacent to a large plot bought by the purchaser, a smaller block not being covered by a general restrictive covenant forbidding certain commercial activity, the plaintiff was put to the election of having his specific performance bill dismissed or taking specific performance of the agreement with the restrictive covenant applying to all of the property, as the defendant mistakenly thought it did. In another case,[77] the plaintiff sued for an injunction to restrain the breach of an agreement for the sale of a patent. There was some ambiguity as to whether the agreement covered use only in England or elsewhere, and as the defendant thought that only England was involved, the plaintiff was granted an interlocutory injunction on that basis.

823   Specific performance may also be awarded *cy près* where the plaintiff is unable to comply literally with particular details, such as the

---

[73] *Supra*, §§711-725.

[74] In addition to the cases cited, *infra*, footnotes 76, 77, see: *Watson v. Marston* (1853), 4 De G.M. & G. 230, 43 E.R. 495; *De Rosiers v. De Calles* (1906), 8 O.W.R. 91; *Fife v. Clayton* (1807), 13 Ves. Jun. 546, 33 E.R. 398. *Cf. Manser v. Back* (1948), 6 Hare 443, 67 E.R. 1239, and *Re Hare and O'More's Contract*, [1901] 1 Ch. 93, both refusing such relief to a plaintiff who did not hear terms announced at an auction.

[75] A similar technique is sometimes used in suits for rectification: *Harris v. Pepperell* (1867), L.R. 5 Eq. 1 (defendant given option of having the contract rescinded or performed on terms as understood by the plaintiff). Compare, however, the categorization of certain terms as conditions which cannot be waived: *Turney v. Zhilka*, [1959] S.C.R. 578, 18 D.L.R. (2d) 447; *Barnett v. Harrison*, [1976] 2 S.C.R. 531, 57 D.L.R. (3d) 255. *Cf. McCauley v. McVey*, [1980] 1 S.C.R. 165, 98 D.L.R. (3d) 577 (similar term held not to be a "true condition precedent").

[76] *Baskcomb v. Beckwith* (1869), L.R. 8 Eq. 100.

[77] *Preston v. Luck* (1884), 27 Ch. D. 497 (C.A.).

method or mode of payment, or where the defendant is not in a position to comply exactly with the contract's terms, but where the court is satisfied that an order can be fashioned which will result in substantial compliance with the spirit of the agreement.[78] A good example of this is the decision of the Supreme Court of Canada in *Webb and Reeves v. Dipenta*.[79] Webb had a partial interest in a property, and agreed to sell it to Dipenta for $1,000. However, Webb sold his interest to Reeves for $4,000, and received $1,125 in part payment. Dipenta sued for specific performance, but the court held that the conveyance to Reeves had been in good faith and could not be set aside. However, the court went on to hold that Dipenta was entitled to get whatever Webb got from the sale, and ordered Webb to pay Dipenta the amount he had already received, and Reeves to pay Dipenta the balance.

824   Another example of modified performance occurs where the plaintiff is acquiring a property or an interest which is subject to a contingent claim. Abatement or compensation for the contingency may be less appropriate than modifying the terms of performance by requiring the defendant to provide security. The leading Canadian example is *Mason v. Freedman*,[80] where a vendor of real estate claimed to be unable to procure his wife's bar of her dower interest. Abatement of the price could be unjust to the vendor, as the wife's right was inchoate and might never become consummate, just as an order which took no account of her possible claim would unfairly expose the plaintiff purchaser to the risk of paying for a clear title but later having it cut down. The appropriate solution was found to be an order requiring the vendor to pay into court as security that portion of the purchase price which reflected the value of the wife's interest, and which could be paid out to secure the purchaser in the event that the wife claimed her interest in possession, or could be returned to the vendor if she predeceased him or released her interest.[81]

---

[78] *Raaber v. Coll-In-Wood Farms Ltd.* (1970), 14 D.L.R. (3d) 234 (Alta. S.C. App. Div.), affd [1971] S.C.R. v, 22 D.L.R. (3d) 128n; *Punch v. Chisholm* (1874), 9 N.S.R. 469 (C.A.); *Jones v. Dale* (1888), 16 O.R. 717 (Ch.); *McCauley v. McVey*, *supra*, footnote 75.

[79] [1925] S.C.R. 565, [1925] 1 D.L.R. 216.

[80] [1958] S.C.R. 483, 14 D.L.R. (2d) 529.

[81] See also *Skinner v. Ainsworth* (1876), 24 Gr. 148; *Wilson v. Williams* (1857), 3 Jur. N.S. 810. *Cf. Kendrew v. Shewan* (1854), 4 Gr. 578, ordering specific performance with an abatement to take into account the value of the dower interest; *Shuter v. Patten* (1921), 67 D.L.R. 577, 51 O.L.R. 281 (S.C.); *Van Norman v. Beaupre* (1856), 5 Gr. 599.

5. Interest and Adjustments

825   When specific performance is ordered, the date the transaction is actually completed will almost always be later than the date agreed to. An issue which has received surprisingly little attention in the case-law is the date to which interest and other charges are to be adjusted.

826   In most cases, it is perhaps most convenient simply to complete the transaction on exactly the same terms as would be appropriate for the date set for closing by the agreement. The vendor will have had the use and any income from the land during the period prior to judgment, and if the purchaser were to compensate the vendor for carrying charges during that period, it would only be fair to require the vendor to bring into account benefits of ownership or occupation. Complex calculations of these amounts (which will usually balance each other out) can be avoided by the simple practice of adjusting to the original contract date.

827   However, it has been forcefully argued that where there is rapid inflation in land values, especially where vacant land held for investment is concerned, there is a serious risk of over-compensating the purchaser if account is not taken of the interest attributable to the purchase price during the period between the contract date for closing and the actual date of closing.[82] The argument has received mixed reception in the courts,[83] and is surely worthy of further consideration. The point may be illustrated by the following example. Assume that A purchases land from B at an agreed price of $100,000. By the date set by agreement for closing, the land is worth $150,000; by the date of actual closing (say two years later), after A has sued and obtained a specific performance decree, it is worth $200,000. Had B kept his promise, A would have got a property worth $150,000 for $100,000. However, A would then have paid or forgone interest on the purchase price (depending on whether he paid cash or borrowed to finance the purchase) during the time the property rose to a value of $200,000. Similarly, B would have had use of the money during that period. Thus, unless some adjustment is made to take into account the fact that the transaction closed two years later than agreed,

---

[82] Swan, "Damages, Specific Performance, Inflation and Interest" (1980), 10 R.P.R. 267.

[83] The approach outlined below was rejected in *306793 Ontario Ltd. v. Rimes* (1979), 100 D.L.R. (3d) 350, 25 O.R. (2d) 79 (C.A.), leave to appeal to S.C.C. refused December 3, 1979, and *Ribic v. Weinstein* (1982), 140 D.L.R. (3d) 258 (Ont. H.C.J.), but applied in *Tanu v. Ray* (1981), 20 R.P.R. 22 (B.C.S.C.).

A will be in a substantially better position having sued for specific performance than had the agreement been completed as agreed. A will, in this sense, be over-compensated by the amount of two years' interest on the purchase price, $100,000, and similarly, B will be worse off by that amount than if he had kept his bargain, on the assumption that the land was vacant, held for investment, and yielded B no benefits or profits. While in one sense, B's refusal to complete produced this situation, remedial contract rules are not normally designed to punish contract breakers or to do anything more than place the parties in the position they would have been in had the contract been performed.[84]

---

[84] *Supra*, §537.

INDEX

Note: References are to paragraph numbers

ABATEMENT. *See* COMPENSATION, SPECIFIC PERFORMANCE WITH

ABORTION
declaration as to constitutionality, 300
injunction to restrain, 117*n*, 272

ABUSE OF PROCESS, 343, 478-9, 481, 489

ACQUIESCENCE. *See* DELAY

ADJUSTMENTS, FOLLOWING SPECIFIC
    PERFORMANCE, 825-7

ADMINISTRATIVE BOARDS
matters within jurisdiction of, 183, 193, 313, 330
non-suable entity, 344-8, 358, 586

ANNUITY CONTRACTS, 556-7, 609*n*

ANTICIPATORY BREACH, 773, 779-80

ANTON PILLER ORDER, 116, 233-48
abuse, potential for, 245-8
disclosure required, 237-42
privilege, 237-42
search warrant, relation to, 247
strength of case, 235, 243-5

ARBITRATION
consensual, 482
injunction to restrain, 118, 482-90
labour, 583
statutory, 482
stay of action, 482*n*

ATTACHMENT. *See* CONTEMPT

References are to paragraph numbers

References are to paragraph numbers

References are to paragraph numbers

References are to paragraph numbers

References are to paragraph numbers

References are to paragraph numbers

NUISANCE — *Continued*
order defining level of activity, 395-6
public authorities, 384, 385, 403
public interest, 380-89, 378-403, 406
pulp mill, 384, 402-3
prematurity, 70-6
riparian, 384, 402-3, 406
roots, 387n
sporting activities, 387-9, 395
stay, 392-4
suspended injunction, 392-4, 384n
trifling harm, 376, 390
vibrations, 375

OBSCENITY, 109, 273n, 281, 299, 358

ORDER, FORM OF, 39-46
defamation, 444n
Mareva, 219-20
non-parties, 516-20
nuisance, 395-6, 507
successor in title, 518-20
vague, 509, 576

OUTPUT CONTRACTS. *See* LONG TERM SUPPLY CONTRACTS

PARENS PATRIAE, 253-4, 286

PARLIAMENT. *See* LEGISLATURE

PARTY STIPULATION. *See* STIPULATED REMEDY

PASSING OFF, 117
(*See also* ANTON PILLER)
foreign defendant, 123n

PATENTS. *See* INDUSTRIAL PROPERTY

PENALTY CLAUSE. *See* STIPULATED REMEDY

PERSONAL SERVICE CONTRACTS, 463, 471
agreement not to terminate, 674

References are to paragraph numbers

References are to paragraph numbers

References are to paragraph numbers

References are to paragraph numbers

References are to paragraph numbers

TRADE ASSOCIATION, 653, 687

TRADE LIBEL. *See* DEFAMATION

TRADE MARKS. *See* INDUSTRIAL PROPERTY

TRADE, RIGHT TO, 460, 473

TRADE UNIONS
(*See also* LABOUR LAW)
breach of rules, 464
contract theory, 461-2
elections, 464
property right required, 460-1
wrongful expulsion, 459-63

TRESPASS, 367, 425-36
(*See also* PROPERTY RIGHTS)
access to neigbouring land, 426-9
air space, 426-7
burden and benefit, 425
conditional order, 434
damage, want of, 426-30, 432-4
defective expropriation proceedings, 433*n*
deliberateness, 434
encroachments, 55, 434, 370*n*
necessity, 430
pre-Judicature Act practice, 431
public interest, 427, 428-30, 434
suspended injunction, 426-34
temporary, 426-30

ULTRA VIRES. *See* COMPANIES; CONSTITUTIONAL LAW; CROWN;
    JUDICIAL REVIEW; PUBLIC AUTHORITIES

UNCERTAINTY, AS DEFENCE TO SPECIFIC PERFORMANCE,
    770-1
(*See also* SUPERVISION)

UNCONSCIONABILITY, 527
(*See also* UNFAIRNESS; HARDSHIP)
discretionary defence to specific performance, 704-10